OCEAN
TRANSPORTATION

OCEAN TRANSPORTATION

CARL E. McDOWELL
AND HELEN M. GIBBS

BeardBooks
Washington, D.C.

Copyright 1954 by McGraw-Hill Book Company, Inc.
Reprinted 1999 by Beard Books, Washington, D.C.
ISBN 1-893122-45-X

Printed in the United States of America

*To the men of America's merchant marine,
afloat and ashore, as represented by*
CAPTAIN NILS E. CARLSON

FOREWORD

An active merchant marine and the knowledge required to operate merchant ships are essential national assets that must be preserved. Twice within the memory of living man, this nation has been called upon to build a great fleet of merchant ships at great cost. During World War I, between two and a half and three billion dollars was spent in constructing ships, most of which were not completed in time to have a bearing on the outcome of the war. This figure was dwarfed by the 12 billion dollars spent building merchant ships during World War II. Furthermore, the pressure of the conflict, in which the United States was called upon to furnish transport not only for her own needs but for those of her allies, impelled the nation to construct several thousand emergency ships—the Liberties—that could be mass-produced but that were of marginal design at their launching.

The World War I ships were built collectively by citizens of the United States, and they were collectively owned by them. But the fleet never became theirs for private commercial operation because the American people did not have the inclination or the understanding necessary to turn a government-owned fleet into a great national asset—a powerful merchant marine. The post-World War II situation has shown considerable improvement. Of the government-owned World War II fleet of over 4,000 vessels, approximately 43 million deadweight tons and equal to two-thirds of the world's total oceangoing tonnage before the war, American shipowners replenished their privately owned fleets so that by 1952 they owned close to 1,300 ships. These are backed up by the roughly 2,000 ships in the government's national-defense reserve fleet. Although the United States has today the greatest peacetime merchant fleet in its history, the nation must not be lulled into complacency on maritime matters. To maintain and bolster our economic and military position we need a constant flow of efficient and speedy ships.

The authors of this book emphasize the necessity for the United States to maintain, as required by the Merchant Marine Act of 1936, a merchant fleet adequate for the commerce and defense of the nation. Their book, however, is primarily concerned with the techniques, practices, and problems of private ownership and operation. In this respect, it should perhaps be pointed out that the Act of 1936 also stipulated that the American merchant marine should be owned and operated by citizens of the United States in so far as practicable. Furthermore, fleet ownership presupposed knowledge of ship operation.

The appearance of a book on ship operation is most timely. Not only has shipping become an integral part of the national and foreign policy of this country in its dangerous and unsought role of leader of the free world; the shipping industry itself has undergone great changes. The United States fleet of pre-World War II days was composed of old and slow vessels. Not only are postwar ships larger, faster, and more complicated, but the postwar ship operator is confronted with problems that, though they are not new, have taken on different aspects. Inflation, particularly since 1948, has greatly enhanced the problem of block obsolescence for the American ship operator, while trade dislocations and the greatly increased costs of cargo handling complicate the shipping process.

Although the need for a book on ocean transportation has been great, it must be admitted that those who undertake to write such a book need courage. Many aspects of the shipping process have their roots in history and have for decades remained with little change, but there is nevertheless the danger that what is written may be out of date before it is printed. Furthermore, ocean transportation or the shipping industry is an extremely complex subject. It embraces not only ships of varied type, design, and employment but also the cargoes they carry, the origins and destinations of those cargoes, the routes traveled, the men who operate them afloat and ashore, laws relating both to seamen and to the ship, insurance, and government. Although the development of shipping has been motivated traditionally by private enterprise and initiative, the nature and problems of the industry inject the government into regulation, shipping finance, and other matters.

For one man to possess, or for that matter to acquire, the specialized knowledge necessary to write with authority on the many aspects of shipping covered in this book, including maritime law, marine insurance, shipping finance, and rates and regulations, would be a virtual impossibility. This may account, at least in part, for the dearth of books in the field of ocean transportation. It seems to me that the authors of this book have worked out a happy and adequate solution by drawing upon specialists in some of the more technical and specialized fields of shipping. This plan has permitted the publisher to offer, for the first time in two decades, a book that discusses the principal aspects of ocean transportation.

E. L. Cochrane
Vice Admiral, USN (Ret.)
Dean of Engineering
Massachusetts Institute of Technology

ACKNOWLEDGMENTS

Many men participate in the preparation of a book of this nature. The authors are particularly grateful to the contributors, who have written eight of the chapters, for their willingness to join in this shipping venture. None of these men bears any responsibility for any part of the book except his own.

In addition to the contributors, specialists in various fields related to shipping and international trade have assisted greatly in the preparation of this book, either by providing technical information or by reading certain chapters carefully. To them the authors are much indebted and wish to express their great appreciation. Special thanks are due to the numerous executives of the American President Lines, Ltd. Whatever errors of omission or commission appear in this book are, however, the authors' responsibility, not theirs.

Captain Henry C. Blackstone
Member, Board of Governors
California Maritime Academy

Captain C. T. Bonney, USN (Ret.)
Dean of Instruction
California Maritime Academy

Eugene Burdick
Associate Professor of Political Science
University of California

Joseph K. Carson, Jr.
Attorney, formerly Maritime Commissioner

Vice Admiral E. L. Cochrane, USN (Ret.)
Dean of Engineering
Massachusetts Institute of Technology
Maritime Administrator and chairman of the Federal Maritime Board, 1950–1952

John C. Coles
Senior Member
New York Adjusting Department
Marsh & McLennan

Bent Damsgaard
Director of Research
Pacific Maritime Association

J. S. Davis, Director Emeritus
Food Research Institute
Stanford University

Herbert E. Dougall
Professor of Finance
Graduate School of Business
Stanford University

Gerald A. Dundon
Vice President and Director
Bowring & Company, New York

Lloyd C. Fleming
Regional Director
Maritime Administration, San Francisco

Frank P. Foisie
Executive Vice President
Federated Employers of San Francisco

ACKNOWLEDGMENTS

Captain A. G. Ford
Officer-in-charge
San Francisco District Office
Office of Maritime Training
Maritime Administration
U.S. Department of Commerce

Joseph J. Geary
Senior Partner
Lillick, Geary, Olson, Adams & Charles

Franklin Howland
Oceanic Forwarding Company
San Francisco and Oakland

E. N. W. Hunter
Assistant to the President, Vice President
Pope & Talbot, Inc.

Commodore Russell Irhig, USN (Ret.)
Superintendent
California Maritime Academy

R. C. King
Chief, Division of Trade Routes
Office of Subsidy and Government Aid
Maritime Administration
U.S. Department of Commerce

Serge G. Koushnareff
Deputy Director, Transportation, Communications, and Utilities Division
Office of International Trade
U.S. Department of Commerce

Walter E. Maloney
President
American Merchant Marine Institute, Inc.

John Mason
District Counsel
Maritime Administration, San Francisco

Captain R. T. Merrill, USCG (Ret.)
Adviser, Shipping Policy Staff
Office of Transport and Communication
U.S. Department of State

Huntington T. Morse
Former Special Assistant to the Administrator, Maritime Administration, and Chairman, Federal Maritime Board, U.S. Department of Commerce

Ralph I. Schneider
Assistant Chief, Division of Trade Routes
Office of Subsidy and Government Aid
Maritime Administration
U.S. Department of Commerce

Alberto Scott, Jr.
Alberto Scott & Co., Inc.
San Francisco

T. J. Smith
Terminal Manager
Farrell Lines, Inc.

Charles L. Wheeler
Executive Vice President, Pope & Talbot, Inc.
Member, International Development Advisory Board

CONTENTS

FOREWORD, by Vice Admiral E. L. Cochrane, USN (Ret.)   vii
ACKNOWLEDGMENTS   ix
INTRODUCTION   1

PART ONE. SHIPPING IN THE WORLD ECONOMY

1. SHIPPING—SEA POWER AND NATIONAL POWER, by Helen M. Gibbs   7

   The Sea and Shipping to the Age of Columbus   7
   Spain and Portugal   9
   Growth of Dutch, English, and French Trade, 1500 to 1800   11
   The Struggle for Asia and America   17
   American Trade to the Civil War   20
   Rise of British Commercial Supremacy   24
   The Steamship   27
   Sea Power and National Power—What They Consist of   30

2. OVERSEAS TRADE AND SHIPPING SERVICES, by Helen M. Gibbs   34

   Growth of International Trade after 1849   34
   Trade in Wheat and Cotton   37
   The World's Tramp Fleet and Its Operations   43
   Berth or Liner Service   47
   Coal—Key to the British Carrying Trade   51

3. OVERSEAS TRADE AND SHIPPING SERVICES (CONTINUED), by Helen M. Gibbs   53

   Petroleum and the Tanker   53
   The Industrial Carrier and Its Cargoes   59
   Nongeographical Factors Influencing Trade   61
   The Postwar Situation   71

4. TRADE ROUTES AND SERVICES, by Helen M. Gibbs   76

   Physical Factors Influencing Trade Routes   76

Definition of Terms	81
United States Foreign Trade Routes	83

5. THE UNITED STATES DOMESTIC FLEET AND ITS EMPLOYMENT, by Carl E. McDowell — 92

Nature and Importance of Domestic Shipping	92
Development of Domestic Routes and Services	95
The Postwar Operator and His Problems	98

6. MERCHANT FLEETS OF THE WORLD, by Carl E. McDowell — 104

Size and Ownership of World's Merchant Fleet	104
Active Merchant Tonnage and the Quantum of World Trade	107
Characteristics of Modern Ships	111
The American Merchant Marine	115

PART TWO. THE SHIPPING PROCESS

7. TRAFFIC MANAGEMENT, by Carl E. McDowell — 127

Explanation of Traffic Management	127
Functions of the Traffic Department	129
Obtaining and Booking Cargo	130
Shipper's Papers	133
Establishing Remunerative Rates	140
Interdepartmental Relations	140
Promotion of Domestic and Foreign Commerce	142
The Traffic Department	143

8. FREIGHT FORWARDING AND FREIGHT BROKERAGE, by John H. Frederick — 145

General Nature of Forwarding	145
Forwarding Functions	147
Forwarding Organization	151
Forwarding and Brokerage Fees	152
Federal Regulation	153

9. SHIP OPERATION: THE SHIP, by Carl E. McDowell — 156

Components of Ship Operation	157
The Ship	158
The Terminal	166
Supervision and Administration	173
The Operational Process	175
Claims Division	181
Purchasing Division	183

CONTENTS

10. SHIP OPERATION: CHARTERS, *by Frank J. Zito*	185
Charter Parties Defined	185
Demise or Bareboat Charters	187
Time Charters	190
Voyage Charters	193
Operation and Brokerage	201
11. SHIP OPERATION: THE MEN, *by Helen M. Gibbs*	204
Officers and Crew	204
Provisions under Which Ships Operate	210
Certificates, Licenses, and Training	213
Wages, Hours, and Working Conditions	215
Labor Costs in the Total Cost of Ship Operation	217
12. ORGANIZATION AND MANAGEMENT, *by Helen M. Gibbs*	221
Company Control	222
Freight Traffic Department	225
Passenger Traffic Department	229
Operating Department	230
Finance Department	234
Public-relations Department	236
Claims Department	237
Service and Supply Department	239
General and Research Departments	240
Agents and Agencies	240
Variations in Organizational Structure	241
Precedent and Conservatism	243

PART THREE. THE FINANCE OF SHIPPING

13. GOVERNMENT AID, *by Helen M. Gibbs*	247
Nineteenth-century Mail Subsidies	248
Ineffective Aid to World War I	250
Benefits under the Merchant Marine Acts of 1920 and 1928	253
The Merchant Marine Act of 1936	257
Ship Sales after World War II	259
Construction-differential Subsidies	260
Operating-differential Subsidies	267
Reserve Funds	270
The Long-range Shipping Act of 1952	271

14. THE PROBLEM OF SHIPPING, *by Carl E. McDowell*   274
    Characteristics of Shipping Capital   274
    Handicaps of American Shipping Capital   278
    Block Obsolescence   282
    Need for Public-relations Program   286

15. ACCOUNTING POLICY AND PRACTICE, *by Arthur B. Poole*   288
    Accounts Related to Operating Statements   289
    Accounts Related to Balance Sheet   296
    Steamship Accounting Methods and Procedures   298
    Steamship Cost Accounting   302
    Contrasts   306

PART FOUR. ADMIRALTY, INSURANCE, AND REGULATION

16. SEAMEN'S LAW, *by Harry L. Haehl, Jr.*   309
    Seaman Defined   310
    The Seaman's Special Status   310
    Compensation for Personal Injury or Death   313
    Longshore Workers   320
    Workmen's Compensation versus Employers' Liability   322

17. THE LAW OF VESSELS, *by Harry L. Haehl, Jr.*   325
    Vessels in General   325
    Control and Regulation   328
    Maritime Liens and Mortgages   330
    General Average   332
    Carriage of Cargo and Passengers   334
    Collision   338
    Salvage and Towage   341
    Pilotage   344
    Limitation of Shipowner's Liability   345

18. MARINE LOSSES AND MARINE INSURANCE, *by Walter G. Hays*   349
    General Nature of Marine Underwriting   349
    Forms of Marine Insurance Policies   351
    Perils Insured against   357
    Duration of the Coverage   359
    Adjustment of Losses   360
    Total-loss and Constructive Total-loss Claims   362
    Particular Average or Partial Losses   364
    General-average Claims   367
    Salvage Claims   **372**

Collision Claims	373
Protection and Indemnity Claims	374
The Marine Insurance Program and Its Cost	375

19. RATES AND PRACTICES AND THEIR REGULATION, by *Ramond F. Burley*   380

Nature of Ocean Freight Rates	380
Factors Determining Rates	385
Origin of Conferences	389
United States and the Conferences	390
The Conference System	394
Regulation of Carriers in Domestic Trades	399

PART FIVE. THE ROLE OF GOVERNMENT

20. LAWS AND AGENCIES GOVERNING SHIPPING, by *J. Monroe Sullivan*   409

Legislation to 1890	410
The Situation, 1890 to 1916	411
United States Shipping Board	412
United States Maritime Commission	415
Federal Maritime Board and Maritime Administration	419
Powers and Functions of the Executive Branch	424

21. INTERNATIONAL CONVENTIONS AND TREATIES, by *Carl E. McDowell*   430

Limited Accomplishment of International Agreement	430
Politico-Economic Agreements	432
Juridical Agreements	433
Technical Agreements	434
International Maritime Organizations	440

22. MERCHANT SHIPPING IN WARTIME AND EMERGENCY, by *Carl E. McDowell*   444

Unique Position of Merchant Shipping in War	444
Wartime Administration of Merchant Shipping	446
Function of the Shipping Industry in Wartime	451
Government Control of Merchant Shipping	452
North Atlantic Treaty Organization	458
Military Sea Transportation Service	458
Defense Mobilization and Korea	459
Conclusion	460

INDEX   461

INTRODUCTION

The flow of civilization, of national power, and of commerce over the sea lanes of the world has been charted by historians, economists, political scientists, and novelists. At times, these writers have captured the essence of merchant shipping and its impact on the world; but, in the main, because of their objectives, shipping has not been for them an entity. The world's merchant marine, or its shipping industry, has seldom been the subject of a book.

POINT OF VIEW

Ocean shipping is an industry characterized by great complexity and by a magnitude of interests. These interests include the designers of the ship, the shipbuilder, the vessel owner or operator, the cargo owner, the holder of the mortgage on the ship, the creditor of the cargo owner, other creditors, agents and trustees, and the consignee. To these must be added the men who serve the ship afloat and ashore—the officers and crew and shore labor—both of which groups bear a somewhat different relationship to the shipping process than do workers in a manufacturing industry. Furthermore, there is the interest of government, for governments have been interested in shipping ever since ships began to sail the seven seas. Not only is there nothing more international than a ship engaged in foreign trade, but no industry is more vital to the welfare of nations and international good will or more essential in time of emergency or war.

The vital core of the shipping industry, however, is the ship, and, at least in certain respects, the vital interest is the shipowner or operator. Although his interests coincide or overlap at times with other interests, it is not possible, within the scope of such a book as this, to present the point of view of the many interests involved.

It therefore seems expedient to concentrate on the ship and on ship operation and management primarily from the point of view of the ship operator. Naturally, activities auxiliary to ship operation affect the owner, but their presentation has been determined by their relationship to ship operation and management. As a result, such matters as admiralty law, marine insurance, and freight rates have been discussed primarily as they affect the shipowner rather than as they affect other interests such as the shipper, the consignee, or the public in general. This explains why such aspects of the over-all shipping industry as ports and terminals and their operation, shipbuilding and ship repair, and passenger traffic have been subordinated to the major components of the shipping industry that are more directly associated with ship ownership. Our cubic capacity was, of necessity, limited, and we have sought to stow our cargo so that the book would be full and down, stable and trimmed.

OCEAN TRANSPORTATION AS A FORM OF TRANSPORTATION

For centuries, the ship was the main instrument of commerce and communications between nations. Today, three-fourths of the trade among nations is transported by water. To this would be added an enormous additional tonnage if inland waterway, river and canal, and Great Lakes traffic were included. Many countries and geographical areas are noncontiguous, separated by broad expanses of water, and the principal means of contact remains the ships.

The question immediately arises concerning the inroads of the plane on waterborne commerce. In October, 1951, Vice Admiral E. L. Cochrane, at the time Maritime Administrator, wrote as follows:

> Air transportation's speedy growth has yet had little effect on the ship as the number one carrier of the world's commerce. It appears unlikely that planes—in the foreseeable future, at any rate—will be able to compete with shipping in this field on an economical basis. Thus merchant ships remain as a powerful force in world economy today.

Rear Admiral D. V. Gallery, chief of Naval Air Reserve Training, wrote in the May, 1953, issue of *Reader's Digest:*

> It is not belittling air power to say that it can never replace sea power as the world's basic means of transportation. It is simply stating one of the economic facts of life. It costs $36 to send a ton of cargo to England by sea. The air rate may run as high as $1700 per ton. But the cost in dollars means less than the cost to the world's limited fuel reserves. It takes 30 pounds of black oil to haul a ton of freight across the Atlantic. It takes two tons of high-test gasoline to do it by air. If it were possible to organize a gigantic airlift capable of handling all our imports, we would soon devour the world's whole supply of oil.

Water has long been considered the most economical form of mass transport, though few studies have been made to support this claim. However, during World War II, the U.S. Office of Defense Transportation developed figures on the costs of moving crude petroleum per thousand ton-miles. The results were as follows: truck, $61.25; railroad,

$16.95; pipeline, $3.44; and ocean tanker, $.82. The spread between the costs of moving petroleum by land and water are striking, but the reason is evident to anyone who understands tanker operations. Because tankers are loaded and unloaded by suction, handling costs, which the ship operator usually pays and which represent a high proportion of the costs of ship operation with general cargo, are a minor item. The figures illustrate the great efficiency (and resultant savings) that can be attained from specialized shipping operations—savings that may be applied in the movement of other commodities, as will be shown later in this book.

NATURE OF THE INDUSTRY

Ocean transportation is a broad term that is often used synonymously with the *shipping industry*. The latter, we feel, is broader than the former. Academically, the general term *transportation* may refer either to the act of transporting or to the system of transportation, *i.e.*, the means of conveyance. In shipping circles, the term *transportation* has a more limited usage, for it refers only to the carriage of goods by water—the service afloat. In contrast, the term *shipping industry* embraces not only the ship afloat and her cargo but also the many shore activities that service the ship. Although the term *merchant marine* is usually defined as "commercial ships of a nation, privately or publicly owned, as distinct from the Navy," shipping men, who are the persons responsible for the operation of a nation's merchant fleet, usually use the terms *shipping industry* and *merchant marine* interchangeably.

The sole function of merchant shipping is to provide a service; it does not produce anything; it has no factory. Only recently have its salesmen been called salesmen, probably in part because salesmen have usually been occupied with selling an object that can change hands. Service, on the other hand, is something intangible. The only thing that the industry offers, and the source from which it derives its revenue, is the service of transporting goods and passengers.

We do not wish to oversimplify the shipping industry, for it is a complex assemblage of many interests and elements. Steamship companies are composed of men, ships, and piers. Paramount in importance is the human element—the men who manage the affairs of the steamship companies and the men who man the ships and shore facilities. The ships may operate in foreign trade services or on domestic coastal routes, or they may give the irregular services of tramps. Also their operations combine, in varying degrees, public and private interests, including those of the military.

Although shipbuilding has always been an art and a science, shipping management as such is a more or less recent development. Until not much more than a hundred years ago, the ship was a means to an end—a means by which the merchant-trader or the shipowner-merchant earned money. Actual ship management in terms of controlled costs, aggressive development of revenues, budgeting and long-range planning, and so forth was of secondary importance.

Today, much of the earnings in ship management and operation is derived, first, from the wise building or purchase of the ship that is best suited to the service in which she will be operated, and second, from the trading instincts of the ship's owners and operators. Perhaps one of the most outstanding lessons we can draw from history to apply to the future is this: the successful shipping company will combine skillful management with an aggressive trading instinct. The size of ships and the amount of capital invested in fleets, together with the more complete separation of ship management and commodity trading, have placed a greater premium on scientific ship management.

At times, it is difficult to see clearly the signs that illustrate this conclusive lesson. To many people, shipping has ceased to be a business and has become merely an "instrument of national policy."

Because it is a service function, shipping is a key element in a country's commercial policy as well as in the inventory of a country's military strength. As the narrow pipeline through which passes the tremendous volume of world trade, merchant shipping is a means by which a nation or a people influences the movement of the goods produced or needed by its economy. Shipping is, therefore, in peacetime, a strategic commercial asset, and in time of war or emergency, an element of combat by which the warmaking capacity of the country is applied to front-line action. Until about a hundred and fifty years ago, the functions of the merchant ship and the naval ship were considered somewhat identical, and much of the fighting done at sea was between armed merchant ships. The steamship separated the functions of shipping and defense when it created an iron and steel vessel for which the merchantman, with a few guns on her deck, was no match. Nevertheless, global warfare requires that merchant shipping be the "fourth arm" of the military services on land, sea, and air.

In this compact One World of harsh realities, merchant shipping and national security are more closely correlated than ever before. Because shipping by its very nature spans the 70 percent of the world that is covered by water, it not only provides access to sources of vital materials and to markets for products, but also the only secure means of safeguarding a major country's warmaking capacity and its ability to project that capacity to the war fronts of the world. In this sense, history proves that shipping has a dual personality—a builder of economic strength in peace and a warrior in time of emergency.

PART ONE

SHIPPING IN THE WORLD ECONOMY

CHAPTER 1

SHIPPING—SEA POWER AND NATIONAL POWER

From the time the Egyptians first took to ships about three thousand years before the birth of Christ until the age of exploration, commercial shipping was confined to the Mediterranean Sea. After an oceangoing ship was evolved, ocean transportation came into its own. If we disregard the isolated ocean voyages of the Phoenicians and the Vikings, ocean transportation is less than five centuries old.

After the astrolabe and compass appeared to help the mariner to find his way, and a seaworthy and manageable ship had evolved, there came an "era of shipping" that revolutionized not only the mental attitude but also the political, social, and economic life of all mankind. Today's fleets are the results of developments extending over thousands of years—years during which maritime strength has moved steadily westward.

THE SEA AND SHIPPING TO THE AGE OF COLUMBUS

The Egyptians, who started to trade their grain and papyrus for timber from the Lebanon about 3000 B.C., were the first people to use the open sea for commercial shipping. For two thousand years before Christ and probably longer, the Phoenicians roamed the shores of Europe, Asia, and Africa in search of the precious cargoes for their flourishing trade.

Greece. Greek maritime supremacy was based on her defeat of the Persians, the greatest power in the then-known world, and on her commerce. Three times, between 492 and 480 B.C., Persia invaded Greece in the world's first campaigns in which the control of the sea was vital. For more than a century, Greece enjoyed a period of commercial prosperity that has been compared to Great Britain's prior to World War I. At the docks of such trading cities as Piraeus, Greek ships from Pontus (the area south of the Black Sea), laden with grain and fish, moored alongside Egyptian grain ships and ships carrying mixed cargoes from the Greek trading settlement of Syracuse in Sicily. To ensure the success of his campaigns against the Persians, Alexander the Great (ruled 336–323 B.C.) liquidated a large Persian fleet, conscripted Phoenician sea power, changed the name of Naucratis ("Mistress of the Seas") to Alexandria, and converted that port into a naval base for his operations.

Rome. Historians who have dealt with the Punic Wars (264–146 B.C.) have sometimes failed to stress the part that the sea played in ultimate victory. In 265 B.C., Carthage closed the Straits of Messina between the toe of the Italian boot and Sicily to Roman trading ships. War ensued. Rome won the second Carthaginian War (218–201 B.C.) because she had secured and never lost control of the basin between Italy, Spain, and Africa. During the third war, she used her sea power to transport an army to Africa to sack and burn Carthage. As a result of these wars, a people of Western and not Eastern origin controlled the Mediterranean.

For Imperial Rome, *navigare est* ("sail we must") might very well be translated "sail or die." To encourage the trade imperative for the preservation of the empire, Rome kept the sea lanes free of pirates; built lighthouses and beacons at such places as Ostia, Boulogne, and Dover; improved ports; dredged the old Egyptian canal between the Nile and the Red Sea; and issued a book of sailing instructions. A martial, not a trading city, Rome was at one and the same time the world's greatest importer and smallest exporter. No Roman of the upper classes was permitted to engage in trade, and only noncitizens were admitted to the navy.

The Ancient Ship. In addition to the plank ship, the Egyptians are given credit for the sail (it was of use in navigating the Nile since the prevailing winds assist craft moving upstream). Improving on the Egyptian models, the Phoenicians evolved two types of ships.

The warship or galley was of shallow draft, with a long, narrow hull, built for speed and maneuverability. The Egyptian wooden snout used for ramming (ramming and boarding were the principal naval tactics for centuries) was replaced with an iron one. Since oars were more reliable than sails and speed a necessity for fighting at close quarters, oars were the main means of propulsion, although sails were used in cruising. The Phoenicians evolved the bireme, and to man bigger ships—the trireme, quatreme, and quinquireme—the Romans merely added more banks of oars. The oar-driven galley remained the world's principal fighting ship until gunpowder came in. The last important naval battle in which such craft were used was Lepanto, in 1571, in which Spain and Venice joined forces to defeat the Turks. So little change had occurred in the fighting ship between the battle of Salamis in 480 B.C. and Lepanto that a sailor who had served under Themistocles could have stepped into one of Don Juan's galleys at Lepanto.

To cope with the calms that a ship might encounter in the Red Sea, many Egyptian merchant ships had been equipped with oars as well as sails. Because oarsmen took up valuable cargo space and had to be rested,

Phoenician merchantmen took to sail, a development that made sailing at night possible. The Greeks and Romans followed Phoenician models, adding more sail as their ships increased in size. It was, however, the old Egyptian square sail increased in width, since too tall a sail was dangerous. Navigation was limited, and many ships were beached in winter. Without the aid of compasses, charts, and lighthouses, and in almost constant danger of pirates, seamen rarely ventured away from the sight of land.

Merchantmen continued to lumber before the breeze. If the wind was unfavorable, they had to wait until it changed or take to oars. Until seafaring men learned how to "beat to windward" or to "sail into the wind" by tacking (that is, to zigzag with the wind first on one bow and then on the other), they were never able to venture out into the open sea.

Medieval Trading Cities. After the fall of Rome, A.D. 476, trade was an extremely hazardous undertaking as likely to result in death at the hands of pirates as in a handsome profit. By about A.D. 1000, a number of city-states had arisen whose prosperity was based on a revival of trade—Venice, Florence, Genoa, Pisa, Marseille, and Barcelona on the Mediterranean, and the Hansa cities in northern Europe.

By far the wealthiest of these was Venice, whose traders were able to furnish the ships for the Crusades (A.D. 1095-1270). Venetian traders were thus in a position to demand commercial privileges in the reopened Syrian ports. About 1400, Venice had 3,300 ships in her merchant fleet and navy, manned by 36,000 men.[1] Venice and other trading cities opened up the old trade routes; they organized the financial institutions to finance their operations, and the later explorations and trade; they suppressed piracy; and they held in check the Moslem tide. Their decline was contemporary with the rise of the national powers, England and the Netherlands, to which the ship and commercial power were to move by way of the Iberian Peninsula.

SPAIN AND PORTUGAL

Before men could sail on long offshore ocean voyages, a new type of ship was necessary—one that could sail close-hauled and therefore make headway against an adverse wind, one sufficiently seaworthy to deal with ocean gales, and at the same time suited to running before a steady trade wind. For this, the Mediterranean ship was not suited.

The Vikings are supposed to have been able to sail close-hauled in the

[1] By this time, Venice and other Mediterranean trading cities used oar-driven galleys for commercial purposes, because freights had risen so high that the additional expense was justified.

one-masters in which they crossed the Atlantic. When trade increased and the traders of northern Europe needed a bigger vessel with more sail, they added a second mast. With this mast square-rigged, the ship lost most if not all of her ability to sail close-hauled; lateen-rigged, she was hard to steer. To achieve a balance, another mast was added in front of the mainmast (the northern Europeans had always placed the mainmast amidships or aft while the Mediterraneans placed it forward), which they square-rigged. This was the type of vessel used by Columbus, Vasco da Gama, Cabot, and Drake.

It was not by accident that the early explorers sailed in Spanish and Portuguese ships. Located on the Iberian Peninsula, these two countries stood at a crossroads between the learning of the Mediterranean and the practical knowledge of northern Europe. The Renaissance had stimulated interest in astronomy, navigation, and map making; the compass had come into general use about 1300; and travelers such as Marco Polo, a Genoese merchant who had been "detained" at the court of Kublai Khan from A.D. 1276 to 1292, had stimulated interest in the Orient. Furthermore, European traders and merchants were straining under the Italian-Arabian monopoly of trade, with its countless middlemen ready and able to exact their fees and thereby add to the cost of goods imported into Europe. On precious cargoes such as spices, freights were so high that the commodities were twice as expensive in Flanders as in Venice.

By the early 1500's, Spain and Portugal were recognized as the maritime powers of the world, but neither was fitted to exploit its position. Little more than a century after Vasco da Gama had visited the Spice Islands and "Calicut" to establish Portugal's claims there, that nation was unable to defend her sea lanes against the energetic Dutch. Since Portugal and Spain were rolled into one under a Spanish king from 1580 to 1640, she shared also in Spain's downward commercial path.

A feudal state, Spain had little on which to build an overseas commerce. During the Inquisition, she had liquidated her most productive agricultural workers, she had little industry and a negligible merchant class, and her explorers were gentlemen adventurers, not traders. The Spanish were forced to pour out their treasure from America—to the English and Dutch for goods and services that they should have been producing at home, to German and Italian bankers from whom their kings borrowed money continually, and to mercenaries who waged their ceaseless wars.

From 1516 to 1556, Spain was a part of the realm of the Hapsburg Emperor Charles, whose noncontiguous dominions, including the Spanish Netherlands (our Benelux countries), Austria, and holdings in Italy, had to be held together by force. Both Charles and his son Philip (1556–1598) waged ceaseless wars with France over the control of Italy, with the Moslems over the control of the Mediterranean, and with Protestant

Europe, for each considered himself the commander-in-chief of the Counter Reformation. When Philip, who was supposed to have been as rich as Croesus, died, there was not enough in the royal treasury to meet the immediate needs of the royal household. Spain's government had "depended for its support, not upon a wide-spread healthy commerce and industry that could survive many a staggering blow, but upon a narrow stream of silver trickling through a few treasure-ships from America, easily and frequently intercepted by an enemy's cruisers."[2] In the hands of two impertinent young upstarts to the north, the Dutch and the English, commerce was being made of sturdier stuff.

GROWTH OF DUTCH, ENGLISH, AND FRENCH TRADE, 1500 TO 1800

Tudor England. While the Spanish were trafficking in bullion and the Portuguese trying to keep their spice trade routes secret, the English, under a Tudor monarchy, were evolving a policy that was to serve as the germ of their later commercial success. According to his first biographer, Sir Francis Bacon, Henry VII (1485–1509) "could not endure to see trade sick." English trade at the time was indeed sick, for England had few seamen and fewer ships, her tiny craft were inferior to the galleys and carracks of Genoa and Venice, and most of her waterborne trade was carried in the hulks of the Hanseatic trading cities. Henry displayed "a grasp of commerce, finance, and the principles of economic power such as no European sovereign had evinced before"[3] and few for centuries thereafter. He passed navigation laws favoring English vessels; strengthened the Royal Navy by building the *Regent* and *Sovereign*, two of the most powerful ships afloat, and by establishing a naval dock at Portsmouth; and promulgated commercial treaties with the Hanseatic cities, the Dutch, and the Spanish. Under Henry, and backed more by his ubiquitous diplomacy than his navy, English ships began trade over their first long route—through "Juberaltar" to Cyprus and Alexandria.

After the early explorations, all overseas trade was to be controlled, so the Spanish and Portuguese thought, by various papal edicts of the 1490's, which had divided all heathen lands discovered and still to be discovered between Spain and Portugal. In other words, the whole non-European world was prescribed as Spanish and Portuguese property with no consideration of the rights and claims of other nations.

Although he was a religious man and friendly to Spain, Henry VII

---

[2] A. T. Mahan, *The Influence of Sea Power upon History, 1660–1783*, 25th ed., Little, Brown & Company, Boston, 1918, pp. 41–42.

[3] J. A. Williamson, *The Evolution of England*, 2d ed., Oxford University Press, New York, 1944, p. 164. This chapter is much indebted to this and other studies by Williamson.

never accepted this; and he laid down the doctrine of effective occupation, which has since become a part of international law. In accord with his principle that he would respect the rights of others only to lands actually in their possession, he stayed out of Spanish territory and sent John Cabot over the western ocean to open up a new and northern route for the spice trade. Cabot found "New Found Land" instead.

Under Henry's successors, who were not bound by ties of religion and alliances, English adventurer-mariners such as Sir John Hawkins attempted to engage in legitimate trade with the West Indies. When their efforts led to accusations of smuggling and piracy and at times to capture and imprisonment, English navigators turned to plundering. Sir Francis Drake's round-the-world voyage of 1577 to 1580 was probably undertaken at Elizabeth's behest to search for a new route to the Far East, and the plundering was his own unauthorized contribution to the plan. By the 1570's, relations between England and Spain had deteriorated, and in 1585, the war broke out that is remembered mainly for the English defeat of the Spanish Armada.

The reign of Elizabeth (1558–1603) was characterized by commercial activity and explorations. In 1553, Sir Hugh Willoughby had lost his life searching for a northeast passage to India via the cold Murman Coast, but his second in command arrived in Moscow, where he made the treaty with Czar Ivan the Terrible that led to the valuable trade of the British Muscovy Company. The best known of the many trading companies formed under Elizabeth was the British East India Company, and its first expedition was on the way home when she died in 1603. This company brought in larger profits on greater amounts of capital than any other trade in which the English had previously engaged. In America, English ships were prying into every coast on the Atlantic seeking in all its quarters for a northwest passage.[4] Men had some time earlier become convinced that America was a barrier that must be sailed around to get to Asia. They wanted to break the Portuguese-Spanish monopoly of the Cape of Good Hope route and to find a shorter way to India and Cathay —unknown places that took unto themselves the whole mystery of Shangri-La with great cities, emperors, and rare wealth added. This was the driving force that sent out dozens of English expeditions, headed by such famous names as Sebastian Cabot, Frobisher, Davis, Baffin, Gilbert, and Hudson.

England was not really a commercially independent country until 1598, when Elizabeth canceled the special privileges of the Hanseatic traders and closed up their great London warehouses of the Steelyard.

[4] The Northwest Passage was not established until 1845, when ships sent out to rescue Sir John Franklin passed through the labyrinth of the Arctic Archipelago to meet in Viscount Melville Sound.

The commercial power of Europe, however, was not England, but Holland, a tiny nation whose people generations earlier had wrested their country from the sea.

Dutch Commercial Supremacy, 1600 to 1660. If the English were drawn to the sea, the Dutch were driven to it, for the land could not produce enough to support their population. Nonetheless, they took to it with zest, for they were then the world's best fighters, navigators, and traders. They could build ships more cheaply and sail them better than any other people in Europe. As the seaboard outlets for the commerce of central Europe's river system, Dutch ports had long carried on a thriving shipping business in that day of negligible land transport. Their country was strategically located between the Baltic with its timber, wheat, and naval stores and the Iberian Peninsula, where their ships called at Lisbon for Portuguese spices to be redistributed throughout Europe. By 1550, the Dutch were monopolizing Europe's coasting trade, and their wealth made Amsterdam, Leiden, Rotterdam, Bruges, and Lille the envy of all Europe. They had inherited the waterborne commerce of the declining Hanseatic cities, and having perfected a method of preserving fish, they made their herring industry the cornerstone of a flourishing commerce with the Catholic Mediterranean.

By the opening of the seventeenth century, Dutch merchant-traders were ready to enter the deep-water trades to Asia and to America. There was no effective force to stop them. Between 1568 and 1580, they had defeated one of Spain's best generals, the Duke of Alva, and had wrung their freedom from King Philip of Spain. In 1595, when Philip seized between 400 and 500 Dutch ships then in Spanish and Portuguese ports, they acted quickly; their first expedition to the Far East left later that year. To eliminate the destructive competition that developed among various trading groups, the States-General chartered the Dutch East India Company in 1602. It was enormously successful: between 1607 and 1620, earnings of investors were between 80 and 250 percent annually.

By about 1610, the Dutch fishing and trading fleet is said to have numbered over 16,000 sail of more than 910,000 tons and to have offered employment to 158,000 crewmen. The Dutch West Indies Company, formed to trade in the Caribbean, alone controlled 800 ships. Dutch ships were soon trading over all the seas, legally and illegally, smuggling and slaving. In 1628, they captured an entire silver fleet returning from New Spain, and the bells of Amsterdam rang out in celebration. A French biographer of Jan De Witt, a Dutch statesman who died in 1672, reported that their herring industry produced 350,000 tons of salt fish annually and supported one-fifth of the population, that their trade with the Far East reached a value of 16 million francs annually, that their "importation" trade ran to 36 million francs annually, and that the total value of merchandise shipped in Dutch bottoms amounted to over one billion francs a year.

In the hands of these new entrepreneurs of world commerce, thrifty burghers of the rising middle class, waterborne trade began to come into its own. Whereas earlier traders such as the wealthy and aristocratic Italian merchant-shipowners, the Spanish, and the Portuguese had been content to deal primarily in exotic, high-value merchandise, the practical Dutch did not scorn traffic in lowly goods. A little pepper went a long way, one cargo of gold represented great value, but hundreds of shiploads were required to carry the wheat, timber, hemp, fish, wax, tar, leather, and iron that the Dutch transported. They appear to have recognized that no one segment of their maritime enterprise was self-sufficient. Even after their overseas trade had developed to a considerable volume and value, they did not neglect their coasting trade or fisheries industry. From the very nature of their commerce, it is evident that the Dutch concept of trade embodied ideas that are today looked upon as modern: that trade must benefit more than the rich and the powerful, that it must be a two-way affair, and that the carrier performs a service.

By about 1650, Holland occupied a shipping position in many respects analogous to that of Great Britain just before World War I. Her prosperity depended primarily on the ownership of the world's largest merchant fleet and a virtual monopoly of the world's carrying trade. But the Dutch, unlike the British of a later date who shipped coal and manufactured goods, had little of their own to export. In the face of a growing world commerce and effective competition, it was inevitable that Holland should not be able to continue her monopoly of the world's shipping.

The English-Dutch Trade Wars. During most of Elizabeth's reign, Holland and England had been allied against Spain; whenever the Dutch lagged in their fight for freedom, Elizabeth lent a helping hand. Throughout history England has repeatedly expended her strength to keep the Low Countries free. But, between 1652 and 1674, England went to war with Holland three times. This reversal of the traditional policy resulted from clashes over colonies and trade.

Although Sir Walter Raleigh had shown keen recognition of the worth of colonies in North America, the average Englishman could see little of commercial value there except the fisheries in Newfoundland. As everyone knows, the first permanent English colonies in the New World were settled during the early seventeenth century; and by the late 1640's, some of those colonies, particularly the plantations in the West Indies, were producing for export. But the British did little to service these colonies. In that day of smuggling, piracy, and armed merchantmen, King Charles sent not a single man-of-war across the Atlantic during his entire reign (1625–1649). Less energetic people than the Dutch would have seized the opportunity, and Dutch merchantmen almost completely monopolized the trade of such British-settled islands as Barbados, Antigua, and St. Kitts and of the southern colonies in North America, buying their sugar and tobacco and selling them slaves. It almost seemed, so the English complained, that they had established colonies so that the Dutch could grow rich on their trade.

Commonwealth statesmen set out to change the situation when they passed the Navigation Act of 1651, which required that goods produced in their colonies be shipped in British ships. War followed in 1652. Because the parsimonious Dutch burghers had failed to provide themselves with a navy adequate to protect their far-flung merchant fleets, Cromwell's powerful ships-of-the-line were able to blockade the coast of Holland. Grass grew in the streets of Amsterdam; the Zuider Zee was a forest of masts. In the peace of 1654, the Dutch acknowledged the right of England to control her own trade and colonies. English military might at sea had proved the stronger, but Dutch commerce remained almost intact. During the war, the English had taken as prizes of war some 1,500 merchant ships, probably double the British merchant fleet at the beginning of the war. Estimates of the Dutch fleet at this date vary. One source gives 10,000 ships about 1660, but, of course, these vessels were much larger than those of about 1610.

With the peace, the Dutch continued to trade and to trade with British plantation owners, who were ready and willing to accept their services because Dutch ships operated much more cheaply than English ships. Clashes occurred between English and Dutch traders in the Indies, both East and West. The war that broke out in 1664 was England's first colonial war, but it soon spread to Europe. This was a commercial war, pure and simple, although it was supported by King Charles of England, who hated the Dutch, their energy and enterprise, and their democracy. Holland's navy was in much better shape than it had been in 1654. The fighting was indecisive though bitter; in the peace of 1667, the honors were divided. The English acquired New Amsterdam, which they renamed New York, but gave up Surinam in New Guiana. In the Far East, the Dutch agreed to confine their trade to the islands, leaving India to the English.

The third war was caused by European politics, for Charles and Louis XIV of France plotted Holland's destruction. When the French invaded and the Dutch as a last resort opened their dikes to create a barrier between the enemy's armies and their cities, British sympathies turned, and Charles was forced to conclude the war. Within a short time, England and Holland were in an alliance designed to check France. England furnished sea forces and some 40,000 troops, while Holland was committed to maintain an army of 120,000 men. Holland's secondary position as a sea power was determined, not on the high seas, but on the battlefields of Europe.

Early French Commerce. France was rather a late arrival in the world of commercial shipping. Quebec was settled in 1608, and Richelieu, who was the real ruler of France from 1624 to 1642, adopted a decisive commercial policy. He encouraged shipping and founded the famed Company of One Hundred Associates to compete with the British and Dutch in America and also trading companies to settle islands in the West Indies. However, his maritime objective was soon overshadowed by one that he regarded as far more important—to break the power of the Austrian Hapsburgs. At his death, France was the supreme power on the Continent, and the king's power was absolute in France. Succeeding Bourbon monarchs had it within their power to develop France as a maritime nation.

Soon after Louis XIV started his regime in 1660, his financial minister Colbert promulgated a policy embodying three means of strengthening France as a commercial and maritime power: (1) increased production both agricultural and industrial, (2) shipping both merchant and navy, and (3) markets and colonies, which were identical because of the navigation laws of the day. A French East India Company was organized as well as a West India Company. The merchant fleet was expanded far beyond anything France had ever owned previously, and the navy increased to exceed Britain's in size. Colbert's efforts had just begun to be felt when Louis, embarking on a policy aimed at continental expansion at the expense of his neighbors, invaded the Spanish Netherlands in 1667. From that year until his death in 1715, France was almost continually at war. Hostilities not only swallowed up the resources of the country but were doubly injurious, because they left France's commerce and colonies defenseless. After 1667, no great French merchant fleet put to sea during Louis's reign.

Eighteenth-century Commerce. When the War of the Spanish Succession started in 1701, England was one of the sea powers. When peace came in 1713, she was recognized as *the* power on the seas. England's commercial growth, however, was steady and plodding, practically lacking in the spectacular achievement of the Dutch between 1600 and 1660 and the glamour and dash of the days of Sir Francis Drake. Statistics of that day are notable for their incompleteness, and the few that are available cannot be accorded the credence of modern efforts. However, they can be trusted to give a general indication of the growth of trade.

Even during the war of 1701 to 1713, British trade flourished. More than 3,550 ships, most of them English, cleared English ports in 1710, while in 1713 clearances had risen to 5,800. By this time the population of Britain's overseas colonies was doubling every twenty years, and her trade grew in proportion. In 1698, trade with the colonies is estimated to have been worth 1.7 million pounds (contemporary value), or 15 percent of her total trade. By 1775, the value of colonial trade had risen to 9.5 million pounds, to represent 33 percent of the total. Furthermore, colonial goods furnished a large share of the cargoes reexported to other European countries, particularly the Baltic and Mediterranean areas. That the colonies had developed into important markets for English exports is evident from the accompanying figures for value of shipments in contemporary pounds sterling. Although English trade with India was con-

Colony	Value of exports	Colony	Value of exports
Jamaica	£467,133	Carolina	£244,093
Virginia and Maryland	437,628	Barbados	145,083
New York	417,957	Antigua	119,740
New England	406,081	St. Christopher	106,162
Pennsylvania	371,830		

siderable, figures were not included since India was not a colony. In 1682, imports of cotton cloth from Surat alone had amounted to over 1.4 million pieces, and the competition offered the English textile industries led to restrictions of the cotton trade.

The only country that could offer England effective commercial competition was France; Dutch commerce had passed its zenith, and the Spanish *flotas*, or annual fleets, were becoming smaller and smaller. From about 1660 to 1815, French commerce fluctuated in accordance with the whims of her monarchs and the vicissitudes of almost continual warfare, and we cannot follow its ups and downs. In 1715, in reflection of Louis XIV's policies, her total commerce is estimated at a value of 72 million dollars (1940 dollars). In 1785, French commerce is estimated at roughly 330 million dollars, in comparison with England's 265 million dollars. The explanation is mainly threefold: France's population was three times that of England; France held Martinique, Guadaloupe, and St. Domingo, the best sugar islands in the West Indies; and commercial wealth then lay in the tropics. British trade had undoubtedly expanded more consistently throughout the century than had French. Owing to popular demand after the wreck of the colonial empire in the Seven Years' War which ended in 1763, the French navy and merchant marine had been rebuilt, and both were at a peak of efficiency during the 1780's, while British trade still suffered from the effects of the Revolutionary War.

THE STRUGGLE FOR ASIA AND AMERICA

In 1650, England's overseas possessions consisted of a strip on the Atlantic seaboard of North America, secured by the effective occupation of the three colonies of Massachusetts, Maryland, and Virginia; islands in the West Indies, of which Barbados, Antigua, and St. Kitts were the most important; and scattered factories or trading posts in the Far East at such places as Surat, in India. These were dwarfed by the overseas holdings of Spain, France, and Holland. At the close of the Napoleonic Wars in 1815, although the British had lost possession of their 13 colonies, their overseas empire had increased to include Canada and Jamaica in America; Gibraltar, Minorca, and Malta in the Mediterranean; Cape Colony in Africa; and all of India, Australia, and New Zealand. These were British prizes in the struggle for the control of Asia and America, a struggle in which the main contestants were the English and French, with the Dutch and Spanish as junior partners.

The Caribbean. The contest opened early in the Caribbean. During the French-Spanish wars over the control of Italy, from about 1520 on, the French attacked the Spanish again and again, sacking the West Indies from one end to the other. After 1570, French seamen were mainly Huguenots, and the fighting became more fierce. After about 1610, the struggle took on a different aspect, for the English, Dutch, and French were all engaged in an island-snatching contest, in which they took from Spain or from each other territories that were not firmly held. If the peace that Cromwell made with the Dutch in 1654 appears soft, there were reasons. Cromwell was preparing to send an expedition into the Spanish West Indies, where the English later took and held Jamaica. As a Puritan, he felt it his duty to strike at England's ancient enemy, Spain; if he had used foresight, he would have realized that leadership in Europe had passed to France.

French-English Wars, 1701 to 1815. In 1701, when England's exiled King James died in Saint-Germain, Louis XIV publicly recognized his son the Pretender as King of England. He meant this only as a polite form, but for the English, who had already had enough of Louis's effrontery, it added the touch of sentiment necessary to consolidate material interests. By then, the English hated and feared Louis XIV's France and everything it stood for: Louis's expansionist ambitions; a Catholicism that owed no more allegiance to Rome than had Henry VIII and that used priestcraft as an engine of rule; and Colbert's pronouncements, which took ideas that the British themselves held on commerce and enunciated them as mathematical propositions to be enforced "to the last detail with the authority that absolute power alone can confer."[5] Anglican England, which had within less than one hundred and fifty years beheaded one king and exiled another, was then ruled by a king who held power not by "divine right" but because Parliament had placed him on the throne. More free than any other people in the world, they were ready to fight for their trade.

[5] Williamson, *op. cit.*, p. 273.

In 1701, the conflict known as the War of the Spanish Succession was brewing. The King of Spain had died, and Louis sent his grandson, who had been bequeathed the throne, to Madrid to assume rule of Spain. For Britain, the issues were clearly drawn. In Spanish hands, the Spanish Netherlands with its splendid port of Antwerp on the Schlecht was no threat to London; Minorca and Gibraltar harbored nothing except innocuous Spanish warships; and the colonies in Central and South America slumbered. Place these in the hands of competent and disciplined Frenchmen, and the situation would be far different. Hence, England fought with Austria, Holland, and Prussia against France and Spain in a war that lasted from 1701 to 1713 and extended from the Mediterranean to northern Europe and into the Americas. At the Peace of Utrecht, England retained possession of Minorca and Gibraltar, both of which she had seized during hostilities, and France conceded her interests in Nova Scotia, Newfoundland, and the Hudson Bay territories.

The Anglo-French struggle for India started in the 1740's. The French East India Company, founded by Colbert, had undergone several reorganizations. By the 1730's, it was flourishing, with Pondichéry as the base for a trade extending into Siam and China. The struggle, in which Clive became a national hero, went on until 1754, ending with the British stronger and the French weaker than at the outset. The future of India was decided in the Seven Years' War, which began officially in 1756. Since incidents had occurred in all overseas theaters for several decades, this date means little except a drift to more intense hostilities.

As far as Great Britain and France are concerned, the Seven Years' War was a struggle for sea power and colonial empire in America, the West Indies, West Africa, and India; and the struggle was world-wide. The French at sea were woefully inadequate. As a result, British trade actually increased during the war under the shield of naval supremacy, and the British took such far-flung posts as Florida, Havana in Cuba, and Manila in the Philippines. At the peace, Britain kept Canada and Florida and all territory east of the Mississippi, returning to Spain her islands and to France the best of her sugar colonies. The French influence in India was restricted in that they could trade but were not permitted any political organization.

To say that "Napoleon's power ended at the shore" is an oversimplification, for Mahan has written a two-volume study of sea power during this period in French history. After Trafalgar, the battle in which Lord Nelson lost his life but succeeded in crushing two-thirds of Napoleon's fleet before the other third could come into action, the British controlled the sea, and their control was never challenged. In this, as in other wars of the century, Britain furnished the naval strength. At the close of the war, the British retained islands and territories that they had occupied during the war, including Cape Colony in South Africa, Ceylon, Malta, and Helgoland—all important as outposts of empire for a nation that was soon to need a world-wide network of coaling stations.

The American Revolution. England's only serious setback during the period 1660 to 1815 was the loss of the 13 colonies in America. As everyone knows, the overt cause of the war was George III's insistence on his right to tax American trade. But the real issue was deeper: the colonies had become a nation, and no nation can consent to be governed from without. Hardly a man in England understood that the crux of the matter was a new sense of nationality, and certainly the colonists did not, for they were "hot for their rights as Englishmen."

From the viewpoint of British sea power, the war was indeed stupid. At the time the colonies had over 2 million people as opposed to about 7.5 million in the British Isles. Given that population, the extent of their territory, coupled with the distance from England, there was little hope of holding them by force if any powerful nations were willing to help. Spain, smarting under the loss of Jamaica and Gibraltar, and France, smarting under the war of 1756 to 1763 and the loss of Canada, were certain to strike their ancient enemy sooner or later. England had won the Seven Years' War without the aid of an important Continental ally, but she had done so with the help of her colonies, and between 25 and 30 percent of the ships under the British flag were owned in her North American colonies. Without detracting from Bunker Hill, Valley Forge, and Yorktown, it is evident that Spanish and French sea power helped to decide American freedom. Three times after 1779, their combined fleets sailed into the English Channel, once in the force of 66 ships-of-the-line, to send the British fleet scurrying to cover of home ports like rabbits. The French fleet, revived from its low ebb of 1756 to 1763, was at a high peak of efficiency, and a large force came to America under command of the Comte de Grasse. The 13 colonies gained their freedom, so Mahan points out, because the British fleet was not equal to the task placed upon it.

AMERICAN TRADE TO THE CIVIL WAR

Although the Revolutionary War had virtually eliminated the merchant fleet of the 13 colonies, the new country started life with a very important maritime asset—a shipbuilding industry that consisted of hundreds of small yards dotting the coast from Maine to Georgia, manned by skilled craftsmen and backed up by the most abundant and easily accessible supplies of shipbuilding timber in the world. Colonial shipbuilders had been furnishing not only colonial-owned tonnage but also

English tonnage. Out of a total of 600,000 gross tons of British-owned tonnage in the 1770's, 210,000 tons had been constructed in the colonies, most of it in North America.

Soon after the war was over, an American merchant fleet was again at sea. The years from 1800 to 1840 have been called the "most glorious period in American maritime history." Throughout these four decades, American ships carried 90 percent or more of the country's imports and exports. During the next two decades, American-owned bottoms carried a decreasing proportion of the nation's trade, but in 1860, only two countries, Great Britain and the United States, owned large merchant marines. Britain's fleet of 5.7 million gross tons was slightly larger than the American fleet of 5.3 million tons, but the greater speed and carrying capacity of American ships more than compensated for the difference in tonnage.

American-built Ships. In 1791, Tench Coxe wrote that the best double-decked American ships could be produced for about $34 per ton, while such a vessel could not be purchased in Great Britain, France, or Holland for under $55 to $60 per ton. The only vessels that could compete on a cost basis with American ships were those constructed in such places as Hamburg, Bremen, Lübeck, and Danzig, which had easy access to Baltic lumber. As late as the 1840's, when shipbuilding costs in the United States had risen far above their earlier levels, British shipowners testified at Parliamentary hearings that, because of the capital charges on high-cost British-built vessels, they could not compete in the North Atlantic with the flash packets of the American Black Ball, Swallow Tail, and Red Star lines. Costs, however, were not the only factor, for American shipbuilders had built ships that could "go" with such speed that they could cross the Atlantic in little more than half the time taken by British vessels. To speed was added prestige. At the Liverpool docks, an Englishman named W. N. Blane wrote in 1824, a man "will see the American ships, long, sharp built, beautifully painted and rigged, and remarkable for their appearance and white canvas. He will see the English vessels, short, round and dirty, resembling great black tubs."[6]

The packets were not the only superior American ships. During the first half of the nineteenth century, American shipbuilders contributed as much to the development of the sailing ship as other countries had in three centuries. Noteworthy changes in rig, design, carrying capacity, and handling of vessels occurred between 1815 and 1850. American builders took the fore-and-aft rig, for which the Dutch were probably responsible, and built a vessel of sharp hull lines called the schooner.

---

[6] Quoted from S. E. Morison, *The Growth of the American Republic*, 3d ed., Oxford University Press, New York, 1942, Vol. 1, p. 499. This section is also indebted to Morison's *Maritime History of Massachusetts, 1783–1860* (Houghton Mifflin Company, Boston, 1921) and to J. G. B. Hutchins, *The American Maritime Industries and Public Policy, 1789–1914* (Harvard University Press, Cambridge, Mass., 1941).

This rig, which has been the favored one for cruising yachts, was particularly adaptable for their coasting trade.

The greatest improvements, however, were in square-riggers. Morison tells of a shipmaster, retired in 1819, who took passage in 1834 on a Boston-built vessel. He was astonished at her ability to carry sail, to beat to windward, and to "tack in a pint o'water." Medford builders had evolved a ship of 450 tons, which, handled by 18 officers and men, could carry half as much freight as a 1,500-ton British East Indiaman with a crew of 125, and could sail half again as fast. Elsewhere we tell of the cotton freighters that doubled the carrying capacity of earlier carriers ton for ton. The sailing ship reached a peak of perfection in the American clipper.

This new type of sailing vessel—characterized by great length in proportion to breadth of beam, an enormous sail area, and long concave bows ending in a gracefully curved cutwater—had been devised for the China–New York tea trade. The voyage of the *Sea Witch* [to San Francisco in 1850] showed its possibilities. Her record was broken by the *Surprise* within a year, and in 1851, the *Flying Cloud* made 'Frisco in eighty-nine days from New York, a record never surpassed. As California then afforded no return cargo save gold dust (the export of wheat began only in 1855), the Yankee clippers proceeded in ballast to the China treaty ports, where they came into competition with the British marine; and the result was more impressive than the victory of the yacht *America*. Crack East-Indiamen humbly waited for a cargo weeks on end, while one American clipper after another sailed off with a cargo of tea at double the ordinary freights. When the *Oriental* of New York appeared at London, ninety-seven days from Hong-Kong, crowds thronged the West India docks to admire her beautiful hull, lofty rig, and patent fittings; the Admiralty took off her lines in dry dock, and the *Times* came out with a leader challenging British shipbuilders to set their "long practised skill, steady industry and dogged determination" against the "youth, ingenuity and ardour" of the United States.[7]

The British answer was the British-built clippers *Stornoway* and *Chrysolite*, but, by the time they were built, Donald McKay had launched his *Sovereign of the Seas*, the largest merchant ship yet built. After gold was discovered in Australia in 1853, McKay built four clippers for the Australian Black Ball Line. One of the reasons for repeal of the British Navigation Acts was that British shipowners wished to employ superior American ships.

Trading. During the period from 1789 to the Civil War, American trade did not develop evenly, but nevertheless it expanded rapidly enough to furnish employment to a fleet second in size only to that of Great Britain. European countries relaxed their navigation laws in favor of American-flag ships (usually in reciprocal arrangements for similar

---

[7] Morison, *The Growth of the American Republic*, Vol. 1, pp. 615–616.

privileges in American ports); peculiarities in those navigation laws made certain commerce available for American bottoms; and on many routes, international competition was not an important factor. Because American shipping enjoyed low construction costs and reasonable operating costs, shipowners could offer superior service at lower rates. Moreover, they prosecuted their business with vigor and energy, and maintained well-established trading connections. Although it should be remembered that foreign trade was then triangular, American ships traded in six broad groupings: Europe, South America, the West Indies, the Mediterranean, the Baltic, and the Far East.

From 1817 on, the direct carrying trade between England and the United States was on the same level of competition as far as the laws of the two countries were concerned, and, as will be shown later, the cotton trade gave American-flag ships a most decided advantage. Brazilian ports were opened to foreign ships in 1808, and the revolutions that started in 1810 made the carrying trade of South America available to fast American ships. The West Indies trade, extremely important as the third point on the triangular European-American trade, was opened gradually. By 1830, United States ships had entry to all European possessions there. New England merchantmen used southern cotton, rice, and tobacco; sugar and molasses from the West Indies; coffee from Brazil; and wool, hair, hides, sheepskins, and tallow from the River Plate area as the cornerstones of a flourishing three-cornered trade between Boston, South America, and Continental Europe and the British Isles.

The China trade had been opened in 1784 with the *Empress of China*, a "commodious and elegant ship" of 360 tons. The heyday of the East Indiamen was from 1792 to 1800. By the latter date, those ships had made Salem, Massachusetts, one of the wealthiest towns in the world for its size. In the Oriental trade, American ships were second only to the British, and a large share of the cargoes were for reexport. Because American shipowners could supply the Baltic cities with Indian shawls and Chinese silks, and because they could supply Russian and Swedish merchants with sugar and other West Indian products, American shipping occupied a dominant position in the Baltic. Around 1809, when Napoleon had closed the ports of western Europe to all neutral vessels, 200 American ships were trading with Russia. In 1840, 64 New England vessels visited St. Petersburg, which imported much of its Far Eastern goods via Boston. During that era of tramping, trading, and reexporting, American trader-shipowners were important in world commerce. American shipping declined when those trading techniques became anachronisms and when the steamship replaced the sailing vessel.[8]

[8] For a discussion of the decline of the American merchant marine after the Civil War, see Ineffective Aid to World War I in Chap. 13.

RISE OF BRITISH COMMERCIAL SUPREMACY

Although Britain had been recognized as the world's sea power since about 1715, her trade at the close of the Napoleonic Wars was still confined primarily to a limited number of shipping lanes over which commodities moved in limited quantities, mainly to the British Isles or British possessions. Between 1815 and 1850, the British took steps to furnish the commercial leadership that was to make the empire supreme in overseas trade for approximately a century.[9]

Freedom to Trade. British shipowners, who were anxious to keep their ships moving and earning, had become convinced that the protection afforded them under the Navigation Acts made it difficult to man the ships. They were also convinced that protection raised freight rates, thereby restricting trade. They were joined by industrialists who pointed out that free trade was absolutely necessary for an island kingdom that imported a large share of its foodstuffs and raw materials from overseas. Consequently, in 1849, the British opened their ports to the ships of all nations that granted British ships similar rights.

The next step was to revise tariffs downward. In 1823, England had in effect over 1,500 customs laws. During the 1820's, duties were lowered on a number of manufactured articles and raw materials, among them metals, wool, silk, and timber. But when the British tried to export their manufactured goods, European countries countered by saying that as long as the corn laws were in force, prohibiting the flow of wheat from the Continent to the British Isles, they had no means of paying for larger British exports. The real break occurred in 1846, when the tariff on wheat was revised downward on a sliding scale. After 1869, it entered the British Isles duty free, and the British adhered to their policy of free wheat until 1932, when the Wheat Act implemented empire preference. So fundamental to the British customs system and trade policy was free wheat that duties on other basic commodities were also removed. Other countries followed the British lead, and, though no European country felt that it could adopt a free-trade policy during the process of industrial development, international trade was more nearly free from 1850 to World War I than ever before or since.

An International Credit System. One of the reasons why Britain was so interested in free trade and the growth of world commerce was that she had become a creditor nation. When Alexander Hamilton sought a loan abroad for the United States, he turned to the Netherlands, the only nation at that time from which loans could be obtained. By 1815, the financial capital of the world was London, not Amsterdam. Since the

[9] This section is much indebted to J. B. Condliffe, *The Commerce of Nations*, W. W. Norton & Company, Inc., New York, 1950.

days of the Commonwealth, the British had been steadily accumulating capital from trade. Increased agricultural production, trafficking in loans with the home government, and marine insurance added to British capital. Because capital chooses to operate from a safe place, such enterprising and international financiers as Alexander Baring and Nathan Rothschild had been attracted to London during the wars. These immigrants were of considerable value in mobilizing Britain's increasing capital resources. The Barings floated loans to pay French reparations and occupation costs at the close of the wars, and the Rothschilds financed the acquisition of the Suez Canal for Britain.

To purchase increasing amounts of equipment and larger and varied amounts of supplies of raw materials and to pay for the services of foreign experts and technicians, newly settled and developing areas needed foreign loans and ownership investments by foreign capitalists. During the century 1815 to 1914, millions of British pounds were loaned abroad to promote land settlement; to develop mining; and to build railroads, factories, public utilities, roads, canals, and docks. Sooner or later, these credit transactions were translated into movements of goods between countries, and, as the principal source of supply for manufactured goods and the world's carrier, Britain benefited.

Hence, a large share of international business was transacted in sterling, to the further benefit of London. As the world's leading money market, the city early developed facilities for short-term international loans for clearing payments on international transactions—both functions necessary to the system of multilateral trade. At London, the money of every nation of the world could be made the basis of credit, and the foundations were laid for the discount market where bills of exchange from the whole trading world were dealt with so as to provide a revolving fund that enabled world trade to be financed on an expanding basis.

The Market and Surpluses. By 1800, the Industrial Revolution was well under way in the British Isles, and from the very beginning of the industrial era, Britain needed certain imports. Her industrial development was founded on abundant supplies of cheap coal, good coke, and iron ore; on a large and efficient body of laborers; and on large numbers of skilled artisans. To produce the machines, engines, locomotives, and steamships that the British manufactured at relatively low cost, the heavy industries imported high-grade ores from Sweden to mix with their low-grade ores. The wool-textile industry early outstripped domestic supplies, and its growth depended on imports. The entire cotton industry of Lancashire was developed because supplies of cotton were available, chiefly from the United States.

Over the years, the only basic commodity in which the British have been self-sufficient is coal. All of her cotton and petroleum are now and have always been imported from overseas. By the 1930's, nine-tenths of the wool and timber and one-third of the iron ores used by British industry arrived by ship. Ships also brought to the United Kingdom four-fifths of her wheat, two-fifths of her meat, and all of her rice, tea, coffee, bananas, and citrus fruits.

The basic foodstuffs to feed Europe's industrial workers and the raw materials for the factories came primarily from the United States, Canada, Argentina, Australia, and New Zealand. These countries were, for the most part, closely tied to Britain economically, culturally, and politically. The largest stream of overseas trade was fed into world commerce not by the regions of colonial exploitation but from areas of settled government and efficient economic production. Trade with Europe developed these areas, for agricultural exports provided an excellent way of paying interest on and eventually amortizing debts to Europe.

Peace and Security. Peace and security are great promoters of commerce among nations and also of the productivity which makes that commerce possible. Between 1815 and 1914, the English people were not engaged in any great war. Both the Crimean and Boer wars were localized conflicts in which hostilities were far removed from the British Isles. Free of the fear of invasion, the British devoted themselves to social, economic, and political changes and reforms in which they far surpassed the rest of the world. In 1815, no country in Europe was in a position to work out such reforms.

At the conference table where the peace of 1815 was formulated, the geographical boundaries of three European countries were extended in recognition of their part in helping to defeat Napoleon—Russia, Prussia, and Austria-Hungary. None of these was then even a minor influence on the sea, though the way was prepared for Prussia later to force her will on surrounding Germanic provinces, to seize France's Alsace-Lorraine district, and as Imperial Germany to challenge Britain's mastery of the sea. France was left an empire with minor adjustments of her boundaries to reduce them in general to pre-Napoleonic dimensions, and her sugar islands of Martinique and Guadeloupe, Pondichéry, and the old French factories were restored to her.

Lying between or around these powers or potential powers of Russia, Germany, Austria-Hungary, and France were the small countries of Europe. Because Castlereagh, whose voice was the deciding one on British policy, thought a strong Dutch kingdom would be a bulwark against French ambitions, the Kingdom of the Netherlands was created to include Belgium, and to the Dutch were restored their rich islands in the Far East and Surinam and a few West Indies islands in America. Denmark, Sweden, and Norway were free, though Norway was joined to

Sweden in a voluntary union. To the south, Italy remained as she had been since the end of the Roman Empire—a country disunited.

To complete the trading map of the world in 1815, Africa was the Dark Continent, as yet little noticed by the countries of Europe except as a source for slaves. The Near or Middle East, still a part of the Turkish Empire, had lost all importance as a link between East and West, waiting for the Suez Canal and petroleum to plunge it back into the vortex of world affairs. India was still governed by the British East India Company; China, a slumbering giant, was yet to be torn by the opium wars; and Japan, a hermit nation, permitted extremely limited trade through the port of Nagasaki to the Dutch. In America, the United States was free, developing a flourishing trade that complemented more than it rivaled Britain's commerce, while Canada remained secure as a British colony. To the south, the vast regions of Central and South America were on the verge of revolt.

Such was the trading world at the beginning of the nineteenth century. History certainly favored the British in their bid for commercial supremacy.

Communications. The nineteenth century witnessed other changes, which, though not caused primarily by British instigation, assisted in the growth of the commerce that Britain was dedicated to promoting. Transportation by land and water and communication between widely separated areas became speedy and cheap. In 1869, the two coasts of the United States were linked by a transcontinental railroad, and railway construction in Argentina, Australia, and India soon proceeded at a rapid pace. Agricultural surpluses produced hundreds of miles inland could be moved to seaboard rapidly and cheaply. Between 1866 and 1895, the first transatlantic submarine cable was laid and the telephone and wireless introduced. International correspondence became inexpensive and reliable when the Universal Postal Union was founded in 1874.

Such communications greatly assisted the growth of trade and naturally that of the country whose overseas commerce was already the largest. Britain's commercial supremacy, however, was completed with the introduction of the steamship.

THE STEAMSHIP

The *Great Britain*, launched in England in 1844 for the Great Western Lines, represents a landmark in the history of the ship, for she was the first iron-hulled, double-bottomed, screw-propelled Atlantic liner. As everyone knows, the wooden-hulled paddle-wheeler, the *Clermont*, which steamed up the Hudson River on Aug. 17, 1807, was the first steamship to engage in commercially successful operations. The wooden, paddle-wheel steamboat, ideal for navigation on rivers and protected waters of sounds and bays, had been an American invention; the oceangoing steamship was born in the tempestuous seas around the British Isles.

After several experimental voyages, effective steamship service was begun between Europe and North America in 1838, the year in which the *Great Western* (1,340 gross tons) and the *British Queen* (1,862 tons) were launched. The British soon added subsidized lines to carry the mails, including Cunard, the Peninsula and Oriental Steam Navigation Company, and the Royal Mail Steam Packet Company. During the 1850's, an American, E. K. Collins, also offered transatlantic service with his steamships, the *Arctic, Atlantic, Baltic,* and *Pacific.*

Although good shipbuilding timber had been in short supply in the British Isles for generations, the iron hull made rather slow progress. The admiralty was ready to accept steam (the Royal Navy had acquired three steamships, the *Comet,* the *Meteor,* and the *Lightning,* between 1820 and 1823), but regarded iron-hulled ships with skepticism, because officials considered them more vulnerable to solid shot than wooden vessels. This stand of the admiralty limited experimentation with iron ships to nonsubsidized operators, or at least to nonsubsidized operations, for the Peninsula and Oriental urged the use of iron for ship construction as early as the 1840's. The leaders, however, were such free operators as the Great Western Railway Lines. Iron gained over wood rapidly after 1846, when the *Great Britain* was stranded off the coast of Ireland and remained on the beach all winter with little damage. Furthermore, the screw propeller had been invented. It was recognized as much more suitable for the rough-and-tumble workaday trade of oceangoing traffic than the cumbersome yet delicate paddle wheels, but its vibrations made wooden hulls leak. In 1854, Lloyd's organized a special committee to draw up rules for the classification of iron ships, both sailers and steamships.

The screw propeller was soon followed by the compound engine, with a great saving of fuel. Next came the surface condenser, which made it unnecessary to carry large quantities of fresh water for the boilers. These changes increased the cruising range of ships, or perhaps it would be more accurate to say their carrying capacity. To save on the coal for bunkers, all early steamships carried auxiliary sails, a practice that was continued up to the 1880's. One of the earliest steamships to cross the Atlantic was the *Sirius,* which loaded 95 passengers and 450 tons of coal at Cork in 1848 and arrived in New York eighteen and a half days later, after having scraped the coalbins and supplemented her coal bunkers with the ship's fittings and furniture. By the 1870's, the British were producing iron steamships of 2,000 gross tons, capable of 7 knots and requiring 40 tons of coal per day.

By the 1860's, the iron steamship had come into its own, and though British shipyards were turning them out as fast as possible, they could not keep up with the demand. By then, approximately 30 percent of the British ships were iron, and 50 percent of those being constructed were iron, many of them iron sailers. This was due in part to limitations of manpower, for a man who had sailed before the mast was not necessarily equipped to serve as a crewman on a steamship, and the navy, by then building only iron steamships, had first call on the services of trained personnel. To meet the demand for vessel tonnage to carry an ever-expanding overseas commerce, British shipyards turned out thousands of iron sailers. The first of these was the bark *Ironsides*, launched in 1838 for trade with Brazil, and the last big year was 1892. British steamships were naturally used on the busiest routes such as the North Atlantic, into the Mediterranean, and to South America, while the iron sailers were used in the Australian wool trade, the grain trade, and so forth. As soon as British yards could furnish replacements, the iron sailing ships were sold abroad—to Germany, the Scandinavian countries, and others then building up their merchant marines.

Prior to 1880, very little steel was used in vessel construction because of the cost. In fact, after the Bessemer process for producing steel plate was perfected, Germany led with the steel ship for a time, but by the 1890's, Britain had turned from iron to steel. At the beginning of that decade, the world's merchant fleet was composed as follows: iron, 10 million gross tons; wood, 7 million tons; and steel, 4 million tons.

The decline of the American merchant marine is contemporary with the development of the steamship. From the vantage point of the 1950's, it is apparent that American shipowners, the American public, and the government had little understanding of the revolutionary changes taking place in the shipping industry. Although the Federal government had subsidized steamships to the extent of 14 million dollars by 1858, the only ships that had been making money were the nonsubsidized transatlantic sailing packets and the California clippers. Present profits blinded shipping men to future prospects and to warnings that they might have heeded. On Mar. 31, 1860, they could have read in the *Scientific American:*

> Three years ago we directed attention to the great increase of foreign screw steamers, and showed clearly how they were rapidly taking away the trade that has been formerly carried by American ships . . . . To-day nearly all the mail and passenger, besides a great deal of the goods, traffic, is carried by foreign ships, the *great majority of which are iron screw steamers* . . . . We have not a single new Atlantic steamship on the stocks, while in Great Britain, there are 16,000 tons of new iron steamers building for the American trade.

From about 1800 to 1840, the United States, a new nation, had been able to challenge Britain's commercial supremacy. (An American steamship, the *Savannah*, which sailed from Savannah, Georgia, on May 22, 1819, was the first ship to use steam in an Atlantic crossing.) As Morison points out, England won it back "in fair competition by the skill of her engineers and the sturdy courage of her shipbuilders. Civil war turned the Yankee mind to other objects; the World War revived the ancient challenge."

SEA POWER AND NATIONAL POWER—WHAT THEY CONSIST OF

In its narrowest sense, sea power means military power at sea, in other words, navies. But no one can study the history of nations in relation to the sea without realizing that the nations that have been maritime forces have usually not depended on naval power alone—a condition that Admiral Mahan recognized when he pointed out, in 1890, that sea power consisted of merchant ships, naval vessels, plus bases from which they could be serviced. As a matter of fact, one condition recognized as fundamental to a nation's being a sea power has been that a great and powerful navy is dependent for its financial support on a large and active merchant marine engaged in a flourishing commerce. The only great nation that has attempted to support a navy without a corresponding merchant marine has been the United States.

For a nation to emerge as a sea power and to retain that status, however, more than ships and bases to serve those ships is involved. A nation's strength on the sea is conditioned by its "national" status and by its ability to absorb imports and to produce for export. The Dutch attained commercial supremacy at sea at a time when their country was little more than a loose federation of seven provinces, and the rich burghers who sat in the provincial legislative bodies were so fearful of central power that they failed to provide for the protection of their commerce. In addition to the Dutch, the early trading nations were the Portuguese, Spanish, English, and French—all of whom emerged as nations before the other peoples of western Europe. Germany, Italy, and Japan did not assume importance on the sea until late in the nineteenth century. It is not surprising that one of the first peoples to evolve as a nation—the British, with their commercial policy, their fleets, and their ability to absorb imports and to produce for export—should have developed as the great maritime and great national power. For almost a century, her navy policed the seas, keeping the sea lanes open not only for her own merchant ships but also for the ships of any nation that were, in the words of His Majesty's Navy, pursuing "their lawful occupations."

National powers may be defined as nations whose policies dominate world affairs economically and politically. Throughout history, world powers have almost always been sea powers. This was true of the ancient world. In more recent times, the only countries not powerful on the sea that could be termed world powers were Austria-Hungary and Imperial Russia, although the "Russo-Japanese War . . . revealed Russia as far less formidable than her size and the multitude of her peoples had caused men to suppose."[10]

Immediately before World War I, the national powers were Austria-Hungary, France, Germany, Great Britain, Italy, Japan, Russia, and the United States. The peace of Europe between 1815 and 1914, or rather the absence of a major war, had rested on a balance of power

. . . which presupposed the existence of France, Germany, Austria-Hungary, and Russia as dominant elements—and all of this flanked by an England instinctively conscious of her stake in the preservation of the balance among them and prepared to hover vigilantly about the fringes of the Continent, tending its equilibrium as one might tend a garden, yet always with due regard for the preservation of her own maritime supremacy and the protection of her overseas empire. In this complicated structure lay concealed not only the peace of Europe but also the security of the United States. Whatever affected it was bound to affect us. And all through the latter part of the nineteenth century things were happening which *were* bound to affect it: primarily the gradual shift of power from Austria-Hungary to Germany. This was particularly important because Austria-Hungary had not had much chance of becoming a naval and commercial rival to England, whereas Germany definitely did have such a chance and was foolish enough to exploit it aggressively . . .[11]

In 1939, there were seven national powers. Great Britain, France, Italy, the United States, and Japan had been among the victors of 1918. Germany, leader of the defeated faction and shorn of her overseas possessions, was nevertheless united and unoccupied, full of energy and confidence. By the 1930's, Germany, Nazi-controlled, was again in the category of national powers. The seventh was Communist Russia. Before World War II began, an overwhelming part of the world's armed strength in land forces and air forces was concentrated in the hands of Soviet Russia, Nazi Germany, and Imperial Japan, with considerable power on the seas, both military and merchant, in the hands of the latter two. For the democracies, strength on the sea lay primarily with Great Britain and secondarily with France and the United States.

After 1945, of that pre-World War I balance of power on which the peace of Europe depended, there is little trace. The greatest western power on the Continent is France, which, with Great Britain, has been faced with rebuilding her economic and political system. The Russia that stares from the steppes is no longer a reliable ally to help France contain Germany, and many of the pathetic little states that resulted from the

---

[10] F. J. C. Hearnshaw, *Sea-power and Empire*, George G. Harrap & Co., Ltd., London, 1940, p. 221.

[11] George F. Kennan, *American Diplomacy, 1900-1950*, University of Chicago Press, Chicago, 1951, pp. 69-70. Copyright 1951, by the University of Chicago.

breaking up of the Austro-Hungarian and Ottoman empires lie within the circle of Soviet domination. Although Britain is still a force to be reckoned with on the seas, much of her might is spent. Only a fleet can tie together her empire, the very life of which is shipping. During the early 1950's, her merchant fleet still represented one-quarter of the world's active merchant marine.

Maritime power, or perhaps we should say the potential for maritime power, has shifted westward. World War I catapulted the United States into a prominent position among maritime countries and transformed it from a debtor to a creditor nation, a position that the people of the United States were unwilling or unready to assume. The years following 1945 stand out in sharp contrast, for by the close of 1951, the United States was not only the leader in the North Atlantic Pact, but had underwritten the sovereignty of most of this world's ninety-odd nations with the exception of those under Soviet domination.

To meet widespread commitments, a powerful navy is not enough. In May, 1952, when Vice Admiral E. L. Cochrane, then Maritime Administrator, testified before the House Merchant Marine Committee, he said:

The events of World War II and those since 1950 have reemphasized that our strength in world affairs is only as great as our maritime strength. Without the means to get cargoes of both men and equipment to the theater of trouble, our remonstrances to threats of communistic aggression in every continent would be but empty words and our resistance a mere gesture . . . There is no dividing line, in my view, between the commercial and military aspects of this problem. A healthy, well-balanced, adequate American merchant marine is essential to economic well-being as well as to national defense.

BIBLIOGRAPHY

American Maritime Council, Inc., *Foreign Trade and Shipping*, McGraw-Hill Book Company, Inc., New York, 1945.
Brodie, Bernard, *Sea Power in the Machine Age*, Princeton University Press, Princeton, N.J., 1941.
———, *Guide to Naval Strategy*, Princeton University Press, Princeton, N.J., 1944.
Clough, S. B., and C. W. Cole, *Economic History of Europe*, rev. ed., D. C. Heath and Company, Boston, 1947.
Condliffe, J. B., *The Commerce of Nations*, W. W. Norton & Company, Inc., New York, 1950.
Hearnshaw, F. J. C., *Sea-power and Empire*, George G. Harrap & Co., Ltd., London, 1940.
Hutchins, J. G. B., *The American Maritime Industries and Public Policy, 1789–1914*, Harvard University Press, Cambridge, Mass., 1941.
James, Sir William M., *The Influence of Sea Power on the History of the British People*, Cambridge University Press, London, 1948.

Mahan, A. T., *The Influence of Sea Power upon History, 1660–1783*, 25th ed., Little, Brown & Company, Boston, 1918.

Morison, S. E., *Maritime History of Massachusetts, 1783–1860*, Houghton Mifflin Company, Boston, 1921.

Richmond, Admiral Sir Herbert, *Sea Power in the Modern World*, George Bell & Sons, Ltd., London, 1934.

Shepard, A. M., *Sea Power in Ancient History*, Little, Brown & Company, Boston, 1924.

Sprout, Harold, and Margaret Sprout, *Foundations of National Power*, 2d ed., D. Van Nostrand Company, Inc., New York, 1951.

―――― and ――――, *Rise of American Naval Power*, Princeton University Press, Princeton, N.J., 1939.

The Shipbuilding Business in the United States of America, Society of Naval Architects and Marine Engineers, New York, 1945, 2 vols.

Williamson, J. A., *Builders of Empire*, Oxford University Press, New York, 1925.

――――, *A Short History of British Expansion*, 2d ed., Macmillan & Co., Ltd., London, 1930, 2 vols.

――――, *The Ocean in English History*, Being the Ford Lectures at Oxford, Oxford University Press, New York, 1941.

――――, *The Evolution of England*, 2d ed., Oxford University Press, New York, 1944.

CHAPTER 2

OVERSEAS TRADE AND SHIPPING SERVICES

The sole function of ocean transportation is to move things from "where they are to where they ought to be." As stated earlier, the shipping industry, the sole business of which is water transport, is a service industry in which the ship is the carrier. Ships in themselves, however, do not constitute the industry; they live *for* and *by* the cargo. As E. G. Mears wrote in 1935: "The shipping industry is essentially a trade problem, and as such its activities are controlled by the requirements of commerce rather than ships .... Shipping is essential to trade, and trade is essential to shipping."[1] Furthermore, the type of shipping service utilized and the route traveled are determined primarily by the commodity and by the country of origin and the region of import. Some understanding of the commodity composition of overseas trade is therefore basic to an understanding of the shipping industry.

GROWTH OF INTERNATIONAL TRADE AFTER 1849

In the following discussion of the growth of overseas trade, the commodities moving, and the routes by which they traveled, we use the year 1849 as a convenient point of departure for the reason that by 1849 —the year in which the British adopted their free-trade policy—the stage was set for the world's waterborne commerce to be transformed as to volume, geographical distribution, and commodity composition. Although world trade statistics for the nineteenth century are not available, it is evident that the tonnage moving started on a sharp upward trend about the middle of the century. Between the two decades 1821 to 1830 and 1861 to 1870, the average volume of British wheat imports increased sixteen times, wool imports nine times, cotton imports five times, and coal exports twenty-nine times. On a value basis, exports of cotton goods increased three and one-half times, iron and steel exports fifteen times,

[1] E. G. Mears, *Maritime Trade of Western United States*, Stanford University Press, Stanford, Calif., 1935, pp. 6–7.

and those of machinery and millwork twenty-two times. Moreover, merchant fleets expand primarily to carry cargoes. Between 1830 and 1860, American-flag tonnage increased from 1.2 million to 5.35 million tons, and British tonnage from 2.5 million to 5.7 million.

To understand the transformation of trade in regard to commodities moving, we need to know what commodities are important and in what volume they move. Although over-all statistics are inadequate for comparisons, it is possible to arrive at certain definite conclusions. From a League of Nations study, published in 1942 and based on a long and careful analysis of the trade of 173 countries and geographical units, Table 1 was compiled. It lists the major commodities moving in international trade in volume of a million metric tons or more during the year 1938 as follows: coal, petroleum and products, iron ore, wheat and wheat flour, sugar, corn, natural phosphates, rice, iron and steel scrap, oils and oilseeds, potash fertilizer, cotton, pig iron, nitrates, bananas, bauxite, manganese ore, citrus fruits, meat, coffee, copper, basic slag, sulphate of ammonia, rubber, and wool.

In 1850, Britain's coal exports amounted to only 3.2 million tons. Trade in petroleum and rubber was nonexistent, for the large-scale development of these industries is a twentieth-century phenomenon. Although some iron ore and pig iron had been exported by England and countries on the Baltic, the large-scale movement of iron ore, iron and steel scrap, and pig iron was dependent on the spread of the Industrial Revolution to countries deficient in these products. The same is true of trade in such metals as bauxite and manganese. Wheat and cotton figure in international trade before 1850, but as will be shown presently, export volume was low until after the steamship made transportation cheap and rapid communications made trading possible. Large-volume international trade in meat products had to wait until countries such as Argentina, Australia, and New Zealand started to produce for the European importing market, and the banana trade was not opened until 1870, when a Boston ship captain formed a forerunner of the United Fruit Company.

In emphasizing the movement of staple or basic commodities, we do not underestimate the importance of manufactured goods. While trade in the latter entails certain advantages to the carrier (such as the capacity of high-value products to absorb higher freight rates), trade in staple, low-value products is of particular importance for ocean transportation. *First*, it is the cargoes of low-value commodities that send out the merchant ships of the world "full and down." Roughly 16,460,000 tons of wheat and flour moved in international trade in 1938, as compared with 431,000 tons of tea. The 25 commodities listed in Table 1 as moving in volume of a million or more tons account for nearly 350 million tons—an ex-

Table 1. World Exports of Important Commodities, 1938

Commodity or commodity grouping	Volume, thousand metric tons	Value, million dollars
Coal	109,953	$ 530
Petroleum and products	107,184	1,140
Crude petroleum	49,690	448
Gas and fuel oil	40,341	298
Petrol (gasoline)	17,153	394
Iron ore	47,000	149
Wheat and flour	16,460	569
Wheat	14,014	442
Flour	2,446	127
Sugar	9,000	340
Corn	8,968	220
Natural phosphates	7,273	
Rice	6,496	197
Iron and steel scrap	5,218	74
Oils and oilseeds	4,554	
Linseed (fat content)	540	
Five other oilseeds (fat content)*	2,439	
Linseed oil	108	
Olive oil	208	
Six other vegetable oils†	1,259	
Potash fertilizer	2,742	
Cotton	2,734	600
Pig iron	2,637	50
Nitrates	2,469	
Bananas	2,394	50
Bauxite	2,383	10
Manganese ore	1,986	21
Citrus fruits	1,913	103
Meat	1,889	438
Beef and mutton	1,352	222
Pork	537	216
Coffee	1,831	263
Copper (unworked)	1,551	325
Basic slag	1,498	
Sulphate of ammonia	1,385	
Rubber	1,032	287
Wool	1,000	435
Lead (unworked)	902	74
Superphosphate	892	
Jute	680	46
Butter	614	304
Tobacco	581	359
Zinc (unworked)	488	34
Tea	431	202
Tin (total)	275	195
Tin ore	132	72
Tin (unworked)	143	123
Silk	36	124

* Groundnuts, palm kernels, copra, soya beans, and cottonseed.
† Groundnut oil, palm oil, palm-kernel oil, coconut oil, soya-bean oil, and cottonseed oil.

SOURCE: *The Network of World Trade,* League of Nations, Geneva, 1942, pp. 32, 71.

tremely high proportion of the world's total foreign trade.[2] *Second*, it is the movement of such raw materials as cotton, iron, and coal and of basic foodstuffs such as wheat that makes possible exports of manufactured goods such as locomotives, adding machines, cotton cloth, and pins and needles.[3] *Third*, the movement of basic commodities has been a major factor not only in expanding world commerce but also in establishing the routes that make up the network of overseas trade.

Their importance to economic life and to the peace of the world was pointed out in a 1932 study by the U.S. Department of Commerce:[4]

International shipping is rooted in the necessity for large-scale exchange of basic commodities between the peoples of the earth. Passenger travel may be curtailed without serious national consequence; interference with the movement of overseas mail may now be mitigated by cable and radio communication and by air transport; stoppage of the transborder movement of finished goods would react unfavorably on both the exporting and importing country; but stoppage of the world flow of basic commodities would have a paralyzing effect on the progress of nations.

TRADE IN WHEAT AND COTTON

Wheat. In the international civilization and overseas trade system built around free trade, the gold standard, and British investments to assist in the development of "new" areas, wheat has been one of the mainstays. "Industrialization and urbanization and the opening of the frontier made wheat one of the most important commodities of international trade."[5]

As the countries of Europe were industrialized, they turned first to agricultural Europe and then to overseas producers for their wheat supplies. Until 1880, wheat was Denmark's principal export,[6] and Russia was one of the major exporting countries until World War I. India, too, exported wheat. A railroad had opened up the Punjab and connected it with the port of Karachi. Because overland transport was not available

---

[2] *United States Statistical Yearbook, 1951* (p. 322) gives 470 million tons as the total for seaborne trade in 1938 (see p. 72).

[3] A League of Nations study found that, from 1876 to 1938 (but omitting the war years 1914 through 1921), the total value of manufactured articles moved in international trade was 60 percent of that of primary products. See *Industrialization and Foreign Trade*, League of Nations, Geneva, 1945, p. 14.

[4] J. E. Saugstad, *Shipping and Shipbuilding Subsidies*, U.S. Department of Commerce, Trade Promotion Series, No. 129, 1932, p. 1.

[5] E. W. Zimmermann, *World Resources and Industries*, rev. ed., Harper & Brothers, New York, 1951, p. 212. This chapter and Chap. 3 are much indebted to Zimmermann's book.

[6] When cheap grain supplies from overseas threatened ruin to Denmark's economy, her farmers started to feed their grain to animals, which were processed into quality foods (butter, cheese, bacon, and hams), which were also exported to countries such as England. Staley has pointed out that "an overseas development which had offered

to carry wheat to food-deficit areas in the interior of India, European buyers were able to outbid native competition for wheat at seaboard.

The main overseas source was the United States. Even before the Civil War, grain shipments had been substantial enough so that the Northerners thought the British might favor their cause, while the Southerners hoped the needs for cotton would swing British sympathies in the opposite direction. Following the Civil War, production increased enormously (the Red River Valley region came into production during the 1870's); the railroads made it possible to ship wheat to seaboard cheaply; and United States grain exports practically flooded the markets of Europe. They increased from 10 million bushels in the crop year 1866–1867 to 89 million in 1873–1874. In certain years, wheat prices fell to a point at which United States wheat was sold as far east as Odessa. As a result, many countries of Continental Europe increased their protective tariffs sharply, and only Great Britain and countries representing such small markets as Belgium, the Netherlands, Switzerland, and Norway continued to accept the cheapened wheat.

Late in the century, the still newer producing regions of Canada, Argentina, and Australia began to be turned into wheat-exporting specialists by the steamship and the railroads. Wheat growing was then, and still appears to be, the most remunerative use of great sections of their vast agricultural lands. Meanwhile exports from the United States had begun to dwindle. Population was increasing more rapidly than wheat production, and the general acceptance of roller milling, which made it possible to mill hard wheats, resulted in a reshuffling of wheat regions in this country.

Thus, by the turn of the century, a pattern of wheat production and trade had evolved in which the old producers (Russia, the Danubian countries, and India) vied with the new and more efficient producers (United States, Canada, Argentina, and Australia). Immediately before World War I (1909–1913), Russia was the main exporter. Her exports of wheat and flour, averaging 162 million bushels a year, accounted for almost one-fourth of the world's total, and were not much below the combined shipments of the United States and Canada (more than 192 million bushels annually). Romanian exports at 52,000,000 bushels exceeded Australia's at 49,000,000, while Hungary exported close to the latter figure. Waterborne shipments of Russian and Danubian wheat reached markets via Black Sea ports and the Mediterranean. Australian wheat joined that from India to pass through the Suez Canal. The main

---

menacing new competition was thus converted . . . into a tremendous new opportunity" and that the result was "one of the highest living standards in the world." See Eugene Staley, *World Economic Development*, International Labour Office, Montreal, 1944, pp. 173–174.

line of the overseas wheat trade was across the North Atlantic to Europe, for the United States and Canada together accounted for close to 30 percent of world trade. A secondary route carried Argentina's 95 million bushels, about 14 percent of the total, from River Plate ports to Europe.

World War I brought about revolutionary changes in this distribution pattern. Russian wheat exports had been possible only because a feudalistic agricultural system had permitted the landlord "to ship out wheat for his own financial benefit even if the people around him were underfed, perhaps actually starving." After 1917, the U.S.S.R. had need of its wheat to feed "the new urban proletariat spawned by the Revolution."[7] India too dropped from the list of exporters, and social changes in Romania and Hungary relegated these countries to very minor roles as wheat exporters. During World War I, Europe needed American wheat at least as much as it needed guns. Wheat acreage in this country was expanded from 45 million acres in 1910 to 75 million in 1919, and the United States was again back in its role of a major wheat exporter. Canadian wheat exports, which had averaged 90 million bushels annually during the years 1909 to 1913, increased to 307 million for the period 1924 to 1928.

As a result, for the years 1924 through 1928, Canada, the United States, Argentina, and Australia furnished more then four-fifths of the world's wheat exports. Canada and the United States provided 57 percent, and the main stream of the wheat trade was across the North Atlantic along what had developed as (and still remains) the main artery for all overseas shipping. United States wheat also left Galveston and Pacific Northwest ports for Europe, while there was a minor movement from western Canadian and American ports for the Orient. Second to the North Atlantic route was the South America–Europe route, for Argentina provided 16 percent of the wheat exports. Australia's share was slightly less (11 percent), most of which went to Europe, with a little to the Orient.

Changes in this pattern occurred during the 1930's, when the world wheat market collapsed. At the close of World War I, many of the countries of Continental Europe reimposed the wheat tariffs that they had abandoned during the war. In addition, many of them adopted control measures to stimulate domestic production and to lessen dependence on imports, including bounties on grain acreage; import quotas, licenses, permits, and certificate systems; a similar battery of regulations to restrict exports; and various schemes for stretching available supplies such as admixture requirements and higher extraction rates. Italy's "battle of the grain" and Hitler's barter agreements, through which he "swapped" German nonessential goods such as cameras for the wheat

[7] Zimmermann, *loc. cit.*

of the Danubian countries, were part of the European campaign to attain self-sufficiency in food grains.

At that point, the U.S.S.R., which had just embarked on her first Five-Year Plan and needed to export in order to pay for capital goods, decided to reenter the world grain market. In both 1930 and 1931, Soviet Russia exported almost 94 million bushels of wheat, more than Australia has exported annually during the years 1924 through 1928. In 1932, the United Kingdom passed the Wheat Act, thereby putting into effect empire preference for wheat as well as stimulating domestic production. Under this Act, Canadian and Australian wheat occupied a preferred position in the British market, which, because of its dependence on imported foodstuffs, continued to purchase more than 200 million bushels of overseas wheat.

With a diminishing market, all the overseas exporters took steps to protect their wheat producers. In the United States, the Agricultural Adjustment Act embodied reduced acreage (and, it was hoped, restricted production) and parity prices for farmers in an effort to make wheat growing profitable. The brunt of the drop in overseas exports was borne by the United States; in certain years during the 1930's, the nation was actually on a net-import basis. This is in sharp contrast to the situation since 1946, when the United States has been furnishing the greater part of the world's "emergency" wheat.

Owing to shifts in the world wheat market during the 1930's and to droughts that reduced North American crops, Argentine and Australian exports represented a higher proportion of the world total.[8] For both of these countries, the long ocean haul is more than compensated for by short rail hauls. However, in part because of their distances from other major shipping regions, the trade of both of these countries is susceptible to breaks in shipping conditions, and a lack of inbound cargoes is liable to raise freight rates and disrupt their export trade. During the 1920 strikes in Britain, when no coal was available for export, wheat ships were diverted to North American ports, to which the British Isles export little if any coal.

Cotton. The geography of world cotton production makes world trade in raw cotton imperative. Production today is concentrated in the United States, India, Egypt, and Brazil, while more than half of the world's cotton is consumed in countries in which it is not produced. Even Egypt, lacking a cotton-milling industry, exports practically her entire crop.

---

[8] For a map of world wheat trade during the 1920's, see Nels B. Bengston and William Van Royen, *Fundamentals of Economic Geography*, 3d ed., Prentice-Hall, Inc., New York, 1950, p. 235; for one for the year 1939, see *Agricultural Geography of Europe and the Near East*, U.S. Department of Agriculture, Miscellaneous Publication 665, 1948, p. 57.

Without trade in cotton, practically every country in Europe with the exception of the U.S.S.R. would be a "have-not" nation.

Statistically, cotton is also important in overseas commerce. Soon after the invention of the cotton gin in 1793, cotton displaced tobacco as the United States' most valuable export, a position it retained until 1937. It was also the chief import of the United Kingdom. The international raw-cotton trade consisted almost wholly of moving cotton from the producing areas to the United Kingdom; to such secondary purchasers as Germany, France, Austria, and Italy; and, particularly after World War I, to Japan. In 1938, world cotton exports of 2.7 million tons were valued at 600 million dollars more than those of any other primary commodity moving in international trade.

Until the Civil War, a very high proportion of the world's cotton exports originated in the United States. This nation's shipments averaged 3.5 million bales during the 1850's. In 1860, United States production totaled 5.2 million bales, equal to seven-eighths of world production, and exports aggregated 4.4 million bales. During the years prior to the Civil War, almost half of the United States foreign fleet was engaged in transporting cotton from Charleston, Savannah, Mobile, and New Orleans, primarily to Liverpool.[9] During the years 1862 to 1865, United States cotton exports shrank to a mere 20,000 bales annually.

European cotton spinners became greatly alarmed. To reduce their dependence on American cotton, France and Germany encouraged cotton production in their African colonies. British efforts in Egypt were far more successful, and a program for irrigated cotton in the Nile Valley made Egypt one of the chief cotton-growing countries of the world. Between 1870 and 1906, the cotton outputs of Egypt and India were tripled. However, the United States still provided more than 60 percent of world exports, while India and Egypt together accounted for roughly one-fourth.

During the 1920's, the Mexican boll weevil, which had crossed into Texas in 1892, completed its invasion of the entire United States cotton belt. On the domestic side, this helped to shift cotton production westward, and the old cotton ports of Charleston, Mobile, and Savannah bowed to New Orleans, which had a hinterland to both the east and the west. Internationally, the damage done to American crops by the boll weevil raised serious doubts concerning the ability of the United States to supply the world demand and thus contributed to the expansion of cotton acreage in various regions, among them Brazil, where planters

---

[9] Liverpool remained, until the beginning of World War II, the principal cotton market for the British Isles and Europe. By the turn of the century, however, such Continental ports as Bremen, Hamburg, Le Havre, and Trieste were important ports of entry for cotton.

were encountering serious difficulties with their coffee-growing industry. The high cotton prices of the 1920's encouraged Brazilians to try their hand at producing commercially a plant that had grown for centuries in their tropical climate. When the United States instituted acreage and production control during the 1930's under the New Deal to support cotton prices, Brazilians were in a position to take advantage of the tempting ratio between the prices of cotton and of coffee on the world market.

The results are reflected in the trade pattern. The United States' share of world cotton exports declined to 41 percent during the years 1934 to 1938. This nation, India, Egypt, and Brazil were furnishing 85 percent of total exports,[10] while 70 percent of world imports were purchased by the United Kingdom, France, Germany, Italy, and Japan. The trade pattern had been changed far more by shifts in demand than by shifts in the suppliers.

In anticipation of war, Germany and Italy had fostered synthetic industries and placed drastic limitations on the consumption of cotton textiles. Germany's regime of barter distorted the whole pattern of usual import trade, and exchange control in Germany, Italy, Czechoslovakia, Hungary, and elsewhere regulated their purchases of cotton. The major change, however, is to be found in the decline of Britain as a raw-cotton importer and the simultaneous rise of the cotton-textile industry in Japan.

Between 1909 and 1913, the United Kingdom purchased 32 percent of the world's cotton imports, but in the years 1934 to 1938, this proportion had shrunk to 20 percent. Britain's spindles had decreased from 56 million to 36 million. After the United Kingdom abandoned the gold standard in 1932, a very high proportion of British imports was purchased in countries with currencies closely linked to sterling.[11] In 1934 to 1938, India supplied close to 14 percent, Egypt over 31 percent, Brazil almost 22 percent, and the United States only slightly more than 20 percent. The British Working Party on Cotton estimated that two-thirds of the decline in British cotton-textile exports was a result of the development of textile industries by British customers and the remaining third of Japanese competition.

Japan's rise as an importer of cotton and an exporter of cotton textiles was simultaneous with her rise as a silk exporter. This can be dated rather definitely as the 1920's (see page 66). Japanese imports of cotton increased from a 1909-to-1913 average of 1.4 million bales to 2.9 million

---

[10] Cotton is also produced in Mexico, Peru, Argentina, and various parts of Africa (the Sudan being the most important). However, total production in these areas during the 1930's was only slightly larger than Brazilian exports in 1938.

[11] On the sterling area or block, see Chap. 3, footnote 19.

during 1924 to 1928, while her exports of raw silk increased from around 10,000 tons to 30,000 tons. By purchasing a large share of her raw cotton from India, Japan was able to secure a market for much of her exported cotton textiles.

THE WORLD'S TRAMP FLEET AND ITS OPERATIONS

The tramp type of ship owes its birth primarily to the movement, in great volume, of grain and cotton. The tramp steamship, which followed the tramp sailer, owes its existence to the movement of these products and to shipments of coal, lumber and logs, ores, phosphates, sulphur, and scrap metal—all bulky, low-value commodities that have tended to move in shipload lots. The whole history of the tramp is an account of efforts to meet the needs of oceangoing commerce.

By about 1850, the wheat trade and the cotton trade demanded a type of service that the merchant-trader of an earlier day could not provide. He had operated his vessel for the owner's account, carried diversified cargoes to spread his risk, and had looked upon his shipping operation as distinctly subordinate to his merchandising. His operations had been similar to those of the later tramp in that his ships were the free-lance operators of the day, adhering to no fixed routes, no constant termini, and no definite time schedule and following cargoes wherever they might be. The keenest businessman of his day, he took a good look at the lucrative cotton-carrying trade and soon recognized that shipping in itself could be a profitable business and that his small vessels-of-all-work were inadequate for the job at hand. Hence, he decided to enter the ship-chartering business and to acquire larger and better vessels.

For the cotton trade, American shipbuilders, especially those in Maine, built a special carrier—a vessel with bluff bow, swollen sides, and a broad, flat bottom for navigating the Mississippi bar. By 1850, these ships were of about 1,400 gross tons in comparison with the 1830 vessel of about 400 tons. They proved to be good sailers and excellent cotton carriers, packing about 2,000 pounds per registered ton in comparison with about 900 pounds for earlier vessels. During the years before the Civil War, American-flag vessels monopolized the cotton trade. In 1852, some 800,000 tons of American shipping were so employed, a figure that represents almost half of the United States foreign fleet.[12]

The cotton trade of that day operated in a triangle: ships sailed out of New England ports or New York for one of the cotton ports, then to Liverpool or Le Havre with cotton, back to a North Atlantic port in the United States with any cargo offered in Europe, and then south again.

[12] See J. G. B. Hutchins, *The American Maritime Industries and Public Policy, 1789–1914*, Harvard University Press, Cambridge, Mass., 1941, pp. 264–265, 321.

Because the coastwise leg of the voyage was closed to foreign ships by United States navigation laws, and because the principal cotton ports (Charleston, Savannah, Mobile, and New Orleans) were not then importing enough to provide cargoes for European ships outbound, the British were unable to compete in this trade until after the Civil War.

The collapse of the United States cotton trade during the Civil War hit the New England shipowners almost as hard as the cotton producers. Many of the big cotton freighters were sold abroad, and those remaining under the American flag were diverted to other uses, such as the carriage of lumber out of mill-town ports on the West Coast of the United States. When the cotton trade revived after the Civil War (it did not reach pre-war levels until about 1879), British and not American vessels dominated, and the typical cotton carrier was an iron vessel, either a screw steamer or a sailing ship, both constructed to navigate the lower Mississippi.[13]

Although the steamship was here to stay by the 1850's, a good but decreasing part of the world's freight was lifted by sailing vessels until the latter part of the nineteenth century—in wooden sailing ships built by such countries as the United States and Canada or the iron sailers produced in British shipyards. These sailers plied to Australia, to the Pacific Coast of the United States, and over other shipping lanes of the world along which the traffic moving in both directions was not sufficient to warrant the regularly scheduled sailings of the steamship offering liner service. Outbound from these regions for Europe, their cargoes were almost always tramp-type cargoes, moved in shipload lots, of cotton, grain, wool, and other foodstuffs or industrial raw material. At Liverpool or another European port, they were usually put "on berth" for some port such as Sydney or San Francisco, and this meant that they would carry any and all cargo offered and that the freight rates would be unusually attractive. Hence, these sailing vessels often offered charter terms (tramp-type service) on one leg of the voyage and berth terms (liner) on the other. By about the turn of the century, the world's shipping lanes were taking more definite shape, and the British, who had built larger and better steamships for liner operations, had retired older carriers into tramp service and had built other tramp-type steamships. Chartered traffic then became the domain of the tramp steamer, and traffic in general merchandise was taken over almost entirely by the scheduled cargo liner.

Tramp Operations. By the very nature of their operations, tramps absorb much of the disproportion between outbound and inbound tonnage. For instance, immediately after the Argentine grain crop is harvested, the tonnage outbound is much greater than that inbound, and the regularly scheduled liner services are not able to take care of the traffic.

---

[13] Since the purchaser usually dictates the means of transport for an "import," this was, in many respects, a logical development.

Consequently, about the close of the Southern Hemisphere crop year (which coincides with the calendar year), the world's tramps tend to congregate at the River Plate.[14] A crop failure would send them scurrying to other parts of the world for cargoes.[15]

The tramp traffic that developed has been called triangular, but it comes nearer to being hexagonal. Many British tramps sailed from home port to be gone for several years. If this seems curious, consider the following voyage, which could be considered representative: Liverpool or Cardiff to Brazil with coal, Brazil to the River Plate in ballast (or she could have sailed directly for Argentina, perhaps Rosario, with coal), Argentina to Rotterdam or Hamburg with wheat or corn, to England for coal to perhaps the River Plate again, grain to South Africa, ballast to the Philippines for copra to be taken to the Pacific Coast of the United States, perhaps San Francisco, and then to the Pacific Northwest for lumber to Europe. This port-to-port movement was possible only because of a wide range of options that permitted an eleventh-hour decision by the charterer as to the exact country and port of destination.[16]

The bulk shipments moving in tramps imply more than shipload lots, for the term *bulk* has come to mean unpackaged. At most of the world's grain ports, grain elevators have been constructed that can load and unload whole shiploads of grain by suction within a few hours. If grain arrives at such an elevator in bags, the sacks are bled before the grain goes into the elevator. Aboard ship bagged grain is placed over the loose grain to keep it from shifting en route. Important bulk-commodity ports such as Baltimore and various Great Lakes ports have special facilities for rapidly loading and discharging coal and ores.

The World's Tramp Fleet. To keep pace with the enormous increase in the overseas movement of the primary products that moved in shipload lots, certain maritime powers acquired sizable tramp fleets. The leader was the British Empire, the parts of which certainly represented the biggest shippers and receivers of bulk cargoes. In 1914, the British tramp fleet aggregated approximately half of that for the entire world (the accompanying table gives figures in thousands of gross tons). Estimates indicate that British ships of all types carried over one-half of the world's seaborne trade and nine-tenths of their own trade.

Between 1914 and 1933, the world's total merchant fleet increased

[14] For information on seasonality, see W. G. Rickman, *The Shipping Seasons of the World's Produce*, published by the author, London, 1930.

[15] This statement needs to be qualified, particularly as to time. Modern crop reporting and modern communications have done much to eliminate the situation described. However, during certain periods, notably the 1920's, Argentina's crop reports were exceptionally poor. Furthermore, it should be noted that since the close of World War II, Argentina has been much less of a factor in the world wheat situation than she was formerly.

[16] See also Chap. 10, "Ship Operation: Charters."

about one-third, but the tramp tonnage remained about the same. In 1933, it represented only 33 percent of the total, as contrasted with 46 percent in 1914. The principal countries that increased their tramp tonnages were those with the cheapest operating costs, such as Greece and Japan. Tramp tonnage continued to decline throughout the 1930's, and just before the war, British tramp tonnage had declined to about 3.4 million gross tons.

	1914			1933		
Country	Total gross tonnage	Estimated tramp tonnage	Percent tramp	Total gross tonnage	Estimated tramp tonnage	Percent tramp
British Empire	21,045	10,800	51	21,820	6,000	27
Norway	2,505	2,100	84	4,080	1,650	40
France	2,319	1,100	48	3,512	1,560	44
Italy	1,668	1,050	65	3,150	1,890	60
Sweden	1,118	800	73	1,675	870	52
Greece	837	700	84	1,417	1,320	93
Spain	899	650	72	1,232	850	69
Denmark	820	600	75	1,168	650	56
Germany	5,459	500	9	3,901	450	12
Japan	1,708	500	29	4,258	2,380	56
Netherlands	1,496	500	33	2,765	650	23
Belgium	352	100	28	456	80	18
United States	5,368	. . . . . .	. .	13,358		
Other countries	3,496	3,300	37	5,128	3,870	21
Total	49,090	22,700	46	67,920	22,220	33

SOURCE: Sir Osborne Mance, *International Sea Transport*, Oxford University Press, New York, 1945, p. 68. The figures for Japan do not include sailing craft, and those for the United States do not include vessels on the Great Lakes.

The decreased importance of the tramp carrier has resulted from a number of causes: (1) the coal trade fell from 171 million tons in 1913 to 142 million in 1937; (2) as established steamship lines offering berth service became stronger, they absorbed tramps gradually and combined by adding new services to the old; (3) tramps that had been kept on a regular beat for some time were converted into regular liners; (4) modern liner trade routes, for example between all California ports and Japan, China, and the Philippines, have provided greater flexibility of berth traffic; (5) dealers have tended to carry smaller inventories and hence to prefer the regular service of the berth operator rather than the bulk service of the tramp; and (6) certain commodities such as petroleum and ores that formerly furnished tramp cargoes have deserted that means of transport for the special industrial carrier. In short, the liner, the tanker, and the ore carrier have all encroached on tramp traffic.

The tramp has lost not only in traffic and numbers of ships but also in prestige. When Mears wrote his *Maritime Trade of the Western United States*, in 1935, he referred to the tramp as "old fashioned." In 1937, because of the inroads on tramp traffic, the U.S. Maritime Commission deemed the tramp "the biggest gamble" of the shipping industry. Since World War II, British tramp tonnage has, according to Lloyd's, stood at 2.9 million gross tons, or less than 20 percent of the British merchant fleet. Furthermore, the British have started to refer to tramp-type ships as "general traders."

As will be shown later, since the war there has been a large but "unnatural" movement of commodities that are transported in bulk, and the United States has figured prominently in this traffic. Owing to the world-wide shortage of bulk carriers, United States government-owned vessels have been put into service; scores of such ships, particularly of the Liberty type, have been employed in an irregular shuttle service of one-way cargoes, largely across the Atlantic. Although in some quarters their operations are considered tramp-like, war-built vessels are generally not considered economically suitable to the bulk trades. Hence, it seems preferable to refer to United States ships in these services as irregular carriers.

BERTH OR LINER SERVICE

The common carrier is a ship that offers the regularly scheduled service called *berth* in the United States and *liner* in Great Britain. It is a vessel engaged in transporting goods for hire and offering space to all who wish to take advantage of the offer, the space being available and the terms mutually satisfactory. The common carrier is available for, and actually carries, a number of shipments received from different shippers consigned for delivery at various points of destination along the vessel's route. The Shipping Act of 1916 defines a common carrier in foreign commerce as a vessel "engaged in the transportation by water of passengers or property between the United States or any of its Districts, Territories, or possessions and a foreign country, whether in the import or export trade." The Act also specifies "that a cargo boat commonly called an ocean tramp shall not be deemed such 'common carrier by water in foreign commerce.'"

The Rise of the Common Carrier. The common carrier was the direct result of the demands of an expanding overseas trade. By the middle of the nineteenth century, the processes involved in ship operation, foreign trade, and merchandising had become far too complex for the individual merchant-trader who had earlier dominated seaborne trade or for his small organization. Ships had increased in size and cargoes increased proportionally. These changes required corresponding increases in capital. Furthermore, the services of specialists such as agents and brokers, by then a necessity in successful ship operation, and the merchandising and distribution facilities necessary to distribute cargoes lay out of the realm of the merchant-trader. Commerce had outgrown his type of service, which had been geared to stagecoach days. On land, people living only short distances apart could not exchange goods until the railroad replaced the stagecoach; on the sea, goods could not move in volume until the merchantman was replaced by the common carrier.

Early Liner Service. The first ships offering the regular service of the liner appeared on the world's most active sea route, the North Atlantic. In 1816, the American Black Ball Line started to operate four 400- and 500-ton swift sailing packets on regular sailing schedules between New York and Liverpool. After the depression of 1819, the Swallow Tail and Red Star added more ships of this type to the American fleet. Within a short time, service had been expanded to include weekly sailings to Liverpool, and also to London, Le Havre, and other Continental ports. Worn ships were sold, often for whalers, to be replaced by larger and better vessels. In 1854, the Morgan Line launched the *Amazon* and *Palestine* of 1,800 tons each, the largest of the American-owned Atlantic packets.

The key to the profitable operation in the North Atlantic was the passenger traffic, for crowded conditions in England and famines in Ireland were sending emigrants to America by the tens of thousands. By 1824, the American packets had, with their regular schedules and hard-driving passages, captured the passenger traffic as well as the express-type freight. As late as 1846, a British emigrants' guide advised passengers to choose an American sailing packet rather than one of the new Cunard steamships that offered liner service after 1840. The packets lost out not to Cunard or Collins steamships but to the low-cost screw steamers that the British Inman Line put on the Atlantic run during the 1850's. They offered a distinctly better service at lower cost.

In part because of American competition but also because of the importance of the West Indies trade, the first British overseas steamship service had been inaugurated, not to North America, but to the West Indies and Central America, when the Royal Mail Steam Packet Company started to operate in 1839. A year later, a company then operating assumed the name Peninsular and Oriental Steam Navigation Company and started to transport passengers and the mail to the Orient via the Mediterranean and a four-day passage across the Isthmus of Suez. By 1865, Europe was connected with every other continent by liner service.

The Modern Carrier. The world has been inclined to regard the passenger vessel with all its magnificence as a liner and anything of lesser size and deck space as a freighter. However, no matter what a vessel carries or what she looks like, if she operates as a common carrier on a regularly scheduled route, she is in liner or berth service. Of the many vessels that carry passengers and freight, there are, broadly speaking, two main categories.

Passenger liners derive the greater part of their income from carrying passengers, although even the finest of them carry the mails and such high-value freight as Paris fashions and other luxury goods. In the Atlantic, vessels of the luxury passenger class include the two Cunard *Queens*, the United States Lines' *America* and *United States*, and the American Export Line's *Independence* and *Constitution*. Passenger traffic in the Pacific Basin is not of sufficient volume to maintain the floating palaces that cater to travelers except for Matson Navigation Company's *Lurline*, which operates between the Pacific Coast of the United States and Hawaii, and the *President Cleveland* and *President Wilson*, operated by American President Lines.

Passenger vessels of lesser magnificence are designed and constructed to carry fewer passengers and more freight. Those that carry 100 passengers can also carry several thousand tons of freight. Many freighters carry up to 12 passengers, and some foreign vessels of this type offer elaborate accommodations. International regulations limit the number of passengers carried by a merchant cargo ship to 12. If more than 12 are carried, the ship is classified as a combination or full passenger ship and must be so licensed. The amount of cargo carried by a freighter depends on the type of ship and the nature of the cargo. American freighters of the Victory class can lift around 10,000 tons and of the C3 class around 13,000 tons.

Liner Cargoes. Liner freighters cater to general cargo.[17] The commodities that comprise the general cargo moving in international trade in any one year could include all items mentioned in a mail-house catalogue plus automobiles (boxed and unboxed), tractors, animals, lumber, fresh fruit, vegetable oils, industrial machinery, and so forth. Certain routes, such as Hong Kong to England through Suez, provide some of the most varied cargoes, including among other things tea, sugar, silk, pepper, spices, rattans, bamboos, rubber, and edible birds' nests for the Chinese population of Liverpool.

Liner cargo is also called dry cargo, in contrast to the liquid, semifluid, or fluid cargoes carried by tankers. Many freighters, however, are now

---

[17] In most trade statistics, general cargo is total cargo minus petroleum and its products moved in tankers and minus lumber. Dry cargo includes lumber. Trade statistics for dry cargo include petroleum moved in containers or in deep tanks aboard dry-cargo carriers.

equipped with deep tanks in one or more holds suitable for transporting bulk liquids such as petroleum products, and coconut and other vegetable oils. By processing some of the raw materials to deep-tank cargoes at point of origin, much space aboard ship can be saved, and the freight charges are consequently lower. Before the last war, cleaning tanks was a dirty, expensive, and time-consuming job, accomplished by men who climbed down into them. Since the war, they can be cleaned with detergents in a matter of minutes.

Liners have always carried such commodities as wheat in parcels. For example, if a British miller had purchased a small quantity of wheat to be used in his blend of flour, he might issue instructions that it be shipped as a parcel rather than wait to have it consolidated with other wheat for a shipload lot. Copra, which has been an important bulk cargo, is now being shipped in bulk (unpackaged) form into the West Coast of the United States, where it is unloaded by suction. Since World War II, about 90 percent of the sugar moving from the Hawaiian Islands to San Francisco Bay has moved in bulk form aboard scheduled freighters. Lumber out of the Pacific Northwest, which formerly moved primarily in shipload lots, now provides partial cargo for many liners. Some shipments are small, but a ship in regular service may carry 4 million or more board feet, as well as general cargo. When liners on voyage after voyage lift a sizable tonnage of such basic cargo, the situation is spoiled for the tramp operator, because the cargo accumulated is not sufficient for shipload lots.

Liner Routes. Passenger liners tend to ply between a few ports at which passengers assemble. For instance, the *America* sails between New York and a number of European ports—Cobh, Ireland; Southampton, England; Le Havre, France; and Bremerhaven, Germany. The *Lurline* alternates her departures from Los Angeles and San Francisco, but calls at both Pacific Coast ports on all voyages. It is common practice for companies operating luxury liners to withdraw one or more of their ships from the North Atlantic run during the winter and schedule them for cruises in the Mediterranean, in the Caribbean, or around the world.

A much wider range of ports is served by freighters. They definitely do not range so far afield as the tramp, but they often operate on triangular or quadrangular routes and almost always between ranges of ports. For instance, a freighter on the North Atlantic–British Isles route may call at New York, Philadelphia, Boston, Baltimore, or all four. In the British Isles, she may call at one port, such as Liverpool, which is really the main seaport for the Manchester-Lancashire industrial region. But other ports of call are often added as cargo offers—Cobh and Belfast in Ireland and perhaps Glasgow in Scotland. Although the schedules of American subsidized operators are fixed in that they have regular ports of call, the option of serving additional ports as cargo offers adds flexibility to their operations.[18]

Steamship companies that undertake triangular and quadrangular routes maintain some flexibility in their service by adding and dropping ports as cargo offers warrant. But the main characteristics of liner service are observed in all of these routings, that is, the carriage of general cargo, the maintenance of schedules subject only to accidents or bad weather on the high seas or port delays, and the same freight rates charged to all shippers regardless of the quantity offered.[19]

COAL—KEY TO THE BRITISH CARRYING TRADE

Iron, steel, and coal revolutionized the world's shipping industry. In that revolutionary change, coal occupied a unique position, for it was at one and the same time the principal cargo outbound from Europe and the chief fuel for Britain's far-flung commercial and naval fleets. Hence, it was with good reason that Zimmermann, writing in 1920, called coal "the key to the carrying trade."[20]

British Exports. As European ships, primarily British, increased in number to transport the foodstuffs and industrial raw materials needed by industrial Europe, shipowners needed an outbound cargo that would move in volume, one to supplement exports of high-value but low-tonnage manufactured goods and thereby to help to balance the volume moving in both directions. Europe could afford to purchase low-value and bulky imports only if freight rates were low. Low inbound rates were contingent on outbound cargoes, for shipowners can offer such rates only when their vessels carry a pay load on both legs of a voyage. The development of overseas trade led the British, who had for generations literally been living on top of some of the world's largest coal reserves, to exploit their natural resource.

In 1850, coal exports from the United Kingdom were 3.2 million tons. From that date, they rose steadily to reach almost 29 million tons in 1890 and nearly 64 million in 1907. The peak came in 1913, when 73.4 million tons were shipped as export cargo. So great were British exports and so wide the market that British trade statistics divided the world into 10 coal markets: (1) Germany and all European countries to the north including Russia; (2) France and all countries to the south including those bordering on the Mediterranean; (3) the west coast of Africa; (4) British South Africa; (5) the east coast of Africa, including Mauritius,

---

[18] On United States "essential" trade routes, see Chap. 4.
[19] Morris S. Rosenthal, *Techniques of International Trade*, McGraw-Hill Book Company, Inc., New York, 1950, p. 36.
[20] E. W. Zimmermann, *Ocean Shipping*, Prentice-Hall, Inc., New York, 1921, Chap. 13.

Bourbon, Arabia, and Persia; (6) India; (7) the rest of Asia; (8) the countries of northern South America; (9) Brazil, Uruguay, and Argentina; and (10) western South America and the western part of the United States.

The only part of the world to which Britain did not ship coal was the Atlantic Coast of North America, a region that was supplied by the United States. United States exports move mainly to Canada (which they usually reach via Great Lakes steamer as a return cargo for the ore carriers), Cuba, Argentina, and Brazil. About the close of World War I, a decline set in for total world coal exports, due primarily to two causes: (1) the introduction of hydroelectric power and of petroleum for industrial purposes and (2) the shift from coal to oil for bunkers.

Coal for Bunkers. Only a far-flung empire could have established and controlled the system of coaling stations necessary for bunkering coal-burning steamships. As the possessor of the world's largest fleet, Britain was the greatest consumer of bunkering coal both at home and at the far corners of the earth. British exports for bunkers increased as did the number of steamships. In 1870, when many of the world's freighters were still sailing ships, they stood at 3.3 million tons, rose to 8.1 million in 1890, and reached their peak in 1913 at 21 million. At that time, they represented more than one-fourth of total British coal exports. Since that date, the use of coal for bunkers has decreased steadily. In 1914, coal accounted for 89 percent of the bunkering fuel, while today it accounts for approximately 25 percent.

Britain led the world in the use of coal for bunkering, but the United States led in the transition from coal to oil. Early in World War I, the British put into effect a licensing (warrant) system as a military measure. Officials of the United States government and shipping men realized that a situation could develop in which the British might use their control of bunkering coal to the disadvantage of the United States. Labor shortages in this country and in Europe during World War I encouraged the building of oil-burning ships. Hence, when the United States was called upon to build millions of tons of ships during World War I, it was to be expected that this country, the leading producer of petroleum, would build oil burners.

BIBLIOGRAPHY

The bibliographical references for this chapter are listed at the end of Chap. 3.

CHAPTER 3

OVERSEAS TRADE AND SHIPPING SERVICES (CONTINUED)

A well-known atomic scientist stated recently that the age of coal is almost past, that the world is now in the petroleum age, and that the future will be an era of atomic power. Until that time comes, petroleum will remain the prime mover for land and sea transport, and overseas trade in petroleum and its products will remain a necessity. Geography and national security so decree. Modern armies and navies move on oil, and control of oil supplies is as vital to national defense as is an iron and steel industry. Two-thirds of the matériel that the United States shipped overseas during the last war consisted of petroleum and its products, and tankers were one of the prime targets of enemy submarines.

PETROLEUM AND THE TANKER

Pound for pound or, if you prefer, cubic foot for cubic foot, gasoline, the major product of petroleum, "packs a much greater punch" than coal. An oil-driven ship can travel three times as far without refueling as one using coal. Specifically, the advantages of oil as a marine fuel are as follows: (1) Because its calorific value is higher than that of coal, oil saves space—in terms of actual weight, about one-third. Moreover, oil can be stored between the double bottoms of modern ships or in other odd places usually not suitable for cargo. (2) An oil burner can take on bunkers in port in a few hours, while a coal burner may require three or four days. Time spent in port adds nothing to a ship's earnings. (3) Fewer crewmen are required aboard ship to pump oil to burners via an enclosed system of piping than to handle coal from bunkers to ship's furnaces. (4) Oil is cleaner than coal, and this affects not only the loading and handling processes but also the equipment that burns it. (5) Oil burners can fuel at sea; and although this is not too important for commercial vessels, it is tremendously so for naval craft, particularly in time of war or emergency. (6) The system of bunkering stations around the world can be stocked with oil more easily and more economically than with coal.

Trade in Petroleum. The prewar trade situation can be described very briefly. The United States, the world's principal producer and consumer of petroleum, was also an important exporter except during the 1920's, when it faced a deficit in crude oil and imports far exceeded exports. This nation has been both an importer and an exporter of oil primarily because of geography—the continental expanse of the country. California found it more economical to export to Asia than to ship through the Panama Canal to the oil-deficit northeastern part of the country. The latter section was generally supplied by oil from the Gulf region, but Venezuela, where American oil companies are prominent, is just as accessible. Petroleum from both Venezuela and the United States was shipped overseas, Middle Eastern oil moved primarily to Europe, while the Far Eastern oil region supplied the limited needs of countries nearby.

Postwar developments are such that anything written may be out of date by the time it gets into print. For example, the world's proved reserves in 1948 were given at slightly more than 71 billion barrels. At the close of 1951, proved reserves were listed at 102 billion barrels, with 26 billion in the United States (see accompanying table). Little more than a month later, it was announced that, as a result of additional prospecting and drilling, United States proved reserves had increased to over 27 billion barrels, or 1,416 million barrels over the 1951 figure.[1]

Area	Proved reserves, thousand barrels	Estimated average daily production, 1951, thousand barrels
North America	29,121,000	6,487
United States	26,121,000	6,143
Mexico	1,400,000	210
Canada	1,600,000	134
South American–Caribbean	11,313,000	1,990
Venezuela	10,000,000	1,700
Middle East	51,320,000	1,909
Iran	13,000,000	350
Iraq	10,000,000	175
Kuwait	15,000,000	545
Saudi Arabia	12,000,000	760
Far East	1,980,000	278
U.S.S.R. and satellites	7,910,000	902
Total	102,320,000	11,701

SOURCE: *Oil and Gas Journal*, Dec. 20, 1951, Vol. 50, pp. 190–191. Statistics are given here for only the major producers and hence do not add up to the totals given. Iranian production was 662,000 barrels daily through June when the industry was shut down.

[1] *Oil and Gas Journal*, Jan. 28, 1952, Vol. 50, p. 218.

The key to understanding oil statistics and also the future of the petroleum trade lies in the words *proved reserves*. The term *reserves* is used at times to apply to potential oil resources as yet to be discovered, while *proved* reserves are those quantities of petroleum "known to be recoverable under existing economic and operating conditions." In the United States, whose surface has been perforated by more than 1.25 million wells and has been prospected and explored far more thoroughly than any other part of the world, oil is still being discovered. Up to 1949, less than 150 wildcat wells had been drilled in the Middle East. At that time, proved reserves there were considered comparable with those of the United States. In considering the problems involved in the trade and transport of petroleum, and the future prospects, the foregoing facts must be borne in mind.

In 1947, the United States shifted from a net-export status to a net-import status. Since the close of the war, emphasis has been not on oil brought in from some producing area bordering the Caribbean but on shipments over the long haul from the Far East. The postwar situation, so characterized, is a result of several developments: (1) the war made demands on domestic reserves;[2] (2) since the war, domestic consumption has increased at a rapid rate owing to a tremendous expansion of our oil-fueled industry, the prosperity of which made it possible for many people to afford for the first time automobiles and clean, easily operated oil burners to replace troublesome and dirty coal burners; and (3) with an economy more dependent on petroleum than that of any other nation, and with newly assumed world-wide responsibilities, the nation *must* be in a position to meet not only its own needs but perhaps those of its allies. The nation is not faced with an oil famine, but rather with diminishing returns from its domestic sources.

This situation is offset (*a*) by increases in the proved reserves within the continental United States and in United States–controlled petroleum in other countries, such as Saudi Arabia and Venezuela, and (*b*) by Canada's potential as an oil producer. Although this country has within its borders approximately one-fourth of the world's proved reserves, it controls at least 60 per cent.[3]

Canada is today one of the great unknowns, or rather one of the greatest potentials. The United States is interested in Canadian oil reserves for both economic and strategic reasons. Canadian proved reserves at the close of 1951 were 1.6 billion barrels. This figure was due

[2] Production was stepped up from 1.25 billion barrels in 1939 to 1.75 barrels in 1945. This was possible because large reserves discovered during the 1930's had been kept underground as a result of controls exercised under proration laws.

[3] A 1938 report estimated that the United States controlled 60 percent of the world's petroleum reserves, British and Dutch interests 26 percent, Russia 8.4 percent, and other countries about 5 percent.

primarily to the discovery of oil at Leduc in Alberta in 1947. Alberta's production that year was 19,000 barrels, but by the beginning of 1952 it had risen to a point where 270,000 barrels could be produced daily if the oil could be handled. Geologists have known for decades that millions of barrels of oil are locked in the asphaltlike beds of northern Canada. The problem is "economic recovery." A Canadian geologist has pointed out that the potential oil area of western Canada is larger than the combined states of California, Texas, Oklahoma, Kansas, and Louisiana. Optimistic estimates place Canadian reserves at 50 billion barrels, and more optimistic ones at 200 billion—double the world's 1951 proved reserves.[4] If reserves approaching even the lower of these estimates should materialize, they would substantially alter the world's petroleum picture. The Western Hemisphere would be self-sufficient in petroleum; pipelines could carry the petroleum directly into the industrial heart of the United States.

The petroleum-exporting regions of the world, regions that produce almost entirely to satisfy the overseas market, are three in number:

1. Of the South American and Caribbean producers, Venezuela is the most important. In 1951, her production at 1.7 million barrels daily was close to the entire production of the Middle East (1.9 million barrels daily).

2. The only oil-producing region of the Far East embraces the islands of Borneo, Java, Sumatra, and New Guinea, all of which have been in the Dutch and British spheres of influence. Their importance as oil producers lies not so much in the quantity produced (in 1951 slightly less than 280,000 barrels daily and about half of Kuwait's production) as in their strategic position at the crossroads of the Indian and Pacific Oceans.

An American oil company, operating in Sumatra since the war, is gearing its plans and production to petroleum needs on the far side of the Pacific Basin, including those of Japan, the Philippines, and Australia. These plans are designed to eliminate the longer haul from the Middle East or from the Pacific Coast of the United States, where the supply is no longer adequate for transpacific exports.

3. The Middle East, including the major producing areas of Iran, Iraq, Kuwait, and Saudi Arabia, and areas of lesser importance such as Bahrein, is now conceded to embrace about one-half of the world's proved reserves, and therefore to be the world's principal oil region. Prior to the close of World War II, it was a sphere of primarily British and French influence, but postwar developments have been primarily American. Needless to say, production has been held down because of limitations on storage facilities and transportation.[5]

---

[4] *Time*, Sept. 24, 1951, pp. 42–48.
[5] For a concise summary of the development of oil interests in the Middle East, see E. W. Zimmermann, *World Resources and Industries*, rev. ed., Harper & Brothers, New York, 1951, pp. 521–22, and *Time*, Mar. 3, 1952, pp. 26–29.

Today, Middle Eastern oil meets not only Europe's needs but is moving to United States Atlantic ports in large quantities. This westbound transatlantic petroleum traffic has led United States oil companies to increase the size and number of tank ships engaged in foreign trade and this increase applies both to United States-flag tankers and to those owned by Americans but registered under foreign flags.

A decisive step was taken in the transport of Middle Eastern oil in 1951, when the Trans-Arabian pipeline connecting Arabia with the Mediterranean was completed. The Persian oil fields are only 1,000 miles from the Mediterranean, but the tanker trek through Suez, around the Arabian Peninsula, and into the Persian Gulf approaches 3,600 miles. The new 30- and 31-inch pipeline has a capacity of 300,000 barrels of crude oil a day. To move this amount would require the services of 62 T2-type tankers of 16,000 tons. Other pipelines of 12 and 16 inches connect Kirkuk with Haifa and Tripoli, and a 30- and 32-inch one runs from Kirkuk to Baniyas, Syria. The latter was completed in late 1952.

Although trade in petroleum is an integral part of waterborne commerce, and although stoppage of the movement of petroleum would paralyze shipping, the traffic in petroleum and its products is a thing apart from the tonnage of dry cargo transported by freighters. This is true not only because oil moves primarily by a special carrier, the tanker, but also because of circumstances inherent in the very nature of the petroleum industry.

1. The international movement of petroleum consists of two phases: exports of crude oil from producing areas to refineries in other countries, such as the movement of crude oil from Venezuela to Dutch refineries in Aruba or Curaçao or to refineries in the Gulf region of the United States; and exports and imports of refined petroleum products.

2. Because the incidence of petroleum is concentrated, the volume of waterborne shipments from some ports and on some routes can, if the petroleum tonnage is included in trade figures, distort the trade picture. In 1938, world exports of crude petroleum, gas and fuel oil, and gasoline alone totaled over 107 million metric tons. Although there is no way of ascertaining just how high a percentage of this was waterborne, the tanker movement must have comprised a high proportion of the world's total seaborne traffic of that year (470 million tons). The situation is even more striking for United States domestic shipping. According to the U.S. Army Engineers, the total domestic tonnage for 1950 was 183 million short tons, of which 141 million tons were petroleum or its products.[6]

The Tanker. To meet the needs of petroleum transport, the world's tanker fleet has grown rapidly in number and size of ships. The first tanker built to handle bulk petroleum was constructed in 1886. By 1911,

[6] The U.S. Army Engineers statistics include all domestic tonnage (coastwise, intercoastal, and noncontiguous) in these figures.

Lloyd's had on register 48 sailing ships and 234 steamers carrying oil in bulk. By 1950, the world's seagoing fleet of merchant tankers had increased to 25.3 million deadweight tons to comprise over 24 percent of the world's active merchant fleet, and tanker tonnage is increasing rapidly as various nations increase their tanker fleets.[7]

When oil was first shipped by water, it moved in 40-gallon barrels.[8] Since a barrel that was not secured tightly could "get a roll on it," this was dangerous. Furthermore, this means of transport was most uneconomical, because close to half of the loading capacity of the ship was lost. The next development was a 5-gallon tin container which, packed either in twos or in fours, transported "oil for the lamps of China" and provided the provident Chinese with a convenient little container for which they found multiple uses. But this too was an expensive way to move a low-value product. At least four days were required to discharge 10,000 barrels, and the expense involved accrued not only from labor costs but from tying up the vessel in port.

The modern industrially owned tankers, some of them 20,000 or more deadweight tons, are the result of trial and error in the carriage of oil and of the efforts of large oil companies to develop an economical and safe carrier. Heating coils in the bottoms of all cargo tanks reduce heavy fuel to a viscosity that permits pumping. The modern tanker can transport 20 or more different types of petroleum products, and an intricate arrangement of pump rooms allows for complicated loading and discharging operations to be performed with safety as regards admixture of cargo.[9] Ullage, the free space allowed in loading (usually 5 percent, depending on the density of the product), permits expansion. Cargo tanks are cleaned with great care. High-pressure jets of hot water remove all trace of previous shipments, and when sensitive products such as lubricating oils have been transported, the tanks are thoroughly dried by hand with clean rags.

This ideal carrier, however, has its drawbacks, for traffic is predominantly a one-way movement. On certain routes, efforts have been made to use such commodities as ores and coconut oil as return cargoes, but the quantity of these products at the termini where petroleum is delivered has not proved sufficient for outbound cargoes.[10] The tanker has proved a successful carrier, primarily because mechanical loading and unloading

[7] On the growth of the world fleet, the United States fleet, and the size of tankers, see Chap. 6.

[8] The barrel (42 gallons) is still the unit of production, but petroleum shipped in containers moves in drums, frequently as deck cargo.

[9] See W. L. Nelson, "Evolution of Tanker Design," *Petroleum*, London, January, 1944, Vol. 7, pp. 9-12. The July, 1952, issue of the *Bulletin*, Standard Oil Company of California, has a loading plan.

[10] However, on the recent movement of liquid chemicals and other unusual liquids such as liquefied petroleum gas in tankers, see *The Bulletin*, American Bureau of Shipping, July, 1950, p. 3.

have resulted in such a fast turn-around for the vessel that the tanker can transport petroleum more economically than a carrier adapted to a variety of cargoes. The success of the system is dependent upon adequate shore installations, including storage tanks at points of departure and receipt and pumps to load or discharge the largest tankers within a few hours.

THE INDUSTRIAL CARRIER AND ITS CARGOES

Although the oil-company tanker is the best-known industrial carrier, fruit companies, packing houses, and steel mills have found it expedient to own and operate their own ships. As owners of the carriers, they are in a position to perfect vessels that are especially adapted to their trade. Fundamentally, the requirements of the product shipped and the economies that may be effected are the determining factors that lead companies to enter the shipping business and to own their own water carriers.

The Ore Ship. Like tankers committed to one-way traffic unless a full or partial load of general merchandise happens to be available, the special ore vessels have nevertheless proved more efficient carriers of ores than freighters. They are built like freighters, with a bluff hull and wide hatches, only more so. Hull design is sacrificed to cargo capacity and to facilities for mechanical loading and unloading. It is common practice for cargo to be loaded or discharged at the rate of 1,000 tons per hour.

The traditional ore carrier has for decades been a part of Great Lakes shipping, but the oceangoing ore carrier was until recently an oddity, for the primary reason that the steel industry has been concentrated at focal points for two products: iron ore and good coking coal.[11] Pittsburgh has been a leader because of geography. Iron ore from the Mesabi Range in Minnesota, the richest, largest, and most easily worked deposit in the world, is shipped to the steel mills by Great Lakes steamer, while good coking coal comes from the nearby Connellsville mines. Birmingham, the world's fifth producing center, is built on a huge ore bed, and coal is available on the western side of Red Mountain.

As early as 1915, the Bethlehem Steel Corporation was importing iron ore for its Sparrows Point plant from Cruz Grande in Chile. At that time, costs of transport and not the domestic-supply situation were the determining factors, because it was cheaper to import ore than to move it by Great Lakes steamer and rail to Baltimore. Since then, and particularly since 1940, the supply position of the United States has changed, for, to

---

[11] This statement is true of the steel industry the world over, for it has achieved its greatest development in countries with adequate or near-adequate iron and coal reserves—in Europe, the United Kingdom, France, and Germany. The development of the steel industries of Italy and Japan was based on what those countries felt to be "security needs" and was dependent on imported supplies.

make this nation the arsenal of democracy, serious inroads in reserves were necessary. Hence, in the postwar world, when the great god steel determines more than ever a nation's warmaking ability and when the United States has assumed great global responsibilities, sources of iron ore within this nation's borders, like those of petroleum, show signs of diminishing returns.

The situation has been offset (1) by a process for beneficiating low-grade deposits and (2) by spectacular discoveries in nearby countries, especially in Labrador and Venezuela (Cerro Bolivar and El Paó). In addition, United States steel companies are importing ores from Cuba, Sweden, and Liberia. As a result of increased dependence on imports, the great steel companies have increased their fleets of ore carriers and now own and operate or charter vessels of, at times, as much as 20,000 or 25,000 tons. Also, the industry shows a tendency to move to seaboard, as indicated by United States Steel's new plant near Trenton, New Jersey.

Nothing can illustrate the necessity for waterborne trade in ores and metals more than the economic dependence of the United States, whose mineral wealth is greater than that of any country in the world. In 1939, the United States steel industry found it necessary to import chromium, cobalt, manganese, nickel, tin, tungsten, and vanadium. According to the *Minerals Yearbook* for 1949, since the last war, this country has been self-sufficient in coal, sulphur, cement, phosphate, potash, molybdenum, and magnesium and nearly so in iron and petroleum. In contrast, most of this country's aluminum, uranium, tin, mercury, and cobalt is processed from foreign ores, and at least 90 percent of the manganese, chromium, nickel, sheet mica, asbestos, radio-grade quartz, tantalum, columbium, and beryllium. Materials that move in shipload lots tend to move aboard special carriers, while those that move in smaller quantities provide partial cargoes for liner freighters.

Refrigerated Ships. Prior to the appearance of refrigerated ships, meat was shipped on the hoof, a singularly expensive manner of transport. One of the earliest refrigerated-meat shipments, consisting of 400 mutton carcasses, went out of Australia for London in 1880. Since that date, shipments of fresh refrigerated meat have increased rapidly. Refrigerated foodstuffs move either in reefer ships or in general-cargo vessels offering reefer service.

Outstanding examples of industrially owned meat and fruit carriers may be found in the fleets of the Blue Star Line and the United Fruit Company. In 1919, the Union Cold Storage Company (the British Beef Trust) bought the fleet of the Blue Star Line, which consisted of 15 steamships with a total capacity of 120,000 deadweight tons. They were originally employed primarily to carry fresh meat from Australia and Argentina to the British Isles, but their operations have been expanded to include a wide variety of activities, such as carrying apples from the Pacific Northwest of the United States to South America.

The banana ships of the United Fruit Company are known in most of the principal ports of the Western world, and the place that the banana occupies in the diet is dependent upon the system used to produce and transport it to market. Bananas are picked green in the producing areas of the Caribbean and Central America and ripen on the voyage. Because carbon dioxide causes premature ripening, bananas cannot be shipped with such fruits as oranges that give off the gas. Furthermore, the temperature must be kept constant at between 50 and 55 degrees.

Hence, to many areas, bananas are the one and only cargo. This is true of shipments to ports on the East Coast of the United States and to Gulf ports. To other ports (those where the marketing area is not broad enough to absorb full cargoes of bananas arriving every few weeks), bananas are shipped in refrigerated holds, while the rest of the cargo may be composed of other fruits, sugar, and coffee. The United Fruit Company, because of the multiplicity of its interests, can usually secure outbound cargo from United States ports to be carried in the insulated holds. For years, the tourist traffic, encouraged by such slogans as "The Great White Fleet serves the Americas," added passenger fares to the company's revenues.

NONGEOGRAPHICAL FACTORS INFLUENCING TRADE

Fundamentally, the location of the producing area in relation to that of the importing region is the most important factor in determining the paths that ships will follow in transporting goods over the seas. However, the movement of waterborne commerce is influenced by other factors, many of which appear to bear little relationship to geography. Perhaps it might be closer to the truth to say that such intangibles as shifts in supplies and demand and competition may substantially alter the geographical pattern of production and trade.

Perhaps the greater influence today is to be found in government decisions and policies, which frequently have a far-reaching effect on supply, demand, and competition. Although the ensuing discussion deals primarily with government decisions and policies as they affect the supply and movement of commodities, governments influence normal commercial patterns in other ways. A clear example is evident in the efforts of certain Latin-American governments to promote national-flag merchant marines through the device of discriminatory legislation.

Government Decisions and Policies. The most common device employed by governments to control and channel their trade is the import duty and, more rarely, the export duty, the composite of which on various commodities comprises a country's tariff system. The tariff, however, is only one of the means utilized by governments to alter the flow of trade. Take, for example, sugar, a newcomer as a staple in the diet of white people and second only to wheat as a major foodstuff in overseas trade. The history of sugar is marked by government interference from the very beginning.

The first overseas sugar imports reached Europe in the early 1600's aboard vessels owned and operated by the companies chartered by their governments and enjoying a virtual monopoly of the trade with the East and West Indies. For almost 250 years, these two areas remained the principal sources of supply. Needless to say, rather limited quantities reached Europe, and sugar was very dear. The expansion of production and trade in sugar is concurrent with the rise in importance of beet sugar.

When Napoleon set out to conquer the world, the British immediately cut off Europe's sugar, much of which had been derived from British-controlled sources and shipped over British-controlled routes. Fearing the results of the British embargo, Napoleon offered a large reward to any scientist who could find a way to extract sugar cheaply from beets or any other source. By 1850, beet sugar accounted for one-seventh of total world production (then only 1.4 million long tons), and during the next few decades the output of beet sugar increased rapidly. Bounties and subsidies stimulated production in such countries as Germany, Russia (including Poland), and Czechoslovakia (then a part of Austria-Hungary), while the sugar-beet industry of the United States was encouraged by a protective tariff. By the close of the century, England's free market had become the dumping ground for the world's sugar surpluses, both beet and cane.[12] As a result, the British were instrumental in calling the Brussels Sugar Convention of 1902, at which the participating countries agreed not to allow open or secret premiums on the production or export of sugar. France served notice of withdrawal early in 1917 and the United Kingdom early the next year. The convention was revoked by Java in 1919, and soon thereafter by the other signatories.

Meanwhile, far-reaching changes had occurred in the world's sugar industry. Beet-sugar production in Europe had been greatly curtailed as a result of World War I. About the turn of the century, a change had set in that was to revolutionize both the management and the techniques of the world's badly organized and haphazard cane-sugar industry. Since the cane-sugar belt, which straddles the equator, lies in a part of the world lacking in capital and know-how, the change was brought about by Americans in Puerto Rico, Hawaii, Cuba, and the Philippines and by

---

[12] Dumping means that a commodity is sold to a foreign buyer for a price lower than that charged the domestic buyer. Obviously dumping is possible only if the offending country has a protective tariff high enough to prevent the commodity from being reimported.

Europeans in Java, Mauritius, Jamaica, and Barbados. Out of the world sugar situation, which involves many problems that cannot be dealt with here, evolved the preference systems that have determined the overseas movement of sugar since the early 1920's and that are certain to affect future developments:

1. The world's largest sugar market is the United States, which consumes over 7 million tons of sugar a year. It relies on domestic supplies of beet sugar (1.5 million tons on the average for 1941 to 1948) and of cane sugar (slightly less than half a million tons for the same years); on duty-free shipments from its possessions, primarily Puerto Rico and Hawaii (close to 2 million tons a year); and on imports from Cuba and the Philippines. Cuba has been assured that the United States will purchase from her a substantial part of this country's total sales. Out of a 1952 quota of 7,700,000 tons, Cuba's quota was 2,425,000 tons, or slightly more than 30 percent. Since the close of the war, the Philippines have proved a negligible source of supply, but a trade act of 1946 granted the new nation a quota of approximately one million tons.

2. The next market is the United Kingdom and Canada, which are grouped together because of the empire sugar policy. Production of beet sugar in the British Isles has been stimulated by subsidies, but during the ten-year period from 1929 to 1938, the two countries imported approximately 2.8 million tons. Such empire sources as Mauritius, British Caribbean possessions, Australia, the Fiji Islands, and South Africa can meet half of the needs of the United Kingdom and Canada; the remaining half is one of the "big prizes of the 'free market.'"[13]

3. Because of their preferential systems, France and Portugal draw their sugar supplies primarily from their colonies, as Japan did also prior to World War II.

In the postwar sugar world appear two unknowns—India, which is automonous in her sugar policy, and the U.S.S.R. Zimmermann classifies both as self-sufficient but adds that "self-sufficiency does not indicate a degree of satiation, but merely implies that a country imports very little sugar, or none at all."[14] Whether these countries remain self-sufficient or become exporters or importers will be determined primarily by government decisions.

Before 1870, India was an exporter. She became a heavy importer and remained so until the early 1930's, when protectionism was introduced. The results were apparent in 1937, when India attained self-sufficiency by producing almost 3.6 million short tons of sugar. This figure was surpassed only by the 4.7 million tons produced by the United States and its possessions. In 1940, India was preparing to reenter the role of exporter,

[13] Zimmermann, *op. cit.*, p. 237.
[14] *Ibid.*

a decision that had not been put into effect as of early 1952. Another great potential is the U.S.S.R., now dominating the sugar-beet areas in Poland and Czechoslovakia. It remains to be seen whether Moscow will deem its surpluses necessary for domestic consumption or whether Soviet Russia will decide to export sugar.[15]

Concerning government interventions such as those affecting trade in sugar, wheat, and other commodities vital in the export trade of certain countries, one statement may be made with certainty. Such interventions are likely to be with us for some time to come. They were initiated because, under the free play of economic forces, the proper adjustment could not be made between two great needs—that of the consumer for an adequate supply at a reasonable price and that of growers and producers for an adequate reward. Sugar controls, as we have seen, were deemed necessary during a period of general prosperity, while the demand for wheat controls originated during the depressed 1930's.[16] In the altered economic structure of the postwar world, one can find scant hope that a balance between producers' and consumers' needs and demands can be met without government trade interference. Furthermore, once initiated, controls may be altered, but they are seldom abandoned completely.

For sugar, the situation involves a complication not present for wheat. The exportable sugar surpluses, consisting primarily of cane sugar, are produced in parts of the world dominated by a one-crop economy. Britain initiated her sugar controls in large part to relieve her cane-growing colonies from a depressed market, while the United States felt it necessary to protect producers within her sphere of interest—in her possessions of Hawaii and Puerto Rico; in Cuba, where the lack of a market for her sugar has resulted in revolution; and in the Philippines. Social planning now occupies a much more important place in national policies than it did earlier in the century, and government interference and intervention are encouraged by the rising concern for social justice.

Supplies, Demand, and Competition. On the world's sugar market, cane sugar from the tropics has had to compete with beet sugar, the product of the temperate zones. Other commodities such as tea and coffee compete or have competed with each other for their place on people's breakfast tables and for their position in transoceanic trade.

Tea and coffee were both introduced into Europe early in the seventeenth century. The first British coffeehouse was opened in England dur-

---

[15] See V. P. Timoshenko, *The Soviet Sugar Industry and Its Postwar Restoration*, War-Peace Pamphlet 13, Food Research Institute, Stanford University Press, Stanford, Calif., August, 1951.

[16] Efforts toward an international wheat agreement proved abortive during the 1930's, but bore fruit in the International Wheat Agreement, signed in the spring of 1949 by the major wheat-exporting countries with the exception of Argentina and the U.S.S.R.

ing the 1650's, when an Indian trader, so it is reported, backed his coachman financially so that he would have an outlet for the coffee he was importing. Coffee soon became the favorite beverage of the English, and it remained so until about 1750. Tea did not begin to attain its present position as the preferred beverage until the reign of Queen Victoria; in fact, the British preference for tea coincides with the rise of the British India Tea Companies, the first of which was formed in 1839. Ceylon leaf had killed the coffee trees that the Dutch had introduced into Ceylon, and the British turned to tea from Assam as a crop for their plantations in India and Ceylon. British preference not only shifted from coffee to tea; it also shifted from the green teas of China to the black ones produced in empire sources.

The center of coffee production meanwhile had shifted from Asia to South America. A native of Abyssinia, the coffee plant had been carried to Arabia by a Mohammedan priest, and the province of Yemen was the main source of supply until about 1690. The Dutch introduced coffee into Java, Ceylon, and the West Indies, from which a Franciscan monk took it to Brazil in 1754. By 1870, the Brazilian industry was important enough to warrant a transatlantic cable to Pernambuco. Le Havre and New York became the world's leading coffee markets to replace London (the main market until about 1830) and Amsterdam and Rotterdam (the distributing centers for Dutch coffee from the Indies). Within recent years, the United States has taken 60 percent of the world's coffee exports and Europe 40 percent.[17]

Hence, it is not a fortuitous circumstance that the main stream of the tea trade is from Ceylon and India to the United Kingdom and that coffee flows primarily from such Latin-American countries as Brazil and Colombia to United States ports and secondarily to Europe. The pattern of production and trade is the definite result of commercial exploitation on the part of commercially aggressive interests.

The Dutch, who introduced both tea and coffee into Europe and who were certainly the world's greatest traders at that time, lost out for reasons that are very evident. Both tea and coffee are today produced in quantity in concentrated areas for a mass market overseas, and that type of market did not exist until the latter part of the nineteenth century. By then, the Dutch were no longer in possession of Ceylon. The British plantation owners, taking advantage of Dutch experience with coffee there, turned to tea, set out to create a market in the British Isles and to produce for that market, and transformed the British people into a nation of tea drinkers.

[17] The loss of the European market during the war and its failure to recover since has led to drastic curtailment of coffee production in Brazil. Coffee, which comprised over 70 percent of the value of total Brazilian exports in 1929, now represents about one-third.

The United States, with no ties to possessions that were tea producers or potential tea producers, turned to coffee, originating not in the small-producing Dutch colonies but in South America, which had been producing for the European market. After 1900 and especially after 1920, United States coffee consumption increased by leaps and bounds. Production in coffee-producing countries kept pace with, and during the 1930's surpassed, demand. The growth of the United States market, however, was probably the result of efforts not on the part of foreign growers so much as on the part of large domestic coffee-roasting companies. Needless to say, they were aided by modern advertising, a rising standard of living, and two wars that did much to promote the coffee-drinking habit.

The story of silk, at least in certain respects, parallels that of tea, for China, the home of silk culture, lost out to a more ambitious competitor. Although carefully guarded, the secret of silk production leaked out around A.D. 300, and silk production spread to India, Iran (then Persia), Syria, France, and Italy. China, however, remained the world's principal supplier, primarily because she had the marginal, and at the same time highly skilled, labor necessary to produce silk and because her mulberry trees yield leaves nearly the year around. But, after disease ravaged the silk industries of the Rhone and Po Valleys in Europe, another country with cheap labor and mulberry trees entered silk culture in earnest.

By 1890, Japan was an important source of silk, and by the 1920's, when demand in the United States shot silk prices to as much as $9 per pound, she dominated the market. In 1929, United States imports were valued at more than 427 million dollars. Cotton fields were turned over to mulberry trees, which soon took up about 10 percent of Japan's arable land. Within less than a decade, nylon has relegated silk to the realm of a has-been, virtually eliminating Japan's most valuable export. Though the transition from silk to nylon was undoubtedly accelerated by the war, this fact makes the final chapter in the history of the Japanese silk industry no less tragic for the more than 2.5 million people who depended on sericulture for their livelihood. Nor does it make matters any easier for those United States officials who are advising the Japanese on economic matters, for the question of what Japan is to export in order to pay for much-needed imports is a pressing problem.

Except for a decision of the United States government, plantation rubber would today have suffered the fate of silk in the United States market, which just before World War II purchased half of the exports of the producing countries.

After World War II the United States found herself with a huge war-born synthetic rubber industry on her hands. It was decided to keep the most efficient half of this capacity in operation, to maintain some of the next best plants on a stand-by basis for emergency use, and to scrap the rest. In reaching this decision, the responsibility of this country as the largest buyer of plantation rubber from the rest of the world in terms of promotion of international trade and good will was definitely recognized. A less enlightened policy might well have aggravated the postwar problems of a sad world engaged in a "cold war," with one-half struggling to restore world trade and the other half fighting against it.[18]

This decision was made in the interest of Ceylon, British Malaya, and Indonesia (formerly the Netherlands Indies), which had acquired the rubber trees for their plantations in the "great seed snatch" of 1878. Although the tree was protected in Brazil, Sir Henry Wickham (who was knighted for his efforts) smuggled several thousand hevea trees from the Amazon region. Later, by way of Kew Gardens in London, some reached Ceylon to become the foundation for the rubber plantations of Southeast Asia. As a result of the aforementioned decision, the United States still purchases a part of her rubber from this area. By 1952, however, because of increased demands, this country was using twice as much synthetic rubber as new.

Balance of Payments. The British postwar experience in an effort to evolve a healthy balance-of-payments equilibrium illustrates the manner in which the balance of payments influences trade, and also presents one of the most perplexing problems today facing the United States' most important ally. The balance-of-payments problem is not new to the British, because for decades they bridged the gap between the cost of their imports and their exports primarily with earnings of a merchant marine that transported close to half of the tonnage moving in overseas trade. By the 1930's, however, British foreign trade was "living beyond its income." During the years 1936 to 1938, Great Britain paid for her imports with income from the following sources: 55 percent from exports, 12 percent from shipping, 23 percent from foreign investments, and 5 percent from commissions, insurance, and similar services. The remaining 5 percent represented a deficit.

The war worsened the situation. The decrease in vessel tonnage due to wartime losses resulted in lowered earnings from the shipping, commission, and other services involved in transportation. Between September, 1939, and June, 1945, the British had liquidated overseas investments worth approximately 4.5 billion dollars. As a result, income on foreign investments dropped from 200 million pounds in 1938 to less than 100 million in 1945. Wartime imports, valued at more than three times exports, had helped to increase Britain's foreign indebtedness from 1.9 billion dollars in August, 1939, to 13.5 billion in June, 1945. Of this total foreign debt, 90 percent consisted of "quick" liabilities.[19] The only way Britain could pay

[18] Zimmermann, *op. cit.*, p. 396.
[19] Most of the 1939-to-1945 increase in Britain's foreign indebtedness was to the sterling countries, because expenses incurred in those countries increased Britain's

her debts was by exporting. In other words, during the early postwar years, when Britain needed imports well above the prewar level to reconstruct her industrial plant, to rebuild bombed-out areas, and to relax in so far as possible the austerity regime under which the civilian population had lived since 1939, the British were called upon to service an enormous foreign debt—and to do so quickly.

Recognizing that world peace and prosperity are not confined by geographical boundaries and that the British balance-of-trade problem was not entirely a British problem, the United States made a loan of 3.75 billion dollars to Britain. It was anticipated on both sides of the Atlantic that this loan would tide the British over to the end of 1951.[20] By mid-1947, it was obvious that the loan would not last beyond the end of that year. In a speech before the House of Commons on Aug. 7, 1947, Mr. Dalton, Chancellor of the Exchequer, gave a complete accounting of the American loan. From that speech certain facts were evident: (1) the British export drive had not lived up to earlier hopes, (2) commodity prices were much higher than had been anticipated, and (3) the large American loan was being depleted rapidly, not only because dollars were being used for purchases in the United States but because Britain was purchasing from other countries in the Americas and from European nations that were unwilling to sell for sterling.

One course only was then open to the British—to draw all imports possible from sterling countries and to reduce those from dollar countries to a minimum. This involved a tightening of exchange controls and other restrictive measures that tend to form isolated blocks or areas of trade and to stifle trade between those two blocks. For decades, Britain had purchased her grains, for both feed and food, from overseas suppliers; but in 1950, the British Ministry of Food concluded a sterling agreement with

---

debt, while United States wartime assistance to Britain took the form of Lend-Lease and Canadian assistance to cover British war expenditures in Canada was treated largely as gifts.

The sterling area is not a wartime or postwar innovation. It consists of a group of countries thrown together during the monetary turmoil and breakdown of the gold standard in 1931. Because of convenience, the tie with the British market and "the long tradition of maintaining exchange reserves in London" led certain countries to join the United Kingdom in a decision to maintain their exchanges stable in terms of sterling, not of gold. Naturally, the members of the Commonwealth, for whose raw materials the British Isles had been the principal market, joined, with the exception of Canada. Other adherents included Portugal, the Scandinavian countries, and Iran. See Paul Bareau, "The Sterling Area—Its Use and Abuse," *The Banker*, London, March, 1945, pp. 131–133.

[20] This was not an ECA transaction or a part of the Lend-Lease program. In 1945, 25 billion dollars of Lend-Lease indebtedness had been canceled, and a loan of 650 million dollars arranged for to settle surplus war property and Lend-Lease deliveries made by the United States after V-J Day. When ECA expired at the end of 1951, Britain had received 2.8 billion dollars from ECA funds. Aid after that date comes under the Mutual Security Agency.

Russia calling for the delivery of 800,000 tons of Russian coarse grain—a contract that accounts for one-fifth of Britain's needs for coarse grain. Argentina was unwilling to sell for sterling, and Britain entered into trade agreements with that nation calling for deliveries of Argentine beef against shipments of petroleum from Iran. In 1950, United States oil companies operating in the Middle East experienced difficulties because sterling-area markets were practically closed to them. Naturally, Britain's situation worsened during the Korean crisis, for many of the commodities necessary in the rearmament program were obtainable only in dollar countries. In June, 1951, the gap between British dollar sales and dollar purchases resulted in a deficit of 420 million dollars, the worst in history, and the trade deficit for the last six months of that year was 394 million pounds, or over 1.3 billion dollars. However, late in 1952, the British were able to announce a surplus of 24 million pounds ($67,200,000) for the first six months of 1952.

Economic Nationalism. The existence of a sterling area is, of course, one facet of economic nationalism, which has taken on various aspects over the centuries. Until the close of the eighteenth century, it was called mercantilism or old-fashioned protectionism. In a sense, economic nationalism went underground during the heyday of the free traders, only to emerge again in the new imperialism of the late nineteenth century. Of that imperialism and its implications for trade, Condliffe[21] has written:

> The new imperialism with which the nineteenth century ended was a struggle to develop the old European empires in south and southeast Asia, and to carve out new empires largely in Africa. Other aspects of this imperialism were the extension of economic influence in the Middle East, in China and in the less developed Latin-American countries with rich mineral resources. In all these regions trade was of the colonial type . . . . Out of the intense struggle from about 1880 to 1914 to secure access to raw materials and markets there came the shipping and naval rivalries which preceded the first World War . . . . The . . . scramble to grab and exploit natural resources brushed aside the weaker peoples and contributed to the tensions that later flared into war. It was not only politically dangerous, it was uneconomic. The largest stream of commodities that was fed into world trade came not from the regions of colonial exploitation, but from areas where settled government and efficient production made an abundant supply of foodstuffs and raw materials both cheap to the consumers and profitable to the producers.

During the uneasy peace from 1918 to 1939, economic nationalism still rested primarily on nationalistic aspirations, but it changed its face to suit the period. For certain nations that the world now knows were preparing for war, "self-sufficiency" became an economic precept. Their

[21] J. B. Condliffe, *The Commerce of Nations*, W. W. Norton & Company, New York, 1950, pp. 292–293.

struggle to free themselves from dependence upon imports cut deep into the trade of all nations and forced other countries to resort to uneconomic production and to construct new trade barriers.

Hand in hand with self-sufficiency went the "have-and-have-not" controversy which received far more credence among thoughtful men than it deserved.

In a free-trade world everybody would be a "have" because everybody would have equal access to all the resources of the globe. In a tariff-ridden world . . . everybody is a have-not—even the United States, as shortages of strategic materials and other goods during the recent war have amply demonstrated. But countries with lesser territory, countries without colonies can present to the world a seemingly plausible case of grievances . . . . Actually, in order to be a successful "have-not," a country must be very powerful. Then it can threaten the world and exact fulfillment of at least some of its demands.[22]

Post-1945 economic nationalism, which Heilperin has called "that fashionable 'young man about town' in the world of contemporary politics and economics," springs from national insecurity and nationalist aspirations on the one hand and from economic collectivism on the other. The main aspect that is new to economic nationalism is the preoccupation of its advocates with full employment. This type of nationalism became prevalent during the depression of the 1930's. It was revived immediately following World War II, when governments anticipated mass unemployment and set up agencies to study the problem of full employment. Its appeal is to the intellects of men, but many believe its logic to be inconclusive.

Anti-depression policies must not be concerned with employment alone; they must embrace the component elements of a well-working economy. If the economy functions smoothly, there is no chronic mass unemployment; if it is conducted with due regard for productivity and yield, standards of living go up; if it maintains trade relations with the rest of the world, there follow all the advantages accruing from an international division of labor.[23]

In general, economic nationalism has been a phenomenon practiced by powerful and wealthy nations, though manifestations have appeared in such countries as India since the turn of the century and in Mexico during the 1930's. But, since the close of World War II, what has been called twentieth-century economic nationalism has risen in some of the least powerful, poorest, and most underdeveloped countries of the world—countries that form almost a solid belt through central and northern South America and across the Moslem world from Gibraltar to the Pacific. This outcropping is, of course, closely associated with the imperialism of certain European countries about the turn of the century and also with

---

[22] M. A. Heilperin, *The Trade of Nations*, Alfred A. Knopf, Inc., New York, 1947, p. 141. This study was of great assistance in writing parts of this chapter.

[23] *Ibid.*, p. 100.

the buccaneering methods of the days of United States dollar diplomacy. In the world of fifty years ago, the demands of such nations would have been given little attention. Recently, and particularly since the close of World War II, the world gives an attentive ear to demands, many of which appear almost childish. The reasons for this change are varied.

The rising tide of social justice dictates that commercial policies should protect the interests of those whose heritage, because of their own limitations, must be exploited by foreigners, as well as the rights of those who invest their capital at considerable risk and who place at the disposal of the underdeveloped countries their knowledge, experience, know-how, and skills. Second, many of the countries now experiencing nationalism in a most extreme form possess resources, primarily mineral, that are in short supply in other parts of the world. Third, with their national income dependent primarily on one resource and one only, with their poverty, disease, and illiteracy, many countries in this group are peculiarly vulnerable to Communist infiltration.

The trade implications of this economic nationalism are everywhere evident. Take only the years 1951 and 1952. Premier Mossadegh and his government assumed control of Iran's oil fields, the world's largest refinery at Abadan was shut down, and Iranian oil ceased to flow to Europe. In Egypt, nationalists are demanding from the British control of the Suez Canal. In a tiny Central American country, a government headed by an army strong man notified one of the world's largest fruit companies that new contracts would embody, among other things, provisions that the company turn over company-built and operated ports to the government and that rates be cut on the company's rail network and on the ships of its fleet. Foreign capital is reluctant to enter countries with unstable governments. After spending more than a million dollars prospecting for oil in one South American country during the war, a large oil company decided to withdraw rather than attempt to operate under the prevailing conditions. Nor is withdrawal or a "hands-off" policy the solution, for this type of economic nationalism will plague the world as long as the conditions that nourish it prevail.

THE POSTWAR SITUATION

Before World War I, a system of overseas trade had developed into a network. While that network did not represent a conscious pattern, nevertheless one existed. The system of trade that moved over triangular or multilateral trade routes was disrupted by the hostilities of World War I. During the 1920's, trade was revived along the lines of prewar years, only to be disrupted again by the depression. Though trade conditions improved during the late 1930's, the seaborne commerce of that decade was hampered by the restrictions of economic warfare.

After World War II, the volume of seaborne trade recovered rapidly. As early as 1946, it was up to 360 million metric tons, or slightly higher than the volume of 1932 and 1933. By 1947, it was well above the level for the "good" years 1928 to 1930. The following year, at 490 million tons, seaborne trade was equal to the commerce of 1937, the peak prewar

Year	Volume, million metric tons	Year	Volume, million metric tons	Year	Volume, million metric tons
1928	430	1931	380	1946	360
1929	470	1932	350	1947	450
1930	440	1933	360	1948	490
Average	437	1934	390	1949	510
		1935	410	1950	550
		1936	430	Average	472
		1937	490		
		1938	470		
		Average	420		

SOURCE: Statistics from *United Nations Statistical Yearbook, 1951*, p. 322.

year. The year 1949 represented an all-time high, only to be surpassed in 1950.

The composition of seaborne trade, however, is another matter, for postwar trade has not been "of a piece." During the months immediately following the war, many of the shipments not only from the United States but also from Canada, Australia, and New Zealand were of a "gift" nature. When the Economic Cooperation Administration (ECA) started to function early in 1948, emphasis shifted to cargoes "to restore economic activity in the modern world." After ECA expired on Dec. 31, 1951, the Mutual Security Agency continued foreign aid, and the key word became "security."

The most striking, but not unexpected, development has been an increase in the importance of the United States in overseas trade. In 1938, this nation purchased only 9 percent of the world's imports on the basis of volume, while in 1947, the percentage was 12. For United States exports, the 1938 figure was 11 percent, as compared with 25 percent in 1947. During 1948 and 1949, this country's share of world exports decreased and her share of imports increased.

Furthermore, since the war, there has been a large volume of seemingly abnormal trade moving. For example, consider the coal trade. Britain, for decades the principal source of coal exports, exported 41 million metric tons on the average between 1935 and 1939, with an additional 12 million tons a year for bunkers. In 1948 and 1949, British exports averaged 14 million tons a year, while bunkers were only a little over 5 million tons annually.[24]

[24] Sara L. Lepman, "Europe's Coal Production and Trade," *Foreign Commerce Weekly*, Apr. 3, 1950, Vol. 39, pp. 3–5.

OVERSEAS TRADE AND SHIPPING SERVICES (CONTINUED)

The decrease in British shipments affected countries of Continental Europe. Scandinavian ships that formerly loaded coal at British ports traveled across the Atlantic to load at United States ports. The failure of the European coal industry to recover "slowed down the convoy" of European industry. The United States attempted to alleviate the situation by unprecedented coal shipments. In 1937, United States exports, exclusive of shipments to Canada and bunkers, were only slightly more than one million short tons. In 1947, they were over 47 million. After dropping in 1950 to 2.5 million tons, shipments in 1951, under the impetus of the defense-mobilization program, rose to 33 million. At one time in the winter of 1951–1952, a 10,000-ton ship loaded with coal left the United States every two hours day and night. United States dry-cargo exports in December, 1951, were 7.4 million short tons, 5 millions tons of which moved by irregular or tramp carrier. The estimate for 1952 coal exports was 42 million, but by April that had been scaled down to 17 million, of which 8 million had already been delivered.

Much the same situation exists for wheat. We have already pointed out that United States exports during the 1930's were at a very low ebb and that this nation was actually a net importer during part of the decade. With this in mind, consider the accompanying figures for the trade and production of the four principal exporters. Because wheat-acreage re-

Year	Argentina	Australia	Canada	United States
Production of wheat, thousand metric tons				
1934–1938 average	6,634	4,200	7,170	19,476
1947	6,664	5,991	9,301	37,209
1948	5,200	5,190	10,515	35,749
1949	5,144	5,939	10,108	31,059
1950	5,796	5,014	12,565	27,744
1951	2,050	4,392	15,041	26,875
Gross exports of wheat and flour, thousand metric tons				
1934–1938 average	3,340	2,787	4,771	1,259
1947	2,305	1,291	6,471	13,194
1948	2,202	3,485	5,114	13,446
1949	1,854	3,193	6,872	11,208
1950	2,783	3,428	5,633	6,812
1951	2,450	3,490	7,871	12,863

SOURCE: The figures tabulated are issued by the Food and Agriculture Organization of the United Nations. Those for 1951 should be regarded as preliminary.

strictions were relaxed and nature smiled on the efforts of the American farmer, postwar United States crops reached peaks that placed this nation in a position to meet the wheat needs of a hungry world.

United States gross exports during the period 1934 to 1938 had averaged less than half of those of Australia, which, over the years, had ranked fourth among the major overseas exporters. In 1947, 1948, and 1949, United States exports averaged 12.6 million metric tons—ten times their prewar level and larger than the Canadian crop harvested during those years.[25] In 1950, they dropped to approximately half of their 1947-to-1949 level, only to shoot up to over 12 million tons again in 1951. Exports for 1951 were swollen not only by demands arising from the Korean conflict but by shipments to India, for Congress authorized a loan for the purpose of financing shipments of one million tons of American wheat to that country.

Wheat exports of late . . . play a major part in the "cold war," the East-West struggle between communistic tyranny and capitalistic or socialistic democracy. To some extent the taxpayer is expected to support them with the same grim determination with which he supports the construction and support of the navy, the army, or the air force.[26]

BIBLIOGRAPHY

Blank, John S., 3d, "The Great White Fleet," *Ships*, May, 1952, pp. 8–15.
"Changes in the Pattern of World Grain Transport," *Transport and Communications Review*, United Nations, October-December, 1948, Vol. I, No. 2, pp. 3–8.
"Changes in the Pattern of the World Movement of Coal, 1937–1947," *Transport and Communications Review*, United Nations, January-March, 1949, Vol. II, No. 1, pp. 3–9.
Condliffe, J. B., *The Commerce of Nations*, W. W. Norton & Company, New York, 1950, especially Chap. 10, "The Network of World Trade."
Fanning, L. M., *American Oil Operations Abroad*, McGraw-Hill Book Company, Inc., New York, 1947.
——— (ed.), *Our Oil Resources*, 2d ed., McGraw-Hill Book Company, Inc., New York, 1950.
Feis, H., *Petroleum and American Foreign Policy*, Food Research Institute, Stanford University Press, Stanford, Calif., 1944.
Hardy, A. C., *Seaways and Sea Trade*, D. Van Nostrand Company, Inc., New York, 1928.
Heilperin, M. A., *The Trade of Nations*, Alfred A. Knopf, Inc., New York, 1947.
Hutchins, J. G. B., *The American Maritime Industries and Public Policy, 1789–1914*, Harvard University Press, Cambridge, Mass., 1941.

[25] Since we are interested in the level of shipments rather than the relationship between crops and exports, exports statistics are for calendar years, not for crop years, which differ in the two hemispheres. Hence, the reader should not attempt to match up the production and trade figures given. For example, United States exports during early 1947 are from the 1946 crop or from carry-overs, and cannot include 1947 wheat until after the crop is harvested.

[26] Zimmermann, *op. cit.*, p. 212.

Johnson, D. G., *Trade and Agriculture*, John Wiley & Sons, Inc., New York, 1950.
Killough, H. B., and Lucy W. Killough, *Economics of International Trade*, 2d ed., McGraw-Hill Book Company, Inc., New York, 1948.
Knorr, K. K., *Tin under Control*, Food Research Institute, Stanford University Press, Stanford, Calif., 1945.
———, *World Rubber and Its Regulation*, Food Research Institute, Stanford University Press, Stanford, Calif., 1945.
League of Nations, *Europe's Trade*, Geneva, 1941.
———, *The Network of World Trade*, Geneva, 1942.
———, *Industrialization and Foreign Trade*, Geneva, 1945.
———, *Raw Materials Problems and Policies*, Geneva, 1946.
Mance, Sir Osborne, *International Sea Transport*, Oxford University Press, New York, 1945.
"Peninsular and Oriental Steam Navigation Company," *Fortune*, October, 1946, pp. 120*ff*.
Pratt, E. E., *International Trade in Staple Commodities*, McGraw-Hill Book Company, Inc., New York, 1928.
"Six Kingdoms of Oil—the Persian Gulf Strikes It Rich," *Time*, Mar. 3, 1952, pp. 26–29.
Staley, Eugene, *World Economic Development*, International Labour Office, Montreal, 1944.
"Steel," *Time*, Nov. 12, 1951, pp. 94–105.
Swerling, B. C., *International Control of Sugar*, Food Research Institute, Stanford University Press, Stanford, Calif., 1949.
Taylor, H. C., and A. D. Taylor, *World Trade in Agricultural Products*, The Macmillan Company, New York, 1938.
United Nations, *World Food Survey*, Washington, D.C., 1947.
———, Food and Agriculture Administration, *World Fiber Survey*, Washington, D.C., 1947.
U.S. Maritime Commission, *A Study of Tramp Shipping under the American Flag*, a report of the Tramp Shipping Committee, Aug. 5, 1949, mimeographed.
Wallace, B. B., and L. R. Edminster, *International Control of Raw Materials*, Brookings Institution, Washington, D.C., 1930.
Wheat Studies of the Food Research Institute, Stanford University Press, Stanford, Calif.
Wickizer, V. D., *Tea under International Regulation*, Food Research Institute, Stanford University Press, Stanford, Calif., 1944.
———, *The World Coffee Economy*, Food Research Institute, Stanford University Press, Stanford, Calif., 1943.
Zimmermann, E. W., *World Resources and Industries*, rev. ed., Harper & Brothers, New York, 1951.

CHAPTER 4

TRADE ROUTES AND SERVICES

Basically, the foremost factor determining the route or path a commodity takes when it moves in oceangoing trade is the location of the exporting or producing area in relation to the overseas market. Other physical factors, however, help to determine the routes that ships will follow.

PHYSICAL FACTORS INFLUENCING TRADE ROUTES

Ports. Waterborne commerce must flow through seaports with facilities for handling the ships and the cargoes. Natural harbors have contributed substantially to the development of such seaports as Boston, New York, Baltimore, San Francisco, Seattle, and Southampton; rivers provided London, Antwerp, New Orleans, and Portland with advantages. The anchorage in quiet water is, however, second to the all-important hinterland. Lacking that hinterland, harbors possessing great natural advantages such as Port Mahon on Minorca, Ireland Island in the Bermudas, and Lyttleton, New Zealand, can possess only strategic value.

When the demands of commerce become strong enough, man sets out to modify geography. Canals made it possible for Manchester, Bruges, Amsterdam, and Houston to become shipping centers, while artificial breakwaters created the ports of Dover, Boulogne, and Los Angeles, the last of which was built only a few decades ago.

Canals. From the vantage point of the mid-twentieth century, it is difficult to evaluate the impact of the Suez and Panama Canals on ocean shipping. The Suez Canal was opened in 1869, prior to the late-nineteenth-century volume increase in overseas trade. Without the shorter haul and resulting lower freight charges, Europe might not have developed into the market that it did for the wheat, jute, rice, tin, rubber, and tobacco of Southeast Asia. Within fifteen years after the canal opened, European prices for certain Eastern products had fallen from 25 to 35 percent.

Between 1869 and the opening of the Panama Canal, the Suez Canal served for a large part of the traffic moving between ports on both sides of the Atlantic and the continent of Asia tributary to the Pacific and Indian

Oceans. The savings in nautical miles on the Suez route as against the Cape of Good Hope route are indicated by the accompanying figures. The saving in distance between Liverpool and Sydney was so small that canal

From	To Bombay	To Batavia	To Hong Kong	To Sydney
Liverpool...........	4,541	2,689	3,410	391
New York..........	3,409	1,557	2,293	−205

dues and the possibility of delay in passing through the canal were usually deciding factors in favor of the Cape route, which had the advantage for traffic between New York and Sydney. Practically the only transpacific trade at that time moved between San Francisco, then the only seaport on the Pacific Coast, and ports in the Orient, principally in China and Japan.

After World War I was over and the Panama Canal opened to commercial shipping, the world's shipping map again underwent a thorough revision. For the United States, the canal eliminated the necessity of two fleets and opened the way for ship operators to resume the intercoastal trade that had flourished from the days of the gold rush until about 1880. The canal cut the distance between New York and San Francisco by over 7,800 miles and that between New Orleans and San Francisco by over 8,800 miles. Prior to the opening of the canal, there had been no waterborne trade between Gulf ports and the Pacific Coast.

To illustrate the savings in distances for overseas shipping, certain ports have been used as representative of the areas they serve. However, it should be remembered that, since trade does not run along unilateral lines, distance savings are not limited to the particular ports mentioned, and also that those savings operate in both directions. For instance, the Panama Canal reduced the distance between Liverpool and San Francisco by over 5,600 miles, to the benefit of all European trade moving to the United States Pacific Coast region via the canal, and vice versa.

Ships sailing from New York and New Orleans, and in fact from all United States Atlantic and Gulf ports, save thousands of miles by using the Panama route on voyages to the Pacific ports of San Francisco, Honolulu, Callao, and Valparaiso. (The tabulation on page 78 presents savings in nautical miles.) To Yokohama, the savings by way of Panama were also substantial. Liverpool benefits by using the Panama Canal on voyages to these ports, except to Yokohama. Savings in distance to Yokohama also apply to all north China ports, such as Shanghai. Hong Kong (and Manila to the south) is nearly equidistant from New York by either canal, while New Orleans can save close to 2,000 miles by using the Panama Canal. For European traffic to and from these points in the Orient, the Suez Canal has the advantage of more than 4,000 miles over the Panama Canal. By using the latter route to Sydney, New York saves over 3,900 miles and New Orleans almost 5,500 miles. Suez, however, offers European traffic to Sydney a slight saving over Panama, while Europe is about 1,500 miles closer to New Zealand going west by Panama rather than east by Suez.

Destination	From New York	From New Orleans	From Liverpool
San Francisco	7,873	8,868	5,666
Honolulu	6,610	7,605	4,403
Callao	6,250	7,245	4,043
Valparaiso	3,747	4,742	1,540
Yokohama	3,768	5,705	− 694
Hong Kong	− 18*	1,919*	−4,172*
Sydney	3,932†	5,444†	− 150*
Wellington	2,493	3,488	1,564*

* Difference between Panama and Suez routes.
† Difference between Panama and Good Hope routes.
Unless otherwise indicated, all savings are from the Panama Canal route compared with those through the Strait of Magellan.

Savings in distance result in appreciable savings in steaming time and hence in lower voyage costs. A freighter outbound from New York for Honolulu saves over 6,600 miles by using the Panama Canal. As the average speed of a C3-type vessel is 16.5 knots, this represents four hundred hours or sixteen and two-thirds days of steaming time one way. Since it costs roughly $2,500 per day to operate an American-flag ship of this type, the resulting operational saving is roughly $41,700. From that amount must be subtracted the canal toll of $7,000, leaving a saving of close to $35,000. To get the total saving for a voyage outbound and inbound, this figure should be doubled. Time saved on voyages results in more voyages over a given period and hence greater earnings. Consequently, the figures used for illustration are inadequate as a measure of the advantages accruing to the ship operator.

The canals did not, and still have not, completely eliminated traffic around the two Capes. Between such points as London or New York and Australasia, the canal routes offer little distance advantage. Between the West Coast of the United States and ports of South America such as Buenos Aires they offer none at all, since Buenos Aires is 1,100 miles closer to San Francisco and Los Angeles via Magellan than it is through the canal. Matters other than distance are considered, including the weather, canal tolls, bunkers, cargo offerings, and intermediate ports of call.

Instead of using the Suez Canal, the sailing freighters that dominated Australia's wool and wheat trade until well after the turn of the century "rounded the Cape" to Australia and "doubled the Horn" back to Europe. Liverpool is only a few hundred miles closer to Sydney via Suez than by the Cape of Good Hope—a distance that is insignificant on a 12,000-mile voyage. Further, using the Cape route, they avoided the doldrums that might have been encountered in the Red Sea, a canal toll and towage fee, and a possible delay in passing through the canal. In contrast, steam freighters were forced to use the canal because bunkers were not available at Capetown or Durban until African coal was marketed.

The Panama Canal also altered the Europe-Australasia trade-route situation. The distance between Liverpool and Wellington is 1,500 miles shorter via Panama than via Suez, but the Panama route is only 500 miles shorter than the Magellan route. Hence, for some traffic, the canal routes offer little if any advantage except weather conditions and possible cargo offerings. Unscheduled carriers would probably sail by way of one or the other of the Capes, while a freighter that was to discharge and load cargo at a number of ports would be scheduled to pass through one of the canals on the route that would probably offer more cargo. In late 1952, a British ship that carried Australian meat to San Francisco in the British-Canadian-Australian meat exchange reached Australia via Good Hope.

Although the proposed St. Lawrence Seaway will not alter the world's map to the extent that the Suez and Panama Canals did, the project is by far the most important enterprise of its kind now under consideration. Such a waterway has been discussed, pressed, and attacked for more than fifty years. In 1951, Canada announced that she would construct the multimillion dollar project alone if the United States did not decide to share in the undertaking. By a system of canals, the seaway will link the St. Lawrence River and the Great Lakes to enable all but the biggest freighters to steam into the industrial heartland of North America.

Sphericity of the Earth. Because the earth is a sphere, a ship operating between western Europe or the United States Atlantic and Gulf ports and Australia and New Zealand may choose a cape route rather than one of the canals. The sphericity of the earth affects the path of practically every ship that sails. From New England, the British Isles are, as Benjamin Franklin pointed out, "down hill all the way." Yokohama is almost due west of San Francisco, but ships sailing between these points swing northward to follow the great circle, which is the shortest distance between them. Steaming due west, the voyage is 4,799 miles, while that toward the Aleutians is 4,536 miles. Seattle, at the western terminus of the great circle, is in an advantageous position in United States trade with Japan and with ports of northern China.

Geography has also contributed to the growth of the port of Los Angeles. Because the earth is a sphere, vessels passing through the Panama Canal for the Orient steam fairly close to the California coast. The effect of the world's shape on trade routes is not made very clear by maps. A globe is better. Use a string, one end at the Panama Canal and the other at Yokohama, and you will see that the most direct ocean path traverses the coast of California. Nature has given Los Angeles another great advantage—oil. San Pedro is one of the ports at which the cost of fuel is so low that it may be worth a few hours of extra steaming to bunker there.

Bunkering Stations. Ever since steamships replaced sail, bunkering stations and their location have influenced the routes of ships. For early steamships, bunkers were of paramount importance. Not only was the system of bunkering stations less far-reaching than today, but the cruising range of ships was not very great. Furthermore, the early engines required so much coal for fuel that the carrying capacity of the ships was greatly reduced. The bunkering situation improved as the network of coaling stations became more widespread and as screw steamers requiring less fuel replaced earlier steamships.

The steamship came into her own, however, when oil replaced coal as the principal fuel. Because of the great saving of space aboard ship and because ships can now bunker frequently on most routes, their cargo-carrying capacity has been greatly increased. If a ship outbound on a 10,000-mile voyage must carry full bunkers, fuel will take up considerable space and lifting capacity; if she can fuel en route, she can carry additional cargo.

Every ship on the high seas, whether a coal or an oil burner, is expected to bunker at the point on its route where bunkers are cheapest. Hence, a vessel headed for the Panama Canal on a voyage to the Orient will inquire whether fuel oil is cheapest at Curaçao, Trinidad, the Canal Zone, or Los Angeles harbor. However, no vessel will steam far off her course to save on the fuel bill, since the extra steaming time and the time lost may cost more than the saving on oil.

Weather, Currents, and Climatic Conditions. Columbus's first voyage to America was, for the most part, over an ocean as smooth as a river and along the northern edge of the northeast trade winds that blow steadily in the late summer between the Canary Islands and America. Homeward bound, sailing as close to the wind as they could, his caravels worked their way northward to about the latitude of Cape Hatteras and went roaring home on the winter westerlies. Columbus had traveled the general route used by future Spanish shipmasters. They learned to take advantage not only of the prevailing winds in the Atlantic but also of ocean currents—sailing outbound on the equatorial current and returning via the Gulf

Stream as far north as Hatteras, from which they launched out into the open Atlantic.[1]

Weather phenomena and currents, which led the captain of a sailing ship to figure a voyage in terms of sailing days rather than nautical miles, also influence the steamship.[2] Big freighters and tankers moving southbound along the Atlantic Coast thread their way surprisingly close to shore between the Florida coast and the Gulf Stream, while northbound they travel with the current. Although a modern ship can make headway even in very adverse weather, she can do so only at a great reduction in speed or a risk of structural damage and with a consequent increase in steaming time and a larger fuel bill. The good-weather route usually shortens the voyage and reduces maintenance costs. Safety, moreover, is a deciding factor in the paths ships travel, particularly passenger vessels.

DEFINITION OF TERMS

Trade Route. Thus far, the term *trade route* has been used in the sense of a "major channel through which trade flows."[3] This definition suffices admirably for a trade route such as that running between North Atlantic ports in North America and Europe—the route that has been called the main artery of overseas trade and one on which a high proportion of the sailings offered is the regularly scheduled service of the berth or liner operator. But even this liner traffic is flexible, since new steamship lines may start to operate and old ones curtail or discontinue their service. Furthermore, any change in world conditions may affect the system, increasing or diminishing the number of ships, adding or eliminating

---

[1] The Gulf Stream, a "river" within the sea 95 miles from bank to bank and the greatest of all ocean currents, was first charted by Benjamin Franklin in 1769. He found that the packets from the British Isles took two weeks longer to cross than did the Rhode Island merchantmen. He sent a chart, based on information furnished by a Nantucket whaler, to England to be used by the captains of the packets, but, he complained, they "slighted it."
Rachel Carson, in *The Sea around Us* (Oxford University Press, New York, 1951, pp. 140–141), presents simple maps of the wind-driven currents of the Atlantic and Pacific Oceans. Her chapters "The Wind, Sun, and Spinning of the Earth" and "The Moving Tides" are informative and delightful reading. The reader with a professional interest will prefer Nathaniel Bowditch, *American Practical Navigator*, U.S. Department of the Navy, Hydrographic Office, Washington, D.C., 1943, or Benjamin Dutton, *Navigation and Nautical Astronomy*, 10th ed., Revisions by the Department of Seamanship and Navigation, U.S. Naval Institute, Annapolis, Md., 1951.

[2] The science of oceanography is usually dated from the work of Matthew Fontaine Maury, whose activities as a young lieutenant in the U.S. Navy led to the publication in 1855 of his book, *The Physical Geography of the Sea*. The monthly *Pilot Charts*, issued by the U.S. Navy Hydrographic Office, carry this notation: "Founded on the researches of Matthew Fontaine Maury while serving as a Lieutenant in the United States Navy."

[3] *Report . . . on the Essential Foreign Trade Routes and Services Recommended for United States Flag Operation*, U.S. Maritime Commission, May 22, 1946, mimeographed.

ports of call, and so forth. None of these qualifications changes or destroys the trade route, however, so long as a considerable number of ships follow the same track over an appreciable period of time for similar purposes.

The term *shipping route* has been employed in the same sense that trade route is used here,[4] and we can see no reason why the terms cannot be used interchangeably. Whatever the term used, a shipping service, which will be explained presently, is the service maintained by a ship operator on a trade route or a shipping route.

The world's major shipping lanes are often designated by broad general terms such as (1) the North Atlantic route, (2) the North Pacific route, (3) the South African route, (4) the South American route, and (5) the South Pacific route. These generic classifications serve admirably in a discussion of shipping in general, for each does possess certain distinctive characteristics.

In the official designations of United States trade routes, as defined by the Maritime Administration of the U.S. Department of Commerce, a more specialized usage of the term *trade route* appears. U.S. Trade Route 12 connects United States Atlantic ports (New York to Jacksonville) and the Far East (the Philippine Islands, China, Japan, Manchuria, Korea, the U.S.S.R. in Asia, French Indochina, Formosa, and Siam). Officially the term refers to a route on which the Federal Maritime Board has determined that American-flag dry-cargo shipping service is essential to further the purposes of the maritime policy of the United States.

Service. In the words of the U.S. Maritime Commission, service is "the means of providing transportation over a trade route, including the itinerary, sailing frequency, and number and type of vessels to be employed."[5] The American-flag ships operating on a trade route designated as essential, such as U.S. Trade Route 12, offer service, as do all other vessels operating on that route. The service of one operator[6] consists of the transportation that he offers over the route, including the itinerary, sailing frequency, and the number and type of vessels employed. The total service on a route consists of all the services of all the operators. In fact, a number of different types of service (passenger, dry-cargo freighter, tanker, tramp, and perhaps reefer) may be needed to furnish adequate transportation over an individual trade route. This will be made clearer by the ensuing discussion of services on United States foreign trade routes.

---

[4] See, for example, Walter A. Radius, *United States Shipping in Transpacific Trade, 1922–1938*, Stanford University Press, Stanford, Calif., 1944, pp. 72*ff.*

[5] See Foreword to *Essential Foreign Trade Routes of the American Merchant Marine*, U.S. Maritime Commission, May, 1949, processed. In the governmental reorganization of 1949, effective May 24, 1950, the Federal Maritime Board and Maritime Administration took over the functions of the former Maritime Commission (see Chap. 20).

[6] The operator is also called the *carrier* (see footnote 7, Chap. 5).

A successful shipping service reflects competent and intelligent analysis of a number of matters including (1) adaptation of ship to the cargo and route, (2) maintenance of adequate service, and (3) achievement of efficient operations. The physical characteristics of the ships employed on a route must reflect the physical characteristics and requirements of the cargo available with respect not only to speed and size but also to the relation of cubic space to deadweight lifting capacity.

Various factors carry different weights with various types of carriers. For such cargoes as ores and grains, speed is not the factor that it is for manufactured goods. The tramp or irregular operator sets "full and down" as his goal for port-to-port movement, except when his ship moves in ballast to the next port. In contrast, the load factor for a liner or berth service operation is related to the availability of two-way cargoes and also to the substantial movement of one or more basic commodities. A liner operator seldom expects to have a load factor of 100 percent on both the outbound and inbound legs of a voyage. Furthermore, on certain routes, the relationship between weight (density) and measurement (cubic) of the commodities handled is of paramount importance. Matters merely mentioned in this section will be discussed more fully in Part Two of this book, in which the shipping operation is discussed.

UNITED STATES FOREIGN TRADE ROUTES

The Merchant Marine Act of 1936, which currently defines United States maritime policy, stipulates not only that the nation should have "an adequate and well balanced merchant fleet" but also that the fleet should include "vessels of all types, to provide shipping service on all routes essential for maintaining the flow of foreign commerce of the United States." The system of routes, now termed *essential trade routes*, has been the result of this Act and its implementation. The essential-trade-route concept was, however, the outgrowth of earlier efforts.

Early Attempts at Establishing Routes. The first instance in which the United States government took steps to inaugurate a trade-route system occurred at the time the Ocean Mail Act of 1891 was passed, providing for subsidy payments to steamships carrying the mails.[7] After a perfunctory investigation that has at times been termed a "study," the Postmaster General called for bids on 53 lines or routes—10 to Great Britain and the continent of Europe, 27 to South America, 3 to China and Japan, 4 to Australia and the Pacific Islands, 7 to the West Indies, and 2 to Mexico. However, as shown elsewhere, American-flag vessels never served on more than 9 of these routes, and the net result could

---

[7] Government aid to shipping is the subject of Chap. 13; here our concern is primarily with routes.

under no circumstances be considered a network of routes for the carriage of the mails and still less of the nation's imports and exports.

The next step occurred after World War I, when the United States was faced with the problem of employing—or disposing of—a large government-owned fleet of merchant ships. To restore shipping to a peacetime basis as soon as possible, the U.S. Shipping Board, under authority conferred upon it by the Merchant Marine Act of 1920, was to place government-owned vessels on trade routes deemed most promising for American shipping and foreign trade.[8] Specifically, the Act of 1920 directed the Shipping Board (1) to ascertain the trade routes "desirable for the promotion, development, expansion, and maintenance of the foreign and coastwise trade of the United States and an adequate mail service" and (2) to sell or charter those ships to responsible "citizens of the United States who would agree to establish and maintain such service."

By June 20, 1920, the Shipping Board had established 209 berth services, 7 of which were wholly between foreign ports. The Act of 1920 had also placed with the Board the responsibility of operating the ships on lines deemed essential "until the business is developed so that such vessels may be sold on satisfactory terms and the service maintained." Hence, when purchasers did not appear to take the government-owned ships off the Board's hands, the agency was required to stay in commercial ship operations. Clearly some further provision was desirable.

In 1923, the Board consolidated its numerous and somewhat heterogeneous network of services into 18 primary groups. On Apr. 8 of that year, it offered to sell both ships and established services at prices below those prevailing prior to that date. This was in essence a package deal, and the terms were restricted in that the purchaser was to guarantee that he would offer regular service over the given route for a given period of time. Nor did this measure have the desired effect of putting "ships and routes" into the hands of private operators.

The next route legislation was embodied in the Merchant Marine Act of 1928, which provided for new ocean-mail subsidy contracts. The Shipping Board was empowered to certify the vessel equipment on the routes established, but the Postmaster General was required to designate the ocean-mail routes that in his opinion should be established. In general, the routes established during the early 1920's were continued under the 1928 Act.

The United States foreign trade routes established and maintained under the Acts of 1920 and 1928 were far from satisfactory. The 209 berth services established in 1920 generally designated only one American

---

[8] It should be pointed out that the functions of the Shipping Board were regulatory and that a subsidiary, the Emergency Fleet Corporation, was the operator (see Chap. 20).

port, though vessels were permitted more leeway in ports of call at foreign destinations. The sales contracts of the 1920's, which restricted operations on a particular trade route for a specified period of time, introduced too great a rigidity into the ship operations of the lines affected. Furthermore, responsibility for determining routes was placed with the Post Office Department, whose primary interest was carriage of the mails and not waterborne commerce. In 1935, the solicitor of that department told a Congressional committee that "ocean-mail contracts have been administered by people of the Post Office Department who had no knowledge . . . of the needs of commerce or whether or not the trade route was essential."

Essential Trade Routes under the 1936 Act. Section 211 of the Merchant Marine Act of 1936 eliminated the ocean-mail subsidy and the Post Office Department as the route-determining agency. The U.S. Maritime Commission, created by the Act to replace the earlier shipping agency, was required to determine and to establish services and routes deemed essential for "the promotion, development, and expansion, and maintenance of the foreign commerce of the United States." Two modifying clauses indicate the growth in the concept of what a trade route actually was and how one should be maintained. The Commission was directed to consider "the probability that any such line cannot be maintained except at a heavy loss disproportionate to the benefit accruing to foreign trade," and to act as a "prudent business man" would act in establishing routes.

Before establishing the system of routes, the Commission considered a multitude of matters, including traffic movement between ports; the nature of that traffic; types of vessels; laws, treaties, and national practices and policies; trade possibilities; and current economic conditions and probable future trends. After a thorough study of United States trade in more than 2,000 commodities and of their movement to and from various American ports, the Commission established over 30 routes.

The over-all scheme of the trade-route system is evident from the map (see Fig. 1). Trade Routes 1 through 4 provide service from Atlantic Coast ports to South America and the Caribbean area, while those numbered 5 through 11 operate between United States Atlantic ports and Europe. Trade Routes 13 through 18 serve both Atlantic and Gulf ports. To complete the swing around the coasts of the United States, Routes 19 through 22 operate from Gulf ports only, and Routes 23 through 30 from ports on the Pacific Coast. Trade Route 31 (Gulf to the west coast of South America) is an added route.

In establishing the trade-route pattern, traffic and geography were prominent factors, and it was recognized that trade usually flows between two trading areas rather than between two ports. To accomplish the desired ends, the United States was divided into the three main coastal areas (Atlantic, Gulf, and Pacific), and then into subdivisions depending on the traffic. For example, ships operating on the routes to South America serve all United States Atlantic ports from Maine to Florida (Boston to Jacksonville), while for commerce moving to and from Europe, the Atlantic Coast is divided so that the western termini of Trade Routes 5 through 10 consist of North Atlantic ports only (that is, those as far south as Cape Hatteras). The counterpart for United States South Atlantic ports (Hampton Roads to Jacksonville) is Trade Route 11. All Atlantic Coast ports are united again on Trade Route 12 for trade with the Far East. For United States waterborne commerce to and from Australia, India, Malaya, and Indonesia, the Atlantic and Gulf areas are combined on Trade Routes 16 through 18 to meet the needs of the traffic.

The Services. To understand the relationship between services and routes, it is desirable to remember that a route is a channel over which trade flows, while a service is the means of providing transportation over that channel. The government-defined services on various trade routes range from the one service (freight) on Route 19 to the five services on Route 10.[9] Services 1 and 2 are both passenger and freight. Service 1 serves a wide range of ports in the Mediterranean, including Marseille, Alexandria, Tel Aviv, and Piraeus. On Service 2 (on which the new 25-knot liners *Constitution* and *Independence* operate), the emphasis is on passenger travel rather than on freight, and calls are confined to the larger Mediterranean ports such as Genoa and Naples. The other three services on Route 10 are freight, distinguished primarily by their Mediterranean termini: ships operating under Service 3 call at a range of ports from Casablanca to Tripoli, those of Service 4 call at French and Italian ports on the Mediterranean, and Service 5 extends to ports in the eastern Mediterranean. Although a service is usually confined to one route, Service 1 on Trade Route 5 provides for calls at ports on that trade route, and also at Le Havre on Trade Route 9. This is currently the passenger service furnished by the liners *United States* and *America*.

The system of services and routes permits far more flexibility than is usually recognized. For example, on Trade Route 19 (United States Gulf to Caribbean ports), the government's outline of essential trade routes provides for only one service, a freight service. But the following note is added:

[9] Details concerning routes and services are available in the May 22, 1946, report of the U.S. Maritime Commission. The information is repeated, with slight modifications, in *Essential Foreign Trade Routes of the American Merchant Marine* (1949), which includes maps for individual routes and termini.

TRADE ROUTES AND SERVICES 87

The Caribbean is covered by many other steamship services, some of which touch at the same ports enroute but most of which ultimately end at different Caribbean termini. Caribbean liner services generally are operated as part of or in conjunction with industrial operations. Many of the services are dependent upon crop conditions and other variable factors so that they do not remain constant year after year as to ships employed, frequency of sailings, or even as to the route followed. As circumstances warrant, services other than the one specified above will be considered for Trade Route No. 19.

Trade routes need continual study. Shortly after the Federal Maritime Board and Maritime Administration became responsible for United States maritime affairs in May, 1950, the Administration's Division of Trade Routes undertook a through investigation.[10] By August, 1951, Criteria to Assist in the Determination of Essential Trade Routes had been developed, and by March, 1952, studies of eight of the established routes had been undertaken. Studies of all routes are expected to be completed in 1953.

American-flag Operators. As will be explained in Chapter 13, United States-flag shipping lines providing services on essential routes may apply for and receive operating-differential subsidies. Table 2 lists the 33 essential routes and the subsidized operators. This listing serves to illustrate steamship lines that may be considered area specialists: the United States Lines, between United States North Atlantic ports and northern Europe (with its American Pioneer Line operating between all Atlantic ports and the Far East and Atlantic and Gulf ports to Australia); American Export Lines, offering service between the Atlantic ports of the United States and the Mediterranean, Red Sea, and Indian Ocean; Moore-McCormack Lines, with operations specializing in service between the Atlantic and Pacific Coasts of the United States and the east coast of South America (and its American Scantic Line on Trade Route 6); the Grace Line, with comparable services to the north and west coasts of South America; and Lykes Bros. Steamship Co., offering services between United States Gulf ports and a variety of foreign destinations.[11]

[10] As explained in Chap. 20, the Board is responsible for quasi-legislative and judicial functions and the Administration for executive functions.
[11] A number of publications are useful in this respect. *United States and Foreign Flag Steamship Lines Which Operated on United States Foreign Trade Routes, Calendar Year 1948 and January–June 1949* (U.S. Maritime Commission, September, 1949, mimeographed) is a little out of date, but valuable because it lists operators under the various trade routes. The annual review issue of the *Log* includes a complete listing of American-flag ships, with owners, types, employment, and so forth. *U.S. Flag Services* (National Federation of American Shipping, Aug. 1, 1952) gives comparable information concerning member lines. In the autumn of 1953, the federation was absorbed by the American Merchant Marine Institute, which represents a major portion of American-flag shipping, including tankers. The AMMI took over all federation functions, including research.

Table 2. United States Essential Trade Routes and Subsidized Operators, Jan. 1, 1953

Route	Description	Subsidized operator
1	Atlantic/east coast South America	Moore-McCormack Lines, Inc.
2	Atlantic/west coast South America	Grace Line, Inc.
3	Atlantic/east coast Mexico	New York & Cuba Mail Steamship Co.
4	Atlantic/Caribbean	Grace Line, Inc.
5	North Atlantic/United Kingdom and Ireland	United States Lines Company
6	North Atlantic/Scandinavia and Baltic Sea	Moore-McCormack Lines, Inc.
7	North Atlantic/Germany (North Sea)	United States Lines Company
8	North Atlantic/Belgium and Netherlands	
9	North Atlantic/Atlantic France and Spain (Vigo to Bilbao)	United States Lines Company
10	North Atlantic/Mediterranean, Black Sea, Portugal, Spain (south of Portugal)	American Export Lines, Inc.
11	South Atlantic/United Kingdom and Ireland, Bordeaux/Hamburg, Scandinavia, and Baltic Sea	
12	Atlantic/Far East	United States Lines Company
13	Gulf and South Atlantic/Mediterranean Black Sea, Portugal, and Atlantic Spain	Lykes Bros. Steamship Co., Inc.
14	Atlantic/west coast Africa Gulf/west coast Africa	Farrell Lines, Incorporated Mississippi Shipping Co., Inc.
15A	Atlantic/South and East Africa and Madagascar	{Farrell Lines, Incorporated {Seas Shipping Company, Inc.
15B	Gulf/South and East Africa and Madagascar	Lykes Bros. Steamship Co., Inc.
16	Atlantic and Gulf/Australia	United States Lines Company
17	Atlantic and Gulf/Straits Settlements and Indonesia	
18	Atlantic and Gulf/India, Persian Gulf, and Red Sea	American Exports Lines, Inc.
19	Gulf/Caribbean	Lykes Bros. Steamship Co., Inc.
20	Gulf/east coast South America	Mississippi Shipping Co., Inc.
21	Gulf/United Kingdom, Ireland, Bordeaux/Hamburg, Scandinavia, and Baltic Sea	Lykes Bros. Steamship Co., Inc.

Table 2. United States Essential Trade Routes and Subsidized Operators, Jan. 1, 1953 *(Continued)*

Route	Description	Subsidized operator
22	Gulf/Far East	Lykes Bros. Steamship Co., Inc.
23	Pacific/Caribbean	
24	Pacific/east coast South America	Moore-McCormack Lines, Inc. / Pacific Argentine Brazil Line, Inc.
25	Pacific/east coasts of South America, Central America, and Mexico	Grace Line, Inc.
26A	Pacific/United Kingdom	
26B	Pacific/Le Havre–Hamburg range	
27	Pacific/Australasia	The Oceanic Steamship Company
28	Pacific/Straits Settlements, Indonesia, India, Persian Gulf, and Red Sea	
29	California/Far East	American President Lines, Ltd. / Pacific Far East Line, Inc. / Pacific Transport Lines, Inc.
30	Washington-Oregon/Far East	American Mail Line, Ltd.
31	Gulf/west coast South America	
Round-the-world		American President Lines, Ltd.

Table 2 does not purport to give a complete picture of American-flag lines operating on various trade routes. Not listed are such companies as the Waterman Steamship Corporation, whose vessels, engaged in nonsubsidized operations, call at United States ports on the Atlantic, Gulf, and Pacific Coasts and a wide range of foreign ports. On some routes, the nonsubsidized lines are numerous. For example, the Grace Line is the subsidized operator on Route 4,[12] but service between United States Atlantic ports and the Caribbean is also offered by a number of lines, including the Bull Line, the Cuba Mail (Ward) Line, the North Atlantic and Gulf Steamship Co. (the Norgulf Line), Seatrain Lines, the Alcoa Steamship Company, and the United Fruit Company.[13]

Furthermore, a number of lines are currently operating on routes, and negotiating for operating-differential subsidies to cover their operations on those routes. This is true of the United States Lines on Route 8, the

---

[12] The Grace Line subsidy contract on Trade Route 4 was effective Oct. 1, 1952. Since the Grace Line's Caribbean service was offered by ships operating between United States and South American ports, the new contract did not increase the number of subsidized ships.

[13] Alcoa and United Fruit operate both American-flag and foreign-flag ships.

South Atlantic Steamship Line on Route 11, and the Gulf & South American Steamship Co. (Gulfsa, jointly owned by Grace and Lykes) on Route 31. In 1951, American President Lines, whose operations around the world and on Trade Route 29 are subsidized, received from the Federal Maritime Board approval of its application to continue unsubsidized operations on Trade Route 17 between United States Atlantic and California ports and Indonesia-Malaya. The company's application for an operating-differential subsidy on this Atlantic-Straits service is under consideration.

Postwar Growth of Subsidized Services. Before the war, the policy was to subsidize only one line per route. The one exception occurred on Trade Route 15, on which the Seas Shipping Company (the Robin Line) and the Farrell Lines, established operators at the time the new operating-differential-subsidy program went into effect in 1937 and 1938, were granted an operating-differential subsidy. Although the Maritime Commission had approved, in 1949, the application of the Pacific Argentine Brazil Line (a subsidiary of Pope & Talbot) for an operating-differential subsidy on Trade Route 24, on which the Moore-McCormack Lines was then a subsidized operator, the question of whether to subsidize more than one line in a trade was not settled until 1952, when a decision was reached concerning the subsidy applications of the Pacific Far East Line and the Pacific Transport Lines.

These two lines were petitioning for an operating-differential subsidy to cover their transpacific services on Trade Route 29, on which American President Lines was already a subsidized operator. After due investigation and hearings on the applications, the Federal Maritime Board, in a report of April, 1952, held that Section 605 of the Act imposed no bar to granting operating-differential subsidies to the two lines involved. Additional hearings were necessary to determine the amount of subsidy and other matters, and the subsidy became effective on Jan. 1, 1953. Pending as of mid-1953 is the application of the Bloomfield Steamship Co. for subsidies on Trade Routes 13 and 21, on which Lykes is already subsidized.

The essential-trade-route concept, as set forth in the Merchant Marine Act of 1936 and carried out by the Maritime Commission and Maritime Administration, has come in for certain criticisms. Charges have been made that the postwar system of routes has not given due consideration to geographical shifts in foreign trade—a charge that the Maritime Administration can answer by pointing to the postwar growth of subsidized services that now support two or even three subsidized lines on the same route. Also, since detailed consideration is given services on which the government supports subsidized liner operations, unsubsidized operators have charged that the Administration is not fair or representative of all American shipping. As pointed out elsewhere, only about 40 percent of the total American foreign fleet was engaged in subsidized operations from 1947 through 1952.

The Maritime Administration's practices, however, embody the first consistent American attempt to arrive at a long-run prediction of the volume and composition of United States trade and of anticipated foreign competition to American-flag ships.[14] Furthermore, they represent the first attempt to arrange balanced services so that operations may be economical and profitable.

BIBLIOGRAPHY

In addition to the references listed in the footnotes, the following may be useful:

"Essential Trade Route Concept," *Shipping Survey*, Association of American Ship Owners, September, 1950, Vol. 6, No. 3.

"World Harbors" (bibliographies), *Transport and Communications Review*, United Nations, January–March, 1950, Vol. 3, pp. 68–81; October–December, 1951, Vol. 4, pp. 64–84.

---

[14] It should be pointed out that the United Kingdom, Canada, and Mexico have undertaken studies of the routes important in their foreign trade.

CHAPTER 5

THE UNITED STATES DOMESTIC FLEET AND ITS EMPLOYMENT

Although the general public is likely to associate shipping with the movement of goods and passengers between countries, the American merchant marine is composed not only of ships in international or foreign trade but of vessels employed in domestic routes and services. Businessmen who ship goods in domestic commerce are aware of domestic water transport and also of alternate means of transportation—rail, highway, and air. As soon as one studies almost any phase of ocean transportation in the United States, the cleavage is apparent between the domestic and offshore branches of the American merchant marine. The differences arise again and again during the development of this book, in the chapters on ship operation, organization of shipping companies, accounting, regulation, and shipping in wartime.

NATURE AND IMPORTANCE OF DOMESTIC SHIPPING

Domestic Routes. The domestic or coastal trades of the United States include all traffic in goods and passengers between ports of the United States. Such transportation is restricted to ships that have been built in the United States, registered under the American flag, and are owned and operated by American citizens.[1] United States domestic shipping should

[1] The limitation of domestic traffic to vessels documented under the flag of a country is called *cabotage*, though in Europe the term is also applied to domestic shipping whether restricted or not. Laws of 1789 and 1817 provided the legislative basis for this limitation in the United States. The limitation is applicable not only to coastwise and intercoastal trade but also to that with the offshore possessions of Alaska, Hawaii, and Puerto Rico. When the United States annexed the Philippine Islands in 1899, there was some agitation to include this possession, though some 6,200 miles distant from our Pacific Coast, in the coastal trade region and to restrict Philippine commerce with the United States to American-flag ships. Certain foreign governments protested, and the matter was dropped when the Tydings-McDuffie Act of 1934 paved the way for the independence of the Philippine Republic in 1946.

Two exceptions to cabotage should be noted. The Merchant Marine Act of 1920, as since amended, permits ore and coal to move between American ports on the

be considered under three separate classifications: (1) coastwise traffic along the Atlantic, Atlantic-Gulf, and Pacific Coasts; (2) intercoastal trade, or that which passes through the Panama Canal to or from ports on the Atlantic or Gulf and ports on the Pacific Coast; and (3) noncontiguous trade, or that between ports in the continental United States and ports in territories and possessions of the United States (principally Alaska, Hawaii, and Puerto Rico) or between ports of those territories and possessions.

People usually think of foreign traffic as moving over the long haul and of shorter distances in connection with domestic traffic. However, a voyage from Boston to Seattle is roughly 6,200 miles, equivalent to the route from Liverpool to Buenos Aires or from San Francisco to Hong Kong. Compare this figure with a service from Norway to the British Isles and ports on the Channel, and then into the Mediterranean as far as Egypt, Israel, Syria, and the Black Sea, covering approximately 6,000 miles and touching perhaps 23 ports in 15 different countries. The distance from Seattle to San Diego is about 1,230 miles and from Boston to the Straits of Florida, 1,380 miles. Other domestic services cover great distances such as New York to Hawaii, 6,700 miles, and Seattle to San Juan, Puerto Rico, 5,050 miles.

Geography, the continental expanse of the country, and its coast line have had much to do with the development of domestic shipping. With a general coast line of 1,888 miles on the Atlantic, 1,629 on the Gulf, and 1,366 on the Pacific (a total of 4,883 miles), the United States has a coast line greater by far than that of any other country. Distance alone is not sufficient reason for waterborne transportation service, but a coast line of such proportions establishes water routes as a most economic means of transportation. The impact of domestic shipping on the geographic and commercial expansion of the United States will be evident from the ensuing discussion of traffic and routes.

The Domestic Fleet in the Total Fleet. Just before the Civil War, the United States fleet was about equally divided between the foreign and domestic services. From then until World War I, foreign tonnage decreased, and domestic tonnage increased to the point where ships employed in the domestic trades represented close to 90 percent of the United States total fleet. American ships participated more heavily in foreign trade after World War I, particularly in the first years while other nations were rebuilding their fleets. The interwar period, however,

---

Great Lakes via Canadian steamers. By act of Congress, approved June 27, 1951, United States citizens may utilize ships of Canadian registry between the Alaskan ports of Haines, Hyder, and Skagway, and between those ports and the continental United States.

was one of a greatly expanding domestic fleet. By 1939, two-thirds of the United States vessels of 1,000 or more tons were in domestic service, whereas by 1950, the reverse was true.

Year		Foreign tonnage		Domestic tonnage	
		Tonnage, thousand tons	Percent of total	Tonnage, thousand tons	Percent of total
1850		1,586	46	1,899	54
1860		2,546	48	2,765	52
1870		1,517	36	2,678	64
1880		1,353	34	2,649	66
1890	100 gross tons and over	947	22	3,392	78
1900		827	16	4,239	84
1910		792	11	6,594	89
1920		9,929	61	6,265	39
1923		9,073	50	9,087	50
1930		6,303	40	9,644	60
1923		3,648	52	3,399	48
1930		3,816	50	3,855	50
1939	1,000 gross tons and over	2,094	33	4,298	67
1950		5,795	62	3,542	38
1951		7,857	70	3,433	30
1952		5,909	65	3,211	35

SOURCE: The figures for 100 tons and over are U.S. Bureau of Navigation data as published in J. E. Saugstad, *Shipping and Shipbuilding Subsidies*, U.S. Department of Commerce, Trade Promotion Series, No. 129, 1932. Those for 1,000 tons and over are from *The Bulletin*, American Bureau of Shipping, September, 1951, p. 41, and September, 1952, p. 40. The use of figures for 100 tons and over for early years (they include commercial vessels and barges) increases the percentage in the domestic trade, because a very high proportion of small ships do not go offshore. Further, the foreign figures for 1950 through 1952 are for "active" tonnage (see Chap. 6).

The importance of the ships in the domestic trades and of the services they render is great indeed. Whether one considers the proportion of tonnage, the relationship of these ships to employment opportunities, shipbuilding and activity in ship-repair yards, purchases of supplies and provisions, or other factors, the conclusion is obvious that the domestic portion of the American merchant marine is vital to the economy of the country. The 490 freighters in the domestic fleet in 1939, totaling 3.4 million deadweight tons,[2] represented a valuable asset during the crucial early years of the war before the emergency shipbuilding program began to launch Liberty ships in large numbers.

[2] See tabulation, p. 98. For an explanation of gross and deadweight tonnage, see pp. 163, 165.

DEVELOPMENT OF DOMESTIC ROUTES AND SERVICES

Coastwise Traffic. Shipping along the coasts of the United States began with settlement. The early commerce of the colonies on the Atlantic Coast was wholly dependent on water transportation because of the lack of, as well as the danger and inconvenience of, land routes. Seaports were usually located on rivers, and paddle-wheel steamboats acted as feeder lines.[3] In 1817, a steamboat managed to go upriver from New Orleans as far as Cincinnati, and two years later about 60 light-draft stern-wheelers plied regularly between New Orleans and Louisville. Freight charges by water via the Mississippi to the upper Ohio were less than half the cost of wagon transport from Philadelphia.

The Pacific Coast coastwise trade had its origin in the movement of lumber from the Puget Sound area southbound—a movement that started immediately after the gold rush and later expanded to furnish lumber for all of California. The small ships returned northbound either with light loads of general cargo or in ballast. The economy of the Pacific Northwest region for decades was almost entirely dependent on the sawmills located at tidewater and the ships that called for lumber. For the domestic segment of this trade, a special lumber carrier was developed, called the steam schooner.[4]

Although domestic shipping had been extremely important in the development of the country from the earliest days of the nation and although two-thirds or more of all American-flag ships from the 1870's on had been engaged in domestic commerce (with the exception of a short period during and following World War I), the actual volume of domestic trade was small in comparison with the traffic of the interwar period ending in 1939. In that year, 244 ships of 1,000 or more tons were employed in the coastwise trades—176 of them in the Atlantic and on the Gulf and 68 in the Pacific. The Atlantic and Atlantic-Gulf coastwise services, consisting of about 33 different companies, were the volume carriers of the interwar period. Their ships moved 30.8 million short tons of dry cargo in 1939, in comparison with 3.7 million tons on the Pacific Coast. The total of coastwise traffic means more if it is compared with the total of all United States foreign trade in dry cargo for that year—49.2 million long tons, only 24 percent of which was carried in American-flag ships.[5]

---

[3] A distinction should be made between domestic ocean commerce, which we are discussing here, and domestic inland waterborne commerce, which would include river traffic and traffic within the Great Lakes.

[4] One of the most informative books on the West Coast lumber traffic is E. T. Coman, Jr., and Helen M. Gibbs, *Time, Tide, and Timber: A Century of Pope & Talbot*, Stanford University Press, Stanford, Calif., 1949.

[5] See *Participation of United States Flag Ships in American Overseas Trade, 1921–1951*, U.S. Department of Commerce, Maritime Administration, June, 1952, processed.

Specifically, about two-thirds of the Atlantic and Atlantic-Gulf traffic consisted of coal and coke, sulphur and phosphates, and other nonmetallic minerals and products. On the Pacific Coast, cargoes southbound consisted largely of lumber and lumber products, while sugar, salt, and miscellaneous general cargo provided northbound tonnage. The load factor southbound was considerably larger than that northbound, a circumstance that introduced difficulties in operation. As will be shown presently, the traffic in petroleum on all coasts moved by tanker far surpassed the movement of dry cargo.

Intercoastal Trade. Modern intercoastal steamship service may be dated from 1914, the year in which the Panama Canal was opened for commercial transits. However, owing to World War I and to slides that closed the canal for long periods of time, the true growth of trade did not begin until after 1919. It increased rapidly to a peak during the late 1920's. Since 1929, it has fluctuated below this early high level.

In 1939, 19 freight companies were in the trade, including common and contract carriers. The number of ships operating during 1939 varies depending on which report one takes, but one government report gives 159 vessels and 7 million short tons of cargo. Intercoastal and coastwise cargoes of such commodities as coal, cement, and sulphur support services largely provided by contract and industrial carriers.

Over the years prior to World War II, eastbound tonnage consisted primarily of lumber (about 40 percent); fruits and vegetables, largely canned (about 20 percent); grain and grain products; and miscellaneous general cargo. In westbound cargoes, iron and steel products provided about 40 percent of the tonnage, while the remaining tonnage was composed of sulphur, phosphate, paper and products, chemicals, food products, and general cargo. Tonnage eastbound from Pacific Coast ports was greater than that westbound from Atlantic to Pacific ports, largely because of the movement of lumber and lumber products. Furthermore, shipments between Pacific Coast ports and Atlantic ports, particularly New York, Philadelphia, Baltimore, and Norfolk, greatly exceeded those between the Pacific Coast and Gulf Coast ports.

Noncontiguous Trade. From the days of the gold rush, trade between San Francisco Bay and Hawaii had flourished. When the territory was annexed in 1898, imports and exports became coastwise shipments. Traffic with the continental United States tended to be limited to that with Pacific Coast ports until after the Panama Canal was opened. Hawaii is now linked by steamship service with the three coastal regions of the United States, and the islands are a port of call for many transpacific liners. A stop at Hawaii takes these vessels a few hundred miles off their course but makes a profitable break in an otherwise long sea voyage. Roughly 90 percent or more of Hawaii's shipments inbound to the United States consist of pineapple, pineapple juice, sugar, and molasses. Outbound shipments reflect Hawaii's plantation economy, for they consist of a wide variety of manufactured goods, consumer goods, and foodstuffs.

Before gold was discovered in the Klondike in 1896, ships occasionally called at Alaska. Thereafter, Seattle became, and still remains, the principal port for United States traffic with this northern possession. During the interwar period, however, certain ships serving the Pacific Coast sailed northward regularly to include Alaska. From 1946 until 1950, the only direct water-carrier service to Alaska was out of Seattle, but in 1950 a line serving the West Coast added Alaskan ports to its schedules. Alaska sends to the United States canned fish, ore concentrates, and fish oils, and receives a large range of manufactured goods and food products. Needless to say, the northbound traffic is heavier than the southbound.

Puerto Rico ships sugar and molasses. Lumber, rice, dried beans, and such canned products as tomato preparations make up the bulk of shipments from the Pacific Coast, while consumer goods and foodstuffs move from the other coastal regions. Puerto Rico's trade is served by American-flag ships operating from all three coasts, including vessels from the Pacific Coast southbound to South America, and by a few of the steamship lines operating intercoastal.

The Movement of Petroleum. As the waterborne movement of petroleum from oil fields to refineries increased in volume, the domestic tanker tonnage increased proportionally. Domestic tanker tonnage increased from 1.4 million gross tons in 1923 to 2.1 million in 1939, when the volume of petroleum moved by tanker was more than double the dry cargo shipped domestically (see accompanying tabulation which gives tonnage figures in terms of millions of short tons). Though pipelines were built

Trade	Total	Dry cargo	Tanker
Coastwise	126.2	34.5	91.7
Intercoastal	8.4	7.0	1.4
Noncontiguous	6.1	5.1	1.0
Alaska	1.0	0.9	0.1
Hawaii	2.9	2.3	0.6
Puerto Rico	2.2	1.9	0.3
Total	140.7	46.6	94.1

SOURCE: Unpublished figures of the U.S. Maritime Commission and originally based on various Commission reports and the annual report of the Chief of Engineers, U.S. Army, Part 2, *Commercial Statistics, Waterborne Commerce of the United States.*

during the war, domestic tanker tonnage has remained at well over 2 million gross tons since 1946. About seven-eighths of the domestic tankers operate on the Gulf and Atlantic seaboard, primarily transporting petroleum and its products from the Gulf region to the oil-deficient Northeast, while the rest operate on the Pacific Coast. The intercoastal movement, primarily from the Los Angeles area eastward, is of minor importance in the over-all volume. Shipments to Alaska and Hawaii, which originate in the West Coast, have been appreciably higher since the close of the war.

THE POSTWAR OPERATOR AND HIS PROBLEMS

The development of domestic routes and services divides itself into three distinct periods: (1) the pre-World War I period, when domestic traffic was largely confined to the coastal ranges; (2) the period 1920 to 1939; and (3) the post-World War II period, which has been one of salvaging what remained of domestic water traffic and of considerable uncertainty as to long-range prospects.

The Postwar Fleet. The domestic fleet, which was comprised of 490 vessels in 1939, numbered only 151 in 1948, or less than one-third of prewar. Because the postwar ships are larger than earlier ones, the decline in ship tonnage from 3.4 million deadweight tons to 1.5 million is not so sharp as for the number of ships.

Trade	1939			1948		
	Dry cargo, millions of short tons	Number of ships	Ship tonnage, deadweight tons	Dry cargo, millions of short tons	Number of ships	Ship tonnage, deadweight tons
Coastwise.......	34.5	244	1.3	17.50	56	0.50
Atlantic-Gulf..	30.8	176	1.0	17.04	52	0.46
Pacific........	3.7	68	0.3	0.45	4	0.03
Intercoastal.....	7.0	159	1.5	3.40	43	0.50
Noncontiguous..	5.1	87	0.6	4.30	52	0.50
Total.........	46.6	490	3.4	25.20	151	1.50

SOURCE: Figures adapted from *Merchant Marine Study and Investigation*, Senate Committee on Interstate and Foreign Commerce, 81st Cong., 2d sess., S. Rept. 2494, 1950, p. 251.

The decline in individual trades is even sharper. The total number of dry-cargo ships on all coasts in coastwise operations dropped from 244 in 1939 to only 56 in 1948. On the Atlantic-Gulf Coasts, where 33 companies had offered service in 1939, there were only 3 in 1951. The intercoastal fleet included 159 ships in 1939; nine years later, it had shrunk to little more than one-quarter of its prewar size. Before the war, 23 ships operating coastwise and 6 operating intercoastal had offered combined passenger-cargo service. Since the war, this has been discontinued entirely. The Pacific Coast coastwise service had 68 vessels in 1939, and only 4 in 1948. This number increased to about 11 or 12 in 1951, some of the vessels extending their operations to Alaska. But in prewar years, some 23 companies had been engaged in Pacific coastwise shipping, while in 1951, 7 contract lumber carriers and only one common carrier offered service.

The number of ships in the noncontiguous trades was 87 in 1939 compared with 52 in 1948. The 1948 tonnage, however, showed only a slight decline from 600,000 deadweight tons to 500,000. The number of passenger-cargo vessels was reduced from 23 to 5. The inroads of airline facilities on passenger travel by water are evident in these figures. Freighters dropped from 64 in 1939 to 47 in 1948, but owing to the larger size of the ships, the decline in dry cargo transported was not so great as the decline in number of ships. By 1951, the number of freighters had increased to 65, and the number of tankers from 7, in 1939, to 10. Of the domestic trades, that with noncontiguous possessions of the United States has been the best maintained.

Problems of Developing the Domestic Fleet. To understand the predicament of the postwar domestic operator, one needs to know certain facts about domestic shipping during the interwar period, especially the 1930's. It was not a happy era for domestic shipping because of ruinous and unregulated competition, the depression, and unsatisfactory labor relations. As a result, much regulatory legislation was introduced, unionism strengthened, and the economic resources of the carriers so weakened that many of them retired from business or were absorbed by other companies. By 1939, the intercoastal fleet, which had numbered 274 vessels in 1923, had shrunk to 159 ships. During the early 1930's, some 140 ships had served Pacific Coast ports, but by 1939, their number had shrunk to 68. The problems confronted by the shipowner operating in domestic commerce did not originate during the years 1940 through 1945, though wartime circumstances have helped to aggravate them.

1. *Ship replacements.* The domestic operators went to war shortly after September, 1939. Their ships were gradually taken from regular service and diverted to emergency requirements and then to all-out war. At the close of hostilities, they were either worn out or lost. The coastwise and intercoastal operators, who had populated their fleets after World War I with ships purchased at costs usually ranging between $50,000 and $250,000, were confronted with the problem of securing replacements for their fleets.

Because the industry was unregulated and highly competitive between the wars, the rate structure had been extremely unstable. This situation, together with the general economic depression and the very unsatisfactory labor-management relations of the 1930's (particularly on the Pacific Coast), had prevented the shipowners who survived from earning enough money to establish reserves in excess of depreciation reserves for the purpose of ship replacement. For example, the 19 companies operating common and contract carriers in the intercoastal route in 1934 were reduced to 13 in 1939; total operations were profitable in only two of the six years; and the six-year record showed a net loss of $8,200,000 for all operators. Consequently, the financial condition of the domestic operators was not favorable to the perpetuation of their routes as early as the 1930's.

Following World War II, the statutory sales prices of the surplus war-built vessels, except for the Liberty-type ship, were approximately double the book value of the vessels owned by intercoastal operators in 1939. These postwar sales prices were, however, modest in comparison with costs during the early 1950's. When Frazer A. Bailey, then president of the National Federation of American Shipping, testified before a Senate committee in April, 1952, he stated that "the average cost of the existing fleet is in the neighborhood of $100 per ton, whereas its reproduction, due to inflation and other expanding costs, will represent approximately $360 to $400 per ton."

Costs of or purchase prices for vessels are linked with their suitability to a particular trade. None of the war-built ships, except the C4, was tailor-made for the intercoastal trade.[6] The Liberty is a good intercoastal ship in so far as cubic space is concerned, but too slow for competitive purposes. The Victory has the necessary speed but lacks a proper ratio of cubic space to deadweight lifting capacity. However, Liberty and Victory-type ships have predominated in the intercoastal trade since World War II.

As far as ships are concerned, the coastwise operator has a more difficult problem than does the intercoastal operator. Intercoastal ships are comparable to the regular oceangoing freighters of 10,000 deadweight tons found in the offshore trades, while the prewar coastal ships were usually of 4,500 deadweight tons or less. Very few small vessels were built during the war, and none was suitable for use on coastwise trade without expensive modification. Some Liberties are to be found on the Pacific Coast, where the coastwise traffic now extends to Alaska, and in 1952, one company was operating four C2 ships in the Atlantic-Gulf coastwise service. Some of the smaller ships that operated before 1939 are still employed. However, one general problem has been the lack of suitable small ships for the coastwise trades.

[6] The C4 was originally designed for the American-Hawaiian Steamship Company, because the C1-, C2-, and C3-type vessels did not fit the packaged-goods trade of the A class intercoastal carrier.

2. *Rates.* In addition to the problem of capital investment, the domestic operators are faced with an unsatisfactory situation with respect to rates, and the postwar rate situation has deterred ship operators from investing in the ever more costly ships for domestic operation. As shown elsewhere (see Chapter 19), while the domestic ships were at war, the railroads and trucks had taken over their traffic. Tariffs for domestic water services, shelved during the war, were six years later dusted off and reexamined. Costs had in the meantime pyramided, and competitors in land transportation had received adjustments in their rates to reflect many of the wartime increases in their costs. The water carriers[7] considered the situation timely to air a long-standing grievance—namely, that over the years the railroads had deliberately depressed rates on most goods that were attractive to the water carriers and for which there was strong competition between rail and water lines. After years of unsatisfactory postponement and delay, the Interstate Commerce Commission, which now regulates the domestic carriers under terms of the Transportation Act of 1940, suggested that the general intercoastal case be laid aside, partly because the evidence had become out of date. The Pacific Coastwise case was decided in favor of the rail lines but on the grounds that "there is considerable doubt as to whether the water lines have the advantage of cost as to any important character of traffic." In the opinion of the water lines, the history of ICC rate regulation since 1940 has cast serious doubts on the justification of the Act.

3. *Handling costs.* As shown elsewhere, costs, mainly those associated with the transfer of goods between ship and shore, have increased to the point where domestic water transportation has been virtually priced out of business.[8] It should be noted that, while the situation is also damaging to foreign trade services, foreign operators do not have to compete with other forms of transportation. Cargo-handling costs, which were formerly about one-third of total costs for the transport of merchandise by water, are now from 40 to 60 percent of total costs. In view of the severe competition with railroads and trucks, water lines cannot increase their rates freely to cover the excessive costs. Domestic operators have had to trim their sails, and many companies have dropped out of the business. Whether new methods of handling cargo and new types of ships and piers can be developed in order to reduce handling costs remains to be seen.

4. *Labor relations.* Unstable labor-management relations in the shipping industry and on the water front for nearly twenty years have shaken the faith of shippers and consignees in the dependability of water service. There has been no improvement in this respect, although the spread of this unsatisfactory experience to the railroads (but to a much lesser

---

[7] The term *carrier* may mean the ship or the owner of the ship.
[8] See Labor Costs in the Total of Ship Operation, in Chap. 11.

extent) has reduced the margin of handicap of the water carriers. Only years of more reasonable labor-management relations and of dependable service will rebuild shipper confidence in domestic ocean-transportation service.

5. *Economic development.* Changes in the location of industry have limited the amount of cargo available to water carriers. The lumber industry in the Pacific Northwest has gradually moved away from tidewater locations, and railroad and truck shipments have increased proportionately. The canning industry of the Pacific Northwest sends about 20 percent of its output to California, and the bulk of it moves by truck. Furthermore, the expansion of population on the Pacific Coast is now sufficient to sustain a more self-sufficient economy in terms of industry and processing of goods, and this development has reduced the quantity of goods attractive to intercoastal commerce.

Outlook. The prospects of a revival of shipping in the domestic services are not encouraging. This situation gravely complicates the over-all problem of strengthening and stabilizing the entire American merchant marine. Before 1941, the domestic fleet was a substantial support of those economic activities that are auxiliary to ship operation—terminal and port management, stevedoring, ship chandlery, ship repairing, and crew employment. The active fleet of ships available for purposes of national security was largely in domestic services, where the ships were more quickly available and convertible to emergency employment than those in foreign waters. For the foreseeable future, all these purposes—economic and security—must be served by the overseas or foreign fleet, the prospects for which are uncertain and to a considerable extent dependent on government support of one kind or another.

The unfortunate aspect of the domestic services is the lack of a strong voice to be raised in their defense. The regulatory and promotional battles of the Atlantic coastwise carriers are remote from those of Pacific coastwise carriers, and the interests concerned with coastal problems are not always associated with intercoastal developments. In addition, while the Transportation Act of 1940 calls upon the ICC to consider national defense as an element in its rate determinations, this factor has never been defined. Hence, the regulatory functions of the ICC have been preponderantly inclined toward the technical aspects of the various rate structures, and no agency of government (or of industry) has adequately assessed the needs of domestic shipping for rehabilitation, stabilization, and perpetuation through ship replacement. Unless this is done and a program implemented by government-industry action, we must conclude that most coastwise and intercoastal shipping, other than the private or industrial carrier, will be of marginal economic value.

BIBLIOGRAPHY

Historical Development of Transport Coordination and Integration in the United States, Interstate Commerce Commission, Bureau of Transport Economics and Statistics, Statement 5015, April, 1950.

Issues Involved in a Unified and Coordinated Federal Program for Transportation, Report to the President from the Secretary of Commerce, Dec. 1, 1949.

Mears, E. G., *Maritime Trade of the Western United States*, Stanford University Press, Stanford, Calif., 1935.

Morgan, C. S., *Problems in the Regulation of Domestic Transportation by Water*, Interstate Commerce Commission Report Regarding *Ex parte* 165, 1946.

Sound Transportation for the National Welfare, Transportation Association of America, Chicago, February, 1953.

CHAPTER 6

MERCHANT FLEETS OF THE WORLD

By 1950, the world's merchant fleet of steam, motor, and sailing ships and of barges totaled 85.3 million gross tons, or almost three times the 1900 fleet of 28.9 million tons. Nearly two-thirds of the increase had been achieved by 1923, when the shipbuilding programs of World War I were completed. Most of the remaining increase in tonnage of this period (28 percent) came as a result of the World War II shipbuilding program, and the small balance (8 percent) in the interwar period.

SIZE AND OWNERSHIP OF THE WORLD'S MERCHANT FLEET

Increase in Total Tonnage. The world's total merchant fleet of all types of vessels increased from 28.9 million gross tons in 1900 to 49.1 million in 1914 (see Table 4). The percentage increase was 70 percent, larger than that for any other period of the half century. This large increase in vessel tonnage was due primarily to the expansion of the steamer and motor fleet, which increased from 22.4 million gross tons in 1900 to 45.4 million in 1914.[1] By 1923, the proportional increase in steamships had tapered off. Between 1914 and 1923, the steam and motor fleet increased from 45.4 million to 62.3 million gross tons, for an increase of 37.2 percent, as compared with 32.8 percent for the world's total fleet.

During the interwar period, the world's total merchant fleet increased only from 65.2 million gross tons, in 1923, to 69.4 million, in 1939. During those years, many older vessels were retired, and European shipyards developed replacement programs to produce faster and, in many cases, medium-sized ships. As a result of shipbuilding during World War II and thereafter, the world's fleets increased from 69.4 million gross tons, in 1939, to 85.3 million, in 1950. The percentage increase was 22.9.

The shipbuilding situation after 1946 has differed from that at the close of World War I. Whereas when World War I ended, the ship-construction

---

[1] As the steamship fleet increased, sailing vessels were retired. In 1900, sailing vessels and barges represented 22.5 percent of the world's total merchant fleet. By 1914, they had declined to 7.5 percent. By 1939, they represented less than 1 percent.

program took three years to taper off, the aftermath of World War II witnessed (1) an extreme shortage of shipbuilding materials and very low capacity for a short time, (2) a program to dispose of surplus ships in the United States,[2] and (3) a belated but heavy shipbuilding program that began four or five years after hostilities ceased. The effect of the last is evident from tonnage figures. In 1951, the world's fleet, including tankers, totaled 87.2 million gross tons, 1.9 million tons (27 percent) above the 1950 level. When ships under construction or on order in 1952 and 1953 are completed, the world's fleet may well be close to 50 percent larger than it was in 1939, or close to 100 million gross tons.

Ownership of the World's Active Merchant Tonnage. Because such an extremely high proportion of the world's vessel tonnage has been built during wartime, the result has been surplus peacetime tonnage, especially in the United States during the 1920's and again after 1945. Hence, especially since the close of World War II, *active* merchant tonnage is a truer criterion of the industry than *total* vessel tonnage. The situation regarding active tonnage can best be summarized by nations or groups of nations (see also Table 3).

Table 3. Merchant Fleets of the World, by Major Shipowning Countries, Selected Years, 1900 to 1950

(Tonnages in millions of gross tons; percentages of total world fleet)

Owning country	1900		1914		1923		1939		1950	
	Tonnage	Percent	Tonnage	Percent	Tonnage	Percent	Tonnage	Percent	Tonnage	Percent
United States:										
Sea	0.9	4.0	2.0	4.5	7.0	12.9	6.4	9.7	9.3	13.3
Lakes	0.6	2.7	2.3	5.0	2.2	4.0	2.5	3.7	2.3	3.3
Total United States	1.5	6.7	4.3	9.5	9.2	16.9	8.9	13.4	11.6	16.6
United Kingdom	11.5	51.4	18.9	41.7	19.1	35.3	17.9	26.9	18.2	26.0
British Commonwealth	0.6	2.7	1.6	3.6	2.6	4.8	3.1	4.6	3.9	5.6
Total British Empire	12.1	54.1	20.5	45.3	21.7	40.1	21.0	31.5	22.1	31.6
Germany, Japan, and Italy	3.2	14.3	8.3	18.3	9.0	16.6	13.5	20.3	5.1	7.3
Norway, Sweden, and Denmark	1.6	7.1	3.8	8.2	4.4	8.0	7.6	11.4	8.8	12.6
Holland, France	1.6	7.1	3.4	7.5	6.1	11.2	5.9	8.8	6.3	9.0
Panama	n.a.	n.a.	n.a.	n.a.	0.1	0.2	0.7	1.0	3.4	4.9
Total	20.0	89.3	40.3	88.8	50.5	93.0	57.6	86.4	57.3	82.0
Other countries	2.4	10.7	5.1	11.2	3.8	7.0	9.2	13.6	12.7	18.0
Grand total	22.4	100.0	45.4	100.0	54.3	100.0	66.8	100.0	70.0	100.0

Source: All tonnage figures are as of July 1 and are from Lloyd's *Register*, 1951, Sec. 7. For a number of reasons, the position of the United States is understated: (1) tonnage figures for 1900 and 1914 include steam and motor tonnage only and omit sail and barge, (2) 1950 figures do not include 0.5 million tons under Lend-Lease to Soviet Russia, and (3) 1950 figures are for the active (private and government-owned) fleet only and do not include inactive vessels. Furthermore, figures for the United States do not account for American-owned tonnage under foreign flags (see footnote 17, this chapter).

[2] The ship-sales program is discussed in Chap. 13.

1. The United States active fleet of steam and motor ships has shown substantial gains since 1900. At the turn of the century, this nation owned less than one million (0.9) gross tons of seagoing tonnage, plus 0.6 million tons on the Great Lakes. The total of 1.5 million tons represented 6.7 percent of the world's total. In 1950, American-flag ships on the Great Lakes and the high seas comprised 11.6 million tons, or 16.6 percent of the world's total. Concerning the over-all shipping position of the United States, improvement was substantial after both wars, and, while the country lost ground after each war, there was, in each case, a net gain over the prewar position.

2. The relative position of the United Kingdom has declined steadily since 1900, when British ships represented more than 51 percent of the world's total fleet. By 1939, the British fleet represented 26.9 percent of the world's active ships. Since 1946, the United Kingdom has held its prewar position, because it still owns 26 percent of the world's active vessels.

3. The fleets of nations that were defeated in the two wars suffered, particularly after World War II. However, the policy of the wartime allies now is to permit these countries to expand their shipping. Germany's tonnage increased from roughly 500,000 gross tons in 1950 to a million tons in 1951, Japan's from 2.6 million tons to 2.9 million, and Italy's from 2.6 million to 2.9 million.[3]

4. The maritime position of the Scandinavian countries shows steady improvement. In 1950, Norway, Denmark, and Sweden owned approximately one-eighth of the world's merchant ships. Norway in particular is noteworthy as a seafaring nation. In 1950, her merchant fleet at 5.5 million gross tons was exceeded only by the fleets of Great Britain and the United States. Norway pays for approximately 33 percent of her imports with the earnings of foreign exchange by her merchant fleet. In this respect, the country leads the world. Historically the Scandinavian countries as a group have been second in importance to the United Kingdom, but since 1945, the United States has assumed second position and Scandinavia third.

5. Holland and France maintained roughly the same relative position in 1950 that they had occupied in 1939, although Dutch activity since 1945 has been greater than that of the French. In 1950, they owned 6.3 million gross tons of merchant shipping or 9 percent of the world's total.

---

[3] Figures for 1951 were not used in Table 3, the purpose of which is to present an overview of the growth of the world's merchant marines over half a century, because 1950 statistics are more representative. United States seagoing tonnage increased from 9.3 million gross tons in 1950 to 11.3 million in 1951 and to 11.6 million in 1952 (see Table 5) primarily because of the reactivation of government-owned ships. Although a number of foreign fleets increased tonnagewise, on a comparative basis the increase was small.

6. Panamanian-flag ships, particularly since 1945, have made Panama a factor in fleet ownership. With a merchant fleet of 3.4 million gross tons, in 1950 Panama ranked fourth among the world's shipowning nations. Much of the tonnage is owned by individuals who are not citizens of Panama but who register their ships in that country in order to benefit from lower crew and other operating costs and fewer restrictions.[4] Many American- and Greek-controlled firms do business under this flag as well as under the Honduran and Liberian flags. These three countries together have 4.6 million gross tons of shipping.

7. Although the nations included in the table as "other" countries did expand their fleets after 1900, they only increased from 10.7 percent of the world's total at the turn of the century to 13.6 percent in 1939. The greatest change has been since 1939, for their merchant ships rose to over 18 percent of the total in 1950.[5] At that time, the countries maintaining the largest fleets were as follows: Honduras and certain Latin-American nations other than Panama, the U.S.S.R., Spain, Portugal, Belgium, Finland, China, Liberia, and Turkey.

ACTIVE MERCHANT TONNAGE AND THE QUANTUM OF WORLD TRADE

A chronic surplus of merchant tonnage is generally considered to exist in the world in "normal" times—a belief that has been held since the turn of the century. Wartime construction has contributed substantially to expanding the world's total fleets, and building programs in the United States led to large laid-up fleets after both wars. The existence of such surplus tonnage confuses efforts to correlate merchant-shipping activity with the economic demand for ships.

Although the problem can be resolved to a certain extent by discussing active rather than total tonnage in relation to the volume of world trade, certain difficulties must be recognized. Unless a surplus vessel is "sterilized" and permanently removed as a commercial unit, its presence, even when laid up, exerts an influence on the world charter and ship-sales market. Laid-up ships are potentially available.

Since 1936, however, surplus American-flag vessels have been considered withheld from the commercial market except under emergency conditions. This policy has been followed in directives applicable to the government's postwar reserve fleet, from which many ships were reac-

[4] On the ownership of the Panamanian fleet, see *The Merchant Fleets of the World, September 1, 1939–December 31, 1951*, U.S. Department of Commerce, Maritime Administration, November, 1952, processed.

[5] Fourteen nations whose merchant marines were nonexistent in 1939 have acquired fleets since the war. These are Burma, Colombia, Costa Rica, Ecuador, Guatemala, Iceland, Indonesia, Iran, Ireland, Israel, Korea, Liberia, Switzerland, and Syria.

tivated following the opening of the Korean crisis. By December, 1951, some 693 government-owned ships were in active service. After grain shipments to India and coal shipments to Europe tapered off in early 1952, most of these vessels were rapidly returned to moth balls. Many of the remaining active government-owned ships were used primarily to carry military cargoes for the armed forces overseas.

Table 4. Total and Active Merchant Fleets of the World, and Percentage Increases, Compared with Increases in Quantum of World Trade, Selected Years, 1900 to 1950
(Tonnages in millions of gross tons)

Year	World merchant fleets						Percentage change in quantum of world trade
	All types of ships	Percent increase	Steam and motor only	Percent increase	Active fleet	Percent increase	
1900	28.9	....	22.4	.....	28.9		
1914	49.1	70.0	45.4	102.7	49.1	70.0	+62.2
1923	65.2	32.8	62.3	37.2	54.3	10.6	− 9.4
1939	69.4	6.4	68.5	10.0	66.8	23.0	+33.5
1950	85.3	22.9	84.6	23.5	70.0	4.8	+ 4.2

SOURCE: All types of ships include steam and motor and also sailing ships and barges. All tonnage figures are as of July 1, and, except as indicated below, are from Lloyd's *Register*, 1951, Sec. 7.

For 1900 and 1914, the figures given for the active fleet are the same as for ships of all types. This was based on the assumption that there was a reasonably full degree of employment in mid-1914. There are obvious faults to this assumption, but these are the best figures available. Taking the total fleet in 1914 and only the active fleet in 1923 may understate the percentage-increase figure for the active fleet as of 1923. The active fleet for 1923, 1939, and 1950 was derived by deducting laid-up American-flag ships (the figures are for vessels of 1,000 gross tons and over) from the world fleet of steamships and motor ships. There was probably no foreign-flag tonnage idle in either 1939 or 1950. The figures for laid-up American-flag tonnage used in these calculations were from the following sources:

For 1923, from a special report of the U.S. Maritime Commission, Division of Economics and Statistics, May, 1943. For 1939 (as of June 30), from *The Bulletin*, American Bureau of Shipping, November, 1948, p. 23 (figures here were converted from 2,390,000 deadweight tons of inactive American-flag shipping). For 1950 (as of Dec. 31, from figures supplied by the Maritime Administration), from *The Bulletin*, American Bureau of Shipping, May, 1951, p. 38. The 1950 figures for all types of ships and for steam and motor only include the reserve fleet and also the temporarily inactive fleet.

Estimates of the volume of international trade, which served in the calculations of quantum of world trade, were taken from the following sources: through 1939, from the 1943 special Maritime Commission study cited above; for 1950, from a series for seaborne international trade in *United Nations Statistical Yearbook, 1949–50*.

Since shipping and trade figures for years prior to 1900 are not available, it is difficult to achieve much perspective of a trend up to World War I. One authority has written: "Shipping has suffered from low rates and excess tonnage from the turn of the century to 1914, except for a temporary boom in 1912 and 1913." However, there is reason to believe that this situation reflects the transition from wooden sailing vessels to iron and steel ships and not a chronic surplus of ship tonnage. Although excess tonnage may have existed at the turn of the century, there has been a reasonably good correlation between the growth of the world's active merchant fleet and the volume of seaborne international trade (see Table 4).

Between 1900 and 1914, shipping tonnage increased 70 percent and international trade 62.2 percent. Comparison of 1914 and 1923 indicates an increase of 10.6 percent in active ships and a decrease of 9.4 percent in trade. However, the tonnage of merchant ships was rather stable from 1923 to 1926, whereas world trade expanded. If statistics for 1924 instead of 1923 are compared with 1914, the comparable figures would be increases of 12.8 percent for ships and 2.5 percent for trade. Between 1923 and 1939, active shipping tonnage increased only 23 percent, while world seaborne trade in 1939 was 33.5 percent greater than in 1923.

In 1950, the tonnage of the world's active fleet at 70 million gross tons was 4.8 percent larger than the fleet of 1939, while the quantum of world trade had increased by 4.2 percent. These figures indicate a close correlation between the increases in vessel tonnage and trade. The postwar situation, however, is particularly difficult to appraise because of the large volume of seemingly abnormal trade moving. We have already given an account of the enormous tonnages of such bulk cargoes as coal, wheat, and so forth that have been moving primarily from the United States aboard war-built vessels that carry one-way cargoes in an irregular shuttle service, largely across the Atlantic.

The World Tanker Fleet. The foregoing comparison fails to take into consideration the tremendous growth of tanker tonnage and of world trade in petroleum and petroleum products, a development resulting from the opening of petroleum fields in the Middle East and from the greater dependence of the United States on imported crude oil. Between 1939 and 1950, the world's tanker fleet rose from 16.9 million to 25.3 million deadweight tons, for an increase of 50 percent.[6] In 1939, tankers represented

---

[6] "U.S. Tanker Fleet Prospects," *Shipping Survey*, Association of American Ship Owners, March, 1951, Vol. 7, No. 1. Attention should be called to various tonnage figures and to the distinction between gross tonnage (the volume of a vessel's enclosed spaces, in which the cubical contents are divided by 100 on the basis that 100 cubic feet of space is equal to 1 ton) and deadweight tonnage (based on the weight of fuel, stores, cargo, and water). For more detail on tonnages used in connection with ships, see pp. 163, 165. The tonnage of a C3 is approximately 7,940 gross tons or roughly

16.6 percent of the world's active merchant fleet, and in 1950, over 24 percent. Even more striking is the situation in prospect for 1954 and 1955. As of October, 1952, tankers constituted 60 percent of the ships being built or contracted for in the world. By 1955, some 30 percent or more of all active vessels in the world may be tankers.

The Dry-cargo Fleet. If we isolate tanker trade and consider only freighters engaged in carrying dry cargo, we find that vessel tonnage and the volume of trade have been roughly in balance since 1939. One study made in 1948 compared employed dry-cargo vessels from year to year and reported 61.7 million deadweight tons as of Sept. 1, 1939, and 60 million tons on June 30, 1948.[7] Another study set this figure at 63.5 million deadweight tons on July 1, 1951, and gave 66.4 million tons as the potential for 1954–1955.[8] The 1954–1955 estimate was made on the assumption that United States surplus war-built vessels would not then be in service. This may well be a maximum figure for that date, because scrapping and marine losses could easily reduce the figure to the July, 1951, level. Further, if economic conditions in the future favor the retirement of older vessels, the figure could even be below the July, 1951, level.

Hence, if world trading conditions should become at all stabilized, it seems reasonably certain that for several years the world merchant fleet of active dry-cargo vessels will be in balance with the economic demand for ships. This conclusion is based on two assumptions: (1) that United States surplus war-built vessels will be withheld from the commercial market when they are no longer required for emergency purposes and (2) that large-scale warfare will be avoided.

The relationship of active shipping tonnage to world seaborne trade is affected, however, by factors not revealed by the statistics. Although the increase in size and speed of the average vessel has materially increased the potential annual carrying capacity of freighters, the turn-around time of ships in port, particularly since the depression of the 1930's, has been so increased that it has probably more than offset all advantages resulting

---

12,100 deadweight tons. The British use gross tonnage, while the tendency in the United States is to use deadweight tonnage. Tonnage figures for the United States used later in this chapter, if deadweight, have been converted to gross in order that they may be comparable with figures for other countries.

[7] *Shipping Survey*, Association of American Ship Owners, December, 1948, Vol. 4, No. 8.

[8] Research Report 51-12, National Federation of American Shipping, Inc., Oct. 17, 1951. The federation's monthly reports and special supplements are valuable for timely information on the status of the American merchant marine and allied subjects. Similar publications that may be consulted are *The Bulletin*, American Bureau of Shipping (monthly), for statistics on shipbuilding and the size and employment of merchant fleets; *Bulletin*, American Merchant Marine Institute, Inc. (weekly), for summaries of current information about the shipping industry; and *Transport and Communications Review*, United Nations (quarterly), for special articles on ocean transportation.

from greater size and speed of ships. One British authority has stated that, because of slower turn-arounds, five ships are now needed to do the work of four before the war. Since 1945, port congestion, as well as slow working of vessels in port, has often been a factor.

Furthermore, trade in manufactured and semimanufactured or processed goods, which run to a higher cubic measurement per weight ton than most raw materials and foodstuffs, has increased. This development has tended to increase the space requirements per ton of world trade. This factor is particularly applicable to a series of statistics based on gross tonnage, which is a space measurement (i.e., 100 cubic feet per ton). Still other factors that may have caused a faster rate of increase include the following: (1) an increased movement of bulk cargoes such as ores, liquid chemicals, asphalt, and so forth has led to the construction of many special carriers, most of which carry one-way cargoes, and (2) the increasing proportion of shipping in liner services has placed a greater value on frequency and regularity of service, leading at times to a somewhat less proportionate emphasis on complete utilization of space and lifting capacity of the vessel.

CHARACTERISTICS OF MODERN SHIPS

Steel, which did not come into general use in ship construction until late in the nineteenth century, has made possible considerable improvement in the structure and marine engineering of steam-propelled ships and also in their economic possibilities. Superior strength, rigidity, and buoyancy; greater size and net space for cargo; and greater length of life and dependability under all weather conditions—these are important factors in the increased value of ships. During the twenties and thirties, many other technical improvements were made in hull design, propulsion, and construction, including cargo-carrying capacity, speed, crews' quarters, refrigeration, and navigation appliances.[9] Since activity in American shipyards was very limited during the interwar period, most of these improvements were found in British, Scandinavian, German, Italian, and Dutch yards.

Size, Speed, and Propulsion. In spite of the claim from time to time that ships had reached the optimum in size and speed, merchant ships have continued to be constructed larger and of greater speed. In 1914, there were 3,608 vessels of 4,000 or more tons, 6,952 in 1939, and 8,842 in 1950. Since shipbuilding in the United States has been concentrated in wartime building programs, American war-built ships reflect increases in size and speed.

[9] Charles H. Hughes, *Handbook of Ship Calculations, Construction, and Operation,* 3d ed., McGraw-Hill Book Company, Inc., New York, 1942.

American cargo ships built during World War I averaged 4,300 gross tons, and tankers 6,500 gross tons. World War II cargo carriers had increased to an average of 7,200 tons and tankers to 9,800 tons. Of American ships of 1,000 gross tons and over, in 1939, 71 percent were of 5,000 or more tons. By 1951, the proportion had increased to 95 percent. The standard Type A vessel built during World War I at the Hog Island shipyard was of roughly 7,800 deadweight tons and had a speed of about 11.5 knots (later rated at about 10 knots). The standard cargo vessel of World War II was the Liberty ship of about 10,790 deadweight tons, with a steam-reciprocating engine, a cruising speed of about 10 knots, and a cruising radius of 9,000 miles. The 10,850-ton Victory, turbine powered, had a speed ranging from 15 to 17 knots and a cruising radius of 20,500 miles. The new Mariner, a C4 type, is of 12,900 deadweight tons. Powered by double reduction geared turbines, developing 17,500 shaft horsepower, they are expected to be capable of sustained speeds of 20 knots. In 1951, the Maritime Administration contracted for 35 of these vessels, and the first, the *Keystone Mariner*, was launched on Feb. 29, 1952.[10]

Foreign-flag ships are also larger. During the 1940's, *Fairplay*, the outstanding British shipping weekly, revised its "standard" ship from a 7,500-tonner, which had been used for many years, to a 9,500-ton vessel. The average speed was increased from 10 to 12.5 knots. Since the war, the trend toward bigger cargo ships and higher speeds is noted in the ships being delivered in foreign yards, particularly in Scandinavia, where ships of 19 knots are reported. However, conservatism continues with respect to the tramp ship, which the British have come to call the *general trader*. A new ship of this type was introduced in May, 1952, when the *Windsor* was launched. She is designed to carry 9,950 tons of cargo and has a service speed of 13 knots.

Tankers have increased in size more than freighters. For nearly thirty years before World War II, they changed little in regard to size and speed, and vessels of 12,000 deadweight tons and of 12-knot speeds proved suitable for most requirements. The typical World War II tanker was the T2 type, of about 16,600 deadweight tons and about 14.5 knots.[11] Three tankers launched in 1950 and 1951 (*Atlantic Seaman, Atlantic Engineer,* and *Atlantic Navigator*) for the Philadelphia Tankers, Inc., a subsidiary of the Atlantic Refining Company, are of over 30,000 dead-

[10] *Fortune*, May, 1952, gives illustrations of the new Mariner and of other American ships. Fig. 8B in Chap. 11 shows the *Keystone Mariner*.
[11] The standard T2-SE-A1 tanker, with a deadweight tonnage of 16,765, is rated to carry 141,000 barrels of petroleum products, which is a ratio of almost 8.5 to 1. The standard T3-S-BZ1 tanker, with a deadweight tonnage of 23,000 tons, is rated to carry 213,000 barrels, which is a ratio of almost 9.3 to 1. One ton of gasoline is equivalent to 8.67 barrels, and 1 ton of fuel oil is equivalent to 6.63 barrels.

weight tons. In early 1952, agents acting for the Greek-controlled World Tankers, Inc., contracted for two 45,000-deadweight-ton tankers to be built in the United States by the Bethlehem Steel Company's shipbuilding division and for two 44,000-ton tankers from a British yard.

The largest merchant ships afloat are passenger liners, and the largest merchant ship ever built in the United States is the *United States*, constructed for service between New York and European ports. The 70-million-dollar ship has 12 decks, is roughly of 52,000 gross tons, 900 feet in length, with a cargo space of 148,000 cubic feet (48,000 cubic feet of which is refrigerated), accommodations for 2,000 passengers, and a crew of 1,000. The keel was laid on Feb. 8, 1950, and she was floated on June 23, 1951, finished for service, and sailed on July 3, 1952, for her maiden voyage. Geared turbines turning quadruple screws are capable of driving her at a sustained speed of over 34 knots.

Factors Influencing Size and Speed. The ships that make the world's fleets are geared to the evolution of the world's shipping economy—the broadening in the types and sources of raw materials and foodstuffs, industrialization, and greater world markets—and also to national policies, the most important of which is today concerned with national security. At the present time, planning for wartime or emergency requirements is the final influence on the size and speed of ships built in the United States. This is especially true of speed, which has become a prerequisite of success in military and naval operation. Speed was the vital element considered when the new United States ships *United States*, *Constitution*, and *Independence* were constructed, but the potential for mass production was also considered when the Maritime Administration ordered the 35 Mariner-type ships. The Mariner is fast enough to travel out of convoy and needs no conversion for peacetime employment. In an emergency, United States shipyards will be counted upon to mass-produce the necessary tonnage, and to this end standardized design is fundamental. This leads to the general design adaptable to wartime use instead of one incorporating the special features that make ships suitable for the specific requirements of selected routes and services.

In addition to security requirements, the psychological aspects of speed and competition should not be overlooked. However, national pride in having the biggest and fastest ship has little place in the fine balance between deadweight carrying capacity, cubic capacity requirements, capital cost, and operating costs. In general, three main economic factors determine the size and speed of merchant ships: (1) the pay load and earning power, (2) the technical aspects of ship construction and marine engineering, and (3) conditions of navigation and port facilities. These are the matters that the shipowner bears in mind when he seeks to determine the commercially most efficient combination of size and speed in relation to the cargo to be handled, the revenues, and the route or service in which the ship will be employed.[12]

First, remembering that the objective of the ship operator is economic utilization of the cubic capacity of his ship and a reasonable freight rate, we can understand the first consideration of the shipowner. He wants a ship to handle the cargo that he expects to carry, as to both type and volume of cargo. For the general-cargo carrier or freighter, consideration must be given to a number of matters, including the average stowage factor as it relates to balance between deadweight and cubic lifting capacity, the amount of refrigerated cargo and of liquids such as vegetable oils, the number of ports of call, the rate of movement of commodities, and the character of competition. The shipowner also estimates the freight-earning character of the cargo—in other words, the potential freight revenues and the earning power of a ship on a voyage. Then, potential cargo volume and freight revenues, together with estimates of time at sea and time in port for the ship, will result in the general requirements for size and speed (and also of the number of ships required to maintain the required frequency of sailings on a route). The next step is for the shipowner to secure estimates of capital cost for the type of ship that he considers essential. From this, he can derive his estimated depreciation charge, fuel, and other operating costs, which will permit him to make his final estimates of revenues and costs and to determine whether he has achieved a commercially feasible balance of size and speed, of capital cost and freight-earning capability.

Recent trends in size and speed of merchant ships undoubtedly reflect recent changes in cargo movement. The loss of British coal cargoes has no doubt had an enormous influence on design and speed of ships, for one of the basic tramp cargoes (coal) and one of the fundamental influences on the development of commodity routes has been diminished, if not almost completely removed. Relocation of sources of supply for ores, oils, grains, and other commodities has led to changes in ships and routes. Postwar bulk buying of commodities in the British Isles may also be influencing ship design. The increased movement of frozen meat, vegetables, and fruits, the expansion in processing vegetable oils at point of origin, and the shipment of vegetable oils in deep tanks are among influences for change. Generally speaking, all these influences have tended to move the general trading ship and former tramp out of the marginal area of such

---

[12] Additional information on the size and speed of modern freighters is available in the following sources: "Economic Speed of Cargo Ships," *Fairplay,* Jan. 10, 1952, pp. 86–87; "Merchant Ship Design," *Lloyd's List & Shipping Gazette,* Apr. 9, 1952, pp. 4*ff.* (summarizing a paper by Sir Wilfrid Ayre before the Institution of Naval Architects, British); and L. Poirier, "Causes of Developments and New Trends in Postwar Merchant Marine Fleets," *Transport and Communications Review,* United Nations, July–September, 1949, Vol. 2, pp. 19–26.

employment and into the area of the cargo liner that operates over a trade route on a schedule. As a result, the tendency has been to increase the cubic capacity of ships in relation to deadweight capacity and to put emphasis on speed.

At the same time, there has been a tendency toward more special or single-purpose ships such as ore carriers, tankers, and refrigerated ships. For ore carriers, there is usually little relation between size and crew requirements. Since they operate on a shuttle basis between source of supply and point of consumption of the raw material, bigness becomes an advantage, dependent only on port facilities and navigational conditions.

Second, increased unit power of propulsion machinery and decreased weight and bulk of machinery per horsepower have done much to permit economic increases in speed of ships. Nevertheless, a basic retarding influence exists in that each knot of increased speed, after a certain limit, calls for a capital investment and a rate of fuel consumption that tends to be of uneconomic size. Other factors have contributed to increase in speed, including the improvement of propellers, the adoption of welding in place of fully riveted ships, and the use of aluminum alloys. Both of the latter factors tend to lighten the structural weight of ships and to increase the effectiveness of the unit power of propulsion machinery. Some of these developments are reflected in the declining size of passenger ships. Furthermore, the emphasis on fast, large passenger liners has been lessened by the increasing speed of cargo liners, which has led to the development of combination passenger-cargo ships.

Two other influences are worth mentioning. The development of air transport and the inroads of airplanes on passenger travel and on certain commodities have encouraged greater speed in ships. On the other hand, the slow turn-around of ships in ports militates against the installation of the propulsion machinery necessary for greater speed. All the advantage in lessening time at sea is lost when the ship lies in port; the capital investment in machinery is not earning much revenue in port.

Third, the depths of harbors and harbor entrances, of channels and canals, the length of piers, and similar physical factors limit the size of ships. For example, the 44,000-ton tankers mentioned earlier will be able to transit the Panama Canal, but their draft, fully loaded, will not permit transit of the Suez Canal at its present depth. The C4 has been limited in intercoastal trade, because so few piers exist in the United States that can handle ships of such length and number of hatches.

THE AMERICAN MERCHANT MARINE

The American merchant marine of the early 1950's bears little resemblance to the industry of 1939 or to that of earlier years, for its composition has been in transition. In 1939, this country's foreign trade was so dependent on foreign tonnage that more than 1,000 Scandinavian ships alone were carrying our exports and imports. World War II left the nation with a residue of over 4,000 war-built ships in the hands of the government. Their total tonnage was equal to two-thirds of the world's total prewar dry-cargo fleet and one-half of the tanker fleet. Many of the problems of the shipping industry today, as well as many of those associated with this nation's shipping policy, are tied to this change. In considering the United States merchant marine, we again use active rather than total tonnage.

The ensuing discussion may be clarified if we recall certain developments. In 1946, the vessel tonnage privately owned was very small, while, out of the war-built fleet of 5,500 ships, the government owned approximately 4,000, the rest having been sunk or so badly damaged that they were scrapped. Between Mar. 8, 1946, when the Merchant Ship Sales Act was passed, and Jan. 15, 1951, when the ship-sales program terminated, these 4,000 ships were offered for sale to citizens and noncitizens under terms described elsewhere.[13] By Jan. 15, 1951, 1,960 ships had been sold (1,113 to noncitizens and 847 to citizens).[14] This left more than 2,000 ships, which, in accordance with the provisions of Section 11 of the 1946 Act, went into the national-defense reserve fleet.

Since 1946, the United States has had the largest peacetime active fleet of seagoing merchant ships in the history of the nation. In June, 1946, before the government's ship-sales program was under way, the active tonnage consisted of 2,332 vessels of 17.2 million gross tons. This included government-owned tonnage but not ships in military service. Four years later, in June, 1950, the commercial fleet numbered 1,251 ships, totaling 9.3 million gross tons. Of these, 1,182 were privately owned, and 69 were government-owned vessels chartered to commercial operators. When the Korean emergency occurred, laid-up government-owned ships were taken from the reserve fleet to transport military, defense-mobilization, and relief cargoes. By mid-1951, active tonnage aggregated 11.3 million gross tons, and by the end of the year, it had risen to 15.3 million tons. As of Dec. 31, 1951, the active fleet numbered 1,955 ships, including 1,262 privately owned and 693 government vessels. As noted earlier, after mid-1952, many government-owned ships were returned to a reserve status.

[13] See Ship Sales after World War II in Chap. 13.
[14] We are here primarily concerned with the American merchant marine, but the following statement of L. Poirier, head of the French Merchant Marine Mission to the United States and Canada, indicates the "foreign-aid" aspects of the ship-sales program: "Further, in 1946, already the United States Government agreed to the sale of more than a third of its surplus shipping—'Liberty' and 'Victory' ships, various cargo ships and large tankers—under financial conditions that were within the reach of all countries. In that way a beneficial transfer took place whereby maritime nations regained powerful means of survival." See *Transport and Communications Review*, United Nations, July–September, 1949, Vol. 2, pp. 19–26.

Tanker Division. The United States tanker fleet reflects the great dependence of this country on oil. Since 1923, when the total United States tanker tonnage engaged in both foreign and domestic movement of petroleum and its products consisted of 2 million gross tons, that tonnage has doubled (see Table 5). Tanker tonnage in 1950 aggregated 3.9 million gross tons, rose in 1951 to 4.2 million, and dropped to 4 million in 1952. Proportionally, tankers represented close to 28 percent of the total tonnage of the American merchant marine in 1923 and, because of greatly increased domestic tonnage, close to 39 percent in 1939. Postwar figures are 42 percent for 1950, 37 percent for 1951, and 34 percent for 1952. These percentage declines were due in part to the reactivation of freighters from the reserve fleet, and in 1952 to a decline in foreign tanker tonnage from 2 million tons in 1951 to 1.5 million in 1952.

The distribution of the tanker fleet between domestic and foreign service reflects the world-wide pattern of petroleum production and transport. From 1923 to 1939, the increase in tanker tonnage was caused largely by expansion of the domestic fleet. As the movement of petroleum from oil fields to refineries by water increased in volume, tonnage rose from 1.4 million gross tons in 1923 to 2.1 million in 1939; in spite of pipeline transport of petroleum, postwar domestic tonnage (the average was 2.3 million gross tons for 1950 to 1952) exceeds that of 1939. In 1952, tankers comprised three-fourths of the total United States domestic fleet. Moreover, the domestic tanker fleet remained larger than that in foreign service in spite of great increases in foreign tonnage.

As explained in Chapter 3, the United States shifted from a net-export to a net-import status with regard to petroleum in 1947, and the Middle East assumed importance as a source for oil. This has had a decided effect on the size and composition of the foreign tanker fleet. Tankers employed in transporting oil from the Middle East are large and fast; many of them are capable of speeds exceeding 16 knots. United States tanker tonnage engaged in foreign trade increased from less than 0.4 million tons in 1939 to 1.6 million in 1950. This represents more than a threefold increase and is roughly three times the wartime estimates of foreign tanker needs (see Table 5). The tonnage rose in 1951 to 2 million tons, and dropped in 1952 to 1.5 million. One does not have to look far for an explanation of the decline.

Operations in the Middle East trade bring the American tanker into direct competition with foreign-flag tankers and in routes that are most favorable to the foreigner. This is true in spite of the fact that about one-third of the proved oil reserves outside the United States are controlled by American companies. The future for American-flag participation in foreign tanker trades is not bright for various reasons. (1) American operating costs are 25 percent greater than for a foreign-flag ship.

Table 5. United States Merchant Marine, by Divisions and by Types of Ships, Selected Years, 1923 to 1952
(In millions of gross tons)

Year as of June 30	Total	Combination	Cargo	Tanker
Total fleet				
1923	7.0	1.1	3.9	2.0
1939	6.4	1.0	2.9	2.5
1950	9.3	0.5	4.9	3.9
1951	11.3	0.5	6.6	4.2
1952	11.6	0.7	6.9	4.0
Privately owned:				
1951*	10.1	0.4	5.4	4.2
1952*	10.2	0.4	5.6	4.2
1944 estimates of postwar privately owned	6.2/9.2	0.2†	4.3/6.4	1.6/2.6
Foreign trade				
1923	3.6	0.7	2.3	0.6
1939	2.1	0.7	1.0	0.4
1950	5.8	0.5	3.7	1.6
1951	7.9	0.5	5.4	2.0
1952	8.2	0.7	6.0	1.5
Privately owned:				
1951	6.6	0.3	4.3	2.0
1952	5.9	0.4	4.0	1.5
1944 estimates of postwar privately owned	3.0/4.1	0.1†	2.6/3.4	0.3/0.6
Domestic trade‡				
1923	3.4	0.4	1.6	1.4
1939	4.3	0.3	1.9	2.1
1950	3.5	…§	1.2	2.3
1951	3.4	…§	1.2	2.2
1952	3.3	…§	0.9	2.4
Privately owned:				
1951	3.3	…	1.0	2.2
1952	3.2	…	0.8	2.4
1944 estimates of postwar privately owned	3.2/5.1	0.1	1.7/3.0	1.4/2.0

* For 1951, privately owned tonnage includes 28 temporarily inactive ships. For 1952, the totals include 113 inactive ships (10 combination, 72 cargo, and 31 tankers).

† Tonnage classified as passenger only.

‡ Tonnage figures include that moving in the intercoastal, coastwise, and noncontiguous trades. For explanation of these terms, see accompanying text.

§ Combination passenger-cargo tonnage in the domestic trades was 45,000 tons in 1950, 41,000 in 1951, and 7,000 in 1952.

SOURCE: All tonnage figures are from *The Bulletin*, American Bureau of Shipping, September, 1951, pp. 40–41, and September, 1952, p. 44. They do not include Great

(2) The cost of constructing tankers in this country is greater than in foreign shipyards,[15] and until mid-1952, tankers were excluded from the benefits of the construction-differential subsidies provided for under the Merchant Marine Act of 1936.[16] (3) Employment in the trades between foreign ports is not attractive to American seamen, who prefer to serve aboard vessels stopping at United States ports. (4) Difficulties involved in foreign exchange induce American oil companies to build ships abroad and to operate them under foreign registry.

As a result, many American-owned tankers are registered under foreign flags. This is one of the main reasons why tanker tonnage under the Panamanian flag increased from 0.7 to 2.8 million deadweight tons between 1939 and 1950. Other American-owned tankers are under the Honduran and Liberian flags.[17]

By building abroad for foreign-flag operation, American owners not only get cheaper ships but also are able to expend accumulated credits that cannot be converted into dollars and returned to the United States. At the same time, they avoid additional accumulation of credits that may not be convertible. Only the congestion of foreign shipyards is now causing tankers to be built in the United States. During the years 1948 to 1950, 51 supertankers were built in American shipyards, many of them for American owners, but only 4 or 5 were for American registry. In December, 1951, British tankers represented 23.3 percent of the world's total fleet, American tankers 23.1 percent, Norwegian 16.2 percent, and Panamanian 9.5 percent.[18] In June, 1952, the British accounted for 40

Lakes vessels and those owned by the U.S. Army and Navy. Because of the rounding, tonnage figures are not always additive. The wartime (1944) estimates of postwar tonnage (these give a range) are from *The Use and Disposition of Ships and Shipyards at the End of World War II*, A Report Prepared for the U.S. Navy Department and the U.S. Maritime Commission by the Graduate School of Business Administration, Harvard University, Government Printing Office, Washington, D.C., June, 1945, p. 120. The American Bureau of Shipping tonnage figures are for ships of 1,000 gross tons or over, while the Harvard estimates are for vessels of 2,000 or more gross tons.

[15] The 44,000-ton tankers ordered for World Tankers, Inc., mentioned earlier, are to cost about 12.6 million dollars, compared with 20 million for the 45,000-ton ships ordered from Bethlehem.

[16] This statement needs clarification. Since the Act provided that ships constructed under the construction-differential subsidy were to be operated on essential trade routes (see Chap. 4) and since no tankers were so engaged, tanker owners did not receive the benefit of the subsidy. The Long-Range Shipping Act of 1952 extends this subsidy to all ships engaged in foreign trade (see Chap. 13).

[17] As of 1950, approximately 200 ships of about 3 million deadweight tons owned or controlled by United States citizens were registered under foreign flags, mostly Panamanian, Honduran, Liberian, and Venezuelan. Of these ships, about three-fourths by number and five-sixths by tonnage were tankers. *Time* (Mar. 24, 1952, p. 95) reports that "at least" 134 United States ships are registered in Panama and 240 under other flags. See also "Foreign Transfers of American Ships," *Shipping Survey*, Association of American Ship Owners, January, 1952, Vol. 8, No. 1.

[18] See *Merchant Fleets of the World, September 1, 1939–December 31, 1951*, p. 58.

percent of the current building and on-order programs, the Swedish for 14.8 percent, Germans for 9.3 percent, and Americans for only 8.7 percent.[19] The United States position is certain to become substantially weaker.

Foreign Trade Division of Dry-cargo Vessels. Offshore activity since the war is much greater than in 1939. In mid-1951, the privately owned freighter tonnage in foreign operations (4.6 million gross tons) was more than four times the 1939 figure and almost 50 percent greater than the forecasts made during the war. In mid-1951, the privately owned dry-cargo fleet consisted of 609 freighters and passenger-cargo ships engaged in foreign trade and another 24 ships in trade between foreign ports. This fleet was slightly smaller in 1952. There were 572 ships in foreign trade and 9 in the category "foreign to foreign."

These were supplemented, as noted earlier, by ships from the government's fleet. As of mid-1951, the active foreign fleet totaled roughly 800 ships, and one year later 870 ships. Many of the operations of this composite fleet of privately owned and government vessels consisted of military types of activity, arising out of the Korean affair and the shipping requirements of the North Atlantic Treaty, and of an irregular and non-sustaining type of trade to carry grain and coal to western Europe, grain to India, and other cargoes of this nature.

The Harvard Report, made in 1944 and published in 1945, forecast a maximum foreign trade fleet of 610 freighters and combination ships, provided one-half of the country's exports and imports were carried in American ships.[20] Although the 1951 fleet numbered 800 ships, American freighters carried only 40 percent of this country's foreign trade in dry cargo. It remains to be seen, however, whether a United States-flag fleet of roughly 600 cargo carriers can, under economic conditions that approach what may be termed "normal," maintain their position in competition with foreign ships.

The offshore or foreign trade division of the dry-cargo ships in the American merchant marine is a composite of ships used in the following employments: (1) nearby foreign trade routes, (2) other foreign trade routes, and (3) the carriage of trade between foreign ports. About 8 percent of the ships are employed in nearby trade in the Caribbean Sea or to Canada, Mexico, and Central America. Almost 90 percent is engaged in foreign trade not classed as nearby or interport, and the remainder (less than 3 percent) operates between foreign ports.

---

[19] *The Bulletin*, American Bureau of Shipping, September, 1952, p. 42.

[20] *The Use and Disposition of Ships and Shipyards at the End of World War II*, A Report Prepared for the U.S. Navy Department and the U.S. Maritime Commission by the Graduate School of Business Administration, Harvard University, Government Printing Office, Washington, D.C., June, 1945.

Combination Passenger-Cargo Ships. In 1923 and again in 1939, shipowners in the United States owned 0.7 million tons of combination passenger-cargo ships engaged in foreign service under the American flag. By 1950 and 1951, foreign passenger-cargo tonnage had been reduced to 0.5 million tons. As a result it had declined from 10 or 11 percent of the total United States privately owned merchant fleet in 1923 and 1939 to 5.4 percent in 1950. Because freighters were returned to service from the reserve fleet during 1951, the percentage dropped to 4.4 percent as of June 30, 1951. The United States position with regard to combination passenger-cargo ships improved when the *Constitution* and *Independence* of 23,719 gross tons each were put into service, in late 1951, and the 52,000-ton *United States* in July, 1952.

Subsidized and Nonsubsidized Operators. In 1938, during the period of transition from the old mail-contract-subsidy system to the operating-differential-subsidy program embodied in the Merchant Marine Act of 1936,[21] our foreign trade operations were carried on by 27 companies that owned 295 ships. Sixteen of the companies, having 177 ships, were subsidized, and 11 operators (of 3 or more ships), with a total of 118 ships, were unsubsidized. The subsidized fleet was reduced to 12 companies and 138 ships by 1940. As of January, 1945, the 12 companies subsidized before World War II had 91 ships, and 11 unsubsidized operators had 66 ships, the balance of the prewar fleets having been sold or sunk.

When operating-differential subsidies were reestablished as of Jan. 1, 1947, they covered the operations of 158 ships owned by 10 companies. In mid-1950, 254 ships owned by 13 companies were approved for subsidy. As of early 1953, the 15 subsidized companies owned or had assigned to their routes 268 ships. When the operating-differential subsidy became effective for the Pacific Far East Line and the Pacific Transport Lines, on Jan. 1, 1953, the number of subsidized operators had increased to 15.

Hence, between 1947 and the early 1950's, the unsubsidized foreign fleet ranged between roughly 350 and 450 ships, or better than half of the total foreign freighter fleet. The number of unsubsidized ship operators far exceeds the number of subsidized operators. Since 163 companies, not primarily tanker owners, purchased vessels under the Merchant Ship Sales Act of 1946 for American-flag operation, there are probably 150 unsubsidized companies in existence in domestic and foreign commerce. Only 33 of that number, however, may be termed major operators. The list of companies approved by the Maritime Administration as charterers or agents of the Federal government for purposes of operating government vessels includes 42 unsubsidized operators, several of whom probably cannot be considered major long-range operators.

[21] See Chap. 13.

Great Lakes Shipping. Great Lakes shipping is largely a specialized industrial operation, utilizing carriers that are specially designed for and largely limited to service on the Lakes. They are engaged almost entirely in transporting bulk cargoes of iron ore, coal, limestone, and grain in the amount of about 180,000,000 net tons a year.[22] Shipping is controlled by weather conditions and the Sault Sainte Marie ("Soo") locks; the season usually extends from Apr. 15 to Nov. 30. American-flag tonnage on the Lakes now constitutes 77 percent of the combined United States–Canadian fleet. American tonnage in 1950 consisted of 423 ships of 2,377,000 gross tons, roughly the same as it has been since pre-World War I days.[23] The Canadian fleet of 252 ships totals 711,000 gross tons.

The oceangoing segment of the Great Lakes fleet, which transports primarily grain and wood pulp between ports on the Lakes and ports in western Europe and the Mediterranean via the St. Lawrence River route and which is largely under foreign flags, is expanding. Since this trade was pioneered by a Norwegian line, during the 1930's, it has grown steadily. By 1953, it was served by 51 shallow-draft ships under Dutch, German, French, Swedish, Norwegian, and British flags.

Block Obsolescence. The United States made an important contribution in both world wars with its shipbuilding programs. In each case, the country requisitioned privately owned ships and constructed large fleets. At the close of both wars, the United States government owned a large fleet of merchant vessels. In 1921, when the World War I building program was terminated, the U.S. Shipping Board owned 1,792 ships representing a total of more than 11 million deadweight tons; at the close of World War II, a residue of over 4,000 war-built ships remained in the hands of the government. The problem of block obsolescence has been created by wartime circumstances.

As indicated in Chapter 13, where the ship-sales programs are discussed in more detail, the sale of war-built vessels after World War I proceeded so slowly that the program benefited the American operator very little. Nor did the provisions of the Merchant Marine Act of 1920 or of its successor in 1928, both of which provided funds for building new ships,

---

[22] As Oliver T. Burnham, secretary of the Lake Carriers' Association, Cleveland, explained, "On the Great Lakes most statistics relating to cargo transported are given in net tons with the exception of figures relating to iron ore which are quoted in gross tons. On the other hand, the capacity of Great Lakes vessels is ordinarily shown in gross tons and the size of each cargo is considered to vary only slightly. Usually bulk cargo, such as iron ore, coal, stone or grain, either fill the vessel hold completely or cause the ship to be submerged to its load line marks before the full capacity of the cargo space is reached. About 95 percent of Great Lakes commerce consists of dry bulk cargoes."

[23] For tonnage figures of the United States Great Lakes fleet, 1900 to 1950, see Table 3.

break the bottleneck of obsolescence. Only 57 ships were constructed under the provisions embodied in the two Acts.

As a result, by 1937, nearly 92 percent of this nation's seagoing fleet was fifteen or more years old. In 1938, out of 282 cargo vessels flying the American flag, all but 3 had been built prior to 1923 and had an average speed of 10 to 11 knots. This fleet competed with a foreign fleet 62 percent of which had been built after 1932 and which had an average speed of more than 12 knots. Vessels built after 1932 averaged more than 14 knots.

The Act of 1936 undertook to break the bottleneck of obsolescence, but its influence was largely limited to the subsidized operator who had to agree to a vessel-replacement program in order to obtain an operating subsidy. The government then initiated a building program, but it was based largely on faith that a market would develop. Before that faith could be tested commercially, World War II broke out. American freighters then averaged twenty years of age.

The ship-sales program of 1946 to 1951 did benefit the American merchant marine. Since the Merchant Ship Sales Act of 1946 gave American buyers preference and reserved the best ships for them, the 847 ships purchased by American shipowners were the most desirable of the war-built fleet. Of the unsold surplus (1,502 merchant ships and 571 military auxiliaries), 1,477 are of the Liberty type. But this entire war-built American-flag fleet will be twenty years old between 1962 and 1965.

The problem of block obsolescence could be met by a good replacement program. However, as of mid-1953, the only fixed program involved the ultimate replacement of the 260-odd subsidized ships; and the only building program of seagoing ships for American registry involved a few tankers, 35 Mariner-class freighters for the government, and one seatrain. When one observes the cost of a new Mariner in the eastern yards, approximately $620 per ton, compared with the sales price of $106 per ton for the C4 type, one may legitimately ask how a shipowner is to accumulate, out of depreciation and operating profits, sufficient funds to overcome the differential between the cost and value of his existing fleet and the apparent cost of replacement.[24]

While the American fleet grows old, other countries are rapidly rebuilding their fleets with new and highly competitive ships. In mid-1951, only 5 percent of the American tanker fleet had been constructed since the war, compared with 30 percent for the United Kingdom, 48 percent for Norway, and 29 percent for Panama. Only 102 of the 1,829 oceangoing ships being built in July, 1952, were being constructed in United States shipyards.

[24] The financial problem involved in block obsolescence is discussed more fully in Chap. 14.

Block obsolescence and ship replacements, and methods and costs of cargo handling, are the biggest problems facing the American shipping industry. With these in mind, we now turn to a discussion of the shipping process.

BIBLIOGRAPHY

Because of the nature of the information contained in this chapter, it is not possible to list the usual type of collateral reading. Anyone who wishes to supplement the information presented or to secure up-to-date information should consult current issues of the publications mentioned in the footnotes.

PART TWO

THE SHIPPING PROCESS

CHAPTER 7

TRAFFIC MANAGEMENT

The shipowner offers service for sale to shippers and receivers (consignees) who move goods in foreign and domestic commerce. His business is to provide this market with service and to provide a service that is better than that offered by his competitors. What, then, do the shipper and the consignee want from the ship operator? What does water-carrier service consist of? What does the term *traffic management* mean for the water carrier? This chapter will answer these questions and outline the functions of the traffic department of a steamship company.

EXPLANATION OF TRAFFIC MANAGEMENT

There are several classes of traffic managers and also several phases of traffic management. The broad term *traffic management* embraces all steps or phases in the control of goods in transit. Hence, traffic management includes the following functions: it makes arrangements with land, sea, and air carriers to move goods and to store them temporarily; it arranges charges for that service; it prepares goods for shipment; it receives the goods; and it performs numerous other functions, all of which are associated with the state of transit. The industrial traffic manager is concerned with the movement of goods from the point of view of his own company as a shipper or consignee. The commercial traffic manager is an employee of a trade association or of a chamber of commerce. The traffic manager of the water carrier, who represents one of the forms of transportation, strives to sell to the industrial or the commercial traffic manager a competitive service that will meet his needs.

Traffic Is Sales. Whereas the function of the traffic department in industry is to provide a service, the function of the traffic department of a shipping company is to sell a service. One wonders why ship operators have not adopted the terminology of salesmanship, why they do not refer to freight sales and passenger sales departments, and why they do not call their representatives salesmen instead of solicitors, district freight agents, freight traffic managers, and so forth. The Keeshin Motor Express

Company of Chicago, a motor freight carrier, was among the first carriers to employ the terminology of salesmanship, but there is no general movement in this direction. Perhaps the shipping industry would benefit if it recognized that its traffic function is one of salesmanship. This might clarify the job that the traffic department has to do and the means of accomplishing it. We say that "service is an intangible thing." This failure to define service more clearly may lessen the perspective of management regarding the function of this department. Any sales department needs to be aggressive and to have sharply defined objectives. Therefore, let us see what the ship operator has to sell.

What the Shipper Wants. As one company expresses our topic, its "ships literally are built for the convenience of shippers." A shipper (or a consignee, if he is arranging for the shipment) wants service, and to him service means the following things:

1. A ship available to move his goods safely to destination.
2. A time of departure from point of origin and a time of arrival at destination that will permit him to consummate his sale or purchase of the goods when desired.
3. A price for the service that will allow him to sell or purchase the goods.
4. The friendly assistance of the representatives of the carrier.

To restate these requirements in terms that apply more directly to the ship operator, the shipper wants (1) safe carriage and delivery of his goods, (2) frequency and regularity of sailings and usually speed of transit, (3) reasonable rates that will not unduly burden the cost of the goods when delivered, and (4) good customer relations. The shipper's interest in the carriage and delivery of the goods often extends to well-located and efficiently operated pier facilities.

There are many details to each of these general provisions. For instance, a shipper of fresh fruit from New York to Rio de Janeiro needs refrigerated space, and a shipper moving cottonseed oil from Buenos Aires to New York wants deep-tank space so that he can ship in bulk. The coffee importer does not want his coffee beans stowed next to garlic. Furthermore, the coffee importer, particularly if he imports on a large scale, is interested in frequent and regular sailings of ships, for the reason that he does not want to carry a large inventory that would tie up a large amount of money or credit from a bank. Also, because his money is tied up while the coffee is afloat, he is interested in the length of the voyage, and therefore in the speed of the ship and the route followed. Some other shipper—of bulk grain, for example—is less interested in frequency of service, regularity, and speed.

The shipper not only wants the ship operator to give him the lowest possible rate. More than that, he wants the carrier to take an interest in helping him to complete his sale and delivery of the goods. This involves varying degrees of personal and impersonal relationships between shipper and ship operator. We shall discuss these relationships, as phases of salesmanship, among the functions of the traffic department of a steamship company.

FUNCTIONS OF THE TRAFFIC DEPARTMENT

The functions of the traffic department vary with the type of service to be rendered and the character of the commodities to be carried. The traffic department of an industrial carrier, for example, will be very different from the same department in a liner service across the North Atlantic. The industrial carrier is more concerned with intracompany relationships and particularly with scheduling the movement of materials in order to meet the requirements of the company's operating or production department. While most common carriers operating liner services have well-developed and aggressive traffic departments, some companies rely heavily on the traffic services of freight forwarders. The traffic department of a liner operator often deals with a freight forwarder, an export commission house, or a manufacturer's agent, any one of whom may control the routing of merchandise and therefore be the real shipper or customer. The traffic department of a tramp carrier is, in effect, one or more ship brokers who scour the trade for available cargoes.

Broadly speaking, the traffic department has three major functions, as follows:

1. To fill the ships with cargo
    a. By selling and booking space in the ship.
    b. By issuing various shipper's papers and documents.
    c. By developing general customer relationships and public relations.
2. To establish remunerative rates
    a. By preparing and issuing tariffs (this is generally done jointly with competing carriers through the shipping conference or conferences at which the company is represented by the traffic department).[1]
    b. By handling relations with other water carriers and with other land and air carriers.
    c. By handling those relations with government that have to do with regulation of rates and practices.
3. To develop relations with other departments and the management of the steamship company
    a. By preparing traffic studies and maintaining traffic statistics that will advise those concerned with volume and flow of business and with possible modifications in ship design or the scheduling and routing of ships.

[1] The shipping conference is discussed in Chap. 19.

b. By cooperating with the company's advertising and public-relations program if it is not actually supervised by the traffic department.
   c. By handling, or at least cooperating with the department that is handling, customers' claims for loss or damage to cargo.
   d. By training personnel.

OBTAINING AND BOOKING CARGO

All the principles of industrial sales management are important in the work of the freight traffic department of a ship operator. The traffic sales manager and his staff must accumulate technical knowledge regarding ships and must be thoroughly informed on the characteristics of cargo and the details of the customer's commodity and his distribution program. This information is essential to effective salesmanship. They must be informed on operating costs for steamships, on port conditions, on competition, and on many other factors, all of which contribute to the competitive position of their company and its ability to satisfy customers. When a traffic sales manager and his staff understand this multitude of detail, they do not feel that the service they sell is intangible. Their problem, however, is to translate that service to the shipper, because they do not go to him with so many cubic feet of space in the ship's hold to display as their product nor do they approach him with a catalogue or samples in hand.

General Customer Relationships and Public Relations. If a steamship operator is to be effective, the full force of his promotional effort must be brought to bear not only on the shipping public but also on the general public. To effect both the environment within which the company can grow and prosper and the direct sales of the company's service to shippers, a broad institutional effort is necessary. Because such an effort has a cumulative effect, it must be applied consistently and strongly; it must be carefully planned and directed and amply supported by budgetary appropriations. Because the traffic department is the immediate beneficiary of successful sales-promotion work, quite generally the traffic manager directs, or at least sponsors, publicity, advertising, and even general public relations. The traffic manager should determine the advertising and mediums that best service the company's needs, except those for broad institutional purposes for which the executive department should be responsible.

Selling Space. To sell his company's service is the job of every employee of the steamship company, and the special assignment of the salesmen or district freight agents of the traffic department. Each representative usually has a list of accounts that are his responsibility, and he will be alert to new prospects for himself or for his fellow salesmen. Accounts may be assigned on a geographical basis, that is, one man may cover one-third of a port city if he is located in an area that develops considerable business. He may handle certain industries, such as the canned goods and foodstuffs trade. Or he may handle only inbound business or only outbound accounts. Moreover, salesmen may be assigned territories on any one basis or on a combination of several bases.

Traffic representatives call on the particular representative of the shipper who controls the movement of shipments. Most often this is the traffic manager on outbound shipments, and either the traffic manager or the purchasing agent on inbound shipments. For certain shipments, the traffic representative may have to contact the person who controls the means of shipment. For instance, if a producer in Portland, Oregon, sells 100 cases of tomato sauce to a buyer in Baltimore on f.a.s. (free alongside) terms, the routing of the shipment rests with the buyer or consignee. Then the salesman in the Portland agency of a company operating intercoastal, perhaps the Intercoastal Steamship Company, telegraphs the information to the traffic department in Baltimore, and a representative immediately calls on the consignee to try to sell his company's service. Since the rate from Portland to Baltimore is the same on all lines, speed and efficiency of service will be the deciding factors when the shipper decides which shipping line he will use.

When the district agent at the Baltimore office calls on the buyer of tomato sauce, he will be familiar with rates, transit time, schedules of competing companies' ships, the past performance of his company if the prospective client has shipped via one of its ships previously, and so forth. The traffic salesman, who cannot call on his prospective customer with sample in hand, has what may appear to be rather limited tools. He should have, however, a thorough knowledge of such matters as his own company's ships, port facilities, routes, and schedules; rates and tariff regulations and government regulations applicable to his company's service; competing operators, including their ships, service, and so forth; and the general trend of developments within the shipping industry. Furthermore, his knowledge should include a thorough understanding of (1) the industries and commodities that affect his customer's business, and the competitive position among them, and (2) the technical phases of the customer's business, such as improved packaging, methods of materials handling, claims procedures, and so forth.

In addition to these tools, the salesman will make full use of some card-index system to record his calls on a customer, to accumulate information about his customer's company as well as about the customer personally, and to determine the amount of business developed from the customer and the amount that moved on his company's ships and on those of competing companies. He will also make certain that the customer is on the mailing list to receive announcements of sailing schedules or other literature mailed by his company. He will telephone his customer to pass on information that may be useful to him or to confirm a departure or arrival date if an important shipment is involved. He will endeavor to win over the customer with whatever personal attentions may be helpful to maintain friendly relations, whether it is an occasional luncheon, an acknowledgment of the customer's advancement, or any of the other means by which salesmen seek to establish the mutual interest of shipper and carrier.

Booking Space. Cargo that moves aboard ships originates either within the port area where it is loaded or from the interior. Cargo of local origin can be booked more easily, because the shipper can deal personally and directly with the carrier. The shipper can telephone one or more carriers to inquire about space and sailing dates or changes thereon. The shipper located in the interior must make his arrangements more in advance, unless the carrier has a representative nearby. In fact, the interior shipper is likely to use a freight forwarder or other agent at seaboard to make his arrangements with the carrier.[2]

The three steps involved in booking steamer space (or "engaging" the space) are as follows:

1. To ascertain that space is available within the time desired and to place the booking with the chief clerk or booking clerk of the carrier.
2. To sign a freight contract.
3. To receive a steamer or shipping permit from the ship operator.

Many liner operators, who offer regular sailings and have many regular shippers, minimize the formality of the arrangements. The shipper merely telephones the booking clerk to confirm a shipment, and this oral arrangement is the full extent of the "booking." The booking clerk notes the following information: shipper, consignee, and destination; type of commodity and quantity in terms of weight and cubic measurement (he may even calculate the latter item himself); and any special shipping instructions. The shipper ascertains sailing data and receiving time, that is, the period of time within which he should deliver his goods to the ship operator's pier.

However, both ship operator and shipper—particularly the inland shipper who must arrange to move his merchandise to seaboard by rail or truck—are in a better position if the booking arrangement is formalized by having a freight contract prepared by the shipper and signed by both parties and by having a permit issued by the carrier. The contract commits the carrier to make space available to the shipper, and the permit is the authority for the shipper to deliver his goods to the carrier's pier. If the shipment is available within the permit time specified by the

[2] See Chap. 8, "Freight Forwarding and Freight Brokerage."

carrier and if for some reason the carrier delays the unloading of, say, the rail car, and demurrage is incurred, the permit protects the shipper. It also protects the carrier if a shipper delivers at the pier unauthorized shipments that cannot be handled either because space is lacking or because the shipper has failed to satisfy the numerous government requirements, such as filing an export declaration or obtaining an export license.

Both documents are useful to the ship operator in planning operations and in notifying all departments of future shipments. For example, a copy of the shipping permit is used to advise the receiving clerk at the pier of what goods will be coming forward. He needs to know this, for he must arrange space on the dock at the proper time (unless the merchandise is to be loaded directly aboard ship). This information also helps the operating department to preplan the loading and stowage of cargo aboard the ship.

SHIPPER'S PAPERS

In addition to the freight contract and the shipping permit, there are other documents that are generally referred to as *shipper's papers*. They include the bills of lading, freight bills, dock receipts, arrival notices, and delivery receipts. The traffic department is concerned with the bill of lading and may be responsible for the freight bills if the latter are not issued by the accounting department. It also issues the arrival notices that inform consignees of the expected arrival date of the ship. The dock receipt (acknowledgment by the carrier that goods have been received from the shipper or his agent for loading aboard ship) and the delivery receipt (which acknowledges that the consignee or his agent has received the goods from the carrier at destination) are most likely to be handled by personnel in the operating department.

The Ocean Bill of Lading. The bill of lading, which is a contract between the carrier and the shipper, is a document of fundamental importance, for it embodies the terms and conditions of the contract of carriage.[3] Besides being the contract, it serves as a receipt issued to the shipper by the carrier to acknowledge that the carrier has received the goods. Also, in the case of a negotiable bill of lading, the document is evidence of title to the goods, and is transferable from one party to another when properly endorsed. As a negotiable instrument, it is a prerequisite to financing and credit.

While the bill of lading forms are usually provided by the carrier, they are now generally prepared by the shipper or his agent. The number of copies prepared depends on both the practice of the trade and the wishes of the shipper and other parties involved in the transaction. Usually, 3

[3] For legal aspects, see Chap. 17.

signed "originals" and approximately 12 unsigned copies are prepared. One of the originals must eventually be presented by the consignee to obtain delivery of the goods at destination, after which the other originals become void.

The legal aspects of the bill of lading are important and complicated, and we will not discuss them in detail. The language employed and the construction of the document have evolved through centuries of usage and interpretation in the courts. Unfortunately, those responsible for preparing and using bills of lading seldom stop to consider the all-important nature of the document and the need for careful preparation with close attention to the detail that is called for. There is space for the names of the shipper and the consignee, the address of the consignee, the name of the ship, ports of loading and discharge, the marks and numbers indicated on the packages, the number of packages, description of the packages and goods, their weight, the signature of the carrier, and several other details.

Accuracy in preparing the bill of lading is important for a number of reasons: (1) the information on the bill of lading must correspond with the description of the goods appearing in the letter of credit and in consular documents; (2) the information is used in preparing other documents used by the carrier in arranging for the safe stowage aboard vessel and the ultimate successful delivery of the goods at destination; and (3) in ocean transportation, the carrier can limit his liability to a much greater extent than the rail, highway, or air carrier. Therefore, to protect himself, the shipper must be very specific with respect to the details descriptive of the character and condition of the goods that he has delivered to the carrier. In all cases, shippers may be subject to fines, delays, and embarrassment if the billing is false, either unintentionally or deliberately, or if discrepancies appear between the data on the bill of lading and those on the original order or other documents associated with the shipment. Consular and customs officials may assess penalties or delay the delivery of the goods.

On-board Bill of Lading. Bills of lading are classified as order and straight bills of lading, and as received-for-shipment and on-board bills of lading. As to the latter classification, the on-board bill of lading is the more generally used as it indicates that the goods have actually been placed aboard the ship with every reasonable expectation that the shipment is as good as on its way. A received-for-shipment bill of lading, on the other hand, is merely a receipt to indicate that the goods have reached the pier. This lacks the guarantee that a ship will come on the berth and that space will be provided. Consignees or buyers quite generally specify in their orders, and in the letters of credit used in connection with financing the transaction, that on-board bills of lading shall be used. While separate bills of lading may be printed, generally a regular bill of lading is utilized, and the clerk or cashier stamps or endorses the "on-board" mark on the paper when the goods have been stowed aboard the ship.

Order Bill of Lading. The other classification of bills of lading involves the negotiability of the instrument. A straight bill of lading is drawn directly to the consignee and must be marked or stamped to indicate that it is a "straight bill of lading not negotiable." However, in foreign trade transactions, the order (or to order of) bill of lading is more generally used for purposes of negotiability. Such a paper may be made out to the order of the shipper so that he may retain title to the goods. However, the real purpose of this document is to service the credit and financial aspects of the transaction so that, by endorsement, the shipper can transfer title to the bank that is representing either the buyer or the buyer's bank. If the goods have been paid for in advance or are being shipped on consignment or open account, the bill of lading will be made out to the order of the buyer, and otherwise to the order of a bank or other intermediate party, with instructions noted on the bill of lading to notify the actual consignee. The "notify" part of the address is essential in order that the carrier will know the name and address of the actual consignee to be notified when the goods have arrived at destination.

However, in some countries, particularly in Latin America, order bills of lading are prohibited, and the ship operator should protect himself as well as the shipper and not issue such bills of lading for shipments to those countries.

Clean Bill of Lading. Because of the legal importance of the bill of lading, the ship operator is extremely careful to make certain that the description of the goods accurately indicates their condition when they come within his custody. If a package has obviously been damaged before it is delivered to the pier, the ship operator wishes to disclaim responsibility for that damage. The receiving clerk will then "clause" the dock receipt to indicate the existence of damage (or a shortage if fewer packages are received than are indicated by the shipper). Unless the shipper arranges to correct the situation by repairing or replacing the goods, the ship operator will indicate on the bill of lading the same information that was noted on the dock receipt. A clean bill of lading is one on which no such exception is noted. The shipowner's security depends (1) on rejection of the shipment if the shipper has not provided adequate packaging or has failed to disclose or properly classify the contents of the merchandise (or the extent of damage when delivered) or (2) on a clear notation on the bill of lading of the condition of the goods when accepted for shipment. In some cases, the ship operator should consult the shipper or his agent with respect to the condition of the goods and protect both the shipper and himself by recoopering or otherwise repairing the container.

Short-form Bill of Lading and Correlated Papers. An examination of several shippers' papers discloses that much of the information called for is similar. This suggests the possibility of (1) simplifying the procedures involved in preparing the various documents and (2) trying to combine the clerical operations incident to preparing them. Also, the statement of terms and conditions pertinent to the contract of carriage that appears on the back of bills of lading is very lengthy, and the greater part, if not all, of this statement is standardized. This suggests the possibility of a short-form statement that would refer to the acceptance of the complete statement by both shipper and carrier.

In recent years, great strides have been made in simplifying shipping documents. Alcoa Steamship Company, Inc., is credited with being one of the first carriers to develop the simplified forms. It is now possible to prepare the following with one operation:

1. Short-form bill of lading.
2. Delivery permit (original for office use, duplicate for wharf use, and triplicate for the shipper).
3. Dock receipt (original for the shipper, duplicate for office use, triplicate and quadruplicate for use by pier offices).

On the delivery permit and dock receipt, the name of the consignee and his address are blocked out; this information, because of its confidential nature, could be of value to a competitor or his agent if he were to observe any of the papers in the carrier's offices or on the pier.

Each of the three documents is different in the space below the description of the goods. The delivery permit indicates the time within which the goods must be received, the method of delivery to the pier (such as by truck or lighter), the name of the person who booked the space, and the date and the signature of the person preparing the permit. The following terms and conditions appear on the back of the delivery permit. It will be noted that the responsibility and liability of the carrier is strictly limited:

> We confirm our notice of your intended delivery to us of the shipment described on the reverse side and will arrange to receive it, when tendered in accordance herewith, if circumstances permit. However, in issuing this confirmation at this time for your convenience, we make no representation whatsoever that the shipment can be so received when tendered or, if received, can be carried; and unless and until our regular dock receipt is issued therefor we will not be responsible for any loss, damage, delay, liability or expense whatsoever in connection with any transportation, storage, handling or care of the goods before or after tender or delivery to us, or in consequence of their rejection when tendered or their receipt or holding by us or their return to you, or otherwise.

The dock receipt indicates the time of arrival of the goods, their location on the pier, the name of the clerk who examines the papers and who "permits" the shipment, the number of packages as counted by a checker and the checker's signature, the time that delivery of the goods is completed, and the signature of the receiving clerk, who acknowledges the following statement: "Received the above number of articles and/or packages in apparent good order and condition, except as noted, contents and other particulars unknown, for shipment to port of discharge indicated hereon."

The following terms and conditions appear on the back of the dock receipt:

This receipt is not negotiable and is issued for record purposes only.

Said goods are received subject to delay and default in shipment caused by accumulation of other goods, riots, strikes, labor disturbances, lack of conveyances, room or facilities of any sort and the like. The goods shall be subject to all charges for storing on wharf and/or in warehouse due to any such delays and any such charges shall be paid by shippers, consignees and/or assigns. The Alcoa Steamship Company, Inc. regular bill of lading in use by it for similar shipments (upon the basis of which freight rates are fixed) shall be issued for said goods to the above named shippers. The Alcoa Steamship Company, Inc. shall not become responsible for the goods as carrier until the goods are actually loaded on steamer; until such loading it shall be liable only for loss or damage occasioned by its fault, such as ordinary bailee is liable for, but subject also to the conditions, exceptions and limitations of liability and value contained in said regular bill of lading with which shippers are understood to have acquainted themselves and to assent to. If the value of any of the goods exceeds $500.00 per package, or in case of goods not shipped in packages, per customary freight unit, a rate of freight based thereon must be arranged before tender of the goods for shipment and the value of the goods declared on delivery at the dock and inserted herein, failing which, the goods shall be conclusively deemed received subject to the bill of lading limitation of value and liability of not exceeding $500.00 per package or customary freight unit.

Shipper's weights as inserted herein will be relied on in handling the goods, and if incorrect, shipper and/or consignee shall be responsible for any loss or damage to carrier or others resulting therefrom.

Attention of shippers is directed to Sections 235 and 236 of the United States Criminal Code, as amended, and Section 4472 of the United States Revised Statutes, as amended, and to regulations made in pursuance thereof, regulating the delivery or tender for shipment of explosives and any other dangerous articles, and the marking therof, and imposing penalties for violation up to $10,000 or ten years imprisonment, or both.

Below these terms and conditions there is space for a record of marks and numbers, type and number of packages, and calculation of the cubic measurement required for the merchandise listed on the reverse side of the receipt.

TR. 5 250M 1-49
PRINTED IN U.S.A.

(SPACES IMMEDIATELY BELOW FOR SHIPPERS MEMORANDA—NOT PART OF BILL OF LADING)

FORWARDING AGENT—SHIPPERS REFERENCES	EXPORT DEC. No.
DELIVERING CARRIER TO STEAMER:	*CAR NUMBER — REFERENCE *New Orleans Tollage (not) absorbed

ALCOA STEAMSHIP COMPANY, INC.
SHORT FORM BILL OF LADING

SHIP FLAG	PIER PORT OF LOADING
PORT OF DISCHARGE FROM SHIP	STEAMSHIP CONTRACT No.

SHIPPER..

CONSIGNEE:.. DESTINATION OF GOODS ....

(If goods are to be transshipped or forwarded after discharge from ship See Clause 11 Long Form Bill of Lading)

ADDRESS ARRIVAL NOTICE TO..

DESCRIPTION OF GOODS				
MARKS AND NUMBERS	NO. OF PKGS.	SHIPPER'S DESCRIPTION OF CLASS AND CONTENTS OF PACKAGES	SHIPPER'S GROSS WEIGHT KILOS	POUNDS
		(Only six items may be listed in this space)		
		SHIPPERS: DO NOT WRITE BELOW THIS LINE.		

ATTENTION OF SHIPPERS is especially directed to Secs. 235-236 U. S. Criminal Code (18 U. S. Code 285-6). Sec. 4472 U. S. Revised Statutes (46 U. S. Code 170). Sec. 16 Shipping Act, 1916 (46 U. S. Code 815). Sec. 3, subdiv. 5, also Sec. 4, subdivs. 5 and 6, of the Carriage of Goods by Sea Act, 1936 (46 U. S. Code 1303, subsec. 5, 46 U. S. Code 1304, subsecs. 5 and 6) which provisions of law subject shippers to substantial penalties, liabilities and disabilities for false classification, misdescription or insufficient description of goods, etc.

Received, from the above-named shipper, the goods, or packages said to contain goods, hereinabove described, in apparent good order and condition unless otherwise noted hereon, to be held and transported subject to all the written, typed, printed and stamped provisions of this bill of lading, on this and on the reverse side hereof, to the port or place of discharge named above or so near thereunto as the ship can always safely get and leave, always afloat at all stages and conditions of water and weather, and there to be delivered or transshipped on payment of the charges thereon, with liberty to proceed via any port or ports in any order as more fully specified and provided in the regular long form of bill of lading of Alcoa Steamship Company, Inc., currently in effect, and with liberty before or after loading to forward the whole or any portion of the goods by any other ship or ships, whether prior or subsequent, and whether of the carrier's own line or of any other line, or otherwise as provided herein, or in said long form bill of lading.

It is agreed that the custody and carriage of the goods are subject to the terms and conditions on this and on the reverse side hereof, which shall govern the relations whatsoever they may be between the carrier, master and ship and the shipper, consignee and goods in every contingency, wheresoever and whensoever occurring, and also in the event of deviation, or abandonment of the voyage, or unseaworthiness of the ship at the time of loading or inception of the voyage or subsequently; and none of the terms of this bill of lading shall be deemed to have been waived by the carrier unless by express waiver in writing duly signed by a duly authorized agent of the carrier.

In Witness Whereof, the master or agent of the said vessel has signed **3** bills of lading, all of this tenor and date, and if one is accomplished, the others shall be void.

ALCOA STEAMSHIP COMPANY, INC.
As Agents for the Master

ITEM	WEIGHT	CUBIC FEET	RATE	STEAMSHIP FREIGHT
1				
2				
3				
4				
5				
6				
HEAVY LIFT AND EXTRA LENGTH CHARGES				
SURCHARGES & LANDING CHARGES				
TOTAL VESSEL FREIGHT				
MISCELLANEOUS CHARGES				
TOTAL FREIGHT & CHARGES U. S. CURRENCY				

Dated at..

PREPAID By______________________ B/L No.__________

FIG. 2. Bill of lading, Alcoa Steamship Company, Inc.

FIG. 2. (*Continued*)

ESTABLISHING REMUNERATIVE RATES

In connection with rates and arrangements with other carriers, the traffic department has the following functions:

1. Many steamship companies belong to steamship conferences that determine rates for their membership and prepare and issue tariffs.[4] If a particular company is not a member of the conference, the traffic department, working on an individual basis, performs this function.

2. The traffic department is responsible for developing relationships with other carriers—sea, land, and air. For example, a company operating on the east coast of South America–Pacific Coast of the United States route can obtain some northbound cargo (such as canned corned beef from Buenos Aires) destined for Yokohama and Manila. This cargo will move under a transshipment agreement between the northbound carrier and a connecting carrier out of, say, San Francisco, westbound to the ultimate port of destination in the Orient. Arrangements for such transshipments are agreed on in advance, and through rates and divisions of revenue between the carriers are established. Also, in the domestic trades, ship operators arrange joint through rates and divisions of revenue with rail and truck lines, and they issue joint rail-water, truck-water, and even rail-water-rail rates.

3. The traffic department is also responsible for handling relations, in connection with the regulation of rates and practices, with governmental regulatory agencies such as the Interstate Commerce Commission and the Federal Maritime Board. While the representatives and legal staff of the steamship conferences either handle these matters or participate in handling them, the traffic department of the steamship company is responsible for preparing data and exhibits for them to use. The traffic manager and one or more of his assistants should be qualified to practice before the regulatory bodies. If that is not possible, they should at least be able to serve as competent witnesses.

INTERDEPARTMENTAL RELATIONS

The traffic department works closely with the other departments of the company, particularly in connection with the following matters:

1. The traffic department should, at all times, know the volume of business being developed by port of origin and port of destination, by shipper and consignee, and by commodity. It should also know the

---

[4] The history and functions of steamship conferences are explained in Chap. 19, as are tariffs. Rates are usually quoted on specific commodities or groups of commodities, and the composite of a company's rates makes up its tariff, including procedures for rate making.

revenue received. A good commodity-tonnage-revenue report is essential to an intelligent analysis of a traffic department's activity. Some type of punch-card or automatic-machine method of collecting and collating the data is generally economical in the long run.

The results of this work are useful in determining frequency of service, ports of call, strong and weak customer accounts, and high- and low-revenue commodities. They are also useful in correlating claims and in studying the seasonality of the movements of various commodities, and so forth. One all-important phase of the statistical record is that it is useful in connection with reports to regulatory and other agencies of government and in connection with applications for rate adjustments, and so forth. Companies that fail regularly to maintain statistical records are at a costly disadvantage when they are called upon to produce information, for then they must, if possible, pull together past records.

2. Traffic studies (for which the main subjects are traffic statistics and rate matters) are frequently prepared for use by the executive, operating, and other departments, as well as by the traffic department itself. The general manager wishes to be informed regularly—perhaps on a weekly basis—of the volume of business being handled by the company. He, in turn, will pass the information on in his reports to the board of directors. The comptroller is interested in the trend of revenues, for much of the cargo moves on a prepaid freight basis and the weekly report on tonnages and revenues indicates to him the immediate financial condition of the operation. The operating department finds that the record indicates the work load of the piers and the personnel associated with the transfer of cargo between ship and land transportation. The operating department may also find commodities for which the revenues are inadequate in comparison with operating costs. Special studies may be requested of the traffic department in connection with all these matters, particularly in relation to costs and revenues.

3. The handling of claims for loss of or damage to the shippers' cargo requires much tact in order to protect the company's revenues and at the same time to maintain the good will of the customer, whether shipper or consignee. Because the traffic department is interested in protecting its relationship with the customer, claims are usually handled by another department. For purposes of maintaining customer good will, it is all important that the closest working relationship exist between claims and traffic. This is particularly true when there is a possibility of suggesting to the customer that improved packaging or some other adjustment would avoid a repetition of a claim on future shipments.

4. Training of personnel is of interest to the traffic department, because a long period of apprenticeship and indoctrination is required to develop good salesmen, rate experts, booking clerks, and administrative per-

sonnel. Accuracy, alertness, aggressiveness, the ability to assimilate and coordinate considerable detail, and a liking for working with people are all-important assets in this department. A person who has these characteristics to begin with and is willing to devote himself to accumulating experience and knowledge should find himself in one of the most satisfying departments of a shipping company. However, there should be, either within the traffic department or in the personnel department to cooperate with traffic, one or more administrative people who are consciously training junior employees to increase their technical ability and capacity for greater responsibility. If you are thinking of seeking employment in the shipping industry, take a good look at the character and quality of the traffic department of the company you approach. If management has failed to appreciate and to sponsor the continuous development of its traffic personnel, if there are evidences of dead rot there, you have good reason to reexamine the field.

PROMOTION OF DOMESTIC AND FOREIGN COMMERCE

The Congress of the United States has stated that this country shall have a merchant marine for the "development of its foreign and domestic commerce." Traffic departments of shipping companies contribute to the promotion of this commerce. The competition to obtain more business makes traffic men alert to all opportunities for expanding the business of their potential shippers. Some traffic departments have formed their own trade-development sections, designed to offer shippers and prospective shippers services similar to those available from the Office of International Trade of the U.S. Department of Commerce or from the world trade department of a local chamber of commerce. One company is credited with developing the cashew-nut trade into the United States; another introduced a movement of filtering earth from California to Argentina; and the babassu-nut trade from Brazil to the United States has also been greatly encouraged.

Furthermore, the trade-promotion work of steamship companies contributes to the balancing of the export and import trade of the United States. The economical operation of ships calls for two-way cargoes. Hence, when traffic departments seek not only to get more cargo but to get it for both the outbound and inbound legs of the ships' voyages, their efforts help to eliminate the disparity between exports and imports.

One company serving African ports issued "a comprehensive handbook for American importers." The foreword states:

Africa has vast resources of vital materials needed by the United States today. This booklet, to the best of our knowledge, is the only current survey describing, country by country, the principal resources which East, South, and West Africa have in abundance. The following pages may enable American manufacturers and importers to find dependable new sources of supplies . . . [and] may also suggest promising new markets to American exporters.

Another company, operating on seven trade routes from Gulf ports, has used full-page advertisements in leading magazines to tell the public how its ships "can serve your export and import requirements" and that "your inquiries concerning export and import ocean transportation will receive prompt, careful attention."

The force behind the trade development of the American merchant marine is the desire to develop those rates and services that are adequate to meet the needs of shippers, exporters, and importers. This developmental work establishes a community of interest with world traders, the international departments of banks, the government, and all others who contribute to the development of strong and healthy trade. Largely from this intangible and intimate association of interests stems the consistent and aggressive promotion of both foreign and domestic waterborne commerce.

THE TRAFFIC DEPARTMENT

The organization of the traffic department of a particular company reflects the functions to be performed, including salesmanship, rate making, participation in conferences, freight booking, preparation of shipper's and related papers, public relations, and departmental administration.[5] It also reflects the geographical distribution of the steamship company's activities, for the traffic department will probably have some representation in each port served.

The position of the traffic department in the over-all organization of the steamship company depends on circumstances pertinent to the individual company. However, the head of freight traffic is generally an executive and is usually at a level of executive responsibility and authority directly under the general manager or chief executive officer of the company. In many companies, he is of vice-presidential rank, responsible directly to the company's top executive. In others, he may carry the title of traffic manager, with responsibility to the chief executive in charge of steamship operations. This is frequently true of companies that are affiliates or subsidiaries of corporations engaged in a variety of operations.

The head of freight traffic, no matter what his title, is located at the head or home office of the company. In a number of other major ports of call, the company will have a district manager in charge who is, in turn, responsible for traffic-representation personnel in his particular

[5] The organization of the traffic department of a particular steamship company (American President Lines, Ltd.) is discussed in Chap. 12. See especially Figs. 9 and 10.

area. For a company engaged in world-wide operations, traffic representation must be on a commensurate scale. As indicated elsewhere, one major shipping line has offices or agents in 246 locations throughout the world.

For administrative purposes, the district traffic manager will report to the district manager; for operational purposes, he will report to the head of freight traffic in the head office. Obviously such a situation creates the need for coordinating programs, and this cannot be accomplished solely by distributing carbon copies of letters. The smooth coordination of administrative and operational detail, within the district office and with the head office, requires the type of cooperation that is almost as automatic as the meshing of gears in a complicated machine. Not only the urge to cooperate is needed, but also the equipment of coordination—occasional department-head meetings; reports issued regularly; frequent exchange of information by personal discussion, telephone calls, teletype messages; and so forth. While perfection is not possible, a constant alertness and an ability to work together will promote the atmosphere essential to efficient operation.

BIBLIOGRAPHY

Because of the nature of this chapter, it is not possible to list the usual bibliographical references. For more information than could be included in this chapter on ocean bills of lading, the following references will be useful.

Knauth, Arnold W., *Ocean Bills of Lading*, 4th ed., American Marine Cases, Inc., Baltimore, 1952.

Rosenthal, Morris S., *Techniques of International Trade*, McGraw-Hill Book Company, Inc., New York, 1950, Chap. 9.

U.S. War Shipping Administration, *Insurance Policies, Charter Parties, Bills of Lading*, edited by Arnold W. Knauth and E. H. Miles, American Maritime Cases, Inc., Baltimore, 1942.

CHAPTER 8

FREIGHT FORWARDING AND FREIGHT BROKERAGE*

The previous chapter emphasized the direct shipper-carrier relationship. Such a relationship does not always exist. Quite often a freight forwarder or broker is an intermediary. The practice in this regard varies from coast to coast and from shipper to shipper. In the intricate procedure of foreign trade, the freight forwarder is a middleman who serves either the shipper or the ship operator or both. He offers a highly specialized service to those who need his assistance, and the functions he stands ready to perform are varied and complex. Export shipments involve much technical detail and much specialized paper work, and often the exporter relies on a freight forwarder as a specialist in his trade. Importers may be clients of the freight forwarder if the forwarder also acts as a customhouse broker.

The freight forwarder represents the shipper more often than the ship operator, and if he serves the latter, he is functioning in the capacity of a freight broker or ship broker. A freight-forwarding company may and does represent a variety of interests, performing diverse functions in behalf of those interests. Its primary functions are to supervise the movement of goods, to prepare the shipping and customs documents involved in the movement of those goods, and to perform miscellaneous services in the interests of its clients.

GENERAL NATURE OF FORWARDING

Shippers utilize the services of freight forwarders for a variety of reasons. Some exporters located at seaboard do not have the facilities or personnel to take care of the multitude of details involved in export shipments, while others whose offices and factories are located at inland points do not have branch offices at the port areas through which exports move. Importers who need a freight forwarder's services fall primarily

* This chapter was written by John H. Frederick, professor of transportation, University of Maryland, and transportation consultant.

into two categories: those who import goods through ports other than the ones in which they are located and those who have factories or carry their wares at inland centers.

In addition, freight forwarders handle overseas shipments for a number of large companies whose volume of traffic, either export or import, is not sufficient to warrant traffic departments in their own organization. Because they are always in close contact with steamship companies and with other transportation agencies, and because they are specialists in the field of international shipping, freight forwarders are able to give merchants and manufacturers the "benefit of their detailed knowledge of traffic conditions, government regulations, and other factors that enter into the efficient and economical handling of goods."[1]

Definition of a Foreign Freight Forwarder. In a brief prepared for the Joint Committee on Foreign Freight Forwarders Associations,[2] a freight forwarder has been defined as follows:

Any individual, partnership, or corporation engaged in (a) the booking of or arranging for cargo space for export shipments on ocean carriers, or (b) the preparation and/or processing of any necessary shipping papers in connection with export ocean transportation, or (c) the clearance of export shipments in accordance with the regulations of the United States Government, or (d) the arranging for certification of consular documents.

From this definition, it is evident that little similarity exists between the activities of foreign freight forwarders and those of domestic freight forwarders. The essential difference to be noted is that the international freight forwarder has none of the characteristics of a carrier. He receives goods for transportation and delivers them to the carrier by which they are to be transported, but he does not assume, and is not paid for, the transportation.

The Foreign versus the Domestic Forwarder. In domestic transport, whether by land or by sea, the freight forwarder assembles numerous small shipments from different shippers and consolidates them into larger shipments, called carload lots in the case of railroads. Since the railroads and the motor carriers offer lower rates per pound for large shipments than for small ones, the forwarder receives the advantage of the lower volume rates on his traffic. He usually charges the shipper the same rate that the latter would pay the underlying carrier on small lots, and therefore receives the amount of difference between the low volume rate and that which he himself has to pay the carrier. In domestic transportation, the term *freight forwarding* does not carry the connotation of

---

[1] See the chapter on freight forwarding in Morris S. Rosenthal, *Techniques of International Trade*, McGraw-Hill Book Company, Inc., New York, 1950, pp. 115–121.

[2] *Port of New York Freight Forwarding Investigations*, U.S. Maritime Commission, Docket 621.

consolidation of functions that it does for international trade. Freight forwarding in the domestic sense implies merely the grouping of a few shipments to meet minimum requirements as to weights.

In contrast, the foreign freight forwarder acts as an agent of the shipper or carrier, a capacity in which he perfoms functions in regard to customs, prepares waybills, books cargo space, advises on export and import quotas and licenses, or prepares consular invoices. When he reserves or books space on a specific carrier, the foreign forwarder usually does so for the shipper and not for himself, and he usually does not issue his own bill of lading.[3] His compensation is an agency fee, paid by the shipper-exporter or by the carrier and, as will be shown later, sometimes by both. Basically, therefore, the freight forwarder acts as an agent of the exporter (he is then a forwarder, strictly speaking), of the ocean carrier (in which case he serves as a freight broker or steamship broker), or of the importer (customhouse broker).

The definition cited lists the four essential characteristics of freight forwarding. If the forwarder performs only the four forwarding functions, he is ordinarily considered an agent. But a person engaged in the business of forwarding may also engage in rendering accessorial services, the most important of which are trucking, warehousing, and obtaining marine insurance. If so, he may be termed an independent contractor. In any event, the freight forwarder is not considered a common carrier, even though he is subject to the regulatory provisions of the Shipping Act of 1916.

FORWARDING FUNCTIONS

Basically, then, the international freight forwarder is responsible for the following functions:

1. To trace the inland movement of the shipment to seaboard and to eliminate all avoidable delays in transit.

2. To book in advance cargo space on the earliest or on a specified vessel.

3. To execute, approve, and submit all shipping documents necessary to the particular shipment.

Tracing the Shipment. For a shipment originating inland, one of the most important functions of a freight forwarder is to expedite its movement to seaboard. If he is to operate efficiently, he must have complete information and instructions concerning a particular shipment. To assure himself of that information and to obviate mistakes on the part of the shipper, caused either by carelessness or by misunderstanding of what is required, the forwarder supplies his exporter client with a "letter of

---

[3] He does, however, issue his own bill of lading for assembled export shipments, which will be discussed later.

instruction," which the shipper should fill out in detail and return to the forwarder. Since the letter includes exact details of the inland routing, including car numbers when known, the forwarder can trace the shipment daily if he wishes. The letter also includes particulars of the shipment such as (1) the number and types of packages and the symbols thereon, (2) an exact description of the merchandise as it will appear on the bill of lading consular invoice, and so forth, (3) instructions regarding payment of the ocean freight charges, (4) instructions regarding marine insurance, (5) the gross, legal, and net weights and the cubic measurements of the packages, and (6) the way the goods are to be consigned to the importer abroad. Since this letter of instruction is mailed to the forwarder as soon as the goods or merchandise leaves the factory or warehouse, he receives it before the shipment arrives at seaboard and is therefore in a position to proceed with the documentation necessary at an early date.

Booking Cargo. As soon as the freight forwarder has received the information concerning the shipment, he books or reserves space on a specific vessel for the shipment, a detail that he usually takes care of by telephoning a steamship agent. Since misunderstandings can easily arise from such arrangements, the forwarder protects himself by securing from the steamship line or its agent a "booking memo" (or freight contract). This document, countersigned by the agent of the steamship company, is sent to the shipper to confirm the reservation.

Activities at the Port. At the port of export, the freight forwarder takes complete charge of the shipment. If the exporter is located at seaboard, the forwarder may supervise the movement of the goods or merchandise to dockside. His primary function, however, is to take care of all documentation, a function which he also performs for the inland shipper.

In case the shipment originates inland, the freight forwarder as the consignee is notified as soon as the merchandise arrives in the port area. The forwarder then secures from the steamship company, or from the agent of the vessel on which he has reserved space, a shipping permit and blank forms for the dock receipt and for the ocean bill of lading. If an export declaration is required, the forwarder presents it to the steamship company when he obtains the shipping permit. This permit not only instructs the receiving clerk at the pier to accept the goods for loading aboard ship but also specifies the name of the vessel, her port of destination, and the date on or before which the merchandise is to be delivered to dockside. Shipping permits are handled in different ways at various ports, but the freight forwarder will know the particular procedure required.

The forwarder usually sends the shipping permit and the prepared dock receipt to the land carrier, with a letter of instructions for delivering the merchandise to dockside. If the shipment consists of several carloads or truckloads, which may not all arrive at the pier at the same time, the forwarder sends the shipping permit to the steamship company's receiving clerk and so notifies the inland carrier. In this case, he informs the carrier that the shipment is to be delivered within the time specified in the permit. No matter what the practice, the forwarder should follow up the shipment to see that it is delivered on time and loaded aboard the vessel.

After executing all shipping documents (including the bill of lading and consular invoices of the country of import) and processing them through the steamship companies, the customs, and the consulates, the forwarder assembles these documents duly signed. He may dispose of them in a number of ways. If a letter of credit or financing is involved, they are usually sent to a local bank. In this case, the exporter sends his invoice and a draft to cover freight charges to the forwarder. This procedure is economical because it involves a minimum of handling of documents. If the export shipper is local or if he is located in the interior and has taken care of his own financing, the forwarder may be instructed to send the documents to the exporter. Under different circumstances, he may send the papers abroad.

Financial Assistance. Usually the responsibility of the international freight forwarder is terminated when the shipment is loaded aboard the ship and the documents are assembled and taken care of. His responsibility does not end then, however, if he has aided the exporter in his financing, although it should be pointed out that relatively few foreign-freight-forwarding companies have adequate capital for this. Freight-forwarding companies are primarily service organizations that derive their earnings from agency fees paid by their clients, and the conduct of their business does not require much capital. Hence, if an exporter wishes financial assistance, he should make special arrangements for it.

Ocean carriers generally insist upon prepayment of freight charges, and a shipper may wish these charges to be collected from the consignee at destination. In that event, the forwarder prepays the freight demanded by the steamship company and forwards the shipment on a collect basis. Thus, he carries the shipper until his own foreign agent can collect the freight from the consignee at destination. Some freight forwarders also assist exporters in the United States and foreign consignees in their financing. At a shipper's request, a forwarder may advance the invoice price of the shipment. He then collects from the consignee either through his foreign agent at destination or by means of drafts handled through regular banking channels. In addition, forwarders endeavor to handle, to the best interests of the export shipper, such goods as may occasionally be refused by consignees.

Consolidated Shipments. Since the rates quoted by shipping companies generally do not vary on account of volume (except as to minimum shipments), there is far less incentive to assemble foreign than domestic shipments. At times, however, packaged goods move in such small quantities that the danger of pilferage is greatly increased, or a shipment goes forward that is too small to warrant the minimum bill-of-lading fee. Also an exporter may wish his merchandise cleared through customs to be delivered duty paid to the customer. Under such circumstances, freight forwarders combine shipments.

The consolidation services that forwarders perform are of two types. (1) Several shipments destined for a single consignee abroad may be consolidated and sent forward on one bill of lading. This type of consolidation may take place when a buyer abroad has ordered goods simultaneously from several exporters, and when the routing orders he has issued to the exporters will permit consolidation of the shipments by a freight forwarder. (2) A number of shipments for different consignees may be assembled and sent forward on one bill of lading to an agent abroad for distribution. In this case, the consignee is usually a correspondent freight forwarder in the country of import. He receives the shipment, enters the merchandise through customs, and distributes it in accord with the instructions of the United States forwarder.

Additional Activities. In addition to the functions already discussed, a number of freight forwarders obtain insurance for the exporter whose volume of business is not sufficient to warrant his carrying a policy of his own. They also at times quote through rates from point of origin to interior foreign destination for clients who desire such service. With regard to forwarders and their functions, recent thinking has fostered such advances that it is now generally understood that the following are important phases of forwarder activity: (1) to furnish information, particularly to new businesses; (2) to assist in interpreting tariffs and in procuring the most favorable freight rates, consular fees, and duties applicable to the products; (3) to offer suggestions concerning packaging of the product in the light of freight rates and product safety; (4) to compute and furnish information to be used in computing prices; (5) to act ethically to further the sale of products and to expand the markets of principals; and (6) to act as a competent service representative in order to keep the name and reputation of the shipper always foremost in the minds of railroads, steamship companies, customs officials, foreign consuls, and port authorities.

Import Shipments. The most important function that a freight forwarder performs for importers is to clear shipments through customs. A forwarder, however, can offer this service only if he is a customhouse broker, and he can carry on this activity only under license from the U.S. Department of the Treasury. Therefore, an importer who wishes all phases of the shipment taken care of by a single agent should select a freight forwarder who is also a customhouse broker.

When a shipment arrives in the United States from a foreign country, it remains in the custody of the customs officials until the importer or his representative secures possession of the merchandise through a procedure that is known as the *customs entry*. The requirements of the port and the laws of customs procedure must be complied with, and a release must be secured either from the collector of customs or from other customs officials. Since the routine involved requires a more thorough knowledge of the laws of customs than most importers have, they usually employ the services of an agent.

When a forwarder is to handle an incoming foreign shipment, the importer sends him the shipping documents so that he will receive them several days before the vessel docks. The importer should send a check sufficient to cover the estimated amount of duty, the freight charges if the shipment is collect, and other charges that the forwarder may be asked to meet. If the goods are to be stored, the importer should give specific instructions. If they are to be moved immediately, the importer should designate the route and the way the bill of lading is to be written. On a shipment moving directly to the importer's customer, the forwarder should notify the customer when the merchandise leaves the port of entry.

FORWARDING ORGANIZATION

To carry on such widely diversified functions and to be prepared to meet any contingency that may arise, the freight forwarder's organization must be flexible. Since that organization depends on the volume and nature of the business handled, the degree of specialization, the competition, and the personal views of the forwarder himself and of his shipper clients, there is no single pattern for an international freight-forwarding company. Usually the main office is at seaboard, where a staff is maintained adequate to carry on all details of the services offered and to develop and hold the company's clients. Additional personnel may include inland representatives to solicit trade and to attend to shipments from inland points, representatives at other domestic ports, and correspondent representatives abroad.

The organization may be built on a geographical basis, or the clientele may be divided among the staff. If the former, the various staff members specialize in European, South American, Australasian, transpacific, or some other trade. Since the freight forwarder represents the shipper at the port and conducts all transactions in his behalf as he himself would do if he were present, there are certain advantages inherent in the division of clientele. A staff member who takes care of all forwarding accounts for an individual customer has more opportunity to become thoroughly familiar with the shipper's products, his policies, and the ends to which he aspires so that every action furthers those ends and in no instance reflects discredit on them.

FORWARDING AND BROKERAGE FEES

International freight forwarders derive their profits primarily from two sources: fees paid them by exporters and importers for services rendered and freight brokerage. Charges for services to shippers vary among forwarders operating at a particular port and among those at different ports, but a single forwarder usually charges flat or fixed fees for the various services rendered, such as filing application for an import license, taking care of an export declaration, or preparing a consular invoice. If the forwarder examines a shipment at a pier before it is loaded, he may charge a single fee or per package, depending on the amount of work required. Such incidental expenses as postage, telephone bills, and carfare are charged to the shipper.

As explained earlier, when a freight forwarder books space on a vessel for a particular shipment, he usually does so as an agent for a particular shipper. Nevertheless, the carrier and not the shipper pays the freight brokerage, which usually amounts to 1.25 percent of the freight charges. Members of practically all steamship conferences except those on the West Coast pay the brokerage fee. The practice is regulated so that the forwarder cannot refund any part of the brokerage to his client.

Hence, when a freight forwarder handles an export shipment, it is common practice for him to collect fees from two sources on the shipment —one from the shipper for booking space and preparing documents and another from the steamship company for freight brokerage.[4] In practice, these two are closely related. If the forwarder received no brokerage, the charge for forwarding services would, in many instances, not be adequate compensation for services rendered. Forwarding fees are held down by competition and by the fact that shippers usually can, if they wish, do their own work. Furthermore, forwarders at times greatly expedite the work of the carrier. For example, four or five forwarders might handle cargo involving as many as 400 to 500 shippers, each of whom would have to be dealt with individually if no forwarders were employed.

[4] Although importers find ocean freight forwarders and brokers a convenient source of information regarding ocean freights on imported cargoes, forwarders do not generally represent either the exporter abroad or the domestic importer in connection with freight contracts with the steamship conferences. An importer who buys f.a.s. vessel or f.o.b. vessel makes his own contract with the steamship conference. Exporters abroad who make contracts may or may not make them through local freight forwarders.

Occasionally freight forwarders assist the steamship companies directly. When ocean carriers have no difficulty in obtaining cargoes, they prefer to book cargoes without using forwarder-brokers, thereby saving the brokerage fees. But when cargoes are not readily available, many carriers find the services of freight forwarders helpful.

In addition to forwarding and brokerage fees, the forwarder receives revenues from other sources. A freight forwarder who obtains insurance for his client may receive the standard insurance brokerage of 10 percent (if he is an insurance broker, he receives this from the insurance company), or he may charge the shipper a fee for this service. Fees for assisting an importer vary for the different services performed, such as inspecting merchandise and arranging for storage and for inland transportation. Fees for customhouse brokerage are not uniform but do not vary widely.

When an international freight forwarder assembles shipments because of the high minimum freights per ocean bill of lading charged by many steamship lines, he receives his normal fee for handling the shipment. But his main profit is derived from the difference between the freight charges he collects from the shipper and those of the ocean carrier. He pays the steamship line for transporting a combined cargo made up of the small shipments of a number of shippers. He, in turn, charges each individual shipper rates that are lower than the high minimum rate per bill of lading demanded by the shipper, but sufficiently high to include a forwarding profit.

The freight forwarder who quotes a shipper a through freight charge to an interior foreign destination may make a profit. The railroad rate from point of origin to the American port of export can be obtained from railroad tariffs, and the ocean freight rate to the foreign port of entry can be obtained from the steamship company, but the actual inland freight charges beyond the port of entry to a particular inland destination are not always readily ascertainable until after delivery has been made. If the through charge that the forwarder quotes his export clients proves to be higher than the actual rates that he pays the various carriers, he makes a profit. In other instances, his expenses may exceed his revenue. Forwarders, when possible, use the actual foreign rate tariffs showing charges to interior foreign destinations or obtain advice from their foreign agents. If such tariffs or advices are not at hand, a forwarder may refuse to quote a through rate.

FEDERAL REGULATION

The Shipping Act of 1916 gave to the Federal regulatory agency (then the U.S. Shipping Board) the power to regulate freight forwarders. The measures applicable were similar to those applying to steamship conferences; that is, they were designed to ensure equal treatment for shippers. Section 217, which was added to the Merchant Marine Act of 1936 by act of Congress in March, 1942, charged the U.S. Maritime Commission with coordinating forwarding and other services utilized in United States foreign commerce. After the war, information on close to 400 freight forwarders was assembled and transmitted to various government agencies that were handling export relief and emergency shipments. On May 24, 1950, the Federal Maritime Board issued General Order 72, which greatly strengthened regulation of the practices of freight forwarders.

General Order 72[5] requires the registration of all forwarders, that is, of all persons

> . . . engaged in the business of dispatching shipments on behalf of other persons, for a consideration, by oceangoing vessels in commerce from the United States, its territories and possessions to foreign countries, or between the United States and its territories and possessions, or between such territories and possessions; and of handling the formalities incident to such shipments.

It also forbids forwarders to engage in business prior to registration, requires that their registration numbers be set forth in communications and business documents, and provides that violation of the order or of the provisions embodied in the Shipping Act of 1916 may result in cancellation or suspension of the registration.

The order requires forwarders to use invoices that state the following, separately and specifically concerning each shipment: (1) the amount of ocean freight assessed by the carrier, (2) the amount of consular fees paid to consular authorities, (3) the amount of insurance premiums actually disbursed for insurance purchased in the name of the shipper or consignee, (4) the amount charged for each accessorial service performed in connection with the shipment, and (5) other charges.

General Order 72 declares that only registered forwarders may collect brokerage from a water carrier, but that registration does not entitle a forwarder to brokerage in cases when payment thereof would constitute a rebate. In order words, the forwarder is not entitled to freight brokerage (1) if he himself is the shipper or consignee, is the seller or purchaser of the shipment, or has a beneficial interest therein; or (2) if the forwarder directly or indirectly controls or is controlled by the shipper or consignee, or by any person having a beneficial interest in the shipment. The order also provides that forwarders shall not share any part of the brokerage received from a water carrier with a shipper or consignee.

[5] For the "1st Revised List of Independent Foreign Freight Forwarders" registered with the Board in compliance with the order, see *American Import & Export Bulletin*, October, 1951, pp. 777-814.

Other provisions concern (a) the invoicing of consolidated shipments, (b) the freedom from itemizing the components of uniform charges filed with the regulatory authority and stated in advance of shipment and accepted by the shipper, and (c) the duty to extend special agreements with individual shippers or consignees to all such persons similarly situated.

Despite the fact that General Order 72 eliminates some of the possibilities for irregularities practiced by some forwarders, it still fails to afford the public the assurance that the proposed operations of a forwarder will be in, or consistent with, the public interest, or that the level of rates, charges, and practices of forwarders are reasonable and not unjustly discriminatory or unduly preferential. In effect, forwarders' rates and charges are those that will promote adequate, economical, and efficient forwarder service and meet the needs of our foreign commerce. On the other hand, forwarders themselves are not protected against unfair and destructive competitive practices.

BIBLIOGRAPHY

Hansen, O. C., *Guide to World Business*, Caravel Press, San Francisco, 1951.

Moran, Charles J., *Handbook of Export Traffic*, Duell, Sloan & Pearce, Inc., New York, 1949, Chap. 7.

Murr, Alfred, *The Foreign Freight Forwarder*, New York University, School of Commerce, Accounts, and Finance, New York, 1947.

Rosenthal, Morris S., *Techniques of International Trade*, McGraw-Hill Book Company, Inc. New York, 1950, Chap. 8.

CHAPTER 9

SHIP OPERATION: THE SHIP

The final test of a shipping company's success is the actual operation of its ships. Management may invest wisely in the right type of ship, at reasonable cost, and select an economic trade route and good terminals. The traffic department may effectively sell the service, provide substantial revenues, and have ample cargoes to utilize fully the ship's capacity. Then, it is up to the operating department to man and operate the ship, to load and stow as well as discharge the cargoes, to establish and maintain schedules, to repair and maintain the ship, and to accomplish efficiently the multitude of details assigned to that department.

The key position of the operating department comes from the fact that, handling these duties, the department spends a major part of the revenues of the company. The expenditures are so large and so difficult to control that companies generally find it hard to maintain cost controls on each voyage. They await the result of the voyage accounts to determine the net profit. These matters are discussed in more detail in Chapter 15.

The purpose of this chapter is to examine the elements of good ship operation. The limited space available restricts the discussion of practical aspects. Moreover, experience and judgment are essential for those who would control the multitude of intangibles that make up "ship operations."

There is often a thin dividing line between expert operation and intelligent opportunism and adaptability born of experience. This is reflected in an outturn report on the discharge of a deckload of polo ponies:

The outturn report is complete as to the condition of cargo. The only thing that I can add to it is that on account of receiving no papers or documents on shipment of horses, and with the strict customs regulations reference importations of animals, it not only caused delay, but as horses were more or less under quarantine, we had to keep them inside of dock with all doors closed until some place could be found that was isolated from other animals. Even though each horse was held by a man, every so often one got loose and ran like hell amongst piles of cargo, slipping and falling down sometimes. It was just bare luck that none of the horses suffered any injury.

COMPONENTS OF SHIP OPERATION

The components of ship operation are the ship and its crew, the terminal facilities, and supervision and administration. A tremendous investment is involved, and an enormous amount of detail must be integrated and controlled. The detail can be visualized by running down the list of cost items for a voyage:

Wages (straight time, overtime, and bonuses; for deck, engine, steward's, and purser's departments).
Subsistence and provisions.
Stores, supplies, and equipment:
    Deck department: consumable stores, rope (manila and sisal rope and wire), expendable equipment.
    Engine department: consumable stores, expendable equipment, and lubricants.
    Steward's department: consumable stores, crockery, silverware, glassware, linen, etc.
Miscellaneous maintenance expense not classified above (such as shore gang labor and loading of stores).
Fuel.
Repairs (hull and deck department; boilers and condensers; main engines; deck and auxiliary machinery; radio and electric; steward's department; extraordinary dry-dock repairs).
Insurance (marine, P & I, other).[1]
Charter hire (if applicable).
Fresh water.
Launch hire and sundry vessel expenses.
Wharfage and dockage.
Pilotage, tug hire, towage.
Dues; quarantine, customs, and consular fees.
Stevedoring and rehandling of cargo.
Dunnage.
Clerk hire.
Cleaning holds and cargo tanks.
Lighterage.[2]

---

[1] See Chap. 18, "Marine Losses and Marine Insurance."

[2] *Lighterage* is the charge for moving cargo from railhead to shipside when small vessels (lighters) are used for loading or discharging vessels that do not dock or for moving cargo to the pier where the ship is docked. The term is also used to mean the function itself. In some harbor areas where there are several ports, it is more economical to use lighterage than to have the vessel shift to other piers.

THE SHIP

The value of a ship is in its ability to render effective service. The company analyzes its ships from the point of view of such items as modern refrigeration compartments, a new type of cargo oil tanks with smooth interiors, improvements in stowage and handling, improvements in air-circulating systems to reduce cargo damage, special cargo lockers and specie tanks to protect packages, and heavy-lift booms to handle almost any piece of equipment that may be offered for shipment. Speed or other factors might be added to these service features of the ship.

However, the basic construction of a hull and the providing of propulsion machinery are prerequisite to these details. From an operator's point of view, cargo ships involve (1) hull construction, including holds and cargo hatches and decks; (2) tonnage and cubic capacity; (3) cargo-handling gear; and (4) propulsion machinery and speed. Propulsion machinery is a special topic for the marine engineer and will not be dealt with here. Based on construction, there are the following types of ships: (a) liner and tramp (general trading) freighter; (b) combination cargo freighter and passenger ship; (c) passenger vessel; (d) bulk cargo carrier (tanker, ore ship, etc.); and (e) special-design ship (refrigerated banana and meat ships, seatrain, etc.).[3]

Naval architects and shipowners are constantly making thorough analyses to achieve the best design of ship to meet the individual needs of shipowners. For example, in early 1952, a new design of the general trader was reported in shipping journals with "fore and aft deck girders which were incorporated in the hatch coamings, and similar fore and aft girders fitted in the double bottom between the intercostals, thus ensuring great longitudinal strength." Early in 1952, six ore carriers of special design were planned to be jointly owned by Houlder Brothers and the British steel industry. The *New York Journal of Commerce* reported that "these vessels will be of 8,000 tons capacity and 9,000 tons deadweight, and their design is based on studies by the British Iron and Steel Research Association."

Ship design is closely related to service characteristics with due regard to the technical limitations of marine architecture. There is no one standard design of ship. A vessel is a functional unit that needs to be tailored to the needs of the service that the owner intends to operate. The objective of the operator in purchasing a ship is to ensure maximum

---

[3] This chapter is primarily concerned with the operations of liners carrying general cargo. Mention has already been made of bulk operations—of wheat ships that usually ply between ports with elevators equipped for bulk loading or discharge by suction and of ore and coal carriers and tankers that load or discharge in a matter of hours. The success of such operations depends on adequate shore installations.

earning power. Therefore he analyzes navigating conditions along the route. Shallow harbors or a bar to be crossed in entering an important port may affect the allowable draft of his vessel. Competition may require a ship capable of making 16 knots instead of 12 knots. The rate of accumulation of potential cargo along the route or the characteristics of the cargo may require a medium-sized vessel capable of lifting 7,500 tons of cargo instead of 12,500 tons. As a result of his analysis of the volume and characteristics of potential cargo, his competition, the conditions of navigation, and so forth, the operator determines the most economical type of vessel as to lifting capacity, speed, and other characteristics. From his experience at the various ports of call and with the type of cargo on the route, he has specifications with respect to the cargo-handling gear, the number and size of holds, the number of decks, and so forth.

The carrier employs a naval (marine) architect to help him work out the design for his ship. This specialist is familiar with the requirements and regulations of governmental and private agencies as well as the costs of building. Costs are of paramount importance since they must govern the ultimate plan that will be submitted to shipyards for bid.

While the vessel needs to be adapted to the service characteristics of the route, there is considerable advantage in achieving as standard a design as possible. The characteristics of cargo moving on a route change and the ship's ability to handle all cargo offered are vital to the success of the venture. Furthermore, a degree of flexibility is desirable so that if business falls off and it becomes desirable to place a vessel on charter, that vessel will be attractive to potential charterers. Norwegian shipowners have been particularly successful in building ships that are sufficiently standard to attract good charters and sufficiently equipped to be suitable for liner operation. One always bears in mind that in the event of a possible sale of the ship, the more standard she is the broader will be her market.[4]

The naval architect is concerned with the seaworthiness of the ship—its buoyance and stability in the water, its strength and endurance, its steering qualities, and the relation of its design to the efficiency of the propulsion machinery (*i.e.*, minimizing the resistance of the hull to propulsion through the water). Having taken from the prospective owner the requirements with respect to desired lifting capacity, size of

[4] The reader is reminded that the owners of the American merchant marine have been greatly influenced in the purchasing of ships by the availability of war-built surplus merchant ships after World Wars I and II (see Chap. 13). The production of standardized designs of ships during wartime thus carries over into relative standardization of commercial ships under the American flag in peacetime. This situation is also discussed elsewhere in connection with block obsolescence of the merchant marine.

holds, speed, draft limitations if any, and so forth, the designer also must keep in mind the second concern or objective, which is the earning power of his ship. His third objective is to conform to all the regulations affecting his plans, so that the ship will pass the inspection of the classification society, such as the American Bureau of Shipping (A.B.S.) in the United States, the Maritime Administration if that agency is concerned, the U.S. Coast Guard, and other interested agencies.

Classification. Classification societies such as the A.B.S. have played an important part in the history of merchant shipbuilding. The history of Lloyd's Register (British) can be traced back to about 1760. Originally established as a convenience to insurance underwriters to classify and rate the merits of various ships and to pool information on ships and their owners and masters, the functions of classification are now (1) to provide a register of ships which gives essential particulars of the hull and machinery, (2) to prepare rules for the construction of new vessels and their machinery, and (3) to provide for testing materials. The A.B.S. assigns load lines, measures tonnage capacities, issues safety certificates, and so forth. In order to do business today, the practical shipowner must provide each ship with a classification certificate from one of the recognized classification societies, and then keep the ship "in class."[5] To be retained in class, a ship must undergo repairs as required and undergo inspection periodically. Ships classed by A.B.S. are inspected every four years. In addition to A.B.S., the societies include Lloyd's Register of Shipping (British), Bureau Veritas (French), Registro Italiano Naval (Italian), and Det Norske Veritas (Norwegian). The A.B.S. is officially recognized by the United States government in the Merchant Marine Act of 1920, which directs government bureaus to recognize the A.B.S. as "their Agency" for classification purposes.

Hull, Holds, Hatches, Decks. A ship may be divided roughly into hull and propulsion machinery. The hull is the shell of the ship, from keel and bottom to top deck and superstructure and rigging, as well as from bow to stern, including the frames that support the shell plating. Bulkheads and decks in turn support the framing. The highest complete deck is the main or weather deck. The next deck below is the upper deck, and, if there is another, it is called the second deck. The space between main and upper deck is the upper 'tween deck and that between upper and second deck becomes the lower 'tween deck. The area between the lowest deck and the bottom of the inside of the ship (above the double-bottom tanks generally required in cargo ships), and lying between two bulkheads, is known as a hold. The ordinary cargo ship has only one or two decks below the highest continuous exposed deck and will therefore

---

[5] Class is the degree of seaworthiness accorded a vessel by the classification society, depending on her construction and kind of materials used.

have holds and either single 'tween decks or lower and upper 'tween decks.

The space between decks of a 'tween-deck compartment may be 8 to 10 feet. The depth of a hold might be 20 feet. The shape and size of cargo compartments are designed for economic and convenient utilization in the handling and stowage of cargo, although structural requirements of the ship affect the design. The number of bulkheads, other than those

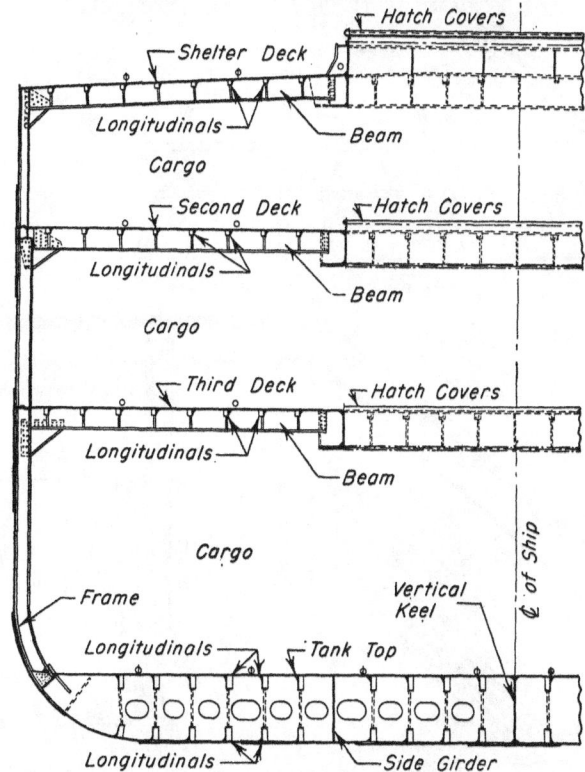

FIG. 3. Midship section of C3-type ship. (*Charles H. Hughes, Handbook of Ship Calculations, Construction, and Operation, 3d ed., McGraw-Hill Book Company, Inc., New York, 1942, p. 249.*)

that separate the machinery space from the rest of the ship, determine the number of holds. The cargo compartment spaces are numbered from bow to stern. The whole of the space between the two forward bulkheads is No. 1 hold (that is, No. 1 upper and lower 'tween decks and No. 1 hold or lower hold), and so on, moving aft, with an average total of four to six holds. The openings in the decks through which cargo can be handled are called cargo hatches.

Some dry-cargo ships or freighters carry deep tank compartments in

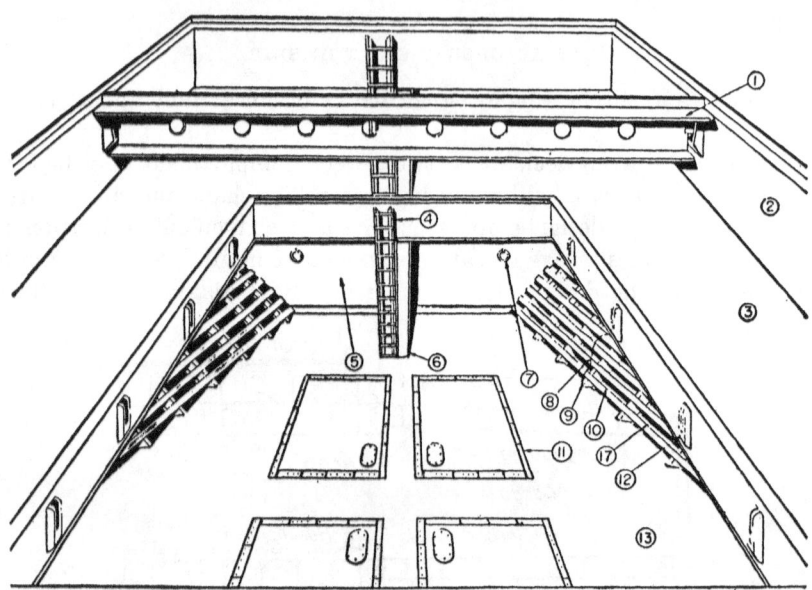

FIG. 4A. Forward hold showing tank tops.

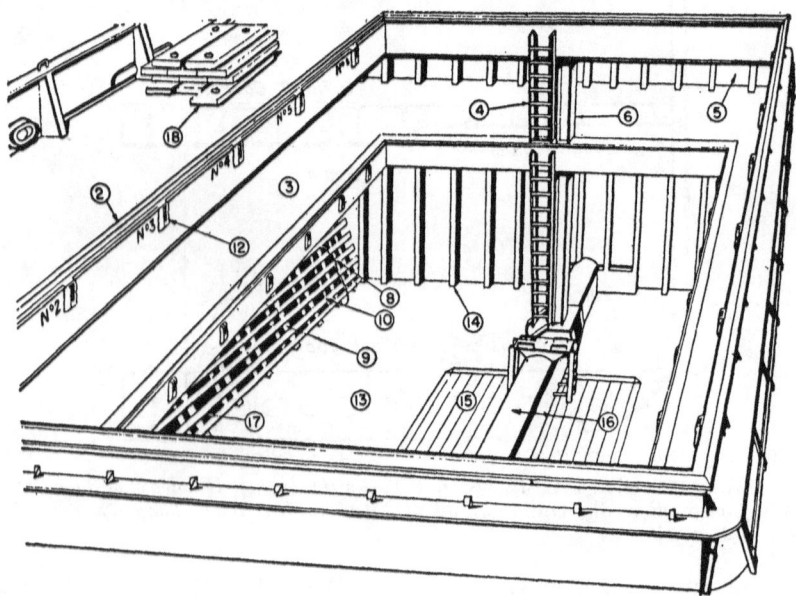

FIG. 4B. After hold showing shaft alley. (*Cargo Handling, U.S. Department of the Navy, Bureau of Naval Personnel, Navpers 10124, 1948, pp. 46–47.*)
Explanation:

1. Beam
2. Coaming
3. 'Tween deck
4. Hatch ladder
5. Bulkhead
6. Stanchion
7. Ring
8. Flare
9. Frame
10. Sweat batten
11. Tank top
12. Beam socket
13. Lower hold
14. Stiffener
15. Ceiling planks
16. Shaft tunnel
17. Skin
18. Hatchboards

one or more of the holds, such as in Nos. 2, 4, and 5 in the C3-type vessel. While often capable of handling packaged cargo, they are primarily intended for liquid cargo in bulk, such as vegetable oils, petroleum products, or other liquids. Their cubic capacity will vary from a few thousand feet to 20,160 cubic feet (grain measure) in the No. 4 starboard deep tank of the C3-type, which would be equivalent to approximately 500-ton capacity. When the entire ship is devoted to handling bulk liquids, the holds become tanks of varying sizes and the vessel is a tanker. On the other hand, some ships are specifically designed to handle either a limited amount or a complete refrigerated cargo. In the latter case, the ship is a refrigerated vessel, or *reefer*. Other vessels are specially designed to carry ores, grain, sugar, and other commodities.

Cubic Capacity and Tonnage. References to the weights and carrying capacities of ships have led to much confusion. The usual reference to the cubical space of a cargo ship has to do with the bale cubic capacity. This has been defined as "the space available for cargo measured in cubic feet to the inside of the cargo battens, on the frames, and to the under side of the beams."[6] The grain cubic capacity of a ship is measured to the shell plating and the top of the beams. A grain cargo occupies the maximum space available. If a ship's bale cubic capacity is 392,000 cubic feet, the grain cubic might amount to 428,000 cubic feet. A typical C3-type ship has a bale cubic capacity of 657,730 cubic feet and a grain cubic capacity of 714,790 cubic feet.

The principal tonnages used in connection with ships are space tons (gross, net, register, underdeck, Suez and Panama Canal tonnages) and weight tons. The different types are as follows:[7]

Gross tonnage is the entire internal cubic capacity of the holds and erections on and/or above the upper deck to the hull of the ship expressed in tons of 100 cubic feet, except certain spaces which are exempted, such as the following: peak and other tanks for water ballast; open forecastle, bridge, and poop; excess of hatchways; certain light and air spaces; domes and skylights; condenser; anchor gear; steering gear; wheelhouse; galley; and cabins for passengers (when on decks not to the hull).

Net tonnage is the tonnage of a ship remaining after certain deductions have been made from the gross tonnage expressed in tons of 100 cubic feet. Among the deductions are crew spaces; master's cabin; navigation spaces; donkey engine and boiler; shaft trunks; and allowance for propelling power.

Register tonnage is applicable to both gross and net; in other words, it can be expressed as gross register tonnage or net register tonnage. How-

[6] Joseph Leeming, *Modern Ship Stowage*, U.S. Department of Commerce, Industrial Series, No. 1, 1942, p. 691.
[7] Taken from *ibid.*, p. 693.

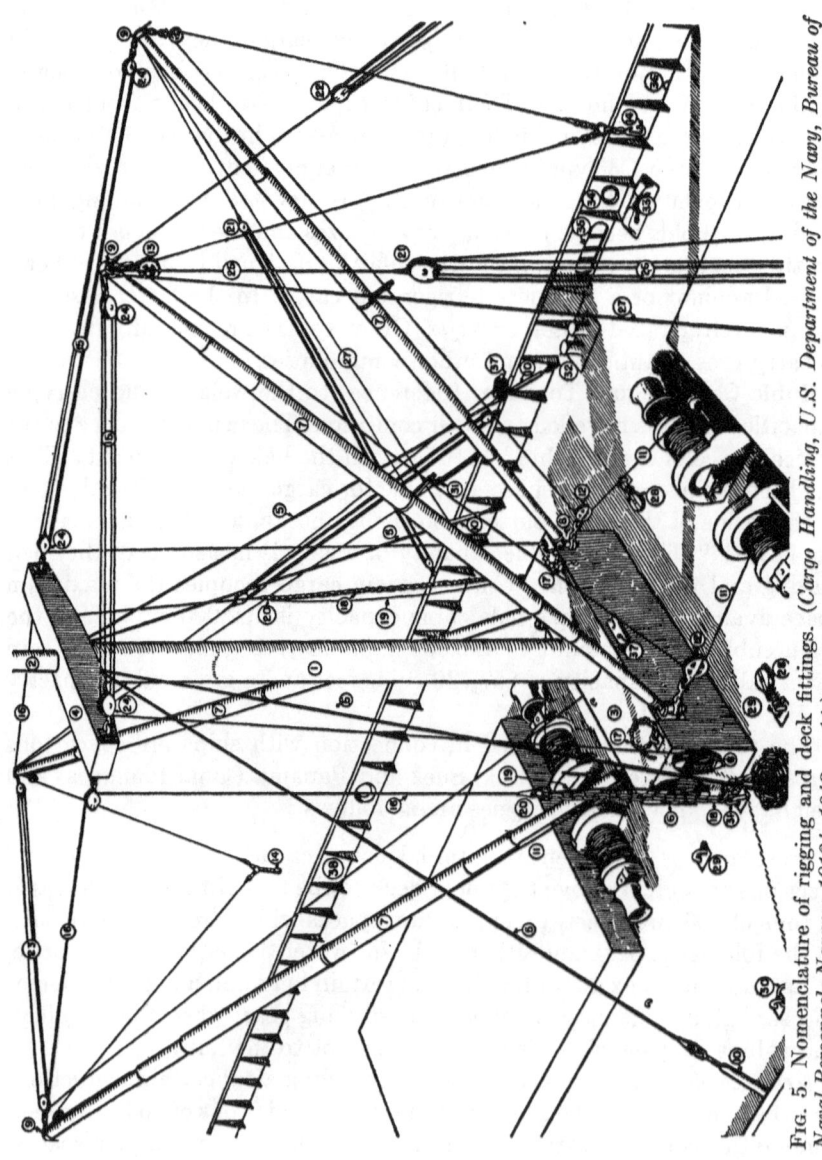

FIG. 5. Nomenclature of rigging and deck fittings. (*Cargo Handling*, U.S. Department of the Navy, Bureau of Naval Personnel, Navpers 10124, 1948, p. 11.)
For descriptive legend see opposite page.

ever, it is ordinarily used to refer to net register tonnage. Register tonnages are so named because they are the tonnages shown on the documents of registration issued for each vessel in its home country.

Underdeck tonnage is a measure of the internal space between the top of the ceiling or double bottom in the hold and the undersurface of the tonnage deck. The unit of measurement is a ton of 100 cubic feet.

Suez and Panama Canal tonnages (for purpose of assessing canal tolls) are arrived at along the same lines as are the gross and net tonnages. Each is, as a rule, larger than the register tonnage because of the inclusion of space which, under national measurement rules, is exempted.

Displacement tonnage, light, is the weight of the ship excluding cargo, passengers, fuel, water, stores, dunnage, and other items which are necessary for use on a voyage.

Displacement tonnage, loaded, is the weight of the ship including cargo, passengers, fuel, water, stores, dunnage, and other items necessary for use on a voyage, which brings the vessel down to its maximum draft. Displacement tonnage, light or loaded, may also be defined as the total quantity of water displaced by the vessel when in the particular condition.

Deadweight tonnage is the carrying capacity of a ship in tons of 2,240 pounds, that is, the difference between the displacement light and the displacement loaded.

Cargo deadweight tonnage is the number of tons (2,240 pounds per ton) which remain after deducting fuel, water, stores, dunnage, and other items necessary for use on a voyage from the deadweight tonnage of the vessel.

Cargo-handling Equipment and Gear. A general-cargo ship must under almost all circumstances be self-sufficient. This is particularly true with respect to the loading and discharging of cargo. The principal source of power in this respect is the winch, which contributes to lifting, moving, and lowering the cargo. The most frequent source of power for driving winches is either steam, which has been the most common in the past, or

---

1. Mast
2. Topmast
3. Mast table
4. Crosstree
5. Shroud
6. Topping-lift cleat
7. Boom
8. Gooseneck
9. Link band
10. Turnbuckle
11. Cargo runner
12. Heel block
13. Head block
14. Cargo hook
15. Topping lift (multiple)
16. Topping lift (single)
17. Stopper chain
18. Bull chain
19. Bull line
20. Bale
21. Outboard guy
22. Inboard guy
23. Midship guy
24. Topping-lift block
25. Guy pendant
26. Guy tackle
27. Preventer
28. Snatch block
29. Pad eye
30. Pad eye and ring bolt
31. Shackle
32. Bitts
33. Open chock
34. Closed chock
35. Freeing port
36. Scupper
37. Cleat
38. Bulwark

electricity. Deck fittings in connection with cargo handling include such items as chocks, bitts, and cleats, all of which are employed to secure standing rigging (permanent fixtures of the ship) and running rigging (moving parts of the cargo-handling gear). The winches, the deck fittings, and the rigging are all associated with the cargo booms (the British call them derricks), which are raised and spotted (or topped) in a working position for purposes of the cargo-handling operation. Most booms have a lifting capacity of around 5 tons. Heavy lift or jumbo booms will handle 15 to 50 tons and are usually placed at No. 3, the largest hatch, on a five-hatch ship. Heavy lifts in excess of the capacity of the ship's booms must be handled by shoreside or floating cranes or derricks. The cargo-handling equipment of the vessels is usually referred to as *ship's tackle* (often pronounced *tākle*).

Ships are often equipped with enough winches, booms, and rigging to be double-rigged. That is, two sets of booms and winches (one on the forward and another on the after end of the cargo hatch) can be used simultaneously, thereby permitting two gangs of longshoremen to be employed in one hold and up to twice as much cargo handled into or out of the hold as when single-rigged.

Cargo is also loaded and discharged from ships by equipment ashore such as cranes and belt conveyers. Other equipment, including save-alls (nets placed between pier and ship's side), hatch tents to place over the hatches in foul weather, fork lift trucks, dunnage, and so forth are part of the shore equipment connected with cargo handling.

THE TERMINAL

A ship operator is obligated to provide a place for a shipper to deliver cargo to be loaded aboard a ship as well as a place for a consignee to pick up cargo discharged from a ship. He can do so by operating his own terminal or pier facilities or by utilizing a public or private terminal. Hence, terminal facilities comprise the second component of ship management and operation. They are as important to success as are the ships and their crews. They are the point of interchange of cargo between the ship and land transportation. The operations associated with them absorb from one-third to one-half of the revenues and half of the time of the ships.[8]

The ship operator engaged in handling general cargo examines care-

[8] On costs of cargo handling, see pp. 218–219; on time in port, pp. 110–111. "Freight is paid for goods to be conveyed to their destination—not to be warehoused on board. Delay in ports not only reduces the ship's earnings but also contributes to raising the price of goods themselves, for their delivery is retarded and a higher rate has to be charged." Pierre Garoche, "The Importance of Handling Charges in a Ship's Operating Costs," *Transport and Communications Review*, United Nations, April–June, 1950, Vol. 3, p. 16.

fully these characteristics of his terminals: berthing space, wharf apron, transit shed, rail and motor access, and supporting transportation and storage facilities. Tentative standards for the incorporation of these characteristics into the design of a general-cargo terminal were defined in the following language by the Port Development Section, Research Division, U.S. Maritime Commission, in September, 1946:[9]

Berthing Space. Adequate space to accommodate the length and draft of a vessel would require a berth 600 feet long with an initial dredged depth of 36 feet MLW. The width of dock or slip required between piers (if pier system is used) would be at least 325 feet for single and 420 feet for multiple berths.

Wharf Apron. Sufficient shipside space to facilitate direct transfer of cargo between ship's hold and rail cars, trucks and wheeled materials handling equipment would require an apron 49 feet wide, flush with the shed floor and having a smooth hard surface.

Transit Shed. In order to meet insurance underwriters requirements and facilitate traffic flow the transit shed would be fireproof, free from interior column interference, with 10 foot candles of illumination and would have a smooth floor to facilitate use of mechanical equipment. The structure would be single story 500 feet long by 200 feet wide, having 20 feet vertical clearance and fitted with disappearing doors 20 feet wide by 15 feet high, in alternate panels. In the case of a shore wharf the rear of the shed would have a 20 foot, covered platform extending the length of the shed adjacent to a depressed, paved, loading area. There would be at least two tracks parallel to this rear platform to permit direct transfer to cars on the same level.

Rail and Motor Access. Adequate rail and motor access to sheds including three apron tracks and two platform tracks having ample crossovers would be available. Careful control of paved surfaces of track work expansion joints, sills and drainage devices would obviate unevenness in the shed and apron decks. The location and grades of access ramps would be controlled to permit most efficient utilization of materials handling equipment. All areas adjacent to wharf decks would be adequately paved.

Supporting Transportation and Storage Facilities. Adequate adjoining transit rail yards and motor storage areas, adjacent warehouses, supporting open storage, motor parks and motor service facilities with controlled motor traffic flows would be made an integral part of the terminal layout and equipment.

One of the greatest difficulties encountered in ship operation in the United States is the antiquated condition of most pier facilities. Generally they have not been modernized to keep up with improvements and changes in the average size and design of ships. Nor have the pier facilities kept up with the growth of the trucking business and industrial highways

---

[9] Taken from *Ocean Shipping, Facts and Figures—Handbook*, an unpublished and unofficial document of the U.S. Maritime Commission, Research Division, Feb. 16, 1948, p. 252. Much of the material in this section on the terminal is based on this document; the chapter on "Port Development" was written by and prepared under the direction of Ralph I. Schneider.

that have substituted for the old drayage system for which so many piers were designed. Also, most of the older piers were built before the appearance of modern materials-handling equipment.

The enormous investment involved in water-front facilities has made it difficult for public and private pier owners to remove and adapt old existing structures and to invest in much-needed new facilities. There are important exceptions to this statement, and most water-front cities realize that improvements are necessary.

Types of Piers. Piers may be grouped in the following types: (1) finger or quay, (2) covered or uncovered, and (3) general or specialized. The finger-type pier extends into the harbor so that two sides are generally available to berth ships and lighters. The quay is situated parallel to the shore line so that usually only one side is available to berth a ship. Although the usual pier facility is the covered transit shed of one or two floors, the uncovered pier facility is used where a large storage area is desired (as in the case of a lumber terminal) or where cargo is moved directly to rail car or truck. In contrast to the general-cargo pier, a specialized terminal is one designed to handle a specific commodity such as grain, ores, copra, or bananas.

There are numerous aspects of pier layout that concern the ship operator. We can deal with only a few of them, and briefly at that. For example, in order to control in an orderly manner the accumulation of cargo on the pier, the floor plan can be divided into sections designated, say, by numbers. If so, one entering the dock would find the odd-numbered sections to his right and the even-numbered sections to his left, proceeding from the lower to the higher numbers as he progressed down the dock. Hence, a truck driver would be informed by the receiving clerk at the head of the pier to unload his goods at a specific section, or palletized loads would be moved from the truck to the section. The clerk would know which section to name by his knowledge of the plan for stowing the cargo aboard the ship and of the relationship of the location along the pier to the various holds of the ship once she had been docked. The individual section, depending on its size, would probably be divided into subsections such as left-rear, left-center, and left-front. As we will shortly see, such detailed division of the dock's floor plan facilitates the operations of receiving and delivering cargo, keeping records of its location and movements, and planning the loading of a ship.

Stevedoring. There are many auxiliary or shoreside facilities and operations that are essential to ship and terminal operation. The most important of these are the stevedoring activities, which have to do with the actual handling of cargo between the pier facility and the hold of the ship. While some ship operators do their own stevedoring and employ longshoremen themselves, stevedoring companies have come to specialize in this particular function, maintaining sizable inventories of cargo-handling equipment.

The individual longshoreman is a key factor in ship operation. His employment is casual and likely to be irregular, made available either through a hiring hall or at the pier for a particular job and not for any one employer. Longshoremen work in gangs that vary in size. The average gang costs about $80 an hour. The exact size of the gang will depend upon the commodity handled. Labor unions have specific agreements with ship operators calling for, say, not less than 22 men in a general-cargo gang, or not less than 18 men in a gang loading steel. Some operators may at times use more men than the minimum requirements, because of dock congestion or for other reasons.

A typical longshore gang includes a gang boss, a hatch tender, a winch driver, six hold men (in the hold of the ship), two dock men, and such other men as are required for the specific operation. One gang works at each hold of the ship that is receiving or discharging cargo, and, where ships are equipped with booms and winches at both the forward and after end of the hatch, it is possible to have two gangs working simultaneously.

The two men on the dock are the hook-on men who attach and detach the cargo hooks on the sling loads of cargo that are moved from dock to ship or the reverse. If cargo is not palletized or if, for some other reason, additional handling is required to build up sling loads, more than two longshoremen will be on the dock. Cargo is moved by power-driven winches under the control of the winch driver and hatch tender, the former controlling the cargo-hoisting machine or winch and the hatch tender guiding him by signals.

In addition to longshoremen, the stevedoring operation utilizes equipment drivers to drive vehicles used to transport cargo on the dock and in the hold of the ship; gearmen to maintain stevedoring equipment; carloaders to handle freight in and out of rail cars (see below); ship clerks to tally cargo; coopers to repair cargo that has been damaged in transit and to prevent further damage; auto mechanics to maintain the automotive equipment; and sweepers and handy men to keep the dock clean.

Accident Prevention. One of the important activities of ship operators associated with the stevedoring operation at some United States ports is accident prevention. This generally involves employers' bureaus equipped to inspect safety features at docks and ships while operations are under way; to investigate accidents, make recommendations, and spread safety information designed to reduce accidents to longshoremen and ships' crews during cargo-handling operations; and generally to cooperate with steamship and shipping companies and various official organizations to the end that the safety record of stevedoring operations shall be improved. One such bureau has an annual budget in excess of $100,000.

Carloading. Carloading, already mentioned in connection with stevedoring, is sometimes referred to as car service and means the loading or unloading of railroad cars at steamship piers. There are three ways of accomplishing the movement: (1) *indirect* car service, in which a place of rest on the pier is used to pile, and generally to assort, the commodity pending further movement (in other words, an intermediate stop in the movement of cargo between the vessel and the rail car); (2) *direct* service, in which the cargo is loaded into or unloaded from a car immediately under ship's tackle; and (3) *continuous* car service, in which the commodity is transported directly between a rail car and ship's tackle but without any stop at the point of rest. There are some independent carloading companies, but stevedoring companies and sometimes steamship companies themselves manage the carloading and unloading operation. Under the terms of most bills of lading, cargo must be placed within reach of ship's tackle by the shipper and removed therefrom by the consignee. Hence, carloading and unloading expenses are charges against the cargo, not the terminal.

Port and Terminal Management. Space does not permit us to dwell on the subject of port and terminal management.[10] However, the ship operator is interested not only in the efficiency with which a port and its facilities are operated by the governing authority but in the cost of the various charges associated with the movement of his ships in a port and the ability of the port to develop traffic for his ships.

Generally the management of ports is in the hands of a central public authority, either state or municipal. But the actual development of facilities rests with different groups, sometimes public and sometimes private. Prior to 1910, most terminal development was in the hands of the railroads. While various developments since then have lessened the direct relationship of railroads to ship operations, nevertheless railroads remain an influence on terminal activity. The railroads control many of the piers on the Atlantic Coast and the flow of traffic to the piers. The rail practice of absorbing terminal charges in the freight rate on through traffic has made it difficult for other terminals and ports to establish compensatory rates, and this in turn has delayed undertaking costly terminal improvements. After World War I, there was an increasing awareness of the need for modernizing and coordinating terminal facilities, but little actual progress was made until after World War II.

[10] On port and terminal operation and management, see George Fox Mott, *A Survey of United States Ports*, Arco Publishing Company, Inc., New York, 1951, and pertinent sections of the *Proceedings—American Merchant Marine Conference*, published annually by the Propeller Club of the United States. Interim Report 5 of the American Association of Port Authorities, Inc., Apr. 15, 1953, announced that a research project on port administration, made under the direction of Marvin L. Fair of Tulane University, had been completed and that the study was to be published.

Port authorities are serving to expand those facilities of a port that are beyond the financial capacity of private interest to develop, such as refrigeration terminals; grain elevators; belt railroads; banana, copra, or other special commodity facilities; and perhaps a foreign trade zone. All these facilities not only attract cargo that helps to fill ships but serve to provide the cargo-handling equipment specially adapted to the commodity involved and thereby expedite the turn-around of the ship in port.

Port and Terminal Charges. The ship operator is concerned with the following port and terminal charges, the terminology and application of which vary from port to port. As a general rule, the carrier's degree of interest in the charges, as well as his rates, will depend on the basis of the carrier's contract with the shipper.[11] Those charges that are assessed for services rendered in connection with the charge are heavy-lift, lighterage, and handling charges. A heavy-lift charge is incurred when a floating crane or some other special piece of equipment is necessary to handle an unusually heavy item of cargo. Companies or public facilities that offer this special service assess their own charges. A lighterage charge results as a cost for loading or unloading a vessel by means of barges alongside the ship. Handling charges are assessed to cover the cost of the service for moving freight between ship's gear (the hook) and the place of rest on the pier. Sometimes sorting, piling, and trucking on the pier are included in the service. When cargo is moved between open or closed freight cars direct to the ship's gear, the handling charge becomes a direct-transfer charge. And a loading and unloading charge may be assessed for the transfer of freight between the dock and railroad car.

Other charges for services within the port or at the terminal that are assessed for general purposes and that do not arise out of the specific handling of cargo are service charge, dockage, wharfage, and demurrage or wharf demurrage. These charges are generally assessed by the port or terminal authority or owner. A service charge against the ship operator is usually based on the amount of cargo handled. It is for the use of terminal facilities, for berthage while the ship is alongside, and for various services such as the administrative expense of the port or terminal authority. Dockage is a charge for the use of a pier by the ship operator and is usually assessed on the basis of the tonnage of the ship. Wharfage is charged for the use of the terminal for the movement of cargo over the pier and is therefore assessed on the basis of the amount of cargo handled.

---

[11] For example, freight rates may apply "from place of rest on dock" "to place of rest on dock," which is often the practice in general-cargo domestic trades. Or freight rates may apply from ship's tackle at loading port to ship's tackle at discharging port (*e.g.*, this is the practice in the lumber trades), and in such cases the shipowner is not concerned with terminal charges. Also, rates may stipulate that the cargo is contracted for on the basis of "free in and out," "free load-ship discharge," or "ship load and free discharge."

Demurrage is charged when cargo remains on the pier longer than the free time allowed, which may be five, seven, or ten days, for example.

In addition to the charges already mentioned, there are such costs as pilotage, which will usually be on the basis of the tonnage or draft of the vessel. The Federal government assesses a tonnage tax on vessels arriving from foreign ports and an entrance and clearance fee. Towage fees are paid when tug services are used.

In the Port of New York, loading and unloading charges include charges that vary, as between truck or railroad movement to and from the piers. New York has generally been known as a lighterage port as freight moves from railhead to ship, generally by railroad-owned lighters. The growth of the trucking industry has, of course, introduced a considerable movement of freight to and from piers by truck. In New York, for instance, all import freight delivered to authorized truckmen at steamship piers is handled by public loaders located on the piers. The loaders engage exclusively in loading freight from pier facilities when the freight is accessible to the motor vehicle. For this service, the public loaders are compensated on the basis of an agreed rate promulgated in a schedule of *Official Loading Charges in the Port of New York* issued by the Truck Loading Authority, which was established by agreement between some shippers and truck operators, the International Longshoremen's Association, and the Port Loaders Council 1757 of the ILA.[12]

Unlike most piers in other ports, freight moved to and from steamship piers in the Port of New York by motor vehicle is not usually subject to pier-usage or wharfage charges. There are a few exceptions in which these charges do apply, but this is true only at piers controlled by the railroads and used by steamship lines free of dockage charges. The line-haul rates of the railroads in New York cover many charges that are assessed separately at other ports.

There are other features of port administration and operation that vitally concern the ship operator. For instance, various marine services are important, such as dredging and salvage facilities, pilotage facilities, and the services of customs, health, tugs, police, fire, and similar agencies and departments.

The Marine Exchange. Ship operators also derive benefits from the existence of a marine exchange or maritime association in the ports of call. A marine exchange gives telephone reports on the arrival and departure of vessels, reports on sea and weather conditions for arriving and departing ships, and records ship movements and charters. Through the committee structure of its members, the exchange investigates problems that are of mutual interest to the members. One such marine exchange has recently installed a radar set to penetrate adverse weather conditions and

[12] See the Port of New York Authority, Traffic Advice 7, Aug. 10, 1950.

provide a reliable determination of the position of ships within its range entering or leaving the port. Such a unit facilitates work in the harbor when the weather is bad.

SUPERVISION AND ADMINISTRATION

Effective supervision and administration make up the third component of successful ship operation and management. Over-all management is considered in Chapter 12. This chapter deals with supervision and administration as it applies to the operating department.

One company described effective administration by its operating department in the corporation's annual report to stockholders in the following language:

Marked progress was made in 1950 in increasing the operating efficiency and earning power of your Company's fleet. The 1950 gross revenue was derived from completion of 106 voyages compared with 98 voyages the previous year. By cutting down time spent in ports, reducing turnaround time by expediting supply, repair, loading, and unloading, maintaining faster sailing schedules between ports, and reducing "free space" the vessels produced a larger margin of profit. Specifically, 1950 voyages were shortened enough to save 335 vessel days as compared with the lengths of similar voyages in 1949. Correspondingly, there was an increase of 8 per cent in 1950 as compared with 1949 in the number of revenue tons per cargo vessel-day. So notable an improvement could not have been made without vigorous and enthusiastic cooperation of your Company's officers afloat, and I take this opportunity to commend and thank them for it.

Your Company initiated a voyage cost control system, budgeting each voyage in order to obtain better vessel utilization and lower costs . . . .

One of the prime objects of the Operating Department has been to increase net revenue by reducing voyage turnaround without a reduction in the volume of cargo handled . . . .

A system was established in 1949 for evaluating the operating efficiency of all your Company's vessels. All factors included in the cost of operation were duly appraised and properly weighed. In 1949 the average vessel efficiency was found to be 79 per cent of the standard of acceptable performance. The efficiency gradually improved since that date and, notwithstanding a raising of the standard of acceptable performance in June of 1950, the average of all vessels for the last quarter of 1950 has increased to 94.5 per cent of the standard.

Organization of Department. The operating department of a cargoliner shipping company is organized along the following general lines. The manager of the department is probably a vice-president and ranks high in the policy-making organization of management. His task is to see that corporate policies affecting his department are carried out within the department. To do so, he must coordinate the numerous functions that generally come under the supervision of an operating manager, including ship and terminal operation, purchasing, claims and insurance, labor relations, and chartering.

The department will probably be divided into at least four divisions (the nomenclature will differ from company to company) as well as such other divisions as are necessary to handle the other activities previously mentioned. A detailed assignment of functions might be as follows:

Dock or wharf division:
    Receiving cargo from shippers or agents.
    Loading vessels (may use stevedoring company).
    Discharging cargo (may use stevedoring company).
    Delivering cargo to consignees.
    Perhaps acting as stevedores for other than company ships.
    Maintaining the division's equipment.

Marine division:
    Safeguarding vessels as to seaworthiness.
    Supervising repair work and annual dry-docking.
    Providing for bunkering and stores.
    Preparing shipping articles and other papers.
    Supervising seagoing personnel (deck officers and crew).
    Supervising communications and personnel.

Engineer division:
    Supervising engine-room maintenance and repairs.
    Supervising seagoing personnel (engineer officers and crew).

Steward division:
    Victualing the ship and providing linen, etc.
    Supervising seagoing personnel (steward personnel).
    Perhaps handling labor relations (for steward personnel).

An interesting phase of operating-department organization, as it is of all departments, is the decentralization of authority and responsibility by districts. While over-all authority and supervision are centralized at company headquarters, a certain degree of operating responsibility and authority will be found at each port where the company keeps any kind of staff. In an active port, there will probably be a district operating manager and under him a divisional organization similar to that in the home port. For administrative purposes, this district group will report to the over-all district manager. For purposes of efficient operation, the district group will coordinate its activities with other district groups (such as traffic). However, for purposes of operating authority, the district operating manager and his staff will look to their counterpart at the home office. This situation again illustrates the problem in organization that is of great importance to efficient ship operation.[13]

[13] See Chap. 12.

Scheduling. The life of the operating-department personnel revolves around the schedule of the vessels. Operating efficiency depends on minimizing the number of days of each ship at sea and of the turn-around time in each port. The combination of distance between ports and the ship's speed is the firmest factor in measuring the length of time for a voyage in regular liner service. However, weather conditions at sea, access to passage through a canal, missing arrival at a harbor in daylight hours (where necessary), or adverse tidal or weather conditions for crossing a bar are some of the situations that may upset a schedule. Turn-around time in port will vary with the quantity of cargo to be discharged and loaded and the speed with which the operation can be accomplished. The type of cargo, weather conditions, number of hatches to be worked simultaneously, holidays, and numerous other factors must be taken into account. In many routes, the timing of competitors' sailings is also an important item to be considered in selecting schedules and timing of calls at ports.

Once everything has been taken into account, including necessary time out for dry-docking and repairs, the operating department can lay out a schedule for the complete voyage. The frequency of sailings to be made will then determine the number of ships necessary to maintain the schedule. For example, if the voyage is estimated to require approximately 112 days and a fortnightly sailing frequency is selected, a fleet of eight ships is necessary.

THE OPERATIONAL PROCESS

Booking Cargo. The booking of cargo is a function sometimes found in the traffic department. Whoever has the responsibility must provide close coordination with the operating department in order to book a maximum cargo. The operation commences weeks before the ship actually begins to load cargo. Let us take, for example, a C3 vessel of 12,100 deadweight tons and 657,000-bale cubic capacity. The tonnage must be booked against both the deadweight and the cubic of the ship in order, among other things, to avoid overbooking the vessel or losing out on some choice cargo from the revenue standpoint. The booking department will keep an accurate check of the weight and cubic measurement of all cargo booked or offered. Also, the booking clerk will bear in mind the factor of broken stowage or lost space resulting from use of dunnage, the location of beams, and so forth. This is generally considered to be 10 percent of the ship's cubic space in general-cargo trades. Hence, in the case given, the booking department will deduct about 65,700 feet from the bale cubic to book against. Of course, in certain trades, experience will lead the booking clerk to reduce or increase the safety factor.

Receiving Cargo. The first step by which goods to be transported come within the jurisdiction of the operating department is the receipt of the goods at the loading pier. The shipper has received a shipping permit or has otherwise been advised that his goods will be received at the pier. He has also been informed of the days for receiving cargo for the ship. A receiving clerk at the dock signs a dock receipt (usually prepared in advance by the shipper) for the goods. They are then tallied, measured, and recorded on dock sheets.

The dock sheets indicate the number of packages received, their marks and description of contents, dimensions and cubical content of the packages, weight and shipping marks, the shipping permit and dock-receipt number, name of the shipper, the ship and port of destination, and any damage to the freight that has been noted by the receiving clerk. Copies of the dock sheets are used by the terminal staff and by the bill-of-lading clerks to check against bills of lading presented by the shippers. The goods are spotted in one of the sections on the dock, as already mentioned.

Loading the Ship. Cargo must be loaded into a ship with a view to the safety of the ship, the cargo, and the personnel. The shipper of goods is responsible for providing satisfactory packing of his goods. But the ship operator (carrier) is responsible for damage to the goods if such damage results from improper or bad stowage. Cargo is also stowed with an eye to the speed with which cargo can be loaded and discharged at the various ports of call of the ship. For these reasons, preplanning the distribution of cargo to be stowed aboard the ship is an extremely important function of the operating department.

One objective of preplanning is to guarantee that the required stability and trim of the ship are achieved. The stability of a ship is its ability to right itself when rolled to one side. This involves the relation of the ship's center of gravity and the center of buoyancy. A ship with too low a center of gravity when loaded will snap when it rolls and endanger both ship and cargo, and a tender ship will roll excessively. The preplanner must be familiar with the basic characteristics of the ship which are provided by the designer and builder. He will also have available to him the capacity, by estimated weight and cubic measurement, of each of the cargo compartments of the ship and the capacity of the deck. By calculating the distribution of the goods, the preplanner can calculate the location of the metacentric height (or GM), which is the height of the metacenter above the center of gravity, and thereby determine whether the ship will be properly loaded and seaworthy. He must also determine that he has made a proper distribution of weight fore and aft, so that the vessel will be in proper trim and not be down or trimmed by the head or have too much of a drag (*i.e.*, be trimmed by the stern).

For all these purposes, the preplanner must know the characteristics of the cargo to be loaded, as to weight and cubic measurement of all of the shipments, and the stowage factor.[14] As a result of this knowledge, he divides his cargo between "bottom" cargo and other goods. Heavy merchandise that will not break makes good bottom cargo—for example, steel rails, lumber, rubber, tin, coal, and sacked beans or seed. Cargo with a low stowage factor (greater density of weight) will tend to be placed in the lower parts of the ship and where the beam of the ship is narrowest, thus leaving the larger cubic areas of the vessel for packages having a higher stowage factor. If such planning reaches its ideal conclusion, a ship will be full and down, utilizing the entire cubic space of the ship and putting the ship down to its maximum allowable draft, or *marks*. Maximum revenue, of course, is more important than the ideal of full and down.

Separation of cargo is also an important factor for the preplanner to consider. He must bear in mind regulations of the U.S. Coast Guard that govern the manner and location of stowage of hazardous goods and bulk grain that is liable to shift in the hold. He must consider such matters as moisture, crushing, contamination, and other characteristics. For example, coffee and flour would involve a contamination problem if loaded together. If sulphur is loaded in bulk into a lower hold after general cargo has been placed in the 'tween deck, Coast Guard regulations require that a wooden bulkhead must be erected in the hatch so that sulphur dust will not penetrate the general cargo and create a fire hazard. Cargo of high value and subject to pilferage is protected by stowage in special lockers when possible. Other cargo, because of size (such as rail cars) or hazard (such as some acids), is considered suitable as deck cargo.

The preplanner will utilize a chart giving the ship's characteristics, including a summary of the cargo and tank capacities of all spaces and a deadweight scale that is provided on all ships. The scale will tell him of the deadweight tonnage capacity of the ship for each measurement of the draft of the ship, and usually will also tell him how many tons of cargo are required to lower the ship another inch in the water (or give the ship another inch of draft). He will then proceed to lay out a preliminary stowage plan for the ship.

[14] Stowage factors are of two kinds: (1) a factor showing the actual space occupied by 1 long ton of a commodity as packed for shipment, with no allowance added for broken stowage and the space occupied by dunnage, and (2) a factor which includes such an allowance. The calculation for the first type is to divide 2,240 pounds by the weight, in pounds, of a cubic foot of the commodity as packed.

The stowage factor is also used to indicate the relation of the ability of a vessel to carry weight with its ability to carry cubic. There is a rule of thumb throughout the world that 40 cubic feet equals 1 ton of 2,000 pounds. It is a rule of early origin and is the stowage factor of Russian black wheat. Actually, the stowage factor varies with each type of ship.

Cargo Handling. The next step beyond the preplanning of the stowage of cargo is the actual loading of the cargo into the ship, either from place of rest of preassembled cargo on the dock or direct at ship's side from rail car, lighter, or truck. With regard to general cargo loaded from the dock, there are five successive cycles involved in cargo handling: (1) the dock-gang cycle, at the point of rest on the dock (moving cargo to dollies); (2) the dock-tractor cycle, to move the cargo to ship's side; (3) the front-men cycle, to put the cargo in sling loads and attach to the hook; (4) the ship's-gear cycle, to move the cargo from dock into the hold; and (5) the hold-stowage cycle. Maximum efficiency in cargo-handling operations is achieved when the cargo moves from cycle to cycle at equal speeds. The rate of stowage will vary with the type of general cargo, the type of dock and facilities, the degree of mechanization of the process, weather conditions, and the general attitude of the men involved in the operation.

The loading of cargo, as well as the reverse action of discharging, is the most expensive single phase of ship management and operation. Many things have been done to improve the efficiency of cargo handling. The handling of bulk cargoes, such as ores, sugar, grain, and petroleum products, is much improved. In this regard, there has been an integration of the facilities aboard ship and at the dock, a situation not generally possible in the case of general cargo.

Much has been written about mechanizing the handling of general cargo and the introduction of palletizing. Wartime experience of the armed forces lent much encouragement and provided valuable experience in this regard. However, net progress has been extremely disappointing. Those who have observed the great improvements in materials handling in warehouses and industrial plants will find it difficult to understand why as much has not been accomplished in cargo handling.

One reason for the difference is the great variety of sizes and shapes of commodities handled aboard ship. A ship's cargo is a composite of commodities from many warehouses and factories; it is not readily adaptable to assembly-line processes. Hundreds of shippers and consignees are represented in the commodities loaded and discharged at the several ports of call of a ship. Cases of canned goods, rolls of newsprint, crates of refrigerators, sacks of coffee, and hundreds of other commodities, packaged and unpackaged, will be found aboard the ship. For this reason, it is not usually possible to specialize on cargo-handling gear. The stevedoring company must have handy a large variety of equipment. Also, it is difficult to maintain a fast flow of goods from dock to place of stowage aboard ship, because of the need to change gear, to place the items of cargo securely in the holds, to shore up those items not stowed snug and tight, and to place dunnage or otherwise protect layers or sections of cargo.

Palletizing has its problems as a solution to the need for great efficiency in cargo handling. Not only do sizes and shapes of goods handled vary greatly, but also in commercial operation, it is not practical to take up too much cubic space in the holds of the ship. Moreover, when cargo aboard pallets is lowered into the square of the hatch, the palletized load must still be moved by hand or some means of conveyance to that area within the hold where it is to be stowed. The use of pallets has permitted greater utilization of pier space, increased efficiency on the docks, decreased damage and pilferage, and made for better housekeeping. Where palletizing has increased the cost of cargo handling, there are those who feel that the improvements have more than offset the higher costs.

As previously mentioned, the rate of flow of goods from dock to hold and vice versa depends on integration of the speed of each cycle. The point through which each sling load or draft of cargo must move is the cargo hook, which is the working end of all the ship's gear and all equipment for the handling of cargo. There is a great deal of this equipment—winches and booms, cargo falls, masts and king posts, boom guys, topping lifts, and other items. However, the rate of flow of cargo into and out of the ship is geared basically to the rate of movement at the hook, which is the least flexible of all the cycles in handling cargo.

Paper Work. The paper work involved in loading cargo aboard ship is extremely important and not too complicated except that a great many copies are usually required. The nomenclature and the types of forms vary from company to company. Generally, there are (1) tally sheets, (2) hatch lists, (3) a stowage plan, and (4) the manifest. As the cargo moves aboard ship, tally clerks keep a record of each sling load of goods, checking it against what they have been advised is to be loaded. Thus each shipment is given another examination to safeguard against shortages or damage to the goods. The tally sheets thus compiled become the permanent record of the operating staff at the loading port.

After all cargo has been placed in a hold at each loading port, the pier staff compiles a hatch list for each hold, showing the goods loaded by shipper, commodity, number of units, and place where stowed in the hold. Copies of the hatch list are given to the ship, to each port of destination, and to the staff at the loading port. The hatch list gives the detail necessary to supplement the stowage plan, which is a profile of the ship, on which is drawn the distribution of the cargo. A stowage plan illustrates the actual stowage of cargo rather than the preplanning previously discussed.

Cargo for a specific port of destination is usually designated on the stowage plan by one color to enable anyone at a quick glance to locate the cargo to be discharged at that port regardless of the loading port. As we have previously said, cargo for any one port is distributed throughout the ship because of greater speed in loading and discharging when the opera-

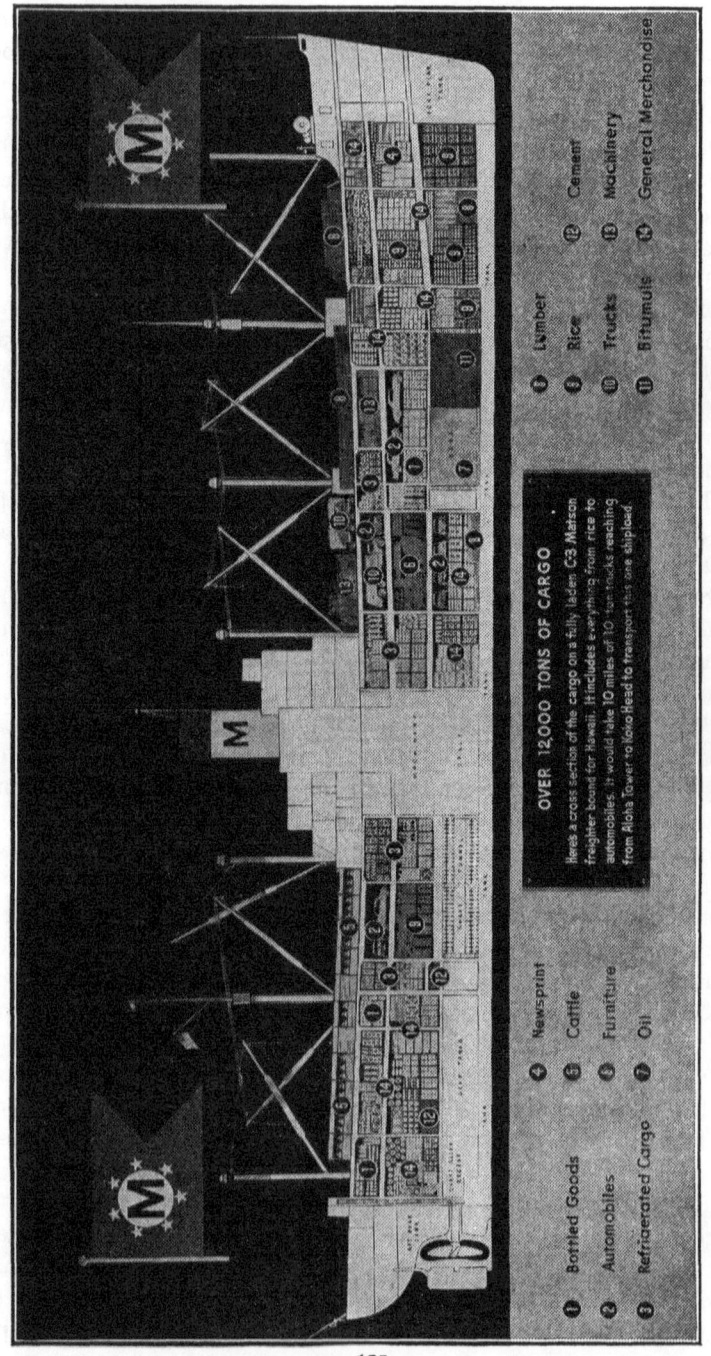

Fig. 7. Profile of a 12,000-ton freighter, loaded. (*Matson Navigation Company.*)

tion can be carried on simultaneously at two or more hatches. It is also distributed to achieve stability and trim of the ship or for other technical reasons.

A stowage plan is constructed as the loading of the ship proceeds. The progress is charted on the profile of the lower holds, which have much more depth than 'tween decks, by building from the bottom of the drawing. The commodity and number of units, port of destination, and physical location in the hold will be written on the plan. Symbols are used to abbreviate reference to the actual location in the hold. For example, "Wgs/P" for one operator will mean "in the wings, port (left) of the square of the hatch"; "A/O" could mean "all over the deck." The layout of the stowage plan of cargo loaded in the 'tween decks is made as though the reader were looking down on the deck, although the same symbols may be employed.

The manifest is the most important single document in the whole shipping operation. Copies must be filed with the U.S. Bureau of Customs, in the records of the company, with each port of destination (at least as to that part of the cargo destined for the port), and with the ship. It is vital that the manifest be prepared accurately. It must be prepared promptly as the cargo is loaded, so that it will be completed for the sailing of the ship. The information recorded on the manifest includes the names of the shipper and consignee, the commodity, the number of units (barrels, boxes, bags, and so forth), the weight and cubic measurement, and the marks of identification on the units. A manifest that also contains information as to ship's revenue and extra charges assessed, and such miscellaneous data as the company requires or desires, is called a "freight sheet."

Discharging and Delivering Cargo. The process of discharging and delivering cargo is generally the reverse of the loading procedure. Again the tallying of the shipments as they come out of the holds is an important step, for purposes of checking the numbers and the condition of the goods. Complete records make it possible to trace shortages and place responsibility for damage or loss. Cargo is placed on the pier for delivery to consignees, who have usually been notified of the expected arrival date of the ship and who have an allowable period of time within which to pick up the shipments before demurrage is assessed. Delivery clerks check off the shipments as they leave the pier and obtain receipts for the goods.

CLAIMS DIVISION

The claims division may be a part of the operating department of the company, and sometimes will be found in the traffic department. However, claims work is often found under a separate department head who reports directly to the general manager of the company.[15] There is a reason

[15] In the company discussed in Chap. 12, claims and purchasing are separate departments, whose directors are responsible to the company's top executives.

for this. A tug of war generally goes on between the traffic department, which wishes not to offend shipper or consignee and would rather absorb the cost of paying a claim than disclaim liability for loss or damage, and the operating department, which may assess the blame against some cause outside of its own jurisdiction.

The function of the claims department is to receive a claim for loss or damage from the cargo owner, usually the consignee, to acknowledge receipt of the claim, to investigate the facts of the case, and to pay part or all of the claim or to reject it. The claims manager and his staff must try to retain the good will of the customer and at the same time be detectives at heart in order to uncover the facts pertinent to the case.

The reader will see the importance of clear and complete records of the company's stewardship in relation to the shipper and consignee, from the time the shipment enters the jurisdiction of the company until it has been delivered to the consignee. Shipments are subjected to many handlings while in transit, as well as to conditions of weather and other factors. Cartons may be torn or dented, the contents may be damaged because of rough handling, sweat damage may occur, damage may be caused by proximity to other commodities, and so forth. Because of concealed damage, goods may reach the consignee without the damage being apparent while in transit; in such cases it is often impossible to determine the cause or the time of occurrence of the damage. The ship operator has definite obligations to cargo owners, and from the standpoint of good will it is most undesirable for an operator to deal lightly with these obligations. This does not mean that the claims division should not resist the payment of undeserved claims, but generally the ship operator is at a distinct disadvantage in proving lack of responsibility for loss or damage.

The ship operator's greatest protection against exorbitant outlays for claims payments is a strong, aggressive claims-prevention program. Sometimes this is called a cargo-protection program, for that is exactly what it is. Each claim is examined thoroughly with a view to determining the cause, and then the cargo-protection program really starts.

A company that is protection minded will not be satisfied just to close the books on payment, either when a claim is rejected or when it is passed along to the insurance company. It will follow through to correct the physical or human failing that permitted the claim to occur. The cause may be a packaging problem, and representations to the shipper will lead him to develop a carton or container that will be more satisfactory for the transport of his goods by ship. The problem may be that the high unit value of the merchandise exposes the goods to pilferage. In such a case, stowage in a special locker aboard ship and on the piers may safeguard the shipment. Perhaps the goods should not have been stowed in No. 3 hold next to the warm bulkhead of the engine room, or should have been given some other kind of designated stowage. Only a thorough investigation of each case will lead to proper indoctrination of personnel and to establishing proper rules and instructions for handling and stowage of the hundreds of commodities that are shipped. In some cases, the shipping company may find that certain goods or the goods of certain shippers are too susceptible to loss or damage or that the special handling required is so costly as to make the goods undesirable from the ship operator's viewpoint. It may then be necessary to recommend an increase in freight rate to cover the total of costs involved.

PURCHASING DIVISION

The purchasing division is an integral part of operations, and this division will usually be found under the jurisdiction of the operating manager. The purchasing agent works closely with the other divisions of the operating department to maintain adequate stores for the ships and to be able to obtain prompt delivery of items required and reported when the ship is in port. The managers of the deck and engine-room divisions will be responsible for expenditures incurred at ship repair yards and for purchases of major items other than ships' stores and provisions. Also, the purchasing agent may not always be responsible for fuel-oil purchases, the size of which usually involves contracts for a year or other long period of time. Such negotiations are often carried on by top executives.

BIBLIOGRAPHY

There are many other phases of ship operation such as passenger operations, tanker operation, ship brokerage, general-agency operation, navigation, and the functioning of the operation department in relation to the ship at sea. For this reason, the bibliography provides guidance to material that could not be included in the chapter.

Defense Transport Administration, *The Ocean Port Story: A Primer for Defense Mobilization*, February, 1953, processed.

Dover, V., *Shipping Industry: Its Constitution and Practice*, Edward W. Sweetman, New York, 1952.

Ebel, F. G., "Notes on Cargo Handling," a talk presented before the Philadelphia section of the Society of Naval Architects and Marine Engineers, January, 1953, mimeographed.

Ford, A. G., and J. K. Webster, *Handling and Stowage of Cargo*, 3d ed., prepared for U.S. Maritime Service, International Textbook Company, Scranton, Pa., 1952.

Garoche, Pierre, *Stowage, Handling, and Transport of Ship Cargoes*, Cornell Maritime Press, Cambridge, Md., 1941.

———, *Dictionary of Commodities Carried by Ship*, Cornell Maritime Press, Cambridge, Md., 1952.

Hughes, Charles H., *Handbook of Ship Calculations, Construction, and Operations*, 3d ed., McGraw-Hill Book Company, Inc., New York, 1942.

Lawrence, Newbold T., "Operating Problems of Transatlantic Liners," *The Log*, October, 1952, pp. 41*ff*.

Lederer, E. H., *Port Terminal Operation*, Cornell Maritime Press, Cambridge, Md., 1945.

Leeming, Joseph, *Modern Ship Stowage*, U.S. Department of Commerce, Industrial Series, No. 1, 1942.

Louis, Edward V., "Simple Form for Calculating Trim and Stability," *The Log*, March, 1948, pp. 60–61*ff*.

Mott, George Fox, *A Survey of United States Ports*, Arco Publishing Company, Inc., New York, 1951.

Ports, Dues, and Charges on Shipping throughout the World, 20th ed., Edward W. Sweetman, New York, 1951.

Quackenbush, L. H., "General Cargo Handling—Developments and Solutions, An Analysis of General Cargo Handling Problems," *The Log*, March, 1948, pp. 44*ff*., and April, 1948, pp. 46*ff*.

"Ship Capacity Charts," *The Log*, June 25, 1952, pp. 189–213.

Stevens, E. F., *Shipping Practice*, Pitman Publishing Corp., New York, 1952.

"Trimming Tables," *The Log*, June 25, 1952, pp. 183–187.

U.S. Bureau of Naval Personnel, *Cargo Handling*, Navpers 10124, 1948.

U.S. Bureau of Naval Personnel, *Principles of Stability in Shiploading*, Navpers 91076, March, 1949.

Washburn, George D., "How Safe Can We Make Our Tankers," *The Log*, January, 1953, pp. 44–50*ff*.

Wooler, R. G., *Tankerman's Handbook*, 2d ed., Edward W. Sweetman, New York, 1950.

CHAPTER 10

SHIP OPERATION: CHARTERS*

As explained in Chapter 2, transportation in ocean commerce may be provided by the common carrier, or general ship, offering berth or liner service, or by the tramp vessel. The common carrier lifts diversified, or package, cargoes. Cargoes that do not fit into the berth-line operation (grain, coal, ore, sulphur, phosphate, and sugar in bulk and at times in bags) move in bulk or shipload lots principally aboard tramp vessels.

In a common-carrier operation, the carrier (the shipowner) issues a bill of lading. Such carriage is now regulated in large measure by the Carriage of Goods by Sea Act (COGSA). This Act affords protection to the shipowner and the shipper and prescribes the issuance of a bill of lading, which serves at the same time as a document of title and a contract of carriage. The forms of bills of lading on a national basis are generally uniform, differing only in the inclusion of special "port clauses."[1]

When cargoes are suited to shipload lots, the whole space of the ship is furnished under a charter party, or, as the document is more generally called, a charter. The contract is one of private carriage, in contrast to the service offered by the common carrier, which offers space to all shippers.

CHARTER PARTIES DEFINED

The term *charter party* is derived from the Latin term *charta partita*, which, translated literally, signifies a divided deed or document. In the very early days of commerce by sea, means of communication were no faster than the vessels that plied between ports; in the case of a particular vessel with the particular cargo covered by the charter, interested parties usually had no word of the vessel between the time she sailed and the time she arrived. Therefore, in order to ensure that the document was genuine and that its contents were authentic, it was the custom to execute the contract in duplicate and to divide the document into two irregular por-

* This chapter was written by Frank J. Zito of Radner, Zito, Kominers & Fort, with the assistance of Robert S. Hope.

[1] For a general discussion of the bill of lading, see Chap. 7; for a discussion of the protection COGSA affords the shipowner and shipper, see Chap. 17.

tions, with each party taking one part. By matching the portions of the charter, they could be assured that it was genuine. Although this custom was not originally confined to contracts involving the use of vessels, the practice survived much longer in sea commerce than in other areas of trade, and the term *charta partita* finally referred by custom only to charter contracts.

Types of Charters. Charter parties, or charters, are contracts for the use of an entire vessel or of its cargo-carrying capacity. There are three forms of charters in general use. Stated in the inverse order of frequency, they are demise (bareboat) charters, time charters, and voyage charters. The three forms embody essential differences that may be stated very simply:

1. A demise or bareboat charter is a contract for the use of a bare boat, and the charterer is required to man, victual, and supply the ship and to perform functions normally performed by the owner. This type of charter was used extensively during both world wars, when the government took over the operation of privately owned ships. Since 1946, many government-owned vessels have been bareboat chartered to privately owned lines which assume complete responsibility for their operation. This program was necessary to handle the economic-aid cargoes that moved all over the world following the last war; since mid-1950, it has been required primarily to supply the United Nations forces in Korea and to carry North Atlantic Treaty Organization (NATO) and Mutual Security Agency (MSA) cargoes to Europe.

2. A time charter is a contract for the use of the cargo-carrying space in a vessel over a specified period of time. The shipowner pays expenses incident to the operation of the vessel (wages for officers and crew, insurance, food, and so forth), while the charterer is responsible for fuel and expenses connected with the cargo. Large steel companies may so contract for the use of ore carriers, and oil companies frequently time-charter tankers. However, if such companies have their own shipping divisions or subsidiaries (and therefore operating departments), they may prefer to charter ships under bareboat terms, which they cover into their owned fleets, and which they man, husband, and operate with their own personnel.

3. As its name implies, a voyage charter, the most frequently used, is a contract for the carriage of cargo not for a period of time but at a stipulated rate per ton, on *one* voyage between two ports or a fixed range of ports. The charterer assumes no responsibility whatever for the navigation of the vessel or the custody or safety of the cargo. Bulk cargoes are usually carried under this type of contract. For instance, a cargo of oil from Texas to the East Coast, coal from Norfolk to South American ports, wheat from the Gulf to Europe, ore from Trinidad to Baltimore, and

lumber from the Pacific Coast to Far Eastern ports are generally transported under this arrangement.

Contractual Nature. A charter party is essentially a contract, subject to the basic requirements of contract law. It must be the result of an offer and acceptance, it must have mutual obligations or promises, and there must be consideration, or mutual benefits.

Because of the historical and traditional development of charter parties as special types of contracts for use in ocean transportation, the decisions of admiralty courts and the customs, usage, and jargon of the sea have had their effect upon certain of the terms and conditions of these contracts, with the result that they defy interpretation except by those familiar with the trade. These terms and clauses have a precise and definite meaning to the owner of a vessel, the charterer or shipper, and the maritime lawyer. This certainty, which often does not exist in other fields of law, makes owners and charterers alike loath to deviate from the fixed forms. With relatively few exceptions, the only significant substantive changes in prescribed charter forms have resulted from governmental operation during wartime. There is considerable difference of opinion as to the "benefits" arising from such major revisions.

DEMISE OR BAREBOAT CHARTERS

Under a demise or bareboat charter, the vessel is normally tendered to the charterer as a dead ship, and the charterer is required to man, victual, and supply the vessel, and to perform every service that would normally be performed by the owner. For all practical purposes, the charterer is substituted for the owner and is designated as the owner *pro hac vice*, that is, "for this turn." Normally a vessel taken under a bareboat charter is included in the charterer's fleet of other vessels, either owned or bareboat chartered, and becomes an integral part of his fleet.

Wartime Development. Prior to World War I, the demise or bareboat charter was rarely used, and even today it is less common than time and voyage charters. This is primarily because it is a contract or method by which the owner "leases" the entire or bare vessel to another operator who desires to use the ship as a carrier. In short, it is usually an arrangement between two carriers rather than between a carrier and a shipper.

When the United States government entered World War I and requisitioned all merchant vessels, the government and the shipowners agreed that these vessels should be operated on a basis that would eliminate undue financial loss to the owner from the extraordinary risks of the war and from anticipated deviations from normal operations. The bareboat charter was peculiarly adapted to this end, since the charterer assumes all risks normally borne by the owner. In order to utilize their experience, the government turned the ships back to the owners, who operated them as agents for the United States.[2] In the interval between the two world wars, there was little need for the demise charter.

After the United States entered World War II, the government once more requisitioned private vessels—at first under time charter, but later under the far more desirable method of bareboat chartering with their owners operating their vessels as agents for the United States. After the war, there was a surplus of government-owned war-built vessels. The Merchant Ship Sales Act of 1946, which authorized the U.S. Maritime Commission (now the Federal Maritime Board) to sell vessels, also authorized the agency to demise-charter them to American private operators. The terms of such charters have been greatly influenced by the standard bareboat form developed by the War Shipping Administration and designated WARSHIP DEMISE. The basic terms have been generally adapted to commercial demise charters.

Nature of the Demise Charter. A bareboat charter may be compared to the lease of an unfurnished building—normally for a period of not less than a year, and at times for periods as long as ten to fifteen years. In most instances, the reasons motivating such a charter operation are the same as those that encourage the rental of "taxpayer" units by large chain stores, retail establishments, or manufacturers. For example, a manufacturer who has decided to stock-pile raw materials might need more warehouse space than he ordinarily maintains. Since he expects to need the facility for a limited time only, his need is not in proportion to the capital expenditure necessary for acquiring the property and for the risk involved in its ultimate disposal.

The bareboat-charter situation is analogous. The charterer needs a facility requiring a substantial capital investment—a whole ship fit for use in his business. A shipowner who charters out a ship is willing to finance the initial expenditure in exchange for a relatively small but no-risk return. The owner thus rids himself of the operation of the vessel and the attendant risks. The operator who charters in the vessel desires a ship that he does not own and does not wish to purchase. He is able to fill out his fleet without large capital outlay and to eliminate the risks of vessel ownership. Therefore, the terms of the demise form of charter are primarily dictated by the economic considerations that motivate such charters and the inherent problems of such an arrangement.

Since the charterer requires a vessel ready for operation and the owner must receive his vessel back at termination of the charter in good condition except for ordinary depreciation, the usual charter form begins with terms to meet these requirements. First, the owner warrants that, so far as due diligence can make it, the vessel is in class and fit for the intended

[2] On wartime operations of ships, see Chap. 22.

operation. To protect both parties, when the vessel is delivered on charter, she must be dry-docked and jointly surveyed by the parties. At that time, a report is made on the condition of the vessel, noting in some detail any deficiencies or damages in the ship or its equipment. In the government form of charter, and more and more in the commercial adaptation, there is a provision that this survey constitutes performance of the owner's warranty as to condition, except as to items noted as deficient or latent defects. In exchange for the owner's warranty, the charterer promises to keep the vessel in class, to perform routine maintenance and repair during the period of the charter, and to redeliver the vessel in the same condition as when delivered, ordinary wear and tear excepted. Therefore, at redelivery, the vessel is again dry-docked and surveyed. Because of these mutual undertakings, the reports of the two surveys assume great importance. If a particular deficiency was noted at delivery, the owner is responsible for it. If, however, it was not noted and did not result from ordinary wear and tear or from latent defect, the charterer is obliged to perform the repairs. At times it is extremely difficult to determine ordinary wear and tear and/or latent defect, and much controversy results. Since these are essentially questions of fact, they probably can never be explicitly spelled out in the terms of the charter.

All vessels have certain equipment aboard that is classed as either expendable or consumable. The expendable equipment such as rope, furniture, linens, bedding, and mattresses is usually included in the rate base and is for the charterer's use. He is liable only for loss or for damage above ordinary wear and tear. However, the consumable items such as food, stores, and fuel oil aboard must be purchased by the charterer upon delivery and by the owner upon redelivery.

The charterer's obligation to return the vessel is, in the event of loss, satisfied by insurance on the vessel. The type of insurance, amount, and underwriter are normally clearly defined in the charter. In the event of total loss, the proceeds are payable to the owner for distribution as the interests may appear, and if for a partial loss, are payable to the charterer. In addition, liability insurance (protection and indemnity) coverage is clearly defined as to type, amount, and underwriter.[3]

The bareboat form of charter will probably continue to perform a significant function in our ocean commerce. The basic form is now fairly well worked out, and has been tried and proved over a representative period. As long as international tensions exist, the government will probably retain ownership of a large reserve defense fleet to which it will add newer and faster vessels from time to time. Since there is fundamental opposition to the government actually operating these vessels, the bareboat-charter device will probably continue to play a major role in keeping

[3] P & I insurance is discussed in more detail in Chap. 18.

these vessels in operation. In addition, private operators have found it expedient to augment their owned fleets during seasonal booms and for special operations with vessels bareboat chartered from owners who have a slack period or who desire to assume as little risk as possible.

The United States demised vessels to operators to carry the UNRRA and ECA cargoes, the coal and grain relief cargoes to Europe and India, and the NATO military-assistance cargoes. Moreover, some intercoastal operators took government-owned ships and placed them on berth in their regularly scheduled common-carrier operations between the East and West Coasts of the United States. At the outbreak of the Korean War, the Maritime Administration bareboat chartered its surplus war-built vessels to steamship companies who manned, equipped, victualed, and operated the ships under time or voyage charter for the Military Sea Transportation Service of the defense establishment.

TIME CHARTERS

A time charter is a contract for the use of cargo-carrying space in a vessel, extending normally for a period of several months or a year or more. The charterer is usually a shipper who contracts for the use of cargo space over a period of time to ensure continuity of shipping space and uniformity of rates. Under this form of charter, the owner remains in complete control of the vessel and its operation, merely placing the ship at the disposal of the charterer. The owner remains responsible for the navigation and safe carriage of the cargo. A time charter may be compared to the lease of quarters in an apartment hotel; it is a relationship in which a completely packaged service may be obtained, as distinguished from the rental of a capital facility for operation, as under a demise charter.

In this form of operation, the charterer is particularly interested in the following factors that constitute characteristics of the vessel:

Speed of the vessel. Inasmuch as hire is paid for the elapsed time, the speed of the vessel is of utmost importance to the charterer.

Fuel consumption. The warranted speed of the vessel is normally coupled with a warranty of fuel consumption for that speed. This warranty obviously is of the utmost importance to the charterer inasmuch as he pays for the fuel.

Deadweight capacity of the vessel. The amount of cargo that the vessel may safely transport on a given voyage is a very important element in the computation of the charter hire payable.

Class of the vessel. The certificate of seaworthiness is important because of the arrangements for cargo insurance.

In addition to the foregoing, there are statements relating to other particulars of the vessel that vary considerably, depending upon the type of vessel and the cargo to be carried. The statements in connection with a tanker are quite different from those pertinent for a dry-cargo vessel. For the former, details are given as to whether she has heating coils and the grades of cargo she may handle and for which she is certified; for the dry-cargo ship, presence or absence of grain fittings and shifting boards, capacity of booms, and the like are important.

The provisions just discussed describe the characteristics of the vessel and outline the undertakings of the owner with respect to the physical state of the vessel. The remaining provisions of the time charter are generally standard. Typical of these are the following:

Duration. Both the owner and the charterer fix the time during which the vessel is at the disposal of the charterer. Except in instances where the duration is tied specifically to a single voyage, the dates are normally conditioned by the word "about." This is necessary because of varying weather conditions and loading and discharging facilities.

Trading limits and cargoes. The owner's insurance arrangements are conditioned upon the type of cargoes to be carried and the trading limits of the vessel. Certain voyage limitations are, therefore, set out in the charter and enumerated cargoes excluded. In addition, and irrespective of the trading limits, voyages are limited to those between two seaports; at times, the privilege is extended to load or discharge at berths having insufficient water to maintain the vessel afloat at all stages of the tide, provided, however, that the vessel may lie safely aground.

In times of international stress or under actual war conditions, there are other variable items of expense which are normally borne by the charterer. Generally, these include the payment of any extra war risk insurance premiums on the vessel or on the crew; bonus payments to seamen necessitated by areas to be traversed; extra insurance premiums necessitated by the trading of the vessel beyond the usual accepted insurance policy limits, and so forth.

Seaworthiness. The usual form of charter warrants that the vessel, upon her delivery, shall be in all respects seaworthy or that due diligence shall have been exercised to render her so. Seaworthiness, of course, is a comparative term, and the vessel may be fitted for the safe and efficient carriage of certain cargoes but totally unfitted for the carriage of other cargoes. This depends upon the nature of the cargo and its stowage requirements. Generally, however, the term means that the vessel must be in such condition as to be fitted for the intended service and to receive cargo with clean-swept holds and with cargo-handling equipment in efficient condition.

Obligation for expenses. The expenses in connection with the operation of the vessel and handling of the cargo are usually allocated to the owner and charterer as follows: (1) The owner is under obligation to pay for wages and expenses in connection with the crew, insurance on the vessel, food, provisions, and all deck and engine-room stores, and the cost of all repairs to and maintenance of the vessel. (2) The charterer is obliged to provide and pay for all fuel, port charges, pilotages, agency fees, and expenses in connection with the cargo.

Orders and directions. The charters provide that the master shall be under the orders and direction of the charterer and that he shall prosecute the voyage with utmost dispatch. The master is obliged to sign bills of lading for the cargo as presented, upon the usual condition that the charterer shall indemnify the owner from any consequences that may arise by reason of the master signing irregular or unlawful bills of lading.

Dissatisfaction with master or crew. Although the owner is under obligation to employ and furnish the master, officers, and crew of the vessel, the charterer reserves the right to demand replacement of the master, officers, or engineers, if he is not satisfied with the manner in which they perform their duties.

Tender of the vessel. Normally, the owner is allowed a range of dates in which to tender the vessel for service under the charter. If there is a breach of this condition, the charterer usually reserves the option of accepting the vessel or rejecting the late tender.

Hire. The charter hire is paid on the basis of the agreed value of the vessel per day and runs continuously from the time the vessel is made available to the charterer until the charter period terminates, except that charter hire is not payable for any time during which the inefficiency of the vessel prevents full operation. It is suspended during such periods unless the charterer was the cause of the inefficiency. The parties usually stipulate the currency in which the hire is payable, the exchange rate, and the terms of payment. Usually, charter hire is payable monthly in advance.

Breakdown clause. Inasmuch as charter hire is payable for the time during which the vessel is at the disposal of the charterer, it is extremely important that the periods during which the vessel is inefficient be excepted from that computation. Because of the importance of this clause, it is desirable to quote one of the generally accepted forms:

That in the event of the loss of time from deficiency of men or stores, fire, breakdown or damage to hull, machinery or equipment, grounding, detention by average accidents to ship or cargo, drydocking for the purpose of examination or painting bottom, or by any other cause preventing the full working of the vessel, the payment of hire shall cease for the time thereby lost; and if upon the voyage speed be reduced by defect in or breakdown of any part of her hull, machinery or equipment, the time so lost, and the cost of any extra fuel consumed in consequence thereof, and all extra expenses shall be deducted from the hire.

Exceptions clause. In a time charter, as in any other contract, the shipowner and charterer are unconditionally bound to perform their respective obligations or run the risk of being sued for damages unless there is an express agreement that the nonperformance of certain conditions will be excused. It is usual to stipulate a mutual release from liability occasioned by the happening of named events peculiar to ocean carriage. Because of the importance of this clause, we quote one of the generally accepted forms: "The act of God, enemies, fire, restraint of Princes, Rulers, and People and all dangers and accidents of the Seas, Rivers, Machinery, Boilers and Steam Navigation, and errors of Navigation throughout this Charter Party, always mutually excepted." Although liability is mutually excepted, the charterer still must pay for payment of charter hire unless the contingency is expressly incorporated in the clause that provides for payment of hire.

Arbitration clause. Because of the relative inexperience of many of the judges before whom the charter disputes would be presented and because of the customs of the industry, most charters contain an arbitration clause providing that commercial men be appointed as arbiters. If either party fails to submit to arbitration, aid by the courts is available.

Lien. The owner reserves a lien for payment of charter hire on the cargo carried and any subfreights due to the charterer; conversely, the charterer retains a lien on the vessel for charter hire paid in advance and not earned and for other overpayments.

Limitation of liability. Various statutory limitations of the owner's liability are customarily incorporated in the charter. In addition, the rights to general average are incorporated, and include not only new York–Antwerp rules[4] but also the Jason clause.[5] The Jason clause reserves to the owner the right to recover general-average contributions despite negligence of the ship's officers or unseaworthiness of the vessel if the owner exercised due diligence to furnish a seaworthy vessel or competent crew at the beginning of the voyage.

It is most important to remember that a time charter is a contract of affreightment in common use and that it is generally employed in situations where the demands of the charterer are for a comparatively long period. This discussion covers only the more important of the time-charter provisions. Other special conditions may be incorporated, depending upon the customs of a particular trade or upon business conditions at the time the contract is made.

VOYAGE CHARTERS

The voyage charter, the most frequently used form, is a contract for the carriage of cargo on one voyage between named ports or a range of

[4] See Chap. 18.
[5] See Chap. 17.

ports for a stipulated rate per ton of cargo carried or contracted for. As previously mentioned, such charters are generally used only in bulk trades, and usually only one shipper engages the whole of a vessel. Although the speed of the vessel is a factor in the choice of a particular ship, transit time does not affect the charter rate. The charterer assumes no responsibility whatever for the navigation of the vessel or for the custody or safety of the cargo. In essence, the charterer of the vessel under voyage charter has the status of a shipper only, as distinguished from a charterer under a time charter who has certain operational responsibilities and is also a shipper.

Because of this difference in relationship, the terms of the voyage charter vary considerably from those of the time charter. The voyage charterer, being a shipper, wants a "package deal." One of the basic differences between voyage and time charters is that the voyage charterer pays for the use of the vessel on the basis of a certain rate per ton of cargo actually carried rather than on a per diem or time basis. This rate is calculated to include all the additional expenses such as the cost of fuel oil, pilotage, and port charges. On the other hand, as mentioned above, under the time form of charter the charterer must pay these expenses in addition to the basic rate of hire. Also, because of the difference in the basic relationship between the charterer and the owner under the voyage charter, the legal rights and obligations of the parties are different. Therefore, in order to understand the distinctions between the two types of charters, it is necessary to discuss the usual terms of the voyage charter so that they may be compared with the provisions of the time charter.

The Form of the Voyage Charter. The two uniform charters in common use were drawn to meet somewhat different emergency situations:

1. *The Gencon form.* International trade increased tremendously after the turn of the century, in respect to both tonnage and variety of cargoes. For a time, established charter forms were employed, but later a form of charter was prepared for carriage of products not covered by one of the approved forms. This charter, designated as the Gencon, was first used in 1924 and revised in 1939. It afforded the shipowner a greater degree of protection than any of the other approved forms. By agreement, it has superseded many of the established forms and is in fairly common use.

2. WARSHIPVOY (Rev.). When all American-flag ships were requisitioned after Pearl Harbor, cargoes were carried by the United States government, represented by the War Shipping Administration (WSA).[6] Vessels were operated by agents (usually privately owned steamship companies), many of whom were experienced only in liner operations and who were not familiar with the multitude of voyage forms in general use. Identical cargoes were being carried under different forms of charters. As a result,

[6] See Chap. 22.

varying measures of liability and loading conditions were imposed. Therefore, a uniform charter, designated as WARSHIPVOY and later revised and known now as WARSHIPVOY (Rev.), was prescribed. This charter admittedly was designed to give the owner (WSA) the maximum control over and use of the vessel and to shield it, to the greatest extent possible, from liability.

Elements of the Voyage Charter. The contract terms may be divided into two major categories. The clauses falling in the first major subdivision define the responsibility in connection with the loading and discharging of cargo in so far as these responsibilities regulate the cost of performing those activities and the time allowed. These may be termed the *working provisions*. The clauses falling in the second major subdivision define the rights and liabilities between the charterer and the vessel in connection with the safe loading, carriage, and discharge of the cargo. For simplicity, these will be termed *legal provisions*.

There are more than a hundred different approved forms of the voyage charter, all carrying code names, and legal and working conditions vary for each. This is true even though there are many different forms of charter for the carriage of the same commodity. In addition, the case in which the approved form is not amended by either deletions or additions is rare indeed. To illustrate, the Chamber of Shipping of the United Kingdom has approved 49 voyage-charter forms for general use. The forms, codified in 1939 by the Chamber, are currently in use, with certain changes. Among the 49 forms approved are 7 for the carriage of wood; 16, ranging in date from a charter prepared in 1896, for the carriage of coal; 11 for the carriage of grain; and so forth.

Working Provisions. In the following discussion of the chartering arrangement, the order will follow that prescribed in the uniform charter approved for use by the War Shipping Administration on Aug. 15, 1944, and designated WARSHIPVOY (Rev.).

1. *Description of the vessel.* The charterer should know the classification of the vessel for purposes of cargo insurance; the draft of the vessel because of possible water limitations at either the loading or the discharging port; the capacity of the vessel for cargo on both a weight and measurement basis; and details concerning the number and size of hatches and the number and capacity of winches and derricks or booms.

2. *Description of the cargo.* This information is necessary to facilitate proper arrangements (*a*) for loading and/or discharging, (*b*) for separation of the cargo, (*c*) for proper receipt of the cargo dependent upon the form in which it is to be shipped (many commodities are shipped both in bulk and in bales or bags); and (*d*) for the attendance of surveyors or inspectors required by certain cargoes, and so forth.

3. *Loading and discharging ports.* A voyage-chartered ship may load

and/or discharge at one port or at a range of ports. If a range of ports, the owner may wish to except certain ports within the range or, because of loading or other conditions, he may, and usually does, prescribe a limitation in connection with the berths at which cargo is to be loaded. He may except those berths where the vessel may, at certain stages of the tide, necessarily lie aground.

4. *Freight rate.* The provision concerning freight is subject to many variations, among which are the following: (*a*) the currency in which freight is payable, (*b*) whether the freight charges are prepaid or collect, and (*c*) the point or time at which freight is earned. If the freight is collect, the owner must take whatever steps are desirable or necessary to ensure that it is collected before he releases the cargo or surrenders possession thereof.

As explained in Chapter 17, under American law, freight is not earned until the cargo is properly delivered at the port of discharge—unless express provision has been made therefor. Nevertheless, the voyage-charter agreement almost universally provides that freight is to be considered earned (*a*) at the time of loading on board the ship, (*b*) upon signing of bills of lading, (*c*) upon departure of the vessel, (*d*) or at some other point in the operation. Government cargo, however, is shipped on a different basis; regardless of charter language, freight is not earned unless the cargo is delivered.

5. *Lay time.*[7] Inasmuch as the use of the vessel is entirely at the disposal of the charterer, the period allowed for loading and the period allowed for discharging must be limited. The time will be fixed to accord with the nature of the cargo, loading or discharging facilities, labor conditions, and customs of the port. Among the various factors to be considered are the following:

a. Although the time allowed for loading and discharge is specific, it is usual to allow the periods to be averaged. It is possible, therefore, to credit the time saved on one operation to any excess of time used in the other. The principle is quite clear, but the means chosen vary considerably. For example, the parties may provide that "working time" shall be credited or that "time saved" may be credited. In the first instance, only the working hours within a working day may be credited, whereas in the latter case, all time (in or out of working hours and including Sundays and holidays) may be credited.

b. Upon arrival of the vessel at the loading or discharge port, the shipowner must serve "notice of readiness" upon the charterer, and the laytime period does not begin until such notice is received. The charterer is allowed sufficient time to make arrangements to bring the cargo alongside

---

[7] Lay time is the period specified in the charter and placed at the disposition of the charterer, for which the costs are considered in the charter hire.

the vessel, to assemble loading or discharging equipment and labor, and so forth. Among the variations in such provisions may be mentioned the following: notice must be in writing; notice must be received; notice must be received within working hours; and so forth.

c. If no provision is especially incorporated in the lay-time conditions—none is incorporated in WARSHIPVOY (Rev.)—any contingency occurring during the lay period that retards or suspends loading is entirely at the risk of the charterer. Examples are such happenings as strikes of stevedores, breakdown of equipment used in connection with loading or discharging the vessel, and fires. This holds true despite the fact that the charter includes a general-exceptions clause expressly stating that neither party will be liable for acts of God, strikes, fires, acts of war, and so forth.

6. *Demurrage.* This may be defined as the measure of payment to the shipowner in the event that the allowed lay time is exceeded. It is in the nature of freight money rather than a penalty. It may be fixed in a number of ways such as a lump sum per day, on a tonnage basis, or on a graduated scale.

7. *Dispatch money.* Generally speaking, the freight rate is based, dependent upon the market conditions, on the anticipated time for the voyage including the time in port. Any saving in that length of time is shared with the charterer in the form of dispatch money. That is, if the vessel is not detained for the full lay time allowed, a sum of money per day is allowed the charterer. Usually this is fixed at half of the demurrage rate. This is sometimes a sizable item.

8. *Stevedoring.* This clause carefully fixes the responsibility, which varies from charter to charter, for obtaining the stevedoring facilities and labor and for their cost. Briefly, provision is made for the following: (a) the responsibility for the supply and cost of dunnage, fittings, shifting boards, heavy-lift gear, and shore cranes; (b) the responsibility for the supply and cost of tally clerks, trimmers, and cleaners; (c) the cost of overtime for stevedores and winchmen, including overtime payable to the vessel's crew; (d) arrangement and expense for wares, samplers, and customs officials.

9. *Dues and wharfage.* The dues or fixed charges imposed by governmental or municipal authorities may be quite burdensome, and the charter should clearly indicate who is responsible for paying them. It is not always clear whether such dues or charges are applicable to the ship or to the cargo. In some instances, charges are based upon the cargo involved, but the dues are levied against the vessel because of ease of collection, since clearance may be held up pending payment. In other cases, an arbitrary charge is assessed against the vessel on a tonnage basis.

Such charges as wharfage, pilotage, or tug hire may be fixed as the responsibility of either the shipowner or the charterer, dependent upon the form of charter and upon the agreed rate. The same is true of lighterage, whether performed as an adjunct to loading at a pier or berth or loading in midstream because of draft, or other limitations.

10. *Canceling date.* The charter usually fixes a date before which the owner must tender the vessel to the charterer ready to load. This is necessary so that the charterer may make arrangements for alternate shipment if the vessel is delayed in arrival, breaks down, or is otherwise incapable of tendering. Although the charter usually provides an option to cancel or continue the time, the charterer must exercise this option within a reasonable time.

Legal Provisions of the Voyage Charter. Unless contract provisions are made to the contrary, a carrier by water is a virtual insurer of the right delivery of cargo. It is important, therefore, to define the limitations, exemptions, and exceptions that relieve the owner from this strict liability. As stated elsewhere, carriage under charter is "private," and the shipowner is not bound by the restrictions to protect shippers that are imposed on the owner of a common carrier. Despite this freedom of contract, the usual liberties and protection afforded the tramp type of carrier under most charters are considerably less than those contained in practically any bill of lading issued by a common carrier. Although some degree of uniformity might be expected to prevail in respect of the legal provisions, this is not the case. The following legal provisions are significant, with WARSHIPVOY (Rev.) again used as the model:

1. *Description of the vessel and voyage.* In the majority of charters commonly used, the vessel is described as being tight, stanch, strong, and in every way fitted for the voyage and service. It would not seem either necessary or desirable to continue that stringent condition, but instead, the conditional warranty applicable to common carriers would seem to be sufficient. The conditional warranty may be expressed in a variety of ways, the net effect of all being that the owner shall exercise due diligence to provide a seaworthy vessel. The advantage of the conditional limitation is obvious and in many cases spells the difference between liability and freedom therefrom.

2. *Limitation of liability.* By this provision, the owner as a rule incorporates most or all of the three primary statutory limitations of liability:

   a. The fire statute, which releases the vessel and owner from liability for loss or damage to cargo by reason of fire unless such fire shall have been caused by the owner's design or neglect. It is proper and desirable to provide for such limitation in respect of goods before loading and after discharge, in addition, of course, to the time during which the goods are actually on the vessel.

   b. Limitation of amount or exoneration from all liability. This provision incorporates the statutory exemption of vessel and owner from liability in excess of the value of the owner's interest in the vessel, in the event that loss or damage is caused without the privity or knowledge of the owner. That is, if the owner establishes to the satisfaction of the court that he exercised due diligence to furnish a seaworthy vessel, including the manning and equipment thereof, then, despite the negligent navigation or management by the officers of the vessel, the owner may limit his liability to the value of his interest in the vessel. In many cases, as in the event of collision or stranding, the owner's interest may be limited to the scrap value of the hull and freight then pending.

c. Limitation of seaworthiness. Many charters in common use effect a modified limitation of the express warranty of seaworthiness by incorporating the Harter Act, which was passed in 1893.[8] The better practice, however, might be to incorporate the Carriage of Goods by Sea Act, which affords the owner greater protection than does the Harter Act, and, inasmuch as its primary purpose was for the regulation of common carriage, there should be no objection on the part of any owner to its inclusion. Since the parties are free to contract as they will, the owner may secure the ultimate in protection by incorporating only those sections of the Carriage of Goods by Sea Act that are most desirable from the owner's point of view, namely, Sections 3(C), 4, and 11.

In any case, it would seem to be good practice to provide that such act should govern before loading and after discharge, in addition to the time the goods are actually on the vessel.

3. *General-average clause.* This provision has for its purpose the general outline of the provisions under which general average shall be adjusted and settled. This subject will be considered in Chapter 18 and need not be discussed at this point, except to caution again that the general-average rules have been recently amended, and as amended, should be incorporated.

4. *Amended Jason clause.* Under the statutory exceptions afforded the owner is exemption from liability due to negligent navigation on the part of the officers. It was decided in an early case, however, that although the owner was excused from liability he could not recover from the cargo owner his proportion of the general-average charges in the event of a general-average situation, such as a stranding resulting from negligent navigation. As a result, the Jason clause was devised to provide for recovery of general-average contributions in such a situation. This result may be accomplished only by express provision therefor. The clause commonly in use prior to the Carriage of Goods by Sea Act has been amended by deleting the condition that due diligence must be exercised to furnish a seaworthy vessel, and the amended clause should be used under all circumstances.

5. *Liberties clauses.* The primary purpose of this provision is to provide

[8] See also Chap. 17.

necessary freedom of movement to the owner of a vessel in the event of situations arising during the course of the voyage which might cause loss or delay—for example, war, insurrection, or strikes. Under the proper set of circumstances, the master may proceed to a substitute port and there discharge cargo or may even, in an extreme case, return to the original port and there discharge the cargo. Such discharge would be deemed a fulfillment of the contract voyage.

6. *Exceptions.* This provision has for its purpose a statement of the situations in which the carrier is excused from liability. In its inception, it was a *force majeure* clause and was limited in the main to acts of God, acts of war, the public enemies, and restraints of princes. Gradually it has been expanded to include latent defects, inherent defect or vice of the cargo, explosions, acts of neglect or default on the part of the master or officers or other servants, and a variety of others. Many of the exceptions formerly stated therein are now contained in the Carriage of Goods by Sea Act. As a result, the better practice recently has been to eliminate such exceptions from the charter provisions.

The foregoing discussion is not intended as a guide to those engaged in the "fixing" of voyage charters, nor is it intended for the student as a complete statement of voyage charter-party essentials. It is simply a brief discussion of some of the elements of such arrangements and a sketchy check list of the fundamentals. It would seem feasible and desirable to effect a general overhaul of the charter forms now in common use to the end that some uniformity in protection to both the charterer and the owner might be achieved and to dispense with the necessity of study of each fixture offered and the necessary correlation of the terms to the rate and amendment to conform with the requirements of the underwriters.

It should be possible to correlate the rights and liabilities so that they are uniformly fixed and adopted by charterers and owners, with the assumption that the terms would be given reasonably uniform effect in the various maritime countries. A uniform voyage charter would also benefit those indirectly involved, such as banks or other commercial institutions and endorsees or transferees of such documents. The desire and need for uniformity in shipping documents are evidenced by the interstate-commerce clause of the Carmack Amendment, the Federal Bills of Lading Act of 1915, which had for its primary purpose uniformity in bills of lading, and adoption subsequently by the various states of uniform bill of lading acts. The Carriage of Goods by Sea Act was the culmination of all such efforts and is, of course, international in scope. Further, there would seem to be little need to point out the advantages of uniformity which have been achieved by reason of the adoption of the York-Antwerp rules, the International Convention for Safety of Life at Sea, the International Salvage Agreement, and so forth.

OPERATION AND BROKERAGE

The operation of ships engaged in tramp activities and operating under charters differs somewhat from the operation of liners as described in Chapter 9. The tramp, to borrow an apt expression, is the "taxicab of the sea" and, of course, operates neither on fixed schedules nor on fixed routes. The berth operator in the liner trades advertises and maintains fixed schedules and employs a high percentage of its personnel in soliciting freight for its service. The representatives of these traffic departments are concerned primarily with dates of departure and arrival of the vessels and, to some extent, with the stowage factors of the package cargo booked.

In the tramp trades, the owner maintains no corresponding department. The peculiar characteristics of bulk cargoes, the adequacy of loading and discharging conditions and facilities, the customs of the different trades, the irregularities not only of departures and arrivals but also of ports involved, and the physical characteristics of such ports demand a degree of training practically impossible to find except in the office of a specialist. The ship broker is that specialist. Because of his accumulated experience, he is in a peculiarly advantageous position to offer help and guidance to the shipowner. In addition, the multiplicity of documents, the variations in them, and the special clauses providing for seasonal or geographic peculiarities require experience far beyond that which could normally be achieved by the personnel of a single steamship company. The ship broker is essentially the traffic representative of the shipowner. He is notified by the owner when a ship is available for the charter, and his first duty is to find a shipper who desires to charter the space in an entire vessel. On the other hand, the shipper who has a shipload of cargo for which he desires to charter a vessel is generally represented by a cargo broker who is, like the ship broker, a highly trained specialist capable of performing the required services for the owner of the cargo.[9]

It has been historically recognized in the tramp trades that the mutual interests of the owner and charterer are best served by a broker on each side representing the primary objectives of each of the parties. Even though the ship broker is the representative of the shipowner and the cargo broker is the representative of the shipper, the fees of both brokers are paid by the shipowner in an amount universally fixed as 1.25 percent of the freight moneys to each. The use of the services of the ship broker and cargo broker eliminates the need for the tramp owner to employ the great number of employees required for the freight solicitation, billing, and other clerical work, who make up the traffic department of the liner

---

[9] A cargo broker differs from a freight forwarder (see Chap. 8) in that the latter does not generally deal with shipload lots.

company. Further, the cost of the composite brokerage function is far less than it would be if such a department were maintained by the operator.

The primary functions performed by the two brokers are the following:

1. To determine the form of charter and special provisions that most nearly meet the needs of the particular transaction.

2. To negotiate the terms and conclude the charter on behalf of the principals.

3. To chart the vessel's position and availability for loading, and to synchronize delivery of cargo to shipside; to supervise the required notices of readiness and election of loading or discharging ports or berths.

4. To supervise preparation of demurrage and lay-days statements, payment of dues and customs at various ports, and settlement, in so far as possible, of disputes arising in this connection. Because of his knowledge of customs of the trade, commercial practice, and charter terms and conditions, the broker's services in this respect are invaluable.

5. To procure certification of freight invoices, arrange for surrender of bills of lading, facilitate collection of freight, and so forth.

6. To arrange for the appointment of outport agents and to issue appropriate instructions.

Since the appearance of the steamship, the United States has not normally engaged in tramp shipping. Foreign-flag tramps, however, have played a significant role in our foreign trade. For example, in 1939, roughly 1,000 Scandinavian ships, many of them tramps, called at United States ports to load and/or discharge cargoes. The wartime and postwar tramp-type operations of United States-flag ships were born of the needs of global warfare and the necessity of transporting postwar relief or emergency cargoes, such as grain or coal to Europe and grain to India. Many postwar emergency cargoes were carried in government-owned vessels chartered to private operators, but, for the first time in the nation's history, the United States has had a privately owned tramp fleet. The size of that fleet depends on what is termed a tramp and what an irregular operator.[10] In 1949, a Congressional committee investigating the American merchant marine estimated that there were 200 tramps operating under the American flag, and in the early 1950's one operating group had as its goal an American-flag fleet of 200 tramps.

The American tramp operator is beset with many problems, the primary ones being the high costs of American-built ships and of operating a vessel under the United States flag as compared with the operating cost of foreign competitors. The tramp owner has received a minimum of assistance from the government, and there has been no provision in existing merchant-marine statutes for the long-range support of this type of operation. As will be explained in Chapter 13, benefit payments, both the

[10] See discussion in Chap. 2.

operating-differential and construction-differential subsidies were limited to line operators serving on essential trade routes. The Long Range Shipping Act, passed in mid-1952, made all American-flag ships engaged in foreign commerce eligible for construction-differential subsidy. Since the close of the last war, tramp owners have thrived because of the large volume of tramp-type cargoes that have moved from the United States, but there is some question of whether an American tramp fleet can maintain itself under conditions that may be termed normal.

During the war and postwar period, the tramp owner and ship broker performed invaluable service to the United States by making available their experienced personnel to assist in the necessary shipping operations. The liner companies, which were also called upon by the government to act as agents and to operate vessels in what would normally be a tramp operation, were highly skilled and competent in so far as the operation and maintenance of vessels were concerned, but they too had to rely upon the ship broker to a large extent.

Emergency periods have well demonstrated the necessity for shipping operations offering the flexibility and availability of the tramp type of service. It is also generally recognized that the tramp operation plays an important role even in normal times. Therefore, knowledge of the three basic types of charter described in this chapter is essential for anyone who is going to be associated with any phase of overseas commerce.

BIBLIOGRAPHY

Benedict, Erastus C., *The Law of American Admiralty*, 6th ed., edited by Arnold W. Knauth, Matthew Bender & Company, Inc., Albany, N.Y., 1940.
Knauth, Arnold W., *Ocean Bills of Lading*, 4th ed., American Maritime Cases, Inc., Baltimore, 1952.
McFee, William, *The Law of the Sea*, J. B. Lippincott Company, Philadelphia, 1950.
Poor, Wharton, *American Law of Charter Parties and Ocean Bills of Lading*, 3d ed., revised by Raymond T. Greene, Matthew Bender & Company, Inc., Albany, N.Y., 1948.
Scrutton, Sir Thomas, *Charter Parties and Ocean Bills of Lading*, 15th ed., Sweet & Maxwell, Ltd., London, 1948.
Sprague, G. C., and N. Nealy, *Cases on the Law of Admiralty*, West Publishing Company, St. Paul, Minn., 1950.

CHAPTER 11

SHIP OPERATION: THE MEN

Ships are only as good as the men who operate them. Without men to load them and take them to sea, the largest and most magnificent of steamships would be little more than monuments to the ingenuity of their designers and builders. The working ship is an awe-inspiring thing, but men make her so.

We are here concerned with ship operation, more specifically with the *man* aspect of that operation, and not with labor problems and labor-management relationships. To discuss union rivalries, strikes and threats of strikes, jurisdictional disputes, and other aspects of what is called the labor problem would shift the emphasis from the men to issues. This chapter has deliberately been limited to the men's part in ship operation at dockside and at sea and not at bargaining tables.[1]

OFFICERS AND CREW

The duties of crew members are varied and responsible, concerned as they mostly are with the efficient operation and safety of ship, cargo, crew, and passengers. As modern ships have increased in size and complexity, the duties and responsibilities of the crew members have been altered accordingly.

The Master. The commander of a merchant ship, and the sole representative of management aboard ship, is the master, or captain. A master who is senior to all other masters of the line is usually called a commodore and commands the flagship of the fleet. Seafaring men of many nationalities have followed British seamen in calling the ship's master "the old man," although this bears no relation to the man's years or the color of his hair.

During the days of the merchant-shipowner, the master of a ship occupied a unique position. He usually owned all or part of the ship and her cargo. To be successful as a merchant-shipowner, the master had to be not only a skillful navigator and sufficiently adept as a leader of men to

[1] See also Chap. 16, "Seamen's Law."

maintain order and discipline on long, tedious, and often dangerous voyages aboard very small ships; he also had to be a merchant, a trader, and a businessman.

Modern communications have relieved the master of certain "business" responsibilities of the voyage. The traffic department now solicits the cargo and books the passengers. Overseas cable service and, more recently, ship-to-shore communication have enabled him to communicate with the owner of the ship. Although the steamship of today is directed from an office in one of the great commercial cities, and although the man on the bridge has been called a "push button" captain, he is still the master in every sense of the word. His is the ultimate responsibility for bringing the vessel, crew, passengers, and cargo to destination.

For him to discharge his responsibilities, wide authority is vested in the master. A voyage involves common interests, risks, and purposes on the part of persons and property embarked on that voyage. To assure successful completion of the maritime venture, the master must have the legal authority to control all interests. For example, under circumstances described elsewhere, maritime law permits the master to pledge the whole vessel and her cargo to secure repayment of funds borrowed to permit the voyage to proceed. This authority is little used today, when it is usually possible to communicate with the owner. However, the master and the master alone may decide when a general-average sacrifice of vessel or cargo is warranted. If a situation arises in which the venture is imperiled, the man on the bridge has been required to make the decision to jettison cargo or to ground the ship, and not the shipowner in a faraway port who does not know the circumstances. One wonders what effect ship-to-shore telephone may eventually do to this time-honored relationship.

Under maritime law, the master has the power to bind the owner by acts done within the scope of his authority in connection with supplies, pilotage, labor, stevedoring, towage, and so forth. He has definite responsibilities for the crew. He is required to see that they have sufficient provisions, proper medical care, and protection from unlawful violence, and he is criminally liable if he abandons sailors in foreign ports. If a disaster occurs at sea, he is the last man to leave the ship.

The responsibility of the master with respect to a competently manned ship cannot be exaggerated. Although he is first of all in charge of the navigation, care, and management of the vessel, in this age of specialization, most details of navigation and vessel operation are delegated to trained personnel, to whom the orders are relayed by the master's associates, the mates. Nevertheless, the captain bears final responsibility for seeing that all orders are carried out in all departments. The manner in which this responsibility is discharged will, at least in theory, determine whether the vessel is a taut, or well-disciplined, ship.

Although modern communications have relieved the master of certain responsibility, the modern ship has, at least in a sense, increased his responsibility. Today's ships, whether cargo or passenger, are extremely complex and represent an investment of many millions of dollars. Large passenger ships, which are virtually little cities afloat, at times present the master with problems and responsibilities he may not encounter when in command of a freighter. They operate on a tighter schedule than freighters, and since practically all ships now carry some cargo, the master must see that cargo is discharged and taken on without interference with the operating schedule, which has been published in advance and which his passengers expect him to maintain. During such operations, he must see to it that parts of the ship are marked off so that curious passengers do not enter dangerous areas. The passenger shipmaster

... must be a man of many parts. He must be a good housekeeper, a social arbiter, a diplomat, a practitioner of psychology—on occasion of psychoanalysis—a disciplinarian who must know the line beyond which discipline fails. He must, of course, be a navigator and to some extent an engineer, a spokesman at once of the firm that owns his ship and of the men who work aboard her, a student of world history, a man of vast sympathy and a talent of knowing when to say "yes" and when to say "no."[2]

Manning Scales. To ensure vessel safety, the U.S. Coast Guard is required by law to fix minimum manning scales for all ships documented under the American flag.[3] Generally speaking, merchant vessels are required by statute to have on board a minimum complement of licensed officers, able seamen, and qualified members of the engine department. Coast Guard standards do not cover the steward's department, and many merchant ships employ a larger number of men than the law requires in other departments. The size of the crew is dependent on the type of vessel and the service in which it is employed. Since the kind of cargo and number of passengers carried influence the size of the crew, considerable variation in manning practices occurs as between ships of the same specific design type. In a sample study made in 1948, the crews for C3 freighters ranged from 46 to 56, with an average of 51.

The crew of a ship is divided into three departments—deck, engine, and steward's—and into licensed and unlicensed personnel. As will be explained later, officers must have government-issued licenses, while unlicensed personnel must have certificates of service or efficiency.

---

[2] Commodore Robert C. Lee, then executive vice-president of Moore-McCormack Lines, at the American Merchant Marine Conference, sponsored by the Propeller Club of the United States, New York, Oct. 21, 1949.

[3] With respect to vessels having operating-differential subsidies, Sec. 301 of the Merchant Marine Act of 1936 empowers the Maritime Administration to incorporate in the subsidy contracts certain requirements as to minimum manning scales and wage and reasonable working conditions.

Deck Department. In addition to the master, the licensed deck department includes the mates. Before World War II, most freighters carried three mates, though the requirements of the large passenger liners called for larger deck departments. Since the war, a C-type freighter or vessel of comparable tonnage carries four mates—a chief or first mate, and second, third, and junior third mates. These officers assume responsibility according to their rank, and by the same token succeed the master in case of emergency. For example, if the master is unable to carry out his duties, the first mate assumes those functions.

The addition of a fourth mate to the deck-officer complement has made an executive officer of the chief mate, and he is in charge of the deck department's work and personnel. He is responsible for maintenance of the ship except for the engine and steward's departments. The other three mates serve as watch officers, with the second mate usually serving from four to eight both morning and evening, the third from twelve to four, and the junior third from eight to twelve, depending on the wishes of the master. On a four-mate ship, the chief mate is the cargo officer, the second mate is the navigating officer, the third mate has charge of the cargo plans, and the junior third is in charge of the ship's log.

The final responsibility for safe loading and stowage is the master's, and he has full authority to see that cargo is stowed in accordance with regulations and sound practices and that his ship is not overloaded. The details of this function, however, are delegated to the mates. In port, the chief mate works closely with the port captain, who is responsible for the dockside part of cargo planning. The other three mates work "cargo watches," which differ from sea watches in that they are eight-hour stretches. The mate on watch is in charge, but, if any emergency or deviation from the cargo plan should arise, he is expected to call the first mate, who remains aboard ship at all times when cargo is being handled.[4]

The unlicensed men of the deck department of an average C3 include a boatswain (or bosun), a carpenter, a deck-maintenance man, and nine seamen—six AB's and three ordinary seamen. The boatswain receives his work orders from the first mate and is responsible to him for the proper execution of orders and for the performance of work done by the seamen. The carpenter operates the windlass (anchor mechanism), sounds bilges, is responsible for battening down the hatches, and does general carpenter work. The able-bodied seamen steer the ship, stand lookout, splice, and do general work such as painting, cleaning, and scaling the ship. Both the deck-maintenance man and the ordinary seamen have maintenance duties on deck.

[4] If a ship is merely tied up at the dock or in the stream, relief mates may be put aboard to give the ship's regular mates time off.

Other Officers. Large passenger liners usually complement the deck officers listed with special staff captains, navigators, cadet officers, and so forth. All oceangoing commercial ships, even those equipped with ship-to-shore communications, are required to carry a radio operator licensed by the Federal Communications Commission. This operator, an officer so classified by act of Congress though not included in the deck department, is accountable only to the captain or to the officer of the watch. He is responsible not only for radio equipment but also for the communication system aboard ship, but not for visual signaling.[5] On some freighters, the operator also serves as purser and receives additional compensation for this work.

The purser is a staff officer whom the layman usually associates with passenger vessels; and indeed, large liners require organizations with a chief purser and a number of assistants. A purser is now frequently a member of the crew of freighters. Paper work for operating purposes has become so voluminous that masters and mates do not have time to handle it. Also certain countries require numerous and elaborate records, attaching a fine for missing or inaccurate documents. Whether the ship is a passenger vessel, a freighter, or a combination, the purser serves as the ship's clerk. On a passenger ship, however, his duties go beyond this, for he serves as custodian and as adviser on immigration and customs matters and assists the master in entertainment. His responsibility afloat is to the master of the ship and ashore to the accounting department of the steamship company.

Engine Department. The extremely complicated machinery and mechanical and electrical equipment aboard a modern liner have made the engine department very important. Steam and electricity have not only eliminated much of the manual labor but also have made ships more efficient and better places to live. Switches, levers, and buttons now do most of the work formerly performed by muscles. Manning the pumps used to be a backbreaking job for all hands. Today it means pushing a button, turning a valve, or throwing a switch.

The intricate and vital mechanical department of virtually the entire vessel is the charge of the chief engineer, who is responsible to the captain and the shipping company. His responsibilities include the main propulsion machinery and boilers, high-pressure and combustion control, water conditioning, refrigeration plant, electrical equipment and wiring, plumbing and piping, galley equipment, ventilating systems, and evaporators. He is responsible for the vessel's machinery both at sea and in repair yards in port. To do his job well, the chief engineer should be familiar with the stability requirements of the vessel and with the struc-

---

[5] Ship-to-shore radio communication, operated from the navigating bridge, was for a time in dispute as between the master and deck officers and the radio operator.

FIG. 8A. *Steel Designer.* Commissioned as the *Sea Hydra* in July, 1945, this C3 cargo vessel was assigned by the U.S. Maritime Commission to the Isthmian Steamship Company on a general agency agreement. The company purchased the vessel on Mar. 14, 1947, and renamed her the *Steel Designer.* She is employed in Isthmian's Far East round-the-world trade.

FIG. 8B. *Keystone Mariner.* Since she was delivered in 1952, the *Keystone Mariner,* the first of the 35 Mariners, has been operated for the Maritime Administration by the Waterman Steamship Corp. under a general agency agreement. She has been employed in the transportation of military supplies for our troops overseas and for our allies.

tural strength of the ship and machinery. "The chief" and his four or five assistants comprise the vessel's licensed engine department and supervise the work of the unlicensed engine personnel.

The engine room is operated by a licensed engineer who stands a four-hour watch. He is assisted by other qualified members of the engine department such as oilers, water tenders, firemen, wipers, junior engineers, electricians, and so forth, depending upon the size of the ship.

Steward's Department. The head of the steward's department is the chief steward, to whom the master delegates supervision of the food served, of supplies and galley, and of the cleanliness of living quarters. The master, however, must see that the steward and his staff "come through." The master of a passenger liner is particularly aware that the food served must meet the highest standards, for he knows that his ship is judged more by the quality of the table set than by any other one standard. The steward's department aboard a passenger liner may outnumber the rest of the crew. A C-type freighter with a total crew of roughly 47 or 48 men usually carries 10 men, including a chief steward, chief cook, second cook and baker, assistant cook, and 6 messmen and utility men.

The chief steward is responsible for supplies aboard ship and for fresh supplies bought at ports of call. With the chief cook, he prepares work sheets for meals, usually planned a week in advance. These include not only three meals a day but also coffee and a buffet. His responsibilities do not end with meals for the crew and passengers carried. He must keep count of the ship's laundry, check the clean linen issued weekly to the men, see that safety precautions are observed in handling galley equipment and hot foods, and on some ships supervise the "slop chest," which contains small stores to be sold to the crew.

PROVISIONS UNDER WHICH SHIPS OPERATE

As everyone knows, seafaring men are highly unionized, and their unions represent a variety of affiliations. Deck officers may belong to the National Organization of Masters, Mates, and Pilots (AFL), while radio operators belong either to the American Radio Association (CIO) or the Radio Officers Union (AFL) and pursers to the American Merchant Marine Staff Officers Association (AFL) or the Staff Officers' Association (AFL). Licensed personnel in the engine department belong to the CIO National Marine Engineers Beneficial Association or the AFL Brotherhood of Marine Engineers. Unlicensed personnel on the East Coast may be affiliated with the National Maritime Union (CIO) or the Seafarers International Union (AFL). On the West Coast, there is the independent Pacific Coast Marine Firemen, Oilers, Watertenders, and Wipers, and the AFL Sailors Union of the Pacific. The stewards are represented by the independent National Union of Marine Cooks and Stewards[6] or by the recently organized AFL Marine Cooks and Stewards.

Because the unions ordinarily are far stronger than individual employers, employers of maritime labor, including not only the steamship companies but stevedoring and terminal companies, have formed associations to represent them in their dealings with the maritime unions. On the East Coast, a committee functioning through the American Merchant Marine Institute negotiates with seagoing personnel for the bulk of the steamship companies on the Atlantic and Gulf Coasts, while the New York Shipping Association serves a like function with longshoremen. On the Pacific Coast, the Pacific Maritime Association negotiates for its membership with both seagoing and shore unions.[7]

The Contracts. Ships operate under the terms of standing agreements or contracts negotiated periodically by the parties concerned. Union contracts stipulate in minute detail the duties of men in the various ratings, and include working rules, provisions for base pay, overtime and penalty pay, and benefits. These various agreements are more properly the subject of industrial relations than of ocean transportation, but certain aspects need to be noted as they concern the shipowner.

First, before an American-flag ship can sail, her owner must have reached agreement with not one but a number of maritime unions, some of which are AFL, some CIO, and some independent.[8] This presents opportunities for jurisdictional rivalries and conflicting political ideologies —opportunities that are not present at least in so acute a form in industries employing labor affiliated with one labor group. Second, men with comparable ratings in different departments vie for parity. Efforts of the men to achieve and to maintain parity extend to base wages, working rules, overtime and penalty pay rates, opportunities to earn overtime pay, working conditions, and fringe benefits.

Hiring. The company owning or operating the steamship hires the masters, chief engineers, first officers, and first assistant engineers.

---

[6] The Marine Cooks and Stewards, formerly CIO, were expelled from that organization on Aug. 29, 1950, for alleged Communist leanings. The International Longshoremen's and Warehousemen's Union was expelled at the same time and for the same reason.

[7] Formed in 1949, this association took over the functions of two earlier associations —the Pacific American Shipowners Association, formed in 1936 to negotiate with seagoing unions, and the Waterfront Employers Association of the Pacific Coast, incorporated in 1937 to deal with shoreside labor.

[8] In early 1953, some of the unions were seriously considering amalgamating. For example, the AFL Masters, Mates, and Pilots and CIO Marine Engineers Beneficial Association signed a mutual-assistance pact calling for a merger under one charter, either AFL or CIO. The President of the CIO American Radio Association announced that his union would also be interested, if "the merger would mean more strength for the officers' unions."

Lower grades are usually hired through the union hiring halls, which supply crews by rotation.

In all Atlantic and Gulf ports, the predominant method of hiring longshore labor is the "shape-up,"[9] while on the Pacific Coast men are hired through union hiring halls. Opinions concerning hiring halls vary. Before a subcommittee appointed to investigate the problems of labor-management relations, Cyrus S. Ching,[10] director of the Federal Mediation and Conciliation Service, stated that he believed it fair to make two generalizations:

(a) All of the important unions in the industry excepting that representing the longshoremen on the east and Gulf coasts regard hiring halls as essential and indispensable to their security and survival as effective unions, and to maintaining that responsibility and discipline which a union should observe under collective-bargaining agreements.

(b) Employers in the maritime industry, excepting those engaged in stevedoring operations on the east coast and the Gulf coast regard well-run union hiring halls as either essential or significantly important for industrial stability in the industry. They express criticisms of some of the practices in vogue in such halls, desire to eliminate them, primarily by bargaining, but wish to continue to resort to union hiring halls as their source of manpower. Their attitude is most generally expressed by the phrase, "We do not want to go back to the 'shape-up.'"

An important effect of the union hiring hall is that it is designed to distribute such work as is available evenly among those registered for the purpose of obtaining it. This is important in an industry in which employment, both afloat and ashore, is highly casual. The constantly changing and intricate needs of the ships for crewmen mean that, even in time of high employment, some men will be "on the beach." By the very nature of ship movements, wide variations occur in the record of loading and discharging operations at a particular port. Every sizable port must have a longshore reserve, for a labor force that is adequate from 80 to 90 percent of the time may be inadequate during a peak period, particularly if it occurs over a week end.

The hiring hall has made a substantial contribution to the elimination of the worst aspects of casual employment. The closest approximation to the purely rotary system is probably to be found in the longshore-

[9] Under the shape-up system, men are hired twice a day, in the morning and at noon. See *Final Report to the Industrial Commissioner, State of New York from the Board of Inquiry on Longshore Industry Work Stoppage, October–November 1951, Port of New York*, Jan. 22, 1952, especially pp. 48–49. In early 1953, the unions took a vote, and the decision was against the shape-up. This followed the investigation (December, 1952, through February, 1953) of the Crime Commission of New York City. As of Dec. 1, 1953, at the Port of New York, longshoremen are required by law to be hired through "employment information" centers.

[10] *Maritime Hiring Halls*, Report of the Senate Committee on Labor and Public Welfare, 81st Cong., 2d sess., S. Rept. 1827, 1950.

men's hall on the Pacific Coast, where men are sent out to work on the basis of the principle first come, first served. Cargo handling is recognized as among the most highly casual of employments, for men are hired by the hour, not by the day.

Although seamen sign ship's articles for a particular voyage, they need not reregister and go through the hall after each voyage but may serve on the same ship continuously for as many voyages as they and the employer wish. Many men serving on ships employed on deep-sea routes serve two or three voyages and then lay over, after which they ship out again. After the war, opportunities for maritime employment were such that men who wished to sail were able to do so. An exception occurred during early 1950, when the West Coast unions representing unlicensed seamen "rotated" the jobs after a man had served two or more voyages. There are definite advantages to a low turnover in the ship's personnel. After several voyages, officers get to know their ship; although two steamships may have been constructed from identical plans, they differ in dozens of small but highly important ways. On the other hand, when the same crew has served aboard a ship over a long period, ship operators have found that "beefs" may bear little relationship to the situation aboard ship.

CERTIFICATES, LICENSES, AND TRAINING

The U.S. Coast Guard issues the licenses required for licensed personnel and the certificates required of unlicensed seamen. The Coast Guard also gives the examinations through which men obtain licenses or certificates. For example, a man who is at least nineteen years old can qualify for the certificate that marks him as a "blue-ticket" AB by serving a minimum of one year in the deck department and passing physical, written, and performance tests given by the Board of Merchant Marine Inspectors of the Coast Guard.[11] He may become a "green-ticket" AB by serving three years at sea or on the Great Lakes on a merchant ship of 100 gross tons or over and passing a practical test or by graduating from a school ship and serving twelve months at sea.

The Merchant Marine Act of 1936 provided that the United States merchant marine should be "manned with a trained and efficient citizen personnel." In 1938, Section 216 was added to that Act, authorizing and directing the Maritime Commission "to establish and maintain the United States Maritime Service as a voluntary organization for the training of citizens of the United States to serve as licensed and unlicensed personnel in American merchant vessels." The training program, started in 1938, was greatly expanded during the war years, and has been con-

[11] Only one-quarter of the AB's on a ship may be blue-ticket men.

tinued on a reduced basis since the war. The training program, currently under the Maritime Administration in the Department of Commerce, is divided into two categories identified as cadet training and maritime-service training.[12]

Cadet midshipmen, so called because each cadet is appointed as a midshipman in the United States Naval Reserve, are trained at the Merchant Marine Academy at Kings Point, Long Island, a permanent institution established in 1942. Candidates are selected from each state and territory on a quota basis and are required to pass examinations based on college-entrance requirements. During the four-year course, one year is spent in fundamental education, the second in active service on merchant ships of various types, and the last two at the academy. Graduates now receive bachelor of science degrees, are licensed either as third mates or third assistant engineers, and are appointed as ensigns in the Merchant Marine Reserve of the United States Naval Reserve and as ensigns in the United States Maritime Service. They may seek employment as deck or engineering officers on merchant ships, may apply for active duty with the Navy, may seek employment in the shipping industry, or may be employed by the Maritime Administration.

Cadet midshipmen are also trained at four state marine schools in California, Maine, Massachusetts, and New York, which are operated partially with state funds supplemented by Federal grants. These schools, three of which have a three-year course and one a four-year course, train licensed deck and engineering officers. Upon completion of the course, graduates receive degrees and are commissioned ensigns. Training at sea is conducted aboard training ships supplied by the Maritime Administration.

The Maritime Service provides retraining, upgrading, and refresher and specialist courses in all duties aboard ship for both licensed officers and unlicensed seamen at two training stations—Sheepshead Bay, New York, and Alameda, California. These courses assist officers and seamen to improve their skills and to achieve advance ratings. The men receive board and room plus all training and the use of recreational facilities at government expense. The United States Maritime Service Institute, also located at Sheepshead Bay, offers correspondence courses covering 46 deck, engine, radio, and basic subjects for the benefit of those eligible.

In the year 1952, 140 cadets graduated from the Merchant Marine Academy at Kings Point, Long Island, and 205 men from the four state maritime schools. A total of 4,609 completed refresher, upgrading, and specialist courses offered by the Maritime Service, and 908 registrants

[12] The reports of the Maritime Administration give current information on the training program.

completed 1,211 correspondence courses with the Maritime Service Institute.

WAGES, HOURS, AND WORKING CONDITIONS

Although the United States government has a substantial interest in the American merchant marine, it collects and issues virtually no statistics on the earnings of seamen. To make such information available, the Association of American Ship Owners made a careful study of earnings of seamen on 18 separate and representative voyages. The investigation covered the earnings of 630 crew members for a total of 27,871 voyage man-days. Total earnings ranged from $342.90 per month for the wiper, the lowest rating in the engine department, to $630 per month for the chief electrician (see Table 6).

Neither these earnings nor the percentage that overtime adds to the base pay are unusual. The Sept. 21, 1951, issue of *The Seafarers Log*, official publication of the Sailors International Union, printed pay vouchers for an able seaman who served for thirty-seven days aboard a tanker. He earned a total of $777.70, of which $456.09, or 58.6 percent, was in overtime pay. *West Coast Sailors*, published by the Sailors Union of the Pacific, reported that a boatswain on a forty-five-day voyage earned $946.50 monthly, while an able seaman earned at a rate of $593.90 monthly. Seamen's wages compare very favorably with those for shoreside workers. In January, 1952, the average wage for workers in all manufacturing was, according to the Bureau of Labor Statistics, $287.87. Earnings of the ordinary seamen, the wipers, and the messmen—ratings that require no previous sea experience and no training—were above that level.

The base wage of a seaman cannot be taken as a measure of his earnings, because overtime may add 50 percent or more. On Dec. 15, 1951, the work week at sea was reduced from forty-four to forty hours. This meant that watch standers (mates, seamen, firemen–water tenders, and oilers), who had previously been paid overtime for watches on Sundays and holidays, were also paid overtime for Saturday watches. To maintain parity for the so-called dayworkers, amounts ranging between $15 and $30 per month were added to their base pay in lieu of the extra overtime earned by watch standers.[13]

Maritime wage contracts are a maze of overtime, penalty pay, and bonus provisions. Seamen are entitled to penalty pay under a variety of circumstances such as missing part of a meal hour or performing a number of unpleasant tasks. A seaman is entitled to penalty pay when

[13] A dayworker aboard ship is a crewman who does not work watch hours. The eight-hour day of dayworkers in the deck and engine departments usually starts at 8 A.M. and finishes at 5 P.M., Monday through Friday, while the hours of men in the steward's department must, of necessity, be broken.

he is called upon to perform such unpleasant work as cleaning tanks for transporting fluid cargo; cleaning holds used to transport penalty cargo (fertilizer, sulphur, carbonblack, arsenic, and creosoted lumber); cleaning major oil spills; going on the dock to handle, connect, or disconnect hose;

Table 6. Average Gross Earnings of Unlicensed Ratings on 18 Voyages, 1951 and 1952

Ratings	Monthly base pay	Average monthly earnings	Overtime as percentage of base pay
Deck department:			
Boatswain	$333.73	$518.70	55.43
Chief electrician	418.72	630.00	50.46
Assistant electrician	329.48	484.20	46.96
Carpenter	299.51	477.60	59.46
Plumber/machinist	342.14	461.10	34.77
Deck maintenance	276.21	419.10	51.73
Able seaman	262.89	414.30	57.59
Ordinary seaman	226.26	378.60	67.33
Engine department:			
Junior engineer (dayworker)	332.81	512.70	55.40
Engine maintenance (dayworker)	332.81	455.10	36.74
Junior engineer	299.51	432.30	44.34
Deck engineer	299.51	391.80	30.81
Engineer, utility	299.51	370.20	23.60
Fireman	262.89	409.20	55.65
Oiler	262.89	398.70	51.66
Wiper	259.56	342.90	32.11
Steward's department:			
Steward	325.63	507.30	55.79
Chief cook	299.51	465.90	55.55
Second cook and baker	272.87	411.90	50.95
Assistant cook	259.56	395.10	52.22
Utility man	226.26	365.10	61.36
Messman	226.26	358.80	58.58
All unlicensed ratings	267.71	411.00	53.75

SOURCE: *Shipping Survey*, Association of American Ship Owners, March, 1952, Vol. 8, No. 2. Average gross earnings were adjusted to give effect to the additional overtime that would have been earned on voyages before Dec. 15, 1951, the date when the forty-hour week became effective and the $30- and $15-per-month increases recently negotiated for dayworkers (in lieu of additional overtime watch standers may earn under the forty-hour week) so as to make earnings figures completely current.

or cleaning bilges. If this work is done during his regular working hours, the penalty rate is added to his base pay.

These earnings, moreover, do not include the total benefits to the ship's crewmen. They may purchase supplies from the ship's slop chest at prices considerably lower than those charged ashore. Additional expenses that benefit the men and add substantially to the total labor cost of ship operation include board and lodging valued conservatively for tax purposes at $1.20 per day per man, but costing substantially more;[14] paid vacations of two to three weeks per year for each seaman; 50 to 60 cents per day per seaman to jointly administered welfare and pension funds; social-security payments; and various other allowances and payments to which the seaman is entitled by virtue of his maritime employment.

In addition, as of early 1953, war bonuses are still paid on all ships entering European or Mediterranean waters ($2.50 per day per man) and west of the 180th meridian in the Pacific. Further war bonuses, amounting to 100 percent of monthly wages, are paid while ships are in the area of the China coast or Korea. Crews of ships entering any of these areas are covered by war risk life and injury insurance. Also, penalties of 10 percent of basic wages are paid when explosive or other penalty cargoes such as hides or sulphur are carried.

For a number of years after the close of World War II, cargo movements were heavy enough to permit American shipowners to absorb the high and rising costs of maritime labor. The government absorbed, and will continue to absorb, the difference between wages on American ships and on foreign-flag competitors for subsidized operators. However, when conditions again become competitive, prospects are indeed grim for the nonsubsidized American-flag common carrier. Nor are the prospects bright for the domestic coastwise and intercoastal operator, whose very existence depends on lower rates, which cannot be achieved without lower operating costs.

LABOR COSTS IN THE TOTAL COST OF SHIP OPERATION

In 1950, Captain P. Garoche of the French Line published in a United Nations publication figures indicating that 43.5 percent of cargo receipts go to pay labor costs involved in ship operation.[15] Because the costs of manning an American ship are higher than those for a foreign ship, the crew's wages aboard an American-flag ship are considerably higher than the 13.5 percent listed in the tabulation, which is obviously for a foreign-flag ship.

---

[14] The unions themselves in their contracts place values of from $8 to $10.50 per day on meals and lodging, and ask for that amount in cash whenever a shipowner is unable to supply meals and lodging in port. See "Wage Trends in the Maritime Industry," *Shipping Survey*, Association of American Ship Owners, November, 1951, Vol. 7, No. 4.

[15] "Importance of Handling Charges in a Ship's Operating Costs," *Transport and Communications Review*, United Nations, April–June, 1950, Vol. 3, pp. 15–18.

Expense item	Percentage of cargo receipts
Crew	13.5
Supplies	2.0
Repairs and maintenance	4.0
Fuel	5.5
Ship insurance	3.0
Cargo insurance	1.0
Other operating costs	1.0
Agents' fees and commissions	1.5
Port charges and wharf dues	3.0
Other port charges	2.0
Handling	30.0
Other freight charges	13.0
Brokerage	1.5
Amortization	7.0
Interest on invested capital	5.0
Dues and taxes	2.0
Administrative expenses	3.0
Publicity	1.0
Reserves	1.0

A study made in 1949 by the Pacific American Steamship Association indicated that the wages of seagoing labor were responsible for 22 percent of the costs of ship operation for West Coast operators and that total labor costs amounted to more than 50 percent. Both sea-going and shore labor have received several pay increases since 1949.

In 1952, a study was made of 1938 and 1952 operating costs covering the intercoastal operations of one company. Crew wages represented 8.5 percent of revenue in 1938 and 9 percent in 1952. In 1938, cargo handling used up approximately 31 percent of revenue, to rise in 1952 to 51 percent.[16] The company found that increases in revenue had kept pace with increases in costs except the cost of cargo handling. Such high handling charges are understood only in the perspective of the shipping operation. Cargo is moved a few hundred feet in port in order that it may be transported perhaps 2,000 to 7,000 miles by water. For every foot it is moved in port, it moves from 10 to 35 miles at sea.

The costs of cargo handling are accounted for only in part by increases in the hourly wage rate (longshoremen received 95 cents per hour in 1935; by 1952, they got $2.10 for straight-time work). As the cost curve has tended upward steadily, the output curve has gone equally steadily downward. If a ratio of 1 to 1 is taken for costs in relation to output

---

[16] Increases in revenue of 1952 are due not only to increases in rates but also to a decrease in the movement of low-rated cargo and to other factors.

Another cost study of an intercoastal operation showed that the stevedoring cost was $3.32 per ton in 1939 and $10.62 in 1951. See *Shipping Survey*, Association of American Ship Owners, November, 1951, Vol. 7, No. 4.

for the late 1930's, the ratio is now at least 3 to 1 and probably closer to 4 to 1.

Some ports and companies have greatly increased their investments and facilities, but output has nevertheless decreased. Performance on the prewar level, which ship operators then did not think was good, would mean a saving of roughly $6 per ton. Responsibility for the current situation must be shared by labor and management. Management has not always shown the desired initiative. For the workers' part, there are such factors as limitations on the size of sling loads and on the number of sling loads per hour as well as an unwillingness, born of depression-days thinking that "work" could and should be made, to accept improved methods.[17] Unless such conditions can be remedied, they destroy the incentive to improve equipment. Some innovations such as palletizing and the use of reusable metal containers have occurred, but the costs of cargo handling remain one of the greatest problems faced by the industry today.

Much of the continuous increase in hourly wage rates in the United States has occurred because of increased productivity of labor per hour of manpower. This increased productivity has been dependent upon machines to increase production per man-hour. It needs to be recognized that, when the general upward tendency of wages has carried with it the wage level of workers in an industry of low productivity, that industry tends to become marginal in nature.

BIBLIOGRAPHY

In addition to sources mentioned in the footnotes, the following may be of interest.

Eliel, Paul, "Labor Peace in Pacific Ports," *Harvard Business Review*, July, 1941, Vol. 19, pp. 429–437.

Labor-Management Relations, West Coast Maritime Industry, Report of the Joint Committee on Labor-Management Relations, 80th Cong., 2d sess., Rept. 986, Part 5, 1948.

Lawler, P. F., "Crisis in the Domestic Shipping Industry," *Harvard Business Review*, January, 1946, Vol. 24, pp. 258–276.

Phelan, Edward, "ILO Activities in the Field of Transport," *Transport and Communications Review*, United Nations, October-December, 1948, Vol. 1, pp. 35–38.

Powell, L. H., "Industrial Relations in the British Shipping Industry," *International Labour Review*, June, 1952, Vol. 65, pp. 681–702.

Riesenberg, Felix, *Standard Seamanship for the Merchant Marine*, 2d ed., D. Van Nostrand Company, Inc., New York, 1936.

---

[17] For example, when standard-unit loads of lumber were loaded and discharged by West Coast water carriers and the output per gang thereby increased from 8,000 board feet to 80,000 board feet per hour, the carriers met with union opposition.

———, *Seamanship Studies for Young Officers*, D. Van Nostrand Company, Inc., New York, 1939, 6 booklets.

Spector, E. P., "Manpower Problems in the American Merchant Marine," *Monthly Labor Review*, November, 1951, Vol. 73, pp. 564–567.

"The Maritime Unions," *Fortune*, September, 1937, Vol. 16, pp. 123–128*ff*.

Wissmann, R. W., *The Maritime Industry—Federal Regulation in Establishing Labor and Safety Standards*, Cornell Maritime Press, Cambridge, Md., 1942.

CHAPTER 12

ORGANIZATION AND MANAGEMENT

The prevailing form of operating concern in the United States shipping industry is the corporation. Sole proprietorship of one or more vessels and partnerships, both of which were popular and common in the United States and Great Britain during the nineteenth century, became inadequate as regards capital and service when liner operations replaced the services of the merchant-trader-shipowner. The joint-stock company or association is a far more common form of business ownership in Britain than in the United States, because it places a special burden on the owners and the shares and embodies practically no advantages over the corporation.[1]

The company whose organization and management setup is used as an example operates in the Atlantic, Pacific, and Indian Oceans; carries both passengers and cargo; engages in subsidized and unsubsidized operations; serves in foreign and domestic commerce; and belongs to more than 60 shipping conferences and at least 8 maritime trade associations. To maintain its services, the company operated 22 vessels as of October, 1952—of which 17 were company owned and 5 chartered.[2]

Management of a steamship company is faced with many problems that do not arise for a nonregulated industry. Because the company serves on certain subsidized routes, the Maritime Administration often

[1] The reader who is not familiar with some of the terminology used in this chapter may wish to consult W. H. Newman, *Administrative Action: The Techniques of Organization and Management*, Prentice-Hall, Inc., New York, 1951, or Paul E. Holden and others, *Top-management Organization and Control*, McGraw-Hill Book Company, Inc., New York, 1951.

[2] In this discussion of organization and management for liner operations, a well-known American company, the American President Lines, Ltd., is used. Company organization is described as of late 1952. It should be recognized that the organization and management of a company are never static; shifts in operations are certain to result in changes in organizational structure, and special arrangements are frequently made to utilize the abilities and talents of exceptional men.

It should be noted that during 1953 the departmental organization of the company discussed underwent change. The trend appears to be toward greater centralization of control—a development that would lead to fewer departments than the nine discussed here.

has a good deal to say on such matters as scheduling, accounting, construction of new ships, and the reports required.[3] In domestic operations, the Interstate Commerce Commission is the regulatory body.[4] Moreover, various agencies of the United States government have promulgated laws and regulations that affect the shipowner, and other countries dictate limits and procedures with which a company engaged in foreign commerce must comply. Membership in associations and conferences means that the company must join in adhering to and supporting the over-all policies established by those organizations. Contracts with other parties, particularly with the unions, provide a framework within which the business of the company must be carried on. In the steamship business, management must be particularly aware of the framework within which it must operate to carry out its day-to-day decisions and routine.

COMPANY CONTROL

Our organization is a carrier by water of freight, passengers, and mail. As in any corporate enterprise, the stockholders elect the directors, and the directors in turn elect the officers responsible for administering company policies.

Nine Departments. To carry out the various functions of its steamship operations, the company has set up nine departments, each presided over by an executive: freight traffic, passenger traffic, operating, finance, public relations, claims, service and supply, general, and research. The freight and passenger traffic departments are the revenue-producing departments, while the operating department is the so-called production department of the company. Since a very high proportion of the company's total expenditures is to defray costs of activities carried on by the operating department, its degree of efficiency and economy is a major factor in determining whether the business reflects a profit. The finance department is responsible for all financial and accounting aspects of the business. Without proper control over its moneys and assets, a company may find itself in dangerous shoals, if not upon the rocks.

The claims department investigates claims for damaged and lost cargo, ascertains the extent of the company's liability, and negotiates settlement of all claims except those in which a wide divergence of view requires court action for determination. In addition, it analyzes past claims and recommends corrective action against future losses. The service and supply and general departments are common-service organizations, the first of which is for central procurement and the latter for

[3] For a discussion of the Maritime Administration and its functions, see Chap. 20.
[4] A company engaged in common-carrier operations in domestic waterborne commerce must obtain a "certificate of convenience and necessity" from the ICC. The regulation of domestic water carriers is discussed in Chap. 19.

general office management and shoreside industrial-relations work. The over-all functions of the research and public-relations departments are obvious from their names.

Five of the nine departments (freight traffic, passenger traffic, operating, finance, and public relations) are presided over by vice-presidents. A vice-president is located in Washington, D.C., and three area divisions (the Eastern division, Far Eastern division, and Southwestern division) are headed by men of vice-presidential rank.

One matter to be borne firmly in mind when studying the organization and management of a steamship company is that the geographical scope of operations has a profound effect on organizational structure. In the case of the company under discussion, operations are world wide, and management is required to assure adequate representation throughout most of the world. The company's executive office (San Francisco) is headquarters for the nine departments organized for operational purposes and from which basic company policies are promulgated. Offices are also maintained in Boston, New York, Cleveland, Washington, Chicago, Los Angeles, Honolulu, Tokyo, Yokohama, Kobe, Osaka, Manila, Hong Kong, Singapore, and Genoa. In addition, the company has owner's representatives in Djakarta in Java and Colombo in Ceylon and is represented by commercial agents throughout most of the globe.

At Manila, headquarters for the Far Eastern division and for over-all operations in the Orient, a vice-president heads a divisional organization that is in many respects a diminutive replica of the principal executive office. Much the same is true of the office at Genoa, headquarters for the European division, which is under the supervision of a managing director. Manila and Genoa may be termed focal points for operations in broad geographical areas, and the structure of the divisional organization reflects their importance. At other points of lesser importance, management's representation reflects the scope and nature of operations as to both size and nature of personnel.

Authority and Responsibility. Throughout the company, a line, staff, and functional organization has been adhered to. Each department is organized on a functional basis and exercises line authority within the scope of departmental authority. Executives who administer the company's policies and activities in their particular areas have been delegated line authority, and personnel working in those areas report to their superiors administratively. Functionally, however, key personnel may report to San Francisco. For example, a key man dealing with passenger traffic in the company's Far Eastern division reports administratively to the vice-president of that division but functionally to the vice-president in charge of passenger traffic in San Francisco. When he communicates directly with headquarters in San Francisco, he keeps the vice-president

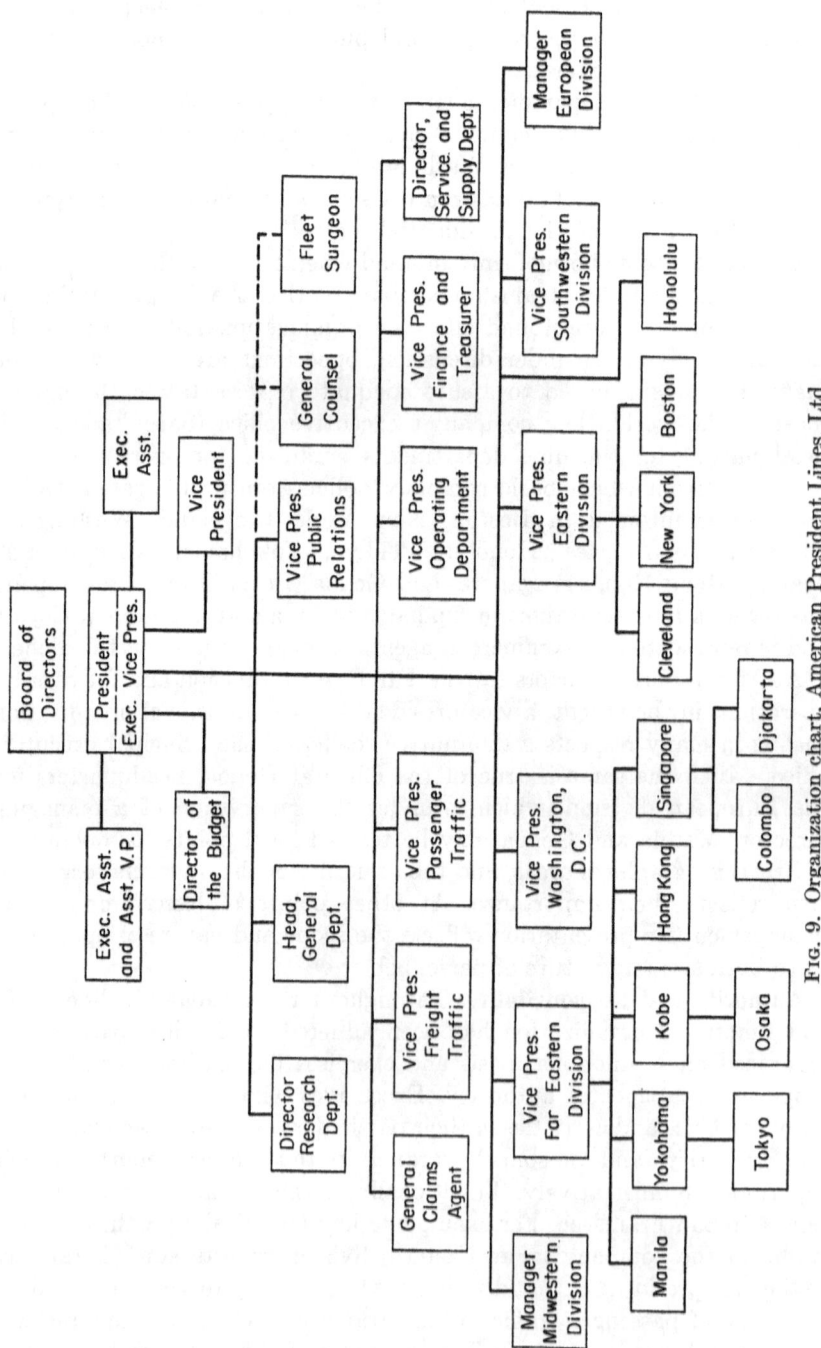

FIG. 9. Organization chart, American President Lines, Ltd.

of the Far Eastern division informed by copies of communications. Similarly, headquarters in San Francisco may communicate directly with passenger traffic personnel in the Far Eastern division, keeping the vice-president of that division informed by copies of communications.

Executive Branch. The president of a large company is responsible for company-wide operations. The president of a steamship company is also responsible for coordinating a great variety of matters that either are peculiar to the shipping business or take on greater importance for a steamship company, including governmental relations, regulatory affairs, the geographical spread of operations, and labor relations. To assist the president in his over-all direction of the administrative and operational affairs of the company, the executive branch includes various assistants to the president. In late 1952, the heads of the nine departments discussed in this chapter reported to an executive vice-president (see Fig. 9).

FREIGHT TRAFFIC DEPARTMENT

Chapter 7 has already discussed the problems of freight traffic management, not only of securing volume of cargo but also of securing well-balanced cargoes offering the best possible average rate per ton from a company-wide point of view, consistent with company policy and shipper requirements. Here we are concerned with the organization of the department that carries on this phase of the company's business and its relationship to the rest of the organizational structure.

The activities of the department are centered around the vice-president in charge of freight traffic, who is also a member of the board of directors. Because his duties are large, he devotes himself in so far as possible to administrative work, leaving the detail work to personnel of his department.

He confers with the vice-presidents in charge of operations and passenger traffic on all matters relating to sailing schedules, utilization or modification of ships, design of new ships, and acquisition or release of ships. From the operating department he obtains advice on vessel expenses, cargo-handling costs, port charges, dispatch conditions, and other factors pertaining to the physical operation of the vessels. Close liaison exists between freight traffic and operations, because these two departments together carry out the contractual agreements with shippers. The vice-president of freight traffic consults the finance department for date and statistics in regard to net operations and for cashier's services in collecting and disbursing moneys. Although claims are the province of the claims department, the vice-president of freight traffic takes an active part in the settlement of claims and works closely with the manager of that department to ensure fair, prompt, and friendly treatment of shipper claimants.

To administer the detailed work, the freight traffic department has three major subdivisions: sales, traffic, and traffic administration, each of which is headed by an assistant vice-president directly responsible to the vice-president of freight traffic. These three divisions function on a company-wide basis; that is, they coordinate all sales and traffic functions of, and exercise functional jurisdiction over, the sales and traffic of local offices and agencies located throughout the world.

Freight personnel are located at all of the company offices mentioned earlier. In addition, there are agents located throughout the United States in such places as Dallas, Galveston, Houston, Memphis, New Orleans, Seattle, Detroit, Baltimore, Norfolk, Philadelphia, Rochester, and San Diego. Overseas, the company has agents located in many places, including Japan, the Philippines, Formosa, Indonesia, Malaya, French Indochina, Ceylon, India, Burma, Pakistan, the Near East, Egypt, Palestine, Lebanon, Greece, Italy, Spain, France, the United Kingdom, Cuba, Panama, and Guam. In total, the company has 246 offices and agents rendering freight service to shippers in many corners of the globe.

Freight Sales Division. The assistant vice-president in charge of freight sales is responsible for a modernized freight sales program that establishes specific freight sales quotas for each company office and agent. He prepares and issues instructions concerning these sales quotas, and instructs company offices and agents in the steps to be taken in assigning the quotas to individual sales representatives. He plans and directs an educational program that is administered at the local level by the head of the freight sales staff, maintains a constant review of the performance of all local freight offices, and coordinates the sales activities of all offices. He also directs a company-wide survey of all shippers and consignees to furnish the information required to develop fully existing and potential freight accounts.

Traffic Division. The assistant vice-president who heads the traffic division is in reality responsible for the physical handling of the fleet and cargo. It is true that the operating department runs the ships, but the ships follow the cargo. The most important function of this division is to coordinate the freight service operations throughout the company's system and to do so in a manner that will obtain maximum utilization of various ships. Usually these operations fall within the framework of established rates and sailing schedules, but the traffic division is often called upon to consider and act upon requests from freight divisions that call for (1) special calls at nonscheduled ports, (2) handling unusual cargoes, (3) booking unusual amounts, (4) detaining ships for additional revenue, and so forth. To assist the assistant vice-president in charge of the traffic division, the traffic division at company headquarters includes three sections.

The rates and conference section maintains appropriate records of all freight tariffs used throughout the company's system and formulates, prepares, and issues those tariffs when they are not issued by conferences.[5] It serves as a main link between the company and the various conferences of which the company is a member, and keeps management constantly advised on all conference matters, relationships, and rulings—a function

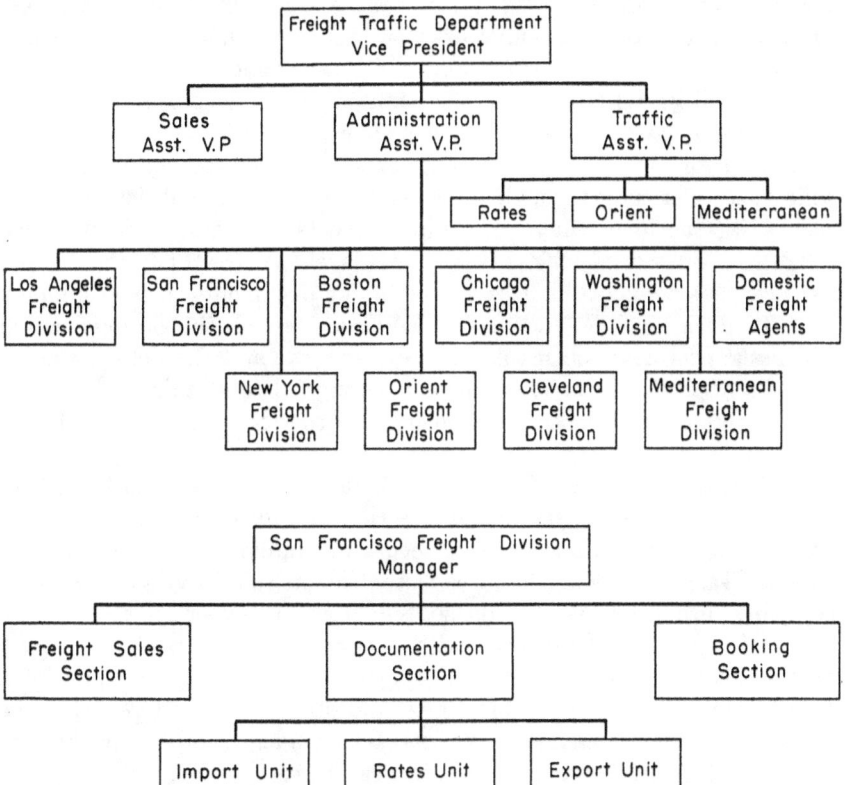

FIG. 10. Organization of traffic department, American President Lines, Ltd.

quite necessary if top management is to implement company policies within the orbit of steamship conferences.

The other two sections—the Orient section (Japan through Pakistan) and the Mediterranean section (Suez through Gibraltar)—are organized to achieve efficient traffic administration in broad geographical areas. Personnel in these sections constantly review sailing schedules, with a view to recommending action when conditions require changes in schedule, and maintain (at the request of management) data concerning various

---

[5] As explained elsewhere, a freight tariff is the composite of freight rates. For a discussion of rates and conferences, see Chap. 19.

services and trade routes. Operationally, they prepare instructions for the local freight divisions concerned with respect to company policy and procedure on various freight matters, and review and analyze the masters' voyage reports.

Traffic Administration Division. The assistant vice-president in charge of the traffic administration division occupies a coordinating position. The man who holds this position is in charge of certain personnel matters, prepares special reports, and works out special assignments. He works very closely with the vice-president of freight traffic.

The Local Freight Division. The three assistant vice-presidents mentioned promulgate regulations, plans, policies, and procedures for soliciting cargo and for moving it in the most expeditious matter on a company-wide basis. Carrying through these regulations, plans, policies, and procedures at the level where the shipper meets the carrier are the local freight divisions or agencies. It is at this level that freight traffic is solicited; cargo is booked; the necessary shipping documents such as shipping permits, dock receipts, and bills of lading are issued; the cargo is routed and assigned rates; the manifests are prepared; and the delivery documents and final carrier documents covering inbound shipments, along with forwarding orders, warehousing instructions, and so forth are handled.

1. *Freight sales section.* The local freight division is divided into three sections. The first is the freight sales section, to which the freight solicitors are attached. Their function is to secure maximum cargo in accordance with the sales quotas and policies of the freight sales division located at company headquarters. To do so, solicitors are expected to establish and maintain cordial relations with exporters, importers, local United States government agencies, foreign governments, manufacturers, brokers, forwarders, transportation companies, and other parties interested in the movement of merchandise in international trade. In order for them to function efficiently, standard procedures are set up. For example, systematic records are kept to record the status of each account.

2. *The booking section.* The booking section is responsible for the allotment and control of cargo space. Booking of cargo for liners loading and discharging a wide variety of freight at a range of ports is no task for amateurs. To do this work, the man who is booking cargo must know how to utilize and control properly the cargo space assigned him. He must possess a broad knowledge of many matters—freight rates, the characteristics and stowage factors applicable to the commodities offering, the characteristics of commodities not suitable to vessels requested by the shipper (such as dangerous or obnoxious cargo on vessels carrying passengers), the lifting capacity of the ship's booms, the measurement of the hatches, the dimensions of the various compartments, Coast Guard regulations relating to such matters as dangerous cargo, port terminal and

stevedoring costs, and terminal facilities. The work of booking personnel is carefully supervised, for their day-to-day decisions accepting and rejecting cargo can be the basis of a profit or a loss and of building up good will of shippers.

The booking desks maintain data for each ship showing, among other things, the available deadweight and cubic capacity. A preliminary load list (showing ports of call, commodities booked, and their deadweight and stowed tons) is prepared about ten days before the arrival of a ship. The final load list is prepared shortly before the vessel arrives. This is used by the operating department to "lay out" the space on the pier for cargo to be received and to enable the port captain to lay out the vessel's cargo plan.

Nor is the booking desk through when the ship is loaded. The sailing report must be prepared, giving the capacity of the ship, cargo loaded, free space, and other pertinent remarks. This is prepared for the vice-president of the traffic department and for the executive department.

3. *Documentation section.* The documentation section has three units: export, import, and rates. Personnel in the export unit are responsible for the shipping papers required for exports; in the import unit, for the documents required in importing. The rate unit quotes rates for outbound and inbound cargo, and either applies and/or checks rates on the bills of lading.

PASSENGER TRAFFIC DEPARTMENT

The passenger traffic department is headed by the vice-president of passenger traffic, who is aided by the assistant vice-president. The former is responsible for the over-all planning and direction of the passenger phases of the company's business. The assistant vice-president serves as acting head of the department in the absence of the vice-president. He is also administrative head of the passenger department, administration division.

Passenger Administration Division. The assistant vice-president implements the policies established by the vice-president by developing procedures, regulations, systems, and controls required for the efficient discharge of passenger matters. To assist him, he has a staff divided into four sections:

1. The traffic section is responsible for studies regarding passenger traffic and its requirements, analysis of competition, fares, agency commissions, and revenues. In addition, it may recommend improved utilization of vessels, handles budgetary matters pertaining to the passenger traffic department, and prepares and distributes the "General Passenger Tariff" and the "General Instructions—Passenger Traffic."[6]

[6] These are only two of the procedural manuals issued by the company to ensure compliance with management's policies.

2. The clearance section maintains liaison with customs, immigration, and public-health authorities and works closely with the operating department to ensure smooth functioning of the arrival of passengers.

3. The booking section maintains the master berth lists for each vessel and voyage and sends space-release messages to all offices. It keeps those offices advised regarding space on future sailing. This section prepares the documentation for passengers on each sailing, including waybills and immigration manifests and several listings of passengers for various purposes. The booking of passengers is, in many respects, similar to the booking of cargo, although in passenger bookings, options are granted more extensively. Bookings are made through the company's branch passenger offices and through travel agencies, either by correspondence or by direct contact.

4. The refunds and prepays section handles the numerous details involved in prepaid transactions and refunds in a manner that will protect the company's financial interests, while maintaining sound public relations.

Other Divisions. In addition to the passenger administration division, the passenger traffic department includes a sales promotion and a service development division. The former is responsible for developing the promotion of maximum passenger sales, including the originating and carrying out of programs for the development of new business. The latter is responsible for the maintenance of a high standard of performance in the servicing of passengers and travel agents. This division reports directly to the vice-president in charge of passenger traffic.

The operation of a local passenger office may be illustrated by the one in New York, which is under the supervision of a general passenger agent. His responsibility is to the vice-president in charge of the Eastern division on office administrative matters and to the vice-president in charge of passenger traffic for the promotion of passenger sales. The New York office is divided into two organizational segments, a sales section and an administrative section. The latter is divided into three units: booking, clearance, and correspondence.

OPERATING DEPARTMENT

The vice-president of operations is directly responsible to the executive department for all phases of the multifarious activities of his department. These include operating the company's ships, administering all seagoing personnel,[7] maintaining the ships (including repairs and alterations),

---

[7] Labor relations are handled by the vice-president of operations in conjunction with the executive department. As indicated in Chap. 11, seagoing and shore personnel are employed under collective-bargaining agreements entered into by associations representing the shipowners.

supervising new construction, determining requirements and needs for stores and equipment, operating the company's terminal facilities, and handling all cargo. To carry out such diverse activities, he must maintain effective and satisfactory working relationships not only with other departments of the company but also with government agencies, other steamship companies, employer associations, labor unions, classification societies, and stevedoring companies.

With such large and varied responsibilities, the vice-president in charge of operations has duties and functions primarily of an executive nature, aimed at formulating policies that will give maximum efficiency to the organization and physical facilities under his control. Under him, he has an administrative or executive operations staff and four primary subdivisions: marine division, engineering division, cargo-handling and terminal division, and port steward division.

Office of the Vice-president of Operations. An assistant to the vice-president serves in a capacity resembling a chief of staff. One of his primary responsibilities is to keep in close touch with all activities of the operating department to single out matters requiring the vice-president's personal attention or action. He is charged with the responsibility of administering and supervising all activities of the immediate staff in the office of the vice-president, with specified functions such as compiling reports and keeping apprised of all regulations and rulings of the Maritime Administration that affect the company, and with such other activities as may be delegated to him by the vice-president.

The office of the vice-president of operations includes, among other personnel, the schedules coordinator. He is responsible for preparing all schedules issued by the operating department showing the movements of all vessels in the company's fleet. He works these out in conjunction with appropriate personnel in the freight traffic and passenger traffic departments. The operating analyst is responsible for developing, and for keeping current, serviceable standards of vessels and vessel-department performance that may be readily compared with actual voyage results. He also prepares standard reports on the essential features of such performance for the use of the operating department and other departments of the company. He works in close collaboration with the heads of the operating divisions.

Marine Division. The marine superintendent, who is directly responsible to the vice-president in charge of operations, is charged with control of all vessels and all personnel employed aboard ship; with appointing all masters and all licensed deck officers; with approving the appointments of all other licensed officers and staff officers to be appointed by other departments; and with maintaining satisfactory relations with other divisions of the operating department, other departments of the company, government agencies, applicable labor unions, and any other outside agencies.

Specifically, some of the more important general duties of the marine superintendent are to prepare sailing letters to masters of all vessels in the company fleet; to review ships' logs, masters' correspondence, and minutes of the conferences that masters are required to hold aboard ship with departmental heads; to maintain a manual of operating instructions; and to prepare inspection reports after inspection of maintenance work aboard ships.

A number of the detailed functions for which the marine superintendent is responsible are delegated to his administrative assistant, labor-relations personnel, and the chief port purser and shipping master.

Engineering Division. This division is headed by the repair superintendent engineer. He and his staff are responsible for the operation, maintenance, inspection, and repair of the ships' machinery and other floating equipment as well as for the material condition of all mechanical equipment. He also coordinates all new construction or conversion programs entered into by the company. He screens requisitions, selects licensed engine personnel, and examines the ship's engine-room logs in a manner similar to that of the marine superintendent.

Personnel in the engineering division includes an administrative assistant to the superintendent engineer, senior and junior port engineers, a port electrician, and naval architects. By judicious selection of officers and constant supervision of engine-operating performance, the repair superintendent engineer strives to produce propelling and auxiliary power economically and to reduce repair costs to a minimum. In order better to control this phase of operations, statistics are kept for evaluating vessel performance.

Cargo-handling and Terminal Division. Cargo-handling and marine terminal functions are under the direction of the superintendent of cargo operations. He is responsible for the following functions: (1) to initiate and promote coordination of duties and efforts of department sections applicable to activities of port, terminal, and cargo-handling operations; (2) to control and evaluate the employment of stevedoring, terminal, and ship-service organizations;[8] (3) to develop procedure and maintain records of performance, productivity, and costs in all phases of cargo handling; (4) to study and promote improved layout and use of terminal facilities; and (5) to initiate the adoption of economical and the best practical methods of cargo handling, clerking, stevedoring, forwarding claims prevention, and security.

[8] For some companies, the man in charge of cargo-handling and terminal operations also negotiates and administers the contracts. For the company being discussed, the vice-president of operations takes care of this function.

Since cargo-handling costs absorb a very high proportion of the revenue from steamship operation, the operations of the cargo-handling and terminal division play an important part in maintaining the efficiency of the operating department. In order to give service in the most economical manner, supervision and methods must be used that will reduce costs to a minimum. Terminal operating costs must be watched with keen judgment to avoid delays, stoppages, or interruptions of the movement of cargo. Moreover, cargo-handling operations at the piers must be closely coordinated with the booking section of the freight department, the marine superintendent, the stevedoring company, and others involved in making arrangements for the efficient and speedy loading and discharge of ships. To assist him in carrying out his duties, the head of this division has under him the terminal superintendent, the port captain, and security personnel.

The terminal superintendent is responsible for the supervision, control, and administration of all terminals and piers and for all activities incidental to the use of those facilities. Stevedoring is handled by contract stevedores, because it is believed that the stevedoring company, which serves more than one steamship line and thereby utilizes its equipment and personnel better, can offer more economical service.

The primary job of the port captain is the stowage of cargo aboard ship, a complicated process explained earlier (see Chapter 9). The position of port captain has been established at ports where large amounts of cargo are handled in order to expedite the turn-around of vessels in port and to assist the mates. The port captain at a particular port knows what is on the dock and committed for stowage, matters that the mates cannot know until arrival.[9]

To plan the stowage, the port captain secures from the booking section of the traffic department certain essential information, including the items booked, their ports of destination, their weight and stowed tonnage, and the type of stowage required. He also needs information concerning the amount and kind of in-transit cargo, its ports of destination, and where it is stowed. This information he obtains from stowage plans for other ports and from letters and dispatches received from the port captains at the ship's prior ports of call. As loading progresses, he may have to revise the schedule and modify the number of longshore gangs accordingly. In this connection, the port captain needs a good knowledge of union contracts.

Port Steward's Division. The chief port steward is charged with responsibility for determining company policy as to meals and service for passengers and crew. On passenger liners, the steward's department is often referred to as the hotel section, and marked similarity exists between the management of a liner's housekeeping functions and those of a hotel. The

[9] On the mates' responsibilities, see Chap. 11.

company recognizes the importance of this department on freighters also, for there is nothing aboard ship more likely to promote satisfaction and improve morale than good food, properly prepared and served.

FINANCE DEPARTMENT

Finance exercises a major role in carrying out the objectives of the company. If the company did not plan adequately for cash requirements or overspent budgeted costs, a profit, if one accrued, would be the result of circumstances or good luck rather than of scientific planning; and without a profit, no private enterprise can last long. The financial and accounting phases serve the same broad function in business management that the chart and compass provide for the mariner—they not only give present location but also serve as a guide to future developments.

Traditionally, the financial activities of a company are the responsibility of a treasurer, often with a comptroller responsible for examining and certifying the accounts. The relationship between these two officers is usually a staff one, and both men are responsible to a higher company official, either the president or the executive vice-president. The importance to the financial function in the shipping industry as reflected in our model organization is reflected in the organization of the finance department. The administrative head is the vice-president of finance, who is also treasurer and a member of the board of directors.

For a steamship company, and particularly for a subsidized operator, finance takes on an aspect that differs somewhat from that of many industries. For that part of the company's fleet in subsidized operations, the Maritime Administration prescribes accounting practices and procedures.[10] Then there is always the problem of investing additional capital in new steamships and in reconstructing ships already in the fleet. The decisions involved need to be made at the top levels of management, and many matters are involved on which the vice-president of finance needs to have broad knowledge and experience, especially when the company decides to make application for construction-differential aid in purchasing or reconditioning ships.

The finance department is responsible for the following functions: keeping the corporate records of the company; establishing systems of internal audit; maintaining cost records of all operations, particularly in regard to subsidy payments; maintaining the insurance program of the company; administering the budget program of the company; and maintaining

[10] See also Chap. 15. Because of the interrelationships and the allocation of sundry income and expenses and because it is inconvenient to keep different portions of the accounts on different bases, for all practical purposes, the Maritime Administration accounting practices and procedures must be utilized to the full by subsidized operators.

property records. To assist the vice-president, the finance department is divided into three major divisions (insurance, assistant treasurer, and accounting). Reporting directly to the vice-president of finance are also an assistant to the vice-president and the subsidy analyst. The former assists the vice-president in matters delegated to him and is also responsible for the confidential payrolls and the dock paymaster unit. The subsidy analyst develops operating-differential rates for subsidy purposes.[11]

Insurance Division. Not only does the operation of a fleet of ships require that the company carry a variety of insurances, but the adjustment of claims arising under policies must be closely followed and expertly handled. Shore activities likewise entail insurance protection of many kinds, including workmen's compensation and group life insurance on behalf of the employees.

The primary types of marine insurance are discussed in Chapter 18. But there are other miscellaneous types used to cover situations not customarily covered by the basic policies, such as deviation of the cargo or vessel, bullion and specie shipments, bill of lading insurance providing shippers in the intercoastal trade with insurance coverage by means of stamping the bill of lading, and cargo insurance for offshore shipments of cargo for exporters who arrange with the company instead of through an insurance broker. This last is also applicable for property of the company that is transhipped to other ports. Further, the types and amounts of insurance taken out vary with the type of vessel and her employment. The insurance manager, who is responsible for the company's insurance program, needs a detailed knowledge of each situation.

In addition, the insurance division works with the security section of the operating department on safety programs designed to prevent or reduce accidents. Handling personal-injury claims for damages alleged to have been sustained by personnel afloat and ashore requires time, and the detail involved may prove costly.

Assistant Treasurer. The head of this division has as his primary responsibility the company's funds and securities. These include receipt and disbursement of cash in the home office and elsewhere, marshaling of funds where they are most useful, contacts with banks, transactions in foreign exchange; investment of funds temporarily idle, maintenance of statutory reserve funds, and safeguarding of cash and securities. At the present time, and it is stated probably not for the long-time future, he also supervises the audit of, and the preparation of journal vouchers for, freight and passenger revenue and vessel payrolls. He also serves as the corporate secretary.

Accounting Division. The administrative head of the accounting division is the chief accountant. He is responsible for maintaining all general

[11] See Chap. 13, pp. 267–270, and Chap. 15, pp. 279–281.

and subsidiary ledgers, for making regular reports and tax returns therefrom, and for preparing all special studies and reports using the financial accounts as a base. He is the official conservator of accounting records, and at present supervises the audit of, and the preparation of journal vouchers for, expenditures other than on vessel payrolls.

PUBLIC-RELATIONS DEPARTMENT

The fifth department headed by a man of vice-presidential rank is the public-relations department, the objective of which has been defined as "always trying to put our best foot forward." The staff maintained at headquarters is not large, particularly in view of the world-wide coverage needed to carry out the department's public-relations and advertising program. A good part of the program, however, is possible because the vice-president in charge of public relations works with and through other company personnel. For example, in the training program for pursers afloat, the chief port purser attempts to instruct pursers and their staffs concerning the type of "lead" information that may be of use to the public-relations department.

The vice-president of public relations is responsible for the company's advertising program and for the expenditure of a carefully prepared and duly approved advertising appropriation. This involves working closely with both the passenger traffic and freight traffic departments to integrate the publicity activities for both departments and for the company generally. Working with the company's advertising agency, the administrative head of public relations supervises the preparation of copy and layouts, the selection of mediums, and the preparation and production of all sales-promotion material, including folders, posters, and miscellaneous display material.

Opportunities for furthering good public relations are virtually unlimited, and the activities of the public-relations department are as broad and varied as time and the limitations of the budget permit. Certain procedures have been established in what can be called routine, as, for example, the company's efforts to go above and beyond the normal contract requirements of providing proper food, shelter, and transportation service for passengers aboard company ships. To make for good will, the company, through the public-relations department, has a supply of personalized company stationery in each passenger's stateroom, with his name imprinted at the top; arranges for his home-town newspaper to reach him air mail at various overseas ports where his vessel calls; provides him with a special, personalized mailing schedule so that he can inform his friends and relatives where mail will reach him at certain dates; and gives him a personalized folder, imprinted with his name in gold, for his ticket and passport. He is given an appropriate souvenir, as a memento of his voyage, and a personal letter from the president of the company. The arrival and departure of passenger liners are covered as a routine matter. Moreover, the interviews and photographs are not confined entirely to well-known and important persons; little-known people may furnish excellent copy for good-will publicity.

Freighters are also covered if the cargo warrants. For example, a pregnant elephant was recently shipped out of Hong Kong for this country on one of the company's ships. The handling of this unusual cargo required skill and attention on the part of the ship's officers and men. Public relations took this shipment, stressing the human-interest aspects as well as the technical difficulties of the operating department, and developed favorable publicity carrying the underlying theme that the company "can handle any kind of cargo, no matter how delicate the condition."

The entire public-relations program is founded on the premise that the company's public relations are no better than the service offered. The integrated advertising, promotion, and publicity program is conceived in an effort to persuade people generally that they can safely trust their persons and their cargoes to company ships. Activities are planned to reach various segments of the company's public—customers and potential customers, both passengers and shippers; company employees, which number more than 900 ashore and roughly 2,500 afloat, depending on the number of ships in service; stockholders; the hundreds of vendors and suppliers with whom the company deals in supplying and maintaining its fleet; the general public; and community groups, associations, and specialized interests. In an effort to carry out this program, the vice-president looks to top management for news concerning plans for new ships, changes in routes or schedules, improvements in service, and constructive announcements. He looks to the captains of the ships, officers, and crewmen for news on such matters as heroism at sea, and to overseas offices and agencies for information on unusual cargoes.

CLAIMS DEPARTMENT

To handle all claims for lost and damaged cargo on a world-wide basis, the claims department has been set up under the charge of the general claims agent who, from company headquarters, coordinates and administers the over-all claims activities both domestic and foreign.

District Offices. At various points around the world, the company has established district claims offices where district claims agents have limited authority to handle claims filed against the company. Each district agent has an area over which he exercises control. When a claim originates, it is assigned a claim number, which is transmitted to the general claims agent at the home office. The district office is also responsible for notifying headquarters on all actions taken on each claim. This is necessary so that claims policies and statistics can be coordinated.

It is the duty of the district office to work with agencies and commercial representatives adjacent to them who have been vested with limited authority to settle claims. Each office must operate on a current basis without time lag in the disposition of claims. Standardized forms, records, and procedures have been developed so that the claims agent can complete his work efficiently and thoroughly and in conformity with company policies.

Claims Procedure. A claims investigation gets underway as soon as the company learns of loss or damage to cargo. This information may be obtained from reports of the ship's mates or from a shipper's notice of intent to file a claim. Each day the claims agent reviews the notices and refers them to a claims investigator for prompt action. Either the consignee or his insurance company is informed concerning the documents that must be submitted in support of the formal claim when filed.

Cargo claims are divided into two categories. The first, called *petty claims*, are for less than a stipulated dollar value. They are handled in an informal manner and as expeditiously as possible. The claims agent will first ensure that the cargo in question did move on the vessel and then request a check from the finance department. This amount is charged to the operating account of the vessel and voyage involved. At the end of the month, the claims office sends to the general claims agent at headquarters a report of petty claims so paid.

Claims that have been filed for an amount in excess of the stipulated dollar value must be routed to and recorded in the cargo-claims ledger, claimants index file. This is done so that the essential information may be recorded for statistical control and analysis, utilizing punch-card machines.

The claims investigator uses the following documents: dock receipt or boat note, discharge records, cargo surveys, and inspection reports. He must know how to sift the information he has assembled and when to probe deeper into the background of the claim. He must learn to recognize situations in which tallies and surveys have to be supplemented by statements from the ship's officers, surveyor, checker, or guard. For example, the logbook may not mention that a situation existed. The absence of such a statement may not be sufficient, and the investigator must judge whether a direct statement from the master or mate is necessary. If so, he should secure it before the ship sails.

After his investigation, the claims investigator should be in a position to recommend the action that should be taken on a claim. Then the claims agent reviews the information submitted to determine whether he agrees with the investigator. Claims are paid when there is a legal liability with the company, and they are declined when there is a valid legal defense.

The claims agent must be prepared to defend the position he takes, whether he approves or disapproves the claim. He must bear in mind two important results that may follow his action: (1) if he denies the claim, a suit may be filed against the company, and (2) if the claim is paid, the company's insurance carrier may determine that there was no legal liability to the claimant and therefore no coverage, and may refuse to reimburse the company for the expenditure.

Additional Duties of District Claims Agent. The primary responsibility of the district claims agent is the settlement of claims, and his other duties are associated with that function. He is responsible for salvaging cargo that is damaged or unclaimed. If responsibility for the loss can be attached to stevedoring companies, terminal operators, or a transshipping carrier, he should initiate collections and recoveries for claims paid originally by the company. He should analyze the monthly statistical reports and take action to reduce the amount of claims and should assist the company's lawyers in claims that have gone to the litigation stage. In addition, he should establish and maintain an efficient and expedient tracing system. When cargo is discharged in port, one or more packages may be either short-landed or over-landed, a situation that results when cargo is not accessible or when it has been mixed with cargo destined for other ports. Shortages and overages are listed on an "over and short report," which gives details for one port, one vessel, and one voyage. The district claims agent sends copies of this report to all ports on the vessel's itinerary so that cargo can be returned to the post of destination as soon as possible.

SERVICE AND SUPPLY DEPARTMENT

The service and supply department is a common-service organization, the function of which is central procurement. The department performs all functions involved in procurement and is charged with the custody and control of all vessel stores and spare parts placed ashore. The department spends several million dollars a year.

Although the department is responsible for the purchasing function, actually what is to be purchased and in what quantity rests primarily with the heads of the deck, engine, steward's, purser's, and medical departments of the company's ships. The requirements for a particular ship are screened by various members of the operating department ashore, such as the port captain, port engineer, and port steward. Requirements are screened against a "standard allowance list" that provides statistical data on the use and consumption of shipboard equipment, stores, and supplies.

The executive head of the service and supply department is the director. The assistant director supervises ship services provided by all concessionaires. The department is divided into four organization segments: purchasing, receiving, inventory, and stores. The purchasing function is performed by buyers who specialize in one of six fields. For example, the purchaser of steward's sundries buys pots, pans, ranges, and cooking and serving utensils, while the subsistence purchaser buys what goes into the pots and pans. The functions of the other organizational segments are obvious from their names.

GENERAL AND RESEARCH DEPARTMENTS

The general department is headed by the general office manager. This, a staff department, renders certain common services to all departments, including the operation of the mail room, the cable room, the telephone switchboard, and the company's automotive equipment. It also administers or aids in executing all company policies in regard to shoreside personnel, both domestic and foreign, as to the following personnel functions: (1) employment of new personnel, (2) compensation of employees, (3) past employment of personnel, (4) working conditions, (5) benefits and services, (6) training, (7) grievance procedure, (8) collective bargaining, and (9) records and statistics affecting personnel.

Research was originally included in the executive department, but it was decided to give the department separate status. The department of research and development is now under a director, who is assisted by an associate director, three research associates, four research assistants, and a secretary. The company library is maintained by the research department. With the consent of the executive branch and the departmental heads, the research department undertakes projects of vital concern to the company's shipping activities. Although specific reports are frequently undertaken at the request of one of the departments, interest is rather generally company-wide, with various departments more interested in the aspects that affect them directly. In a commodity study, for example, the freight traffic department is likely to be interested in tonnages, both moving and potential, the finance department in the revenue aspects, and the operating department in problems involved in the handling of the particular commodity.

AGENTS AND AGENCIES

The shipping company used here as representative both serves as an agent and utilizes the services of agents. At San Francisco, Los Angeles, and other ports, the company serves as agent for Lykes Bros. Steamship Co., Inc. As noted earlier, the company has offices in a number of key locations throughout the world; to fill in this network, it utilizes commercial agents to bring the total of locations where the company is represented to 246. For example, Forbes, Forbes, Campbell & Co., Ltd., is the agent at Bombay; Whittall & Co., at Colombo, Ceylon; and Di Luggo Wood & Co., at Naples. Company ships call regularly at these ports, and the agents perform all functions involved in steamship operation including husbanding the ships, soliciting cargo, and loading and discharging cargo.

If a steamship company arranges for a ship to call at a port at which it maintains no facilities or personnel, the company will gladly and necessarily make use of agency representation. The privately owned ships requisitioned by the United States government at the beginning of World War II as well as the war-built fleet were operated by American shipowners acting as agents and subagents for the government.

Agency representation is an economical way to provide services at ports where a shipping company finds it uneconomical to maintain facilities or personnel. Conversely, where a shipping company does maintain offices, it can often, by providing agency services to other companies, make fuller and more economical use of its facilities and personnel.

The shipping agencies that serve as agents only and do not own and operate their own ships are also vital to agency representation. They may limit their operations to one port or to several. They have traffic and operating divisions, passenger departments, and so forth, with the organization depending on the extent of their operations.

VARIATIONS IN ORGANIZATIONAL STRUCTURE

The shipping company used here as a model is engaged, as noted earlier, in the transportation of freight, mail, and passengers. In other words, its activities are confined primarily to the steamship business.

Other shipping companies, such as the Grace Line, Inc., are wholly owned subsidiaries of other companies. If an organization chart were prepared for the parent organization (in the case of the Grace Line, W. R. Grace & Co.), the shipping company would represent only one part of that chart.[12] Further, if the shipping company engaged in the transportation of passengers and freight and offered common-carrier service, as does the Grace Line, its organizational structure would be similar to that of any other shipping company engaged in comparable operations. In other words, the company would have divisions to cover operations, solicitation of freight and passenger traffic, claims, finance, and so forth.

[12] The Grace Line represents the largest single item in the Grace portfolio. See the April, May, and June, 1952, issues of *Fortune* for articles on the Grace interests.

The operation of a fleet of industrial carriers, such as tankers, requires a simpler organizational structure, because such ships usually engage in transporting for owner's account. They may be owned outright by the industrial company or by subsidiaries or affiliates. The large fleet of tankers operated by the Gulf Oil Corp. (40 ships in 1952) is an example of an industrial fleet owned by an oil company. The organization segment responsible for operating such ships is usually called a marine department, or marine division, and is responsible for all phases of ship operation. Needless to say, a department to solicit cargo is unnecessary, and since industrial carriers are constructed with special equipment for loading and discharging, "operations" are much more simple than for the common carrier that transports packaged cargo.

Such shipping lines as the Alcoa Steamship Co., Inc., and the United Fruit Steamship Corp. fall midway between the common carrier and the industrial operator, at least in certain respects, for both lines were organized to serve as auxiliary to an industry that found it desirable to furnish its own transportation. Furthermore, although both companies now offer common-carrier service, ores from the Caribbean and fruits, sugar, and so forth from Central America furnish a nucleus of cargoes for the ships employed. This has an effect on organization. For such companies, the department or division responsible for traffic solicitation must work closely with the associated industry, and, since passenger traffic is of minor importance, passenger solicitation may be handled by the same division that deals with freight solicitation.

Further variation in organizational structure is to be found with steamship companies whose ships engage in tramp or irregular operations. Although it has been said that the office of a shipowner engaged in such shipping activity can be "where he hangs his hat," that is an oversimplification. The organization and administrative staff that is maintained, moreover, depend on the type of charter operations employed (see Chapter 10). A shipowner who demise-chartered his ships would need the smallest staff, because the charterer acquires the use of a bare ship and is himself responsible for husbanding it. Under a time charter (the owner is responsible for wages of officers and crew, insurance, and food) and under a voyage charter (the owner is usually responsible for additional expenses such as fuel oil, pilotage, and port charges), the owner would have to have an operating division suitable to the extent of his operations. Under charter operations, however, the shipowner is not responsible for loading and discharging cargo, functions that are extremely important to successful liner operations. Vital to the success of charter operations are ship brokers, through whom vessels are usually chartered. The steamship company offering its vessels for hire would therefore have a well-qualified and effective organizational segment to deal with charters.

PRECEDENT AND CONSERVATISM

Although the shipping industry is very old, the general outline of a vessel's shape and the method of handling cargo in and out of a ship have undergone little change. When this is contrasted with the rapid rate of change and development of railways, trucks, buses, and more recently airplanes, the contrast is striking. Some explanation, however, is to be found in the nature of the shipping industry itself: (1) A voyage is a joint venture in which many parties participate to the extent of their interest—namely, vessel owner and operator, cargo owner, holder of a mortgage on the ship, creditor of the cargo owner, and other creditors, agents, and trustees. (2) The shipping industry is one that involves tremendous investments per ship and exposure to sudden and violent disasters. It is small wonder then that the shipowner, as well as the shipbuilder, stresses security and is reluctant to experiment with changes.

The net result of the complexity of relationships of the interests involved and of the enormous values at stake, as well as the tremendous forces of the seas and the elements that must be considered by the builders and owners, is to introduce into shipping management a strain of conservatism. Tradition, precedent, and the time-tested practices of building and operation provide security and certainty. There is a natural reluctance to introduce change, for even the simplest modification of a bill of lading, of an accounting procedure, or of a structural characteristic of a ship may open up a variety of unprecedented situations with respect to legal interpretations and responsibilities. One simple change may have repercussions through many phases of ship operation, pier management, government relations, and so forth.

It is easy to be impatient with and critical of the slowly changing characteristics of ships and shipping management. There is a constant balancing between management's ability to recognize the need for change and the values of conservatism. One of the greatest rewards of sound shipping management will be the opportunity to measure scientifically the greater net returns to be realized from an investment in change. Such an approach will provide management and ownership with the courage to advance. Shipping management must take the lead from the shipbuilder and the commodity trader.

Shipping management as such is a more or less recent development. Shipbuilding, on the other hand, has always been an art and a science, and also most conservative. The modern ship is in most respects merely an adaptation of its smaller and less complicated predecessors. Until not much more than one hundred years ago, the ship was a means to an end—a means by which the merchant-trader of commodities or the shipowner-merchant earned money. Much of today's profit in ship management and operation is derived, first, from the wise building or purchase of the ship that is best suited to the service in which it will operate, and second, from the trading instincts of the ship's owners and operators. Actual ship management in terms of controlled costs, aggressive development of revenues, budgeting and long-range planning, and so forth, is of secondary importance.

Perhaps the most outstanding lesson we can draw from history to apply to the future is this: the successful shipping company will combine skillful ship management with an aggressive trading instinct. The size of ships and of capital invested in fleets, together with the more complete separation of ship management and commodity trading, has placed a greater premium on scientific ship management.

BIBLIOGRAPHY

Because of the nature of this chapter, it is not possible to list the usual bibliographical references.

PART THREE

THE FINANCE OF SHIPPING

CHAPTER 13

GOVERNMENT AID

The United States government has given financial aid to the American merchant marine for one purpose—to maintain a shipping industry able to meet the nation's minimum economic and military needs for ocean transportation. The limitations and restrictions that accompany that aid are designed primarily for the purpose of protecting or securing the government's interest and not for regulatory purposes. Hence, government aid is more a matter of shipping finance than a role of government.

Historically, the United States merchant marine needed no financial aid during the fifty-odd years following independence. The American shipowner could buy the best-constructed and more durable ships being built in the world from domestic shipbuilders at prices lower than those paid by his foreign competitor. All he asked of Congress was protection from the discriminatory laws then common among all the maritime nations of the world. That protection given, he was perfectly able to take care of himself. However, just before the Civil War, when the metal ship appeared, the American shipowner lost this construction-cost advantage, and the United States merchant marine began to decline.

For about one century, roughly from 1845 to 1936, the American merchant marine operated under conditions that at times virtually removed the American flag from the seas. At intervals, various programs of government assistance were initiated and tried, but all of them failed at their primary objective of maintaining an adequate merchant marine. One difficulty was that government financial aid was an on-again, off-again affair that did little to assure shipowners that American-flag ships were a sound investment. Another was that aid to the merchant marine was tied to the ocean-mail subsidy, a device that must have seemed very logical in 1845 but which should have been discarded long before 1936.

The Merchant Marine Act of 1936 recognized in a very realistic manner that construction and operating costs were greater for American-flag ships than for those of foreign registry, and the measures for government aid embodied in that Act and in subsequent legislation were designed to compensate for the differentials. Although the greater part of this chapter will deal with developments since 1936, it should be remembered that the policy, and also the philosophy, underlying the present program of financial aid to American-flag shipping has been more than a century in the making.

NINETEENTH-CENTURY MAIL SUBSIDIES

When governments first set out to give direct aid to their shipping industries, they connected that aid with the overseas mail service.[1] Throughout the civilized world, the transport of the mails, both on land and by sea, has developed as a government function. By about the 1840's, overseas mail was taking on a volume and assuming an importance previously unknown, and ships were the only means of overseas communication. To transport ocean mails, governments therefore had to utilize the services of shipowners. This brought them into direct working contact with the shipping companies at a time when those companies were in need of assistance because of the impending transition from wood and sail to metal and steam. Hence, it must have seemed very logical to utilize that close working contact to effect two ends—carriage of the mails and government aid to merchant shipping.

The Period 1845 to 1858. By a law passed on Mar. 3, 1845, Congress authorized the Postmaster General to advertise for bids to provide for carriage of the mails between the United States and foreign countries. The first service offered under provisions of this Act, that to Bremen starting in 1847, was not entirely an American undertaking. In 1845, a representative of the Bremen Senate had come to this country to assist in the organization of a direct steamship service to Continental Europe. The German states, which had been sending thousands of emigrants to the United States, were dissatisfied with the Boston-Liverpool service and with the high postal rates of the British Cunard Line. When difficulty was encountered in raising the necessary capital, Bremen and the German states raised $289,000, which represented more than one-third of the sum used to capitalize the Ocean Steam Navigation Company.

In 1847, E. K. Collins was authorized to offer subsidized service between the United States and Liverpool. Before he completed the vessels called for in his contract, he encountered financial difficulties, and Congress

[1] The British had granted mail subsidies before the United States did. Although this chapter is devoted to government aid to the American merchant marine, it should be understood that government aid to, or participation in, the shipping industry is not a phenomenon peculiar to the United States but a national characteristic of practically all countries that have found it expedient politically, economically, or militarily to have a shipping industry. A good study of shipping and shipbuilding subsidies among the maritime nations of the world, to date of publication, is J. E. Saugstad, *Shipping and Shipbuilding Subsidies*, U.S. Department of Commerce, Trade Promotion Series, No. 129, 1932.

authorized advance payments totaling $385,000, a sum equal to his yearly mail subsidy under his 1847 contract. Moreover, when the Collins ships came into direct competition with the Cunard Line and transatlantic freight rates dropped from $35 to $20 per ton, Congress increased the subsidy from $19,250 per round voyage to $33,000 and raised the number of voyages from 20 to 26 per year.

The third service inaugurated under provisions of the Act of 1845 was the Atlantic-Pacific service. The national interest demanded not only that adequate communications be maintained between the Eastern seaboard and the Pacific Coast, but also that the service be regular and dependable. The Atlantic portion of this service, operating between New York and Panama (with calls at Charleston, Savannah, and Havana and with service to New Orleans), was offered by the United States Mail Steamship Company, while the Pacific extension was served by the Pacific Mail Line, also called Aspinwall's Line.

Government payments to the four shipping companies from the time service was inaugurated until aid was withdrawn in 1858 totaled $14,400,000, distributed as follows:

Line	Period of operation	Amount
New York–Bremen..............	1847–1857	$2,000,000
New York–Havre...............	1852–1857	750,000
New York–Liverpool............	1850–1858	4,500,000
New York–Panama..............	1848–1858	2,900,000
Astoria–Panama................	1848–1858	3,750,000
Charleston–Havana.............	1848–1858	500,000

Mail Contracts, 1864 to 1877. A second group of ocean-mail contracts was made possible by a law passed by Congress on May 28, 1864. A contract with the United States and Brazil Mail Steamship Company called for 12 voyages a year between the United States and South America over a ten-year period. Of the $250,000 annual subsidy, the United States paid $150,000 and Brazil $100,000. In 1865, an annual payment of $500,000 was authorized to the Pacific Mail Line for monthly service to China and Japan. Before the transpacific service was inaugurated, Pacific Mail petitioned to be released from the requirement that the ships stop at Honolulu, and this service was taken over by the California, Oregon & Mexican Line in 1869. Additional subsidies were granted Pacific Mail in 1872 for extra service.

Total government expenditures for mail service between 1864 and 1877 amounted to roughly $6,500,000, of which $1,500,000 went to the Brazil

Line, $4,580,000 to the Pacific Mail Line, and $425,000 to the California, Oregon & Mexican Line.

The Ocean Mail Act of 1891. In 1890, Congress considered two distinct types of aid to shipping: (1) a bounty bill that provided for payments of 30 cents per gross registered ton per thousand miles sailed outbound and inbound by all ships of over 500 tons built and owned in the United States and operating in foreign trade and (2) a mail-subsidy bill providing for payments to four classes of subsidized steamers. The latter was passed in an emasculated form. In July, 1891, the Postmaster General called for bids on 53 lines. Up to April, 1893, bids were received and contracts awarded on nine routes or lines, but a year later, contracts were in force on only four of those routes. An additional route was added in 1895, when regular sailings started between New York and Southampton. In 1899, when service was instituted between Boston and Philadelphia and Jamaica, five routes were in operation; in 1905, eight routes. Contract payments between 1892 and 1923 under the Ocean Mail Act of 1891 totaled $29,630,000, approximately half of which went to the American Line, operating between New York and Europe.

INEFFECTIVE AID TO WORLD WAR I

With the appearance of the metal steamship, the United States needed new shipping companies and new ships. In an era of greatly expanding world trade, the merchant-trader-shipowner of the New England towns was inadequate in respect to both his activities and the capital at his disposal. Therefore, the success of the ocean-mail subsidies may be judged, in large part, by their effects on American companies and on the United States merchant fleet.

Both of the companies operating in the Atlantic under the 1845-to-1858 subsidy arrangements ceased to exist after Congress withdrew aid. When the Ocean Steam Navigation Company was liquidated, with the consent of the German states, the German interests that had been influential in helping to organize the first steamship service under United States registry then became instrumental in forming the great Bremen shipping company, the North German Lloyd. The lines operating to Panama, Oregon, and the West Indies were able to survive even though the compensation for carrying the mails on a weight basis was lower than the subsidy payments.

The only link between operations during the 1850's and the present is to be found in the Pacific Mail Company, which also benefited from the subsidy of 1864 to 1877. That company operated continuously until 1925, except for a brief period after the Seamen's Law of 1915 was passed. In 1925, when the Dollar Steamship Lines (now American President) succeeded to the transpacific and Oriental business of the company, Dollar obtained the services of a number of experienced shipping men who had received their training and experience in the Pacific Mail Company.

The United States and Brazil Mail Steamship Company, formed to transport mails between this country and Brazil, survived withdrawal of the United States subsidy in 1875 and entered into a ten-year contract with Brazil. However, the company ceased to operate after 1893.

Nor was the Act of 1891 any more successful as far as shipping companies were concerned. The only new line established between 1891 and 1898 was the American Line, which was organized by American capitalists who had purchased the British Inman Line. In 1894 and 1895, this company launched the *St. Louis* and *St. Paul*, the first transatlantic liners built in United States shipyards in twenty years. Although men were reluctant to invest money in American-flag ships, this reluctance did not extent to all ships. In 1901, after J. P. Morgan had purchased the Leyland Line, 136 ships of 672,456 gross tons were owned or controlled by American capital and operated under the British, Belgian, and Norwegian flags. In 1900, total United States flag tonnage engaged in foreign trade was slightly less than 827,000 gross tons, of which only 341,000 tons was power driven.

The account of new ships is no more encouraging. As mentioned in Chapter 1, in 1860, the United States owned 5.3 million gross tons of shipping, in comparison with Britain's 5.7 million, and American ships more than compensated for difference in tonnage by their greater speed and carrying capacity. Also the British, who had had trouble producing competitive ships as long as wooden-hulled sailing ships held sway, were soon able to construct the world's best and cheapest ships, while the United States virtually rejected the metal steam-propelled vessel. This is reflected in the composition of the fleets of the two countries.

In 1885, approximately 75 percent of Britain's total fleet was steam, while the United States fleet was divided approximately half and half—50 percent steam and 50 percent sail. But the power-driven craft was concentrated in the domestic fleet. Of the registered foreign trade fleet of 1,287,999 gross tons, only 186,406 tons were steamships. This is less than 15 percent. As late as the period 1910 to 1914, roughly one-third of the American-flag ships engaged in foreign trade were still sailing ships. In 1914, United States oceangoing and Great Lakes steam tonnage was 4.3 million gross tons, while the United Kingdom's was 18.9 million tons.

The composition of the United States fleet naturally affected the carriage of the nation's foreign commerce. In 1850, American-flag ships carried between 72 and 73 percent of the nation's foreign commerce. By 1900, this had dropped to 10 percent; it dropped to 8.7 percent in 1910.

Of the United States total fleet of steam vessels in 1910 (4,829,000 gross tons), over 4,272,000 tons were engaged in domestic trade. Much of this domestic tonnage should not be dignified with the name of steamship, for it consisted of stern- and side-wheelers utterly inadequate for oceangoing commerce.

There are reasons, both social and economic, why American shipyards concentrated on such craft. Honors were heaped upon the shipbuilders who produced sailing ships—vessels that were commercially obsolete practically as soon as they left the ways, while the men who worked with iron were considered ironmasters and ironmongers. It takes a well-established iron and steel industry and a good shipbuilding industry to turn such men into skilled workmen, and at the time the United States had neither.

Navigation laws and the tariff policy contributed their full share to the decline of the American merchant marine. Although shipowners repeatedly asked for "free ships," Congress made no change in the registry laws, on the statute books since 1789, that limited documentation under the American flag to ships built in the United States. After the Civil War, the high tariff rates of the Morrill Act of 1861 were retained and in some cases raised to even higher levels. An Act of June 6, 1872, provided some minor concessions, but iron plate and other materials essential to shipbuilding were not included in the free list. Steel plate was finally added to that list in 1890, and other materials in a tariff passed in 1894. However, successive acts embodied provisions that ships built in whole or in part of foreign materials imported duty free could not engage in the coasting trade for more than two months of the year. With such restrictions to curtail their domestic activities, shipowners were unwilling to purchase vessels for foreign trade.

Neither the Congress nor the country was marine minded. During the Civil War, roughly 750,000 gross tons of ships had fled the flag. In 1866, Congress denied owners of those ships readmittance to American registry. Although the merchant marine was considered by Congress again and again, the only maritime legislation enacted provided for the disguised or indirect aid of the ocean-mail subsidy—a means of aid less distasteful to its constituency than paying money directly from the public treasury.

It is, however, the people on whom the responsibility rests, and a change had certainly occurred in their attitude toward the country's merchant marine. Whereas shipping had been during the early days of the republic the nation's one industry and the principal occupation in which a man could hope, with hard work and a few strokes of good luck, to gain a competence or perhaps lay the basis for a family fortune, industrialization changed that. New opportunities for employment and investment drew upon the nation's capital and man power. Furthermore, immigration was altering the nature of the population. By the 1840's, immigration had reached 1.5 million annually, of which 75 percent were Irish and German people, with little tradition of the sea. They were later followed by people from central and southern Europe, many of them from the peasant class. It is not surprising that these people had little appreciation of a merchant marine as a national asset.

BENEFITS UNDER THE MERCHANT MARINE ACTS OF 1920 AND 1928

In early 1914, the only statute on the books purporting to benefit the nation's merchant marine was the Ocean Mail Act of 1891, which stipulated that mail contracts should be let in a manner best to "subserve and promote the postal and commercial interests of the United States." This policy of linking maritime affairs to carriage of the mails was certainly open to question during the next few years.

A Merchant-marine Policy. In the autumn of 1914, Congress relaxed the law regarding the registration of foreign-built ships, but no major piece of shipping legislation was enacted until September, 1916, when the Shipping Act was passed. Although the language of the preamble to this Act could be construed to embrace a "policy," such was not the case, for the Act was primarily a piece of emergency legislation creating the U.S. Shipping Board and authorizing that agency through a corporation to be formed for that purpose (which became the Emergency Fleet Corporation) to purchase, construct, equip, lease, charter, maintain, and operate the merchant ships necessary to meet the emergency.[2] Section 11 of the Act provided that this corporation should be dissolved "at the expiration of five years from the conclusion of the present European war." Furthermore, the Act embodied no measures designed to aid the privately owned merchant marine.

The preamble to the Merchant Marine Act of 1920 states simply that the purpose of the Act is "to provide for the promotion and maintenance of the American merchant marine, to repeal certain emergency legislation, and provide for the disposition, regulation, and use of property acquired thereunder." Section 1 of the Act is, however, far more specific, for it provides:

It is necessary for the national defense and for the proper growth of its foreign and domestic commerce that the United States shall have a merchant marine of the best equipped and most suitable types of vessels sufficient to carry the greater part of its commerce and serve as a naval or military auxiliary in time of war or

[2] The Act also embodied certain regulatory provisions, which are discussed in Chap. 19. For more detail on the Shipping Board and the Emergency Fleet Corporation, see Chap. 20.

national emergency, . . . and it is hereby declared to be the policy of the United States to do whatever may be necessary to develop and encourage the maintenance of such a merchant marine . . .

The Merchant Marine Act of 1928 reaffirmed this policy. Hence, the Merchant Marine Act of 1920 embodied the first definitive statement of government policy under which aid could be given the American merchant marine. As we shall see, the Act of 1928 was the first statute that granted substantial financial aid to private shipping in peacetime to enable it to modernize its fleet.

Ship-sales Program after World War I. In 1916, while the Shipping Act was being debated, the Chamber of Commerce of the United States had proposed that the government should aid merchant shipping by subsidies to compensate private operators for the construction-cost and operating differentials as between American and foreign costs (both provisions were later embodied in the Merchant Marine Act of 1936). After World War I, the United States government could have disposed of the war-built fleet in a manner that would have benefited the American merchant marine simply by selling ships to American shipowners at prices they could afford to pay.[3] In other words, the ship-sales program could have absorbed the construction-cost differential. However, the program was administered in such a way that it not only failed to benefit shipowners but left in the hands of the government agency a fleet that involved substantial losses.

The Act of 1916 had given broad, general powers for disposing of the emergency fleet, but no specific instructions. Furthermore, the disposition of the government-owned fleet, which had cost the nation approximately 3 billion dollars (roughly $200 per ton), was a matter on which legislators, chambers of commerce, shipping executives, civic groups, and others had definite and conflicting opinions. Although he was willing to sell wooden vessels and to return requisitioned ships, Mr. Hurley, chairman of the Shipping Board, was not willing to take the responsibility for putting on an extensive sales campaign to sell the more desirable steel ships. This attitude is very understandable, inasmuch as it had been proposed on the floor of Congress that the war-built fleet be retained by the government and operated for its profit.

The Shipping Board got its first legislative guidance concerning ship-

---

[3] The size of the government-owned fleet depends on the date chosen, for the shipbuilding program did not terminate in 1918. According to the Harvard Report, the peak of cargo-vessel ownership was in 1921, when the U.S. Shipping Board owned 1,792 vessels of 11 million deadweight tons. Through June 30, 1924, the Board had owned a total of 2,541 ships of 14,706,000 deadweight tons. See *The Use and Disposition of Ships and Shipyards at the End of World War II*, A Report Prepared for the U.S. Navy Department and the U.S. Maritime Commission by the Graduate School of Business Administration, Harvard University, Government Printing Office, Washington, D.C., June, 1945, pp. 218–219.

disposal policies when the Merchant Marine Act of 1920 was passed in June of that year. Although this Act provided the Board with the machinery to sell ships, neither the provisions of this Act nor those of subsequent legislation recognized the government-owned fleet as "surplus," a good share of the cost of which should be charged off to the war effort. In fact, the Act of 1920 directed the Board that it should be influenced by the factors and conditions "that would influence a prudent, solvent business man in the sale of similar ships or property that he is *not* forced to sell."[4]

The Act of 1920 was passed on June 5. The Board settled matters concerning pricing, terms of sale, the market, and so forth, and prices of between $160 and $185 per deadweight ton were set for good steel ships. By June, however, freight rates were on the downgrade from their postwar high levels. Throughout 1921, they ranged between 30 and 40 percent of their Jan. 1, 1920, levels; from 1922 to 1925, between 20 and 30 percent. In a 1921 study, the Board found that world market prices had averaged $110 per deadweight ton in 1919, $99 in 1920, and $26.87 in 1921. About $30 was decided upon as a fair price. This lack of a fixed price did nothing to stabilize the market for government-owned ships, and it also involved the Board in problems of granting relief to purchasers who had bought vessels earlier at higher prices.[5]

As indicated earlier (see Chapter 4), the Board established service on trade routes deemed desirable with government-owned ships, and offered the ships and the routes for sale on a "restricted-price" basis. Sales of ships and routes proceeded slowly during the next five years. In 1928, the Merchant Marine Act of 1928 was added to the statute books to provide for new ocean-mail contracts and for the first effective aid in ship construction and in modernizing the nation's merchant fleet.

Ocean-mail Contracts. The Merchant Marine Act of 1920 left the Ocean Mail Act of 1891 on the statute books, modifying its provisions only to the extent that the U.S. Shipping Board and the Postmaster General were jointly to determine rates, terms of the contract, and so forth. Since the contracts already let under the 1891 Act did not expire until 1923, payments under the law of 1920 cover only the years 1924 through 1929, for the 1891 law was repealed by the Merchant Marine Act of 1928. Mail-contract payments between 1923 and 1929, totaling $4,800,000, benefited six lines only.

The Merchant Marine Act of 1928 set forth three processes that were to precede the award of an ocean-mail contract under terms of the Act: (1) the Postmaster General was to certify to the Shipping Board the

[4] Italics added.
[5] For more detail concerning ship sales, 1920 through 1933, see the Harvard Report, pp. 219–261.

ocean-mail routes that in his opinion should be established, including the advisable dates for sailings and the volume of mail; (2) the Shipping Board was to certify the required vessel equipment for service on such routes (that is, the type, size, and speed of the vessels so employed and the frequency of sailings); and (3) the Postmaster General was then directed to advertise for bids and to conclude contracts with United States citizens. For each route, a contract was to be awarded the lowest bidder who, in the judgment of the Postmaster General, was qualified to ensure performance under terms of the agreement. Contracts were to be for periods not exceeding ten years.

Vessels employed in the mail service were to be (a) steel, (b) built in the United States, and (c) registered under the American flag not later than Feb. 1, 1928, or (d) ordered and under construction prior to that date. All licensed officers serving aboard ships operating under mail contracts were to be United States citizens. For four years after passage of the Act, one-half of the crewmen were to be citizens, and thereafter two-thirds. To determine compensation, vessels were classified into seven groups, and the maximum rates varied from $12 per ton per nautical mile for ships of 20,000 or more gross tons and 24-knot speed to $1.50 per nautical mile for small, slow ships.

Immediately after the 1928 Act went into effect, the Postmaster General certified 27 itineraries as essential ocean-mail routes, and the Shipping Board certified the necessary equipment. The routes were advertised, and 25 contracts awarded to successful bidders. In 1929, President Hoover appointed the Interdepartmental Mail Contract Committee, which undertook a study of primary movements in United States oceanborne trade. The committee recommended additional routes, with the result that 46 contracts were negotiated with 31 steamship companies. The various contracts embodied varying requirements depending on the permanency of the service undertaken; the construction of new vessels; and reconditioning, substitutions, or improvements of then current equipment. According to a Maritime Commission report of Mar. 26, 1937, the Post Office Department paid out about 200 million dollars in mail subsidies, of which about 25 million represented normal rates for mail actually carried.

Construction-loan Fund. The Merchant Marine Act of 1920 had authorized a construction-loan fund of 125 million dollars. This, however, did little to stimulate shipbuilding; between 1922 and 1928 not a ship was constructed in the United States for transoceanic service.

The Act of 1928 increased the construction-loan fund to 250 million dollars, which was to remain a revolving fund. Many of the ocean-mail contracts awarded after the 1928 Act was passed were conditioned on replacement of old tonnage and provisions requiring a certain degree of expansion of the commercial fleet. Hence, vessel construction or reconditioning was closely allied with ocean-mail payments. Loans were not to exceed three-fourths of the cost of construction or remodeling and were to be repaid in twenty years. During any period that a vessel operated in foreign trade, the interest rate was to be the lowest rate of yield of any government obligation issued subsequent to Apr. 6, 1917, but during any period in which the vessel operated exclusively in the coastwise trade or was inactive, the rate was not less than 5.25 percent per year. Vessels on which loans had been made were to remain under the American flag, and the government's equity was to be secured by a preferred mortgage and by insurance. While the 1928 Act was in force, 31 new ships were built and 41 reconstructed or reconditioned.

THE MERCHANT MARINE ACT OF 1936

While the 1928 Act was a substantial improvement over earlier legislation, it had several serious defects, which were summarized in a 1950 report by the so-called Magnuson committee:[6]

First the compensation granted American lines was not based upon actual conditions encountered on the particular route served, so that some lines got more than they needed, while others competing with subsidized foreign companies were given too little aid. Second, the ship replacement provisions were somewhat too laxly enforced. Third, loans for shipbuilding were made at varying rates, so that lucky lines got money at almost nominal interest charges, while others paid several times as much, creating an element of unfairness. This, however, was not due to favoritism, but to legal interpretation of a carelessly worded section of the act . . . Fourth, there was inadequate supervision over the use to which subsidy money was put by the lines, officers of one or two companies paying themselves huge bonuses and dividends when their companies were almost going bankrupt. Fifth, there was complaint that in violation of law, contracts were so worded that public bidding was frustrated and only a predetermined line could comply.

On Mar. 4, 1935, President Franklin D. Roosevelt sent a message to Congress on the American merchant marine, in which he stated:

In many instances in our history Congress has provided for various kinds of disguised subsidies to American shipping . . .

I propose that we end this subterfuge. If the Congress decides that it will maintain a reasonably adequate American Merchant Marine I believe that it can well afford honestly to call a subsidy by its right name.

Approached in this way a subsidy amounts to a comparatively simple thing. It must be based upon providing for American shipping Government aid to make up the differential between American and foreign shipping costs.

[6] *Merchant Marine Study and Investigation*, Senate Committee on Interstate and Foreign Commerce, 81st Cong., 2d sess., S. Rept. 2494, 1950, p. 109.

The resulting legislation was the Merchant Marine Act of 1936, effective Oct. 26 of that year. It created a new Federal regulatory agency, the U.S. Maritime Commission,[7] and provided that the Commission was to carry out the purposes of the Act through the following:

1. Construction-differential subsidies on vessels built in the United States for use on essential foreign trade routes.
2. Operating-differential subsidies on vessels utilized on essential foreign trade routes.
3. Financial aid in the construction of vessels, either with or without construction-differential subsidies, by deferment of a portion of the purchase price (granting loans).
4. Applying to the purchase price of new vessels an allowance of credit for obsolete vessels taken in exchange.
5. Restrictions on the sale or use of vessels owned or acquired by the Commission.
6. Payment for national-defense features incorporated in the vessels.
7. Low interest rates on construction loans.
8. Establishment of reserve funds with attendant income tax benefits to the vessel operators.
9. Construction of vessels for chartering to private operators.
10. Additional subsidies to offset the effect of governmental aid paid to foreign competitors.
11. Guarantee of ship mortgages.
12. Training of citizens to serve on American merchant vessels.
13. Prescribing of minimum manning scales, minimum wage scales, and minimum working conditions for all officers and crews employed on vessels receiving an operating-differential subsidy, and other benefits to American seamen.
14. Authority to requisition or purchase vessels when advisable for the security of the national defense or during national emergencies.[8]

The Maritime Commission had little more than started to put into effect the long-range program provided for in the 1936 Act when war intervened and the United States embarked on a shipbuilding program that produced 5,500 merchant ships. This war-built fleet was superimposed on, and altered, the long-range program commenced under the 1936 Act. In 1946, Congress passed the Merchant Ship Sales Act, to direct the Maritime Commission as to procedures and prices for disposing of this government-owned fleet. As pointed out by the Maritime Commission, the sale of these ships had the immediate effect of providing the American merchant marine with "an almost adequate number of cargo vessels to carry out the initial objectives of the 1936 Act."

[7] In 1933, the membership of the U.S. Shipping Board had been reduced to three members, and the agency, known as the U.S. Shipping Board Bureau, had been transferred to the Department of Commerce. For more detail, see Chap. 20.

[8] *Report on Audit of United States Maritime Commission,* Letter from the Comptroller General of the United States, 81st Cong., 2d sess., H. Doc. 465, 1950, p. 2.

SHIP SALES AFTER WORLD WAR II

Under authority given to it by the 1946 Act, the U.S. Maritime Commission offered for sale more than 4,000 ships, representing a deadweight tonnage of 43 million tons. They included nearly 3,500 dry-cargo ships and 563 tankers. Although sales were permitted to noncitizens, the best ships were reserved for American purchasers, and they were given preference with respect to priority of application.[9] By Jan. 15, 1951, when sales were terminated, American shipowners had purchased 581 dry-cargo vessels and 266 tankers.

The Act established a firm pricing policy in that it fixed statutory prices. These varied from $59 per deadweight ton ($639,000 per ship) for the Liberty to $106 per ton ($1,650,000 per ship) for a C4 and $121 per ton ($2,026,500) for a T2 tanker. These prices, based on a percentage of the prewar domestic costs of producing the particular type of vessel (dry-cargo ships 50 percent and tankers 87.5 percent), were adjusted to take account of (1) the cost of putting the vessel in class, (2) the absence of standard features, (3) the presence of desirable features, and (4) normal depreciation. The Act, however, provided for a floor price equivalent to $50 per deadweight ton for Liberty ships and $99 for the C4. At the time of the sale, purchasers were required to pay at least 25 percent of the statutory price, with the balance payable in not more than 20 equal installments, and with interest fixed at the rate of 3.5 percent annually.[10] The government's interest in the ship is secured by a preferred mortgage.

By Jan. 15, 1951, the government's reserve fleet was down to roughly 2,100 ships, of which 1,477 were Liberties. A year earlier, the Magnuson committee[11] had pointed out:

> There is little need for further extension of sales authority because ample private tonnage is now available to meet commercial and military cargo requirements, and further, because a continuation of the sales program would only serve to hold a large group of cheap ships over the market which would have the inevitable effect of holding back building programs of private companies. Block obsolescence is a prime problem in the merchant marine today, and the sooner the sales program comes to an end the sooner the orderly replacement of war-built ships can begin.

---

[9] The Act permitted noncitizens to make application to purchase any war-built ship "other than a P-2 type or other passenger type and other than a Liberty type collier or tanker." When sales to noncitizens were terminated on Mar. 1, 1948, 897 dry-cargo ships and 216 tankers had been sold to noncitizens. Most of the figures appearing in this section are from *Shipping Survey*, Association of American Ship Owners, June, 1951, Vol. 7, No. 3.

[10] These conditions applied only to sales to American citizens.

[11] *Merchant Marine Study and Investigation*, p. 52.

CONSTRUCTION-DIFFERENTIAL SUBSIDIES

The Merchant Marine Act of 1936 had laid down certain provisions that had to be met before a construction-differential subsidy would be granted. The U.S. Maritime Commission had to determine (1) that the new vessel was to be used on a foreign trade route termed essential,[12] (2) that the proposed ship was of a type adequate to meet foreign competition on the specified route, (3) that the vessel met certain specifications with regard to Navy requirements for rapid conversion as a military or naval auxiliary, and (4) that the operator possessed the ability, experience, and financial resources requisite not only to operate the proposed vessel but also to continue adequate service on the essential route. Subsidies were limited, except in special cases, to $33\frac{1}{3}$ percent of the cost of the ship, though defense features might be incorporated at government expense. Ships so financed were to be built in yards within the continental United States.

The size of the subsidy was to be determined by a careful study of the cost of building a similar ship in a foreign yard, and the contracts were to be let on a competitive basis. Further safeguards were included when the vessel was completed: (1) the shipbuilder was required to file a report showing the contract price, the cost of meeting the contract, overhead, and net profits; (2) in computing the cost of building the ship, no salary of more than $25,000 a year was to be considered; and (3) earnings in a year in excess of 10 percent of the contract price should revert to the government unless the shipbuilder had incurred deficits in the preceding year. Then the deficit would be allowed as a credit in determining the excess profit.

In November, 1937, the Maritime Commission submitted to Congress an economic report disclosing that 88 percent of the ships in the merchant fleet were either obsolescent or approaching obsolescence. The first construction-subsidy agreement had been signed in October. (This was for the passenger ship *America*, the largest merchant ship so far built in a United States shipyard.) Private enterprise, however, was reluctant to finance the ships necessary for replacements and for expansion of the merchant fleet. In 1938, Congress authorized the Maritime Commission to proceed with a construction program calling for 50 ships a year over a ten-year period, without any clear idea of the ultimate disposition of the ships. This program was under way in 1939, when the needs of the world-wide shipping emergency led to stepping up the program. In that year, the construction of 150 ships was approved over a two-year period. By October, 1941, 112 ships had already been completed and 771 were on the ways. Most of these were C1's, C2's, and C3's—ships of standardized

[12] The essential-trade-route concept was discussed in Chap. 4.

design developed by the Commission's technical staff and incorporating the Navy's requirements for national defense. The construction program not only furnished the United States with a nucleus of modern freighters for use during World War II but provided the basic machinery for the shipbuilding program of 1940 through 1945.

Postwar Passenger Ships. The postwar ship-sales program took care of the immediate needs of United States ship operators for good freighters. The situation regarding passenger vessels, however, was far less favorable. In 1947, the President's Advisory Committee on the Merchant Marine[13] reported:

Because of present pressing demands for overseas transportation, war-built troopships, with almost primitive passenger accommodations, are transporting Americans and other nationals under conditions which can be justified and permitted only because no more suitable ships are available. These ships not only fail to meet the standards of safety at sea prescribed by the United States Coast Guard regulations, but in some cases fall short of meeting the requirements established by the International Convention of Safety of Life at Sea.

Other agencies concerned with the condition of American ships, including the Trade Route Committee of the U.S. Maritime Commission, concurred on the need for passenger ships. The wartime records of the *Queen Mary* and *Queen Elizabeth* had made it clear that such ships had great defense value. Furthermore, the United States had lost many passenger ships during the war.

On Aug. 9, 1948, the Maritime Commission unanimously approved the application of American Export Lines, Inc. for construction-differential aid in building two fast passenger ships, the *Constitution* and *Independence*, capable of carrying 972 passengers on the route between New York and the Mediterranean. In a contract of Aug. 11, 1948, the application of American President Lines, Ltd., was approved for aid in constructing three combination passenger-cargo ships to be used in round-the-world service. They were designed to carry 188 passengers and 7,800 tons of freight at a speed of 19 knots. The sixth postwar passenger vessel contracted for is the United States Lines' superliner, the *United States*, which entered service in July, 1952. The three American President vessels were never completed for private account, and the sale of the other three involved "sudden shifts in policy," which *Time* magazine blandly states "would hardly encourage shipbuilding."[14] This will be clarified by details of the manner in which the construction-differential subsidy is administered.

[13] This committee consisted of K. T. Keller, Marion B. Folsom, Andrew W. Robertson, James B. Black, and E. L. Cochrane.
[14] *Time*, Mar. 24, 1952, p. 95.

The mechanics of the construction-subsidy arrangement are such that the subsidies are not paid to the ship operator. Instead, the government agency (the Maritime Commission until May, 1950, and thereafter the Federal Maritime Board) is authorized to contract with a United States shipbuilder for the construction of the ship, and concurrently to contract with a ship operator to sell him the ship at its estimated foreign cost exclusive of national-defense features. In 1948, the total costs of the two liners *Constitution* and *Independence* were determined at $23,415,000 for each ship, with the selling price to the applicant, $11,956,285. The government subsidy was, hence, to be $11,458,715, which included various national-defense features. At the time the contracts were entered into among the Maritime Commission, American Export Lines, and the shipbuilder (Bethlehem Steel), the formal purchase price was still to be determined.[15]

On July 11, 1949, the Comptroller General of the United States submitted a report[16] in which it was charged (1) that the foreign-cost estimate of $11,945,285 per ship had not been founded on the "convincing evidence" required by Section 502 of the Act of 1936, if the subsidy is over $33\frac{1}{3}$ percent of the ship's cost, and (2) that the allowance of more than $1,676,000 per ship for national-defense features was in his judgment an allowance, at least to some extent, for certain features sought by American Export for commercial purposes. When the *Independence* was ready for delivery on Jan. 11, 1951, the Federal Maritime Board, successor to certain powers, duties, and unfinished business of the former U.S. Maritime Commission, was confronted with the problem of formalizing the prior informal sales agreement.

Hence, following January, 1951, the Federal Maritime Board was confronted with the task of determining what it would have cost in 1948 to build the *Independence* in the selected foreign shipbuilding center, Holland. In the report[17] embodying its decision, dated Feb. 25, 1952, the Board pointed out:

---

[15] The contract and the ones for the other passenger ships discussed in this section are all on an "adjusted-price" basis. "Under that form of contract, the shipyard and the Commission agree on a base price as of a certain date. That price is subject to increase or decrease based on the movement of indices published by the U.S. Department of Labor for selected shipyard straight time hourly earnings and prices of metals and metal products. The estimates of foreign costs used in the determination of the selling prices to the applicants likewise are on an 'adjusted price' basis. Accordingly, in order for the subsidy to be properly determined, the initial sales price to the applicants should be subject to escalation." *Report on Audit of United States Maritime Commission*.

[16] 81st Cong., 2d sess., H. Rept. 1423.

[17] *In the Matter of the Review and Redetermination of the Vessel Sales Prices of the SS Independence and SS Constitution to American Export Lines, Inc., Pursuant to Title V of the Merchant Marine Act, 1936, as Amended*. Much of the information in this section is from this mimeographed report of the Federal Maritime Board.

The staff of the former Maritime Commission and the present staff were confronted with the fundamental problems of properly evaluating foreign costs, with the handicapping knowledge that the sources of information divulged much of it, if at all, reluctantly and usually anonymously. We encountered some difficulties in making recalculations after a considerable lapse of time, but had the advantage of official publications, industrial indices, and a wealth of new material as to conditions in 1948, which information was not in existence at the time of the Commission's computation in that year.

The Board's decision was that the foreign cost of both ships (the estimates were on a two-ship basis) would have been $17,308,000 per ship in 1948. Since the total construction cost in the United States shipyard had been estimated at $23,733,000, the subsidy should have been $6,425,000 per ship—or 27.7 percent of the total cost of construction rather than the 48.9 percent of the 1948 contract. In other words, the Board set more than $17,000,000 each as the purchase price for ships that the company had contracted for at roughly $12,000,000.

Meanwhile, the two ships had been delivered to American Export Lines under a contract that permitted the government to "make a redetermination of the vessels' sales prices." The steamship company was to have thirty days to accept or refuse the redetermined price. Furthermore, under its operating-differential agreement dated June 6, 1951, if American Export Lines failed to accept the Board's redetermination of the sales prices on the two ships, the company's operating-subsidy contract "shall terminate automatically on December 31, 1952." American Export Lines appealed the Board's February decision. In preparation for further hearings, the three members of the Federal Maritime Board, technical personnel of the Maritime Administration, and representatives of the Comptroller General went to the Netherlands in July, 1952. Later that year, the Board set $14,036,751 as the purchase price of the *Independence* and $14,436,956 as that for the *Constitution*, and the sales contract was signed in November, 1952.[18]

When the superliner *United States* was delivered to the United States Lines, the matter of financing her cost of construction was not settled. On May 12, 1952, Secretary of Commerce Charles Sawyer wrote to the Comptroller General:

The decision made by the former Maritime Commission was not made by me or by anyone under my control. It may or may not have been sound. That question, it seems to me, is beside the point. There is no suggestion that the contract was affected by fraud of any kind, and to me the opinion of my counsel that it is a valid and binding contract is persuasive. If I should refuse to go through with this contract the United States would immediately have a ship on its hands and would be forced to try to make some prompt arrangements for its use. I

[18] The *Independence* had cost $26,479,000, and the *Constitution* $27,218,000.

prefer not to strain at a gnat and swallow a camel. From the standpoint of the taxpayer and his ultimate situation, and from a practical commonsense standpoint, it seems to me more important for the United States to carry out its contract already entered into than that the Government be saddled with a ship which it cannot run and a lawsuit which it cannot win.

Soon after the opening of hostilities in Korea, the Department of Defense took the three vessels being constructed for American President Lines' round-the-world operations; as of early 1953, no contracts had been entered into for the construction of other vessels in place of these three; and the company had canceled its 1950 application for aid in building four other combination passenger-cargo ships.

Postwar Freighters. The first postwar freighter was the *Schuyler Otis Bland*, an experimental ship, which the Maritime Administration bareboat-chartered to the American President Lines for operation in its round-the-world service from July, 1951, to July, 1952, when she was redelivered to the Administration and chartered to the Waterman Lines.[19] A number of her experimental features were incorporated into the design of the Mariner, the first new class of cargo ship to be built in the United States since the war.

In 1950, the Maritime Administration requested, and Congress appropriated, 350 million dollars to build 35 Mariners. The first Mariners entered service during the latter part of 1952. Since the cargo carriers in the government's reserve fleet were frozen when the ship-sales program terminated on Jan. 15, 1951, these ships are the only ones that can be sold to private operators. In this respect, it is again worth noting that the only postwar freighters constructed for United States-flag operations have been the government-built ships.

After the launching of the first Mariners, the government had inquiries from several prospective purchasers, and the first sales were announced late in August, 1953. Pacific Far East Line had signed contracts with the Federal Maritime Board for the purchase of three Mariners to be delivered in mid-1954. At the time the announcement was made, Louis S. Rothschild, chairman of the Board and Maritime Administrator, estimated that the purchase price per freighter would be between $5,460,000 and $6,625,000. Even the lower of these two figures is somewhat higher than a previously mentioned sales price of roughly $4,500,000 (approximately half of their cost, which ranges between $8,250,000 and $10,000,000), but the "fixed" sales price, as determined by the Board, will include special features required by Pacific Far East Line, which will operate the ships in its transpacific service over U.S. Trade Route 29.

National-defense Features. Although the Act of 1920 provided that the

[19] The Maritime Administration handles administrative matters, and the Federal Maritime Board regulatory matters. See Chap. 20.

nation's merchant marine should be sufficient to "serve as a naval and military auxiliary in time of war or national emergency," construction loans under that Act and the Act of 1928 were not contingent upon the inclusion of national-defense features. Furthermore, since subsidy payments were tied to the carriage of the mails, both laws tended to benefit the operators of passenger and combination vessels rather than those of freighters.

Since 1936, but more particularly since 1946, national-defense features have been of paramount importance in the construction of United States ships. The Act of 1936 called for a "well balanced" fleet of vessels "suitable for economical and speedy conversion into naval or military" auxiliaries. As the international situation has developed since 1946, those responsible for the nation's maritime policy and its implementation have considered it absolutely necessary that better and faster ships be added to the American merchant marine, for, as Admiral William M. Callaghan, then commander, Military Sea Transportation Service, pointed out, "slow speed may be quick death in a future war."[20] The Maritime Administration's answer to the needed freighters was the Mariner—a type of ship designed to be mass produced, fast enough to travel out of convoy during wartime, and needing no conversion for wartime employment.

The need for fast passenger ships that can be converted into troopships was a deciding factor in the construction of the *Constitution, Independence,* and *United States.*[21] The latter can transport an entire division— 14,000 men—from the United States to Europe in ninety hours, and put them ashore with equipment and supplies for initial maintenance. Or she can take them on a 10,000-mile voyage without additional supplies of fuel, water, or food.

To ensure that a ship that is to be constructed under a construction-differential subsidy meets national-defense requirements, the Act of 1936 (Section 501b) requires that the plans and specifications for the proposed vessel be submitted to the Navy Department "for examination thereof and suggestions for such changes as may be deemed necessary or proper." Further, the Secretary of the Navy is required to certify approval of the plans as submitted or as modified. Then, the selling price to the private operator (that is, the cost of construction minus the construction-differential subsidy) is further reduced by excluding the "cost of any features incorporated in the vessel for national-defense uses."

National-defense features include not only increased speed (that of the *Constitution* and *Independence* was increased from 22.5 to 25 knots, and

[20] Speech delivered at the American Merchant Marine Conference, sponsored by the Propeller Club of the United States, Los Angeles, Calif., Oct. 8, 1952.

[21] Before the war, the United States had had 162 passenger ships as compared with 62 in late 1952, after the *United States* entered service.

the Mariners are capable of sustained speeds of 20 knots) and materials used (no inflammable materials were employed in constructing the *United States*, and the only wood used is in the butcher's block in the galley and the pianos) but also such features as the extra cost of strengthening a deck so that it is capable of supporting a gun tub in the event the vessel is armed during wartime.

The construction of ships for dual purposes poses certain problems for private commercial operators, who are in the shipping business for the very laudable purpose of making a profit. Regarding cargo ships, Admiral Callaghan said, in his speech mentioned earlier:

> ... we come face to face with one of those conflicts between what is best for commerce and the optimum requirement for military purposes. Unfortunately the high speed desired for military use is not necessarily a requirement for commercial trade. It may, in fact, constitute an economic handicap to the private operator who gains a few days' time at sea at much higher operating costs and is not able to realize any overall savings because of the slow turnaround time in port.

Under present circumstances, it is important that the people and the press take a realistic attitude toward the national-defense aspects of the country's shipbuilding program.

Administration of Construction Differential—A Summary. The Merchant Marine Act of 1936, as Vice Admiral E. L. Cochrane, Maritime Administrator in 1952, pointed out, was drafted during the period of recovery following the depression of 1933; and its promulgators envisaged an era of world-wide economic stability in which "fair and reasonable" estimates might be possible. Congress recognized that war conditions made reliable foreign construction costs virtually unobtainable, and on June 11, 1940, Joint Resolution 82 established the foreign costs prior to Sept. 3, 1939, as the basis for computing construction-differential subsidies. This situation was given statutory recognition through July 25, 1947. In 1947, the President's Advisory Committee on the Merchant Marine recognized the continuing instability and predicted the difficulty that has developed. The 1952 decision of the Federal Maritime Board, with the Maritime Administrator concurring, summarized the situation:

> Estimating the cost of building a large ship of a new design is a difficult job even by the management of the shipyard concerned, which over the years accumulates files of carefully analyzed data based on its own methods of recording actual cost returns and upon the shrewd use of quotations from various vendors of materials and parts. . . .
>
> The spread of the bids received 31 January 1951 from ten (10) American shipyards for building of the new Mariner Class in blocks of five identical sister ships . . . ran from $7,775,000 for each of five to $10,526,000. . . . Any one of these bids would clearly qualify as a "fair and reasonable estimate of the cost"

etc., but the result in determining a construction-differential subsidy for another ship on these figures assuming they were from a foreign yard would vary correspondingly.

In short, while the 1936 Act in section 502 (b) purports to present a precise, mathematical formula for determining construction-differential subsidy for a new ship, it actually presents a practical impossibility from the administrative point of view. . . .

I recommend most earnestly . . . that the law be amended to permit a predetermination from time to time of the subsidy rate which can be approved objectively and free from specific application if possible; so that future contracts can be negotiated with confidence and promptness and with fairness and reasonableness both to the Government and to the prospective shipowner. . . .

OPERATING-DIFFERENTIAL SUBSIDIES

Title V of the Merchant Marine Act of 1936 had recognized frankly that American-built ships cost more than foreign ships. Title VI of that Act gave the same recognition to operating costs; it provided for operating-differential payments representing the difference between the costs of the American-flag operator and his foreign-flag competitor or competitors. Operating aid was, like the construction-differential subsidy, tied to the essential-trade-route concept,[22] for the Act provided that operating-differential subsidies were limited to "the operation of a vessel or vessels, which are to be used in the essential service in the foreign commerce of the United States." Before an application was to be approved, the Federal administering agency had to determine (1) that the service to be rendered was required to meet foreign-flag competition and to promote the foreign commerce of the United States, (2) that the applicant either owned or was in a position to acquire suitable vessel or vessels, (3) that the applicant possessed the ability, experience, and financial resources to enable him to meet competitive conditions (that is, to offer service over a specified time), and (4) that the aid was necessary to place the operator on a parity with foreign competitors. The Act provides that contracts may be executed for a period of not more than twenty years. However, though the purchaser of a vessel undertakes a twenty-year obligation, operating-differential-subsidy contracts have been let for periods of ten to twelve years.

The Contracts. The ocean-mail contracts entered into by the Postmaster General with 31 companies under terms of the Act of 1928 were terminated as of June 30, 1937. The following day (July 1), the first operating-differential-subsidy contracts were effective. To the end of 1937, the Maritime Commission had made 17 contracts, but a number of these operators were not able to qualify under terms of the 1936 Act. On

[22] See Chap. 4.

Jan. 1, 1938, 7 long-term contracts were effective, and 2 more were added during 1938 and 1939. During 1940, 2 long-term agreements were canceled and 2 more executed. Hence for the fiscal years 1940, 1941, and 1942, the number of subsidized operators was 12.

By 1941, wartime conditions had virtually assured United States operators capacity cargoes, and effective June 1 of that year, 9 subsidized operators agreed to substantial cuts in the subsidy payments. Practically all ships were requisitioned in 1942, and subsidy payments were suspended until Jan. 1, 1947.

The first postwar contracts were effective Jan. 1, 1947, when 10 operators resumed subsidized operations. By 1949, 13 contracts were in effect. After the operating-differential-subsidy contracts effective Jan. 1, 1953, became operative covering the operations of Pacific Far East Line and Pacific Transport Lines on Trade Route 29, the number of subsidized operators was increased to 15.[23]

Determination of Operating-subsidy Rates. The law of 1936 provides that the operating-differential subsidy shall be determined on the basis of the difference between the costs of American-flag operation and those of foreign-flag operation. Items considered in determining subsidy rates include (1) wages and subsistence of officers and crew, (2) insurance, (3) maintenance, (4) repairs not compensated for by insurance, and (5) "any other items" determined by the Federal administering agency. Since a separate rate is determined for each type of expense, and separate rates are determined for each type of vessel on each trade route, the task of determining the subsidy rate is not an easy one. For example, if an operator employing two different types of ships on a route had five foreign competitors, 25 vessel calculations would be necessary for each vessel type, or a total of 50 for that company. To estimate what his subsidy payments will be on the subsidizable portion of his operations, a ship operator considers domestic and foreign costs of scores of individual items of food, repair, maintenance, wages, insurance, and so forth.

Because of the difficulties in determining rates for subsidy payments, most of the postwar contracts have not embodied approved rates, and the rates included have usually been considered tentative by the Federal Maritime Board and subject to recalculation. The first postwar payments were not made until 1950, and then they were limited to 75 percent of the estimated subsidy for portions of the years 1947 and 1948. Even after recalculation by the Board and ultimate payment of a subsidy, that amount is only an estimate of what the steamship operator may receive from the government due to the recapture provisions of the 1936 Act.

Recapture Provisions. Section 606 of the Act requires subsidized operators to repay operating-differential subsidies to the extent of one-half of

[23] See Table 2 (Chap. 4) for a listing of the companies by routes.

net profit in excess of 10 percent per annum of capital necessarily employed by the contractor in the operation of subsidized vessels.[24] It also permits profits and losses to be averaged over a ten-year period and provides for the recapture of subsidies only at the end of each ten-year period unless the contract is terminated. Hence, the net subsidy payments indicated in the accompanying table for postwar years are in reality estimates. The final accounting cannot take place until, at the close of the ten-year

Fiscal year	Accruals	Recapture	Net subsidy paid
1938	$ 8,741,222	....	....
1939	11,408,683	....	....
1940	12,794,876	....	....
1941	13,845,542	....	....
1942	4,602,085	....	....
Subtotal.....	51,392,408	$31,193,231	$20,199,177
1947	9,470,000	7,889,450	1,580,550
1948	25,736,000	18,014,425	7,721,575
1949	40,906,958	51,131,183	25,775,775
1950	54,090,970	9,576,588	44,514,382
Subtotal.....	130,203,928	50,611,646	79,592,282
Total........	181,596,336	81,804,877	99,791,459

SOURCE: These figures were published in *Merchant Marine Study and Investigation*, Senate Committee on Interstate and Foreign Commerce, 81st Cong., 2d sess., S. Rept. 2494, 1950, p. 44.

period, the accounts of the subsidized operator have been audited by the General Accounting Office.

Restrictions on Operations of Subsidized Contractors. Much could be written about the restrictions, obligations, and limitations that circumscribe the steamship company operating under an operating-differential subsidy. What the contractor must not do, without the consent of the Maritime Board, may be summarized as follows:

1. Operate any chartered vessel under subsidized contract.
2. Operate any vessel over twenty years old under subsidized contract.
3. Engage in any auxiliary services directly or indirectly connected with the operation of subsidized vessels, such as stevedoring, ship repairing, ship chandlering, towboat, or kindred services.
4. Operate unsubsidized vessels in competition with other subsidized lines.
5. While operating a subsidized service, engage through ownership operation or charter of any vessel in the protected noncontiguous, inter-

[24] The Act provides that the recapture shall, in no case, be more than the amount of subsidy payments received theretofore by the operator.

coastal, or coastwise trades of the United States, either directly or through affiliates, or hold any pecuniary interest in any person or vessel in such service.

6. Effect any merger or consolidation, or directly or indirectly embark upon any new enterprise or business activity not connected with the business of shipping.

7. Own, charter, or act as agent or broker for, or operate, any foreign-flag vessel competing with any American-flag service determined by the Maritime Administration to be essential.

8. Operate any unsubsidized vessel in the subsidized service of the contractor.

9. Dispose of any interest in the subsidy agreement or make any arrangement for maintenance, management, or operation of the service of others.[25]

RESERVE FUNDS

Title VI of the 1936 Act also provides that all subsidized operators shall maintain both a *capital reserve* fund and a *special reserve* fund. They are designed to stabilize the financial condition of the subsidized merchant marine and to ensure that the contractors have funds available for their vessel-replacement programs. Both funds are exempt from Federal tax.

The subsidized operator is required to place, out of his gross earnings, the following items in his capital reserve fund: depreciation, insurance indemnities, amounts realized from the sale of vessels, and profits that the operator intends to use for vessel-replacement purposes.[26] The capital reserve fund is a replacement fund, while the special reserve fund may be termed a *shock absorber*. Into it, the subsidized operator must place excess profits (that is, over 10 percent of the capital necessarily employed) and also such funds as may be placed in the reserve fund by mutual consent. The subsidized operator may utilize the special reserve fund (1) to reimburse his general funds as a result of losses or previous or current voyages or (2) to pay the government recapture. With the Maritime Administration's permission, any excess in the special reserve fund, over accrued government recapture and a basic balance equal to 5 percent of capital necessarily employed in the subsidized operations, may be transferred to general funds and used without restriction (unless previously tax paid, earnings so withdrawn become subject to income tax). This 5 percent is required to be maintained as a minimum reserve balance to meet future recapture obligations.

[25] For the "response" of the unsubsidized operators, see *Shipping Survey*, Association of American Ship Owners, August, 1952, Vol. 8, No. 3.

[26] The last two items were added to the original Act by later amendment.

GOVERNMENT AID 271

As on June 30, 1951, the subsidized operators had in their capital reserve funds $48,125,032 and in their special reserve funds $39,560,066, or a total of $87,685,098.

Any shipowner can maintain a construction reserve fund. Within the last few years, numerous bills have been introduced into Congress that would extend to the nonsubsidized operator the tax benefits now enjoyed by subsidized operators. This provision was embodied in the so-called Long-Range Shipping Bill, but it was eliminated before that bill was enacted into law on July 18, 1952.

THE LONG-RANGE SHIPPING ACT OF 1952

The construction-differential subsidies embodied in the Merchant Marine Act of 1936 provided that the government would absorb the difference between construction costs in the United States and those in foreign countries only on vessels constructed in the United States and owned by steamship companies operating those ships on foreign trade routes deemed essential by the government. This meant that the only steamship companies eligible for construction-differential subsidies were those whose ships were engaged in subsidized operations—a segment of the United States foreign fleet that, as we have shown elsewhere, represents less than one-half of the American-flag dry-cargo ships engaged in foreign trade.[27] The new law of 1952 extends the construction differentials to all ships operated in the foreign trade of the United States, including tankers and irregular, or tramp-type, vessels.[28]

The Act also amends Sections 503 and 509 of the 1936 Act to provide for nonrecourse loans on passenger ships of not less than 10,000 gross tons or 18-knot speeds. Under the normal interpretation of the former mortgage agreements, a shipowner who owns a ship built with a government subsidy obligates himself to pay not only with the particular ship herself but also with the value of the rest of his fleet.[29] This amendment was designed to apply to the owners of such large passenger vessels as the *Constitution*, *Independence*, and *United States*, the loss of which could, under certain circumstances, jeopardize the company's entire operation, for they may represent as much as 80 percent of the net worth of the company.

Under the 1936 Act, the Maritime Commission could, at its discretion, purchase a vessel seventeen or more years old if that ship were to be

---

[27] In addition, other ships including tankers and ore carriers have been constructed with mortgage-loan aid under Title XI, added to the 1936 Act by Act of June 23, 1938 (52 Stat. 953, 969).

[28] Public Law 586, 82d Cong.

[29] However, the mortgagor of a ship (excluding the passenger-ship mortgages described) must discharge his obligations out of any or all assets he holds, not merely out of the mortgaged vessel and the rest of his fleet.

replaced by a new vessel. In other words, the ship either obsolete or approaching obsolescence was traded in on a new ship. The 1952 law reduces the trade-in age from seventeen to twelve years. It also broadens the availability of construction reserve funds for use in the reconstruction and reconditioning of vessels and provides for recomputation of the life expectancy of the reconstructed or modernized merchant ship.

The provision of the 1936 Act limiting the salaries of all employees of companies receiving government aid to $25,000 has long been under attack on the grounds that the shipping industry needs the best men available and that the $25,000 limitation makes it difficult to attract top-flight men. This has been particularly true since 1939, with the upward trend of salary levels. The new law removes the salary limitation but provides that, for purposes of determining the government's right under the subsidy contracts, the $25,000 maximum still applies. In other words, subsidized companies may pay executives more than $25,000 per year, but the increase must be borne exclusively by the private operator as far as subsidy recapture and "additional charter hire" are concerned, but not so far as income tax is concerned.

The 1952 law is a decided step forward, particularly in overcoming the greatest weakness of the American merchant marine—ship obsolescence. The workability of the law will depend on its application. Increasing consideration is being given to a complete overhauling of the 1936 Act.

BIBLIOGRAPHY

Bailey, Frazer A., *Shipping Subsidies: Government Aid to Industry in a Free Enterprise Economy*, National Federation of American Shipping, Inc., Washington, D.C., Aug. 1, 1951.

Dearing, Charles L., and Wilfred Own, *National Transportation Policy*, Brookings Institution, Washington, D.C., 1949.

"Government Policy in the Ship Sales Market," *Shipping Survey*, Association of American Ship Owners, June, 1951, Vol. 7, No. 3.

Hutchins, J. G. B., *The American Maritime Industries and Public Policy, 1789–1914*, Harvard University Press, Cambridge, Mass., 1941.

Saugstad, J. E., *Shipping and Shipbuilding Subsidies*, U.S. Department of Commerce, Trade Promotion Series, No. 129, 1932.

The Use and Disposition of Ships and Shipyards at the End of World War II, A Report Prepared for the U.S. Navy Department and the U.S. Maritime Commission by the Graduate School of Business Administration, Harvard University, Government Printing Office, Washington, D.C., June, 1945.

U.S. Comptroller General, *Report on Audit of United States Maritime Commission*, 81st Cong., 2d sess., H. Doc. 465, 1950.

———, *Audit of Federal Maritime Board and Maritime Administration, Department of Commerce, and the Predecessor Agency, United States Maritime Commission*, 82d Cong., 1st sess., H. Doc. 93, 1951.

U.S. Congress, Senate Committee on Interstate and Foreign Commerce, *Mer-*

chant Marine Study and Investigation, 81st Cong., 2d sess., S. Rept. 2494, 1950.

U.S. Department of Commerce, Federal Maritime Board and Maritime Administration, *Annual Reports*, 1950, 1951.

U.S. Maritime Commission, *Economic Survey of the American Merchant Marine*, Nov. 10, 1937.

———, Tramp Shipping Committee, *A Study of Tramp Shipping under the American Flag*, Aug. 5, 1949, mimeographed.

What's the Score on American Shipping? Committee of American Shipping Lines Serving Essential Foreign Trade Routes, James A. Farrell, Jr., chairman, New York, April, 1953.

Zeis, Paul M., *American Shipping Policy*, 2d ed., Princeton University Press, Princeton, N.J., 1946.

CHAPTER 14

THE PROBLEM OF SHIPPING FINANCE

A total of more than two billion dollars of private capital is today invested in the ships of the American merchant marine. The process by which this sum was created is not peculiar to the shipping industry, but special characteristics of capital formation in shipping need to be recognized and understood. Many of the basic problems of forming and maintaining this capital arise from the impact of wars and economic troubles on the efforts since 1920 to establish a stronger American shipping industry.

CHARACTERISTICS OF SHIPPING CAPITAL

Large Amount of Investment. The shipping industry in the United States has three basic characteristics of capital. The first of these, not limited to this country, is that the purchase of a ship involves the commitment of a large amount of money and involves that commitment for an extended period of years. Not many industries require so large an investment to provide capital equipment, in proportion to total investment, as does shipping. Ships are the fixed assets of ocean transportation, and there is no ready second-hand market for them, as there is for many other industrial assets. Because service is being sold and this intangible product cannot be stock-piled, inventories are negligible. Also, as will be evident from Chapter 15, the industry works largely on a cash basis, and there are few receivables.

The statutory sales price after World War II of a mass-produced, war-built freighter, the Liberty, was $639,000. The better war-surplus ships sold for as high as $1,280,730 for the C3 type and $1,650,000 for the C4 type. If built at 1952–1953 costs, the cost of the C-type ships would run from at least $3,500,000 for the C1 to at least $6,000,000 for the C4. The new passenger liner *United States* cost over $70,000,000. When the future owners of these ships decide to commit their capital to the purchase, they have in mind a long-range decision extending at least twenty years, which is the period of depreciation established by the 1936 Act.[1] In earlier years,

[1] To this period of time, when building a ship, the owner must add the two or more years involved in designing, building, and outfitting the ship.

twenty-eight- and thirty-three-year periods were generally employed to establish rates of depreciation. In this connection, it should be noted that one difference between a ship as a unit of production and an industrial plant is that the ship cannot be replaced by degrees as is usually the case in industry. Therefore, we see that this first characteristic of capital—the large and long-range commitment—calls for a major decision by the owners of that capital.

Unsatisfactory Earnings Record. The second characteristic of merchant-shipping capital is the industry's history of "boom and bust," with a few years of prosperity in any cycle of time. Good years are associated with world-wide economic prosperity or times of international emergency, when a large volume of cargo bids for the relatively inflexible lifting capacity of the ships available. Long spells of uneconomic or less economic operation coincide with "overtonnaged" trade routes and business recessions. The results of this characteristic are twofold. First, it lessens the attractiveness of the industry to an investor; second, it makes it less certain and more difficult for a steamship company to establish the sound financial reserves necessary for expanding the enterprise and replacing ships.

One shipping executive has emphasized this characteristic of unsatisfactory earnings records in the following words:

Shipping securities are not too popular with the public. This is evidenced by the fact that during the last five years, taking Dow Jones selections, rail securities advanced by some 23 percent and industrials about 25 percent, while shipping securities actually declined. Because shipping earnings during this same period have been very good, the foregoing may sound paradoxical. Not to the investing public. They understand that shipping enterprises make good profits at times, but earnings fluctuate wildly over a long period, and worn out ships make poor dividends. The public is interested in steady income, even at lower rates. It is difficult, if not impossible to forecast a large rebuilding program primarily through the sale of new bonds, Debentures or equity shares.[2]

The prosperity of merchant shipping is volatile and very responsive to fluctuations in the volume of activity in the basic commodities of world trade. Charter rates are a good indication of the condition of the world's shipping. Note the rapid changes in the (British) Chamber of Shipping index numbers of tramp-shipping freights[3] reflected in the accompanying table, in which 1948 equals 100.

[2] From address by James A. Farrell, Jr., president, Farrell Lines, Inc., New Orleans, Feb. 28, 1952.
[3] In shipping, the term *freight* applies to the cost of transportation (the rate), and the merchandise transported is usually referred to as *cargo*.

Month	1949	1950	1951	1952
January	87.1	72.8	151.9	163.9
February	100.5	75.5	164.7	157.3
March	95.0	75.8	180.6	137.7
April	94.6	74.4	176.8	109.4
May	99.7	71.4	203.8	110.9
June	86.7	74.3	179.0	99.1
July	73.3	78.8	179.6	90.2
August	70.6	86.6	149.3	79.2
September	71.6	89.0	165.5	80.7
October	69.8	95.8	190.4	94.2
November	66.5	97.6	172.9	99.0
December	72.8	115.7	168.5	98.8
Year	82.3	84.0	173.7	110.6

SOURCE: *Lloyd's List*, Jan. 17, 1952.

The period between world wars was generally unsatisfactory for merchant shipping. Commenting on the domestic fleet, which comprised two-thirds of the prewar United States fleet, the Harvard Report stated: "Before the outbreak of the war . . . the financial position of the average coastwise and intercoastal shipping company was weak."[4] The combined profits and losses of 14 domestic operators for the years 1934 to 1938 gave total earnings of $366,005, and net losses were registered in two of the five years. Forty-two shipping corporations that reported to the government for the period 1928 to 1937 showed a combined net profit of $54,177,000 for the 10 most successful companies and a combined loss of $19,291,000 for the remaining 32 companies. The average earnings per annum on the investment were 2.8 percent for all the companies.[5]

World War II generally liquefied the capital assets of American operators as a result of the taking of ships by the government, by purchase or charter, or their loss by enemy action and the subsequent receipt of compensation or insurance payments. There was a broad-scale reinvestment of these capital funds by the shipping industry after 1946, except in the domestic routes. The postwar record was generally one of prosperity, tempered by the feeling that the conditions responsible for the prosperity were unhealthy, unrealistic, and temporary. This feeling and other influences have made the holders of shipping capital hesitant to make further commitments of their capital.

Small Amount of Public Participation. The third characteristic of

[4] *The Use and Disposition of Ships and Shipyards at the End of World War II*, A Report Prepared for the U.S. Navy Department and the U.S. Maritime Commission by the Graduate School of Business Administration, Harvard University, Government Printing Office, Washington, D.C., June, 1945, p. 73.

[5] *Ibid*, pp. 73–74.

shipping capital (and this is primarily so in the United States) is the small amount of participation by the general public. This is in direct contrast with the British industry, which we shall discuss presently. It also explains the importance of American public policy with regard to shipping, because the taxpayer's government is the indirect public investor as well as the banker for the great bulk of the American shipping industry.

During the heyday of the American merchant marine in the last century, when ships were owned by individuals who held eighth interests (or shares as low as sixty-fourths), many people owned "parts of a ship." The 2 billion dollars of private capital invested today is of quite a different nature. More than half of it is provided by industry and is invested in the industrial or private carrier. Much of the balance of the private capital comes from shipping families, many of whose names are still associated with their companies.

The Standard Oil Company of New Jersey is the largest shipowner in the United States, and also the owner of the largest fleet of tankers in the world.[6] The fleet of oceangoing freighters owned by Isthmian Steamship Co. and the still larger fleet of Great Lakes ore carriers owned by Pittsburgh Steamship make the United States Steel Corporation one of the nation's important ship operators. Large fleets are owned and operated by such interests as the other oil companies, United Fruit Company, and the Aluminum Corporation of America. The American President Lines stems from the early lumber interests of Captain Robert Dollar, but the divorcement of the early commodity interest is complete, and the company now has a common-carrier operation. Many of the intercoastal carriers are very closely tied to lumber operations in the Pacific Northwest.

The fact that so much of the capital comes from industrial and family sources is reflected in the small number of companies that have common or preferred stock listed on stock exchanges. Companies with stock in the hands of the public include American Export Lines, American-Hawaiian Steamship Company, American Mail Lines, American President Lines, Atlantic Gulf & West Indies Steamship Lines, Matson Navigation Company, Moore-McCormack Lines, and United States Lines.

Because the general public shares little of the risk of steamship ownership, the public has little proprietary interest in the industry's welfare. Its interest is indirect, through government, and remote except in time of emergency or for the romanticist who sees only the luxury liner and is unaware of the plodding freighter that carries his coffee, the lumber for his home, or the crude rubber for his automobile tires.

[6] Standard Oil of New Jersey's tankers are owned by subsidiaries and registered under both American and foreign flags.

Contrast with the United Kingdom. The three characteristics just discussed would not seem sufficient to make a substantial difference in the nature of capital in British and American shipping. Nevertheless, in the United Kingdom, public participation is broad, new capital has always been available, dividends have been paid regularly, and the public's attitude has been one of confidence and positive encouragement. All of this is quite the opposite of American experience. The contrast is sharp. For example, British investors are willing to accept yields as low as 5 percent or less for the stock of a better-known company, whereas yields of 10 percent and more are common in this country. This same contrast is reflected in the political environment within which the maritime policy of the respective countries is determined.

In other words, direct public participation in British shipping ventures is an invigorating, disciplinary influence on the industry, and the industry is directly responsive to the investing policy. The American industry lacks the fullness of this influence and is responsive to many influences, some of which are not so invigorating as is substantial public interest. Legislators, for example, are hardly suitable substitutes for trained and experienced shipping-management specialists who are responsible to private owners. Government is generally cautious and slow moving, a circumstance that too often leads to compromise rather than decisive action. Moreover, its interest in shipping not only fluctuates with administrations and changes in agencies but also is diluted by hundreds of other activities that compete for the attention of legislative committees, for position on legislative calendars, and for appropriations.

HANDICAPS OF AMERICAN SHIPPING CAPITAL

A number of problems bear on the financial situation of the American shipping industry, including the difficulty of achieving an industry policy, lack of legislative understanding that should result in a successful formula for a permanent maritime policy and a virile industry, inconsistent administration of policy, unsatisfactory labor-management relations, and the costly cycle of block obsolescence of the merchant fleet. The total of these problems affects the attractiveness of the industry to capital and has been a negative influence on the development of an American merchant marine.

Effect of Lack of Industry Unity on Policy. The various classes or types of operators in the shipping industry have difficulty in contributing to a strong, constructive statement of over-all transportation policies and needs. The end result cannot be measured in dollars, but the over-all climate is less conducive to profitable operation. The operators seldom reconcile their individual immediate interests, either because of the disinterest of one specialized segment in another or because of direct conflict of interests. The many characteristics and problems in the pattern of the American shipping industry are of varying degrees of importance to individual operators. Each ship operator is particularly concerned with those factors that pertain to his welfare. Moreover, these differences often initiate friction and conflict within the industry. Not only do differences and conflicts serve to prevent unity on industry policy, but they are also confusing to laymen and legislators, some of whom have, at times, used the confusion as an excuse to escape the issues rather than to tackle them.

For example, in the discussion of the 1936 Act, it has been noted that trade-route development and national security are objectives of national maritime policy. The realization of these goals is a particular responsibility of subsidized companies, but cuts across the field of interests of ship operators who are not involved in such direct participation with the government. As indicated in Chapter 13, before mid-1952, an operator who held an operating-differential subsidy was generally eligible to buy a new ship at a lower price than a nonsubsidized operator, by virtue of the construction-differential subsidy. On the other hand, among the 25 or more restrictions on the subsidized operator, there is his limitation to a certain trade route, whereas a nonsubsidized operator has the right to cut in and out of his trade route as cargo conditions warrant, including the right to cut into the trade route of the subsidized operator. An intercoastal operator has a competitive problem with respect to land carriers that is of little concern to most foreign trade operators. The domestic operator's problems are not even administered by the agency of government (the Maritime Administration) that is charged with the responsibility of developing a merchant marine.[7]

The failure of the industry to submerge some portion or degree of its competitiveness and find and expand an area of agreement on major overriding principles has done great harm to the whole industry. The situation has permitted opponents of shipping, in effect, to divide and conquer. Whether their motives stem from economic competition or from political aspiration, the results are the same.

Vagueness of Maritime Policy. The development of policies to accomplish the specific desired results requires an understanding of the nature not only of ship operation but also of the pattern of domestic and world affairs into which shipping fits. Such an understanding is not easily acquired, and very few people outside of the operators concerned have acquired it. Although the entire nation is the beneficiary of a merchant marine, only the people in harbor areas are conscious of shipping as such. The great interior of the country—even the hinterlands of ports—is too remote to feel the vital pulse of commerce. Inhabitants of the interior are

[7] See Chap. 19.

producers and consumers, bound up in the daily affairs of their lives. The problems of shipping, they feel, are someone else's job, even though their representatives in Congress who often reflect this attitude are controllers of public policy.[8] Even people in port areas who see shipping in action are not versed in cargo movements, international economics, obsolescence, and depreciation reserves.

In spite of the valiant efforts of the American Legion, the United States Chamber of Commerce, and similar national organizations, the public in general is too distant from the shipping industry. The public is easily influenced, as a result, by irresponsible charges of favoritism, profiteering, and other negative accusations, as well as by flag waving and other appeals to patriotism, which are at times the final resort of shipping men. Emotion rather than reason has too often been the foundation of legislative policy. As L. R. Sanford, president of the Shipbuilders Council of America, said, the "maritime industry, and the government agency charged with its promotion, have been and continue to be favorite whipping boys for those looking for subjects for public chastisement. Every peacetime transaction seems to be viewed with suspicion by somebody somewhere."[9] Because the public and the legislators generally do not understand the character of shipping, there has been a lack of pressure on Congress to develop legislation to clarify and improve the 1936 Act and other laws and a tendency for vagueness in legislation and administration.

Inconsistent Administration of Maritime Policy. Lack of unity of purpose within the industry and of fundamental support and decisive action by Congress, as well as a long history of inconsistent and weak administration of governmental policy (except in wartime), has contributed to the unattractive character of the shipping industry from the standpoint of capital investment. Inconsistency of administrative interpretation of law and of administrative action has worried private investors and the shipping industry alike.

Many shipping companies that had made mail-subsidy contracts through the U.S. Shipping Board in the 1920's were (some believe recklessly and for reasons of political gain) accused of collusion with the Post Office Department. The contracts were canceled by Congress in the 1936 Act. Some of the companies recommitted themselves by way of operating-differential-subsidy contracts with the new U.S. Maritime Commission. Although the operator is required to commit his capital in a new ship for a twenty-year venture, the Commission on its own initiative committed

[8] The story is told of the legislator who boarded his first ship, walked across the deck, came to a hatch coaming, looked down into the hold, and exclaimed in amazement, "Why, it's hollow!"

[9] From address by L. R. Sanford, before the Mississippi Valley Association, St. Louis, Mo., Feb. 11, 1952.

itself for a twelve-year subsidy contract. Further, from 1937 to 1940, subsidized companies had entered into contracts with the understanding that the deposit money they were required to place in the reserve funds was tax-exempt. In 1940, they were confronted by a contention of the Bureau of Internal Revenue that their understanding was wrong and that deposits in such funds were only tax-deferred. An agreement with the Treasury Department was eventually entered into in July, 1947. This departmental interpretation of the intent of Congress, originally forced upon the operators in 1940, was never reviewed by Congress.

Moreover, since World War II, certain companies committed capital to build new ships only to have a Congressional committee (not the committee that has cognizance of merchant-marine matters) accuse the parties involved of improper determination of the percentages of the construction-differential subsidy. As discussed in Chapter 13, a lengthy review by the Federal Maritime Board of the decision in this respect by its predecessor, the U.S. Maritime Commission, resulted first in the Board's finding that the percentages of differential as to two ships (the *Constitution* and *Independence*) had not been properly determined. The American Export Lines, which operates the ships, was faced with the decision of whether to invest several million dollars more or to return the ships to the government. A later decision of the Board materially lessened the amount that the company would have to add to its original investment, and the funds were obligated.

These matters are not here reviewed for the purpose of determining whether the facts of each case favor one party or another. They are reviewed for one purpose: any shipping investment that is dependent on government policies or contracts is speculative in character and therefore lacks attractiveness for the private investor, who compares degrees of security of investment, as well as for the shipowner.

One of the difficulties in this situation is that influence on policy and administration is distributed among many agencies and branches of government—Commerce, State, Defense, Bureau of the Budget, Treasury, Comptroller General, committees of Congress, and so forth. Another difficulty has been the constant change of basic administration. Since 1920, there has been (1) an independent Shipping Board, (2) a Shipping Board Bureau of the Department of Commerce, (3) a Maritime Commission, (4) divorcement of regulatory control of domestic carriers from the Maritime Commission and transfer to the Interstate Commerce Commission, (5) abolition of the Maritime Commission, and (6) the setting up of a Federal Maritime Board and a Maritime Administration in the Department of Commerce. Now the determination of clear-cut policy and administration, as between the Congress and the administrative agency, is in danger of confusion because the administrative agency is a subordinate bureau within the Department of Commerce.[10] Few people sense the potential disaster to the shipping industry, both in peace and in war, of this subordination of shipping administration in government. Under the cloak of security, many commitments can be made without the industry becoming aware of the degree to which its interests become prejudiced. One man has said:[11]

The [Maritime] Administration is subordinate to the Secretary of Commerce through an Under Secretary for Transportation, its policies or program are subject to modification and virtual control by the Bureau of the Budget, and it does not have independent direct access to the White House that the Chairman of an independent agency like the Maritime Commission should have. Furthermore it is continually handicapped in carrying out the national policy and its activities pursuant thereto are curtailed by limiting legislation attached to appropriation acts, contrary to proper legislative procedure, and sponsored by certain individuals apparently not friendly to the Merchant Marine.

Only the strong leadership by the Maritime Administrator and the Federal Maritime Board, and effective teamwork by the Secretary and Undersecretary of Commerce and the Administrator, will safeguard the national maritime interests under the existing arrangement.

Unsatisfactory Labor-Management Relations. The difficult character of labor relations in the maritime industry includes lengthy tie-ups of ships, innumerable quickie strikes, sad records of pilferage, loss and damage, seriously reduced output of labor, drastically increased wages and supplementary pay charges, and resistance of labor to introduction of labor-reducing machines and methods. All these things have lessened the value of the shipping industry in the eyes of those who might risk their investment capital and thereby produce jobs for labor and a healthier industry.

BLOCK OBSOLESCENCE

Bottleneck. Block obsolescence of the merchant fleet under the American flag is one of the most troublesome problems of the American merchant marine. While its effect is felt in legislative misunderstandings, administrative difficulties, and other ways, there is a specific aspect that concerns capital investment. We have already discussed the effect on ship supply of mass production of ships during the two world wars.[12] This type of production not only creates a surplus-disposal problem, with prices adjusted accordingly, but also standardizes the type of design so that ships cannot

---

[10] For details on the Shipping Board, U.S. Maritime Commission, and Federal Maritime Board, see Chap. 20. The regulatory control of domestic carriers is discussed in Chap. 19.

[11] From address by L. R. Sanford.

[12] See Chap. 6, pp. 122–124; and Chap. 13, pp. 254–255, 258–259.

be tailor-made to suit the specific requirements of various trade routes. The competitive value of such ships is seriously reduced. .

Block obsolescence of the World War I fleet created a capital-investment problem; the same situation has resulted from World War II. The cost of replacing ships in each case is much greater than the purchase price of the war-built ships. Ships purchased for $50 a ton or less after 1920 would have cost up to $200 a ton to replace, but the earnings of the 1920's and 1930's did not produce replacement reserves to supplement depreciation reserves. Improvements in ship design and propulsion would have made it possible for two new ships generally to do the work of three old ones, but even this technical betterment did not offset the cost-of-replacement problem. Nor did cheap construction loans authorized by the 1920 and 1928 Acts solve the difficulty. By 1935, there were many ship operators who could see only liquidation of their business as the solution, the problem being aggravated by depression and labor-relations difficulties as well as by the uncertainties associated with various government investigations.

Out of the studies and investigations there came the Merchant Marine Act of 1936. By that time, the great majority of the ships in the merchant marine were approaching or had reached twenty years of age. The portion of the Act (Title V) directed to the solution of block obsolescence was intelligently designed.[13] As explained in Chapter 13, it introduced the construction-differential subsidy, designed to provide a ship operator with a vessel at as little as one-half of its construction cost. However, the advantages of this building subsidy were limited in application to dry-cargo-ship operators who guaranteed to operate these ships on essential foreign trade routes. Other foreign trade operators, tanker operators, and those in domestic trade routes were not granted the cost differential. Construction-loan funds at low interest rates were their only recourse.

What would have happened to nonsubsidized operators is anyone's guess. Domestic dry-cargo operators might have struggled along until ships were lost or sold. Foreign traders would have been more and more at a competitive disadvantage. Tanker operators would probably have survived. However, World War II ended all speculation as to the future, because the entire American-flag fleet that was not sold abroad during 1939 to 1941 was transferred to the government, either for ownership or for use. In 1946, American operators who wished to reestablish their business were able to buy surplus war-built ships from the U.S. Maritime Commission at standard prices.

The great bulk of the war-built fleet is now eight to twelve years old. Only a few passenger ships, the Mariner-class ships, and some tankers have been built since 1946 to improve the general status of the fleet. This

[13] It has, however, serious technical faults, as will be shown presently.

fleet competes with an ever-increasing supply of tailor-made, fully modern, foreign-built ships. The cost of replacement is once again a main stumbling block from the investor's standpoint—a stumbling block induced not alone by inflation and high costs of labor. The problem was summarized by the president of an American company early in 1952:

The present privately owned merchant fleet of about 1,300 ships, including tank ships, cost their owners about $120 a ton. Today the replacement cost of this fleet is close to $360 a ton. The existing fleet would cost more than seven billions to replace. Accruing depreciation will finance only between one-fourth and one-third of such a rebuilding program.[14]

A ship purchased in 1946 for $100 a ton would cost between $400 and $500 a ton to replace in 1953. And prior to the passage of the Long-Range Shipping Act in the summer of 1952, the only shipowners in a position to benefit from a construction-differential subsidy were the 13 operators who, as of Feb. 1, 1952, had 260 ships employed in subsidized operations, or approximately 30 percent of the 838 privately owned oceangoing American dry-cargo fleet.

Solution. The easiest solution to block obsolescence and ship-replacement problems is to extend the construction differential to all shipbuilding in the United States. If the subsidy were extended to all shipbuilding, parity would result for all operators, including those in domestic trades.

A collateral and more difficult solution is to extend tax savings on earnings and reserves to all ship operators provided they will dedicate their financial resources so gained to an orderly program of shipbuilding and replacement. A system of accelerated depreciation could also be permitted, as is done in some other countries, so that the building of depreciation reserves could be expedited during years of good earnings. Until the shipping industry can be made more attractive to the public investor, the suggestions made in this paragraph seem to provide the only means of accumulating replacement reserves in addition to the depreciation reserves of the industry.

The alternative to encouraging the building up of replacement reserves is to permit shipowners to buy ships on the world market and register them under the American flag if they conform to American standards of construction. The decision here is whether or not the American people want to support the shipbuilding industry for reasons of national security. So far, the ship-operating aspect of the maritime industry has borne the brunt of the public's apathy about this problem. It is basically a shipbuilding problem and a matter of continuing what is, in effect, a protective tariff for shipbuilding.

The construction-differential-subsidy phase of the 1936 Act, while in

[14] From address by James A. Farrell, Jr.

the right direction, is almost impossible to administer. It calls for a fine determination of the cost of building a ship in a foreign yard. This means that American representatives must determine costs of labor, materials, supplies, and equipment in a competitor's yard. One can imagine the willingness with which a competitor parts with these data. Moreover, the determination may vary percentagewise from one year to the next, although the final cost of the ship to the American operator is fixed for the life of the ship. A more forthright recognition of the basic capital problem would seem to call for a flat construction subsidy, selected perhaps somewhere between 35 and 50 percent of total cost, excluding national-defense features, depending on the ship and conditions relative to each case. If the subsidy were so determined, this would eliminate much uncertainty and interagency squabbling.

Other aspects of block obsolescence and ship replacement have to do with the foreign-flag transfer (ship sale) problem, a trade-in-and-build program, and the use of the capital and construction reserve funds provided by the 1936 Act, as amended. The foreign selling situation has whipped up a lot of emotion, particularly from the labor front. Certainly, under some conditions, a matter of patriotism is involved; if national security were endangered by the removal of a ship from United States jurisdiction, an owner should not be permitted to transfer his ship from United States registry to registry under another flag. There is, however, a legal question whether the interference with the right of an owner to dispose of his ship where he wishes constitutes confiscation of the owner's property rights.

As matters now stand, Section 9 of the Shipping Act of 1916 establishes the requirement that "it shall be unlawful" to sell or otherwise transfer any vessel owned by an American citizen or documented under American laws without the approval of the Federal Maritime Board. While efforts are being directed toward the determination of a set of principles to govern the decision to grant approval of flag transfer, heretofore each case has been decided on its own merits. In so far as the capital situation in the industry is concerned, efforts to tighten up on flag transfers are in the wrong direction. Unless a realistic and reasonable approach is made to the subject, the problem of obsolescence will be all the more serious. Investors in the industry will be prevented—or at least discouraged—from liquidating their capital by selling older ships to reinvest in newer ships. Such a situation will discourage initial investment of fresh capital in the industry.[15]

The alternative, at least in part, to a sound foreign-selling or flag-transfer program is to establish a realistic trade-in-and-build arrange-

[15] *Shipping Survey*, Association of American Ship Owners, January, 1952, Vol. 8, No. 1.

ment. Methods of pricing and various procedures would have to be established by the government. This would substitute the government as the market for ships instead of the world-wide commercial market. This situation has obvious disadvantages—a monopoly by the government, a political determination of values with all of its attendant investigations and accusations, and so forth. Efforts in this direction in the past have been neither successful nor harmonious.

The various reserve funds provided by the 1936 Act were explained in Chapter 13. One of the most unfortunate developments in shipping legislation, as it relates to investor confidence in and governmental control of the industry, has been the attack on these reserve funds and their purpose by certain elements in government. The 1936 Act was created in the atmosphere of calling a spade a spade. Title V was framed in order to attack the problem of block obsolescence and the threat to capital formation within the industry. The objective of the reserve-fund provisions is to secure adequate capital funds to perpetuate the American merchant marine, in other words, to dedicate to the maintenance of the industry those capital funds that are at risk. At best, the effort is limited to those few operators who undertake the many obligations and rights of partnership with the government. The partnership since 1946 has not been a happy one, largely because of the lack of positive interest by the great majority of government forces and because of the bitter and often insidious attacks on the program by small but strongly organized minority groups.

NEED FOR PUBLIC-RELATIONS PROGRAM

Those most interested in solving the problems of shipping capital are the shipowners and operators. They need a strong, unified public-relations program. They need to pound home the basic truths of the service function of their industry. They need to organize their program on an industry-wide, nationwide basis. They need to resolve their lack of unity into a solid front. There are many in industry who seek to fill these needs. In 1942, the American Maritime Council was formed, conceived as a counterpart of the British Chamber of Shipping and having the goal of broad representation of all phases of the maritime industry. The Council produced a book in 1945, *Foreign Trade and Shipping*, and died from lack of support and the pressures of war. Then there came the National Federation of American Shipping, Inc., which has been a federation of regional shipping associations. However, its effectiveness has dwindled, and the organization disbanded.

There is a tremendous challenge to the shipping industry to merge its mixture of special interests and to unite in a program of research, indoctrination, and public relations. To concentrate on lobbying is not enough. Constant direct work to explain the function of ocean transportation at the grass-roots level and to policy makers is essential.[16] The function of shipping in the American economy is difficult to understand. Only a dedication to the purpose of creating and maintaining such a function will permit it to endure. Reliance on flag waving will not provide a substantial or enduring foundation.

We have built up an imposing and seemingly hopeless set of problems that bear on the capital structure of the shipping industry under the American flag. An earnings record, in so far as volume of cargo and the fortunes of general economic conditions are concerned, is not a subject for us to discuss here. However, industry, labor, and legislators can do much to stabilize the economic condition of the merchant marine and to overcome the difficulties stemming from block obsolescence. There are, of course, certain prerequisites, and they include the achievement of unity of policy and action by the various segments of the industry and the redefinition of national maritime policy and the dedication of all branches of the government and industry to the realization of that policy. The capital structure of the industry that requires safeguarding is largely dependent on government financing, industrial carriers, and the maintenance and preservation of existing private-capital commitments. Only a consistent, unified attack on the problems that beset this capital structure—an attack by men in business and government who have a broad concept of the economies of merchant shipping and of America's position in world affairs—will preserve the opportunities to achieve the desired goal. The effort needs men who recognize the need of overcoming the usual competitive sparring for position because of their being clothed with a peculiar and special degree of public interest. It needs men who are not intellectually muddled by a missionary concept of international economic relations.

BIBLIOGRAPHY

Because of the nature of this chapter, it is not possible to list the usual bibliographical references.

---

[16] The writer is indebted to Congressman John F. Shelley of California, a member of the House Committee on Merchant Marine and Fisheries, for the strength and clarity of his statement on the need for public relations in an address in San Francisco late in 1951.

CHAPTER 15

ACCOUNTING POLICY AND PRACTICE*

The steamship industry has two main divisions that are convenient to have in mind. One is the unsubsidized portion of the industry, which includes steamship lines operating in the domestic (noncontiguous, intercoastal, and coastwise) trades and some lines running to foreign ports. The subsidized steamship industry is wholly composed of so-called offshore or deep-sea lines, operating to foreign ports. As explained elsewhere, an operating-differential subsidy is paid to these lines, after their routes have been determined essential in the foreign trade of the United States and after other findings and determinations have been made by the Federal Maritime Board showing that their applications meet all the requirements of the Merchant Marine Act of 1936.[1] This subsidy is intended to compensate for extra costs imposed on the companies by United States laws. Costs include the use of Americans in crews and of "only articles, materials, and supplies of the growth, production, and manufacture of the United States . . . except when it is necessary to purchase supplies and equipment outside the United States to enable such vessel to continue and complete her voyage, and the operator shall perform repairs to subsidized vessels within the continental limits of the United States, except in an emergency."

These subsidized lines have certain accounting problems that do not devolve upon nonsubsidized lines. On the other hand, the accounting problems of the nonsubsidized lines are completely shared by the subsidized lines. Accordingly, this chapter discusses the special accounting and auditing problems and techniques of the subsidized lines, thereby automatically covering most of the accounting problems and techniques of the nonsubsidized lines. More specifically, the discussion is confined largely to the accounting problems and techniques of American President Lines, Ltd., which is one of the very few steamship companies that com-

* This chapter was written by Arthur B. Poole, vice-president in charge of finance, treasurer, and member of the board of directors, American President Lines, Ltd.
[1] Essential trade routes were discussed in Chap. 4, and the operating-differential subsidy in Chap. 13.

bine domestic (and nonsubsidized) business with both subsidized and unsubsidized foreign business. The organization and management of this company have already been discussed in Chapter 12.

ACCOUNTS RELATED TO OPERATING STATEMENTS

The Voyage as the Accounting Unit. From the oldest known days of ocean traffic down to the present, it has been customary to account for vessel operations on what is called a *venture* basis. For this purpose, the round voyage has been the unit. A round voyage is a voyage from a given port back usually to the same port, and customarily ends with the discharge of the homebound cargo, the new voyage picking up when loading for the next voyage begins. For practical reasons, the end of a voyage is normally taken as midnight of the day on which inward operations are finished. In early days, when ownership of vessels was calculated in sixty-fourths, there might be changes in ownership from one voyage to another. In the present day of corporate ownership of vessels, changes occur infrequently, but the voyage has continued to be the convenient and logical unit for accounting for profits. Thus a statement of income includes only the operating profits or losses of voyages completed during the accounting period, although depreciation, interest and overhead are accrued to the date of the statement; and no allowance is made for the operating income or expenses of voyages not yet completed at that date.[2]

The basic unit of the income statement is the *voyage profit*. This is the profit of a voyage after vessel and voyage expenses but before subsidy, depreciation, mortgage interest, advertising, overhead, subsidy recapture, and taxes. Vessel expense constitutes the direct cost of operating the vessel, including wages, fuel, lubricants, repairs, expendable equipment, vessel insurance–premium amortization, loss and damage claims, charter hire, stores, water, and provisions. Voyage expense comprises stevedoring, cargo checking, port charges, canal tolls, brokerage, and other direct expenses not actually a part of operating the vessel itself.

In 1938, the U.S. Maritime Commission, through its General Order 22, promulgated a complete system of numbered accounts to which subsidized lines must adhere in rendering quarterly and annual reports to the Commission.[3] Steamship lines engaged in coastwise and intercoastal traffic in competition with railroad and truck lines have been, since 1940, under the jurisdiction of the Interstate Commerce Commission[4] and

---

[2] For purposes of public statements, generally accepted accounting principles would require provision in some form for a material loss on an unterminated voyage, if it were improbable that the remainder of the voyage would substantially reduce the loss.

[3] In 1950, the functions of the Maritime Commission were taken over by the Maritime Administration and Federal Maritime Board. See Chap. 20.

[4] The ICC's regulation of domestic water carriers is discussed more fully in Chap. 19.

must render accounts in accord with the ICC system of accounts for water carriers. In recent years, the Maritime Administration and ICC have collaborated in a revision of their respective accounting requirements, resulting in what they describe as "Uniform System of Accounts for Maritime Carriers, Issue of 1950." This system of accounts went into effect Jan. 1, 1951. Statements prepared from these accounts, together with such other information as is required, are filed annually in an elaborate form of report. The basic report is the same for both regulatory bodies, but each requires a few pages of additional information not required by the other. The industry was consulted in the development of the uniform system of accounts, and finds it generally sound and appropriate.

Tables 7 and 8 present a form of voyage report, one sheet for direct accounting data and one sheet for certain statistical and unit-cost data. The pegboard form is especially convenient for voyages, because it makes readily possible a consistent comparison between any given voyage of a vessel and other voyages of the same vessel, similar voyages of sister ships, or any other voyages with which comparisons may be useful. Tables 7 and 8 contain less detail on some revenue items, and more

Table 7. Analysis of Revenue and Expenses for the *President Pierce*, a C3-type Vessel, Operating Transpacific, Voyage 32, Ended Nov. 8, 1952

Revenue

Freight (including ad valorem $0)		$318,947.68
Charter		0
Mail:		
United States	$ 0	
Foreign	789.82	789.82
Passenger:		
First class	7,362.50	
Third class	0	7,362.50
Baggage		28.63
Refreshments		0
Slop chest		104.84
Concessions		0
Laundry		0
Other		36.48
Total revenue		$327,269.95

Operating expenses

Wages[a]	S/T	O/T	Bonus 41 days	
Deck	$21,694.13	$ 9,787.52	$2,050.00	$ 33,531.65
Engine	22,165.41	8,998.88	2,050.00	33,214.29
Steward	8,315.16	5,133.67	1,207.50	14,656.33
Purser	1,278.11	212.40	102.50	1,593.01
Total	$53,452.81	$24,132.47	$5,410.00	$ 82,995.28

Table 7. Analysis of Revenue and Expenses for the *President Pierce*, a C3-type Vessel, Operating Transpacific, Voyage 32, Ended Nov. 8, 1952 (*Continued*)

P/R taxes[b]		$ 2,299.81
Welfare plans		2,480.40
Subsistence—provisions		9,197.40
Deck:		
Consumable stores	$3,258.13	
Rope—manila/sisal	136.71	
Wire	152.53	
Expendable equipment	391.91	$ 3,939.28
Engine:		
Consumable stores	2,910.73	
Lubricants	77.21	
Expendable equipment	449.69	3,437.63
Steward:		
Consumable stores	358.78	
Crockery, silverware, glassware	60.11	
Linen—table, bedding, etc	446.03	
Other expendable equipment	177.28	1,042.20
Medical—supplies and equipment		79.42
Stationery and office supplies		154.61
Total stores, supplies, and equipment		$ 8,653.14
Repairs to expendable equipment		$ 371.05
Shore gang:		
Contract jobs	$2,903.17	
Company labor (including P/R charges)	1,510.54	
Other	132.53	4,546.24
Laundry		858.60
Loading stores		580.04
Sundry		371.29
Total other maintenance expense		$ 6,727.22
Fuel		$ 25,914.52
Repairs:		
Restoration	$11,777.45	
Alterations	3,121.07	
Periodicals (detail on reverse side)[c]	5,877.60	$ 20,776.12
Insurance:		
Marine (including reserve $1,200.00)	$10,748.35	
P & I (including reserve $1,000.00)	3,528.31	
Other	242.94	$ 14,519.60
Charter hire—basic		$ 0
Fresh water		73.28
Launch hire		73.10
Sundry		8,647.29[d]
Total other vessel expense		$ 8,793.67
Total vessel expense		**$182,357.16**

Table 7. Analysis of Revenue and Expenses for the *President Pierce*, a C3-type Vessel, Operating Transpacific, Voyage 32, Ended Nov. 8, 1952 (*Continued*)

	Freight and mail	Passenger	
Agency fees...			$ 0
Commissions...........................	$2,875.84	$ 0	2,875.84
Brokerage.............................	343.66	379.69	723.35
Total agency fees, commissions, and brokerage....................			$ 3,599.19
Wharfage and dockage..			$ 6,197.48
Pilotage, tug hire, and towage.................................			2,755.70
Other port dues and fees.....................................			1,627.27
Sundry...			3,675.17
Total port expense......................................			$ 14,255.62
Stevedoring...			$ 36,635.25
Dunnage..			2,197.39
Clerk hire...			7,898.36
Cleaning holds and cargo tanks................................			1,238.19
Sundry...			6,083.53
Total cargo expense.....................................			$ 54,052.72
Canal tolls...			$ 0
Other voyage expense.......................................			216.30
Total other voyage expense...............................			$ 216.30
Total operating expense................................			$254,480.99
Net earnings (loss)...			$ 72,788.96
Subsidy..	$66,228.18[e]		

[a] Straight time (S/T), overtime (O/T), and bonus days were explained in Chap. 11. Wages include provision for wage increases then being considered by the Wage Stabilization Board.

[b] Payroll taxes.

[c] The explanatory comments on this item given on the reverse side are as follows:

Type of reserve	Reserve accrued prior voyages	Repair job costs		Reserves accrued this voyage
		For period	This voyage	
Dry-docking (9 months)......	....	....	....	$3,950.00
Tailshaft (3 years)..........	$ 1,121.46	....	....	354.71
Special survey (4 years).....	15,173.14	....	....	1,572.89
				$5,877.60

[d] This item includes $8,215 estimated stevedores' overtime differential incurred at Oakland in connection with loading 6,581 tons Military Sea Transportation Service general cargo carried F.I.O. (free in and out) to expedite dispatch of vessel.

[e] Although an addendum to the company's operating-differential-subsidy agreement was executed on Oct. 5, 1951, no final rates covering freighter-type vessels have as yet been incorporated therein. The estimated subsidy accrual for this voyage is based on differential rates used for accrual of subsidy for 1952 terminations in the "prospectus" filed with the Securities and Exchange Commission and effective Oct. 7, 1952.

detail on other revenue items, expenses, and statistics, than is required by the "Uniform System of Accounts for Maritime Carriers."

It might be thought logical from what has been said about operating-differential subsidy that subsidy earned would be deducted from the specific vessel expense accounts on which the subsidy was calculated. As a matter of fact, it has been found more convenient and useful to calculate voyage profit on actual revenue and gross expense, and then to add to the voyage profit thus calculated the amount of the subsidy, giving rise to a new amount of voyage profit after subsidy. This method has been crystallized by its incorporation into the uniform system of accounts previously described.

Charges against Voyage Profits. Until recent years, the vessel depreciation taken by steamship companies and recognized by the U.S. Department of the Treasury usually ranged between 2 and 4 percent, except for tankers and other vessels that carried corrosive cargo. The Merchant Marine Act of 1936 requires for its purposes that depreciation on vessels be figured on twenty-year useful life, after deducting from cost a small arbitrary residual value. Probably 4 percent comes nearest the rate that experience in this and other nations has shown to be a safe and appropriate average. The Act of 1936 was designed to err a little on the conservative side so as to call for earlier replacement of vessels which may not have worn out but which may have become obsolescent by comparison with vessels under other flags. The Department of the Treasury accepted the 5 percent depreciation rate provided in that Act.

Administrative and general expense, the principal element of overhead, differs little in a steamship company from the same expense in other industries. Agency fees and commissions earned, unless so substantial as in the opinion of the Maritime Administration to require separate allocation of overhead to them, must be deducted from administrative and general expense before such expense is ready for inclusion in overhead.

Advertising and interest expense are accounts that differ in no respect from similar accounts in other industries. Although a steamship company often has mortgages against individual vessels, the interest cost is nevertheless not included in computing the voyage profits of those vessels. This is sound because, for no reason related to earning power, one vessel may be heavily mortgaged and another lightly mortgaged, while at some other date, the borrowed capital may be nonexistent or held instead on an unsecured bank loan.

Steamship-company taxes differ greatly from those of a manufacturing or trading company. Deep-sea vessels, because of their location, are usually not subjected to a property tax at all. Furthermore, in order to encourage investment in an industry that was not attractive in former years and that had been the victim of changing and uncertain government policies, Section 607(h) of the Merchant Marine Act of 1936 provides that

Table 8. Voyage Statistics for the *President Pierce*, a C3-type Vessel, Operating Transpacific, Voyage 32, Ended Nov. 8, 1952

Service (F—freighter, F & P—freight and passenger)	F
Date voyage began	8/22/52
Date voyage ended	11/ 8/52
Number of nautical miles traveled	16,398
Running time—days	41
Port time—days	38
Total number of days	79
Vessel expense—cost per day	$2,308.32
Number of passengers:	
First class	20
Third class	0
Number of nonrevenue passengers	4
Total number of passengers	24
Meals served:	
Passengers, first class	1,294
Passengers, third class	0
Officers	3,330
Crew	8,630
Free..........117 Paid..........0	117
Total meals served	13,371
Subsistence—cost per meal day	$2.06
Subsistence and lodging paid to crew	$6.00
Number in crew:	
Deck department	20
Engine department	20
Steward department	12
Purser department	1
Total crew	53

"the earnings of any contractor receiving an operating-differential subsidy under authority of this Act, which are deposited in the contractor's [Capital and Special] Reserve Funds . . . except earnings withdrawn from the Special Reserve Funds and paid into the contractor's general funds or distributed as dividends or bonuses . . . shall be exempt from all Federal taxes." Accordingly, the tax charges in steamship company statements at times are lower than might otherwise be expected. It may be of interest to note that in settling matters of controversy with the U.S. Department of the Treasury, the subsidized lines agreed that, commencing with the postwar resumption of subsidized operations, such earnings (including capital gains) deposited in reserve funds would be deemed tax-deferred rather than tax-exempt.

Offshore steamship companies do have considerable difficulty with income taxes in foreign countries. It has been generally recognized by those engaged in international trade that taxation of international car-

Table 8. Voyage Statistics for the *President Pierce*, a C3-type Vessel, Operating Transpacific, Voyage 32, Ended Nov. 8, 1952 (*Continued*)

Fuel purchases and consumption:
Barrels on hand, beginning of voyage................................. 50
Barrels purchased:

Port	Barrel price	Number of barrels
Los Angeles (B/L)..........................	$1.70	10,306
Los Angeles...............................	1.75	5,458
San Francisco (B/L)........................	1.96	481

Total barrels, on hand, start of voyage, and purchased............... 16,295
Barrels on hand, end of voyage.................................. 1,270

Barrels consumed during voyage................................... 15,025
Barrels consumed:
Running.. 13,078
Port... 1,947
Fuel expense—average cost per barrel............................... $1.72
Revenue cargo tons:
General—N.O.S. 5,138
M.S.T.S. general.. 6,581
M.S.T.S. reefer... 795
Tallow—bulk.. 98
Lumber... 300

Total revenue cargo tons...................................... 12,912
Nonrevenue cargo tons.. 0

Total cargo tons... 12,912
Revenue ton rate:
General—N.O.S. $31.50
M.S.T.S. general.. 17.48
M.S.T.S. reefer... 29.78
Tallow—bulk.. 31.83
Lumber... 50.77

Stevedoring expense—cost per ton.................................. $ 6.62
Other cargo expense—cost per ton.................................. 3.14

Total cargo expense—cost per ton (excludes 6,581 tons M.S.T.S. general
cargo and 795 tons M.S.T.S. reefer cargo carried F.I.O.).............. $ 9.76
Percent total operating expense of total revenue....................... 77.76

riers should be confined to the nations to which the carriers belong. Some progress in this direction has been made by way of treaties, and the Department of State has in hand the matter of negotiating similar treaties affecting other nations and colonies. Of course, American steamship companies, like all other American companies doing business in foreign countries, may deduct from their United States income tax an amount actually paid in income tax to a foreign country, to the extent that such tax does not exceed the amount that would otherwise have been payable on the same income to the United States government. Regardless of such deduction, dealing with the tax laws of many countries, differing tax concepts, rates, definitions, dates, languages, and public attitudes is time-consuming and expensive work.

Income Items Applicable to Prior Years. It is considered good practice for most non-public-utility companies to absorb in the current year's income statement small adjustments and newly discovered or determined items that pertain to prior years, leaving only large or otherwise significant items to be set forth separately as surplus entries or as nonrecurring-income items. This is only partially true under the Maritime Administration's uniform systems of accounts. All amendments and adjustments to the operations of a prior accounting period must be recorded by the period to which they relate and in the exact detail in which they would have been recorded in that earlier period. Thus a given year's operations are in effect held open indefinitely. Although statements issued to the public may not disclose these additions and revisions as applicable to prior years, ledger accounts and reports to the Maritime Administration must show them.

ACCOUNTS RELATED TO BALANCE SHEET

Asset Accounts. As a rule, transportation is not furnished on credit terms; in fact, the bulk of waterborne shipments is prepaid at time of shipment.[5] Accordingly, a steamship company is likely to have accounts receivable relatively smaller in total than those of a typical manufacturing or merchandising corporation. Such receivables as exist, other than accrued operating-differential subsidy, are likely to arise from interline accounts with other carriers, government bills of lading unaccomplished,[6] cargo on pier awaiting delivery, a few due bills from consignees, and sundry amounts other than those due from customers.

A subsidized operator will have a *capital reserve fund* on his balance sheet.[7] Into that fund go all earned depreciation on the subsidized vessels and the proceeds of all subsidized vessels either sold or lost. The Maritime Administration may permit voluntary deposits of earnings to go into this fund.

From this fund are paid out the purchase prices of new vessels (including purchase-price mortgage-note maturities) and the cost of reconstructing or reconditioning old vessels—all under the control of the

---

[5] See Chap. 17, p. 336.

[6] For example, if a company carries merchandise for the government to Formosa, the freight is not paid until the merchandise is delivered to the government warehouse in Formosa and the papers involved endorsed and cleared through proper channels.

[7] For more detail on the reserve funds discussed here, see Chap. 13.

Maritime Administration. The capital reserve fund in part serves the same uses as a construction reserve fund for an unsubsidized operator, or as a replacement fund under Section 112(f) of the Internal Revenue Code for owners of property in general. In case of financial need and the prior exhaustion of the special reserve fund, the capital reserve fund may be drawn on to cover operating losses.

The *special reserve fund* is another item peculiar to the balance sheet of a subsidized operator. Into this fund go all earnings in excess of 10 percent on "capital necessarily employed" in the subsidized operations, as defined and determined by the Maritime Administration. Voluntary deposits of earnings may also, with permission, be made into this fund, which is available to meet any subsidy recapture not covered by direct deduction from subsidy theretofore received and to maintain the operator's financial strength by means of withdrawals to cover operating losses. The Maritime Administration aims to keep in any operator's special reserve fund an amount that is (exclusive of recapture obligation) not less than 5 percent of capital necessarily employed in the business. Additional amounts may be permitted by the Maritime Administration to be transferred to the capital reserve fund, or even withdrawn for other corporate uses. Upon such withdrawals, any earnings not previously tax-paid become taxable at the rates then applicable.

Under Section 511 of the Merchant Marine Act of 1936, either a non-subsidized or a subsidized operator may have a construction reserve fund, into which may be paid the proceeds of nonsubsidized vessels. Such a fund resembles the replacement fund provided for in the Internal Revenue Code. The tax thus deferred is ultimately paid as the result of depreciation deductions limited to those calculated on the tax base of the vessel sold or lost (exclusive of any capital gain deposited in the fund). The advantages that a construction reserve fund offers over a replacement fund are (1) the fact that it is open to the proceeds of vessels lost or sold voluntarily as well as involuntarily and (2) the advantages, if any, of administration jointly by the Maritime Administration and the Department of the Treasury instead of the Department of the Treasury alone.

The capital asset accounts of a steamship company usually reflect chiefly owned vessels. As mentioned earlier, subsidized operators now use a conservative useful life (twenty years) in calculating depreciation. Thus, barring unexpectedly large obsolescence, the fleet is likely to have an unamortized value on the balance sheet somewhat less than might otherwise remain to be spread over the rest of its life.

Another asset account that does not differ from the related account in other balance sheets, but is likely to be disproportionately large in comparison, is unearned insurance premiums. The values of individual steamships are large, the risks of loss and damage and of liability to passengers, crew members, and the public are substantial, and the premiums consequently are a major element both in the balance sheet and in the calculation of voyage profit. Steamship companies usually find it wise to cover the vessel risks with policies extensive both in their breadth of coverage and in the amounts of protection.

Liabilities. On the liability side of a passenger-carrying steamship company balance sheet, it is normal to have large balances for tickets sold for voyages both not yet commenced and commenced but not terminated. Also, it is normal on many ocean trade routes for most freight to be prepaid. Accordingly, there may be large amounts of freight moneys received on voyages commenced but not terminated. Since the wage and repair obligations are not determined until the end of the voyage, and the stevedoring and certain other costs accrue only as the voyage proceeds, there is to be expected at any one time a substantial balance of deferred revenue over the amount of vessel and voyage expenses incurred on unterminated voyages. In fact, one could say that in the steamship business, instead of financing your customers, your customers may supply a substantial part of your net working capital.

A steamship company customarily stores its vessels directly from wholesale dealers and maintains only small inventories of stores and spare parts. Hence usual credit terms are short, payments are prompt, and trade accounts payable are comparatively small in total.

No other balance-sheet account seems to require comment except that a subsidized operator may have a liability to the Maritime Administration for operating-differential-subsidy recapture, as previously described. He may also have a small amount due the Maritime Administration as refund of construction-differential subsidy on account of revenue earned between domestic ports located on his trade route to a foreign country or countries. Since domestic carryings are protected from foreign-flag competition, any construction-differential subsidy received to equalize construction costs with those of foreign competitors must be refunded to the Maritime Administration in the same proportion that revenue from domestic carryings bears to total revenue. Reports and payments of construction-differential-subsidy refund are due annually.

STEAMSHIP ACCOUNTING METHODS AND PROCEDURES

Accounts Receivable and Revenue Collections. From the preceding description of accounts, certain procedures typical of steamship accounting may readily be inferred. Thus, no customers' accounts receivable ledgers are kept. Instead, bills of lading and reports of serially numbered tickets issued from stock form the basis of collection of revenue; the freight cashier and passenger-ticket issuers, respectively, are held primarily responsible for revenue collections.

Freight revenue arises from revenue tons determined by the weighers and measurers of cargo at the dock and from rates specified by special rate clerks who know the large and complicated tariffs. The tonnage and rates are entered on the bills of lading issued for the given voyage. The freight cashier is required within a short period to account for all moneys indicated on the manifest as collectible from shippers or consignees at his port on the voyage in question.

Passenger revenue arises almost wholly from space assigned in the shoreside passenger office to a person who has purchased a ticket before he embarks. Collection of passenger revenue is assured by holding a passenger office responsible for ticket stock delivered to it. The passenger manifest, prepared by the vessel's purser and showing space occupied and ticket numbers, serves as a check on the periodic reports of tickets issued by the several passenger offices.

Accounts Payable. Another inference from what has already been said is that steamship companies' trade accounts payable are rather closely current, that no trade accounts payable ledgers of the usual type are maintained, that the accounts payable at the end of an accounting period are ascertained by the mechanical listing of unpaid invoices, and that the cumulative volume of business with a given supplier (useful wherever "reciprocity" is practiced) is ascertained by the same mechanical means.

Traffic Analysis. A successful steamship company must watch with care the average freight rates earned on a voyage, must keep a keen eye to notice dwindling commodity movements, and must be alert to see possible movements of new commodities and possible movements of old commodities to new ports. Thus it is important that the bills of lading be analyzed in a number of ways. The commodity itself, the shipper, the consignee, the port of loading, the port of discharge, the freight rate, the total freight, the soliciting freight office, and the weight and measurement tonnage are all factors of interest. Fortunately, the average bill of lading covers enough freight fully to justify the use of a punched card, and punched cards are extensively used for freight-traffic analysis. Some use is also made in the industry of punched cards for similar analysis of passenger tickets sold, but this use of punched cards is up to now less extensive than that for bills of lading.

Controlling Accounts in Voyage Accounting. The most elaborate system of controlling accounts found in steamship companies is that having to do with voyage profit. Such controlling accounts are supported by a recapitulation of terminated voyage revenues like this:

| | Route X |||||| |
| Revenue | Vessel type A ||| Vessel type B ||| All vessels and voyages |
	Voyage 1	Voyage 2	All voyages	Voyage 1	Voyage 2	All voyages	
Freight revenue............	xx	xx	xxx	xx	xx	xxx	xxxx
1st-class passenger revenue	xx	xx	xxx	xx	xx	xxx	xxxx
3d-class passenger revenue	xx	xx	xxx	xx	xx	xxx	xxxx
Other revenue.............	xx	xx	xxx	xx	xx	xxx	xxxx
Total revenue..........	xxx	xxx	xxxx	xxx	xxx	xxxx	xxxxx

The recapitulation then goes on to provide the same for other routes, and finally the totals for all routes. Vessel and voyage expenses are recapitulated in the same way, so that one maintains complete details for what the controlling accounts supply in terse form:

Terminated voyage revenues... xxxxxx
Terminated voyage expenses... xxxxxx
Terminated voyage profit (before overhead, depreciation, interest, subsidy recapture, and taxes)... xxxxx

While actual ledger accounts for more detailed control of voyage costs are not essential, information providing such detail by voyage is important. One of the remarkable things about steamship operation is the wide area over which certain voyage expenses may range on ships that at first blush may seem to be operated similarly. It is a fact that unnecessary spoilage, breakage, obsolescence, extravagance in use, overstocking of supplies, careless authorization of overtime, inefficient fuel combustion, poor cargo handling and stowage, and inexpert handling of mechanisms can easily turn a profitable voyage into a substantial loss. Any operator with a fleet large enough to lose the intimate personal contact of owner-manager with vessel operation cannot afford to do without accounting controls that will pin-point the areas in which economy is present or lacking.

Each voyage expense requires a form of control especially adapted to it. A sample may illustrate this point—the cost per diem of stores, supplies, and expendable equipment. Any ship not carefully supervised will be found to have a much larger diversity of items than is necessary and to have quantities of numerous items far greater than the prospective voyage requires. The first logical step is to pare down the number of items to real needs. At that point an interim quantity of each may be determined and a combination form of inventory requisition devised. Each item requisitioned thereafter is required to be related to the inventory on hand and to the standard allowance. By coding purchases, it will be possible to watch the expenditures in convenient subclassifications of stores, supplies, and expendable equipment. By a process of selecting the most economical ships and voyages, along with careful supervision of operating-department officials and personal discussions with ships' officers, there will eventually be determined definitive quantities of each item to be provided for a given voyage and a satisfactory allowance per diem of cost for each subclassification of the expense for stores, supplies, and expendable equipment.

This example involves a development of control by cooperation among departments. In it, the accountant or comptroller will be especially involved in coding the subclassifications and in seeing that the code numbers are used by the purchasing agent and the vendors. He will accumulate costs per voyage by these subclassifications. He will see that inventories are made at unexpected intervals to verify those turned in by ships' officers on their requisition forms. He will provide specific data as to the supplies purchased that caused any particular subclassification to exceed substantially its per diem allowance.

The accountant or comptroller will find punched-hole cards almost a necessity for the kind of analysis described and for the desired analysis of certain other voyage expenses.

Accounts in Foreign Currencies. Naturally, many steamship companies have to deal very largely in foreign exchange. They have been able so far, however, to require payment of freight and passenger revenue in United States dollars or other stable currency or their equivalent. The "other stable currency" or the "equivalent" is, in the case of experienced American steamship companies, almost instantly converted into United States dollars, thus removing both the risk of foreign-exchange fluctuations and much of the work of maintaining and converting accounts kept in foreign currencies.

Home-office Concentration of Accounting Work. Steamship companies get financial data from a very large number of domestic and foreign branches, agents, vessel pursers, and connecting lines. It is the uniform practice to require straight factual reports from all these sources and to perform nearly all bookkeeping and auditing duties at the home office. Needless to say, it is quite a task to secure and fit together all these reports in order to provide promptly the complete and accurate story of the voyages terminated during the month, each voyage account being composed of transactions in as many as 15 to 30 calls at 6 to 25 different ports, in nearly as many different countries.

Crew Payrolls. Because of the elaborate nature of crew payrolls, steamship companies must maintain capable and alert crew-payroll-audit sections. Added to the accrual of basic wages for the odd periods of voyage duration, there are the complications of overtime, area bonuses, penalty wage additions, allotments, money advances, "slop-chest" charges, fines by the master, and earned vacation credits, not to mention the usual tax deductions and withholdings. Allowance for the value of meals and lodging furnished must be made for certain deductions but not for others. Added to all this is the necessity that the crew be paid off almost immediately upon arrival at the last port of the voyage, although the purser may not have been able to complete his payroll ready for submission to the auditor, and quick shoreside assistance to him is required.

Invoices. Frequently the operating manager of a steamship company will want, when he gets his voyage report from the accounting office, personally to review all the costs of the voyage. For this reason, it is important to have voucher files in such condition that the invoices charged to a given voyage, or perhaps the invoices supporting certain expenses of a given voyage, may be readily assembled for examination or audit by representatives of the Maritime Administration.

Income-Tax Accruals. Despite the fact that for certain Maritime Administration reports and computations, ledger entries involving revenues and expenses must be related back to the year to which they belong, no matter how many years may have intervened, it is not necessary to hold income-tax liabilities open for this purpose. Once accruals on subsidy and subsidy recapture have become capable of reasonably close approximation, the Department of the Treasury will in general accept later items of any kind as applying to the year in which recorded.

STEAMSHIP COST ACCOUNTING

Three items on this subject appear to merit attention in this chapter: unit revenues and costs as calculated from voyage statements, allocation of costs as between freight and passenger traffic, and allocation of overhead to the voyage.

Voyage Costs and Statistics. The second sheet of the voyage statement (see Table 8) shows certain of the unit costs that one large steamship company finds it worth while to present uniformly: cost per meal day in each passenger class, average cost of fuel per barrel, fuel consumption in port and while steaming, average revenue per freight ton, cargo expense (chiefly stevedoring) per ton, and operating ratio (the sum of vessel and voyage expense, divided by revenue). These unit costs are amplified by somewhat more elaborate analyses of these and other voyage expenses, contained in separate sheets.

All these unit costs need to be mentally or actually adjusted to meet the applicable conditions. For example, if fuel cost was high, was the higher cost occasioned by purchasing fuel in out-of-the way ports in order meanwhile to gain more deadweight capacity for high-rate cargo? If the fuel consumption was light, is that fact traceable to the low deadweight on that voyage? If the revenue per freight ton was low, was a considerable portion of the cargo of a liquid nature, requiring almost no loading or discharge expense? Conversely, if the cargo costs were high, was the average freight rate sufficiently high to more than cover them?

These examples suffice to illustrate the point, which is that nearly all unit costs are good or bad only in relation to the other factors with which they are interrelated. A good cost accountant can contribute a great deal by helping to develop the real significance of the unit costs of almost any steamship voyage.

As explained elsewhere, revenue tonnage is the tonnage on which freight is computed. A weight ton is usually 2,240 pounds in foreign trade, frequently 2,000 pounds in domestic trade. A metric ton is almost the same as a long ton of 2,240 pounds. A cubic ton is usually 40 cubic feet, though there are exceptions; rubber from Singapore, for example, is measured at 50 cubic feet to the ton. It is usual for foreign freight to be computed, at the carrier's option, on weight or measurement, whichever will give the larger revenue. Thus, it is possible for the revenue tonnage on a given voyage, ignoring even an allowance for broken stowage, to exceed both the cubic tonnage and the cargo deadweight tonnage. The cargo bookers naturally try to secure balanced cargoes, so that the ship will be as nearly as practicable full and down; that is, with both cubic and deadweight capacity fully used.

Before leaving the question of unit costs, it will be of interest to note the controversy over the use of ton-mile costs. Some persons feel that a steamship operator is in the dark until he knows how much it costs to move a ton of freight one mile. Others are skeptical of the significance of such a figure—or rather, they say it is useless to know the cost of moving an average ton of freight an average mile, when so little cargo is close to average and a mile in a 600-mile haul is quite different in point of cost from a mile in a 14,000-mile haul. Some cargo (liquid) requires no stevedoring expense; other cargo (certain chemicals) may be "penalty" cargo, involving premium payments to stevedores. Some cargo may be easily and simply stowed; other cargo may require much dunnage and leave "broken stowage" free spaces. Some cargo may require careful treatment, clear of humidity, odors, dust, and abrasion; other cargo may be practically invulnerable to damage. Some cargo may handle easily in efficient sling loads; other cargo may require special loading preparation and be slower to move and pile. It may be that ton-mile costs are useful in specialized trades and on a route like the intercoastal, where the 2,000-pound ton is the uniform revenue unit, but that it is a deceptive bit of information in more diverse operations. One thing is clear. There is much room for competent and practical cost accountants in further study of unit revenues and costs in the steamship industry.

Joint Passenger and Freight Costs. One of the most interesting things to me in my steamship accounting experience is that I have never yet run across a serious, fully developed set of cost accounts setting forth the relative net profit of the passenger and freight traffic carried on a given vessel or group of vessels. Obviously such cost accounts, if available, would be useful in developing the rate structure and in the design of new vessels, and might lead on occasion to major alterations in vessels in service.

Of course, the revenue from the sale of passenger tickets and transport of excess baggage is accurately known, and so is the revenue for carryings of cargo and mail. It is on the cost side that analysis bogs down. In the first place, the entire design of the vessel is affected by passenger facilities. The cubic space occupied by passengers and by the extra crew members who care for them is provided partly by taking space from what would otherwise be cargo space and partly by enlarging the superstructure. The cargo deadweight capacity is affected by a change in the safe load line, by the weight of the superstructure, by the change of the center of gravity, and by the weight of additional compartmentation bulkheads. The higher speed required for passenger service involves heavier and larger propulsion equipment, heavier loads of fuel oil, and finer hull lines affecting the cubic cargo capacity of the hull. The factors affecting cargo cubic capacity may be disproportionate to the factors affecting cargo deadweight capacity. With all these factors, who would undertake to estimate, in terms of vessel depreciation and insurance and of cargo revenue lost, the cost of carrying passengers?

Again, a passenger vessel must adhere to a regular schedule of sailing hours and piers. A freight vessel may delay a sailing, shift to another pier in the port, or even make calls at unscheduled ports, in order to get desirable cargo that a passenger vessel must forgo. Also, a freight vessel may on occasion omit a call at a lesser port when traffic offerings are light and may regularly omit calls at a port that a passenger vessel must serve. But an itinerary of a passenger-carrying vessel needs to be regular. A transpacific passenger vessel, for example, must call at Honolulu both ways, more because the pleasure of the passengers demands it than because the volume of business requires it, though otherwise it might profitably bypass Honolulu by as much as 2,000 miles.

Further, passengers load and unload themselves, and the operation requires that the vessel remain at a pier or dock for only a limited stay. The volume of cargo to be delivered or picked up determines time in port for a freighter, except possibly for storing and repairing at the end of a voyage; as shown elsewhere, modern freighters spend roughly half their time in port. Moreover, at point of origin, cargo must be received and stored (usually before arrival of the vessel), loaded aboard the vessel, and then unloaded, restored, and delivered at point of destination.

The costs of terminal operations are indeed of diverse natures. Who could with reasonable accuracy allocate those costs to passenger traffic and freight traffic? What kind of pier would a steamship company occupy if its operations were entirely passenger or entirely freight, and how does one separate the costs of a terminal staff whose services are joint as to passenger and freight traffic?

Enough has been said to indicate the difficulties of calculating relative passenger and freight net income. The result of these difficulties is that typically a vessel is taken as the unit; its profit in terms of investment, gross revenue, and required administrative overhead is judged as a unit. The passenger and freight revenues and expenses are considered joint in the same manner that joint revenues and costs are treated in many manufacturing industries. Someone who enters the steamship industry may bring a fresh approach to this problem. Perhaps he will yet show us how to arrive at a reasonable approximation of the separate results of carrying passengers and cargo on the same vessel. At the same time, he might keep in mind that some of the passenger lines look upon their passenger traffic as an important factor in establishing their prestige and public acceptance and that they deem it to have a substantial effect on the volume of cargo obtained.

Allocations of Overhead. Frequently, it is desirable to attempt an approximation of net profit from a voyage, or at least the profit after allocation of overhead. There is no standard formula for allocating overhead to voyages. The allocation might be made by gross tonnage, for passenger vessels, or by deadweight tons, for freight vessels.[8] Sometimes overhead is taken as a charge against voyage profits, on the theory that management does, or should, expend efforts in proportion to the voyage profit obtainable. The nature of the accounting problem, not to mention the result desired, may influence the method decided upon for overhead allocation.

The Maritime Administration uses the vessel-day as the unit for the allocation of overhead in calculating profits on vessels chartered bareboat from the United States, raising or lowering the vessel-days in the cases of unusual vessels requiring substantially more or less than normal operating supervision. The Maritime Administration uses gross revenue as

---

[8] As noted elsewhere, a gross ton is 100 cubic feet of a vessel's enclosed space, while a deadweight ton is 2,240 pounds of carrying capacity available for cargo, fuel, lubricants, water, or stores.

the principal basis for allocation of overhead in computing subsidy recapture. An operator may use other bases of allocation for his special purposes.

CONTRASTS

It may be useful to set down a few of the high lights of steamship accounting as it differs from accounting likely to be found in another industry.

1. The accounting unit of operations is the terminated voyage. Cost accounting for the terminated voyage is a pleasure or a burden for an accountant, depending upon how deeply he likes to get into the most tangled mass of interrelated cost factors imaginable.

2. The problem of assembling promptly the voyage revenues, expenses, and physical data, related, for example, to a round-the-world voyage of about 25 port calls, is enough to keep an accountant on his mettle. The vessel pursers, branch offices, agents at ports "on line" and on the lines of connecting carriers, and the connecting carriers themselves—all these together constitute an extraordinarily large number of sources of the financial data relating to the terminated voyage. These data must be assembled rapidly if the voyage results are to be known with reasonable promptness.

3. The operating-differential subsidy, construction-differential subsidy, recapture of the former and refund of the latter, capital reserve funds, special reserve funds, and construction reserve funds are all peculiar to the steamship industry and all require understanding of the Merchant Marine Act of 1936 and its application.

4. Subsidized steamship companies are largely consistent with each other in the terminology, form, and fleet valuations in their financial statements; nonsubsidized companies, if not subject to General Order 22, are much less consistent with each other.

5. Federal taxation of subsidized steamship companies varies substantially from ordinary Federal taxation on corporations.

6. Punched cards are well adapted to the analysis of freight and passenger revenues and of vessel-operating costs.

7. Federal statutes, collective bargaining, and established steamship practices combine to make crew payrolls among the most elaborate that are prepared anywhere.

BIBLIOGRAPHY

Because of the nature of this chapter, it is not possible to list the usual bibliographical references.

PART FOUR

ADMIRALTY, INSURANCE, AND REGULATION

CHAPTER 16

SEAMEN'S LAW*

The laws relating to seamen reflect the peculiar nature, hazards, and historical hardship of seamen's employment—circumstances that find no real counterpart among land occupations. Many of these laws were enacted in days, not long past, when seamen were among the worst-treated, lowest-paid, and least-privileged employees in all industry. Often shanghaied from the human dregs of the water front, they were required to live in cramped, unhealthy quarters and to subsist on food that few, if any, other workers would have tolerated.

The vessel in which a seaman served was a small, isolated community where he was subject to the most severe discipline and completely at the doubtful mercy of sometimes brutal superior officers. His obligations to the ship were rigidly enforced not only by the ship's officers but also by a society that treated a deserting seaman as a criminal and forced him to return, against his will, to the employment he sought to escape. Once in port, temporarily released from the harsh discipline and the confinement inherent in shipboard life, the seaman was fair prey for any who would part him from his wages. Since his earnings disappeared almost immediately, he was soon forced to return to the sea.

Within the last three decades, a wide variety of laws have been enacted to protect the seaman, and collective-bargaining groups have grown. As a result, the seafarer's life has gradually improved to the point where legislative protections on such matters as living conditions, wages, health, and safety are now less vitally important than in earlier years. These matters are today more frequently the subject of union-management negotiations than of legislation. In recent years, statutes have been directed principally to the legal remedies of seamen for personal injury or death.

Despite these improvements, the seaman's calling remains widely different from land employment, and it retains many characteristics peculiar to, and inherent in, employment at sea. It lacks the continuity found in most land service. The seaman's contract of employment, the

* This chapter was written by Harry L. Haehl, Jr., partner, Lillick, Geary, Olson, Adams & Charles.

ship's *articles*, apply to only one described voyage. The seaman is employed thereafter only if he signs new articles for the following voyage. The personal relationships between employer and employee of the type developed over a long period of continuous employment on land are virtually unknown to the seafarer.

The seaman, his fellow officers and crew members, the vessel herself, her passengers, and her cargo—all these embark on a common venture in which the rights and obligations of each are intimately identified with and affected by the rights and obligations of the others. All are jointly subject to many hazards peculiar to the sea. To complete the venture successfully, relative rights, obligations, and restraints must be enforced, for no one person or interest in the joint undertaking should be allowed to jeopardize the safety of the whole. These special circumstances have given rise to special laws to restrict and protect the seaman in the performance of his part in the maritime venture.

SEAMAN DEFINED

Originally, the term *seaman* was limited to one who could handle the lines and sails of a sailing vessel and stand watch at the wheel—a true mariner. Gradually this definition has been expanded, and the term now includes many who can scarcely be called mariners. The United States Code defines a seaman as any person, other than an apprentice, who is employed or engaged in any capacity on board any vessel belonging to any citizen of the United States.[1] Under this definition, the master himself has been held to be a seaman for the purposes of some statutes. While serving on board an American-owned vessel, surgeons, firemen, switchboard and radio operators, bartenders, cooks, stewards, and even muleteers and members of an orchestra have been held to be seamen. Longshoremen have also been considered seamen within the meaning of some statutes, though in many respects their rights are quite different, as will be mentioned later.

THE SEAMAN'S SPECIAL STATUS

Probably no other employees are regulated in such minute detail or are the subject of so many statutes as are seamen on American vessels. These statutory regulations begin to operate the moment the seamen-employer relationship is created.

The Ship's Articles. In substantially all cases, the ship's articles must be signed in the presence of a United States shipping commissioner or, if

[1] Title 46, *U.S. Code Annotated*, West Publishing Company, St. Paul, Minn., 1944, Secs. 541–713. Because this chapter is not intended to be used by lawyers, footnote citations will be held to a minimum.

executed in a foreign port, before a United States consul. The exact form of the contract is prescribed by statute. Additional terms may be added to the articles if not contrary to law. This is customarily done either by attaching "riders" relating to matters not covered in the standard printed form of the articles or by separate collective-bargaining agreements.

A legible copy of the articles must be posted in a place accessible to the crew. It must name and describe the vessel, her owners, the nature and duration of the voyage, and the port or country where it is to end. The standard form specifies the daily issues of fruit juice or other antiscorbutics and the exact amount of each type of food to be allowed each day of the week. It must also describe the capacity in which each seaman is employed, the wages to be paid him, and the time when he must be on board the vessel. Statutory penalties are imposed on the master if he fails to post the articles and have them properly executed. Disciplinary regulations must be included in the agreement. Special provisions apply to the coastal trade, as distinguished from intercoastal or foreign trade.

Similarly, elaborate regulations apply to the signing off, or discharge, of seamen. If this occurs in the United States, the seaman must be discharged and paid his wages before a United States shipping commissioner; if abroad, before the United States consul. Before discharge, the seaman must be given a certificate of service and conduct. Many statutes relate to the discharging process.

The ship's articles contain only a fraction of the agreement that the law implies as a part of the employer-employee relationship thus created. These "relational" rights arise in part from general maritime law, which the United States has inherited from other maritime nations and has adopted as a part of its own law by judicial decision and by statute.[2] They also arise from special statutes enacted from time to time to prevent specific abuses or to grant particular benefits. A discussion of a few of the statutes will illustrate the detailed control that Congress has exercised over the smallest incidents of the seaman's employment.

Control of the Seaman's Life. The crew can question the seaworthiness of the vessel and compel examination. Designated government officials are required to make regular inspections of the crew's quarters and to satisfy themselves that the quarters are of the required size, properly ventilated, clean, and sanitary. Detailed regulations cover the size of the crew's quarters (specified in exact cubic feet of air space and square feet of deck space), the sanitary conditions, washing facilities, plumbing and mechanical appliances, and hospital spaces to be maintained.

A proved complaint about the quantity or quality of the provisions and water furnished the crew entitles them to collect penalty payments

[2] See Gustavus H. Robinson, *Handbook of Admiralty Law in the United States*, West Publishing Company, St. Paul, Minn., 1939, Chap. 1.

for each day of deficiency. Medicines and antiscorbutics, even the heat in the seamen's rooms, and the slop chest, or store where the crew may purchase clothing, tobacco, blankets, and other materials, are the subjects of Federal legislation. The number of hours in a day's work and the division of watches are also prescribed. Destitute American seamen in foreign ports are given rights to be provided return transportation to the United States by consular officers, and other United States vessels are required to furnish transportation for this purpose.[3]

The seaman's traditional inability to care for himself financially has brought forth elaborate legislation to help him collect and retain the wages that must be paid him when he is discharged. If a seaman exercises his right to demand discharge in a foreign port because of some justifiable and proved complaint on his part, he is entitled to be paid an extra month's wages and to be furnished employment on another ship or to be provided passage back to the United States. If he is improperly discharged before he has been employed a month, he must be paid a full month's wages, for the ancient adage that "freight is the mother of wages" has no application to American seamen. If payment of his wages at discharge is delayed without sufficient cause, he may have two days' pay for every day of delay. At each intermediate port during the voyage, he is entitled to a "draw" of one-half his then accrued wages; if this is not paid him, he may "jump ship" without losing his right to accrued wages and may, in fact, be entitled to receive wages for the balance of the voyage payable when the voyage ends.

The seaman is given special remedies to collect his wages from the ship. To secure payment of the wages due him, he may sue the shipowner personally, or he may seize the ship herself in a suit *in rem* based upon the maritime lien given him by traditional maritime law. When he commences his suit in a Federal court, he is not required to prepay costs or filing fees and need not post the security for costs of suit that the law requires of other litigants in admiralty cases. His remedy for receiving his wages, and also his lien upon the ship to secure that recovery, are doubly protected, for a statute invalidates any agreement by which these rights are contracted away. He is also protected against almost any attachment of his wages, and his employer is permitted to pay wages to him despite any sale, assignment, attachment, or encumbrance then outstanding. The master may not advance unearned wages either to the seaman or to others; any allotments to dependents must be in writing, noted on the articles; and no assignment of unearned wages is valid.

It is easy to see why the seaman has frequently been described as the ward of courts and legislatures. While some of the reasons for the special

[3] The qualifications for officers and crew and the Maritime Administration's training program were discussed in Chap. 11.

protection given him are attributable to historical conditions now past, his situation remains in many respects sufficiently unique to justify continuing his special rights. Unlike other workers, he is peculiarly dependent on the vessel and his employer for his job, food, and care. A seaman cannot quit in mid-voyage. If his physical surroundings are dangerous, unhealthy, or inadequate, his legal remedies cannot relieve him of them immediately. He is tied to his job, even though the protection he has gained from collective action has now brought him privileges outstripping the imagination of his predecessors of only a few years ago.

In order to enforce the seaman's obligations in the maritime venture, punishments must be available if he wrongfully fails to do his duty. Actually, much of the legislation on this subject has been devoted to lessening the great severity of the punishments formerly given to the recalcitrant seaman. For instance, up to 1898 a deserting seaman could be arrested by shore authorities and kept in jail until just before the vessel sailed, when he was delivered to the ship. This procedure was upheld in the courts despite the provision of the Constitution abolishing involuntary servitude. The statute permitting this has since been repealed, and flogging and all other forms of corporal punishment are now prohibited on all vessels. Statutes enumerate in great detail the offenses and the particular punishments that may be inflicted for each. A record of each offense must be entered in the vessel's official log, signed by the master and another member of the crew. A copy of the log entry must be furnished to the seaman and must be read to him, after which he may make a reply.

The special rights of seamen are not limited to the court decisions and statutes of the United States. On June 13, 1938, the Senate ratified conventions adopted by the International Labour Conference at Geneva in October, 1936. These relate to minimum requirements concerning the professional capacity of merchant-marine officers; the liability of shipowners in cases of sickness, injury, or death of seamen; shipboard hours of work; maintenance; and the minimum age for child workers at sea. In general, the international requirements and benefits are less than those already established by corresponding American rules.

COMPENSATION FOR PERSONAL INJURY OR DEATH

Legislation has not only improved seamen's shipboard conditions but also expanded their rights of indemnification for personal injury and the rights of their personal representatives or heirs in case of death. The centuries old rights of seamen were accepted by the United States as a part of its general maritime law. These rights were enumerated in 1903 by the United States Supreme Court in the *Osceola* case.[4] This important

[4] 189 U.S. 158, 23 Sup. Ct. 483, 47 L. Ed. 760.

decision settled American law on the subject. Four basic principles were listed:

1. That the vessel and her owners are liable in case a seaman falls sick, or is wounded, in the service of the ship, to the extent of his maintenance and cure, and to his wages, at least so long as the voyage is continued.
2. That the vessel and her owners are, both by English and American law, liable to an indemnity for injuries received by seamen in consequence of the unseaworthiness of his ship, or a failure to supply and keep in order the proper appliances appurtenant to the ship.
3. That all the members of the crew, except perhaps the master, are, as between themselves, fellow servants, and hence seamen cannot recover injuries sustained through the negligence of another member of the crew beyond the expense of their maintenance and cure.
4. That a seaman is not allowed to recover an indemnity for the negligence of the master, or any member of the crew, but is entitled to maintenance and cure, whether the injuries were received by negligence or accident.

Wages, Maintenance, and Cure. The shipowner's obligation to the seaman for "wages, maintenance, and cure" is an absolute right given to the seaman as an implied part of his contract and rising out of the relationship of seaman and employer.[5] It does not arise because of any negligence. No matter whose fault may cause the injury or sickness, if that injury or illness occurs "while in the service of the ship" and is not caused by the seaman's own gross misconduct or willful desire to injure himself, he cannot be abandoned and deprived of the opportunity to maintain and cure himself. Neither can he be deprived of the wages he would have earned if he had completed the voyage. The right extends to all the ship's company, including the master; it is not limited to injury sustained on board the vessel. The seaman's employment need not be the cause of the injury or illness.

Efforts to determine the exact limits of the right to wages, maintenance, and cure have presented problems that are reflected in many court decisions. The maintenance required is comparable to that which the seaman is furnished at sea. The amount paid varies from time to time, and is designed to cover the cost of room and board.

The question of cure has been more difficult. The word is used in its original meaning of *care;* an absolute cure, which in some cases may be impossible, is not required. How long the cure must be furnished has been a particularly perplexing problem. In the case of incurable diseases, it has

---

[5] The shipowner's obligation to furnish the seaman maintenance, cure, and medical service is often discharged by making the facilities of a marine hospital, now part of the U.S. Public Health Service, available to him. These hospitals were originally established in 1798. They were maintained by taxes deducted from seamen's wages until 1884, but are now supported by Federal appropriation of funds raised by tonnage taxes paid by shipowners.

finally been determined that cure must be furnished until the patient's condition becomes static or until he has been cured as far as medical science can then help him. The resulting condition may leave him considerably worse off than he was before, perhaps a hopeless invalid or cripple. For this permanent disability, other rights are given him, but the obligation to furnish maintenance and cure has ended. Thus, the obligation to pay wages is always determined by the length of the voyage, but the obligation to furnish maintenance and cure may extend for a longer or a shorter period, depending on the circumstances of the individual case.

Other Rights under General Maritime Law. The protection afforded the injured seaman by furnishing wages, maintenance, and cure obviously cannot fully compensate him for injuries of a permanent nature. Therefore, on the theory that the shipowner, as a part of his contract with the seaman, undertakes a duty (1) to furnish a seaworthy vessel, equipped with safe and proper appliances, in good order and condition, and (2) to furnish proper food and housing, the courts in England, and later those in the United States, granted additional rights to the seafarer. For breach of any of these duties, the shipowner is required to indemnify the seaman to the extent that illness or injury results. The seaman's right is secured by a maritime lien that he may exercise by seizing the vessel in an action *in rem* in the admiralty court.

The obligation to furnish a seaworthy vessel extends not only to the condition of the vessel's hull itself but also to her equipment, the stowage of cargo, and the presence of a crew both numerically adequate and technically competent. This obligation commences at the beginning of the voyage and continues until the voyage is completed. The shipowner cannot avoid responsibility for the consequence of unseaworthiness merely because the condition arose after the vessel was at sea. Nor can he delegate away responsibility for this duty. If a breach of duty occurs, the seaman has the right of indemnity regardless of whether the unseaworthy condition was created by the negligence of the shipowner or of his employees.

Under general maritime law, however, the seaman formerly had no remedy for illness or injury caused by the negligence of his fellow employees provided no defect of the vessel or of her tools or appliances contributed to the result. If the injury was caused by the deliberate brutality of an officer, it was considered to have been caused by unseaworthiness arising from the shipowner's failure to have proper officers aboard, but mere carelessness or negligence on the part of an officer or crew member did not give the seaman any right of action for resulting injuries.[6]

[6] The seaman's right of recovery for injury or illness caused by a fellow crew member and his rights for redress of an injury resulting from the use of nondefective appliances have been the subject of legislation. This is discussed later in this chapter.

The standard of care to which the shipowner is held with respect to the tools and appliances furnished the seaman is rather higher than comparable standards by which employers on land are judged. This difference arises from the facts that the tools and appliances used by seaman cannot be exchanged while the vessel is at sea and that the seaman cannot walk off the ship because they are dangerous. Even though a seaman may use tools or appliances that he knows are defective and unseaworthy, this circumstance affords no defense to the shipowner. But if a seaman voluntarily assumes risk through the careless use of proper appliances, or if he is negligent in other respects, his contributary negligence may be considered and the indemnity awarded to him reduced proportionately.

The same considerations apply when a seaman is injured or is made ill because of unwholesome food or improper housing. The seaman has no alternative but to accept the food and quarters assigned. If the shipowner fails in his duty and if illness or injury results, the seaman is entitled to indemnification under general maritime law in addition to wages, maintenance, and cure.

Rights Given by Statute. The rights of seamen under general maritime law discussed above were inadequate in several important respects. The principles laid down by the Supreme Court in the *Osceola* case prevented recovery of any indemnity for injury or illness caused by the negligence of the master or any fellow member of the crew—the "fellow-servant doctrine." Further, the seaman was held to have assumed the risk of any injury to himself caused by the ship's appliances if the appliances themselves were not defective.

The first effort to cure the defects in the seaman's right to indemnity was the La Follette Act of 1915. It provided that in suits for damages for injury sustained on a vessel or in her service, seamen having command should not be held to be the fellow servants of those under their authority. In the Chelentis case (1918),[7] the United States Supreme Court had occasion to determine whether this statute changed the rules previously announced in the *Osceola* case. The Court, however, held the prior rules unchanged, stating that whether the negligent other employee was a fellow servant or not made no difference and that the language of the La Follette Act "disclosed no intention to impose on the shipowners the same measure of liability for injuries suffered by the crew at sea as the common law prescribes for employers in respect to their employees on shore."

Because of the Supreme Court's decision in the Chelentis case, and other decisions like it, pressure began to build up to correct the disparity between the liability of the maritime employer and of the land employer for injuries to employees. The opportunity to make the correction arose

[7] *Chelentis v. Luckenbach S.S. Co.*, 247 U.S. 370, 38 Sup. Ct. 501, 62 L. Ed. 1171.

when, shortly after World War I, legislation was considered to promote and maintain American shipping. The completed legislative effort was the Merchant Marine Act of 1920, commonly called the Jones Act. Section 33 of the Act granted seamen new rights by amending the earlier La Follette Act. Then, for the first time, seamen were given rights for personal injury or death resulting from negligence and were put on an equal footing with land employees.

The new legislation provided that any seaman injured in the course of his employment could elect to maintain an action for damages at law, with the right to a jury trial, and that in this action "all statutes of the United States modifying or extending the common-law right or remedy in cases of personal injury to railway employees shall apply." It also provided that, in cases of death, the personal representatives of deceased seamen could exercise the same rights enjoyed by railroad employees.

The rights of railroad employees are those given by the Federal Employers' Liability Act of 1908 and its amendments. Under this Act, the employer was liable for damages to any employee injured while in his employ (or, in case of death, to the employee's personal representative) for injury or death due wholly or in part to the negligence of the employer's officers, agents, or employees or to the employer's negligence in the care of equipment, cars, engines, appliances, etc. After the Jones Act was passed, these rights became a part of the maritime law of the United States.

The Federal Employers' Liability Act had abolished the defense of contributory negligence in any case where the employer had violated the Federal Safety Appliance Act of 1893 or its amendments. If there had been no such violation, the Employers' Liability Act followed the comparative-negligence rule (which had long applied in maritime law), under which the employee's negligence merely reduced his award in proportion to his relative fault but did not bar recovery entirely, as contributory negligence does at common law. The Act also abolished the defense of "assumption of risk" if the injury or death resulted from the employer's violation of the Federal Safety Appliance Act.

To prevent the employees from losing these valuable rights, the Act of 1908 further provided that no contract, rule, or "device whatsoever" could avail to exempt the employer from its statutory liability. In case of death, the rights survive and may be enforced by the personal representative for the benefit "of the surviving widow or husband and children of such employee, and if none, then of such employee's parents; and if none, then of the next of kin dependent upon such employee." If the survivor for whose benefit the suit is brought is not one of the relatives listed, actual dependency must be shown.

The rights of the Jones Act did not eliminate the seaman's prior rights

(1) to wages, maintenance, and cure or (2) to indemnity for the consequences of unseaworthiness or faulty appliances. These prior rights did not depend upon negligence, as the Jones Act rights did, but were considered more in the nature of remedies for the breach of implied terms of the ship's articles or of incidents of the shipowner-seaman relationship. The Jones Act rights were additional ones based upon the negligent act of the employer or of those for whom he was responsible.

The Jones Act gave the seaman rights "at his election," and a question soon arose whether the seaman's election was between the old *maritime* rights and the new *nonmaritime* ones. The courts held the new rights to be simply additional maritime rights that Congress had added to American maritime law. However, a single injury could give rise to only one claim, whether it was asserted under the old rights or under the new ones. The employee was not entitled to be compensated twice for the same injury, once for unseaworthiness and again for negligence. It was therefore held that the seaman's "election," made when he decides to enforce the liability imposed on shipowners by the Jones Act, is between the right to damages for negligence, on the one hand, and the right to indemnity for unseaworthiness or defective appliances under general maritime law, on the other. He need not choose between either of these rights and the right to wages, maintenance, and cure. He is entitled to the latter, in addition to whichever of the other two—Jones Act or indemnity for unseaworthiness—he chooses.

Before statutes designed for railroad employees could be incorporated into maritime law, they had to be modified and adapted. This was done by court decisions in the many cases that soon arose under the Jones Act.

In so far as suits under the Jones Act are concerned, the fellow-servant defense under general maritime law has been abolished, and a seaman can recover damages for injuries resulting from negligence of a fellow crew member. The seaman is also given a right of action based on negligence for injuries or death due to defects or insufficiency in the vessel herself or in her equipment or appurtenances. The former effect of contributory negligence of the employee has not been changed, since it had never been an absolute bar under maritime law. The courts have interpreted the Jones Act in such a way as to eliminate the prior defense of "assumption of risk." As a result, if the seaman uses appliances that he knows are defective or dangerous or if he exposes himself to other obvious or known risks, this cannot bar his recovery under the Jones Act entirely, though his negligence in this regard, as in any other, can be considered in proportionate reduction of the damages awarded him.

One of the distinguishing features of an action under the Jones Act, as compared to the former remedies, is that such an action can succeed only if negligence is proved, regardless of seaworthiness or the condition of appliances. This actionable negligence could result in unseaworthiness, as well, but proof of the latter without proof of negligence, while sufficient to allow recovery under general maritime law for indemnity, will not support a Jones Act suit. Another difference is that actions under the Jones Act are always *in personam* and always against the employer. They are not *in rem* against the vessel. They may be brought at law in state or Federal courts with trial by jury, or in admiralty; but if the employer is the United States, the action can only be brought in the Federal courts under the Suits in Admiralty Act, or in some circumstances, under the Public Vessels Act.

The Jones Act gives the seaman no rights against persons other than his employer. The reference in the Act to "any seaman" is construed, under another statute, to mean any person who is employed on board any vessel owned by a citizen of the United States. Any American-owned vessel is included, even if registered under a foreign flag. The term includes the master and all others who sign the ship's articles, and also a pilot employed on the vessel. Further, it includes civilian seamen on government-owned merchant-type vessels, but not personnel serving on Navy, Coast Guard, or other public vessels. In addition, it covers seamen of any nationality serving on American vessels, regardless of whether the accident occurred on the high seas or in the waters of a foreign country. But American seamen serving on foreign vessels are not included unless the accident occurs in American waters.

Wrongful Death. Under general maritime law, as adopted by the United States, if a seaman died, no cause of action survived him or arose because of his death even if unseaworthiness was the cause. The Judiciary Act of 1789, which granted exclusive jurisdiction over admiralty and maritime actions to the district courts of the United States, contained an exception "saving to suitors in all cases, the right of a common-law remedy, where the common law is competent to give it." Hence, death actions permitted by state or foreign death statutes could be enforced in maritime cases. But these local statutes were by no means uniform and were available only if death happened to occur in the territorial waters of a nation or state having a death statute or on a vessel flying the flag of such a nation or belonging to a citizen of such a state. This type of remedy was uncertain and inadequate.

The Jones Act of 1920 created a right of action for seamen's survivors. This Act superseded the Federal and the various state acts. But, since the Jones Act grants rights only against the employer, it superseded other legislation only in so far as actions against the deceased seaman's employer are concerned. Actions against any wrongdoer other than the employer are covered by the Federal Death on the High Seas Act or various state death acts. This Act, also enacted in 1920, provides for a general right of action for death, not limited to seamen.

LONGSHORE WORKERS

Brief discussion of the laws governing longshoremen may be instructive to illustrate the sometimes tortuous development of the laws affecting maritime and semimaritime workers.[8] The discussion will also give a background for a comparison of the two significantly different methods of compensating employees for the injuries that befall them in the course of their employment, (1) employers' liability for negligence and (2) workmen's compensation.

The earliest efforts to make compensation for employee's injuries a direct charge upon industry are found in the various state workmen's compensation laws. As shore workers assumed more and more of the tasks previously performed by the ship's crew (such as loading and discharging cargo, mechanical and electrical repairs, and similar matters unrelated to actual navigation), the disparities in the laws affecting them drew attention. If injured ashore, shore workers received workmen's compensation; if injured on board a vessel prior to the passage of the Jones Act, they could gain relief only by resort to the incomplete and unfamiliar remedies afforded seamen by maritime law.

Early efforts to enforce state workmen's compensation laws as the remedy for a longshoreman's injury on board a vessel were defeated in May, 1947, by the United States Supreme Court on the ground that workmen's compensation was not the type of "common law remedy" that the Judiciary Act had preserved as enforceable in maritime actions. A few months after this decision, Congress amended the Judicial Code to remove claims under state workmen's compensation laws from the area of exclusive Federal jurisdiction. But in early 1920, the Supreme Court held this legislation unconstitutional. Congress promptly tried again in the same year, but this second effort met the same fate in 1924. In its second decision, the Supreme Court broadly hinted that the answer to the problem was a Federal workmen's compensation law.[9]

After the Jones Act was passed in 1920, a longshoreman who had been injured on a vessel sued his employer, a stevedoring company, claiming

---

[8] This development is more fully described in the excellent "Commentary on Maritime Workers" by James Henry Willock, which is published in Title 46, *U.S. Code Annotated*, Vol. 2, pp. 211*ff*.

[9] The three decisions involved were *Southern Pacific Co. v. Jensen*, 244 U.S. 205, 37 Sup. Ct. 524, 61 L. Ed. 1086; *Knickerbocker Ice Co. v. Stewart*, 253 U.S. 149, 40 Sup. Ct. 438, 64 L. Ed. 834; and *State of Washington v. W. C. Dawson & Co.*, 264 U.S. 219, 44 Sup. Ct. 302, 68 L. Ed. 646.

he was a "seaman" within the meaning of that Act. The Supreme Court held that he was, pointing out that he was doing work formerly done by a ship's crew and that he should not be penalized for the chance circumstance that a stevedoring company rather than a shipowner had hired him.[10] Longshoremen continued to have seamen's rights under the Jones Act until 1927.

In 1927, Congress enacted the Longshoremen's and Harbor Workers' Compensation Act, under which personal injuries or death, whether due to employer's or employee's negligence, are compensated according to predetermined standards. This Act is exclusive in its delineated field. It does not apply to the master or members of the crew of any vessel, to a stevedore or repairman employed directly by the master on small vessels, or to government officers or employees. It also excludes claims for which compensation is available under state workmen's compensation laws, and it operates only on the navigable waters of the United States, as defined in the Act.

This Act gave longshoremen and other harbor workers who were not subject to state legislation the benefits of a uniform system of compulsory industrial insurance to protect them against disability or death caused by injuries or accidents in the course of their employment. If the circumstances are such that the Longshoremen's and Harbor Workers' Compensation Act applies, it is the exclusive remedy for such workers, and they are no longer entitled, as they were between 1920 and 1927, to sue their employers under the Jones Act. However, they do have an entirely separate right of action against the shipowner for injuries caused by defective conditions aboard ship if the shipowner has not furnished a safe place to work and proper appliances. This is not a matter of workmen's compensation at all, and can only be asserted by suit against the shipowner.

The longshoreman or harbor worker therefore has a basis of compensation for personal injury or death entirely different from that applicable to the merchant seaman. The former is compensated, regardless of negligence, according to a predetermined scale of awards for death or for disability, whether temporary or permanent, partial or total, which results from accident or disease. The employer ordinarily insures his obligation to make these payments. Claims under the Longshoremen's and Harbor Worker's Compensation Act are heard and determined by the United States Employee's Compensation Commission.

Seamen have the right to wages, maintenance, and cure in any case, plus (1) either the indemnity rights under general maritime law or (2) the Jones Act rights based upon negligence, whichever they choose. In either event, common-law defenses are modified and restricted in the employee's favor. There is no predetermined scale of awards. Unless a settlement is

[10] *International Stevedoring Co. v. Haverty*, 272 U.S. 50, 47 Sup. Ct. 19, 71 L. Ed. 157.

made, these rights are enforced by court actions. The employee's recovery in each case depends upon whether the court or jury finds unseaworthiness or negligence creating liability on the employer, and, if it does, upon how much the particular court or jury believes is necessary to compensate for the harm. A lump sum is awarded rather than a continuing disability payment, and sometimes the judgments in these cases are very large. The ultimate benefit the seaman receives must depend on his ability to invest or spend it wisely. In many instances, failure in this regard materially reduces the benefits actually realized.

WORKMEN'S COMPENSATION VERSUS EMPLOYERS' LIABILITY

Before the longshoreman was given workmen's compensation, his rights differed greatly depending upon whether he was injured on land or on a vessel, even though his employment might require him to move from one situs to the other many times in a single hour's work. This anomaly has been cured by the Longshoremen's and Harbor Workers' Compensation Act. But, as we have seen, two widely divergent systems still operate simultaneously on a single vessel, one applying to a merchant seaman and the other to a longshoreman although both may be injured at the same time and by the same cause. Although the logic of resolving this difference and of applying one system to both workers is apparent, this has not yet been done, and efforts to do so have created bitter legislative conflicts.

The first state workmen's compensation law was enacted by New York in 1910, and similar laws were soon passed in most other states.[11] The system appealed to seamen, who, as early as 1913, began to demand equal rights with other classes of labor and recognition of their right to workmen's compensation. The legislative efforts toward this end were continued until World War I, but without any real success. After the war, some effort was made to provide workmen's compensation for seamen as a partial substitute for the rights they then had. The seamen's unions were not enthusiastic about this, since they did not wish to give up any of their existing rights but only to have the new ones supplement them.

The seaman's remedial position, in comparison with that of other workers, changed greatly when the Jones Act was passed in 1920, though the seamen's unions and representatives did not at first realize how great the change was. As late as 1923, the legislative committee of the International Seamen's Union reported that the right to sue under the Jones Act was of only theoretical value, and the committee even recommended legislation that would surrender the right in exchange for workmen's

[11] For a detailed discussion of the history of such legislation and a statistical comparison of the benefits under the different systems, see *Workmen's Compensation and the Protection of Seamen*, U.S. Bureau of Labor Statistics, Bulletin 869, 1946.

compensation. However, as the value of the right to sue and of the restrictions on defenses available to employers under the Jones Act gradually became apparent, the unions began to change their position. They still wanted workmen's compensation, but only if it was added to and did not disturb Jones Act rights. Employers also observed the effect of the Jones Act, and they began to insist more and more strongly on workmen's compensation as a substitute for the Act.

These divergent views were sharply defined when the Longshoremen's and Harbor Workers' Compensation Act was being considered in 1926 and 1927. As originally drafted, it included seamen, but they opposed this unless their other remedies were left intact. The employers wanted the seamen included but only if the remedy was made exclusive, as it was for others under the Act. The conflict could not be resolved, so seamen were excluded from the Compensation Act entirely.

In 1936, the International Labour Conference at Geneva adopted several draft conventions, including one that created a modified form of workmen's compensation covering injury or death of merchant seamen. This convention was ratified by the United States Senate in June, 1938, and became effective for this country in October, 1939. Since the convention was not self-executing, legislation to implement it was necessary. Such legislation was introduced in Congress in 1939 and was considered simultaneously with another bill to extend the Longshoremen's and Harbor Workers' Compensation Act to seamen. The implementing legislation not only gave effect to the convention but also expressly preserved all the seamen's existing rights, thus gaining them much and losing them nothing. The shipowners objected strongly to this bill, and supported the bill to bring seamen under the Longshoremen's and Harbor Workers' Compensation Act. The unions opposed the latter but were willing to accept the former. The interested government agencies could not agree among themselves.

As a result of this disagreement, an interdepartmental committee was appointed, comprised of representatives from the U.S. Departments of Commerce and Labor, the U.S. Maritime Commission, the United States Employee's Compensation Commission, and the Maritime Labor Board. This committee concluded (1) that workmen's compensation is in principle a more desirable and satisfactory method of providing recovery for injured workers than a system of liability based on negligence and (2) that a workmen's compensation system could be devised which would retain the desirable features of this kind of remedial legislation and at the same time preserve the seaman's traditional right to wages, maintenance, and cure.

The committee then considered whether such a modified workmen's compensation plan would be desirable and advantageous from the standpoint of the seamen, the industry, and the public. It pointed out that, unlike the situation in other industries, labor opposed and management supported such legislation. The seamen opposed because under the Jones Act they enjoyed remedial rights and relative freedom from defenses that other industrial employees did not have. The committee recognized that if workmen's compensation were given to seamen without reduction in the rights they already enjoyed, the system would have to be somewhat different from other compensation statutes.

The committee could not accurately judge the comparative cost to industry of the proposed compensation system but found that the employers believed it would improve labor-management relations and that they were prepared to bear the additional cost if need be. Because of the growing feeling of public responsibility for the care of the indigent and because the compensation system would probably reduce the number of seamen or their dependents forced to public relief or charity (inasmuch as awards would not be limited to cases where negligence was proved), the committee felt the public interest would best be served by a workmen's compensation system applicable to seamen and modified to fit their particular needs.

Despite these findings and the historical trend toward workmen's compensation, no such system has been made applicable to seamen to date, and perhaps none will ever be. The reason is obvious: the employees themselves do not want it. This situation, the opposite of that in nearly every other industry, points up the fact that seamen, once so badly treated and so lacking in legal remedies to protect them, now enjoy a position just the reverse of that of a few years ago. Instead of having remedies generally inferior to those of other industrial workers, seamen now have remedies so superior to those applicable to their fellow workers that they resist any effort to reduce their status to the common level. Since the days before World War I, the merchant seaman has come a long way.

BIBLIOGRAPHY

Benedict, Erastus C., *The Law of American Admiralty*, 6th ed., edited by Arnold W. Knauth, Matthew Bender & Company, Inc., Albany, N.Y., 1940.
Norris, Martin J., *The Law of Seamen*, Baker, Voorhis & Company, Inc., New York, 2 vols., 1951, 1952.
Robinson, Gustavus H., *Handbook of Admiralty Law in the United States*, West Publishing Company, St. Paul, Minn., 1939.
U.S. Bureau of Labor Statistics, *Workmen's Compensation and the Protection of Seamen*, 1946.
Willock, James Henry, "Commentary on Maritime Workers," Title 46, *U.S. Code Annotated*, West Publishing Company, St. Paul, Minn., 1944, Vol. 2, pp. 211*ff*.

CHAPTER 17

THE LAW OF VESSELS*

Vessels, and the rights and obligations of those who own, use, serve, or deal with them, are subject to a great number of regulations and rules of law, most of which are enforced in the United States in the Federal admiralty courts.[1] Several important subjects in the law of vessels—including freight forwarding and brokerage, charters, seamen's law, marine insurance, rates and regulation, Federal agencies governing shipping, and international conventions and treaties—are all treated separately in other chapters of this book.

VESSELS IN GENERAL

Before embarking on a discussion of particular regulations and rules of law applicable to vessel operations, some general observations are needed about vessels themselves.

Identity. Congress has defined the term *vessel* to include "every description of water craft or other artificial contrivance used, or capable of being used, as a means of transportation on water." The size, form, and means of propulsion or lack of it are not determining factors. All that is important is the purpose for which the object was constructed and the business in which it is engaged. A partially completed structure, although intended eventually to be used as a means of water transportation, is not a vessel until it becomes employable as such. Structures that may at one time have been used as vessels lose that identity when they are converted to other uses. Old hulls used as dance halls, wharves, or hotels come within this category. Scows, barges, and similar craft, capable of many uses, are

---

* This chapter was written by Harry L. Haehl, Jr., partner, Lillick, Geary, Olson, Adams & Charles.

[1] To cover merely the principal rules, without any discussion at all of various refinements and exceptions, requires oversimplification of a complex subject. The reader should bear in mind that this chapter can at most touch only on the high lights of the principal subjects comprising the law of vessels. Such a statement of broad principles, lacking the detail needed for technical accuracy, may give a nodding acquaintance, but certainly no intimate familiarity, with the subject.

considered vessels only when used as such. While being towed with a cargo on board, they are vessels, but not when they are held stationary and used as a wharf or landing, even though still afloat. The term *vessel* includes not only the hull but also the auxiliary boats, tackle, furniture, supplies, machinery, and other kinds of equipment that are the normal appurtenances of an operating ship. When operated on the surface of navigable water, even a seaplane may be held to be a vessel for some purposes.

Nationality. Vessels have a national character of their own. Under international law, this is recognized as that of the nation whose flag they are entitled to fly. In many respects, commercial vessels, wherever they may be, are considered a part of the nation to which they belong. Warships and other public vessels have an even greater degree of extraterritorial right. As a general rule, when a vessel is in water foreign to her flag, the rules of the local sovereign control her external liability to persons or property and prescribe the rules of navigation and conduct in relation to nationals of the foreign country or of other countries. Matters affecting the vessel's own crew, cargo, or passengers, however, and those relating to the internal management of the ship are generally governed by the law of the ship's flag. These rules are not uniformly applied in the courts of all nations, for differences exist in the views of various national courts in this as in other fields of international law.

Most maritime nations extend certain privileges to their own vessels and impose duties and obligations upon them. Before qualifying his vessel as one of a particular nation, the shipowner must comply with that nation's requirements for formal registry or other identification of the vessel.

Registry, Enrollment, and License. For any vessel, other than a very small one, to be entitled to the rights and privileges granted by the laws of the United States and to be considered an American vessel, one or more of several official documents issued by the government to identify the particular vessel and to show her national character must be obtained. Vessels engaged in foreign trade must have a certificate of registry, and those engaged in domestic trading along or between the coasts of the United States must have a certificate of enrollment and license if they are larger than 20 tons, or a certificate of license if smaller. These documents are issued by the U.S. Treasury Department, Bureau of Customs, and are the official proof of the vessel's identity and nationality. They serve purposes roughly comparable to those of a combined birth certificate, health certificate, and passport of an individual citizen.

These documents must be kept up to date. Any material changes in structure, equipment, or ownership of the vessel must be endorsed on them. The original is filed in the customhouse at the home port of the vessel, and a certified copy is kept on board. The home port is considered the vessel's official residence. It need not be the place where the vessel's owner resides but should be the port nearest his residence.

Title and Ownership. Vessels are personal property and are subject to the usual rules of law relating to this type of property. Like other personalty, title is normally transferred by bill of sale which, as to American vessels, must include a verbatim recital of the vessel's certificate of registry or of enrollment and license. Forms printed by the Bureau of Customs are usually used. Because of the perambulatory nature of the ship, a sale is not wholly effective until the buyer is given possession. Title is normally established by recording the bill of sale and by having a new certificate of registry or of enrollment and license issued to the new owner.

In the absence of particular agreement to the contrary, if several persons own interests in a vessel, they are considered to be tenants in common, not joint tenants or partners. If one owner dies, his interest normally passes to his heirs rather than to the surviving coowners. When several persons own a vessel, one of them is usually designated managing owner, or *ship's husband*, with authority to act as the agent for all in making the necessary contracts for the vessel and in directing her operations. His authority is subject to any specific limitations imposed by law or by the other owners.

Security Devices. The traditional security devices of maritime law were bottomry and respondentia bonds. The bottomry bond was used to pledge the vessel and created a lien upon her, enforceable in admiralty, if she arrived safely at destination. The respondentia bond was a similar hypothecation of the cargo made by the master as the implied agent of the cargo owner. These bonds were common in the days when the master could not communicate quickly or adequately with the shipowner to request help in raising funds for needed repairs, supplies, or services. If money was required to continue the voyage, the master was given the authority to pledge the ship herself and if necessary the cargo to secure the repayment of money borrowed.

The bonds could be validly given only when a ship was in a foreign port and only when the money raised was essential for repairs, supplies, or services without which the voyage could not be continued or the safety of the ship could not be assured. These extraordinary bonds could be used to obtain funds only as a last resort. If it could be shown that the money could have been raised in another way (for instance, by communicating with the owner), this would destroy their validity. The master who gave respondentia bonds acted as the involuntary agent of the cargo owners. Because they needed special protection against abuse of this authority, proof of real necessity was particularly required for this type of bond.

A peculiarity of both the bottomry and respondentia bonds was that each became absolutely void if the pledged object—vessel or cargo—was lost before arrival at destination. Since the lender assumed the risk of safe arrival, these bonds customarily carried extraordinary interest, known as *marine interest*, which could far exceed the rate otherwise considered usurious.

Early maritime law did not recognize mortgages or other common-law security devices that give the lender the personal credit of the borrower, as well as the security of the pledged object. However, maritime law did recognize the validity of mortgages executed under state laws when these became common; but, since such obligations were not maritime in nature, they were given no relative priorities among maritime obligations or liens. They could not be enforced in admiralty courts and were treated as junior to all maritime liens. This kind of security gave the lender inadequate protection and made investment in maritime ventures unattractive.

To remedy this defect and to furnish an inducement for private capital to invest in shipping, the Federal Ship Mortgage Act was enacted in 1920.[2] This Act recognized a security device like the common-law mortgage but truly maritime in character, and assigned it a relative priority among other maritime obligations. If it qualified as a preferred ship mortgage, it was placed ahead of many maritime liens.

CONTROL AND REGULATION

Government Authority. The United States Constitution gives Congress power "to regulate Commerce with foreign Nations and amongst the several States . . . " This power includes the right to regulate not only the commerce itself but also the instrumentalities and persons engaged in it. The superior power of the Federal government in this field is not necessarily exclusive. Within limits, the states may regulate the instrumentalities and persons engaged in foreign or interstate commerce so long as they do not discriminate against or unduly burden them. The power of the states to legislate is limited to fields in which Congress has not acted, since action by the Federal government in a given field thereafter excludes the operation of state laws.

The Judiciary Act of 1789 granted exclusive original jurisdiction in admiralty matters to the Federal district courts, "saving to suitors in all cases, the right of a common-law remedy, where the common law is competent to give it." This provision had the effect of preserving common-law rights and remedies existing in 1789 but did not preserve new remedies such as state workmen's compensation laws, which arose subsequently. The latter cannot be enforced in the admiralty courts.

[2] This is Sec. 30 of the Merchant Marine Act of 1920.

Customs, Quarantine, and Health Regulations. Federal statutes govern the clearance and entry of a vessel at American ports. A clearance is a certificate given by the collector of the port stating that the master of the vessel, bound for a named port and having on board the goods described, has entered and cleared his vessel according to law. It establishes the vessel's right to depart on her voyage and, in a sense, is a permission to sail. *Entry* of a vessel denotes that the master has exhibited or deposited with the collector of the port the various papers required by law, which include a detailed list of the cargo the vessel is to discharge.

The term *quarantine* originally applied to the period of forty days that had to elapse before persons coming from foreign ports afflicted with the plague would be permitted to land. The term now applies to a wide variety of restrictions enforced upon vessels which may have contagious plant, animal, or other diseases on board. Although the Federal government has paramount authority, state and local governments may enforce reasonable and nondiscriminatory quarantine and health regulations for their own safety. Such local rules must be primarily designed for self-protection and may not injuriously affect foreign or interstate commerce. Congress has enacted additional health and quarantine regulations.

Inspection and Survey. A defective vessel, unsound in hull or machinery or lacking the equipment needed to navigate her properly, is a peril to herself and to her crew, passengers, and cargo. She is also a peril to other vessels and to bridges, wharves, and other structures on or near the waters she navigates. To reduce this peril, Federal legislation has created an elaborate system, administered by the U.S. Coast Guard, for inspection and survey of all American and some foreign stream vessels as to hull, machinery, boilers, and other appurtenances. Detailed statutes cover the time, scope, and effect of these inspections and lay down regulations covering the issuance and use of certificates of inspection and penalties for violations of the rules.

If the owner fails to submit his vessel for the required inspections at the prescribed times, he is severely penalized. However, even if the vessel is inspected as required, and if proper certificates of inspection and survey are obtained, this does not conclusively establish the seaworthy condition of the vessel. It does not relieve the shipowner of responsibility for defective conditions that may exist even though they are not discovered by the inspectors.

The inspection laws relate generally to all American vessels propelled in whole or in part by steam that navigate waters of the United States, with the exception of public vessels and certain designated canal boats and other craft specifically excluded from the regulations. The states may also enforce similar regulations so long as they do not encroach on the paramount authority of the Federal government or unreasonably burden commerce.

Taxes, Duties, and Penalties. Vessels and their owners and operators are subject to most of the duties and taxes imposed on any other personal property or on the ownership or operation of it. In addition, vessels and their operations are subject to a considerable number of other taxes, duties, and penalties.

The Federal government imposes tonnage taxes on all vessels entering American ports from foreign places.[3] Foreign vessels are also subject to a somewhat similar duty, called *light money*. Furthermore, the Federal government imposes various penalties and forfeitures for violating (1) registry, enrollment, and license rules and (2) inspection laws, safety regulations concerning passengers, customs clearance, and entry; and for committing a variety of other offenses, even including engaging in the slave trade.

The states may levy taxes on companies that own and operate vessels as on any other business concern. Their power to tax is limited, however, in that they may not discriminate against or unnecessarily burden sea commerce, either interstate or foreign. States may tax vessels as property, but they may not levy any "duty of tonnage." A state may, however, require vessels to pay for specific services that they actually receive or for facilities that they actually use, and these charges may be measured by tonnage.

MARITIME LIENS AND MORTGAGES

The true maritime lien must be distinguished from the familiar common-law lien. The latter arises from and is dependent upon possession of the thing on which the lien is claimed. It usually comes into being because the lien holder has repaired, manufactured, or performed some other service for the thing to which his lien attaches. Such a common-law lien may attach to a vessel as well as to any other personal property, but it lasts only while the lien holder retains possession.

The true maritime lien, on the other hand, can arise in many ways unknown to common law and is considered to have been created by the vessel herself. It gives the lien holder a property right in the ship—one that is not dependent upon possession but that follows the ship wherever she goes. The maritime lien does not require affirmative action of the shipowner or anyone acting for her to bring it into being. Its original purpose was the same as the one that gave rise to several other rules discussed in this chapter. The maritime lien was intended to make it possible for a master in a foreign port to obtain the supplies and services necessary to complete the voyage successfully. Obviously, the supplier could not retain

[3] As the term implies, tonnage taxes or duties are those measured by the tonnage of the vessel or by her cargo or carrying capacity.

possession of the vessel as security and still allow her to continue her voyage. Unless a foreign supplier could have a lien independent of possession he would not be likely to give credit to the ship or master.

The same considerations gave rise to the general rule that maritime liens, unlike common-law liens, rank among themselves in the inverse order of creation. That is, among maritime liens of the same class, the lien incurred last in time takes precedence over those created earlier. Only in this way could a vessel in a foreign port obtain credit from a supplier who had no way of knowing what liens already existed. The maritime lien is the basis of all actions *in rem* against the vessel herself in the admiralty courts. The interest in the vessel created by a maritime lien follows the vessel wherever she goes and is not extinguished by a change of title or possession, by sale to a bona fide purchaser without notice of the lien, or by the death or insolvency of the shipowner.

Maritime liens arise, as a general rule, out of any truly maritime contract. They secure the faithful performance of that contract. If the transaction is not of a peculiarly maritime character, the lien arises only if the contract so provides. The maritime lien may also arise because of a wrongful act of the vessel or of those in charge of her. These liens arising from wrongful acts are based on the theory that the ship herself, as distinguished from those who own or operate her, is considered the wrongdoer.

One who advances money for the payment of claims secured by maritime liens becomes entitled to the same liens and preferences, but one advancing money or furnishing materials or services to a vessel is not entitled to a maritime lien unless these acts are done on the credit of the vessel rather than on the personal credit of the owner, agent, or charterer. In the absence of a contrary showing, advances made to a master in a foreign port (at his request, to pay either for repairs or supplies necessary to prosecute the voyage or for services rendered to the vessel) are presumed to have been made upon the credit of the vessel. To create a maritime lien, the repairs or supplies must be ordered by someone authorized to act for the vessel. The Federal Maritime Lien Act of 1910 (reenacted in 1920) specifies the persons who are presumed to have such authority.[4]

Before the question was settled by Federal legislation, a great deal of confusion existed as to whether the furnishing of repairs or supplies to a vessel in her home port, where the credit of her owner was presumably available, would give rise to a maritime lien. Conflicting state laws had been held applicable on this question until the matter was settled by the Federal Maritime Lien Act specifying the liens that could arise at the home port of a vessel.

[4] This Federal legislation also removed prior uncertainties in the maritime law arising out of conflicting state statutes concerning what liens could arise in the vessel's home port.

Liens for repairs, advances, supplies, and services furnished to keep the vessel fit for sea, and to make it possible for her to continue the voyage, take precedence over all prior claims on her except those for seamen's wages or for salvage. Because the vessel herself, including the interests of all previous lien holders, is considered responsible for her wrongful acts, the lien granted to an injured party (for collision or personal injury) takes precedence over all former liens other than those for crew's wages or for salvage, which are given a unique priority.

The vessel also has a lien on her cargo for freight, general-average contribution, damage, or other obligations arising out of the transportation furnished. This lien is reciprocal to the lien the cargo has on the vessel for damage caused by the ship or those operating her. The ship's lien on cargo is, however, more similar to a common-law lien and, in the absence of agreement to the contrary, depends on possession of the cargo.

The lien holder normally enforces his lien by an action *in rem* in an admiralty court. He is not required to do so, however, and he may waive his lien and sue the owner of the vessel or the cargo personally, or he may resort to a common-law remedy in the state courts if the transaction creates such a remedy.

GENERAL AVERAGE

The principal of general average is one of the most ancient in admiralty law. It is found in the laws of Rhodes,[5] in the Roman Justinian codes, and in all subsequent statements of maritime law.

In connection with marine insurance, the term *average* means loss.[6] A *general-average* loss is a loss of concern to all interests in the maritime adventure—the vessel, the cargo, and the freight. The basic principle is that all interests contribute to make good the loss suffered by one due to a sacrifice voluntarily made, or to an extraordinary expense incurred to save the voyage and to protect or benefit all the interests, in the face of a common danger. For example, when the entire venture is imperiled, the master may jettison part or all of the cargo or may deliberately ground the vessel to keep her from sinking. These are typical general-average sacrifices. To make good the general-average sacrifices, each of the interests contributes in proportion to the value of each that was at risk and was saved.

In contrast to a general-average loss, *particular-average* loss is one that falls on one of the interests alone. It is consequently borne by the owner of that interest or by his underwriters. A loss suffered as a result of a voluntary act of the master in an effort to avoid or minimize a threatened

---

[5] A fine academic dispute exists over the authenticity of these laws—a matter that does not need to concern us here.

[6] Chap. 18 explains the insurance arrangements for general-average and particular-average losses. See especially pp. 364–371.

loss of concern to all property interests involved in the sea voyage is classified as a general-average loss, while a loss arising directly from accident rather than from the voluntary decision of the master would be classified as a particular-average loss. By centuries-old usage and the precedence of numberless cases, certain essential requirements have been established for a claim for general average.

The first of these is the common peril that makes the sacrifice or expenditure necessary. The peril must be common to all interests in the maritime adventure, for only those imperiled and saved can properly be required to contribute. The peril must be imminent and apparently inevitable unless averted or diminished by an act of sacrifice or expenditure. Under American law, the general rule is that no one may claim general-average contribution to make good his loss if the peril arose due to his own fault or the fault of those for whose acts he is responsible.

The shipowner is not liable for damage occasioned by the master's or crew's faults or by errors in the management or navigation of the vessel.[7] Shipowners therefore contended that they could claim contribution in general average from the cargo even though the peril arose due to the fault of their own employees if that fault related to management or navigation of the vessel. The Supreme Court held, however, that the exoneration from liability to cargo for loss occasioned by errors in management or navigation would not be extended to authorize an affirmative recovery of general-average contribution from the cargo unless the ship and cargo contracted for such a result in the bill of lading or other contract of affreightment. Because of that decision, it has been uniform practice for shipowners to include in their bills of lading a Jason clause, named after the vessel involved in a Supreme Court case upholding the validity of such a claim. This clause contains an agreement by the cargo to contribute in general average even though the loss may be occasioned by the fault of the shipowner, if it is the kind of fault that would not give the cargo the right to recover damages from the shipowner.

The second basic element of general average is the sacrifice, or expenditure. The sacrifice must be for the benefit of all interests and not for any other purpose. If any one interest is not really imperiled, the sacrifice is not for its benefit and it need not contribute to make good the loss.

Third, the sacrifice must be to some practical extent successful, for the other interests contribute only to the extent that they are actually benefited or saved. If the disaster is simply delayed, but not avoided, no claim for general average arises. If the sacrifice is made involuntarily or accidentally, or if it is inevitable and cannot be avoided, no general-average contribution can be claimed. The sacrifice must be ordered by the master or other person lawfully in command of the vessel or responsible

[7] The carrier's liability for cargo loss is discussed later in this chapter.

for the cargo, for otherwise it cannot be considered the voluntary act of the owner of the interest or of one authorized to act for him. In making a sacrifice, the master acts under implied authority of the cargo owner and as the direct agent of the shipowner.

Another important consideration in general average is to determine which interests contribute, in what amounts, and how these contributions are to be collected. This is primarily a matter of general-average adjusting and is the proper concern of the chapter on marine insurance (Chapter 18), where it is treated at some length.

CARRIAGE OF CARGO AND PASSENGERS

The rights, duties, and liabilities of an ocean carrier when transporting goods or persons for hire at sea are treated together because there are many similarities in the rules governing them.

Cargo. The common carrier was described in Chapter 2. Many government shipping regulations apply only to common carriers. They are prohibited from unfair discrimination among shippers or others dealing with them and are required to obtain government approval of, and adhere to, published schedules of freight rates and service charges, called *tariffs*. The liabilities of a common carrier to a cargo owner are quite different from those of a private carrier. The latter may, within rather loose limits, contract with the shipper for freedom or exoneration from almost all types of liability.[8] The common carrier may not.

At common law, the common carrier was considered a bailee of the goods entrusted into his custody and was as completely responsible as an insurer of their safe delivery against all risks except those entirely beyond his control, such as act of God, of war, or of public enemies, arrest or restraint by public authorities, or the fault of the shipper or inherent vice of his goods. Common law did not prevent the carrier from reducing this heavy liability by contract if the shipper would agree to the modification. Common carriers therefore insisted on elaborate exonerating provisions in their contracts with shippers.[9] In England, where shipowners have always been more powerful than shippers or consignees of cargo, common carriers were allowed to contract for wide freedom from liability, even from the consequences of their own negligence. In the United States, cargo interests were stronger, and bill-of-lading contract provisions freeing the carrier from liability for negligence were held to be against public policy because they lessened the incentive to care for the cargo properly.

The rights and liabilities between ship and cargo are now regulated by

---

[8] See also Chap. 10, "Ship Operation: Charters."
[9] The contract between ship and cargo is the bill of lading, which was described in Chap. 7.

statutes that have both reduced the carrier's common-law liability as an insurer and prohibited bill-of-lading clauses exonerating him from liability for his own negligence. These statutes have proceeded on the theory that, while the shipowner must properly outfit, man, supply, and equip his vessel and must exercise due diligence to make her seaworthy, he cannot personally do more, and after she has sailed, he must necessarily rely solely on his master, officers, and crew to protect, care for, and deliver the cargo.

The shipowner's liability for loss or damage to cargo is governed by the Harter Act of 1893 and the Carriage of Goods by Sea Act of 1936. These statutes distinguished between loss or damage due to (1) unseaworthiness or failure of the shipowner to outfit, man, supply, and equip the vessel for her voyage; (2) negligence of her master, officers, or crew during the voyage; and (3) causes entirely beyond the carrier's control, such as an act of God or of war.

Concerning (1), the Harter Act prohibited any contract provision lessening the shipowner's obligation to exercise due diligence to prepare the ship properly for her voyage. Even though the shipowner had exercised due diligence to make the vessel in all respects seaworthy, this would not prevent liability if she was found to be actually unseaworthy unless the cargo agreed to this result in the bill-of-lading contract. Concerning (2), the Harter Act prohibited the shipowner from contracting away liability for his employees' negligence in the loading, stowage, care, custody, or delivery of the cargo. Faults or errors of the master or crew in the navigation or management of the vessel herself were not included in this prohibition, and any resulting damage or loss was treated as arising from a cause outside the shipowner's control. The shipowner was freed from liability for these causes, plus the others referred to in (3), but this exoneration was given him only if he had previously discharged his duty of due diligence to make the vessel in all respects seaworthy and to prepare her properly for the voyage. If he had not, he forfeited his protection.

For many years after the Harter Act was passed in 1893, the rules in other maritime nations governing a common carrier's liability differed widely, and they were usually more favorable to the shipowner. In the United States, since most of the shipowner's protections from liability were granted only if he had exercised due diligence to make the vessel seaworthy in all respects, trials of cargo cases were unduly complicated by tedious evidence. For, if cargo was damaged on a vessel which had not been made seaworthy when the voyage started, the shipowner was held liable even though the unseaworthiness and the lack of due diligence had not caused or contributed to the particular damage actually suffered by the cargo.

For many years, the maritime nations tried to reach uniformity in the rules governing the rights and liabilities of ship and cargo. They finally succeeded in 1924, at Brussels, when the International Convention for the Unification of Certain Rules Relating to Bills of Lading was approved. The terms of this Convention were subsequently enacted as domestic legislation in substantially every maritime nation. The American enactment is the Carriage of Goods by Sea Act of 1936, commonly referred to as COGSA.

The Brussels Convention and COGSA established standards generally similar to those of the Harter Act, which still remains in force. The principal difference is that the shipowner's right to rely upon the defenses given him is no longer conditional upon his exercise of due diligence to make the vessel in all respects seaworthy at the start of the voyage. If he fails in this regard, COGSA holds him liable, but only if the failure actually causes or contributes to the damage to the cargo.

COGSA gives the shipowner many defenses that the Harter Act merely permitted the shipowner to contract for but did not affirmatively grant him. On the other hand, under the Harter Act the shipowner could provide in the bill of lading for strict monetary limits on his liability for each package or unit of cargo and could specify relatively short times within which the cargo owner must present his claim for loss or damage and must commence suit upon penalty of having his claim time-barred. COGSA itself states minimum limitations on value and on time for claim and suit that are more fair to the cargo owner. It invalidates any agreement lessening these limits. For most purposes, COGSA has supplanted the Harter Act in foreign trade, but it does not apply in domestic commerce unless the parties to the bill of lading agree that it shall apply.

Despite all the legislation on the subject, the carriage of cargo remains basically a matter of agreement whereby the shipowner agrees to transport the cargo in return for a specified payment, called *freight*. If the ship's voyage differs materially from the one agreed upon in course, time, or risks to which the cargo is exposed, the shipowner breaches his agreement. He is then held guilty of a "deviation," and thereby loses protections granted him in the contract and possibly some of those granted by statute, unless he can prove that the variance was a reasonable one.

In the absence of special agreement, he does not become entitled to his freight payment until he has earned it by delivering the cargo at destination. Many bills of lading and charters, however, provide that freight is to be prepaid, and most of them also provide that the freight is earned, whether prepaid or not, when the voyage begins or the goods are received, regardless of final delivery. In the latter case, the payment is called *earned freight*. The claim of the shipowner for freight and the claim of the cargo owner for loss or damage to his cargo are secured by reciprocal maritime liens, the former upon the cargo and the latter upon the ship.

Passengers. As in the case of cargo, the rights and liabilities of a maritime carrier in relation to passengers carried for hire are governed by the contract with the passenger, subject to statutory regulation of some of its terms. This contract is the passenger ticket, which usually contains detailed provisions governing and limiting the duties and obligations of the carrier. The rights of the passenger and the protections due him apply not only on shipboard but also on the wharf or dock he uses to board, or to land from, the vessel. They also apply in launches or other means of going to or from the ship.

The common law does not make the shipowner an insurer of the passenger's safety but merely holds him liable for negligence. Hence, common law imposed greater responsibility on the carrier for cargo than for passengers. The difference is no doubt based on the premise that an animate passenger can protect himself better than inanimate cargo can. However, the carrier owes a very high duty of care to a passenger, and is held almost an insurer in so far as assaults or insults by the crew are concerned.

Statutes affecting the shipowner's liability are in some respects similar to those governing liability to cargo. They restrict the carrier's right to limit the time for filing claim and commencing suit. They prohibit any contractual limitation on the carrier's responsibility for negligence or on the momentary amount of his liability for personal injury or death. They do not grant the carrier specific exemption from liability for damage arising from errors in management or navigation of the vessel as is done with respect to cargo. The proscriptions in the American statutes are based upon public policy. For this reason, American courts refuse to give effect to contractual provisions reducing responsibility for negligence or limiting recovery for personal injury or death, even though the contract may have been made in a country such as England, where such provisions are allowed.

Peculiarly enough, passengers at sea have been legislatively more favored than those traveling by air. In 1934, the United States adhered to an international convention signed in 1929, at Warsaw, which placed monetary limits on the liability of international air carriers on claims for death, personal injury, and loss or damage to personal effects. Our laws have made the air traveler share some of the risk of the means of travel he selects but do not require sea travelers to do so.

Liabilities for loss or damage to passengers' baggage are different from those concerning commercial cargo or passengers and are substantially unaffected by legislation. *Baggage* cannot be exactly defined. It comprises the belongings a passenger is entitled to take with him by virtue of his ticket and is limited to the things commonly taken for his personal use on the trip. The quantity, type, and value vary with the destination, length, and purpose of the voyage and with the financial status of the traveler.

Baggage does not include household goods, excess articles of great value, or merchandise not to be consumed or used during the voyage. The carrier's liability for loss or damage to baggage retained on board in the passenger's possession or in his stateroom is limited to negligence, but the carrier becomes an insurer of baggage entrusted to his possession and care during the voyage. Both of these liabilities can be, and customarily are, limited in the ticket contract, both as to time for claim and suit and as to momentary amount. Excess baggage or other possessions of the passenger that are shipped under a bill of lading are, of course, governed by the terms of that contract and by the statutes applicable to cargo.

COLLISION

The most important and bitterly contested cases in admiralty are those arising from marine collisions. Liability of a vessel for collision with another vessel or object is usually established by showing a violation of the "rules of the road," that is, the written rules of navigation prescribed by statutes, or regulations issued under them. These are the traffic rules for ships. Collision liability does not have to be based on violation of a specific rule. It can be established by showing general negligence in navigation or lack of due skill and care or, occasionally, by showing a violation of some lawful custom or usage in navigation which is so well established in a particular locality as to have the effect of law. No matter what type of fault is charged, causal connection with the collision must always be proved.

The rules governing vessel navigation by which the conduct of colliding vessels is measured are both international and domestic in character. General maritime law—the "common law of the sea"—establishes rules of international character applying on the high seas. They are given effect by maritime countries to the extent that each adopts these international rules as a part of its own laws and usage. After a long period when the rules of navigation on the high seas were composed of some universally recognized rules and a number of divergent rules peculiar to various nations, the need for uniformity was recognized, and a series of international meetings culminated in a conference at Washington in 1889, where the International Rules for the Prevention of Collisions at Sea were formulated. Since then the International Rules, as modified in subsequent conferences, have been recognized as the standard of navigation on the high seas by substantially all maritime nations.

Each nation may enact supplemental rules not in conflict with the basic International Rules on the high seas. American examples of such individual action are found in the limitation of liability statutes, which are treated later in this chapter, and in the Death on the High Seas Act, which was mentioned in Chapter 16. Unless specifically made to apply to inland waters of a particular nation, the International Rules govern only on the high seas. In the United States, as in many other nations, inland rules are prescribed for inland or national waters.

The Inland Rules apply to all vessels in harbors and in the waters of the United States except on the Great Lakes and their tributary waters and on certain rivers. They govern up to a point where, by American regulation, the area of the International Rules begins. The Inland Rules are generally, but not entirely, similar to the International Rules, and the Great Lakes Rules and the Western Rivers Rules differ from both. These differences create obvious disadvantages and confusion for vessels navigating near the invisible boundaries where the rules change.

Space does not allow any attempt to specify the particular obligations imposed upon vessels by the rules of navigation. They provide in great detail how vessels must navigate with respect to each other; what lights, whistles, or other visual or sound identifications and signals must be given; what speed is proper; and what modifications of conduct are required because of darkness, fog, or other impairment of the vessel's ability to see others or to control her own actions. The relative rights and obligations of vessels differ depending upon whether they are meeting each other, whether one is overtaking another, or whether they are running on crossing courses. Enforcement is so strict that a vessel guilty of violating a statutory rule is held at fault unless she proves not only that her fault did not cause the collision but also that her fault could not have caused it.

In nearly every situation except when vessels are meeting head to head, one vessel is considered "privileged" and the other "burdened." A sailing vessel is privileged over a steam vessel. When crossing, the vessel having the other on her port, or left, side is privileged and the other burdened. An overtaken vessel is privileged, and the overtaking vessel burdened.

In navigating with respect to another vessel, certain assumptions must or may be made. For instance, if the bearing of the other vessel remains constant, it must be assumed that danger of collision exists and appropriate steps must be taken to avoid it. However, a vessel is entitled to assume that the other will navigate properly until there is some indication to the contrary.

The burdened vessel must keep out of the way and avoid collision. The privileged vessel is entitled and required to maintain her course and speed so that the burdened vessel may predict her movements and thereby avoid collision. The "privilege" to maintain course and speed does not, however, allow stubborn adherence to the rule into the jaws of collision. When the privileged vessel observes that collision will result if she continues to hold on, she is then obliged to take whatever action is necessary to avoid the disaster. Raymond Farwell, who was one of the greatest authorities on navigation in the United States and the author of *The Rules of the Nautical Road*, once humorously described the "privilege" as one continuing "up to, but not into or through the burdened vessel."

Risk of collision increases greatly when darkness, fog, snow, or rain reduces a vessel's ability to see others approaching or to judge their character, position, course, or speed. The identifying lights required by the navigation rules and the opportunity to take repeated bearings on them decrease the risk if the night is clear. But fog is a serious hazard because it plays tricks with sound, sometimes muffling fog signals close at hand or making them seem to come from the wrong direction. When in fog, snow, or heavy rain, the rules require a vessel to stop her engines and "navigate with caution" whenever a fog signal is heard from an unseen vessel apparently forward of her beam. In such "thick weather" she must operate at moderate speed, which is usually held to be such as will permit her to stop within half of the visible distance. The use of radar on merchant ships has decreased the hazards of reduced visibility, but the courts have refused to relax the precautionary requirements of the navigation laws for vessels so equipped and have, in fact, held them more strictly accountable for collisions because they should be better able to avoid them.

In American law, responsibility for any collision between vessels must be decided in one of four ways: (1) sole fault of one vessel, (2) sole fault of the other, (3) mutual fault of both vessels, or (4) inevitable accident, the fault of neither. Cases of the last type are very rare. In case of mutual fault, the total damages suffered by both vessels (including their liabilities for damage to cargo and for personal injury or death claims) are divided equally between them—a result quite different from the common-law rule of contributory negligence that requires each party to bear its own loss regardless of how unevenly it is distributed.

When both vessels are at fault, but not equally so, the English courts allocate the damages in proportion to relative fault, such as 80 percent on one vessel and 20 percent on the other. American courts do not have similar latitude. Except in case of inevitable accident, they must divide the total damage equally or fix it all on one of the vessels alone. As a result, where both vessels are at fault, but the errors of one are far more serious and reprehensible than those of the other, the guiltier vessel is sometimes held solely liable under the "major-and-minor-fault" rule, which justifies overlooking small or technical faults on one side if glaring ones appear on the other and if equal division of damage would be unjust.

SALVAGE AND TOWAGE

Salvage. Collisions, fires, and other casualties occurring at sea create a much greater danger of total loss than similar accidents do on land. Following an accident, an automobile can be taken off to the side of the road to await repairs, but there is no such haven for a stricken vessel at sea. If seriously damaged, she may sink before help arrives. Because vessels, cargoes, and persons at sea are exposed to such risks, for centuries it has been a tradition of the sea that vessels will divert from their appointed voyages and speed to help another in distress. To encourage vessels to help one another in need, the rescuer, or *salvor*, is well rewarded when his voluntary assistance to a vessel or her cargo either saves or recovers it from an actually impending sea peril.[10] The arrangements for such assistance, the persons entitled to the reward, and the amount properly due are the subjects of the law of salvage.

Salvage services are either voluntary or contractual. The latter arise when the shipowner or master employs another to render the service and agrees upon the compensation for it. Such contracts may differ widely, depending upon the circumstances. Sometimes payment depends upon success in the salvage operation—"no cure—no pay." Those negotiating the contract for the ship faced with imminent peril of great loss are scarcely in a bargaining position and are sometimes forced to accept grossly unfair terms. As a result, admiralty courts scrutinize such contracts closely and revise the payment if moral duress, fraud, or gross overreaching is proved. But the mere fact that the time, expense, and risk actually encountered by the salvor is much less than was supposed when the agreement was made is not a ground for revision or refusal to enforce the contract. The salvor who accepts the risk of a "no cure—no pay" agreement is entitled to insist on a much higher reward if he succeeds than if he had not gambled on success.

Voluntary salvage is performed without prior agreement on terms. There must be a real and imminent marine peril to the salved vessel or her cargo or both. A peril is marine if it threatens a waterborne vessel, even though it originates from a cause on land. The service can consist of extinguishing a fire; repairing, towing, or recapturing a vessel or cargo; saving a life if property is also saved; or any number of other protective acts.

Since the service must be voluntary, no reward is earned by those who merely perform duties already imposed on them by law. Frequent disputes arise on this issue. The master, officers, and crew to whom the vessel is entrusted and whose duty it is to bring her safely to port cannot claim

[10] A salvor receives no award for saving lives alone, but his reward for saving a vessel or cargo is increased if lives are also saved.

an award for saving their own vessel while thus employed. They are, however, entitled to compensation for salvage services performed for the vessel after their employment ends. If a vessel is completely abandoned after an accident without hope of returning to her, and if this is done in good faith to save life and at the master's order, the crew's employment has ended and they are free to claim salvage for subsequent successful efforts to save the ship or her cargo. The operator of a tug towing a vessel in a normal operation is in a generally similar position. If an accident occurs, the tug is obligated to protect her tow as a part of her regular service under the towing contract. Unless unanticipated circumstances arise which would justify the tug in abandoning the contract, she may not claim salvage for saving her own tow.

Success is another most important element in voluntary salvage or under a "no cure—no pay" contract. In the absence of agreement to the contrary, the salvor has no personal claim against the owner of the salved property. He does have a maritime-lien right of high priority in the property itself, but this right is worthless if nothing is saved. No matter how valiant an unsuccessful effort may have been, an award is not earned unless the property is completely or partially saved.

A passenger is also obligated to help save the ship, but he can earn a salvage award if his services are so extraordinary that they exceed his obligation. Crew members also are sometimes given compensation "in the nature of salvage" for particularly exceptional, brave, or meritorious service beyond their normal duties. The person or vessel whose fault creates the peril and the need for salvage cannot, however, earn an award even by later successfully averting or minimizing the threatened loss.

The law imposes a strict obligation of good faith and devotion to duty on salvors. Any plundering, fraud, or other misconduct defeats the right to a salvage award. If the salvor voluntarily and permanently abandons the effort, he has no right to an award even though others who later succeed are helped by his uncompleted work. However, if he abandons the undertaking according to agreement whereby a cosalvor continues the work, he does have the right. Two or more vessels can cooperate in the salvage effort and are entitled to awards in proportion to their merit. By Federal statute and by customary provisions in charters and bills of lading, common ownership of the salvaging and the salved vessel does not bar appropriate salvage recovery.

The salvor does not, however, acquire legal title to the salved vessel, even after she has been completely abandoned by the crew, including the master. He is only entitled to assert a lien against her for a salvage award, which in such a case would probably be very large. In the much publicized case of the *Flying Enterprise*, the newspapers described the master's courageous and lonely vigil on his ship as a protective measure to keep others from acquiring title to her as a derelict. This was entirely incorrect, though many believed it at the time.

Public policy favors liberal salvage awards. The only definite rules in determining awards are that they must be fairly compensatory and cannot, of course, exceed the value of the property saved. In fixing the amount, a number of different factors are considered. These include the values of the salvor's property employed and of the property in peril, the degree of danger threatening these respective properties, the risks to the lives of salvors and of the persons saved, the time consumed and skill shown by the salvor, and the degree to which assistance of cosalvors was available or contributed to the result.

Towage. Towage service is rendered when one vessel is used to propel or maneuver another or to expedite the latter's voyage. Such services are sometimes required to save a vessel from peril, in which case the services are salvage and are rewarded as such. True towage services are those rendered according to prior agreement, not because of any accident or peril threatening the assisted vessel, or *tow*. The towing vessel is usually, but not always, a small steamer or tug especially designed for the purpose.

By undertaking to perform a towing service, the tower assumes certain duties and responsibilities imposed by law. He must use his best efforts to accomplish the operation successfully and is excused for failure to complete it only if unforeseen hazards or accidents make further performance impossible. He must bring to the task a seaworthy tug of sufficient power for the intended job, a competent crew, and such adequate towing hawsers, pads, and other tackle and equipment, in good condition, as are reasonably to be expected of such a class of vessel.

The responsibilities of the tug master are affected by the nature of the tow. If the tow is not equipped with, or does not intend to use, its power of self-propulsion, normally the tug master controls the operation of both tug and tow. This is called a *dead*, or flat, tow. If the tow is to use its own self-propelling power, the activities of the tug are normally controlled by directions from the master or pilot on the tow. Such "live" tows are usually of short duration, as when a tug or several tugs move a vessel to or from her berth or assist her movement in a river or harbor. If a vessel is being moved as a dead tow, the tug master frequently directs the operation from the bridge of the tow. The towage contract often provides that the tug master, when directing the operation from the tow, acts as the employee of the owner of the tow, and any errors he makes create no liability on the tug or her owner.

In any towing operation where the tug is in charge, the tower is responsible for the make-up of the tow, which often consists of several barges, scows, or small vessels. Even if others actually secure the lashings or set the length of hawsers connecting parts of the tow, the tower is ultimately responsible for the safety and seaworthiness of the whole tow. He must check and satisfy himself that all is in order and make such corrections as safety and good seamanship require before or during the towing operation. He is also responsible for the navigation of the tow he controls. He sets the course and speed and must properly gauge the weather, wind, tide, and channel currents, courses, and depths.

The assisted vessel also has responsibilities. If her master is in control, he must see that the tugs are not endangered by the maneuvers he orders. Even when the tug is in control, the tow must take all reasonable steps to avoid injury to the tug and to facilitate the operation. If equipped with steering, propelling, or signaling gear, she must obey orders promptly and with reasonable skill. She must steer to follow the tug's track and in emergency must cast off or otherwise act to avoid danger to the tug as well as to herself.

A tug and tow must display the required lights and give the other signals prescribed to identify themselves to others. For purposes of the rules of navigation, the two are considered as one vessel, but other vessels must make due allowance for their relative awkwardness in maneuvering.

Under American law, the tower is considered an independent contractor and not the agent of the tow. Consequently, a tug in control is normally held responsible for any collision involving the assisted vessel unless the tow has contributed to the accident through some actual fault of her own. In England, the tug is more commonly treated as the tow's agent, whose faults create liability on the tow as principal.

The owner of the assisted vessel can normally hold the tower liable for damage sustained by his vessel. In case of collision, the tow can also recover from the other colliding vessel if the latter is at fault. If the tug is at fault in a collision, its errors are attributed to the tow because of the identity of the tug and tow under navigation laws. However, whatever portion of recovery is denied the tow from the other vessel because of the tug's imputed faults can normally be recovered from the tug as the only other malefactor.

PILOTAGE

A pilot, in the usual sense of the term, is one who holds himself out as particularly skilled in navigating vessels into or out of a port; through a river, channel, or roadstead; or along a particular coast. A vessel takes him aboard to gain the benefit of his personal knowledge of the waters and their hazards. He supersedes the master in command of the ship in directing speed, course, stopping, reversing, use of anchors, and similar navigational matters. If he is a licensed pilot, he must refuse to act unless he is given effective control of the ship in these regards. The master, however, always remains ultimately responsible for the ship's safety.

If the pilot's acts are putting her in peril, the master must resume command.

In many waters, state laws make employment of pilots compulsory upon penalty of having to pay full or half the pilotage fee if the pilot is declined. A pilot voluntarily engaged is considered merely an employee of the shipowner, but a compulsory pilot has a status more like that of an independent contractor. The latter may be held liable to the shipowner for failure to use reasonable care and skill. The negligence of a voluntary pilot is imputed to the shipowner as in the case of any other employee, but the doctrine of *respondeat superior* does not apply to the acts of a compulsory pilot. However, since a compulsory pilot is lawfully in charge of the vessel, an action *in rem* can be brought against the vessel on the theory that she is the offender, even though the compulsory pilot's negligence does not create personal liability on the shipowner.

Pilots, like others performing maritime services for a vessel, normally have a maritime lien on the vessel for the fees due them. They often group together into pilots' associations, some of which are highly organized, with rigid control of earnings and membership. Other associations are loosely formed, with little or no control of membership, and merely provide for sharing certain common expenses.

Both state and Federal regulations apply to pilots and pilotage, and both governments issue pilots' licenses. Despite the fact that the subject is an integral part of maritime commerce, over which the Federal government may exercise exclusive control, Congress has specifically recognized the need for state action in regulating pilotage in local ports and has invoked its right to assume exclusive control only as to those phases of the subject affecting more than one state.

LIMITATION OF SHIPOWNER'S LIABILITY

By common-law principles, the personal liability of a shipowner for damage or injury caused by his ship or resulting from her operation was limited only by the amount of the loss suffered and the owner's ability to pay. Ships are costly instruments of trade, and often the cargo carried is even more valuable than the ship. Because of the hazards inherent in shipping, one who invested capital in a ship always ran the risk of liabilities far exceeding his initial investment if his ship was lost with valuable cargo on board or if she was to blame for a collision causing the loss of another vessel of even greater value. If that other vessel also carried valuable cargo and if lives were lost in the collision, the liability resulting from a single accident could easily bankrupt the owner of the offending ship no matter how solvent he had been. Insurance against such unlimited risks could be obtained only at excessive costs.

Potential investors were reluctant to risk capital in such an undertaking, and nations dependent upon merchant shipping suffered from the lack of private investment in the industry. Early in the eighteenth century, laws were enacted in Continental European countries and in England to encourage capital investment in shipping by limiting the total liability of a shipowner for a single accident to his financial interest in his ship plus the pending freight she was earning at the time of the accident. No matter how great the liability would otherwise have been, all claimants were required to accept pro rata satisfaction from this single "limitation fund." In order to permit Americans to compete with foreign shipowners on equal terms of liability and insurance cost, the same general principles were made a part of the American law by the Limited Liability Act of 1851. This Act has been amended a number of times, usually reducing the shipowner's protection in one regard or another.

The limitation of liability statutes have never absolved the shipowner from responsibility for his own personal faults. They only protect him against imputed liability for the acts of subordinate employees or crew members if the owner is not in "privity" and has no personal knowledge of the acts or other cause of the loss. The right to limit liability disappears if the owner himself, or a principal officer of a corporate owner, is at fault. The owner's obligation to use proper care to furnish a seaworthy vessel, properly equipped, and a competent master and crew is personal to him. Failure in any of these regards forfeits his right to limit liability.

A major modification in the American law was made following the terrible disaster in 1934, when the *Morro Castle* burned and sank off the New Jersey coast, killing 134 and injuring 224 persons. While Congress was still not disturbed about limiting liabilities to insured cargo owners, cutting off the rights of individuals to recover for personal injury and death was quite a different matter. The difference was tragically spotlighted in this case where death and personal-injury claims were more than ten times as great as cargo claims. The limitation to which all claimants would have been restricted, except for facts peculiar to the individual case, was less than 1.5 percent of the total claims.

Consequently, Congress changed the limit of liability for death and personal-injury claims and provided that it could not be less than $60 per ton of the vessel. Further, as to such claims, the privity or knowledge of the master, or of the superintendent or managing agent of the owner, was made conclusively the "privity or knowledge of the owner," which would defeat the right to limit liability at all. As to all types of liabilities, a bareboat charterer is given the same rights as the owner. The liabilities subject to limitation include contractual obligations as well as torts, but do not include claims for seamen's wages or obligations on contracts which the owner makes personally, as distinguished from those made in his name by subordinate agents or employees.

In the United States, a shipowner seeking to limit his liability can surrender the vessel and assign her pending freight to a trustee for the benefit of the claimants, since it is the value of each at the end of the voyage that measures his responsibility.[11] If no freight is pending and the vessel is a total loss, he pays nothing on claims other than those for personal injury or death.

The shipowner's right to limit liability can be asserted as a defense to a suit brought by a claimant in any court, or in the form of a separate petition filed by the shipowner in a Federal admiralty court either before or after claimants have sued. The shipowner's petition must be filed within six months after the first written notice of claim is received and he must then either surrender the vessel and freight to a trustee or deposit either cash security or a surety bond in the amount of their value. Normally the shipowner's petition seeks a decree exonerating him from any responsibility at all or, alternatively, limiting his liability as allowed by statute if he is ultimately found to be liable.[12] Claimants are notified to file their claims and answers to the petition in this proceeding, and any other actions in Federal or state courts are abated. The issues of the shipowner's initial responsibility, his right to limitation, the amount of the limited-liability fund, the validity and amount of the claims, and the proportionate distribution among claimants are then all determined in the one proceeding. This means of marshaling claims and determining the issues of fault, damage, and award in a single forum has the obvious advantages of judicial economy and uniformity.

BIBLIOGRAPHY

In addition to the books listed below, those by Benedict and Robinson in the bibliography for Chapter 16 apply here.

Farwell, Raymond F., *The Rules of the Nautical Road*, 2d ed., United States Naval Institute, Annapolis, Md., 1944.
Griffin, John W., *The American Law of Collision*, American Maritime Cases, Inc., Baltimore, 1949.
Henderson, James S., and Sanford D. Cole, *Carver's Carriage of Goods by Sea*, 8th ed., Baker, Voorhis & Company, Inc., New York, 1938.
Hodgson, A. J., and G. R. Rudolf, *Loundes and Rudolf's Law of General Average*, 4th ed., Baker, Voorhis & Company, Inc., New York, 1952.

[11] In England, the measure of liability is the value of the vessel before the accident but not exceeding a fixed amount per ton.
[12] In England, a shipowner cannot seek such alternative relief. He may petition to limit his liability only after he has first admitted responsibility.

Knauth, Arnold W., *Ocean Bills of Lading*, 4th ed., American Maritime Cases, Inc., Baltimore, 1952.

Koushnareff, Serge G., *Liability of Carriers of Goods by Sea*, Delphic Press, New York, 1943.

Poor, Wharton, *American Law of Charter Parties and Bills of Lading*, 3d ed., Matthew Bender & Company, Inc., Albany, N.Y., 1948.

Roscoe, Edward S., *The Measure of Damages in Actions in Maritime Collisions*, 3d ed., Stevens and Sons, Ltd., London, 1929.

Scrutton, Sir Thomas E., *Charter Parties and Ocean Bills of Lading*, 15th ed., Sweet & Maxwell, Ltd., London, 1948.

CHAPTER 18

MARINE LOSSES AND MARINE INSURANCE*

Most of the expenses of steamship operation can be estimated and budgeted by customary accounting procedures. However, fortuitous happenings to which ships and their cargoes and crews are exposed may, in the absence of a proper program of marine insurance, result in losses or liabilities of such magnitude as to upset completely the most carefully prepared budget. By using the facilities of the marine insurance market and by paying insurance premiums, the shipowner can make certain the cost of these accidental occurrences during a specified period of time. Insurers, in turn, agree to indemnify him against losses and liabilities that result from insured perils.

An adequate and fully integrated program of marine insurance is therefore a vital part of the financing of ocean shipping and of efficient and successful steamship operation. Practically all mortgage contracts and most charter parties and other contracts involving ships and ship operation make reference to the responsibilities of the contracting parties with respect to marine insurance.[1]

GENERAL NATURE OF MARINE UNDERWRITING

Insuring the risks involved in ocean transportation was one of the earliest developments in the broad field of insurance. The earliest known marine insurance policies antedate even the first known fire or life insur-

* This chapter was written by Walter G. Hays, chief average adjuster, Marsh & McLennan, San Francisco.

[1] This chapter, like the ones on seamen's law and the law of vessels, can deal only with broad principles; the reader seeking technical accuracy should consult one of the sources listed at the end of the chapter. Moreover, the discussion deals entirely with the major features of a vessel owner's marine insurance program and does not discuss the various forms of marine insurance policies available to shippers, consignees, or owners of cargo. For a comparable discussion of cargo insurance, see Philip MacDonald, "Cargo Insurance," *Practical Exporting*, The Ronald Press Company, New York, 1949, or Morris S. Rosenthal, *Techniques of International Trade*, McGraw-Hill Book Company, Inc., New York, 1950, pp. 219–288. It is suggested that the student read Chap. 17 before this one.

ance policy. Because it has a history of several hundred years, the marine insurance business is regulated, to a very considerable degree, by precedents and practices of long standing. The wording of some clauses of modern marine insurance policies is so antiquated that the clauses are almost unintelligible unless one examines the record of court decisions interpreting them.

The so-called perils clause, the basic insuring clause in all hull, increased value, and freight insurance policies, is an example. This clause, developed by underwriters at Lloyd's, London, about the time of the American Revolution, reads as follows:

Touching the Adventures and Perils which we, the Assurers, are contented to bear and do take upon us, they are of the Seas, Men-of-War, Fire, Enemies, Pirates, Rovers, Thieves, Jettisons, Letters of Mart and Counter-Mart, Surprisals, Takings at Sea, Arrests, Restraints and Detainments of all Kings, Princes and Peoples, of what nation, condition or quality soever, Barratry of the Master and Mariners and of all other like Perils, Losses and Misfortunes that have or shall come to the Hurt, Detriment or Damage of the said Vessel, &c., or any part thereof; . . .

The form used today is practically identical with that of one hundred and fifty years ago. It has been preserved, with its archaic spelling and antiquated and illogical arrangement, because the court decisions of decades have given practically every word a definite legal meaning. It is contended that, if a revised and modernized perils clause were adopted, the industry would be subject to the vagaries of court interpretation for a long period of time during which the element of certainty of meaning that now exists would be missing.

Other clauses, such as the Inchmaree clause and the collision clause, both of which are also included in the modern hull policy, represent later additions to marine insurance policies. They were made necessary by the development of new types of vessels, new practices in ship operation, and new exposures to loss resulting from changes in the law of the sea. In December, 1951, the American Institute of Marine Underwriters and the American Marine Hull Insurance Syndicate effected a complete revision of their time hull clauses. One of the principal changes was the addition of a new peril to be insured against: "breakdown of motor generators and other electrical machinery." The voyage clause was completely revised to meet more adequately the conditions of present-day navigation.

The history of marine insurance reflects the evolution of ocean shipping, in the development not only of new clauses but also of certain divisions of marine insurance operations. The shipowner who would have a proper marine insurance program must have some knowledge and understanding of the general divisions of marine insurance, their historical background, and the conditions prevailing in them.

FORMS OF MARINE INSURANCE POLICIES

The main divisions of marine insurance for the vessel owner are as follows: hull, increased value, freight, protection and indemnity (usually called P & I), and war risk.

Hull Insurance. Hull insurance protects the shipowner against the physical loss of, or damage to, his vessel (including its machinery, appurtenances, and equipment) and against the liabilities arising out of the collision of his vessel with another vessel. Hull underwriters reimburse the shipowner for the following types of losses, all of which will be explained later in this chapter: (1) total loss or constructive total loss, (2) partial loss or particular-average damage, (3) general average and salvage assessments, and (4) certain liabilities arising out of the collision of the insured vessel with another vessel.

Increased Value Insurance. To provide himself with additional protection against the risk of total loss of his vessel, the shipowner purchases increased value insurance (sometimes called disbursement insurance). If the vessel is a total loss, the shipowner loses not only the vessel herself as a physical and salable property but also suffers certain intangible losses such as the earnings of the vessel until he can find a replacement. His shoreside personnel and his shoreside facilities may be geared to the operation of a fleet of a given size. Hence, the loss of one vessel from the fleet may result in temporarily unbalancing the shoreside factor in his over-all operations. Increased value insurance protects the owner for these exposures by providing that his insurers will pay him an additional sum—beyond the amount of hull insurance—in case of total or constructive total loss of his vessel.

Increased value insurance also may insure against the risks covered by the excess-liabilities clauses usually added to this type of policy. This coverage has two facets, both related to the value of the vessel.

First, as will be explained later, in a general-average or salvage adjustment, the vessel's contribution may be assessed on the basis of a value higher than that which is agreed in the hull policy. The hull underwriters would then respond for only a proportionate part of the ship's general-average or salvage assessment. To protect himself against assessments because of undervaluation that are not recoverable under the basic hull policy, the shipowner adds the excess-liabilities clauses of the increased value policy. Differences between the hull insurance value and the contributory value of a ship in a general-average or salvage adjustment are understandable, since there is no spot market for ships as there is for commodities such as grain and coffee. Furthermore, expert appraisers differ in their opinions as to the value of a vessel, and, during the hull policy period (usually one year), the market value of ship tonnage may rise or fall owing to changes in economic conditions.

Second, although hull policies protect the vessel owner against collision liabilities, the limit of that protection is the amount of hull insurance, and in some circumstances the owner's liability may exceed that amount. Under the Limitation of Liability Statute, a shipowner may limit his liability arising from collision to the value of his vessel and her pending freight.[2] If, however, the "limitation fund" should exceed the amount of hull insurance for any of the reasons suggested in the previous paragraph, the owner would be unprotected as respects the amount of his liability in excess of his hull insurance. Also, the benefits of the Limitation of Liability Statute may be defeated if the cause of the collision may be charged to the "fault and privity" of the vessel owner personally. In such event, his liability could well exceed the amount of hull insurance. The excess-liabilities clauses of the increased-value policy give the vessel owner additional protection against collision liability in excess of the amount of hull insurance. It will be appreciated that this additional protection against excess general-average and collision liabilities is limited to the amount of the increased value insurance purchased and that, in the event of a major and fast rise in ship values, the combined protection of the hull and increased-value policies might not be adequate to cover the vessel owner's total liability.

Because the increased-value policy insures intangible and indefinite interests, underwriters specifically waive the usual requirements that the assured prove his insurable interest in the subject matter of insurance before a loss is paid.[3] This feature of the increased-value policy makes it legally unenforceable as a gambling or wagering contract, so that the vessel owner must rely solely on the honor of the underwriter to comply with the terms of contract. However, vessel owners do not discount the value of the policy on this account, since marine underwriters are particularly careful to protect their reputations by discharging the written terms of the policy promptly and fully.

Freight Insurance. Freight insurance protects the vessel owner against the loss of the earnings of his vessel as a result of the destruction of the vessel or of its cargo. A vessel derives its value primarily from its earning capacity as a carrier of cargo or passengers. The ship's revenue, called *freight*, represents the compensation that the owner earns under such contracts as the bill of lading or the charter party. The freight money contracted for represents an intangible property interest, the loss of which the vessel owner may insure against under a freight insurance policy.

The earning of freight under a bill of lading is dependent upon the

---

[2] An exception exists if there is loss of life or injury to persons—a matter that is discussed elsewhere in this chapter.

[3] Policies incorporating provisions waiving proof of interest are variously described as honor, P.P.I. (policy proof of interest), or F.I.A. (full interest admitted) policies.

delivery of the cargo at destination, unless the bill of lading provides for "earned freight." It is permissible legally, and now common practice, for the vessel owner to incorporate in his bill-of-lading contract a provision that freight moneys shall be considered earned when the cargo is loaded on board the vessel and that they are not returnable to the shipper regardless of whether the cargo is delivered at destination or not. Such a provision is referred to as a guaranteed-freight clause. Under such a contract, the shipowner has no freight "at risk" and needs no freight insurance.

If, on the other hand, the bill of lading embodies no provision for earned freight, the shipowner must bear the risk that the cargo may be lost before arrival at destination or that the vessel may not be able to deliver the cargo at destination, and consequently the risk that he will not earn the freight moneys. Since he makes considerable outlays in loading costs, wages of crew, fuel and stores for the voyage, canal dues, and so forth in anticipation of earning such freight, the shipowner with freight moneys at risk usually insures himself against the loss of those moneys owing to marine casualties.

Contracts of affreightment coming under the classification of charter parties are so numerous and varied in form that it is desirable to discuss them in a general way only.[4] The earnings of a vessel owner derived from operations under various charter-party contracts may often be defeated by the total loss of the vessel or of its cargo as a result of marine disaster. For example, under one form of "lump-sum voyage charter," the compensation to the vessel owner for carrying a cargo on a single voyage is defined as a given lump sum, payable upon delivery of the cargo at destination. If the vessel and cargo are totally lost before arrival, the owner is deprived of his right to collect his charter hire. Losses of this character and similar losses under other charter parties may be insured under a policy on freight.

Protection and Indemnity Insurance. The three forms of marine insurance already discussed protect the vessel owner against the legal liabilities arising out of tort or negligence in the operation of his vessel only in the case of collision with another vessel. The P & I policy, a relatively modern development in marine insurance, protects the shipowner against practically all other forms of tort (negligence) liabilities. It offers protection against liabilities for loss of life or personal injury or for damage to cargo or to other properties. Such liabilities may, on occasion, exceed the losses resulting from the total loss of the vessel by marine perils.

Protection and indemnity insurance represents a separate division of marine underwriting, with its own policy forms. It partakes of the nature of casualty insurance rather than of property insurance, and is generally offered and written by a different group of insurers from those who insure

[4] See Chap. 10, "Ship Operation: Charters."

against physical loss or damage.[5] The reasons for this, and for the exclusion from the P & I policy of tort liabilities arising out of collision, are purely historical.

When shipowners first demanded protection against tort liabilities arising from collision, the underwriters insuring traditional marine risks were the only ones qualified to write any form of ocean transportation insurance. Later, when shipowners demanded insurance against other tort liabilities, the traditional marine insurance market was not prepared to engage in insuring these risks. To meet the situation, ship operators organized into mutual protection and indemnity insurance associations. These mutuals, or P & I clubs, as they are commonly called, were developed primarily in England, where they are still the major underwriters of protection and indemnity insurance. In recent years, several stock insurance companies have gone into this field, both in the United States and in the United Kingdom.

Considerable variation exists among the P & I contracts offered by the various English clubs and particularly between the policy forms of the English clubs and those issued by American stock companies. However, the basic coverages granted by the various forms are substantially the same, and may be summarized as follows:

1. *Loss of life, or personal injury or illness.* As indicated in Chapter 16, the law imposes on the shipowner certain obligations for crew members and also protects longshoremen who load and discharge cargoes. The law courts and legislative bodies have been solicitous for the welfare of seamen; very heavy liabilities are often imposed upon vessel owners as a result of illness, injury, or death of seamen while employed on vessels. In addition, repairmen, suppliers, passengers, and others who come aboard ships in the ordinary conduct of the ship's business may suffer injuries that give rise to heavy damage claims against the vessel owner. All these forms of liability are insured under the usual P & I policy, subject to a prescribed deductible.[6]

2. *Damage to cargo, baggage, and personal effects of passengers.* The shipowner's obligations to respond for loss of, or damage to, cargo, baggage, and personal effects of passengers are very complex (see Chapter 17). Vessel owners generally have made efforts to limit the extent and amount of their liability under their bills of lading or other contracts of affreightment and have received considerable relief by legislation, but very heavy

---

[5] In general, hull, increased value, and freight insurance are written by the same group of underwriters.

[6] Different deductibles are generally applied to claims falling into different classifications, *e.g.*, to the total of claims for loss of life or personal injury arising from each separate accident, to the total of all cargo claims filed in connection with each one-way voyage, and to "all other claims."

penalties may still be assessed. These various liabilities are insured under the P & I policy.

3. *Damage to shore properties.* Claims against vessel owners for damage due to collision with such shore facilities as docks, piers, and bridges generally arise from negligence in the navigation of the vessel. Claims in this class also arise from dropping anchors on submarine cables or other shore properties. Losses of this type can impose heavy liabilities on the shipowner.

4. *Customs, immigration, or other fines or penalties.* If alien stowaways are found on board ships entering United States ports, if oil is spilled in harbor waters, or if irregularities appear in manifests, government authorities impose fines and penalties against a vessel. The losses falling under this type of claim are seldom heavy, but the P & I policy recognizes and insures against the possibility of fines or penalties.

5. *Damage to another vessel, not caused by collision.* Negligent navigation of a vessel in harbor waters sometimes causes accidental damage, by stranding or collision, to another vessel or to property carried on another vessel, without there being any actual contact between the two vessels. In such circumstances, the owner of the negligently operated vessel may be liable to respond for damages. If a fire or explosion aboard the insured vessel damages another vessel, or if cargo or gear is dropped from the insured vessel onto the deck of another vessel, whatever claim arises will fall into this classification.

6. *Expenses of repatriating crew.* The laws of some countries require that if a seaman is stranded away from his home country by the total loss of the vessel on which he was employed or by other circumstances, the owner of the vessel must stand the expense of repatriating him. If imposed by statute, liability for such expenses is insured against under the P & I policy. During recent years, contracts of employment between shipowners and maritime labor unions have frequently obligated the owner to repatriate seamen who have been stranded in foreign ports under various circumstances. Liability of this character growing out of the contract of employment is not customarily insured under the P & I policy.

7. *Removal of wreck.* The laws of maritime nations vary considerably in regard to the obligation of the vessel owner to remove from navigable waters the wreck of his ship lost by marine casualty. Under some circumstances, this would be a heavy burden on the owner.

8. *Uncollectible proportions of general average due from cargo.* Most of the casualties that give rise to a general-average adjustment occur in circumstances that make it necessary for the shipowner to expend his own money for salvage or other operations and to look to the cargo interests for recoupment in a general-average adjustment. In some cases, however, where

the casualty is produced by some negligence or failure of the owner, he may be deprived of his right to claim contribution to these extra expenses from the cargo interests. The P & I policy undertakes to reimburse the vessel owner for the general-average contributions that he is unable to collect from cargo interests under such circumstances. This feature of the P & I policy is distinctive in that it does not deal with a liability imposed upon the owner, as do other P & I coverages, but rather it provides that he be reimbursed for his own expenditures made under special circumstances.

War Risk Insurance. In times of war or threatened war, and even in times of peace if a vessel is operating in mine-infested waters, it is extremely important that the owner insure against loss by war perils. Moreover, developments in connection with war risk insurance are unpredictable, and the prudent vessel owner should examine the situation carefully and repeatedly in the light of the international situation and of the conditions existing on his trade routes.

The insuring of war risks presents many special problems to marine underwriters, and the practices and controls that have been developed are so distinctive as to make war risk insurance a special division of the marine underwriting field. During a major hostility, the difficult problems of insuring war risks generally result in the coordination of commercial war risk operations with a government-operated program.

The perils clause gives protection against the risks of war in the following terms: "Men-of-War, . . . Enemies, Pirates, Rovers, . . . Letters of Mart and Counter-Mart, Surprisals, Takings at Sea, Arrests, Restraints and Detainments of all Kings, Princes and Peoples, of what nation, condition or quality soever . . . " In modern times, however, war develops with a suddenness and intensity that can be disastrous to marine underwriting operations unless they are regulated and controlled virtually on a day-to-day basis. But, instead of deleting the war risk features of the perils clause, underwriters have incorporated an exclusion clause, commonly referred to as the F.C. & S. clause (free-of-capture-and-seizure clause). To protect himself against war risks, the vessel owner can have a special endorsement added to the marine insurance policy setting forth in detail the terms and conditions under which the risks of war are to be insured.

The war risk coverage obtainable in the commercial market is, however, subject to major limitations and restrictions. But, because ocean shipping is essential to the conduct of modern warfare, and because an adequate war risk insurance program is a correspondingly essential part of any national war effort, the governments of maritime nations generally enter the field of war risk insurance in wartime. For instance, the United States government insured war risks on all privately owned vessels operated for government account during World War II. In general, the risks that are assumed by the war risk underwriters are those that are excluded from the marine insurance policy by the F.C. & S. clause. During both world wars, efforts to determine the line of distinction between war risk losses and marine risk losses were a major and difficult problem; and the matter has given rise to a considerable amount of litigation between war and marine underwriters. As a result, a large number of changes have been made in the wording of war risk insuring clauses.

PERILS INSURED AGAINST

Basic Perils Clause. "Perils of the Sea," which are listed among the insured perils in Lloyd's perils clause, have been construed by various court decisions to include all the risks of the elements, such as wind and wave and lightning, and most of the navigational hazards of ship operations, such as stranding, collision, striking bottom or rocks, or collision with docks or shore structures.[7] Jettison and the risk of fire are specifically enumerated. "Barratry of the Master and Mariners" consists of any wrongful act of the master or crew of the vessel in violation of the rights of the vessel owner. All the other causes of loss that are specifically enumerated in the clause come under the general classification of war risks, and these perils are excluded from the coverage of the marine policy by the F.C. & S. clause.

Inchmaree Clause. As noted earlier, the perils clause is basic to all hull, increased value, and freight insurance policies in that it defines the basic risks of loss for which the vessel owner will be indemnified under those types of policies. Hull and increased value policies also contain a separate clause, known as the Inchmaree clause, which lists additional perils to be insured against.

The clause takes its title from the name of the vessel on which a type of loss occurred for which marine underwriters had never previously responded under the Lloyd's perils clause—the bursting of a steam boiler. The owner of the *Inchmaree* sued his marine underwriters to recover his damages as a loss by "perils of the sea," but was unsuccessful. This litigation pointed up the necessity of broadening the protection of the hull policy and led to the adoption of the new clause. Many additional perils not involved in the original lawsuit have been added to the clause since it was originally adopted, and the form in most common use at the close of 1951 added the following perils to the policy coverage:

Accidents in loading, discharging or handling cargo, or in bunkering;
Accidents in going on or off, or while on drydocks, graving docks, ways, gridirons or pontoons;

[7] The reference here is to damage to the vessel rather than damage to shoreside facilities covered under the P & I policy.

Explosions on shipboard or elsewhere;
Breakdown of motor generators or other electrical machinery and electrical connections thereto, bursting of boilers, breakage of shafts, or any latent defect in the machinery or hull, (excluding the cost and expense of replacing or repairing the defective part);
Contact with Aircraft or with any land conveyance;
Negligence of Master, Charterers other than an Assured, Mariners, Engineers or Pilots . . .

Considerable difficulty is often encountered in arriving at agreement between shipowners and marine underwriters concerning the proper interpretation of certain words in this clause. This is notably true of such phrases as "breakage of shafts," "any latent defect in the machinery or hull," and "negligence."

Collision Clause. Another addition to the list of perils originally insured against under the basic hull policy is to be found in the collision clause, the basic provisions of which are as follows:

If the vessel hereby insured shall come into collision with any other ship or vessel and the assured . . . in consequence thereof . . . shall become liable to pay and shall pay by way of damages to any other person or persons any sum or sums in respect of such collision, we, the underwriters, will pay the assured . . . such sum or sums . . . provided always that our liability in respect to any one such collision shall not exceed . . . the value of the vessel hereby insured.

This clause is distinctive in the hull policy in that it covers tort liabilities, in contrast with all other coverages in the policy which pertain to loss of or damage to the assured's own vessel. The protection of the clause extends to charterers of the insured vessel and to anyone who may act as surety for either owner or charterer as to the collision liabilities covered by the clause. The liabilities covered by the clause include physical loss and damage to the other vessel and its cargo and loss of profits and detention expenses of the owner of that vessel, but the clause stipulates that hull underwriters assume no liability arising out of collision (1) for injury to harbors, wharves, and similar shore structures; (2) for loss of life and personal injury; or (3) for loss of the cargo or engagements of the insured vessel. These liabilities, except as to the engagements of the insured vessel, are covered by the P & I policy, which has already been discussed. Legal expenses are also included in the coverage, subject to established rules of adjustment, if the liability of the insured vessel is contested with the consent of the underwriters, or an effort is made to limit the liability of either of the vessels.

To provide an equitable basis for adjusting matters in a mutual-fault collision settlement as between (1) underwriters, who assume the physical damages of the insured vessel and all collision liabilities (except as noted above), and (2) the insured vessel owner, who is usually *uninsured* against the damages he may suffer by the detention of his vessel for collision repairs, the collision clause includes a feature commonly referred to as the *cross-liability* provision. Both increased value policies and P & I policies, which can be involved in collision cases, have a corresponding cross-liability collision-claim provision.

The collision clause also provides that "the principles involved in this clause shall apply to the case where both vessels are the property, in part or in whole, of the same owners or charterers," and stipulates that in such cases all questions of responsibility and amount of liability as between the two vessels shall be settled by arbitration. This is known as the *sister-ship* provision.

DURATION OF THE COVERAGE

Most marine insurance policies insuring the interests of the vessel owner (including hull, increased value, freight, and protection and indemnity policies) are written on a time basis, although any of them may be written on a voyage basis if required. By common practice, none of these policies is written for a period of longer than one year; the majority of them are written on a year-to-year basis. Many chartering operations, however, require that vessel insurances be arranged on a voyage basis. In that event, in order to avoid a possible lapse or a possible overlapping of insurance, it is extremely important that the time for the attachment of the insurance and for its expiration be specifically provided for.

When marine insurance is written on a time basis, it is customary to specify both the date and the hour of attachment and expiration. Sometimes the insurance may be extended beyond the specified expiration time, as, for instance, if the vessel is at sea at that time, in distress, or at a port of refuge. Underwriters customarily grant an extension of the insurance until the vessel arrives at her port of destination, provided the owner has given previous notice of his intention to extend the insurance. When insurance is so extended, underwriters charge an additional premium, prorated on a monthly basis.

Hull policies ordinarily provide that the insurance shall continue in effect while the vessel is in port, at sea, and on dry dock, in all places and in all services and trades. However, if the insured vessel undertakes towage or salvage services under a prearranged contract, underwriters customarily charge an additional premium. The same is true if the vessel is towed, other than is customary in harbors or inland waters, or when in need of assistance. If such services or operations are undertaken, the policies are not canceled, but the owner is obligated to pay additional premiums commensurate with the extra risk involved.

To obtain concessions in premium charges, shipowners often agree to confine the operations of their vessels to certain definite geographical limits. In such situations, special "trade-warranty" conditions are incorporated in the marine insurance policies. Such provisions do not ordinarily stipulate that the insurance shall cease if the vessel proceeds out of the specified geographical trade limits but do provide that additional premiums commensurate with the additional risks involved shall be paid.

Since the ownership and operation of a vessel are material factors affecting the underwriter's consideration of the rates and conditions on which he will insure any given vessel, policies usually provide for automatic cancellation of the insurance if the insured vessel is sold, transferred, bareboat chartered, or requisitioned.

ADJUSTMENT OF LOSSES

In spite of the many new devices designed to eliminate marine casualties, such as radio-direction finders, radar, and depth-sounding devices, accidents at sea occur frequently. The most frequent causes of marine loss are fires and heavy weather damages; accidents due to errors in navigation such as collision, stranding, and so forth; and negligence in the operation of the ship's engines and equipment.

Marine underwriters agree to indemnify the shipowner only for losses caused by the specific perils enumerated in their policies, and the burden of establishing that any loss claimed has been caused by the perils named in the policy rests with the assured. The law of marine insurance recognizes that few marine casualties are caused by a single peril but that most casualties are the result of a series or chain of causes. Our law courts have laid down the rule that, to recover a loss from marine underwriters, the shipowner must establish that the *proximate* (also variously defined as *paramount, real,* and *effective*) cause of the loss was one of the perils specifically insured against. When an effort is made to determine the proximate cause, various problems arise. Losses due to "wear and tear" are to be distinguished from losses caused accidentally, and losses by insured perils must be distinguished from losses resulting (1) from an error in the design of the vessel or its equipment or (2) from negligence of shipyard workers, as distinguished from negligence of the ship's crew.

The pattern for handling a shipowner's claims against his marine underwriters is well established. When a loss occurs, or when damage that is believed to be recoverable is discovered, it is incumbent upon the owner to give prompt notice in writing to the marine underwriters to advise them when and where the damage may be surveyed by their representatives. American hull underwriters have organized the United States Salvage Association, Inc., which maintains a staff of surveyors at all principal

United States ports and at many foreign ports. The English counterpart, the Salvage Association, London (maintained by Lloyd's and other London underwriters), maintains a staff of surveyors at all major ports in the British Isles and at many ports on the continent of Europe and throughout the world, including the United States. These surveyors are in effect the fact-finding agents of the marine underwriters, for they examine vessel damages, investigate the circumstances under which the loss occurred, and make written reports of their findings.

The vessel owner should be properly represented at the time the survey is made. His representative, usually the port engineer or other member of the operating staff, should make a preliminary investigation of the facts. After consulting with the insurance department, and possibly with the average adjuster who is to handle the claim against the underwriters, he should, wherever possible, make specific allegations as to the cause and extent of the damage that is to be claimed. These allegations are ordinarily made verbally to the underwriters' surveyors at the time of the survey.

The owner's representative and the underwriters' surveyor usually make every effort to reach an agreement on all pertinent factual matters relating to the loss. However, the surveyor is not the underwriters' settling agent, because he has no authority to admit or deny liability for a specific loss. Underwriters, of course, rely heavily on the advice and opinions of their surveyors. When the representatives of owners and underwriters are not able to agree on factual matters at the time of the survey, questions of the underwriters' liability should be left open to be determined through direct negotiation between the vessel owner and his marine underwriter. Such negotiations are ordinarily conducted for the shipowner's account by the average adjuster.

The proper handling of claims against marine underwriters for these losses, and for general-average and salvage losses, is important in the over-all efficiency of any shipping operation. These matters are ordinarily the responsibility of a claims and insurance department, but if marine insurance claims are to be settled properly and satisfactorily, that department must have the full cooperation of all departments of the shipowner's organization, and especially of the operating and freight departments. To handle most claims under P & I policies, as well as collision and general-average claims, the services of a competent admiralty counsel will be required.

Also essential are the services of an average adjuster (1) to assist in the development of factual data to substantiate marine insurance claims, (2) to prepare general-average and salvage adjustments, and (3) to assist in the presentation of these claims and adjustments to underwriters and to other contributing interests. The average adjuster, a specialist whose business it is to know the laws and practices concerning the adjustment of shipping and marine insurance losses, is technically a professional adjuster of general-average losses. In this country, however, most average-adjusting offices are associated with marine insurance brokerage firms and are prepared to handle other insurance claims as well as general-average adjustments. The charges for the services of the average adjuster are paid by the marine underwriters as part of the loss, or are included in a general-average adjustment.

The factual data required to substantiate a claim against marine underwriters are ordinarily submitted in the following forms: affidavits or statements by the master or officers of the crew; certified extracts from the vessel's log books; notes of protest or extended notes of protest by the master and crew of the vessel; survey reports of underwriters' surveyors, of classification surveyors such as those representing the American Bureau of Shipping or Lloyd's Register of Shipping, and in some instances of a special surveyor acting on behalf of the owner. The average adjuster ordinarily assumes the responsibility of preparing the documentary evidence required to substantiate a claim.

TOTAL-LOSS AND CONSTRUCTIVE TOTAL-LOSS CLAIMS

Occasionally, as a result of some major disaster such as sinking at sea, a vessel may be lost completely. One may be so badly burned that nothing is left but wreckage. A vessel may be stranded and break up in the surf before salvage equipment can be dispatched to bring her into a safe port. Whenever the disaster is such that the owner is permanently and irretrievably deprived of possession and use of his ship by perils insured against, he may claim on his underwriters for an actual total loss. The underwriters then pay the face value or the total-loss value of their policies.

Occasionally, a serious marine disaster may occur that does not result in the actual total loss of the vessel but in which it can be demonstrated that the cost of salvaging and repairing the vessel would be greater than the value of the vessel when repaired. Under such circumstances, English law permits the shipowner to abandon the wreck of his vessel to his underwriters as a constructive total loss and to file claim for the face values of their policies, or their total-loss values, as in the case of actual total loss. Upon payment of such claim, the marine underwriters ordinarily take title to the wreck or to whatever proceeds may be realized from its sale.

To substantiate a constructive total-loss claim in the United States, common law and the statutes in many states require that the cost of recovering and repairing the vessel exceed only one-half of the repaired value. However, hull underwriters almost always stipulate specifically that "no recovery for constructive total loss shall be made hereunder unless the expense of recovering and repairing the vessel shall exceed the insured value," and they thereby establish the English rule by contract.

The hull provision just quoted sets the "insured value" rather than the "repaired value" as the figure to be compared with the expense of recovering and repairing the ship. The provision is so worded to obviate the difficulty involved if the underwriter and assured were required to come to agreement on the repaired value of the vessel. In a constructive total-loss claim, however, the "expense of recovering and repairing the vessel" is a factor that often must be established by estimate or agreement, and this may present serious practical difficulties. The expense of recovering the vessel should include her proportion of all general-average and salvage expenses, actual or estimated. If the vessel is actually brought to a port of safety, the cost of repairs can be determined fairly accurately by survey or even by taking bids for repairs. Or the costs of repairs can be established by the opinion of experts based on such examination of the vessel as may be possible under the circumstances.

Whenever a casualty occurs that presents the possibility of a constructive total-loss claim, the shipowner must proceed with care and caution but, at the same time, with some dispatch. The general law of insurance imposes upon the assured the obligation of taking all reasonable steps possible to minimize or avert a loss claimable from his underwriters. All marine insurance policies include a sue and labor clause, by which the underwriters agree to reimburse the shipowner for costs incurred in the reasonable discharge of this obligation. By virtue of this clause, hull underwriters may become liable for more than the full values of their policies, for they must pay the face value in settlement of the constructive total-loss claim and, in addition, must reimburse the assured for reasonable sue and labor expenses. Underwriters include this clause because they recognize that the vessel owner is in a much more practical position to take active steps to minimize or to avert a threatened loss than are the insurers.

In any situation that may involve a possible constructive total loss, the vessel owner must declare his intentions concerning abandonment within a reasonable time. He is not allowed to prejudice the salvage opportunities of the underwriters by unreasonably delaying his decision. Once having notified the underwriters that he has decided to abandon ship, he must look to them for instructions relative to further salvage operations, always bearing in mind his obligation to continue all reasonable efforts to minimize the loss and his corresponding right to obtain reimbursement for the costs of his efforts in that direction from the insurers.

After they have received notice of abandonment from the owner, the underwriters are under obligation either to accept or to decline the abandonment within a reasonable time. In the majority of cases, they will decline, chiefly because it is not practical for an underwriter to accept title to a vessel with all the responsibilities attending ownership. This does not necessarily mean that they decline to pay the total-loss claim, but rather that they decline to accept title to the wreck. When the underwriters intend to pay the total-loss claim, they ordinarily instruct the owner to sell or otherwise dispose of the vessel, transferring title directly to the purchaser and holding the proceeds from the sale for account of the underwriters.

Whenever an actual or constructive total-loss claim is established under basic hull policies, all underwriters insuring increased value, or other total-loss-only interests, automatically pay the face values of their policies to the shipowner. The sole criterion as to whether a total-loss claim will be paid under such policies is whether an actual or constructive total-loss claim has been paid under the hull policies.

A total-loss claim under a hull policy is not necessarily followed by a total-loss claim under a freight policy, because the casualty causing the total loss of the vessel may not result in the total loss of the cargo. If the cargo could be transferred to another vessel and delivered at destination, the freight underwriter would expect the shipowner to proceed accordingly and would, of course, pay the costs of transfer and forwarding as sue and labor expense. Naturally, if the cost of transferring and forwarding exceeded the value of the freight at risk, the underwriters would expect the shipowner to give notice of abandonment under the freight policy and also to abandon the cargo to its owners.

Increased-value underwriters, or others writing total-loss-only insurance, are not entitled to participate in the proceeds realized from the sale of the wreck of a vessel after a total or constructive total-loss claim has been paid. In this sense, the total-loss-only policies are said to be written "without benefit of salvage."

PARTICULAR AVERAGE OR PARTIAL LOSSES

A general-average loss is one of concern to all interests involved in any common venture, while a particular-average loss is one that falls on a particular interest (see pages 332 to 334). In this sense, the term *average*, which means loss, has a meaning entirely independent of any relation to marine insurance, and in fact was in common use in shipping circles long before marine insurance was first written. General average has been a part of the maritime law of nations for at least three thousand years. It is probable that the first germ of the idea of insurance was a development from the institution of general average, which was a universal feature of the laws of all early maritime peoples. Bottomry and respondentia bonds represent an intermediate development, but the idea of distribution of losses, which is inherent in the practice of marine insurance, undoubtedly had its inception in the institution of general average.

In relation to the marine insurance policy, the term *particular average* is commonly used to describe a partial loss or damage—one that is less than a total or constructive total loss. The term serves to designate losses that are suffered accidentally, as distinguished from the general-average loss that is suffered as a result of a voluntary act of the master. The two types of losses may result from the same casualty, with the former flowing directly from accident and the latter the voluntary act of the master.

Underwriters insuring increased value, or any other excess total-loss-only interests, are never called upon to pay a particular-average or partial-loss claim. Freight underwriters may be called upon to pay a partial or particular-average claim, depending on circumstances. If part of the cargo was lost at some point in the voyage short of destination, the vessel owner would be deprived of his right to earn freight revenue on that part of the cargo that was a total loss, and he would therefore have the right to a claim for a particular-average loss from his freight underwriters. However, if the underwriters were called upon to pay transfer and forwarding charges, as discussed in the previous section on total-loss and constructive total-loss claims, such claims would more properly be classified as claims for sue and labor expense, rather than as particular-average claims.

By far the greatest number of claims that the ordinary vessel owner files with his hull underwriters are particular-average claims. The differences between automobile and marine insurance are considerable, but, in a sense, the claims a vessel owner makes under particular average are similar to those arising from damaged fenders, radiators, and so forth. Such claims (like particular-average claims) arise much more frequently than claims for the total loss of the car (marine total-loss claims). The handling of particular-average claims is of paramount importance to the vessel owner.

When the vessel owner files a particular-average or partial-loss claim with his hull underwriters, he has, first of all, to establish that the damage has been "proximately" caused by a peril insured against under the hull policy. After that, his chief concern is to establish the proper measure of the underwriters' liability for the vessel's damages. Basically, the underwriters are obligated to pay the reasonable cost of such repairs to the vessel as may be necessary to restore her to the same condition of seaworthiness as existed prior to the accident. What constitutes such repairs, and what represents the reasonable cost thereof, are matters that are ordinarily determined at the time the vessel is surveyed.

The hull form of the American Institute of Marine Underwriters provides that the insurers have the right (1) to decide the port to which a damaged vessel shall proceed for docking or repairs, (2) to veto in connection with the place where the repairs are to be made and the repairing firm, and (3) to insist that competitive bids (tenders) be taken from various repair firms before any decision is reached as to where and by whom the repairs will be made. The wishes of the underwriters are generally conveyed to the owner by their surveyors. If the underwriters insist that the vessel be moved for repairs to a port out of the regular course of the voyage on which the vessel is then engaged, they are required to reimburse the shipowner for resultant extra expenses of the voyage.

Underwriters seldom exercise their right to demand that competitive tenders be taken except in connection with major repair jobs. If bids are required, there is certain to be delay in starting the repairs, and most hull policies include a tender clause, which provides that the shipowner receive an allowance partially to reimburse him for the loss of earnings during the interval between the time the survey is completed and the tender accepted.

For the ordinary job to repair damage of a minor nature, the vessel owner and the repair yard, assisted by the underwriters' surveyors, agree on the cost of repairs. This agreement may be reached before the job is started, while it is in progress, or after it is completed, depending on the circumstances and conditions existing in the port of repair, on the wishes of the shipowner, and on the views of the surveyors as to the reasonableness of the program proposed by the owner. For the most part, the underwriters' surveyors are quite willing to accommodate the vessel owner on such matters, unless there is reason to believe that the program proposed will result in unreasonably high costs.

To eliminate a large number of small claims that would otherwise be filed against the underwriters, hull policies usually incorporate a provision that the underwriters will not pay particular-average claims unless they amount to a specified minimum figure customarily referred to as the *franchise*. The franchise most frequently incorporated into hull policies is $4,850 (the one-time practical equivalent of £1,000) or 3 percent of the hull insurance value, whichever is the lesser. However, claims resulting from the so-called major perils of stranding, sinking, fire, and collision are paid regardless of amount. Franchise provisions are not applied on a per accident basis but on the basis of the total of damages suffered on any voyage. For the purpose of application of the franchise provisions, hull policies generally specify in considerable detail what shall constitute a voyage.

Some of the more frequently applied principles and practices governing the adjustment of particular-average claims on hull underwriters are as follows:

1. As underwriters do not insure against loss of profits resulting from

loss of time during a period of repair, they do not respond for overtime bonuses to expedite the completion of repairs.

2. Charges for services necessary both for the completion of repairs that are for underwriters' account and for owner's maintenance work, such as dry-docking charges, tank-cleaning charges, and so forth, are divided equally between owner and underwriters.

3. Allowances are ordinarily not made for depreciation or for betterment realized by substituting new material for old in the process of repairs. This is the effect of the common policy provision that claims shall be paid "without deduction of thirds, new for old."

4. The costs of cleaning and painting a vessel's underwater body by reason of exposure to air are apportioned on a monthly basis under some policy forms, depending on the last previous docking date, and this item is eliminated entirely from the particular-average claim under other forms.

5. Damages that have not been repaired at the time the policy is terminated may be claimed as "unrepaired damage," on the basis of the depreciation in the value of the vessel by reason of the damages, but not exceeding the estimated cost of repairs.

6. Hull underwriters are responsible for all damages suffered during the currency of their policies, without reduction in the amount of insurance and without the payment of additional premiums.[8]

GENERAL-AVERAGE CLAIMS

The legal requirements that must be present to support the declaration of general average may be summarized as follows: (1) there must be a common impending peril; (2) a loss or expense must be incurred as a result of some voluntary act of the master of the vessel; (3) the loss must be extraordinary, that is, beyond the ordinary contractual commitments of the parties involved in the voyage; and (4) something must be saved as a result of the general-average sacrifice or expenditure.

General average is a unique institution of admiralty law that imposes important responsibilities on a vessel owner. As the bailee of the cargo and husband of the venture, he is responsible for meeting the complex problems posed by the development of a general-average situation and for formulating a program to handle these problems. These responsibilities are generally assumed by the shipowner's claims and insurance department. However, as the institution of general average is in no way dependent upon the existence of marine insurance, the shipowner cannot delegate

[8] For a more detailed discussion of the adjustment of particular-average claims, see any of the standard books mentioned at the end of this chapter.

to his marine underwriters the discharge of his obligations in a general-average situation, even though his ultimate loss under a general-average adjustment is recoverable from those underwriters if his insurance program has been properly arranged.

The fourth requirement of the law of general average is of the utmost importance to the vessel owner, for it is he who is obligated to contract for salvage or towage assistance in case of any marine disaster. He is therefore required to expose to the risks of the voyage something beyond the value of the vessel that represented his original stake in the common venture. If the general-average program is unsuccessful, the shipowner loses not only the value of the ship but also whatever additional amounts he may have expended or contracted to pay in the discharge of his duties as the husband of the venture. The inequity of this situation is quite apparent, and is recognized by the general practice of allowing the vessel owner to insure "general-average disbursements" and to charge the premium cost of such insurance to general average if the vessel and the cargo are saved. If the general-average act is unsuccessful, the vessel owner then loses only the amount of the premium paid for the general-average disbursements insurance, rather than the full amount of his general-average expenditures. The subject of general-average disbursements, though of considerable importance to the vessel owner, is beyond the scope of this discussion.

Contributory Values. General-average losses and expenses are made good by a ratable contribution from the owners of those properties that have been saved by virtue of the general-average act. The apportionment of a general average is based on the values saved, since they measure the benefits realized from the success of the general-average act. More specifically, the values that are used in a general-average apportionment (that is, the contributory values) are the market values of the ship, cargo, and freight in the conditions existing at the termination of the voyage. For purposes of the general-average adjustment, many difficulties are posed by the problem of proper contributory values.

1. *Contributory value of ship.* The contributory value of a ship is based on its market value. The difficulties in this assessment arise because no readily ascertainable spot market exists for the sale of any particular ship and because any given ship is a unique element in the theoretical ship-sales market by reason of its individual characteristics such as age, construction, equipment, history, and so forth. The procedure most commonly followed is to obtain from some competent and recognized ship appraiser a certificate showing the value of the specific ship at a specified time and place, *i.e.*, the time and place at which the ship and cargo are separated at the end of the general-average voyage. If appraisal represents the sound value of the vessel, as would be more usual, accidental

damage suffered on the voyage must be deducted to determine the arrived value, which would be the contributory value.

2. *Contributory value of cargo.* Contributory value of the cargo interests are also assessed on the basis of market values, but at destination (or termination of the voyage) on the date of the completion of discharge. If the cargo arrives at destination damaged by some accidental happening rather than as a result of a general-average act, the contributory value of such cargo will be assessed on the basis of the market value of that cargo in the condition in which it arrives at its destination. For reasons of expediency, a practice has been adopted in many trades of taking the invoice value of cargo, plus 10 percent thereof, plus guaranteed ocean freight, as the equivalent of sound market value at destination.

General-average Allowances—Cargo. The rules for the adjustment of general average also provide that allowances made in general average for sacrifices of cargo shall be based upon market values at destination. If the general-average act has resulted in the total loss of all or part of the cargo, allowance is made in the general average on the basis of the sound market value of that cargo at destination, less contingent expenses such as collect freight payable, duties imposed at destination, and so forth. If the general-average act has resulted only in damage to the cargo, allowance is made on the basis of the difference between the sound market value and the damaged market value at destination.

General-average Allowances—Ship Sacrifices. Allowances in general average for sacrifices of the ship or its equipment are generally made on the basis of the cost of repairing the general-average damage or replacing parts or equipment lost or destroyed as the result of the general-average act. The true measure of the recovery for such damages is the reasonable cost of repairing the damages and restoring the ship to the same condition that existed prior to the loss, with proper deductions for depreciation when the repairs involve the replacement of old materials with new. The York-Antwerp rules, which generally govern the adjustment of general average, include a complete schedule of deductions to be made on the principle of "new for old." The deductions are one-third or one-sixth of the cost of replacement, depending on the age of the vessel or of the damaged part.

In any general-average case involving vessel sacrifices, the adjuster must determine what items of vessel damage will be made good and obtain from the attending surveyors the proper segregation of the repair bills to show separately the cost of repairing general-average damages. For this purpose, the adjuster requires the close cooperation of the shipowner's repair department, the underwriters' surveyors, and the repairing contractor. He must often consult with the master and officers of the vessel.

General-average Expenses. The situations in which allowances are most frequently made for general-average expenditures, as distinguished from sacrifices, may be summarized as follows:

1. Port-of-refuge expenses, covering wages, provisions, fuel, and stores, are allowed when they result from the voluntary putting in to a port of refuge to effect repairs necessary for the safe prosecution of the voyage.

2. Costs of discharging, storing, and reloading cargo at a port of refuge are allowed if required to permit repairs that are necessary for the safe prosecution of the voyage.

3. The extra cost of dry-docking with cargo on board, classified as a *substitute expense*, may be allowed in lieu of the costs of discharging cargo; temporary repair costs may be allowed to the extent of any savings realized in port-of-refuge expenses; and the extra costs of towing a vessel from a port of refuge to destination may be allowed for up to the savings in port-of-refuge expenses realized thereby.

Disbursing Commission and Interest. Customary practice allows the vessel owner a 2 percent disbursing commission on all general-average expenditures to compensate him for pledging his credit for the benefit of all the interests involved. Interest is also allowed on all general-average sacrifices and expenses to the date of the completion of the adjustment.

General-average Security by Vessel Owner. The formal adjustment of general average is a complicated operation, the completion of which may take many months or even years. Such being the case, some arrangements must be made to guarantee the payment of the assessments established by the general-average adjustment. To protect the right of the shipowner to collect general-average contributions, the law gives him, as the bailee of the cargo, a possessory lien on that cargo. It is customary, however, for the cargo to be delivered to the consignees or owners after satisfactory security has been posted for the payment of general-average contributions. The taking of such security is generally arranged for by the vessel owner or, more frequently, by the average adjuster. When a general-average situation is declared, all owners of cargo are advised in writing of the requirements for general-average security.

Such security generally consists of the execution of an "average agreement" or "average bond," plus a cash deposit in a specified amount; if the cargo is insured, a separate guarantee in favor of the vessel owner or the average adjuster, and executed by the cargo insurer, may be accepted in lieu of a cash deposit. Certified copies of the invoices or affidavits of value are obtained from the owners of cargo to be used as the basis of assessment of contributory values. Cash deposits, when required, are ordinarily for a specified percentage of the invoice value of the cargo or of its sound market value at destination. The percentage of deposit is determined by a preliminary estimate of the totals of contributory values and of general-average allowances, and by an estimate, based on these figures, of the percentage of contribution that will be required in the final adjustment.

The usual practice in the United States is for the vessel owner to assign to the average adjuster the full responsibility of taking general-average security from cargo and of making a preliminary estimate of the percentage contribution as required in the taking of cash-deposit security. When the average adjuster receives complete security on individual cargo shipments, he issues general-average "release orders" to the vessel owner, who then delivers the cargo to the consignees in the ordinary manner. However, the shipowner is expected to instruct his agents and representatives at the delivery ports not to deliver cargo to the consignees until they have received confirmation that all general-average security requirements have been met.

York-Antwerp Rules. The York-Antwerp rules, which have been mentioned from time to time, are a set of rules for the adjustment of general-average losses promulgated by an international committee. The purpose of the rules is to bring about uniformity of practice on matters on which there is conflict in the laws of various maritime nations. Unless contracts of affreightment provide otherwise, the law of the country where the voyage is terminated controls the adjustment of general-average matters. It will be appreciated, however, that on a single voyage a vessel may be carrying cargo consigned to more than one country. The owners of cargo delivered in one country would be entitled to have their general-average liabilities determined in accordance with the law of that country even though the adjustment might involve other cargo that is consigned to another country where a different law might exist, or its interpretation might differ. Conceivably, any one general average might have to be adjusted in accordance with the laws of several different countries, and this would result in considerable additional expense and inequity in the final settlement.

The York-Antwerp rules do not take effect by legislative act but are designed to be incorporated in the contracts of affreightment. To avoid the complexities and inequities referred to, the vessel owner should incorporate into his bills of lading and charter parties some provision relative to the employment of York-Antwerp rules in general-average matters. This is the almost universal practice of ship operators throughout the world today.

Effect of Negligence on an Adjustment. The basic rule of our admiralty courts is that if a vessel is placed in a position of peril as a result of the negligence of one of the interests involved in a common maritime venture, the party guilty of such negligence cannot claim from the other interests contributions to his general-average sacrifices and expenses. The position of the vessel owner as the carrier and vessel operator is such that this penalty of negligence is more likely to be imposed against him than against any of the other interests. By appropriate provisions in the bill of lading or other contract of affreightment, the shipowner can protect himself to some degree from this penalty. These provisions are commonly found in the Jason clause, which was discussed in Chapter 16.

Relation to Marine Insurance. When the shipowner's general-average or salvage loss has been determined by adjustment,[9] he looks to his hull underwriters, and possibly to the underwriters of his increased value or excess liabilities insurance, to recoup his losses. If the sound value of the vessel as assessed in the adjustment exceeds the value of the vessel as agreed in the hull insurance policies, the hull underwriters pay only that portion of the vessel's general-average or salvage assessment that the insured value bears to the contributory value of the vessel. Standard provisions to this general effect are incorporated in practically all hull insurance policies.[10]

Detailed formulas for determining the hull underwriter's liability for general-average and salvage contributions in case of underinsurance are customarily set forth in detail in the hull insurance policy. The prudent vessel owner ordinarily arranges insurance to protect himself against the possibility that general-average or salvage liabilities may be assessed on the basis of a value in excess of the hull insurance value because of fluctuations in the ship-sales market or for other reasons. This is usually done by adding excess-liabilities clauses to disbursements or increased value policies.

SALVAGE CLAIMS

The legal prerequisites for salvage were described in Chapter 17. Not all awards for maritime salvage, however, are determined by court procedure, for the parties concerned often reach agreement on the amount of the award by negotiation or agree that the amount should be determined by arbitration. Many salvage operations in foreign waters are conducted on the basis of Lloyd's Uniform Salvage Contract, which provides for arbitration of the salvage award under the supervision of the Committee of Lloyd's, London. This contract was promulgated to offer a ready and satisfactory form of salvage contract, and its use eliminates unnecessary loss of time in commencing salvage operations.

While Lloyd's form is used extensively in foreign waters and occasionally in American waters where foreign owners are involved, the form more

---

[9] Salvage losses are included here, because a salvage claim is settled in the same way as a general-average claim.

[10] This is not true, however, of general-average sacrifices of the vessel, which are paid in full by the hull underwriters.

generally used in the United States is that of Merritt-Chapman & Scott Corporation. This form usually provides for settlement at a "later determination." Nearly all Merritt's cases are dealt with by the Salvage Awards Committee of the Board of Underwriters of New York in an amicable "across the table" negotiation. Merritt's form provides protection to the salvors in the event of failure to agree in negotiations by stating that the case shall be settled by arbitration. So far no case has ever had to go to arbitration.

When a salvage operation has been completed successfully, the vessel owner generally assumes the burden of giving satisfactory security to the salvor for the payment of whatever award may eventually be assessed. He, in turn, generally takes security from the various cargo interests for the payment of their proportions of the salvage award. This is done by following much the same procedure prescribed for a general-average situation. Since both the carrying ship and her cargo receive benefit from the salvage service, the award (which is ordinarily paid in full by the vessel owner initially) is apportioned among the ship and cargo interests in exactly the same manner as are general-average losses and expenses.[11] That is, the award is apportioned on the basis of the salved value of the vessel and cargo.

COLLISION CLAIMS

Physical damages suffered by one vessel in collision with another are paid by hull underwriters as particular-average damages, and such claims are processed in the same manner as any other particular-average claim. Liabilities imposed upon the vessel owner as a result of collision, including both physical damages and loss of profits and detention expenses of the other vessel, are also paid by the hull underwriters.[12] When collision claims are settled on a mutual-fault basis, whether by amicable agreement or by litigation, due account must be taken of the "cross-liability" features of the collision clause.

This provision provides that, in the event of a mutual-fault settlement of a collision case, the damages must be adjusted between the insured vessel owner and his underwriters as if the court actually held each liable to the other for one-half of its damages, or such other division of damages as might be appropriate under any out-of-court agreement. Only by this

[11] If this method of settlement is used, the vessel owner is entitled to a disbursing commission and to interest on the salvage payment, as in the case of general-average expenditure.

[12] The collision clause of the hull policy is construed as an additional contract undertaking of the hull underwriters, separate and distinct from his other commitments under the policy. Hence, even though the full amount of the insurance policies may be paid to discharge the obligations of the collision clause, the underwriters are still required to respond for particular-average, general-average, and salvage losses arising from the same collision.

method can uninsured losses of the vessel owner—for loss of use, detention expenses, and so forth—be accounted for equitably.

As explained in Chapter 17, if two vessels collide at sea, under American law, the total damages suffered by both vessels must be divided equally between them; under British law, the total damages are assessed against each vessel in proportion to the degree of fault. Regardless of whether the law in the jurisdiction in which a mutual-fault collision case may be tried divides the damages equally or in proportion to the degree of fault, the courts generally give judgment for a single amount against one vessel owner for the net balance due under its division of damages. That is to say, in this country, in a mutual-fault collision case, the court would not award judgment against vessel A for one-half damages suffered by vessel B and a similar judgment against vessel B for one-half of the damages suffered by vessel A, but would give a single judgment against the vessel with the lesser damages for one-half the difference between the damages suffered by both vessels.

The damages involved in such cases would include detention expenses, loss of profits, and possibly other items of damage that are not insured against under hull policies, as are physical damages. Since these uninsured losses are taken into account by the courts in making its single award in a mutual-fault case, the cross-liability feature of the hull policy is necessary to accomplish a proper adjustment of the losses between owners and underwriters. Similar considerations of equity explain the inclusion of the sister-ship provisions of the collision clause, for obviously in the event of collision between two vessels of the same ownership, the probabilities are that the shipowner will suffer uninsured detention expenses on both vessels. The intention of the sister-ship clause is to put the insured shipowner in the same position he would occupy if there were not common ownership of the two vessels.

Although the handling of most collision claims requires the services of admiralty counsel, the shipowner must assume the responsibility of substantiating any allowance claimed for loss of profits, detention expenses, and so forth. Hull underwriters will expect to be kept informed of developments. The shipowner should obtain their approval before any out-of-court settlement is made and, if the decisions of lower courts are adverse to the insured vessel, before appeal is filed in a higher court. The handling of collision claims requires close cooperation among the vessel owner, his admiralty counsel, the average adjuster, and the hull underwriters.

PROTECTION AND INDEMNITY CLAIMS

Claims that fall under the protection and indemnity policy are generally liability claims and are governed, for the most part, by the laws of negligence and damages. It is appropriate to discuss briefly the mechanics for handling P & I claims both within and outside the shipowner's organization.

If the American vessel owner has placed his P & I insurance with one of the London P & I clubs or stock companies, he and his counsel will have to assume the responsibility of handling and settling claims for personal injuries, cargo damages, and so forth, as the London P & I insurers seldom maintain a resident agent in the United States to handle these matters. If the shipowner's operations are extensive, he will have to maintain a considerable staff of trained claims agents to handle these claims properly. On the other hand, some American P & I underwriters offer an almost complete P & I claims service, including the services of their own counsel and claims representatives, who deal directly with personal-injury or cargo-damage claimants.

Both methods have advantages and disadvantages. The vessel owner must weigh the advantage of reducing overhead by transferring the responsibility to his underwriter against the disadvantage of partial loss of control over the settlement of claims, which, in the aggregate, will control his future costs for the purchase of P & I insurance. In addition, he must consider the effect of these two possible methods of handling P & I claims in his relations with his regular cargo customers and with maritime labor unions, both of which are important factors in the success of a continuing ship operation.

THE MARINE INSURANCE PROGRAM AND ITS COST

The shipowner seeking to protect himself from exposures involved in the operation of steamships is offered a variety of policies providing different types of coverage. Considerable variation in valuation, limits of liability, and restrictive provisions (*i.e.*, trading warranties, deductibles, and so forth) is possible in arranging each of the types of coverage. Moreover, the rates that he will be charged by marine underwriters are not determined by a manual setting forth tariffs or schedules of rates, as is the case in other fields of insurance. Marine insurance costs are the net result of negotiations between the vessel owner and the underwriters, negotiations in which both parties have to consider many factors influencing insurance needs and costs.

Usually, in these negotiations, the vessel owner is represented by a marine insurance broker, and his competence and position in the marine insurance market can have a definite bearing on the ultimate cost of marine insurance. That ultimate cost is, in large part, dependent upon market competition. Competition may exist within the London market, and does exist between English and American underwriters. The marine insurance broker who functions properly is constantly in touch with conditions in all markets so that he can obtain for his principal, the shipowner, such advantages as may be obtainable.

Agreed Valuation. Marine hull insurance policies are written on the basis of an agreed valuation, which is a rather distinctive feature of the marine insurance policy as compared with insurance policies commonly issued in other fields. The shipowner and his hull underwriters agree to the value of the vessel at the time the hull insurance policy is issued. By such agreement, all possible differences of opinion concerning the vessel's value that might otherwise arise in the settlement of total-loss claims are avoided. The agreed valuation is binding on both the underwriter and the assured for all purposes in connection with the hull insurance policy.

The vessel owner is primarily responsible for determining this agreed valuation. In deciding the amount of insurance that should be carried on any given vessel, he should take into consideration not only her value as an operating unit but also her market value and his exposures to liability for the payment of general-average, salvage, and collision liabilities. He should also consider the effect that the agreed valuation will have on his over-all insurance cost.

Valuation and Insurance Rates. When a marine hull underwriter considers what rate should be charged for insurance on a given vessel, he will ordinarily differentiate between the portion of the over-all contemplated premium that can be allocated to the risk of total loss and the portion that must be allocated to particular-average and other claims. The average frequency of occurrence of total-loss claims can be determined fairly accurately, and therefore the rates charged for the risk of total loss do not vary greatly. However, when the underwriter contemplates the particular-average claims that he may have to pay during the policy period, he must consider the size of the vessel, her age, construction, and so forth. In the long run, a greater aggregate amount will be paid as particular-average claims on a large vessel than on a small one. Also more claims will be paid on an old vessel than on a new one.

To make a profit on his underwriting operations, the hull underwriter must promulgate a rate that will earn premiums sufficient to pay the particular-average claims expected and at the same time to compensate him adequately for assuming the risk of total loss. If the amount of insurance proposed by the vessel owner is relatively low, the hull underwriter must nominate a relatively high rate of premium; conversely, if the amount of insurance proposed is relatively high, he can afford to nominate a relatively lower rate. The vessel owner should consider these matters when he determines the amount of insurance and the agreed valuation that he will propose for a particular vessel.

Other Factors Influencing Rates. Vessels that are maintained in a high class in the American Bureau of Shipping or in Lloyd's Register of Shipping are considered better risks than vessels that are not. Vessels equipped with all the modern safety devices such as radar, radio-direction finders, and depth-sounding devices are considered better risks than those not so equipped. The trade in which a vessel is engaged (whether in the carriage of petroleum products, lumber, general cargo, and so forth) is considered to have some effect upon probable loss frequency. Some trade routes are considered more favorable than others. The reputation of the vessel owner as an efficient or inefficient operator also affects the underwriters' thinking in relation to insurance costs. Above all, the recent loss-experience record of the vessel owner, whether good or bad, will have an important bearing on the insurance quotations obtainable from marine underwriters. In this connection, the shipowner should realize that he has within his limited control a very important factor affecting his future insurance costs.

Returned Premiums. It is not uncommon for vessels to be laid up or out of commission because of general trade conditions or out of service for repairs or other reasons. Since the exposure to loss during such lay-up periods is materially reduced, provisions for the return of premiums in the event that the vessel is laid up are a common feature of all marine insurance policies, including P & I policies. Premiums are also returned if a ship is sold.

Rate Concessions. When he negotiates with hull underwriters concerning costs, the shipowner may use various devices to his advantage. Usually a concession in insurance rates may be obtained by placing the insurance on all vessels operated by one company as a fleet. In some circumstances, the shipowner may realize a reduction in cost by agreeing to certain limitations in the form of his policies such as trading limits and deductibles (which are usually applied to the total of all losses arising out of each separate accident) or by relieving the hull underwriter entirely of any obligation to pay particular-average claims, and so forth. Before accepting insurance involving any of the more drastic limitations in coverage, the shipowner should make certain that the concessions in rates obtained are commensurate with the restrictions in coverage. The counsel of an experienced and competent marine insurance broker is essential to the proper evaluation of the advantages and disadvantages of these devices.

Total-loss-only Insurance. Since the value of a vessel to her owner is represented partly by her sale or market value and partly by her anticipated future freight-earning capacity, the owner is faced with the perplexing problem of determining the extent to which he should rely on freight insurance as against hull insurance for indemnification in the event of total loss of the vessel by marine perils. Because total-loss-only insurance is charged lower rates, the vessel owner naturally prefers to carry a minimum of hull insurance and a correspondingly greater amount of total-loss-only insurance on freight, disbursements, and so forth. However, hull underwriters, influenced by other considerations, generally find it desirable to control the amount of total-loss-only insurance. The necessity of developing sufficient hull insurance premiums to pay partial-loss claims, the effect of the amount of hull insurance on constructive total-loss claims, and the moral hazard that might be created if an excessive amount of total-loss insurance exists are all factors that have prompted hull underwriters to control the amount of total-loss-only insurance.

Thus, hull underwriters generally limit the total of excess insurance against the risk of total loss to 25 percent of the amount of hull insurance: 10 percent on "disbursements, commissions, and/or similar interests" and 15 percent on various freight interests. If, however, the actual amount at risk, and deriving from any specific contract of affreightment, exceeds 15 percent of the insured value under the hull policies, the policies permit an insurance on freight at the actual amount at risk on any one voyage. These conditions are incorporated in the hull policy in the form of warranties. A breach of such a warranty would invalidate the hull policy.

P & I Insurance. The amount of insurance that is nominated in a P & I policy is not an "agreed valuation," as in the case of hull insurance, but rather a limit of liability of the P & I underwriter for claims arising out of any single accident. In determining the amount of P & I insurance that he will purchase, the shipowner must therefore consider the greatest liability to which he might be exposed as a result of any single accident. The statutes that permit the vessel owner to limit his liability to the value of the vessel and her pending freight will therefore be an important factor in arriving at the amount of P & I insurance that should be carried. However, since the limitation may be defeated by the "fault and privity" of the owner, some owners will carry P & I insurance in an amount greater than the estimated value of the vessel. Advantages in costs may sometimes be obtained by purchasing "primary" P & I insurance in an amount equal to the approximate value of the vessel and by arranging "excess" P & I insurance to supplement the primary coverage. The rate for such excess insurance is lower than that charged by the primary P & I underwriter.

The cost of P & I insurance is determined primarily by the loss-experience record of the vessel owner and the size of the vessel. Large vessels require more crew members and carry more cargo than small vessels, and for these reasons they present greater exposures to P & I claims. It is therefore customary for both vessel owners and P & I underwriters to deal in terms of cost per gross ton rather than in terms of cost per $100 of insurance protection, as is the case in hull insurance, for example. Regardless of the amount of P & I insurance purchased, the underwriter will be interested primarily in obtaining a premium income sufficient in amount to pay the claims that will be presented. Some variations in policy terms, however, may affect the P & I premium rates that can be negotiated. The most important of these would be the amount of insurance purchased and the size of deductibles to be applied to each class of claims. Since future insurance costs are largely determined by present loss experience, the wisdom of the various accident-prevention and safety programs maintained by many shipowners is obvious.

The same physical characteristics of a proposed risk that affect hull insurance rates also affect the rates charged for increased value, freight, or other total-loss-only insurances, that is, the type and age of the vessel, the trade engaged in, and so forth. As to policy terms, the major factor affecting costs in connection with these types of insurance would be the amount of insurance required, since the rates charged by underwriters will not vary greatly except as a result of differences in the physical aspects of the risk.

BIBLIOGRAPHY

Arnould on the Law of Marine Insurance and Average, 13th ed., edited by Lord Chorley of Kendal, Stevens and Sons, Ltd., London, 2 vols., 1950.

Congdon, E. W., *General Average Principles and Practice in the United States of America*, 2d ed., Baker, Voorhis & Company, Inc., New York, 1923.

Dover, Victor, *Students' Analysis of Insurance Clauses*, rev. ed., Witherby & Co., Ltd., London, 1936.

Eldridge, W. H., *Marine Policies*, Harry Atkins, London, 1938.

Gourlie, John H., Jr., *General Average*, Sherrard's Printing House, Philadelphia, 1881.

Gow, William, *Marine Insurance*, 5th ed., Macmillan & Co., Ltd., London, 1931.

Hodgson, A. J., and G. R. Rudolph, *Loundes and Rudolph's Law of General Average*, 4th ed., Baker, Voorhis & Company, Inc., New York, 1952.

Templeman, Frederick, and C. T. Greenacre, *Marine Insurance*, MacDonald & Evans, London, 1934.

Winter, W. D., *Marine Insurance*, 3d ed., McGraw-Hill Book Company, Inc., New York, 1952.

CHAPTER 19

RATES AND PRACTICES AND THEIR REGULATION*

The ocean-transportation industry has only recently, and then only partially, been clothed with the regulations and controls necessary in the public interest.[1] The first legislation providing for Federal control of steamship lines engaged in foreign and domestic trade was the Shipping Act of 1916, which provided for direct government control over certain phases of operations of the water carriers. The passage of the Intercoastal Shipping Act in 1933 opened an era of Federal regulation of domestic water carriers. This legislation embodied control of the rates charged and provided that intercoastal operators should meet specific requirements in regard to filing and changes in their rates. When the Transportation Act of 1940 was passed, the regulation of domestic operators engaged in both the coastwise and intercoastal trades was placed within the purview of the Interstate Commerce Commission. The charges of domestic water carriers are now regulated in the same manner as are those of the railroads and truck lines.

NATURE OF OCEAN FREIGHT RATES

General Nature. A steamship operator or carrier[2] sells space in a vessel for the transportation of commodities between port of loading and port of discharge. Compensation for the sale of this space is expressed in terms of freight rates. The following are examples of some of the many forms in which ocean freight rates are stated:[3]

* This chapter was written by Ramond F. Burley, chairman, Pacific Coast–Latin American Freight Conferences.
 [1] This chapter is concerned primarily with the regulations applying to all American-flag dry-cargo ships. Government controls of subsidized operators were considered in Chap. 13.
 [2] As explained earlier, the term *carrier* may refer either to the ship or to the shipowner.
 [3] The rates quoted are those in effect as of February, 1952. It should be borne in mind that steamship rates are not static. Changes in conference rates are usually subject to sixty days' notice, while nonconference rates may be subject to change without notice.

1. The rate on canned meats from Argentina to Atlantic Coast ports in the United States is $24 per long ton, and from Brazil $24 per 1,000 kilos.
2. The rate on coffee from Brazil to Atlantic and Gulf ports is $1.75 per bag of 60 kilos net.
3. The rate on Christmas trees from Atlantic and Gulf ports to Balboa, Canal Zone, is $101 per short ton.
4. The rate on lumber from the Pacific Coast to Buenos Aires, Argentina, is $50 per 1,000 board feet, net board measurement, when shipped in lots of greater than 200,000 board feet.
5. The carload rate on canned goods from Atlantic Coast ports to Pacific Coast ports is $1.37 per 100 pounds, equivalent to $27.40 per short ton, based on a minimum weight of 20,000 pounds.
6. The rate on wire netting from all Pacific Coast ports to ports on the west coast of Central America is $22 per short ton, weight or measurement.

The foregoing examples (all of which are commodity rates, a term that will be explained presently) illustrate the most common units of weight that serve as bases for freight rates. Whenever the term *ton* is used, it should be indicated whether the unit is a long ton (2,240 pounds) or a short ton (2,000 pounds).

In foreign trade, rates are frequently quoted, as in the sixth example, on the basis of a certain cost "per ton W/M," which means "per ton, weight or measurement, ship's option." The rate applies on a weight basis if the density or stowage factor of the commodity is equivalent to less than 40 cubic feet per ton (or 50 cubic feet, in some routes), and on a measurement basis if the stowage factor is 40 cubic feet or greater per ton. The relationship of stowage factors to the determination of rates is discussed later.

Types of Rates. The rates used in ocean transportation are quoted on many bases. The carrier's *tariff*—his price list for services rendered—is a composite of various rates.[4] As will be explained later, nonconference rates are set by the individual carriers, while conference rates are determined by groups of carriers through the conference. The rates quoted, whether nonconference or conference, reflect the nature of the commodity with respect to its stowage aboard the vessel.

1. *Commodity rates.* Steamship tariffs usually set forth rates for a number of particular commodities, numbering perhaps between 75 and 100 items and depending on the route. The established rates relate to the stowage factor, value of the cargo, the competitive situation, and other factors. They are applicable to the particular commodity only.

For commodities moving regularly and in volume, such as coffee northbound from Latin America and canned goods in the intercoastal trade,

[4] Steamship tariffs are discussed more fully later in this chapter.

commodity rates are usually quoted. Also, if a commodity starts to move in volume in a particular trade, a shipper or shippers may seek and get, either from the individual carrier or from the conference, a rate for that particular commodity. However, in waterborne commerce, there are scores of shipments including commodities that never move in sufficient volume or with enough regularity to warrant the establishment of a commodity rate. To cover such situations, carriers include in their tariffs "catch-all" groupings, which may be called general-cargo rates or class rates.

2. *General-cargo rates.* Many tariffs publish an over-all rate, called a general-cargo rate, to cover all commodities upon which no specific commodity rate is published. These rates are frequently referred to as for cargo n.o.s. (not otherwise specified). Because of the broad range of cargo that might be presented for shipment under such rates, they are held high to protect the carriers. This type of rate is usual in United States foreign trade, domestic trade with offshore possessions, and intercoastal trade.

3. *Class rates.* Class rates have been compared to the rates for postal service, which cover first-, second-, third-, and fourth-class mail and parcel post. In the determination of class rates, commodities are classified in general groupings or categories. This procedure recognizes the variable transportation characteristics of a commodity more closely than does the general-cargo rate. Class rates usually start at class 1 and continue to classes 6 to 10, depending on the trade route. The highest rate is for the first class, and the rate becomes lower as the number of the class increases. Commodities of heavier density and lesser value are in the lower classifications. This procedure is comparable to the universal practice of the railroads. The class rate is widely used in the coastwise and many of the Latin-American trades.

4. *Arbitrary rates.* To the commodity, general-cargo, or class rates (which may be termed *basic ocean freight rates*), additional charges are sometimes added, such as an arbitrary rate. This rate may be included in the contract for ocean transport if the merchandise is delivered at a port where transshipment is necessary, if shallow water or other conditions make navigation difficult, or if the quantities of cargo available for loading or discharge are small.

5. *Ad valorem rates.* Rates predicated on the declared value of the merchandise only are termed ad valorem rates. Such rates are charged for commodities that are high in value, light in weight, and compact in bulk. An ad valorem rate may be added to the normal rate when the value is considered excessive.

6. *Refrigerated-cargo rates.* Such rates are higher than ordinary stowage rates, because the carrier must be responsible for providing special reefer

stowage and for maintaining the necessary temperatures to ensure the proper outturn of the cargo.

7. *Deck cargo.* Some cargo is accepted only for on-deck stowage when the commodity is dangerous or offensive in relation to other cargo. Explosives and certain acids may come in this category. Lumber is a commodity particularly adapted to on-deck stowage.

8. *Minimum rates.* A minimum rate is one that sets a floor below which the carrier may not quote. It permits flexibility of maintaining a rate higher than the minimum.

9. *Parcel rates.* On small packages that are forwarded in the care of ship personnel and that, because of their size, are not stored in the vessel's holds, parcel rates apply.

10. *Open rates.* An open freight rate is one that is free to competitive forces. In other words, rather than setting and publishing an established rate, the carriers agree to leave the rate on a particular commodity open, so that each line may quote whatever rate it determines upon. Open rates are rather rare and are utilized when the common carrier is very competitive with full-cargo charters or nonconference berth-service competition.

Application of Rates. An ocean carrier's rate is the charge for moving a commodity between "port of loading and port of discharge." The application of that rate is clearly expressed in the carrier's tariff, and the structure or application of the rate is dependent upon the trade route involved and particularly on whether the service is in foreign or in domestic commerce.

In foreign trade, the practice is to publish rates as applying from the end of ship's tackle at the loading piers of the individual carrier to the end of ship's tackle at the port of destination. The term *end of ship's tackle* means a position alongside the ship where the cargo is to be picked up and lifted aboard by the ship's gear (tackle) or by whatever loading gear is provided, or where the cargo has been deposited by the ship's or other unloading gear. The language means that the rate does not include or cover any labor cost involved in moving the goods alongside the ship, either from the place of rest on the steamship terminal (in the case of cargo accumulated before the ship commences to load) or from railroad car or truck. Nor does it include any labor expense at destination to move the goods beyond the ship's tackle.

There are exceptions to this general practice where the rates may include some or all of these additional costs. On the Pacific Coast, in many trade routes, carriers assess a handling charge that specifically covers the labor cost for moving cargo between place of rest on the carrier's terminal and ship's tackle.

In domestic trades, the usual practice is to name freight rates that apply between place of rest on the loading terminal and place of rest on the discharging terminal. However, when the vessel moves to a steamship terminal other than that designated as its regular terminal, the rate terminates at the end of, or commences at the beginning of, ship's tackle.

At many ports of loading and discharging, there are various terminal charges, often called *accessorial charges*, that apply against the cargo and are in addition to the freight rate. The handling charge mentioned above is considered as supplementary to the freight rate and cannot be considered as a terminal charge. Terminal charges include wharfage, which is to defray some of the cost of maintaining a terminal; car loading and car unloading, which service is performed by stevedoring organizations; and other charges such as service, heavy lift, and lighterage charges. At foreign ports, there are also miscellaneous charges described as port charges, landing charges, cargo taxes, port dues, stamp charges, and so forth. In the United States, however, port charges cover pilotage, dockage, towage, and so forth. These are charged to the vessel rather than to the cargo.

During periods of emergency, it is not unusual for carriers to assess a percentage surcharge over the freight rate to cover additional costs that suddenly arise and are expected to be temporary in nature, such as crew bonuses, increased cost of fuel oil, war risk insurance, and delays to voyage turn-around because of port congestion.

The Carrier in Relation to Rates. What has just been said concerning ocean freight rates and their application applies to the operations of common carriers, vessels offering berth or liner services. These generally comprise the membership of the many steamship conferences.

Because common carriers transport a diversified cargo, their rate structure is more or less complex. In contrast, the ocean tramp carrier, operated on charter and usually transporting one cargo between few ports, has a very simple rate structure. Tramps usually act independently, competing freely with one another for cargoes and charging whatever rates can be obtained in view of the supply and demand for ship tonnage.[5] Private industrial carriers (tankers and many ore, coal, and lumber carriers) assess operating costs more by intracompany accounting methods than by the law of supply and demand. Private operators are not subject to the types of regulation discussed in this chapter.

Hence, our primary interest in this chapter is the common carrier operating in foreign or domestic commerce. Not only is the type of ship important in the study of rates and practices, but the trade is also. The rate agreements of common carriers operating to foreign ports are today a matter of conference agreement, while those of the domestic operator

[5] See Chap. 10, "Ship Operation: Charters."

(both the common and the contract carrier)[6] have been, since 1940, under the jurisdiction of the Interstate Commerce Commission. Therefore, special attention will be given to the differences that exist between the domestic and foreign sections of the industry with respect to regulation of rates and practices. In the ensuing discussion, it should be remembered, however, that not all common carriers operating in foreign trade are members of conferences.

FACTORS DETERMINING RATES

Liner rates, usually the result of conference agreement, are based upon the recommendations of traffic officials of the member lines. When rates are established, numerous factors must be considered, factors that carry varying consequences for different routes.[7]

Volume and Character of the Cargo. The qualities and natural characteristics of each commodity in the form in which it will be offered to the carrier, and the carrier's obligations as to the circumstances and conditions under which delivery must be made to fulfill the shipping contract, must be carefully considered.

1. *Volume.* Suitable cargo offering in large and steady volume enables a common carrier to be reasonably certain that he can fill his vessels and that he has a dependable revenue to be earned over the period of a number of voyages. Volume of traffic is so essential to successful steamship operation that one of the principal objectives in rate making is to encourage and maintain volume at its maximum.

2. *Availability.* The basic rates of a steamship tariff are created on the premise that the cargo is available for movement over the regular terminal facility of the carrier at port of loading and port of discharge. When the vessel is required to move to another terminal location for loading or discharging, such additional cost may be reflected in the rate.

3. *Susceptibility to damage or pilferage.* Certain commodities are more susceptible to damage than others. For such commodities, a greater pro-

[6] The common carrier has already been defined (see Chap. 3). Part III of the Interstate Commerce Act of 1940 defines the "contract carrier by water" as any person who engages in the transportation by water of passengers or property for compensation under individual contracts or agreements. Contract carriers do not engage in the movement of all commodities offering, as do common carriers, but restrict themselves to commodity movements under a specific contract or agreement.

[7] This discussion is adapted from one published in *Inter-American Maritime Conference, Washington, D.C., November 25, 1940, to December 2, 1940,* Report of the Delegates of the United States, 1941, pp. 25–28. The theory of rate making is out of the scope of this book. Anyone interested should consult pertinent chapters in M. L. Fair and E. W. Williams, *Economics of Transportation,* Harper & Brothers, New York, 1950, or T. C. Bigham and M. J. Roberts, *Transportation; Principles and Practices,* 2d ed., McGraw-Hill Book Company, Inc., New York, 1952.

portion of the freight money will go into the settlement of claims; this is taken into account when the rate is made. Also, such commodities as wearing apparel, edibles, liquor, and luxury items present the opportunity for pilferage during transit. This situation leads to claims and other extra expense. For this type of commodity, the carrier often provides special stowage (*e.g.*, a strong room). The claims record for losses and the additional expenses of handling are considered when rates are made on such items.

4. *Value.* The carrier assumes greater responsibility for goods of high value than for goods of lower value, and the freight rates usually reflect this situation. However, consideration is customarily given to the relationship between freight charges and the value of the goods. On the basis of value added to a commodity at destination by virtue of the transportation service, a high-value commodity can bear a greater share of the total transportation cost than can a low-value commodity. Although it may cost the ship as much to handle each commodity, identical freight rates might discourage or even prevent the movement of low-value items. An ad valorem charge is established at times to cover goods of very high valuation, or a scale of rates is determined upon actual or released value of the goods.[8]

Packaging. Well-packaged goods facilitate handling, conserve the carrier's space, and reduce the possibility of claims. The nature of the packing, therefore, is considered when a rate is made. Strapped or unstrapped packages and new or second-hand containers are examples of variable conditions considered.

Stowage. Some commodities are desirable from a stowage viewpoint as weight or stiffening cargo. Some are useful for topping off, and others in blocking off or protecting fragile goods. Other commodities are of great bulk but little weight and are difficult to stow. While some can be quickly handled, others cause delay. There are commodities that require special stowage because of their odor or because of their susceptibility to contamination by others. For instance, flour may not be stowed in the same compartment with sulphur because of the danger of flour becoming tainted through the absorption of odors. Onions may not be stowed with rice for the same reason. All these characteristics must be considered when a rate is established.

Relationship of Weight to Measure. To operate to the greatest advantage, a ship should be loaded to her full deadweight capacity and at the same time to her full cubic capacity. That ultimate desire in booking a vessel is best described by the phrase: "The vessel must be full and down." To accomplish this requires a proper balance between *weight* cargo and

[8] A released value is established when a shipper sets a value and agrees not to hold the carrier liable for any higher value.

measurement cargo. For example, a vessel of 500,000 cubic feet cargo space, 10,000 tons deadweight capacity, 2,500 long tons of fuel, water, and stores (*i.e.*, 7,500 long tons of deadweight cargo-carrying capacity), and having a load of cargo measuring 100 cubic feet to the ton at a rate of $10 per ton weight would earn a revenue as follows:

500,000 cubic feet of cargo at 100 cubic feet per ton is equivalent to 5,000 tons weight at $10 per ton, or $50,000.

On the other hand, give this vessel 4,000 tons of weight cargo measuring 40 cubic feet per ton at a rate of only $7.50 per ton and fill the remainder of the space with cargo measuring 100 cubic feet at $10 per ton, and the revenue would be earned as follows:

160,000 cubic feet of weight cargo at 40 cubic feet per ton is equivalent to 4,000 tons at $7.50 per ton, or $30,000, and 340,000 cubic feet of measurement cargo at 100 cubic feet per ton is equivalent to 3,400 tons weight at $10 per ton, or $34,000. In other words, a total of 500,000 cubic feet and 7,400 weight tons produces a total revenue of $64,000.

Proper rate making encourages the movement of all classes of goods and permits the best possible balance of cargo from the point of view of both revenue and vessel utilization.

Heavy Lifts and Extra Lengths. Some cargo cannot be handled by the ship's gear. If it is necessary to hire floating derricks or other special harbor equipment, an extra charge is made. Some vessels equipped with special rigging may be able to handle such goods with their own cargo-handling gear, but extra expense is usually involved. The carriers generally establish an additional scale of rates to cover costs for heavy lifts, and the scale is graduated upward as the weight of the piece increases.

Because of their extra length, some commodities require special handling and special stowage or facilities. Extra-length charges are assessed accordingly, with the rate graduated upward in proportion to the length of the article.

Costs of Operation. A remunerative ocean freight rate should cover the direct costs of ship operation, which include such items as fuel, water, food, supplies, crew's wages, maintenance, and repair. Distance between port of loading and port of discharge affects these factors.

1. *Costs of handling.* This includes receiving and delivering, checking, watching, coopering, sorting, loading and discharging, and other expenses incurred by the carrier in the physical handling of cargo. The major costs are in connection with loading and discharging cargo, and also include cargo claims.

2. *Lighterage.* In some trades it is necessary for vessels to lighter the goods from or to shore. This extra expense may be an added charge. If not, it is considered when freight rates are determined.

3. *Fixed charges.* Fixed charges against operation include amortization, depreciation, interests, taxes, and shore staff (including general overhead expenses such as executive personnel and office rent, piers, and terminals), all of which must be earned from freight revenue for the continuous successful operation of a steamship line. Also to be included under this heading is a contemplated profit, without which there is no business incentive.

4. *Insurance.* Ordinary marine insurance on the vessel and P & I insurance, discussed in Chapter 18, are usually regarded as fixed charges. However, extraordinary conditions which require the placing of additional insurance on the vessel, such as war risk insurance, add materially to the operating costs of the vessel and are usually reflected either in increases in freight rates or in surcharges added to the freight rate.

5. *Canal tolls.* In some trades (for example, Atlantic or Gulf ports to the West Coast of South America), vessels transit canals, and the expense of canal tolls must be considered in rate making. In early 1953, it cost roughly $7,000 for a C3 to transit the Panama Canal.

6. *Port charges and dues.* Port charges, port dues, dockage, lighthouse, and other governmental or port-authority charges against the vessel add to the expenses that the vessel, and hence the freight, has to bear. The efficiency of port operation is generally reflected in the dues and charges.

Port Location, Facilities, and Regulations. Some ports are difficult of access because they are located up rivers or inside bars or because the vessel must traverse dangerous channels during restricted hours. These conditions involve delay and consequent extra expense. The availability of docks, equipment, berths, labor, and other facilities involved in port operations (as well as labor costs, prompt dispatch, and so forth) affects the costs incurred in connection with the receipt and delivery of cargo. Port regulations that permit a ship to enter or clear at all hours facilitate handling of a vessel and thereby contribute to economy of operation. When the situation is reversed, the operation becomes more expensive. All these matters are considered in connection with determining rates.

Return Cargoes. An economically sound trade is one in which vessels secure full or substantial cargoes on both outward and inward legs of a voyage. The availability or lack of full cargoes in one direction materially affects the measure of freight rates. If a ship is operating in a trade in which she can be filled both outward and inward, the carrying (or earning) capacity of the ship is double that of a ship which goes out full but returns light. This means a better round-voyage revenue. The prospects of filling for the round voyage are of necessity given full consideration when the general level of rates is decided.

Competitive Matters. When rates are determined, the carriers consider potential competition from other carriers that operate either as nonconference lines or as tramps. Therefore, conference carriers endeavor to maintain rates at reasonable levels so that shippers will not favor or encourage other carriers.

Competition with goods from other sources is one of the foremost factors that carriers consider in making freight rates. Through the element of transportation cost, they endeavor to place the American exporter or importer on a competitive basis in his markets with respect to his foreign competition in that market.

Cargo from certain interior points in the United States can move via any one of several widely separated ports to a given destination. For example, goods originating in Middle Western states can often move via either Atlantic, Gulf, or Pacific ports. The carriers that serve these various gateways endeavor to equalize the competitive transportation conditions through the rate structure. If lower inland-transportation costs favor one gateway, carriers serving other ports sometimes equalize the situation by establishing proportionally lower ocean rates applying only on cargo from that inland point of origin.

ORIGIN OF CONFERENCES

Ever since the steamship began to replace the sailing vessel as the principal carrier in overseas transport, the shipping industry has been threatened with self-destruction by rate wars and uncontrolled competition. The requirements of commercial trade make regular sailings desirable, and this involves the maintenance of schedules regardless of whether the space of a particular ship was fully booked at the time of the scheduled sailing. This type of operation is often expensive in terms of utilization of vessel space and of loss of flexibility of operation. In other words, there are times when the cost of delaying the sailing of a vessel may be exceeded by the revenue from additional cargo that might be developed for the vessel. The problem of the vessel owner has been to secure rates that will be remunerative under such conditions of operation. Steamship conferences were organized to meet this situation.

The first steamship conference dates from 1875, when the Calcutta conference was formed. As the result of success in developing iron vessels, both sailing craft and steamships, British yards were turning out hundreds of new ships to replace the old wooden sailers. To protect themselves from the resulting ruinous competition, steamship lines engaged in trade between the United Kingdom and India formed the Calcutta conference. They fixed equal rates to be charged and agreed that no preferential rates or concessions should be given to any shipper or group of shippers.

The new conference rulings did not meet with the approval of certain large shippers who had formerly enjoyed special privileges in the form of preferential terms. They placed steamships on berth to operate on the

United Kingdom–India route at cut rates in opposition to the conference ships. The conference lines attempted to meet this new competition by making contracts with shippers for their exclusive patronage, but many refused to bind themselves to the exclusive-patronage conference contract if the conference lines adhered to the principle that all shippers be accorded the same rates.

To meet this difficulty, the conference lines introduced, in 1877, the deferred-rebate policy—a system designed as a means of keeping shippers "loyal" against the inroads of nonconference carriers or tramps that offered lower rates. Shippers were notified that those who confined their traffic to the conference lines during a stipulated period would be granted a refund of a part of the freight, to be paid at the end of a further period of time.

Both the deferred rebate and the exclusive-patronage conference contract were defensive measures, and to them the conference lines added an aggressive measure, "the fighting ship," although the latter never came into the same general use as the former. A fighting ship is one placed on a run to transport merchandise that might form the nucleus of the cargo for a nonconference steamship, and to do so at rates that were wholly unremunerative. The losses from such operations were apportioned among the conference members, with the result that the loss of each was much less than that of the nonconference operator.

UNITED STATES AND THE CONFERENCES

Some United States steamship companies participated in the first transatlantic conferences when they were organized during the early 1900's. However, a legal problem existed concerning whether conference membership violated United States antitrust laws. The American merchant marine was not of sufficient force in our economy prior to World War I to take the matter into the courts, but the problem existed until the Shipping Act of 1916 was passed.

Investigation of 1912. In 1912, a series of resolutions was passed by the House of Representatives calling for an investigation of shipping pools and their practices, particularly in regard to rates; the House Committee on the Merchant Marine and Fisheries conducted a thorough research in the matter. Its final report, compiled by S. S. Huebner, expert to the committee, and published in 1914 as the *Investigation of Shipping Conditions under House Resolution 587*, is known as the Alexander report, because Joshua W. Alexander was chairman of the committee. That report embodied the following statement:[9]

[9] Quoted from *Handbook of Merchant Marine Development and Regulation in the United States*, U.S. Maritime Commission, 1940.

It is the view of the committee that open competition cannot be assured for any length of time by ordering existing agreements terminated. The entire history of steamship agreements shows that in ocean commerce there is no happy medium between war and peace when several lines engage in the same trade. Most of the numerous agreements and conference arrangements discussed in the foregoing report were the outcome of rate wars and represent a truce between the contending lines. To terminate existing agreements would necessarily bring about one of two results: the lines would either engage in rate wars which would mean the elimination of the weak and the survival of the strong, or to avoid a costly struggle, they would consolidate through common ownership. Neither result can be prevented by legislation, and either would mean a monopoly fully as effective, and it is believed more so, than can exist by virtue of an agreement. Moreover, steamship agreements and conferences are not confined to the lines engaging in the foreign trade of the United States. They are as universally used in the foreign trade of other countries as in our own. The merchants of these countries now enjoy the foregoing advantages of cooperative arrangements, and to restore open and cutthroat competition among the lines serving the United States would place American exporters at a disadvantage in many markets as compared with their foreign competitors.

The lengthy investigation contributed to the passage of the Shipping Act of 1916, which opened the way for American steamship operators to participate in shipping conferences.

The Act of 1916 and Subsequent Legislation. Section 15 of the Shipping Act of 1916 was designed expressly to meet the matters referred to in the paragraph quoted from the Alexander report. Every common carrier or person subject to the Act was required, as soon as any agreement pertaining to rates or related matters had been entered into with another carrier or person subject to the Act, to file a "true and complete memorandum" of that agreement with the U.S. Shipping Board. This Board, created by the Act, was vested with the responsibility of administering the regulatory provisions of the Act.[10] Furthermore, the Board was granted the power to "disapprove, approve, cancel, or modify any agreement," and the Act stipulated that all agreements, modifications, or cancellations made after the Board was organized were to be lawful "only when and as long as approved by the board."

The 1916 Act firmly established the legality of shipping conferences, for it conferred on the Board the power to exempt such conferences from the antitrust laws of the United States. It forbade use of the deferred rebate and the fighting ship, but not of the conference-contract system. The United States government did not in 1916, and does not now, exercise any

[10] The regulatory agency remained the Shipping Board until 1933, when it was succeeded by the Shipping Board Bureau. The Bureau was succeeded in turn by the U.S. Maritime Commission in 1936, and in 1950 regulation passed to the Federal Maritime Board of the Department of Commerce (see Chap. 20).

direct control over the establishing of freight rates on waterborne import and export traffic of the United States.

Section 19 of the Merchant Marine Act of 1920 authorized the regulatory agency to make rules and regulations affecting shipping in foreign trade that do not conflict with existing law but that the agency deems necessary to adjust or to meet general or special conditions unfavorable to such shipping. Under this general authority and by order in Docket 128,[11] all common carriers by water in foreign commerce are required to file their export rates from the United States on all commodities, except those carried in bulk without mark or count, within a period of thirty days after they have become effective. The rates on import traffic from the east coast of South America to the Pacific Coast of the United States must also be filed in accordance with the order in Docket 507. No advance filing is required, nor does the governmental regulatory agency have the power to suspend the effective date of such rates. The advantage of this procedure is to keep the regulatory agency advised of developments. As a matter of fact, most of the steamship conferences go beyond the legal requirements, for they both make their tariffs available to the public on a subscription basis and give advance or immediate notice of rate changes both to the public and to the regulatory agency. According to the 1951 report of the Federal Maritime Board, during the fiscal year 1951, a total of 24,945 rate filings were received covering freight and passenger tariffs in the foreign trade, nearly 6,000 more than had been received in any previous year.

The following actions are forbidden to common carriers by water in foreign commerce:

1. To give any undue or unreasonable preference or advantage to any particular person, locality, or description of traffic.

2. To subject any particular person, locality, or description of traffic to any undue or unreasonable prejudice or disadvantage.

3. To allow any person to obtain transportation at less than the regular rates established and enforced on the line of such carrier by means of false billing, false classification, false weighing, or other unjust or unfair devices.

4. To demand, charge, or collect any rate, fare, or charge which is unjustly discriminatory between shippers or ports.

5. To demand, charge, or collect any rate, fare, or charge which is unjustly prejudicial to exporters of the United States as compared with their foreign competitors.

6. To retaliate against a shipper by refusing space accommodations when such are available or to resort to other discriminating or unfair

[11] Decided July 12, 1935, by the U.S. Shipping Board Bureau.

methods because a shipper has patronized another carrier or has filed a complaint.

7. To make any unfair or unjustly discriminatory contract with any shipper based on volume of freight offered.

8. To treat unfairly or to discriminate unjustly against any shipper with respect to cargo space accommodations or other facilities, the loading and landing of freight in proper condition, and the adjustment or settlement of claims.

It is unlawful for any shipper, receiver, forwarder, broker, or other person knowingly and willfully to obtain, or attempt to obtain, transportation by water for property at less than the rates or charges that would otherwise be applicable by means of false classification, false weighing, or other unjust or unfair devices.

Conferences Operating to and from United States Ports. At present, United States ports are served by some 120 conferences, the membership of which ranges from 3 to about 30 steamship lines. Some American lines belong to as many as two dozen conferences. Among the more important conferences operating to and from United States ports are the following:

North Atlantic United Kingdom Freight Conference
Gulf/Mediterranean Ports Conference
U.S. Atlantic & Gulf–Venezuela and Netherlands Antilles Conference
Pacific Coast Caribbean Sea Ports Conference
Far East Conference
Pacific Westbound Conference
Mid Brazil/United States–Canada Freight Conference
Pacific Coast River Plate Brazil Conference
Pacific Coast European Conference
West Coast of South America Northbound Conference
Western Hemisphere Passenger Conference

Conference practices regarding ports of call for loading and discharge vary, but from the names listed it is evident that conference ships sail between a wide range of ports. Also, some conference ships load at only North Atlantic ports, while the ships in another conference may load at South Atlantic Coast ports. Many steamship lines sail their vessels on voyages wherein they might have cargo on board involving two or more conferences. Usually, there are different conferences for outbound and inbound traffic—a fact that is clearly indicated in a number of the conferences named. The first three are outbound conferences. The Far East Conference is outbound from Atlantic and Gulf ports, and the Pacific Westbound Conference is its Pacific Coast counterpart. The Pacific Coast River Plate Brazil Conference is a "between" conference, in that it covers traffic moving in both directions. The Mid Brazil/United States–Canada

Freight Conference is for northbound cargo destined to both United States and Canadian ports. Passenger liners belong to the Western Hemisphere Passenger Conference, which applies between the Atlantic and Gulf Coasts and Bermuda, Cuba, various Caribbean ports, and the west coast of South America.

THE CONFERENCE SYSTEM

Form of Conference Agreement. Most conference agreements follow a general pattern. The more important subject matter usually included is as follows:

1. Name of conference, description of territory to be covered, purpose of agreement.
2. Basis of freight charges and manner of collection.
3. Statement that no undue preference or advantage or unjust or unreasonable discrimination may exist and that the giving or receiving of special rates or other special privileges or advantages is prohibited.
4. Provisions as to brokerage and absorptions.
5. Conference rules and regulations.
6. Provisions as to membership, admission fee, meetings, voting rules and privileges, officers, expenses, meetings with other conferences.
7. Maintenance-of-service clause defining distinction between an active and an inactive member.
8. Method of proceeding if agreement is breached by a member.
9. Approval of governmental regulatory agency as required under Section 15 of the Shipping Act of 1916.
10. Terms required for modification or cancellation.

In short, the conference agreement is the basic document to which all conference members subscribe and which covers their relations in the shipping operation.

Steamship Tariffs. One of the most important functions of a conference organization is to prepare and issue freight tariffs.[12] Because of the constant adjustments that are being made as a result of changing business conditions, these tariffs are issued in loose-leaf form. Some conferences make their tariffs available to the shipping public on a subscription basis, charging a set amount for the initial tariff and a certain amount thereafter, on an annual basis, for all corrections and reissuances. A typical freight tariff is arranged as follows:

1. Title page describing its coverage and ports of application.
2. Correction checking sheet. Each sheet is numbered, and by following

---

[12] Tariffs are also published by individual carriers and, particularly in domestic trade routes where carriers are controlled by the ICC, by agents. Nonconference lines usually published either individual tariffs or rate cards.

the table, one may always ascertain if all corrections have been received and if the tariff is up to date.

3. Table of contents.
4. Index of ports to or from which rates apply.
5. Participating carriers.
6. Reproduction of shippers' rate agreement or whatever rate contract form is applicable.
7. Rules and regulations, including provisions to cover the following: (a) application of rates, protection of rates, effective date of rate changes; (b) provisions of bills of lading and carriers' liability, owner's risk; (c) marine insurance, war clause, and strike clause; (d) payment of freight charges, statement of minimum charge; (e) explosives, dangerous and objectionable cargo; (f) accessorial charges at loading port, various port charges at loading and discharging ports; (g) strapping and sealing of packages, marks and numbers of packages; (h) bills of lading and consular requirements, export declarations; (i) livestock, other animals, poultry, and birds; (j) definitions; and (k) abbreviations.
8. Commodity-rate section. This lists the various commodity items upon which rates are provided. Certain tariffs have different rates to various destination groups, and all such group rates are listed following the commodity description.
9. General-cargo-rate or class-rate section. As explained, in some foreign trades and in the noncontiguous and intercoastal trades, the general-cargo rate takes care of commodities not listed separately, while in the coastwise and Latin-American trades, the class rate is the usual rule. If class rates are included, this section lists hundreds of individual commodities and assigns them to a class for rate-making purposes. The purpose of classification and of class rates is to simplify the process of quoting rates on the many hundreds of items that move in commerce. Commodities having a traffic likeness will tend to be placed in the same class for purposes of rating (i.e., establishing a rate).

Rate Adjustments. Individual merchants or trade associations may negotiate with conferences or shipping lines for the purpose of obtaining rate adjustments. The more generally accepted practice at the present time is to conduct negotiations with the personnel at conference headquarters. Most conferences provide an application form to assist in the securing of all pertinent information required in arriving at a decision. Questions usually asked are the following:

1. Name of commodity, trade name if used, and full description of article.
2. Nature of commodity with respect to being hazardous, inflammable, and liquid or solid.

3. Particulars of shipping package, including material from which made, and shape (*i.e.*, box, barrel, crate, etc.).

4. Length, width, depth, cubic feet, gross weight of package.

5. Cubic feet required per 2,000 or 2,240 pounds, using gross weight and measurements of package.

6. Value per unit—ton, pound, article, etc.

7. Uses of commodity (this information contributes to a better understanding by the conference of the problems involved in the transporting and marketing of the goods).

8. Present and proposed ocean rate, port of origin and destination, and rail rate to port if origin is interior point.

9. Source of foreign competition involved, if any, and particulars as to such matters as rates from source to market in which competition is experienced.

10. Volume in which commodity ordinarily moves and nature of movement with respect to whether it is continuous, seasonal, or sporadic.

11. Reason for the requested change in rate.

Most conferences accord applicants the opportunity of appearing in person before either representatives or committees of the conference and, on occasion, before the full conference membership. Every effort is made by the conferences to avoid delay in the processing of rate matters.

Contract with Shippers. Each conference has a contract for the carriage of goods that it offers to shippers and receivers. Those signing such a contract agree to offer all their business within the area covered by the particular conference exclusively to the members of the conference. In turn, the conference commits its member lines to maintain rates unchanged over a substantial period, to charge only such rates as are published in a conference tariff, to grant advance notice of rate increases, and to treat all shippers alike, large and small. Shippers who sign the contract are not limited to any one shipping line but may choose among conference ships and members, and in fact some conference contracts stipulate that a shipper's business should be divided equitably among all members of the conference. The contract includes numerous provisions as to penalties for nonobservance, cancellation, notification on rate increases, and so forth.

Pros and Cons of the Conference System. The advantages of the conference system, enumerated in the so-called Alexander report, which is now forty years old, are worth repeating:

1. A substantial increase in sailing opportunities.

2. Fixed dependable dates of sailings at regular intervals.

3. Stability of rates over long periods of time, with the result, among others, that shippers are able to quote prices and make contracts for future delivery without fear that instability or violent fluctuation in freight rates will introduce the speculative element.

4. Uniform rates, irrespective of the size of the shipment or the economic power of the shipper.

5. Maintenance of proper relationship between freight rates and various sources of supply to common freight markets.

6. Prevention of the elimination of weaker steamship lines.

On the other hand, carriers not members of a conference, but desiring to compete with the member lines, object to the conference system on the grounds that it is monopolistic, inflexible, and discriminatory against their rights of free competition. The features most frequently attacked are the dual-rate system and pooling and sailing agreements.[13]

The Dual-rate System. Soon after they were organized, conferences found that the practice of fixing rates by mutual agreement and guaranteeing to continue published rates over a fixed period of time left them completely at the mercy of the nonconference lines. The latter can change rates at will, not only from ship to ship but from shipper to shipper on a single ship. As a result, conferences generally adopted the dual-rate system, under which a contract rate applies to all those signing with the conference and a somewhat higher noncontract rate to all other shippers.[14] The Act of 1916 forebade deferred rebates but not the contract-rate system.

Contract rates have not gone unchallenged, especially since World War II. In 1948, Isbrandtsen Company, Inc., filed in the United States District Court a complaint against the United States, two conferences, and their members, requesting that certain agreements approving contract and noncontract rates be enjoined and set aside. The two conferences concerned were the North Atlantic–Continental Freight Conference and the North Atlantic Westbound Freight Conference which, on Oct. 1, 1948, sent notice to all known shippers in the North Atlantic trade that, effective Nov. 1, the exclusive-patronage contract-noncontract-rate system would be inaugurated. The contract rates were to be the ones then prevailing, and the noncontract rates from 20 to 30 percent higher.

The court granted a temporary injunction restraining the carriers from instituting the exclusive-patronage system, but this was conditioned upon Isbrandtsen's diligent prosecution before the Maritime Commission of a complaint challenging the validity of the agreements. Isbrandtsen's complaint was filed with the Maritime Commission and later came before its successor, the Federal Maritime Board. On Dec. 1, 1950, the Board dismissed the complaint on the ground that the agreements were not unfair or discriminatory. Isbrandtsen then filed an amended complaint in the

---

[13] For a discussion of the pros and cons of the conference system, see Daniel Marx, *International Shipping Cartels*, Princeton University Press, Princeton, N.J., 1953.

[14] At the request of the Federal Maritime Board, some conferences have recently adopted the practice of publishing two sets of rates—contract and noncontract.

District Court. In March, 1952, that court ruled that the conference system, as in operation at that time, was illegal, because it was arbitrary and not based on costs, and an injunction was entered against the North Atlantic–Continental Freight Conference. The conference proposed a new contract, providing for a 10 percent differential, to be effective as of Oct. 1, 1952, but the Federal Maritime Board instructed the conference to abstain from sending out the contracts to shippers until the Board had ruled on its merits. In November, the Board ruled that all conferences should justify their contract and noncontract rates. The Federal Maritime Board issued General Order 76, effective the early part of 1953, prescribing certain rules of procedure in connection with establishment of, changes in, or justification of the spread effective by the conferences between their contract and noncontract rates.

Proponents of the conference system have pointed out that the decision in the Isbrandtsen case was not against the conference or the dual-rate system per se but was based on the fact that the spread of 20 percent was arbitrary. They contend that, without the financial benefit of the contract rate, shippers would refuse to sign a conference contract and to use conference lines, and that the inevitable consequence could be a rate war between conference and nonconference carriers and even among individual conference members. Moreover, without the assurance of continuous patronage, conference lines would find it difficult, if not impossible, to maintain the quality of service, including regularity and frequency, that present-day overseas trade demands.

It has been argued that the discounts provided for in conference contracts constitute a discrimination against those not signing such contracts. Each shipper, however, has the choice of signing the contract and securing the lower rate or remaining independent and paying the higher one. Inasmuch as any shipper is free to enter into a contractual relationship with the conference, no discrimination can be ascribed to the conference on this score.

Pools and Rotation-of-sailing Agreements. The Shipping Act of 1916 did not forbid pooling or sailing agreements but provided that the parties involved should file with the regulatory agency every agreement "pooling or apportioning earnings, losses, or traffic; allotting ports or restricting or otherwise regulating the number and character of sailings between ports." Pooling agreements were fairly common in the North Atlantic trade before the war, and immediately before the outbreak of the war in Europe in September, 1939, 10 such arrangements were in effect on various routes between the United States and South American ports. One year later (September, 1940), only 5 such agreements were in effect. War and the consequent disruption of services of belligerent lines had resulted in the withdrawal of many carriers, and the remaining conference members were allowed to put as many ships on berth as they wished. Since 1946, pooling agreements have been rather infrequent.

However, two pooling arrangements (Agreements 7796 and 7797) came up for review by the Federal Maritime Board in 1951. The former will serve to illustrate how such arrangements operate and are regulated. Grace Line, Inc., had, with the consent of the Board, entered into a pooling arrangement with the Chilean company Campania Sud Americana de Vapores covering southbound operations of the two companies between United States Atlantic ports and Chile and all copper northbound. After certain deductions, gross freight earnings accruing on pool tonnage were to be pooled, and the two companies undertook to maintain a minimum of 25 southbound sailings per annum, spaced not more than twenty-five days apart. Agreement 7796, submitted to the Board in compliance with the 1916 Act and approved after minor recommended modifications, became effective on Nov. 1, 1950, and was to continue until Dec. 31, 1960.

The West Coast Line, Inc., and Rederiet Ocean A/S, trading jointly as the West Coast Line, filed a complaint with the Federal Maritime Board charging that the pooling agreement was unjustly discriminatory and unfair. The complainant averred that the original pooling agreements were not in themselves discriminatory and unfair but based their charges on the actual method of operation in combination with other factors, the chief one of which was the Chilean import license system. On May 14, 1951, the Board completed its study of the case, and the complaint was dismissed.[15]

REGULATION OF CARRIERS IN DOMESTIC TRADES

The Federal government is interested in the regulation of carriers engaged in serving three segments of domestic waterborne trade: (1) offshore trade between United States ports and United States territories and possessions, (2) intercoastal trade, and (3) coastwise trade.[16] Carriers operating in the first category, called noncontiguous trade, are regulated by the Federal Maritime Board under provisions of the Intercoastal Shipping Act of 1933, as amended in 1938, and of certain sections of other shipping acts.

The regulation of carriers operating intercoastal and coastwise is somewhat more complex, and the ensuing discussion may be clearer if we indicate at the outset three periods: (1) 1916 to 1933, when domestic con-

[15] Federal Maritime Board Docket 705 also embraced the complaints of Agreement 7797 against Campania Sud Americana and the Gulf and South American Steamship Co., Inc., a Grace–Lykes Bros. enterprise.

[16] Carriers operating on inland waterways also come under ICC jurisdiction. Carriers handling water traffic solely between ports within a state are subject to the individual laws of that state.

ferences attempted to provide industry control; (2) 1933 to 1940, when the conferences still functioned in their rate-making capacity, subject to certain governmental regulation; and (3) the period beginning in 1940, when the Transportation Act transferred control over intercoastal and coastwise shipping to the Interstate Commerce Commission.

Industry Regulation. Although the Shipping Act of 1916 was designed to encourage domestic steamship conferences, the entire interwar period is one of a "long succession of short-lived conferences." The situation was particularly acute in the intercoastal trade, which was heavily overtonnaged by the late 1920's. As a result, the trade between Atlantic and Gulf Coasts and the Pacific Coast suffered from a succession of rate wars, the last of which took place in 1931. After months of complete disruption, the Intercoastal Conference was reorganized in February, 1932.

Conditions improved little if at all. Those who endeavored to maintain a conference agreement either were still harassed by a large number of competing nonconference vessels or were unable to agree among themselves as to an equitable rate structure and rate relationship among the members. Many companies organized for the intercoastal business failed because of the unprofitable return from their operations. This lack of stability in rates was also of great concern to the competing transcontinental land carriers, but most of all to the shipping public. Shippers were unable to determine their own competitive position in the Atlantic and Pacific Coast markets because a variety of rates applied on the same commodity and because such rates were constantly subject to change without notice. The situation was a matter of national concern, since this segment of water traffic accounted for a large number of the vessels making up the American merchant marine. As a result, the regulation of intercoastal water carriers became the subject of special legislation.

The Intercoastal Shipping Act, 1933. The Act of 1933 required that all common and contract carriers must file their actual rates with the regulatory body in charge, that any changes be subject to thirty days' advance notice, that the regulatory body have the power of suspension, and that their rates must stand the test of being reasonable and nondiscriminatory. This type of regulation was patterned after that applicable to the rail carriers under the Interstate Commerce Act.

The results were that the intercoastal carriers created a new agreement including all common carriers operating between the Atlantic and Pacific Coasts and organized the Intercoastal Steamship Freight Association with the head office in New York. There was also a conference of the Gulf intercoastal carriers located in New Orleans. After this legislation passed, rate wars ceased.

In 1938, the Intercoastal Shipping Act was amended to include the operations of domestic coastwise carriers and of those operating between ports of the continental United States and ports in offshore possessions and territories. The carriers serving ports along the Atlantic Coast, between Atlantic and Gulf ports, and along the Pacific Coast had been confronted with the same competitive problems as had the intercoastal lines. It was reasoned that, since more stringent regulation had saved the intercoastal carriers from self-destructive competition, the same remedy should relieve the coastwise operators. It also seemed desirable to include services such as those to Alaska, Hawaii, and Puerto Rico. After 1938, rate wars were prevented, and greater stability in rate structures resulted.

The 1938 amendment to the Intercoastal Shipping Act greatly enhanced the stability of the domestic conferences. The water lines operating Atlantic coastwise, between Atlantic and Gulf ports, Pacific coastwise, and to Puerto Rico, Hawaii, and Alaska all have conferences or tariff bureaus. When control over domestic water rates was transferred to the Interstate Commerce Commission by the Transportation Act of 1940, the domestic carriers were permitted to retain their agreements under Section 15 of the Shipping Act of 1916. This has been a great convenience to those particular steamship lines, as they have not had to concern themselves with the new type of agreement that must be accomplished by the rail and truck lines under the Reed-Bulwinkle legislation.[17] The domestic conferences publish tariffs and represent the carriers in rate and regulatory matters.

While the direct regulation of domestic carriers resulted from the 1933 Act, actually the coastwise carriers on the Pacific Coast had been subject to regulation by indirection since 1930, under the so-called long-and-short-haul clause, which is Part I, Section 4, of the Interstate Commerce Act. For many years, the railroads operating along the Pacific Coast contended that they should be permitted to name lower rates between the ports than were applicable at intermediate points so they might better meet water competitive rates. Although they had received limited long-and-short-haul relief prior to 1930, it was not until that year that the Commission granted such wide-sweeping rate-making permission as it did in its decision in the Pacific Coast Fourth Section case.

The Interstate Commerce Commission granted relief to the rail lines by permitting them to name lower rates between the ports than at intermediate points (*i.e.*, from one port, say San Francisco, to one point, such as Eugene, Oregon, lying intermediate between two ports such as San Francisco and Portland). Such port-to-port rates might be related to the water rates by certain fixed differentials, in cents per hundred pounds, which when added to the water rate of the standard steamer lines would create the rail rate. This process was subject, however, to certain mini-

[17] The Reed-Bulwinkle Act, signed June, 1948, exempted the railroad rate bureaus from antitrust legislation, provided they met certain requirements outlined in the Act.

mum-rate provisions. It was further provided that such rail rates could be increased or decreased at the discretion of the rail carriers to adjust to corresponding changes in the water rates.

Since the rail carriers were a definite competitive factor in the efforts of the Pacific coastwise water lines to secure traffic, there was little the steamship lines could do, ratewise, to improve their volume. Consequently, by necessity, the water carriers' rate structure was stable but unproductive of the needed volume of cargo or of sufficiently high rates to permit continued operation.

Rail-Water Rates. Joint rail and water rates are controlled by Part I of the Interstate Commerce Act. For many years, coastwise carriers on the Atlantic, Great Lakes, Gulf, and Pacific Coasts have maintained a complete network of such joint rates. In some territories, there are also rail-water-rail joint rates. The decline of domestic coastwise services since World War II has greatly depreciated the value of this type of rate making by the water carriers. Such rates have always been related to the competitive all-rail rate by a differential sometimes prescribed by the Interstate Commerce Commission. In the intercoastal trade, only the Gulf intercoastal route has established a rather complete line of rail-water rates, and at present the joint rates in effect on this route apply in connection with the rail carriers at New Orleans, Mobile, and other Gulf ports. There are also some water-barge-rail rates in the Gulf intercoastal trade.

Truck-Water Rates. Through rates have been established in recent years by the water carriers with the motor-truck lines. The carriers in the Gulf intercoastal trade name commodity joint rates on traffic in both directions, and the tendency to establish such rates is increasing. There have been some coastwise rates, generally applicable on less-than-carload traffic, but at present they are of little consequence. Effective June 25, 1953, the Intercoastal Steamship Freight Association established some joint through rates with truck carriers from Pacific Coast ports to interior points in New York, New Jersey, and Pennsylvania. These rates are all regulated by the Interstate Commerce Commission.

Legislation as to Rates at New Ports. While the Intercoastal Shipping Act of 1933 was pending, there was considerable discussion in Congress as to the rights of ports in the initial establishment of rates. The Federal government was spending, and has since spent, large sums of money in port development. There was some feeling that steamship conferences had too great an authority in determining the structure of rates for a new port of call. The failure to establish any rates at all, or the setting of a rate basis which might be noncompetitive with adjacent ports, was a decision solely within the rights of the conferences under their separate agreements. It was possible for a newly created port to be isolated by the nonapplication of a rate basis or by discriminatory rates. Congress inserted a provision in the Intercoastal Act, and later in Section 205 of the Merchant Marine Act of 1936, which makes it unlawful for a conference to prevent any carrier from serving any port located on an improvement project authorized by Congress at the same rates that it charges at the nearest port already served regularly.[18] This action left the matter of establishing rates at such ports entirely subject to the initiative of the individual steamship lines.

Transportation Act of 1940. The keen competition of rail lines and motor-truck lines with the domestic water carriers resulted in many rate differences. There was constant argument between the water lines and land carriers as to the proper rate differential that should be applicable; there was also disagreement as to the carriers' right to make downward rate adjustments which affected the flow of traffic via one or the other form of transportation.

The U.S. Maritime Commission was regulating the water lines, and the Interstate Commerce Commission the rates of the rail and truck lines. Consequently, a great deal of confusion existed on competitive matters. On the belief that the Interstate Commerce Commission should be in a legal position to rule on intercarrier differences, the Transportation Act of 1940 was passed, transferring the regulation of domestic water carriers to the Commission.[19]

This Act contains the following declaration of national transportation policy:

It is hereby declared to be the national transportation policy of the Congress to provide for fair and impartial regulation of all modes of transportation subject to the provisions of this act, so administered as to recognize and preserve the inherent advantages of each; to promote safe, adequate, economical, and efficient service and foster sound economic conditions in transportation and among the several carriers; to encourage the establishment and maintenance of reasonable charges for transportation services, without unjust discriminations, undue preferences or advantages, or unfair or destructive competitive practices; to cooperate with the several States and the duly authorized officials thereof; and to encourage fair wages and equitable working conditions;—all to the end of developing, coordinating, and preserving a national transportation system by water, highway, and rail, as well as other means, adequate to meet the needs of the commerce of the United States, of the postal service, and of the national defense. All of the provisions of this act shall be administered and enforced with a view to carrying out the above declaration of policy.

[18] It should be noted that, when this provision was incorporated with the Merchant Marine Act of 1936, it also became applicable to the rates quoted for foreign commerce.

[19] This Act was Part III of the Interstate Commerce Act of that same year. After its passage, the U.S. Maritime Commission (now the Federal Maritime Board) retained its regulatory power, derived from the 1938 amendment of the Intercoastal Shipping Act, in so far as it related to carriers operating between United States ports and United States territories or possessions.

The 1940 Act provided, among other things, that no common carrier by water shall engage in transportation unless it holds a certificate of public convenience and necessity issued by the Interstate Commerce Commission, provided, however, that if any such carrier was in bona fide operation on Jan. 1, 1940, over the route or routes or between the ports with respect to which the application is made, and has so operated since that time, the Commission shall issue such certificate without requiring further proof that public convenience and necessity will be served by such operation. This provision is commonly known as a "grandfather" clause.

This Act also provides for regulation of contract carriers that are defined as carriers which, under individual contracts or agreements, engage in the transportation by water of property in interstate or foreign commerce for compensation. No person is permitted to engage in the business of a contract carrier by water unless he holds an effective permit, issued by the Commission authorizing such operation, subject to a grandfather clause similar to that applied to the common carriers. While the common carriers by water are required to file their actual going rates on prescribed notice, the contract carriers need only file their minimum rates. The Act does not apply to the transportation by a water carrier of commodities in bulk when the cargo space of the vessel in which such commodities are transported is being used for the carrying of not more than three such commodities. Neither does it apply to the transportation of liquid cargoes in bulk in tank vessels designed for use exclusively in such service.

An innovation for water carriers was the requirement that, before a new company could start in business, it had to prove that the operation would be a public convenience and a necessity. The same requirement applied in connection with efforts to extend a service to include additional ports of call. This provision has tended to prevent overtonnaging of a particular trade route—a restriction that in turn protects the carriers' general rate structure.

The balance of Part III of the Transportation Act, pertaining to such subjects as the filing of tariffs, suspension of rates, handling of formal and informal complaints, and inspection of accounts, is quite similar to the provisions of Part I and Part II, which are applicable respectively to rail and motor carriers.

Relation of Regulation to Postwar Developments. Immediately following the close of World War II, the domestic water carriers were faced with a tremendous problem of rate adjustment and fleet replacement (see pages 99 to 101). In mid-1946, domestic service was resumed, when the War Shipping Administration permitted certificated carriers to operate government-owned vessels on what was termed a *berth-agency* basis, with the Administration absorbing the losses. The War Shipping Administration requested the Interstate Commerce Commission to conduct an investigation as to the level of the competitive rail-rate structure and the relationship between rail and water rates.[20] The investigation was particularly desirable because the government had announced that the subsidized operations and berth-agency agreements would terminate in July, 1947.[21]

The hearings opened in Washington in April, 1947, and were continued into 1950. The water carriers also considered the situation timely to air their long-standing grievance that the railroads had, over the years, deliberately depressed rates on most goods that were attractive to the water carriers and for which there was strong competition between rail and water lines. The coastwise carriers on the Pacific Coast requested reconsideration of the Pacific Coast Fourth Section Order.

While these proceedings were in progress, the rail carriers filed a number of petitions through which they sought percentage increases in their rates to compensate for greatly increased costs of operation. The Interstate Commerce Commission did grant a succession of percentage increases in rail rates, and amended the Pacific Coast Fourth Section Order, eliminating the portion that granted the rail lines permissive rights as to rate increases. The order was later canceled completely. Although ICC rulings did improve the situation for the water lines, the domestic steamship industry feels that the proper relationship between rail and water rates has not been achieved and that the general principle involved in the rail-water rate structure has not been given a satisfactory hearing. After years of unsatisfactory postponement and delay, the ICC suggested that the general intercoastal case be laid aside, partly because the evidence had become out of date. The Pacific coastwise case was decided in favor of the rail lines but on the grounds that "there is considerable doubt as to whether the water lines have the advantage of cost as to any important character of traffic."

The contemplated investigation of the domestic trades by the Interstate Commerce Commission has never taken place in the manner intended, since the needs of the rail carriers for higher rates automatically created an improved water rate structure. There are those who believe that such a rate structure has not restored domestic services to the strength warranted by the economics of water transportation and by standards of a strong American merchant marine in terms of national

---

[20] The functions of the Administration were transferred to the Maritime Commission on Sept. 1, 1946, when the wartime agency was terminated.

[21] The investigation, set by the ICC in *Ex parte* 164, was concerned with rail and water rates as they affected both coastwise and intercoastal service. Two dockets were concerned with the coastwise business: Docket 29721, "All-rail Commodity Rates between California, Oregon, and Washington," and Docket 29722, "Pacific Coastwise Water Rates."

security. The domestic steamship business believes that the national transportation policy stated in the preamble to Part III of the Interstate Commerce Act has not been implemented in so far as their interests are concerned. Without doubt, the intervention of World War II created a situation that has delayed a determination of whether or not the conclusion of 1940 was proper—namely, that all competitive forms of land and water transportation should be regulated by one body.

BIBLIOGRAPHY

Frederick, J. H., "Development of Transport Regulation in the United States of America," *Transport and Communications Review*, United Nations, October–December, 1951, Vol. 4, pp. 41–49.

Furness, Robert, "Steamship Conferences Operating from the Pacific Coast," *The Log, Review and Yearbook Number*, July 1, 1946, Vol. 41, pp. 75–79.

Inter-American Maritime Conference, Washington, D.C., November 25, 1940, to December 2, 1940, Report of the Delegates of the United States, 1941.

Mears, E. G., *Maritime Trade of Western United States*, Stanford University Press, Stanford, Calif., 1935, Chaps. 17 and 18.

Morgan, C. S., *Problems in the Regulation of Domestic Transportation by Water*, Interstate Commerce Commission Report Regarding *Ex parte* 165, 1946.

U.S. Maritime Commission, *Handbook of Merchant Marine Development and Regulation in the United States*, 1940.

Williams, E. W., "Inter-carrier Competition in United States Transportation," *Transport and Communications Review*, United Nations, July–September, 1951, Vol. IV, pp. 39–46.

PART FIVE

THE ROLE OF GOVERNMENT

CHAPTER 20

LAWS AND AGENCIES GOVERNING SHIPPING*

The laws and regulations that govern the shipping industry, and the agencies that administer them, are many and complex. In a paper read before the Society of Naval Architects and Marine Engineers, in 1947, William B. Jupp of the marine-transportation department of Socony-Vacuum Oil Company, New York, noted that there were 23 standing committees in Congress making laws affecting ocean shipping and 67 agencies and bureaus in the executive branch of the government administering those laws and issuing regulations.[1]

An average-size combination passenger and freight vessel requires the delineation of 1,000 to 1,200 plans, most of which are required to be executed in multiple copies. Vessel specifications usually contain a section stating that the ship as delivered shall comply with all the requirements and regulations of all or most of the following: American Bureau of Shipping; U.S. Coast Guard; Revised Statutes, Navigation Laws of the United States; International Load Line Convention, London, 1930; International Convention for the Safety of Life at Sea, London, 1948; U.S. Public Health Service; Senate Report 184, Federal Communications Commission; U.S. Customs Regulations on Admeasurement; Panama Canal Regulations; Suez Canal Regulations; and American Institute of Electrical Engineers Recommended Practice for Electrical Installations on Shipboard. Twelve different government certificates are required for the documentation of a new vessel on delivery, and nine separate papers are needed to clear a vessel from an American port. The latter do not include the bill of lading, dock receipts, and other papers already discussed in Chapter 7 and connected with the actual shipment.

The chapters of Part Four were devoted specifically to laws and agencies dealing with matters involving admiralty, insurance, rates, and regulations. Chapter 16 discussed the laws applicable to maritime labor,

---

* This chapter was written by J. Monroe Sullivan, formerly assistant professor, College of Business Administration, University of San Francisco; currently assistant to the president, Pacific American Steamship Association.
[1] *Marine Engineering*, December, 1947, pp. 90–93.

but it could give only cursory attention to the number of regulatory agencies involved. In 1948, the Waterfront Employers' Association of the Pacific Coast (now Pacific Maritime Association) issued a chart indicating that 21 major Federal departments and agencies affected the character of labor relations in the employment of longshore workers alone. A chart prepared by the American-Hawaiian Steamship Company in 1943, entitled "Outline of United States Departments, Offices, Agencies, and Establishments Affecting the Vessel Owner," lists more than 100 agencies.

Nor does the list of Federal bodies complete the account of regulation. Under the provisions embodied in Section 15 of the Shipping Act of 1916, regulation of certain matters has been granted to non-Federal regulatory agencies. For instance, the California Association of Port Authorities has authority to deal with rate matters of public port terminals, including such charges as wharfage, dockage, and service charges, while the regulation of such rates at private terminals comes under the jurisdiction of the California Public Utilities Commission. Because of the complexity of the subject, this chapter will concentrate on the United States, and more specifically on Federal laws and agencies.

LEGISLATION TO 1890

The second law passed by Congress, on July 4, 1789, provided for discriminatory tonnage taxes and discriminatory import duties in the form of discounts for merchandise arriving in American bottoms and for higher duties for that aboard foreign-flag ships.[2] Another measure enacted in 1789 forbade the documentation of foreign-built vessels under the American flag. Other early legislation reserved the coastwise and intercoastal trade to American-flag ships.[3]

Much of the shipping legislation of the early part of the nineteenth century was defensive, and the measures paralleling enactments in force in other countries were regarded as counteractions. When Britain repealed her old Navigation Acts in 1849, thereby opening the way for the sale of American-built ships abroad, the American trade reciprocity policy, which though opportunistic had nevertheless furthered maritime interests, had

[2] The tariff is outside the scope of this book. The student interested in the early history of the tariff should consult F. W. Taussig, *The Tariff History of the United States*, 7th ed., G. P. Putnam's Sons, New York, 1923. For a more recent study, see Asher Isaacs, *International Trade: Tariff and Commercial Policies*, Richard D. Irwin, Inc., Chicago, 1948. On the reciprocal trade agreements, see J. M. Letische, *Reciprocal Trade Agreements in the World Economy*, King's Crown Press, New York, 1948; Harold P. Macgowan, "Reciprocal Trade Agreements Program," *Foreign Commerce Weekly*, July 30, 1951, Vol. 44, pp. 3–5, 27–28; *Operation of the Trade Agreements Program, June 1934 to April 1948*, U.S. Tariff Commission, Report 160, 2d series, 5 parts, 1949; and *Operation of the Trade Agreements Program, April 1948 to March 1949*, U.S. Tariff Commission, Report 163, 2d series, 1950.

[3] See Chap. 5, footnote 1.

almost achieved its goal. The policy, however, had been based on the false assumption that American shipping operated at a substantial natural advantage, whereas the real advantage had arisen from low costs of American ship construction and the registry laws of European nations. "Earlier measures that had been designed to retaliate rather than to permanently protect the maritime industry" became both protective and monopolistic.[4] When the United States government was for the first time faced with the broad issues of protection or free trade, the choice was protection. Legislation passed during the last half of the nineteenth century was hence of little benefit to maritime enterprise, although ocean-mail subsidies were paid during the years 1847 to 1857 and 1864 to 1877 and tariff duties were relaxed in 1890 and 1894 to permit the free entry of materials used in shipbuilding (see Chapter 13).

THE SITUATION, 1890 TO 1916

Between 1890 and 1916, a number of circumstances made the nation increasingly aware of the inadequacy of its merchant marine. When Secretary of State Olney offered to arbitrate the Venezuelan–British Guianan border dispute in 1895, and threatened war with Great Britain if the incident were not settled satisfactorily, he knew full well that the nation lacked the ships to prosecute such a war and carry essential imports. Three years later, the British, with at least a degree of justification, refused to furnish naval assistance to the United States in the war with Spain, and a shortage of merchant ships could have been a serious problem if the war had been of long duration. In 1893, the United States had annexed Hawaii, and at the close of the Spanish War, the Philippines and Puerto Rico became United States possessions.

When President Theodore Roosevelt decided to send the fleet around the world in 1908, the voyage, which had been intended as a gesture to impress Japan, could have turned into a fiasco. Shortly before the fleet was to sail, it was discovered that provisions for bunkering a force of that size were totally inadequate. The United States government purchased and chartered foreign tramps to accompany the warships, and the ships of the United States Navy sailed for foreign ports accompanied by service vessels flying the flags of foreign nations. In addition, Congress had at first refused an appropriation sufficient to finance the voyage. President Roosevelt informed that legislative body that funds were available to send the fleet into the Pacific, it was going, and it would stay there unless money was forthcoming to bring it home.

In 1912, Congress enacted the Panama Canal Act, which included an

[4] J. G. B. Hutchins, *The American Maritime Industries and Public Policy, 1789–1914*, Harvard University Press, Cambridge, Mass., 1941, p. 313.

amendment to the Interstate Commerce Act of 1887 giving the Interstate Commerce Commission certain powers so that it could prevent the railroads from stifling competition of water carriers. Another measure included in the Act was one providing that foreign-built vessels not exceeding five years of age could be documented under the American flag if wholly owned by citizens of the United States. Although this provision, which represented the first relaxation of the 1789 registry law, was hailed as a culmination of the "free-ship" agitation heard since the Civil War, not one ship was transferred to the American flag until the registry law was further relaxed in 1914.

Under the leadership of Andrew Furuseth, the International Seamen's Union had been striving to secure legislation in behalf of seamen. Legislation passed by both Houses during Taft's administration (1908–1912) had been given a pocket veto. Interest became more widespread after the *Titanic* disaster in 1912, and a new bill was introduced in 1913. It was passed in revised form to become the Seamen's Act of 1915, sometimes called the La Follette Act, because of Senator Robert La Follette's strong advocacy.[5]

The Harvard Report[6] summarizes legislation from 1890 to 1916 thus:

There were several varying motives underlying the legislation or proposed legislation of the twentieth century prior to the First World War. These motives comprised fear of trusts and monopolies; realization of the inadequacy of the United States fleet for commerce, particularly in times of emergency; growing commitments for defense in the Western Hemisphere and beyond; and a realization of the dangers of sea life and the consequent necessity for lessening risks and making occupation at sea sufficiently attractive to secure the services of an able group of men. The passage of legislation to meet these recognized needs was complicated by disagreement as to the methods of attaining the desired ends. Thus, measures for assuring the upbuilding of the merchant fleet were impeded by endless discussions of the relative merits of subsidies or discriminating duties to assist a weak, privately owned fleet. Although investigations were conducted, and many bills were proposed and discussed, the main legislation passed during the period consisted of the Panama Canal Act (1912) and the Seamen's Act (1915). The Investigation of Shipping Combinations occupied many months, but no legislation resulted from this study prior to 1916.

UNITED STATES SHIPPING BOARD

When war broke out in Europe in the late summer of 1914, the United States, which had depended on foreign-flag vessels to carry roughly 90

[5] See Chap. 16.
[6] *The Use and Disposition of Ships and Shipyards at the End of World War II*, A Report Prepared for the U.S. Navy Department and the U.S. Maritime Commission by the Graduate School of Business Administration, Harvard University, Government Printing Office, Washington, D.C., June, 1945, p. 277.

percent of its foreign trade, was confronted with a critical shipping crisis. Grain piled up at the ports of exit, the railroads placed embargoes on further shipments, and cotton exports almost ceased. Since the Department of the Treasury was then financing crop movements and the Federal government had an investment of 34 million dollars in the 1914 grain harvest, Secretary of the Treasury McAdoo was vitally interested in alleviating the shipping crisis.

In August, 1914, Congress passed a bill to repeal the five-year clause of the Panama Canal Act of 1912 and to permit the registry of foreign-built ships. By August, 1915, over 520,000 gross tons of shipping, much of it American owned under foreign flags, had been transferred to American registry. The panic of 1914 was followed by a period of great prosperity for shipowners, and Congress was relieved of pressure from both agricultural interests and shippers. Throughout 1915, the administration continued to press a reluctant Congress for shipping legislation. Finally, in September, the Shipping Act of 1916 was enacted into law, creating the U.S. Shipping Board, an independent agency of five members appointed by the President with the consent of the Senate. Although the Act conferred upon the Board regulatory, promotional, and proprietary functions, the power to acquire, own, and operate ships overshadowed all other functions.[7]

Wartime Activities. A few dates suffice to indicate the wartime task of the Shipping Board. Although the administration had been pressing Congress for shipping legislation throughout 1915 and 1916 and the Shipping Act was passed on Sept. 7, 1916, the first commissioners were not nominated until Dec. 22, 1916; the Board was not organized until Jan. 30, 1917; and it did not receive its full complement of five commissioners until Mar. 15, the date on which President Wilson signed the Selective Military Conscription bill. Under an executive order of Mar. 12, American merchant ships were being armed, and Congress declared war on Apr. 6. The Emergency Fleet Corporation, provided for in the 1916 Act to purchase, construct, lease, charter, and operate merchant ships, was not organized until Apr. 16. Furthermore, to carry out its obligations, the Emergency Fleet Corporation had at the time only the 50 million dollars provided for in the 1916 Act. Emergency legislation on July 17, 1917, provided 750 million dollars for shipbuilding and ship purchasing. Before the World War I fleet was completed, Congress had appropriated well over 3 billion dollars.

The chief accusations against the wartime operations of the Board were extravagance and inefficiency in the construction and operating programs and in the Board's failure to include in the shipbuilding contracts termina-

---

[7] The Harvard Report (p. 283) points out that the Act laid the foundation for "regulation of rates of lasting significance." For more detail on rate regulation, see Chap. 19.

tion clauses. It should be remembered, however, that the purpose of the shipbuilding program was then, as during World War II, to create a large fleet in the shortest possible time.

In our earlier account of the ship-sales program following World War I, we pointed out that the American merchant marine benefited little and that the government failed to realize from the sale of ships what it might have if the war-surplus fleet had been viewed more realistically and the sales program better timed. This was due in part to inadequacies of administration.

Inadequate Administration. Even before the Shipping Board was fully organized, one appointee resigned, and three others followed suit on July 24, 1917. In 1920, Congress passed the Merchant Marine Act of 1920, providing that the number of commissioners should be increased from five to seven, and then quickly adjourned without providing funds to pay salaries. Consequently, there was no Board for a period of several months. The Wilson appointees of late 1920 were not confirmed by the Senate, and the Board appointed by President Harding on Mar. 5, 1921, was a new board except for one man. Between 1917 and 1933, there was a total of 35 different commissioners on the Shipping Board. Only 12 of these served more than three consecutive years. While the Shipping Board was responsible for policies, much of the work was done by the Emergency Fleet Corporation and the Ship Sales Division, charged with the function of negotiating sales. These agencies, too, were subject to personnel changes.

These changes in the membership of the agencies concerned are obviously not due to any one factor. Political influences certainly figured prominently. The salaries of the members of the Shipping Board ($7,500 from 1916 to 1920, and $12,000 after the Act of 1920 was passed) may have militated against securing and holding capable executives. The Harvard Report[8] also mentions that lack of freedom of action imposed by legislation, by other Congressional action, and by public opinion had the effect of discouraging members from serving on the Shipping Board.

Much more probably, however, is that they were frustrated by the failure of Congress to state in clear terms the objectives which they should seek and the actions which they should take in carrying out this work. The whole history of the early years of the Shipping Board and the Emergency Fleet Corporation appears to illustrate the concept that administrative responsibility should not be delegated unless accompanied by adequate administrative authority.

One of the primary reasons that the Shipping Board was not given adequate administrative authority was the prevalence of the mistaken concept that the emergency fleet, financed by government bond issues

[8] P. 254.

and taxation and constructed at wartime prices, would be a valuable national asset for years to come. This, in turn, was associated with government ownership and operation to constitute a problem that was to plague the Shipping Board throughout its entire existence.

Government versus Private Ownership. While the Merchant Marine Act of 1920 was being debated in Congress, a strong faction was of the opinion that the government-owned fleet, built at such great expense, should be retained by the government and operated for its profit. The Act as passed provided for a merchant marine "ultimately to be owned and operated by citizens of the United States," but, as we have seen, the bulk of the government's merchant fleet remained unsold. In July, 1926, the Senate passed a resolution directing the Shipping Board to submit plans for building and maintaining the United States merchant marine through either government ownership or private ownership. After holding hearings in 30 cities, the Board adopted a resolution recommending the continuance of their operation of the fleet for the time being and recommended to the Senate that private ownership be favored. The Act of 1928 did not take a positive stand on private ownership, but its provisions were definitely designed to assist the privately owned merchant marine.

The first concise statement regarding private ownership[9] is to be found in the Merchant Marine Act of 1936, which calls for an "adequate" merchant marine "owned and operated . . . by the citizens of the United States insofar as possible." The Merchant Ship Sales Act of 1946 was even more explicit. Section 11 provided that ships owned by the government after the sales program was terminated on Jan. 15, 1951, should be placed in the national-defense reserve fleet.[10] The Act further provided that "a vessel placed in such reserve shall in no case be used for commercial operation, except that any such vessel may be used during any period in which vessels may be requisitioned under section 902 of the Merchant Marine Act, 1936, as amended."

UNITED STATES MARITIME COMMISSION

As indicated earlier, the Merchant Marine Act of 1920 did not alter the status of the Shipping Board, although it did increase its membership and salaries. Moreover, the Merchant Marine Act of 1928, also known as the Jones-White Act, left the administration of maritime matters in the hands

[9] It is generally recognized that the final version of the 1936 Act was an improvised conference-committee compromise of the House government-ownership bill and the Senate private-ownership bill. Title VII of the Act embodies the authority for government to complete such part of the "long-range program" as private industry does not provide.

[10] The Act originally provided that the sales program should terminate on Dec. 31, 1947. Various amendments extended the period until the beginning of 1951.

of the Board.[11] In 1932, the membership was reduced to three members, and the following year, the agency was transferred to the U.S. Department of Commerce, where it was called the U.S. Shipping Board Bureau. President Franklin D. Roosevelt made it clear not only that he wished ship subsidies stripped of their alleged disguise as ocean-mail contracts but also that he wished matters pertaining to the nation's merchant marine thoroughly investigated with a view to the enactment of effective legislation. There followed a period of the most intensive investigation to which the American merchant marine and its problems had ever been subjected up to that time.[12] With regard to the maritime authority, empowered to supervise the merchant marine in so far as the government was affected, most of the recommendations called for a commission type of agency.

Composition of the Commission. The Merchant Marine Act of 1936 provided for a five-man independent Commission, appointed by the President with the consent of the Senate. After the Commission was constituted, the term of office was to be six years. Not more than three of the members were to be from the same political party. Three members were to be considered a quorum for the transaction of business. Further, no person could be appointed a commissioner if, within three years prior to his appointment, he had been employed by, or had had any pecuniary interest in, any carrier by water, shipbuilder, contractor, or other person, firm, association, or corporation with whom the Commission might have business relations. Their salaries were fixed by law at $12,000 per year. The newly constituted Commission was given all property and contractual obligations of the Shipping Board and Emergency Fleet Corporation. Likewise, all duties and functions of the Board as defined in previous legislation, and the duties and functions of the Postmaster General in respect to ocean-mail contracts, were transferred to the Commission.

As pointed out elsewhere, when the Act of 1936 was written, providing, among other things, for a commission type of Federal shipping agency, a somewhat static situation was envisaged—static as to the level of trade-route requirements, as to cost of ships, and as to demands for, and on, the United States merchant marine. In so far as the Federal shipping agency was concerned, the framers of the 1936 Act directed their efforts to correcting the administrative deficiencies apparent in the old Shipping Board. The purpose of the 1936 Act was to modernize the American merchant marine. The Maritime Commission had made decided steps in that direction when war interrupted a program planned for long-range and peacetime operation. This analysis of the inadequacies of the Maritime

---

[11] The principal features of both the Act of 1920 and the Act of 1928 have already been discussed, notably in Chaps. 13, 16, and 17.

[12] The Harvard Report (pp. 297–310) gives details.

Commission, as constituted by law, needs to be tempered with an understanding of (1) what the Commission was organized to do and (2) the circumstances that developed after the opening of World War II, particularly after Pearl Harbor.

First, owing to wartime shipping demands, the President found it necessary to create by executive order, in February, 1942, the War Shipping Administration (WSA) headed by an administrator, and to vest in him broad authority and responsibility for operation, purchase, charter, insurance, repair, and requisition of merchant ships. As explained in Chapter 22, Vice Admiral Emory S. Land, Chairman of the Maritime Commission, added to his responsibilities those of the Administrator of WSA.

Second, the War Shipping Administration was abolished, in 1946, and its remaining functions returned to the Maritime Commission. Congress made provision for the sale, charter, and lay-up of the war-built fleet, numbering roughly 4,100 ships,[13] by passing the Merchant Ship Sales Act of Mar. 8, 1946. Hence, the Maritime Commission was charged, as President Truman commented in his Mar. 13, 1950, message transmitted to Congress urging the adoption of Reorganization Plan 21, "with the conduct of a variety of large and costly promotional and business-type programs demanding the prompt and vigorous administration for which experience both in Government and in private enterprise has demonstrated that a single executive is essential." Moreover, the postwar Maritime Commission (called upon to assume greatly expanded responsibilities as well as to implement the then somewhat modified, long-range policy instituted in 1936) was composed of men not one of whom had served on the Commission during the peacetime years 1936 to 1939.

Third, the Ship Sales Act of 1946 had been enacted as an interim measure anticipating that the United States would be able to return to a long-range program in regard to the government's relation to the nation's merchant marine. Instead, postwar developments exaggerated rather than ameliorated maritime problems. (*a*) Although foreign aid had been expected to taper off five or six years after the close of the war, it did not. World conditions, particularly after mid-1950, made it necessary for the United States to reactivate hundreds of ships from the national-reserve fleet to carry emergency cargoes. (*b*) Postwar inflation, particularly since 1948, has increased construction costs for ships to the point where ships that cost operators $100 per ton at the close of World War II cost between $400 and $500 per ton in 1953. (*c*) Since such inflation made ship replacements difficult, it "inflated" the problem of block obsolescence—a problem that has been with the American merchant marine since World War I. These and other postwar developments led, as pointed out earlier, to

[13] Of the 5,500 ships built, 700 were lost during the war and some 640 were so badly damaged that they were scrapped.

amendment of the 1936 Act through the enactment into law in July, 1952, of the Long-range Shipping bill. They also enhanced the importance of a more effective Federal shipping agency. When the President's Reorganization Plan 6 went into effect on Aug. 20, 1949, the chairman of the Maritime Commission was made its chief executive and administrative officer. This was, however, an interim arrangement, for various proposals were being considered in regard to the Maritime Commission.

Reorganization Plan 21. From 1947 through 1950, the administration of the Maritime Commission was studied by three different bodies. The first of these, the President's Advisory Committee on the Merchant Marine, stated in its report[14] published in 1947:

> Although the Committee believes the philosophy and operating policies of the Merchant Marine Act of 1936 are fundamentally sound, it appears to the Committee that the organization structure of the Maritime Commission set up in the same Act is wholly inadequate for the multitude of diverse activities for which the Maritime Commission is now responsible. These activities at present range from the preparation of economic studies and research through the technical questions of detailed design. They embrace the construction, ownership, operation, and disposal of ships and of maritime shore facilities. They involve financial or banking relations with the industry, the determination of fitness of the various shipping companies, the training of licensed and unlicensed operating personnel, the establishment of minimum manning and wage scales and of minimum working conditions on subsidized vessels, the issuance of insurance, the setting and regulation of certain freight rates, the determination of fair and reasonable compensation, the distribution of shipbuilding work, and the maintenance of a field organization for the inspection of Government-owned vessels building and in operation, and for the preservation of laid-up reserve fleets and shore facilities.
>
> The deficiencies of the statutory organization for carrying out these widely diversified functions are regarded by the Committee to be the most serious obstacle standing in the way of the development of a sound continuing merchant marine.

A 1949 study of the Maritime Commission, undertaken for the Senate Committee on Expenditures in the Executive Departments, found that the organization of the Commission was "complicated, heterogeneous, and ineffective," and concluded that "the fundamental weakness of the Maritime Commission, as it is now constituted, lies in its prescribed organization." The report pointed out that the Commission had two broad responsibilities: (1) operational and promotional and (2) judicial and regulatory. It recommended that the quasi-judicial and regulatory functions be discharged by an independent commission and that all other functions of the Maritime Commission be made the responsibility of an executive in the Department of Commerce. In general, these recommenda-

[14] *Report of the President's Advisory Committee on the Merchant Marine,* November, 1947, p. 67.

tions agreed with the ones set forth by the President's Advisory Committee, which had recommended a Maritime Administration under a single administrator, who would have charge of the executive and operating functions and who would report to the Secretary of Commerce, and a Maritime Board vested with the quasi-legislative and quasi-judicial functions.

The third study, made in 1949 by the Commission on Organization of the Executive Branch of the Government, stated:

> It is an anomaly that a regulatory commission should also conduct the executive function of managing a huge business; that executive functions should be carried on by an agency that is not subject to Presidential directions; that executive functions should be carried on by a full-time board.

On Mar. 13, 1950, President Truman submitted Reorganization Plan 21 to Congress. This plan called for a small Federal Maritime Board and a Maritime Administration in the Department of Commerce. In May, 1950, the Maritime Commission was abolished, and its functions and duties were transferred to the new organizations.[15]

FEDERAL MARITIME BOARD AND MARITIME ADMINISTRATION

The Federal Maritime Board consists of three members appointed by the President with the consent of the Senate. The President indicates which of the three is to be chairman, and that member is, ex officio, the Maritime Administrator in charge of the Maritime Administration. The members of the Board are appointed for a term of four years, except for terms of the first members, which expire June 30, 1952, 1953, and 1954. Not more than two of the members in office may be from the same political party, any two of the members constitute a quorum, and the affirmative votes of any two members are sufficient for action on any matter that comes under the jurisdiction of the Board. The chairman-administrator receives a salary of $16,000 a year, and the other two members $15,000. The provision of the 1936 Act prohibiting any person who had been employed by a carrier by water from serving on the Maritime Commission is not applicable to the Federal Maritime Board.

The first appointees were Vice Admiral E. L. Cochrane, USN (retired), chief of the Navy's Bureau of Ships during World War II; Albert W. Gatov, formerly president of the Pacific American Steamship Association, San Francisco; and Robert W. Williams, an admiralty attorney, Baltimore. Admiral Cochrane was the first chairman.

---

[15] For a discussion, pro and con, of the reorganization plan, see *Reorganization Plan No. 21 of 1950*, Hearings on S. Res. 265, Senate Committee on Expenditures in Executive Departments, 81st Cong., 2d sess., May 8–9, 1950.

Functions of the Board. The regulatory functions provided for in Section 15 of the Shipping Act of 1916 are vested in the Federal Maritime Board. These involve the review and approval of conference agreements among shipping companies, the prevention of unfair and discriminatory practices on the part of water carriers, and the regulation of shipping rates between the continental United States and its territories and possessions.[16]

Although the Federal Maritime Board is in the Department of Commerce, the Secretary of Commerce has no authority over the handling of regulatory cases, for the plan provided that with respect to regulatory functions the Board and chairman "shall be independent of the Secretary of Commerce." Nor are the Board's decisions and actions subject to review by any other administrative agency. Thus, the Board is guaranteed complete independence in the performance of its regulatory functions. As Frederick J. Lawton, director of the Bureau of the Budget, pointed out, there is "nothing novel in such an arrangement. Reorganization Plan No. IV of 1940 placed the Civil Aeronautics Board in the Department of Commerce and provided that it should exercise its regulatory functions 'independently of the Secretary of Commerce.'"[17]

In performing its subsidy functions, the Board is subject to the general policy guidance of the Secretary of Commerce. However, the Board alone determines to whom subsidies shall be granted, and Section 105 of the plan provides that the Board's action "shall be final." This enables the Secretary of Commerce to delineate general policies, but leaves the final decisions on whether a subsidy should be granted, which applicant should receive it, and how much the subsidy should be, to the Board. The Board's decisions are subject only to court review. In placing responsibility for subsidy arrangements in a bipartisan board rather than in a single official, the plan assures deliberation and protects against hasty or partisan action.

In respect to construction-differential subsidies, the Board is required to determine the suitability of the design of the vessel, the qualifications of the subsidy applicant, the cost of national-defense features, and the amount of the subsidy. The Board enters into the contract with the shipyard for the construction of the ship and with the applicant for the purchase of the vessel. With regard to operating-differential subsidies, the Board determines not only the qualifications and need of the applicant but also the percentage differentials between American and foreign operating costs.

Functions of the Chairman-Administrator. As chief executive and administrative officer of the Board, the chairman has the following specific functions:

[16] See Chap. 19.
[17] *Reorganization Plan No. 21 of 1950*, p. 27.

1. To appoint and supervise, with minor exceptions, all personnel employed by the Board.
2. To distribute business among the Board's personnel and organization units.
3. To use and expend funds for the Board's administrative purposes.

To assist him in performing his functions, the Maritime Administrator has directly under him a deputy maritime administrator appointed by the Secretary of Commerce after consultation with the Administrator. Organizational components of the Federal Maritime Board and Maritime Administration and the lines of control are shown in Figure 11. Not shown in the chart, however, are such employees in the office of the Maritime Administrator as one or more special assistants, advisers, and specialists. Section 302 of the reorganization plan provides for the joint use of personnel "in the interests of efficiency and economy." As of early 1952, the total number of persons employed by the Board and Administration numbered roughly 4,200, a figure that represents a drop from the 4,800 employees of the former Maritime Commission. Other reductions followed in 1953.

Section 204 of the plan transfers all functions of the Maritime Commission except those reserved to the Federal Maritime Board to the Secretary of Commerce, who is instructed to "make such provisions as he shall deem appropriate authorizing the performance by the Maritime Administrator of any function transferred to such Secretary by the provisions of this reorganization plan." The Secretary of Commerce has authorized the Maritime Administrator to perform all functions transferred to him except the following:

1. The authority to take action on the determination or modification of essential trade routes and services.
2. The authority to establish general policies for the guidance of the Maritime Board in exercising its subsidy award and other functions.
3. The authority to establish policies of general application (*a*) for the purchase, acquisition, construction, charter, and sale of vessels and (*b*) for the administration of programs concerning operating subsidies, reserve funds, and transfers to foreign ownership or registry, and charters to foreigners.

The activities and responsibilities of the Maritime Administration, as authorized by the Secretary of Commerce under Reorganization Plan 21 or subsequent legislation, may be summarized as follows:

1. *Subsidy contracts.* Once a subsidy contract has been made by the Board, the decisions and actions involved in carrying out the agreement are, with a few exceptions, the responsibility of the Maritime Administrator. These actions include inspection of subsidized ships under construction and operation, the audit of accounts of shipyards and subsidized

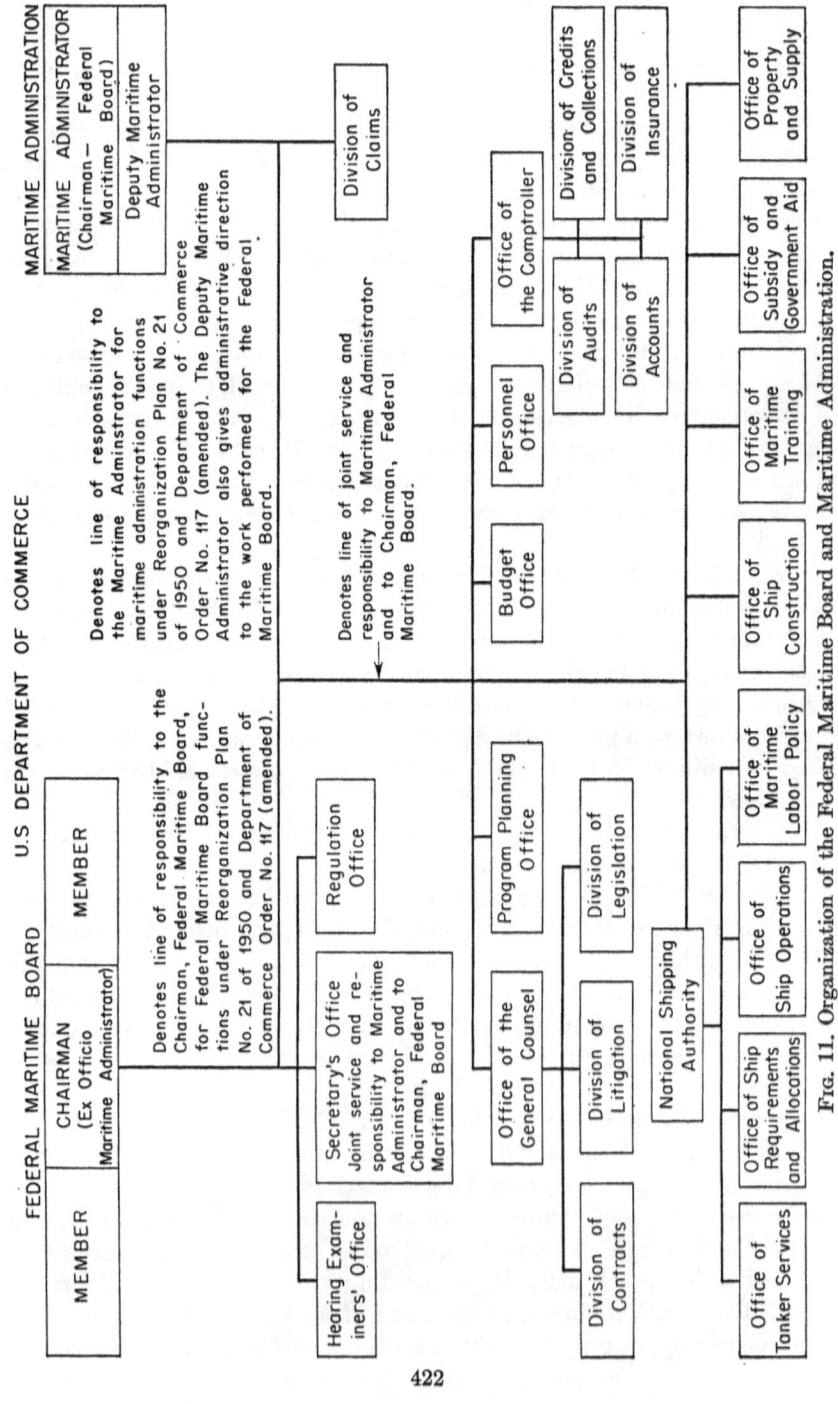

FIG. 11. Organization of the Federal Maritime Board and Maritime Administration.

operators, the actual payment of the subsidies, and checking to determine if the terms of the subsidy contracts have been complied with.

2. *Reserve funds.* The Maritime Administration is responsible for supervising deposits in, and withdrawals from, the reserve funds that the subsidy arrangements require all subsidized operators to maintain.

3. *Construction of vessels.* On Jan. 6, 1951, Congress made approximately 350 million dollars available to the Maritime Administration for construction of 35 prototype postwar dry-cargo carriers, the Mariners. These vessels are not required to be constructed for a specific applicant or for an essential trade route as required under the 1936 Act.

4. *Sale of vessels.* When completed, the Mariners and the *Schuyler Otis Bland* will be the only government-owned ships that can be sold to private operators. However, the Administration was responsible for sales of war-built vessels up to Jan. 15, 1951, when the program was terminated.

In addition, the Administration is responsible for the sale of vessels for scrapping or nonoperational use. As the reserve fleet becomes older, this function will be of more importance.

5. *The National-defense reserve fleet.* The Merchant Ship Sales Act of 1946 required that, at the termination of the sales program, unsold vessels should go into a national-defense reserve fleet, the size of which depends on the number chartered. The maintenance of that fleet became the responsibility of the Maritime Administration in 1950. A Supplemental Appropriation Act of 1951, approved Sept. 27, 1950, contained an appropriation of 18 million dollars for expenses necessary for the repair, activation, and deactivation of vessels in the reserve fleet.

6. *Charters.* The Merchant Ship Sales Act of 1946 contained provisions permitting government-owned ships to be chartered to private operators under certain conditions. This authority was extended beyond June 30, 1950, by Public Law 591, Eighty-first Congress. The same law provided that the Secretary of Commerce could issue charters when required in the public interest and when the service could not be provided by privately owned American-flag vessels at reasonable cost of hire. Under this authority, the Maritime Administration has reactivated Victory-type and Liberty-type ships to be bareboat-chartered to private operators and then rechartered to the Military Sea Transportation Service or the National Shipping Authority.

7. *Training activities.* The training of prospective merchant-marine personnel, inaugurated by the Maritime Commission, has been continued under the Maritime Administration (see Chapter 2).

8. *Other property.* The Maritime Administration has title to or custody of various government-owned shore facilities, including marine terminals, shipyards, and warehouses. When leased to private operators, or main-

tained in a laid-up condition, these facilities are the responsibility of the Administration.

POWERS AND FUNCTIONS OF THE EXECUTIVE BRANCH

Department of Commerce. The transfer of Federal maritime functions to the Department of Commerce centralized in that department the principal nonregulatory agencies dealing with land, air, and water transportation. In 1949, the Commission on Organization of the Executive Branch pointed out: "Transportation activities are scattered over many separate agencies, with consequent waste and overlap," and the Commission recommended a grouping of all major nonregulatory transportation activities of the Federal government. Reorganization Plan 21 provides for an Undersecretary of Commerce for Transportation within the Department of Commerce to lighten the burden of the Secretary and make him better able to meet his responsibilities in the field of transportation.

In addition, the Department of Commerce embraces agencies performing a variety of services related to shipping and foreign trade:

1. The Bureau of the Census, which has existed since the early days of the Republic, has since 1902 functioned as a permanent agency for collecting general statistical information. Over the years, the various statistical series issued have been changed, but since the close of World War II, the Bureau has provided information on export and import shipments by both dollar value and shipping weight. Reports are issued on a monthly and annual basis.[18] Tabulations include detail about commodities shipped, trade with each individual foreign country, trade through individual United States customs districts, commodity totals by port of lading and unlading, flag of vessel, and vessels entered and cleared. By the manipulation of punch cards, the Bureau is able to prepare additional valuable reports in great detail as requested.

2. The Bureau of Foreign and Domestic Commerce, created by act of Congress on Aug. 23, 1912, to foster, promote, and develop the foreign and domestic commerce of the United States, offers businessmen personal and published aids in the fields of international and domestic commerce and industry. It aims to be a storehouse of information and statistics that can be assimilated easily. The Bureau maintains detailed information on over 800,000 foreign firms and individuals engaged in international commerce; will furnish on request special reports, surveys, and information concerning trade opportunities; assists in settling trade disputes; and is a source of information in reciprocal trade agreements, tariff rates, and required shipping documents.

[18] The September, 1953, issue of the *Shipping Survey*, Association of American Ship Owners (Vol. 9, No. 2), discusses the current statistical program of the Bureau of the Census.

One of the Bureau's four major offices, the Office of International Trade, has the specific objectives of encouraging the expansion and balanced growth of international trade, promoting the stability of international economic relations, cooperating with other nations in solving trade and exchange problems, and reducing obstacles and restrictions upon trade. It also exercises control over exports to assure equitable distribution of supplies to serve national-security and foreign-policy objectives.

3. The National Bureau of Standards, established in 1901, sets up standards of Federal specifications. More specifically for shipping, it furnishes technical advice and information on materials, processes, and design of ship construction and shipboard devices. It also attempts to aid in the establishment of international standards.

4. Although Congress authorized a survey of the coast of the United States in 1807, the Coast and Geodetic Survey was not so named until 1878. An act of Aug. 6, 1947, clarified the duties of the agency regarding surveys and so forth. It is responsible for surveying and charting the coast and territorial waters of the United States, for studying tides and currents, and for collecting and exchanging information on coastal charting with other nations. Field offices located in port cities supply information to ships.

5. The Weather Bureau was established in 1870 under the Signal Corps of the Army and transferred to the Department of Agriculture in 1891. In 1940, the President's Reorganization Plan IV transferred the Bureau to the Department of Commerce. The Bureau gathers, analyzes, and publishes information about coastal and ocean areas; receives information from ships at sea; and exchanges weather information internationally.

6. The activities of the Foreign Trade Zones Board, created by act of Congress in June, 1934, are carried on under the jurisdiction of the Department of Commerce (the Secretary of Commerce is board chairman). The Board establishes, maintains, and operates foreign trade zones in New York, New Orleans, San Francisco, Los Angeles, Seattle, and San Antonio, where merchandise may be brought and stored for reshipment to foreign ports or for permissible changes in form without payment of duties and without intervention of customs officials.

Department of State. The Department of State represents the United States at all international meetings such as the International Conference on Safety of Life at Sea, load-line conventions, and International Labour Office maritime conferences. Its consular staffs in port cities are responsible for functions associated with the rights of American seamen in foreign lands.

Under the Assistant Secretary for Economic Affairs of the State Department are the Office of Transport and Communications Policy and the Office of International Trade Policy. The latter, which discharges the responsibility of the Assistant Secretary for Economic Affairs with respect to international trade policy, includes a commercial-policy staff to deal with such matters of commercial policy as preferences, discriminations, certain quantitative restrictions, intergovernmental commodity arrangements, customs, unions, customs procedures and formalities, state trading, reciprocal trade agreements, and the modernization of treaties of friendship, commerce, and navigation. The shipping-policy staff of the Office of Transport and Communications Policy is responsible for matters relating to ocean shipping, including preferences and discriminations, safety at sea, and ocean freight rates.

Department of the Treasury. When the Department of the Treasury was created by act of Congress, Sept. 2, 1789, to superintend and manage national finances, it was natural that customs should be included within its functions, because customs duties were the main source of revenue then available to the new nation. Many acts have figured in the development of the Department and its functions. The Bureau of the Customs was created in 1927 to discharge the duties of the Secretary of the Treasury pertaining to United States imports and exports and to the regulation of certain marine activities.

The main function of the Bureau of Customs is to assess and collect import duties and, incidental to this, to prevent smuggling. It maintains a service that investigates smuggling activities and compliance with navigation laws, and it cooperates with other government agencies in enforcing the preventive, sanitary, and other laws relating to articles brought into the United States and, in some cases, to outgoing articles. Its marine activities embrace a variety of responsibilities, including registry, enrollment, and licensing of vessels; admeasurement of vessels; collection of tonnage taxes; recording of mortgages and sale of vessels; and the remission and mitigation of fines, penalties, and forfeitures incurred under the laws governing these matters.

The Coast Guard now represents an amalgamation into one united service of the activities of the old Revenue Cutter Service, the Life Saving Service, the Light House Service, and the Bureau of Marine Inspection and Navigation (formerly included in the Department of Commerce). Although the structure of the service and its duties and obligations have been altered by legislation over the years, its history dates from 1790. As now constituted, the Coast Guard is a military service and a branch of the armed forces of the United States, operating as an agency in the Department of the Treasury except when operating as a service of the Navy during time of war or when the President directs.

The functions of the Coast Guard are primarily concerned with enforcing maritime law and with the safety of life and property on the high seas and in waters subject to the jurisdiction of the United States. The service is charged with the enforcement of maritime regulations covering all matters not specifically delegated by law to some other executive department. The Coast Guard assists other governmental agencies in the enforcement of laws and regulations that require marine or aviation personnel and facilities for effective enforcement. Into this category fall the Oil Pollution Act; anchorage regulations; and laws relating to internal revenue, customs, immigration, neutrality, and conservation of fisheries and wildlife. The service itself is specifically charged with enforcement of the detailed laws covering vessel inspection.[19] Its powers designed to secure safe navigation are by no means limited to inspection of vessels in port.

The Coast Guard is required to approve of the plans for constructing, repairing, and altering vessels and of the materials used therein. It regulates the carriage of explosives and hazardous goods; administers load-line requirements; controls log books and the numbering of undocumented vessels; and enforces rules for lights, signals, speed, steering, passing, anchorage, movement, and towlines of vessels. Much of its work may be classed as preventive rather than regulatory. It investigates marine disasters and collects statistics relating thereto; removes or destroys derelicts, wrecks, and other hazards to navigation; and opens ice-blocked channels and ports. The Coast Guard ice patrol in the North Atlantic warns ships of dangers and also carries on oceanographic studies. The American seafaring man also comes within the scope of the Coast Guard's jurisdiction.[20]

To carry out its functions of saving life and property, the Coast Guard maintains an established organization of inshore and offshore rescue surface vessels, aircraft, and lifeboat and radio stations. It establishes and maintains aids to navigation such as lighthouses, lightships, radio beacons, direction-finder stations, buoys, and the system of Loran (long-range aid to navigation). The service is also engaged in advancing the use of radar and other modern electronic improvements. Ocean stations are operated and maintained in both the North Atlantic and North Pacific Oceans to provide facilities and meteorological services in the ocean areas that are regularly traversed by United States craft.

Department of Defense. The National Security Act of 1947 created the Department of Defense under a secretary who serves as over-all head of the Department of the Army, the Department of the Navy, the Department of the Air Force, and a group of other agencies created by the Act: the Armed Forces Policy Council, the Joint Chiefs of Staff, the Munitions Board, and the Research and Development Board. The Munitions Board controls certain cargoes imported into the United States for stock-piling purposes.

[19] See also Chap. 17.
[20] See Chap. 11.

Under the 1947 Act, the Secretary of the Army retained his responsibility for the defense, maintenance, and operation of the Panama Canal and for public health and sanitation in the Panama Canal Zone; for the civil-works program of the Corps of Engineers; and for certain other construction projects that affect navigation such as the construction of bridges and the control of power and irrigation developments. The Chief of Engineers, who is responsible to the Secretary of the Army, is in charge of shore protection and administers the laws for protection and preservation of the navigable waters of the United States, including the maintenance of ship channels. The law requires that, before the Corps of Engineers undertakes a new navigational project, local authorities fulfill certain obligations. The Army maintains a large engineering staff, but many large projects are contracted for by private companies.

The Military Sea Transportation Service, created within the Department of the Navy to serve as a unified transportation service for all branches of the armed forces,[21] is responsible for the armed forces' merchant-type ships. To be assured that commercial merchant ships, especially those constructed with government aid, include defense features, MSTS furnishes information to the Navy which consults with and advises the Federal Maritime Board. The naval research of the Bureau of Ships includes studies of merchant ships operating in various waters to obtain information of value to the Navy, and the Bureau of Naval Personnel develops and coordinates plans for the Naval Reserve program, embracing the Merchant Marine Reserve.

Department of Justice. Civil suits on such matters as requisitioning merchant vessels and strategic materials and litigations arising out of war shipping and war risk insurance involve the Claims Division of the Department of Justice. The Customs Division protects the government's interest in reappraisement and classification of imported goods and represents the United States in the Customs Court and in the U.S. Court of Customs and Patent Appeals. The duties of the Immigration and Naturalization Service relate to the admission, exclusion, and deportation of seamen and to other matters.

Post Office Department. Prior to 1936, when the Merchant Marine Act abolished the contract-mail subsidies, the Postmaster General exercised a considerable control over overseas shipping, in that he had the power to enter into contracts for carrying the mails. He still makes provisions for the carriage of the United States mail, and for in-transit mail, but payment is on the basis of the quantity carried. Needless to say, transport of the mails results in considerable revenue for ships on certain routes.

Department of Labor. In its attempts to develop desirable labor standards and desirable earning formulas and to improve working conditions,

[21] See also Chap. 22.

the Department of Labor naturally affects maritime labor. It is specifically charged with administering the Longshoremen and Harbor Workers Compensation Act. The Office of International Labor Affairs had the primary responsibility for United States participation in the International Labour Organisation.

The President. In addition to Cabinet positions, the executive department includes a number of other agencies whose functions have a bearing on United States shipping. Reorganization Plans I and II, effective July 1, 1939, transferred various functions and agencies to the executive office of the President. These included the White House Office, an agency that includes such offices as the President's naval aide, and the Bureau of the Budget, which screens, consults, and advises the President on the budget and all Federal appropriations, including those for the various maritime agencies.

Because security and shipping are inseparable, the functions of the National Security Council and the National Security Resources Board, created by law in 1946 and 1947 respectively, influence American shipping. The National Security Resources Board studies and makes recommendations to the President on strategic matters relating to natural resources in the United States and the world, and its transportation section studies merchant-marine needs. As indicated in Chapter 22, the NSRB assumed an important role in the nation's planning prior to the Korean affair. In March, 1953, NSRB was consolidated with the Office of Defense Mobilization.

The General Accounting Office, created by the Budget and Accounting Act of 1912, is constituted as an agency of the legislative branch of the Federal government, the purpose of which is to perform an independent audit of all government accounts. Its chief officer is the Comptroller General of the United States, who is appointed by the President with the advice and consent of the Senate, and its reports are addressed or submitted to Congress. GAO prescribes accounting principles, practices, and related requirements for executive agencies. It also has the power of disallowance based on the finality of the Comptroller General's settlement of accounts and claims. We have already seen (Chapter 13) that the present Maritime Administration and Federal Maritime Board are confronted with problems in relation to both operating-differential and cost-construction subsidies, because the General Accounting Office questioned the basis for computing the subsidies.

BIBLIOGRAPHY

The references used for this chapter are the same as those listed for Chapter 13.

CHAPTER 21

INTERNATIONAL CONVENTIONS AND TREATIES

International shipping has enjoyed a freedom of growth and competition that seems unusual in this day and age of regulation. It is true that free competition has felt the impact of various forms of government aid and subsidy and, to some extent, of shipping conferences. However, international shipping has experienced only a limited amount of international organization, and that has been decentralized for purposes of technical aids, labor matters, regulation, management aspects, and so forth. The experience with international maritime machinery at either industry or intergovernmental level has been largely concerned with the actual and planned mobilization and employment of ships during wartime. This aspect of international shipping will be discussed in Chapter 22; here we discuss conventions, treaties, and agreements that are applicable to peacetime.

LIMITED ACCOMPLISHMENT OF INTERNATIONAL AGREEMENT

Each state claims complete jurisdiction over all ships in its waters except as it has waived that jurisdiction by agreement. These waivers are usually in the form of treaties. The basic and essential agreement is the Treaty of Friendship, Commerce and Navigation, which sometimes reserves cabotage and fisheries to national vessels but otherwise gives foreign vessels the same privileges that are accorded its own.

The development of the modern concept of freedom of the seas from the British Navigation Acts of 1661 to their final repeal effective Jan. 1, 1850, is a fascinating chapter of history, in which the United States is the chief protagonist of liberality. But the old concept of sovereignty is behind almost all the maritime conventions, as each represents waivers of that sovereignty in specific directions. There is also, as a by-product, the unsettled case of territorial waters, the definition of which for various purposes ranges from the three-mile limit to the doctrine of the continental shelf.

Much of the experience associated with international maritime agreements is limited to the twentieth century and is concentrated largely in Great Britain. As the volume of international commerce expanded and as its mechanics became progressively more complex, a degree of technical competence was necessary if the commercial system was to be able to function smoothly and to avoid chaos; that degree of technical competence required a framework of acceptable principles and rules of the road. Both commercial and political (or public) bodies have contributed to the erection of this framework. They include, for example, the International Maritime Committee[1] and the International Law Association (both legal in nature), the International Shipping Conference (composed of shipowners' organizations), the International Union of Marine Insurance, and the several existing and proposed intergovernmental bodies in or associated with the United Nations. Many of the latter were founded during the existence of the League of Nations.

In the development of international conventions and treaties, two principal problems occur: (1) the difficulty of compromising the different legal systems of the various countries and (2) the fear held by individual nations and their shipowners that competitive advantages will be sacrificed if they agree to adhere to some international common denominator.

The machinery for bringing a convention or treaty into being moves at a painfully slow rate, primarily because, before most conventions are put into effect, they must be ratified by a minimum number of participating nations. For instance, the Safety of Life at Sea Conference of 1914 drew up a document that was signed by all participating nations, but, as noted later, it never went into force as a convention. A second conference, in 1929, drew up a convention, but, since the United States did not deposit its ratification of that convention until 1936, the treaty did not become applicable to this country until that year. For a third convention, promulgated by a conference that convened in 1948, the minimum number of ratifications was not received until November, 1951. By the terms of the act, the new Safety of Life at Sea Convention did not come into being until one year later (Nov. 19, 1952), and then only as to the nations which ratify it, including the United States.

In consequence of the problems involved in erecting international maritime agreements, disaster or crisis has at times impelled nations to strive for agreement. The tragedy of the *Titanic* in 1912 spurred the United States Congress to urge that an international conference be held to develop rules to prevent such disasters, and the International Ice Patrol in the North Atlantic was agreed to at the aforementioned 1914 conference. The *Vestris* incident prompted the 1929 conference leading to the

---

[1] The International Maritime Committee is a voluntary, nongovernmental association founded in 1896. It first met in Belgium, and from this dates the primacy which that country traditionally exercises in the field of international maritime law.

International Convention for the Safety of Life at Sea, 1929, and the *Morro Castle* fire led to the fire-prevention features of the 1948 revision of this Convention. On the other hand, the very practical Maritime Ports Convention was adopted in 1923 and ultimately ratified by more than 20 nations. This was a contribution of the League of Nations to the determination of freedom of the seas.

POLITICO-ECONOMIC AGREEMENTS

The more important international maritime agreements have been variously classified as (1) governmental and (2) nongovernmental. Governmental agreements have been further classified as (*a*) politico-economic, (*b*) juridical, (*c*) technical, and (*d*) welfare or personnel. Some of the agreements are self-executing treaties; some are recommendations for uniform national legislation; and some are recommendations for uniform administrative action. Private agreements cannot affect the sovereignty question and are usually economic in nature, limited in scope, and regional in application. One of the few technical matters is the North Atlantic Track Agreement, which is given governmental recognition in the 1948 Safety-at-Sea-Convention.

Governmental politico-economic law is largely concerned with freedom of the seas, including its application to territorial waters, canals, straits, and ports. While the general rule still holds that a ship on the high seas is subject to the authority of the state whose flag it flies, nevertheless international legal authority has initiated limits to this sovereignty.[2] And, though Great Britain has long sought to have the three-mile limit recognized as the limit of territorial waters for purposes of determining fishing rights and the extent of neutrality and for customs regulations, there is no international agreement as to territorial waters. Efforts of the League of Nations toward such agreement were fruitless.

Ever since the Kiel, Suez, and Panama Canals were constructed they have been affected by treaties and conventions agreed to by various countries, and the Turkish and Danish straits are also the subject of international agreements. The General Convention of Maritime Ports, already mentioned, covers a long list of provisions pertinent to freedom of, access to, and equality in treatment in, ports.

---

[2] For example, there is the case of the S.S. *Lotus*, decided by the Permanent Court of International Justice in 1927, in which the Court concluded "that there is no rule of international law prohibiting the State to which the ship on which the effects of the offence have taken place belongs, from regarding the offence as having been committed in its territory . . . " Ships bearing the flags of Turkey and France were involved in this case, which was submitted to the Court by agreement between the two governments. In effect, the case involved one state exercising sovereignty over a ship of another state, for an occurrence on the high seas.

JURIDICAL AGREEMENTS

The area of commercial or private international agreements encompasses a great deal of important law. It includes conventions[3] dealing with a wide variety of maritime matters, many of which have already been discussed—including assistance and salvage at sea, compensation and jurisdiction arising out of collisions, bills of lading, limitation of shipowners' liability, maritime liens and mortgages, and general average. The Belgian government, the International Maritime Committee, and the International Law Association have made valuable contributions in connection with all these matters.

The International Convention for the Unification of Certain Rules Relating to Bills of Lading has already been mentioned (see page 336). The International Chamber of Commerce and the International Union of Marine Insurance have under consideration a possible convention that would bring into being a uniform through bill of lading for international commerce. Such a document would be of tremendous value. However, the varying national laws and regulations, involving sea, land, and air carriers as well as freight forwarders, present a tangle that is almost impossible to unsnarl.

In connection with other subjects mentioned, there was a Brussels convention (1910) to unify certain laws dealing with assistance and salvage at sea and a Brussels convention (also 1910) to unify certain rules regarding collision. The International Maritime Committee met in Oslo in 1933 and discussed penal jurisdiction and civil jurisdiction in matters of collision. Neither of these matters was ratified by governments, but both were approved by the International Union of Marine Insurance. The Brussels convention of 1924 finally reduced to agreeable form the subject matter of maximum liability of shipowners with respect to compensation for damage, obligations arising out of bills of lading, salvage, general average, and certain contracts connected with a voyage. The topic had been under discussion since 1898. A Brussels convention for the unification of rules on maritime liens and mortgages was signed in 1926 after some twenty years of discussion. It has been ratified by several countries. The United States has accepted only two of the six Brussels conventions—salvage and assistance, and uniform bills of lading.

Regulations of international scope regarding general average were initially prepared at York in 1864 and revised at Antwerp in 1877. They have since been known as the York-Antwerp rules. They were revised beginning in 1890 and, as adopted in 1924, consisted of 7 rules on general principles and 23 rules governing the application of those principles. They

[3] While these conventions were drafted at nongovernmental levels, they were submitted for ratification at diplomatic conferences of governments.

were again revised in 1950. The rules have not been ratified by governments but are generally recognized.

TECHNICAL AGREEMENTS

Safety of Life at Sea. International administrative maritime law embodies all the agreements relating to safety matters as well as to some other technical matters. The first International Conference on Safety of Life at Sea (1914) was attended by the representatives of 13 nations. It provided that passenger vessels should have minimum standards of subdivision, minimum boatage, and lifesaving appliances; required the use of radio; established the International Ice Patrol; and recommended the use of fixed routes on the North Atlantic run. Parts of it were enacted nationally, particularly those parts pertaining to lifesaving appliances. For the United States, which never ratified the Convention, the provisions were largely contained in the La Follette Seaman's Act of Mar. 4, 1915.

Eighteen nations participated in the second conference (1929). The work of this conference placed special emphasis on watertight integrity of ships and on radio communication. The 1929 Convention contained five chapters, dealing with ship construction, radiotelegraphy, safety of navigation, lifesaving appliances, and the issuing of certificates pertaining to the foregoing matters. The Convention also contained an appendix that proposed changes in the regulations for the prevention of collisions at sea.[4] In 1936, when the United States finally ratified, this Convention had been accepted by 43 nations. United States ratification, which bore three reservations, came only after certain fears, said to have been aroused by Andrew Furuseth, then president of the International Seamen's Union, had been resolved in the Senate. Mr. Furuseth was concerned with the effect of the Convention on the legislative powers of Congress and on certain laws relating to the welfare of seamen not coming within the terms of the Convention.[5]

Improved techniques and advances in nautical science made a new conference advisable after World War II. Such a conference was held in 1948 after months of preparation in the various interested countries. In 1945, preparatory to this conference, the Commandant of the U.S. Coast

---

[4] Collision at sea had earlier been the subject of *Revised International Regulations for Preventing Collisions at Sea*, which was apparently based on British regulations that had originally been adopted in 1862. The regulations were effective for this country by an act of 1885. It was superseded by the current rules, International Rules for the Prevention of Collisions at Sea (see p. 338), agreed to at an 1889 convention, which was effective for the United States by national legislation in 1897 and not by acceptance in treaty form.

[5] He was the United States labor representative of the 1914 conference. He walked out in the middle of it and came home; it is said that his opposition was the reason that the United States never ratified the 1914 Convention.

Guard had mobilized a total of 235 representatives of interested government agencies and of shipbuilders, shipowners, underwriters, and the admiralty bar, who joined in the work of various committees.

Delegates of 30 nations and observers of 4 others were present at the 1948 conference, together with observers from the International Civil Aviation Organization, the International Hydrographic Bureau, the International Labour Organisation, the International Meteorological Organization, the International Telecommunication Union, the World Health Organization, and the United Nations. Five technical committees were arranged to consider construction, lifesaving appliances, radio, safety of navigation, and general provisions.

The 1948 Convention consists of 15 articles having to do with the contractual relations among the governments party to it. It is accompanied by 6 chapters of technical regulations. Chapter I contains provisions of general applicability of the technical regulations, including application, general definitions, general exceptions, special exemptions, and the acceptance of equivalents. Chapter II deals with the construction of ships from the standpoint of safety. Its provisions go far beyond those of its 1929 predecessor. For example, the requirements for protection against fire exceed considerably those of the 1929 Convention, and requirements that had previously been limited to passenger ships are extended to cargo ships.

Chapter III deals with lifesaving appliances and emergency musters and drills. It also exceeds the 1929 Convention by extending its provisions to cargo ships of 500 tons and more. Chapter IV covers radiotelegraphy and radiotelephony, while Chapter V deals with safety of navigation and embodies recommendations of governments associated with the International (now World) Meteorological Organization and continues, in general, the International Ice Patrol.[6]

Chapter VI deals with the carriage of dangerous goods, that is, cargoes that are dangerous either because of their inherent nature or because they are liable to shift at sea. Because the 1948 conference lacked the time to make an extensive study of this subject, only basic principles were written into the regulations. The carriage of grain was dealt with in some detail. In respect to inherently dangerous articles, the conference adopted the

[6] Ship operators are vitally concerned not only with having available accurate and complete weather information but also with the technical meteorological aspects of cargo problems. The latter have to do with the effects of varying weather conditions, of water and air temperatures, and of humidity on cargo. Of course, these are purely individual matters and not subject to any international rule or regulation. For example, operating personnel should be aware of the effects that high deck temperatures may have on liquids carried in drums on deck. In connection with canned goods, condensation is particularly troublesome, for rust often results. An excellent article on this general subject is "Meteorology in Relation to the Carriage of Goods by Sea," *Journal of the Honourable Company of Masters Mariners*, April, 1952, pp. 64–70.

existing United States principle that requires the shipper accurately to describe a shipment of dangerous goods and requires the ship to carry a special manifest listing such goods. In the United States, the Coast Guard is responsible for implementing the provisions contained in Chapter VI and for continuing to develop rules and regulations regarding the packaging, marking, and stowing of such goods. Since the list of dangerous goods includes over 1,400 commodities and provides perhaps one-third of total United States exports, these provisions and their subsequent regulation are of particular concern to this country, the greatest producer and shipper of chemical manufactures in the world.

Safety of Goods. Various organizations in the United States have been interested in rules and regulations pertaining to the safety of goods in transit. The Bureau of Explosives has contributed a great deal to this work, as has the U.S. Coast Guard. The Board of Underwriters of New York has, for many years, served shipowners, the government, and marine underwriters through its Bureau of Inspection. This bureau developed recommendations for correct stowage of goods and provided cargo-inspection services on the Atlantic and Gulf Coasts for ship and cargo interests. On May 15, 1952, a new National Cargo Bureau, Inc., was incorporated to satisfy the requirements of the Coast Guard under Chapter VI of the 1948 Convention and to provide a nationwide, non-profit organization to continue the development of rules for stowing grain and dangerous goods and to provide cargo-inspection services for all coasts. The new bureau has taken over the work of the above-mentioned Bureau of Inspection and of Pacific Coast underwriters, and is expected to serve cargo requirements in the same manner as the American Bureau of Shipping serves hulls.

Load Lines. Load-line legislation extends well back in history.

In former days, under the stress of competition, and probably in some cases due to the owner's cupidity, ships both properly and improperly constructed, were overloaded and sent to sea where, in the course of their voyage, gales and hurricanes were encountered, and due to lack of buoyancy, weakness of construction, or improper closing of the openings, many of these ships and crews were lost. Even if the vessel were not lost, a lack of buoyancy of the vessel and nearness of the working platform to the water would oftentimes cause the seas to come aboard and wash men overboard.[7]

England tackled the problem first. As a result of the efforts of Samuel Plimsoll, the British Merchant Shipping Act of 1875 established the first legal requirement for a load line. It became known as the *Plimsoll mark*. In 1882, data gathered by the British government and by classification societies were published in tables of freeboards, which were used as guides

[7] *Proceedings of the Merchant Marine Council,* U.S. Coast Guard, May, 1952, p. 108.

to prevent overloading and by insurers of the ship and cargo. The Merchant Shipping Act of 1890 subsequently provided that the tables be mandatory in fixing load lines. This legislation, and that of other countries since then, provides that the position of the load line be usually determined by a classification society such as the American Bureau of Shipping or Lloyd's Register of Shipping, in accordance with rules approved by the government.[8]

In order to protect the competitive position of British ships, the British Act of 1890 required all foreign ships leaving a British port to be marked and loaded to the same load lines as were required for a British ship. This provision encouraged action by other maritime nations. In 1891, the United States Congress passed an unsatisfactory act, but finally achieved constructive legislation when the Load Line Act of 1929 was adopted.[9] An International Load Line Convention was signed in 1930. It was ratified by 54 nations, including the United States (1931). Its regulations, technical requirements, and formula were promulgated in the United States under the authority contained in the 1929 Act. Again American shipowners, shipbuilders, and government agencies collaborated in contributing to the development of an international convention.

The Convention is applicable to all ships of 150 gross tons and above, engaged in international voyages, except ships of war, fishing vessels, and ships without cargo or passengers. The rules adopted followed the British proposals very closely in regard to cargo ships, but provided for deeper loading of tankers, ships of special type, and those carrying deckloads of lumber. Consideration was given to seasonal and geographic weather variations and provision was made for adjustment of the load line to suit. Whereas the Safety of Life at Sea Convention deals with the construction of ships from the standpoint of safety with special regard to preventing and mitigating casualties, the International Load Line Convention deals with the compliance with rules of classification societies as to strength and seaworthiness of ships under normal operating conditions.

Additional Safety Matters. Other technical and safety questions pertain to buoyage and lighting of coasts, tonnage measurement, preventing accidents to longshoremen, marking weight on heavy packages, oil pollution of the seas, lifeboat services, and refrigeration. In addition to those already discussed, the list of agreements and decisions includes Regulations for Preventing Collisions at Sea, the International Code of Signals, the Brussels Salvage Convention, 1910 (in so far as it refers to assistance to vessels in distress), the Cape Spartel Light Agreement, the proposed Red Sea Lights Convention, the Dockworker's Convention (in so far as it

---

[8] See Chap. 9, p. 160.
[9] This was applicable only to international voyages. The Loadline Act for domestic trade was passed in 1935.

affects the equipment of ships), the Officers' Competency Certificates Convention, the Qualifications of Able-Bodied Seamen's Convention, the World Meteorological Organization Convention (in so far as it affects ships), the Telecommunication Convention (in so far as it applies to vessels), and some of the administrative decisions of the International Hydrographic Bureau. Agreement on admeasurement, which will be discussed next, has been attempted unsuccessfully. Uniform-buoyage agreement is not likely; the United States, with about 80 percent of the buoys of the world, uses a different system from that of Europe. There is, however, a good case for regional uniformity, such as for North European waters.

Negotiations on some of these matters, looking to international agreement, have had a long and frustrating history, first under the auspices of League of Nations agencies and other organizations, and subsequently through the UN. The Joint Maritime Commission of the International Labour Office, acting as a preparatory and advisory committee, has been particularly active in so far as manning scales and other matters of importance to seamen and longshoremen are concerned. There are those who believe that the ILO should restrict its maritime work to the area of welfare and not, apparently, duplicate such work as safety that is handled elsewhere.

In so far as welfare or personnel agreements are concerned, progress has been very limited. One delaying factor has been the relationship of the proposed measure to potentially increased costs of ship operation and the loss of competitive advantage between ships of different flags. The International Chamber of Commerce and other groups have also contributed to such subjects as tonnage measurement.

Admeasurement. The difficulties involved in achieving international uniformity of tonnage measurement illustrate the problems present in most phases of international maritime agreement. The determination is important, because either gross or net tonnage (see page 163) is the basis for assessing dues and charges for port facilities, harbor dues, and canal tolls. The rules for measuring tonnage are complicated, particularly with respect to deductions, and they vary among different nations. The Suez and Panama Canals have their own systems. If every ship were measured under a single set of universally adopted rules, naval architecture and ship construction would be greatly simplified and improved in efficiency.

Before World War II, the lack of uniformity was considered by the League of Nations Technical Committee for Tonnage Measurement and its subcommittee and by the Committee for Ports and Maritime Navigation. The United States participated in some of the work. Subsequently, the League of Nations Transit Section drew up and recommended to governments a set of rules, technical in nature, and including 92 articles, a number of tables, and 124 figures. In 1938, the Norwegian government held a conference, in Oslo, which was attended by the chief surveyors from several countries; the League of Nations held another conference in 1939.

While some people prefer a number of the Oslo rules to present United States admeasurement rules, it is nevertheless generally believed that the latter are more realistic and liberal. An advantage claimed for the United States regulations is to be found in the rules regarding ballast. Since the weight of ship structure and machinery has been constantly reduced, vessels float at lesser draft when without cargo, and therefore require increased ballast capacity. In reference to water ballast, both the United States law and the Panama Canal admeasurement rules permit unlimited ballasting (required for the safety of the ship), but the Oslo rules fix a percentage of ballast that can be provided without tonnage penalty. Consequently, modern cargo ships in ballast (i.e., empty of cargo) would be penalized. Restriction on design through penalties in tonnage rules, according to one source, is damaging to high-speed passenger vessels in the North Atlantic winter route or in other trades where experience indicates that additional ballast is required.

Since World War II, the Norwegian government and the UN have contributed additional efforts on this subject of admeasurement. Conferences were held in Oslo in 1947 and 1948, both of which were attended by observers from the United States. The 1947 conference resulted in a convention signed on behalf of eight governments, establishing uniform regulations for tonnage measurement among these countries. The regulations adopted were based on the 1939 proposals of the League of Nations, which were substantially the British system of admeasurement. The 1948 meeting in Oslo brought tonnage experts of eight countries together in further study. Under the leadership of the United Kingdom there is now being considered a modification of the machinery-space deduction in the present rules.

In 1949, the Economic and Social Council of the UN adopted a resolution on unification of maritime tonnage measurement and invited views on the desirability and practicability of promoting a more general and closer adherence to the Oslo rules. The United States has taken the position that the Oslo rules fail to meet the requirement of not tending to restrict freedom of design leading to increased seaworthiness and safety. While favoring the rules in effect at the Panama Canal, the United States government has, in the meantime, been carrying on a more thorough study of the problem involved, because officials believe that a basis can be found for a uniform system of tonnage measurement that would be simpler, clearer, and more realistic than any of the systems now in effect and that the new system might stand a chance of international adoption.

Under the sponsorship of the interdepartmental Shipping Coordinating Committee,[10] the following government and private agencies have considered the subject: the Maritime Administration, Coast and Geodetic Survey, and the transportation and communications staff of the Department of Commerce; the Departments of Defense, State, and Treasury (Customs Bureau and Coast Guard); Board of Governors of the Panama Canal; American Bureau of Shipping; Lake Carriers' Association; Shipbuilders Council of America; and the National Federation of American Shipping.

INTERNATIONAL MARITIME ORGANIZATIONS

At this writing, there exists no satisfactory world-wide intergovernmental or private maritime agency to which all maritime matters can be referred. Here is an international business, steeped in tradition and experience, highly competitive, and fundamental to the world's commerce. But it lacks a suitable organization to mobilize, resolve, codify, and study matters of international importance, essential to the peace of the world.

The UN concept has brought about an interesting situation. It has collected under one roof, so to speak, a battery of specialized agencies, many of which touch on or have an interest in maritime matters. They include the International Telecommunication Union, Intergovernmental Civil Aviation Organization, World Meteorological Organization, World Health Organization, and International Labour Organisation. Shipping has no organization in being of equal status.

Under the League of Nations, there was a Committee for Communications and Transit, as well as a Communications and Transit Organization, and the League Secretariat had a Communications and Transit Section. The Transit Committee had several subcommittees and special committees, including the Subcommittee (later full Committee) for Ports and Maritime Navigation, which dealt with admeasurement and buoyage systems. While some general maritime matters came up for study and discussion, the League generally was ineffective in the maritime area.

In 1920, the International Labour Office decided to establish a Joint Maritime Commission to deal with maritime labor subjects. It consists of representatives of the shipowners, labor organizations, and the ILO governing body. A great many labor conventions and recommendations have come from the ILO during its years of existence, but very few have been ratified by the United States.

The Pan-American Union, since 1889, and later the current Organization of American States have contributed some discussions and studies on

---

[10] The chairman is the administrator of the Maritime Administration, and the Department of State provides the executive secretary.

consolidation of port dues, shipping documents, legal matters, freight rates and services, and so forth. However, other than general resolutions, and a sanitary code in 1924, there is very limited concrete evidence in the maritime field to show for the years of intermittent association. The hemispheric interests of the member countries call for understanding and firm accomplishment.

Other international maritime organizations in which governments participate include the International Hydrographic Bureau, founded in 1919 and including some 20 nations. By study of charts, sailing directions, tides, and so forth, it serves to coordinate the hydrographic work of the various countries and to lessen the hazards of navigation. There is also the International Ice Patrol, established in 1914, which is an agreement rather than an organization. It is supported financially by about 10 nations; the United States is the managing government for the patrol.

A more complete list of agencies in which governments participate would include the International Commission of the Cape Spartel Light, the International Institute of Refrigeration, the World Health Organization, and the International Telecommunication Union. Various private international maritime organizations include the International Shipping Conference, founded in 1921 and composed of shipowners' organizations; the International Maritime Committee, founded in 1897 to deal with legal matters; the International Shipping Federation, an organization composed of shipowners' representatives, founded in 1909 to deal with labor matters; and the Sea Transport Committee of the International Chamber of Commerce. The International Law Association has already been mentioned. A new organization is the International Cargo Handling Coordination Association, originated in 1950. Its first world meeting, devoted solely to cargo handling, was held in May, 1952, and was attended by 150 delegates.

The time is here for the establishment of a top-level international maritime coordinating organization, to which qualified governmental representatives and industry advisers are assigned. Suggestions for such an agency can be traced to 1888. It was hoped that the League of Nations would provide a medium, and some constructive work was accomplished.

The United Nations inherited the residual responsibilities of the League of Nations, and there is now under the Economic and Social Council of the UN a Transportation and Communications Commission, which has included maritime affairs on its agenda. Simultaneous with the establishment of this Commission and its temporary predecessors after 1945, the seeds of a full-fledged maritime agency were planted in the minds of shipping personnel. As a result, when the United Maritime Authority (see page 457) went out of existence on Mar. 2, 1946, the following day there came into being a provisional United Maritime Consultative Council. This Council was to provide shipping on a voluntary basis for the United Nations Relief and Rehabilitation Administration (UNRRA) and for the needs of areas liberated from war. It was also to provide a forum for a continuing discussion of problems and for exchange of information. At its final meeting in October, 1946, the Council recommended to its 18 member governments that, through the machinery of the UN, a permanent shipping organization be established, and also an interim body to be called a Provisional Maritime Consultative Council. This Council is presently in being. The Secretary General of the UN was notified of this action. Through 1947, the now permanent Transport and Communications Commission and the Provisional Maritime Consultative Council met from time to time, and, while independent, each was aware of the other's work.

The United Nations Maritime Conference met in Geneva early in 1948 at the invitation of the Economic and Social Council. At this conference, the Convention to establish the Intergovernmental Maritime Consultative Organization (IMCO) was concluded, and the Convention included a draft agreement of relationship with the UN.[11] Dr. J. J. Oyevaar of the Netherlands, one of the outstanding maritime statesmen of the world, was chairman of the conference. Thirty-two governments were represented by delegates and four more by observers. In addition, numerous organizations sent observers.

The IMCO convention provides an organization representing shipping interests which can act with the other international organizations in the transport and communications field to effect the coordination necessary in matters of safety procedures at and over the sea, and the planning necessary to work out the effective integration of transport systems throughout the world.[12]

The purposes of the organization, as stated in Part I of the Convention, are as follows:

(a) to provide machinery for co-operation among Governments in the field of governmental regulation and practices relating to technical matters of all kinds affecting shipping engaged in international trade, and to encourage the general adoption of the highest practicable standards in matters concerning maritime safety and efficiency of navigation;

(b) to encourage the removal of discriminatory action and unnecessary restrictions by Governments affecting shipping engaged in international trade so as to promote the availability of shipping services to the commerce of the world without

---

[11] A very complete and valuable record of the background and history of IMCO is contained in *Toward a World Maritime Organization*, U.S. Department of State, Publication 3196, 1948. This publication contains reprints of articles from *Department of State Bulletins*, Jan. 25, Feb. 1, and Apr. 18, 1948.

[12] U.S. Department of State, Publication 3282, 1948, p. 22. *Integration* is perhaps not the appropriate word to be used in this connection.

discrimination; assistance and encouragement given by a Government for the development of its national shipping and for purposes of security does not in itself constitute discrimination, provided that such assistance and encouragement is not based on measures designed to restrict the freedom of shipping of all flags to take part in international trade;

(c) to provide for the consideration by the Organization of matters concerning unfair restrictive practices by shipping concerns in accordance with Part II;

(d) to provide for the consideration by the Organization of any matters concerning shipping that may be referred to it by any organ or Specialized Agency of the United Nations;

(e) to provide for the exchange of information among Governments on matters under consideration by the Organization.

The organization, the functions of which are consultative and advisory, includes a Maritime Safety Committee for purposes of recommending measures affecting maritime safety.[13] Pending the effective establishment of the IMCO, the Safety of Life at Sea Convention provided that the United Kingdom is to act as the "bureau power in all matters," with a few exceptions. Before IMCO can be established, the Convention must be ratified by 21 countries, of which 7 shall be nations having a total of not less than one million gross tons of shipping. To the middle of 1953, ratifications have been disappointingly few. Totaling 13, they include Argentina, Australia, Belgium, Burma, Canada, France, Greece, Haiti, Ireland, Israel, Netherlands, the United Kingdom, and the United States.

When IMCO comes into being, the shipping nations and those that may be called "user" nations will have a forum for the purpose of building a strong and useful framework of mutually acceptable maritime policies. When it does come into being, it will stand as a monument to that small group of maritime statesmen who have worked with understanding, courage, and devotion to the best interests of their own countries and the free world to erect the structure for peacetime (IMCO) and the machinery for wartime.

BIBLIOGRAPHY

Because of the nature of this chapter, it is not possible to list the usual bibliographical references.

---

[13] See the record of the 1948 Safety of Life at Sea Conference, contained in U.S. Department of State, Publication 3282, which gives the report of the United States delegation, including the final act and related documents.

CHAPTER 22

MERCHANT SHIPPING IN WARTIME AND EMERGENCY

In time of war, merchant ships are elements of combat. They make a substantial and vital contribution to the prosecution of war and particularly to the effective application of a nation's warmaking capacity when and where it is needed. The United States Steel Corporation[1] recently pointed out:

Urgent as it was to produce weapons and munitions in mass quantities, they were of no value until they reached the fighting fronts. A bewildering diversity and volume of supplies—700,000 separate articles in all—had to cross the Atlantic and Pacific Oceans to sustain American armies in World War II. Also, through Lend-Lease, the United States helped to fortify the home and fighting fronts of our Allies.

UNIQUE POSITION OF MERCHANT SHIPPING IN WAR

Inadequacy of Supply. The supply of merchant shipping in time of emergency or war has always been inadequate to meet the heavy demands of both military and civilian requirements. The claims made upon the available tonnage are much greater in wartime than in peacetime. Also, in wartime the character of the employment of ships places greater demands upon the capacity of the ships. This problem of inadequacy of supply is directly related to the definition of "adequacy" of the peacetime American merchant marine, because this nation's maritime policy requires "that the United States have an efficient and adequate American-owned merchant marine . . . capable of serving as a naval and military auxiliary in time of war or national emergency." The experience of World War II was that there was never truly an adequate supply of merchant ships.

Nature of Wartime Claims on Ships. One would think offhand that global warfare would bring a stop to the commercial use of shipping and

[1] Douglas A. Fisher, *Steel Serves the Nation, 1901–1951*, United States Steel Corporation, 1951, p. 57.

that therefore all ships afloat would become available to meet the needs of warfare. But war multiplies the claims of civilian agencies as well as those of the military.

A nation's warmaking capacity is dependent on the productive capacity of its fields and factories. The civilian population that furnishes the manpower for industry must be supplied with food, clothing, and the necessities of life, and the many services and activities concomitant with industrialization, such as transportation and other public utilities, must be maintained. Both industrial and civilian requirements necessary to maintain a war economy are dependent upon the supply of raw materials and foodstuffs. The American economy, though the most nearly self-sufficient in the world, is nonetheless dependent upon imports for many items. Although imports of the luxury and nonessential commodities are eliminated or minimized in wartime, the necessary all-out industrial effort leads to expanded imports of a multitude of strategic and essential commodities not available in this country in sufficient supply—iron ores, tin, bauxite for aluminum, chrome and other ores, vegetable oils, vegetable fibers, hardwoods. In other words, war greatly increases the import requirements of the United States.

Furthermore, merchant ships are utilized less efficiently in time of emergency than in normal operation. Hence, more space is needed to move the same tonnage. Convoy operations are an example. Delays attendant upon the assembly of ships and formation of a convoy, the zigzag pattern of the route, and the fact that convoy speed is set by the speed of the slowest ship are likely to add from 10 to 15 percent or more to the voyage time. Port congestion, damage to ships and repair time, waiting for cargoes, and diversion of ships either to new ports of destination or for purposes of loading inbound strategic cargoes—all these factors may slow operations. During World War II, our Army utilized 330 ports of debarkation, more than 7 million troops were sent overseas, and 268 million tons of cargo left our shores—four-fifths of all the supplies and matériel utilized by all the nations fighting Nazi Germany.

Global Aspect of Supply and Demand. Another basic factor that in the past has contributed to the inadequacy of the supply of ships in wartime has been the dependence of the rest of the democratic world on the United States to meet their deficiencies not only of supplies but also of ships in which to carry those supplies. The United States undertook merchant-shipbuilding programs in both world wars. It is clear that the concept of the North Atlantic Treaty embodies a plan to pool the warmaking capacity of the allied nations. Nevertheless, even a pool of all the merchant ships of the participating nations would fall far short of the combined wartime requirements of these nations. The problem, then, becomes one of compensating for deficiencies. The experience of World War II indicates that, in the event of an emergency in the foreseeable future, the main burden would fall on the United States. The United States would have to produce and ship matériel of war to add to the domestic supplies of allied nations and would have to build the bulk of the merchant ships necessary to augment the existing fleet of the democratic world and to replace any ships that might be sunk or otherwise lost.

One wanders into the realm of speculation if he endeavors to forecast the character and demands of a World War III. In terms of ship availability and shipbuilding capacity, we may well wonder, however, whether the steel industry would be able to meet the demands that would be placed on it for munitions and other items, as well as for ship construction. At one time during World War II, over 30 percent of the output of the steel industry went into vessels to meet the requirements for merchant and military ships. Can that be done again? If the answer is no, then our problem of the administration of the inadequate ship supply becomes all the more important.

WARTIME ADMINISTRATION OF MERCHANT SHIPPING

The shipping industry refers to the American merchant marine as the "fourth arm" of the military services. As such, one might expect merchant shipping in wartime to be administered by the military forces in the same manner that the Army, Navy, Air Force, and Coast Guard are administered. However, ships have other than military tasks to perform, and, because of the shortage of ships, there must be some over-all authority which rations ship space to all the claimants. It is not enough to make the statement to which all agree, namely, that the needs of the military come first. The armed forces do and must have top priority, but at times the question becomes one of whether the hen or the egg comes first. Most major military operations could not be launched if the manganese and bauxite had not been imported, the steel and airplane wings produced, and the guns, bullets, and planes put in condition and place of readiness for military operations. This is the nature of the civilian warmaking capacity that must back up the military.

The military services may argue, with some justification, that their needs in the early stages of World War II were thwarted by civilian authority that controlled the available supply of ships. But that is not relevant to the basic necessity, which is to bring into being an overriding central authority to determine relative rights of priority to the use of the limited supply of ships available.

The military concept is perfectly understandable. Its object or urge is to centralize in its hands the control of all the facilities that must be coordinated for purposes of logistics and military supply. Ships are a vital element in this formula of strength and mobilization.

The Over-all Viewpoint. Most shipping men believe that military control of merchant ships in time of emergency would involve an inherent difficulty, for such control does not, and could not, provide the flexibility essential to the fullest possible utilization of the limited supply of ships. There are many essential nonmilitary requirements for shipping space, and they are of such a nature that the military should not be placed in the position of judge of the relative merits of claims of both military and nonmilitary claimants for ships. Hence, the only solution is to establish, at a higher level or in an independent position, one authority with the power to direct the allocation of ships in accordance with the priorities and a second authority to have the responsibility for the manning, storing, fueling, and other aspects of ship operation. The latter is a *service* function which is the sole function of merchant shipping. In wartime, the authority responsible for ship operation is a service organization. Much of the operating activity can be delegated to the shipping industry through the private owners and operators who can function as general agents of the national shipping authority.

Wartime shipping activities call for ships of specific design for special purposes. While a general-cargo ship may be satisfactory to lift the great bulk of military cargoes, the services, particularly the Navy, need a certain number of tankers for fleet operation, other ships for refrigerated cargoes to supply the fleet, supply ships to accompany the fleet, and various other types of vessels or craft, such as submarine-mother ships and repair ships. All these become naval auxiliaries and are usually regularly commissioned vessels flying the Navy ensign and manned by Navy crews.

However, the diverging paths of military and commercial usefulness of cargo ships create a strong influence on estimates of ship requirements. The military, who are constantly devising bigger and better weapons and equipment, are naturally concerned with the problem of adaptability of commercial ships to meet the needs of modern warfare and of the military's ability to have under control a supply of such ships. Therefore, in an emergency, not only will the military make demands on the supply of merchant-type cargo ships, but they will also probably ask for a large supply of specially designed military cargo ships. Vice Admiral William M. Callaghan,[2] then commander, Military Sea Transportation Service, stated in 1952:

To be sure, the great bulk of military supplies, and even most equipment, can presently be transported in conventional-type cargo ships. The time is drawing near, if indeed it is not already at hand, when we will have to give consideration to providing ships to transport special types of equipment which cannot be accommodated in commercial ships. Even if it were practicable to load this

[2] Speech delivered at the American Merchant Marine Conference, sponsored by the Propeller Club of the United States, Los Angeles, Calif., Oct. 8, 1952.

specialized cargo in conventional ships, it cannot be unloaded with the dispatch which military use may require.

Such military cargo ships would not be flexible in their employment, and probably would not be suitable for use in a world-wide pool of merchant-type ships. The problem will obviously be whether the country can afford to stock-pile such special ships in peacetime or to divert steel and shipyard capacity to produce both military and merchant cargo ships in wartime. There is a requirement here for the closest possible cooperation of military and civilian planners to coordinate the size and other characteristics of military weapons and equipment with the characteristics of ships to the end that an economical and efficient ship-construction program will satisfy the optimum requirements of all interests.

Part of the wartime military tonnage will consist of ships in the regular peacetime Navy or of ships held in reserve either by the military itself or by the Federal government. The adequacy of this part of the wartime fleet will depend on how well the Department of Defense and Congress can agree on appropriations and on the shipbuilding program. Additional ships can be obtained by using or converting merchant ships for strictly military purposes, a procedure that will, of course, lower the inventory of merchant ships. (Actually, during World War II, by Dec. 31, 1943, about 500 merchant ships had been assigned and transferred to the control of the Army and Navy.) The remainder of the tonnage necessary to meet emergency requirements must come out of the inventory or pool of ships that are available to meet the needs of all claimants.

There will be certain areas of operation where the military need for a merchant ship or a group of ships is relatively constant. An example is the shuttling of supplies and equipment to Alaska from Seattle or between Pearl Harbor and Guam during the last war. The great bulk of military shipping requirements, however, is not of such a nature. Two general classifications of employment are involved:

1. There is a need for shipping to mount a major offensive or campaign such as the North African campaign and the invasion of the Philippines during World War II. A campaign or assault of this nature requires (a) that a specified tonnage of merchant shipping be mobilized or allotted for the initial assault, and (b) that several echelons of support shipping follow the assault. This involves considerable preplanning and assembling of the necessary tonnage. While a considerable number of ships are likely to be involved in such campaigns *at all times*, there are many bulges in the requirements, and long-range planning by an over-all authority is necessary to map out the rationing of ships over several months ahead in order to satisfy all claimants.

2. In time of war, the military forces will have regular bases in the most

available and useful locations around the world. These, together with newly won bases and fronts, must be supplied regularly, and a certain amount of shipping will be so employed.

Nonmilitary claimants for shipping space include whatever governmental agency or agencies are concerned with importing industrial raw materials, foodstuffs, and other supplies, as well as those agencies responsible for sending supplies to allied nations and to the civilian populations in Puerto Rico, Alaska, and other territories and areas of interest to the United States.

The same general-cargo ship can satisfy any one of these claimants upon the available supply of merchant tonnage. The only requirement is that the ship be at a specific port, and at a certain time when the cargo is there to be lifted. The total of these requirements for lifts can be programed in advance (that is, thirty, sixty, and ninety days ahead), and against these requirements can be balanced the amount of shipping that will be available to lift the total cargo tonnage involved in all programs, both military and nonmilitary. An agency that is familiar with or has records of the characteristics of all ships will know for each ship such characteristics as the following: (a) the cubic capacity, (b) the ratio of cubic capacity to deadweight lifting capacity, (c) the size of the hatches, (d) the lifting capacity of the booms, (e) the fuel capacity, and (f) the speed. Hence, that agency can maintain flexibility in the utilization of ships, allocating each ship to the particular employment that will achieve the most efficient use of the limited shipping capacity. Ships will be allocated in accordance with the prior determination of the relative priorities of the several claimants, such determination having been made by a higher central authority.

This shipping authority, for purposes of allocation of ships, is in a position to collect and collate the statistical information necessary to determine forward requirements and tentative allocations. For example, it would be able to determine that a certain merchant ship (ship A) would be returning to the United States at the Port of Baltimore with a partial cargo of chrome ore from Africa. Outbound this ship had been employed by the military to transport a cargo of equipment and supplies for the armed services in India. At the end of its voyage, control had reverted to the central allocating authority, which had ordered the carrier to proceed homebound via Africa to load there the chromium and certain other commodities that had been assembled for procurement by the national production authority. In the meantime, the military had initiated another program that involved cargo for the Red Sea, and the cargo included several heavy-lift items.

The central allocating authority observes that ship A, inbound for Baltimore, will reach port, discharge, and be available to load outbound two days before the Red Sea cargo will be assembled at the port. It also observes that another vessel (ship B), inbound from the east coast of South America, will be in position approximately when the military cargo is available and (what is equally important) that ship B is better adapted to handle the heavy-lift units.

If each of these ships was frozen in her employment—the first by the military and the second by the central allocating authority—the chances are that ship A would lie idle for at least two days awaiting the Red Sea cargo and that ship B might be utilized for transporting a cargo of small stuff. Furthermore, ship A might be found so inadequate that the military would desire to employ a third ship for the journey to the Red Sea.

Multiply this one instance by the thousands of decisions that must be made daily and revised hourly if the tempo and fluidity of wartime shipping and the pressure of war mobilization are to be maintained, and the need for intelligent central control by experts who know merchant shipping is apparent. It is of paramount importance that no system of control and allocation of oceangoing merchant shipping should be applied which does not ensure, in so far as is possible, the maximum continuous and most efficient employment of all vessels. This can be achieved only by the establishment of a central pool of oceangoing merchant tonnage out of which all requirements, military and nonmilitary, can be met with the greatest flexibility. It is through a master plan of scheduled employment taking into account all approved requirements that wasteful use of tonnage can be avoided. As one man has said, "The game has to be played by ear." But it has to be played by experts. The men who directed merchant shipping in Washington, New York, San Francisco, New Orleans, and other ports at home and overseas, and in the shipping centers of other allied nations, went to war in 1939 as fully and as wholeheartedly as did the men in uniform.

Collateral Problems of Administration. Other phases of the wartime administration of merchant shipping are also said to make it undesirable for the control, allocation, and operation of merchant ships to be assigned to the military command. In the first place, there is the matter of international coordination of the shipping pool. In the event of another war or major emergency, the allied group may organize a central shipping pool. This is a subject for governmental negotiation and administration and, in many instances, would involve negotiation by our government with other governments that maintain civilian control of shipping. In the United Kingdom, the "merchant Navy" has remained under civilian control throughout two wars and during the tenure of Britain's postwar government. The United Kingdom probably would not look kindly on the proposal that it contribute ships to a pool if a military authority were to direct and administer the employment of a substantial number of merchant-type ships over which there was no central control.

In the second place, if the military were to control merchant shipping in wartime, military authorities might find themselves in situations where they would be required to make decisions concerning vessel employment that would involve civilian agencies over which the military has no control. Also, they would have to deal with commercial activities and organizations such as stevedoring companies, ship repair yards, and similar facilities connected with the supplying, maintenance, and operation of ships. To be fully effective and to control all things essential to its authority, the military would have to make more and more inroads on civilian authority. The philosophy of government in the United States involves a proper balance between the military forces and the civilian branches of wartime government. In that balance, the control of merchant shipping should rest with an authority that is independent of all claimants upon ships and that looks only to a higher central authority for its direction.

FUNCTION OF THE SHIPPING INDUSTRY IN WARTIME

During World War II, a major contribution of the shipping industry to the war effort of the United States was to furnish expert personnel to the central shipping authority and to the armed forces to supplement the regular military personnel in matters connected with the operation of ships and of the shore facilities essential to shipping. The main function of the industry, however, was to serve as general agents of the national shipping authority to husband the nation's merchant fleet. Ships owned by all private operators were requisitioned by the Federal government under the war powers of the President. Section 902 of the Merchant Marine Act, 1936, as amended Aug. 7, 1939, reads:

Whenever the President shall proclaim that the security of the national defense makes it advisable or during any national emergency declared by proclamation of the President, it shall be lawful for the Commission[3] to requisition or purchase any vessel or other watercraft owned by citizens of the United States, or under construction within the United States, or for any period during such emergency, to requisition or charter the use of any such property.

The industry speaks of this provision as the authority "to requisition for title or for use." When the provision was invoked during World War II, the American merchant marine "went to war" and ceased to function

[3] Since May 24, 1950, the Maritime Administration of the U.S. Department of Commerce (see Chap. 20).

as a commercial industry. No other industry was so completely affected. Also, the merchant marine was the only civilian industry that was directly exposed to the combat of war. The shore staffs and many of the licensed and unlicensed seagoing personnel, adapting themselves to wartime requirements, continued to function in their normal places of business or occupation; masters of vessels received their sailing orders and routing instructions from the United States Navy; and the commercial operators and longshoremen who loaded the cargo seldom knew the destination of the ship they were handling.

Ship operators, called general agents, were responsible for, among other things, loading, manning, fueling, victualing, storing, and repairing the ships—activities for which they were reimbursed by the national shipping authority. Some of these general agents, appointed by the government and assigned vessels on the basis of quotas that had been determined for the maximum number of ships to be operated by one agent, were generally assigned vessels that were or had been owned by them at the outbreak of the war. In addition, they were also assigned other ships. Other general agents were newly formed companies that mobilized the necessary personnel and facilities to augment the number of supervisory husbanding agents. By the end of 1943, a total of 130 agents were serving the United States government in this capacity. At times, general agents were also designated as *berth subagents* to husband the ships of other general agents when such ships came to a port or were operating in an area where the agent to whom the ship was assigned did not have his own office and facilities.

GOVERNMENT CONTROL OF MERCHANT SHIPPING

The organization of national and international administrative agencies for control of merchant shipping in time of emergency has evolved through the experiences of World War I and World War II and through the defense-mobilization and Korean experiences since 1950. In each case, the mobilization and effective use of ships have been an essential factor in marshalling democratic forces. The major lesson learned from the cumulative experience since 1914 is that the transition from peace to war must be accomplished more and more rapidly and that a high degree of readiness for an emergency is essential to survival and ultimate victory.

World War I. The shock of war in 1914 was devastating to commercial shipping as well as to many related lines of commerce. The enemy's attack was so broad in nature and so utterly ruthless that shipping and other related activities, such as marine insurance, were unprepared for the adjustments and demands that fell upon them. For example, not until January, 1916, did the British appoint a Shipping Control Committee to allocate certain tonnage and to advise with respect to military requirements for ships. The whole of the British mercantile marine was already under some form of control, but not in an organized and centralized sense. The 1916 Shipping Control Committee, a Ship Licensing Committee, the Port and Transit Executive Committee, the Transport Department, the Admiralty, and the War Office were all factors (1) in the allocation of shipping, (2) in the limitations on the direction of employment, and (3) in other actions to effect the fullest utilization of the capacities of the tonnage and the ports. As late as August, 1916, only some 40 percent of British oceangoing ships were armed for defense against submarines. Also, efforts to control freight rates on cargoes had met with only partial success. This was due, in part, to the existence of a volume of neutral tonnage, generally outside the control of the British or their allies.

Finally in December, 1916, the British created a ministry of shipping and appointed a shipping controller. This was just prior to the outbreak of so-called unrestricted warfare in February, 1917. At this point we pick up United States activity in World War I. However, throughout World War I, the control of allied shipping rested primarily with the British. They were instrumental in establishing at London, on Dec. 3, 1916, the Inter-Allied Bureau for the purpose of chartering neutral steamers. Although the Inter-Allied Shipping Committee was set up in January, 1917, with representatives of Great Britain, France, and Italy, the Committee was generally without power and ineffective. The British—at the time the strongest shipping power in the world—rendered assistance to her allies during World War I, including the United States.[4]

During World War I, the United States maritime organization consisted principally of the U.S. Shipping Board, created by the Shipping Act of 1916, and the Emergency Fleet Corporation.[5] The grave shortage of ships under the American flag and under American control placed a tremendous burden on the Shipping Board, and it was necessary for the government to charter and otherwise to control a substantial tonnage of foreign ships. The requisitioning of American ships started in 1917. Although the Emergency Fleet Corporation undertook a huge shipbuilding program for merchant ships, only a few were delivered before the Armistice was declared in November, 1918. Since the shipbuilding contracts did not include a cancellation clause, ships continued to be delivered up to 1921, and the Shipping Board was seriously occupied with terminating agreements and completing the building program. In spite of initial difficulties, confusion, and lack of experience as well as of ships, the

[4] See J. A. Salter, *Allied Shipping Control: An Experiment in International Administration*, Oxford University Press, New York, 1921, 2 vols.
[5] See Chap. 20.

Shipping Board developed a strong organization and cooperated with the allied shipping control authority, from which evolved the Allied Maritime Transport Council and the Allied Maritime Transport Executive.

Perhaps one of the great turning points in maritime history—not appreciated at the time, of course—occurred late in 1917 in Paris at the conference attended by delegates of all the powers active with the Allies. The conference opened on Nov. 29, and a Special Committee for Maritime Transport and General Imports was appointed. For the committee's consideration, the British pointed out that much assistance could be rendered the cause of the Allies by American merchant tonnage, thereby acknowledging indirectly at least the desperate supply situation of Britain, France, and Italy. The United States was urged to undertake an extensive shipbuilding program and to make provision immediately for a large volume of American shipping. (Was this the point in history at which American shipping and shipbuilding assumed the key position relative to the delicate balance of power of democratic nations in time of international emergency?) American participation in World War I, however, was of short duration, and this nation supplied mostly manpower, 50 percent of which had to move overseas in foreign-flag ships.

Out of the Paris Convention of 1917 came the recommendations that led to the formation in December, 1917, of the Allied Maritime Transport Council and the Allied Maritime Transport Executive.[6] Both the Council and the Executive were still in the process of development when the Armistice was declared, but they continued to function in a limited manner until February, 1920. Their cooperative functioning in connection with supply and shipping matters proved that negotiation by specialists, in a common effort, without regard to nationality and with commendable restraint of national interests, is the best means of accomplishing the desired result under the pressure of wartime circumstances.

World War II. As early as 1937, the United States formed the nucleus for the shipping organization necessary in wartime under the Maritime Commission.[7] Men who had gained experience during World War I held responsible positions both in the Commission and in the military departments.

---

[6] The Council was not supposed to perform executive functions; it was expected to influence the various national governments when they determined their policies and when they carried through those policies by subsequent executive action. The Transport Executive was the actual operating body charged with collecting and collating the data and with determining how ships should be utilized in order to meet the demands made upon them.

[7] As explained in Chap. 20, the U.S. Shipping Board and the Emergency Fleet Corporation had been followed by the U.S. Shipping Board Bureau of the Department of Commerce in 1933. This maritime agency was restored to independent status when the Maritime Commission was formed in 1936 as a result of the passage of the Merchant Marine Act in that year.

Prior to December, 1941, the pressure of the war in Europe and the neutrality and other policies of the United States government had led many shipowners to dispose of their ships or transfer them to foreign flags. The world market value of ships was high. In the meantime, the Maritime Commission had augmented its peacetime building program that had as its objective "50 ships a year for ten years." The nucleus shipbuilding industry sponsored by this program and the ship-design experience were important factors in the ability of that industry to expand and to meet the later requirements for ships.

The entrance of the United States into the war in December, 1941, emphasized the need for close coordination of the military and civilian shipping services of the government. Accordingly, later that month, the President established a Strategic Shipping Board, consisting of the Chief of Staff, the Chief of Naval Operations, and the chairman of the Maritime Commission. Mr. Harry Hopkins represented the President. This Board, which was to establish policies for allocating ships, was short-lived. The task was too great for it, and the Maritime Commission, with its multihead organization, was not constituted to handle an emergency program of this nature.

Consequently, in February, 1942, the President established the War Shipping Administration (WSA), and named Vice Admiral Emory S. Land, the then chairman of the Maritime Commission, as administrator. He was empowered to utilize the services of available personnel of the Commission, the military services, and other government departments and agencies. The functions and duties of the administrator were outlined as follows in an executive order from the White House, dated Feb. 7, 1942:

    a. Control the operation, purchase, charter, requisition, and use of all ocean vessels under the flag or control of the United States, except (1) combatant vessels of the Army, Navy, and Coast Guard; fleet auxiliaries of the Navy; and transports owned by the Army and Navy; and (2) vessels engaged in coastwise, intercoastal, and inland transportation under the control of the Director of the Office of Defense Transportation.

    b. Allocate vessels under the flag or control of the United States for use by the Army, Navy, other Federal departments and agencies, and the governments of the United Nations.

    c. Provide marine insurance and reinsurance against loss or damage by the risks of war as authorized by Title II of the Merchant Marine Act, 1936, as amended.

    d. Establish the conditions to be complied with as a condition to receiving priorities and other advantages as provided in Public Law 172, Seventy-Seventh Congress, approved July 14, 1941.

    e. Represent the United States Government in dealing with the British Ministry of War Transport and with similar shipping agencies of nations allied with the

United States in the prosecution of the war, in matters related to the use of shipping.

f. Maintain current data on the availability of shipping in being and under construction and furnish such data on request to the Departments of War and the Navy, and other Federal departments and agencies concerned with the import or export of war materials and commodities.

g. Keep the President informed with regard to the progress made in carrying out this Order and perform such related duties as the President shall from time to time assign or delegate to him.

The organization of the War Shipping Administration evolved throughout the war. Basically, however, it consisted of the following offices and divisions:

Office of the Administrator:
  Legal Division.
  Personnel Management Division.
  Office of the Coordinator of Ship Defense Installations.
Office of the Deputy Administrator for Construction.
Office of the Deputy Administrator for Vessel Utilization, Planning and Policies:
  Port Utilization Committee.
  Office of the Assistant Deputy Administrator for Ship Control.
  Office of the Assistant Deputy Administrator for Allocations.
  Office of the Assistant Deputy Administrator for Shipping Services.
  Office of the Assistant Deputy Administrator for Ship Operations.
  Office of the Assistant Deputy Administrator for Tanker Operations.
  Office of the Assistant Deputy Administrator for Fiscal Affairs.
  Office of the Assistant Deputy Administrator for Maintenance and Repair.
  Office of the Assistant Deputy Administrator for Small Vessels.
  Office of the Assistant Deputy Administrator for Charters and Valuations.
  Office of the Assistant Deputy Administrator for the Pacific Area.
  Office of the Russian Shipping Area.
Office of the Deputy Administrator for Labor Relations, Manning, Training, and Recruitment.
Field Offices:
  Atlantic Coast District Office.
  Gulf Region District Office.
  Regional Office of the Great Lakes Area.

International control of shipping during World War II started as a joint United Kingdom–United States effort, for, in the absence of controls by the governments of occupied countries, these two countries controlled almost all the merchant shipping of the world. The Combined Shipping

Adjustment Board (CSAB) was established by agreement between President Roosevelt and Prime Minister Churchill on Jan. 26, 1942. This Board consisted of officials of the two national shipping authorities—the War Shipping Administration and the Ministry of War Transport. It was created primarily as a planning and liaison body without executive authority, to achieve maximum efficient utilization of the ships available and to coordinate shipping with the activities of other "combined boards" (*e.g.*, Combined Chiefs of Staff, Combined Raw Materials Board, etc.) and of the various national agencies. The CSAB received advice on allocation programs and approval on specific programs, from a Priorities and Allocations Committee, which was composed of representatives of the War Shipping Administration, the Combined Raw Materials Board, the Munitions Assignment Board, the British Food Mission, the Office of Lend-Lease Administration, the Board of Economic Warfare, the State Department, the Office of the Coordinator of Inter-American Affairs, the Combined Food Board, and the Combined Production and Resources Board. Although the CSAB still exists on paper, it is inactive.

As long as many countries were occupied, CSAB provided the collaboration necessary for effective joint shipping effort. However, as soon as the governments of these areas were again able to function, it became clear that there would be a transition in respect of substantial amounts of shipping, from the purely military use through a relief stage and eventually approaching a quasi-commercial status. During this transition period, questions of interest to many nations would be involved in maintaining control over shipping. Even before UNRRA was developed in 1944, a plan was conceived for a central authority to continue the coordinated control of merchant shipping. Such an authority was announced under an *Agreement on Principles* of August, 1944, and went into operation on May 22, 1945.

The United Maritime Authority (UMA), as it became known, consisted of a Maritime Council, which was roughly comparable to the Allied Maritime Transport Council of World War I, and a United Maritime Executive Board. The latter, somewhat comparable to the Allied Transport Executive of World War I, was to operate in two branches and through committees, one in London and one in Washington. The United States was represented through the War Shipping Administration. The 1944 agreement acknowledged the common obligation of the member nations to supply shipping for all necessary military tasks, for provisioning all liberated areas, and for the general service of the United Nations. By the terms of the agreement, UMA was dissolved on Mar. 2, 1946.

The War Shipping Administration (WSA) was terminated as of Sept. 1, 1946, and its work and personnel were either dissolved or absorbed by the Maritime Commission. By virtue of the executive order establishing

WSA, the Maritime Commission had been left only the regulatory and quasi-judicial functions and the responsibility for all phases of construction of merchant ships by private shipyards under government contract. Several units of the Maritime Commission also serviced WSA.

From September, 1946, to May, 1950, when the Federal Maritime Board and Maritime Administration started to function, the Maritime Commission was the principal Federal agency concerned with the United States merchant marine (see Chapter 20). However, because national security and shipping are inseparable, the National Security Resources Board (NSRB), created by the National Security Act of 1947, assumed a leading role in the nation's planning, including the field of merchant shipping. Reorganization Plan 3 of 1953 abolished NSRB and transferred its functions to the Office of Defense Mobilization.

NORTH ATLANTIC TREATY ORGANIZATION

The North Atlantic Treaty (the organization is called NATO) was signed in April, 1949. Under the pressure of events in Europe later that year, and urged along by planning activities stimulated by the National Security Resources Board, early in 1950, there developed within NATO a Planning Board for Ocean Shipping. The programing of our national planning for mobilization of merchant shipping in the event of war was done, after July, 1949, by the Sea Transport Mobilization Survey in the Office of Transportation and Storage of the NSRB. This dovetailed with the work of the NATO Planning Board, which in 1951 announced the broad terms of its plan for an international shipping-control organization in the event of an emergency or war. The organization, to be known as the Defense Shipping Authority, would be comprised of a council and an executive board that would operate (in wartime) in two branches on both sides of the Atlantic. The authority would be open to all nations that wished to contribute their merchant shipping to the central shipping pool, which would be operated in the common effort and from which ships would be allocated to employment.

MILITARY SEA TRANSPORTATION SERVICE

The military organization for the operation of merchant-type ships (not fleet-auxiliary vessels) dates back to 1898. The United States Army founded the Army Transport Service in that year when it purchased six British-owned ships. This occurred in the same year that Admiral Dewey made his expedition to Manila Bay, a voyage that was made possible through the purchase in Hong Kong of a British collier. The Navy formed the Naval Overseas Transportation Service in 1918 to assist in the operation of auxiliary-type vessels. This became the Naval Transportation Service on a permanent basis in 1920, although it was largely inactive from 1921 to 1939. Efforts were made in 1941 to extend the Navy's mission to man and operate the Army Transport Service. This move, however, failed when the Navy was unable to man the Army cargo vessels.

Late in 1949, as a part of the unification of the armed forces, a decision was reached to consolidate all seagoing military transport and supply functions under the Navy; on Oct. 1, 1949, the Military Sea Transportation Service (MSTS) was established. The transfer of Army ships to the Navy began on Mar. 1, 1950, and was completed by Nov. 1, 1950. Under its first commander, Vice Admiral William M. Callaghan, USN, MSTS began a remarkable and efficient job of which the services and shipping industry may be proud.[8]

DEFENSE MOBILIZATION AND KOREA

The outbreak of the Korean hostilities found the United States in this position:

1. The National Security Act of 1947, which had established the National Security Resources Board, contemplated planning for an all-out war. Therefore, most planning for mobilization was of a long-range and all-out nature, and the requirements for a localized emergency were not considered.

2. The Maritime Administration of the Department of Commerce had just come into being and was being operated by a temporary interim administrator. This government shipping agency lacked authority to requisition ships or to appoint general agents to operate government-owned vessels under general agency agreements.

3. The newly established Military Sea Transportation Service was the only agency with the necessary authority and facilities to meet the shipping requirements of the emergency.

Consequently, the MSTS, which had a fleet of 174 ships (50 transports, 48 tankers, 25 cargo ships, and 51 miscellaneous small craft) late in June, 1950, rapidly expanded its fleet by chartering and using over 400 private and government-owned reserve ships. With strong support from private operators, MSTS did a remarkable job in the movement of personnel, equipment, and supplies. In the meantime, the Defense Production Act of 1950 was enacted. Under its provisions, there was established within the Maritime Administration a National Shipping Authority (NSA). The NSA relieved MSTS of a great deal of pressure, initiated a general-agency program, and assumed all the characteristics and functions of a nucleus wartime shipping-control organization.

[8] See H. Morrow, "He's the Stingiest Admiral," *Saturday Evening Post*, July 12, 1952, pp. 26ff.

It can act as the national counterpart of the international Defense Shipping Authority, which was proposed by the North Atlantic Planning Board for Ocean Shipping.

CONCLUSION

The potential demands of emergency exceed the peacetime capacity of the American merchant marine and of the framework of the national shipping agency. National maritime policy, as reiterated and clarified in 1946, calls for a merchant marine adequate for the needs of national security. The substitution of national "security" for national "defense" recognizes that the position of the United States calls for alertness, not a passive attitude toward world affairs. We must be capable of the initiative if we are to lead in peace and survive in war.

Nevertheless, efforts to implement the national maritime policy have been limited. A lack of broad national understanding of the meaning of a merchant shipping industry to the United States is reflected in the attitude of Congress, which is too often passive, even negative and punitive. The shipping industry, composed of numerous segments with diverse special interests and types of employment, has been unable to mobilize a strong, unified program of public relations. Also, the industry has not succeeded in applying, on a broad basis, the principles of research and development to solve such technical problems as the most efficient relationship of the ship to its shore facilities and the possibilities of joint utilization of piers by more than one company. Consequently, the industry lacks attractiveness to private capital, is limited in its ability to apply initiative, and is faced again with the as yet unsolved problem of block obsolescence of its main asset—the fleet.

The Maritime Administration and the Federal Maritime Board, serving under the guidance of the Undersecretary of Commerce for Transportation, together with a few outstanding members of Congress, of the shipping industry, and of the Department of Defense, are making progress in the right direction. Vice Admiral E. L. Cochrane, USN (Ret.), who was appointed Maritime Administrator in June, 1950, initiated a 35-ship building program and has given much encouragement to the whole merchant marine. It is to be hoped that the industry will devote more effort to public relations and research, that Congress will adopt a greater constructive interest in the merchant marine, and that *all* branches of the government will wholeheartedly undertake to implement and not impede the national maritime policy.

The dual function of the merchant marine, as a service industry in peace and an element of combat in war, has led to confusion in legislation and administration in the past. Surely the position of the United States in world affairs dictates that national strength and security must be maintained in a high degree of readiness and efficiency at all times.

INDEX

A

Abandonment, 342–343
ABS (*see* American Bureau of Shipping)
Accessorial charges, 384
Accident prevention, 169, 437–438
Accounting (*see* Steamship accounting)
"Active" vessel tonnage, 105*ff.*
Admeasurement, 409, 438–440
AFL (American Federation of Labor), 210–211
Agencies governing shipping, international, 431, 440–443
  U.S. (*see* specific government agencies)
  during wartime or emergency (*see* Wartime merchant shipping; World War I; World War II)
Agents and agencies, steamship, 226, 240–241, 306
  (*See also* General agency agreements)
Agreements (*see* General agency agreements; International maritime agreements)
Air transport, 2, 92, 99, 115, 337, 433
Alaska, 92–93*n.*, 97, 99, 100, 401
  (*See also* Domestic waterborne trade; Noncontiguous trade)
Alcoa Steamship Company, 89, 136–139, 242, 277
Alexander report, 390–391
Allied Maritime Transport Council (and Executive), 453–454
America, 49, 50, 86, 260
American Bureau of Shipping (ABS), 160, 362, 409, 436, 437, 440
American Export Lines, 49, 87–88, 261–263, 277
  (*See also* Constitution; Independence)
American Federation of Labor (AFL), 210–211
American-Hawaiian Steamship Company, 100*n.*, 277, 410
American Institute of Marine Underwriters, 350, 365–366
American Legion, 280
American Line, 250, 251

American Mail Line, 89, 277
American Marine Hull Insurance Syndicate, 350
American Maritime Council, 286
American Merchant Marine Institute (AMMI), 87*n.*, 211
American President Lines, 49, 89, 90, 221*n.*, 250–251, 261, 264, 277, 288
Arbitration in salvage claims, 372–373
Arbitration clause in charters, 193
Argentina, 26, 27
  as wheat exporter, 38–40, 44–45, 73–74
Army Engineers, U.S., 57, 428
Army Transport Service, 458
Articles, ship's, 213, 310–311
Associations, maritime, American Merchant Marine Institute, 87*n.*, 211
  National Federation of American Shipping, 87*n.*, 100, 440
  New York Shipping Association, 211
  Pacific American Steamship Association, 218
  Pacific Maritime Association, 211, 410
Atlantic Gulf & West Indies Steamship Lines, 277
Atomic power, 53
Australia, 26, 27, 29
  as wheat exporter, 38–40, 73–74

B

Baggage, 337–338
Bailey, Frazer A., 100
Balance of payments, 67–69
Ballast, 439
Baltic trade, early, 17, 23
Banana trade, 26, 35, 36, 60–61
Bareboat (demise) charters, 186–190, 242
  (*See also* Chartering of U.S. government vessels to private operators)
Barges, 325–326
Barratry, 350, 357
Belgium, 26, 46, 433
Berth-agency operations, 404, 452
  (*See also* General agency agreements)

461

INDEX

Berth (liner) service, 47–51, 111
Bibliographies, 32–33, 74–75, 91, 103, 144, 155, 183–184, 203, 219–220, 272–273, 324, 347–348, 379, 406
Bill of lading, 147, 170, 192
  clean, 135–136
  government unaccomplished, 196, 296
  importance of, in shipping operation, 133, 176, 185, 298–299
  ocean, 133–134
  on-board, 134–135
  order, 135
  and shipowner's liability, 334–336, 352–353
  short form of, and correlated papers, 136–139
  uniformity in, efforts to achieve, 200, 335–336, 433
Black Ball Line, 48
Block obsolescence, 123–124, 282–286, 417
Bloomfield Steamship Co., 90
Blue Star Line, 60–61
"Blue-ticket" AB, 213
Board of Underwriters of New York, 373, 436
Booking, of cargo, 132–133, 148, 175, 228–229, 303
  of passengers, 230
Bottom cargo, 177
Bottom tanks, 160–162
  (*See also* Deep tanks)
Bottomry bonds, 327–328, 364
Brazil, 29, 40–42, 65, 249, 251
British Chamber of Shipping, 195, 275–276, 286
Broken stowage, 175, 303
Brokerage, ship operation and, 201–203
  (*See also* Freight forwarding)
Brokers, cargo, 201, 203
  customhouse, 147
  ship, 129, 147, 201–202, 242
  (*See also* Charters)
Bulk carriers (*see* Ore carriers; Tankers; Tramps)
Bulk shipments, 45, 49–50, 185
  contract for carriage of (*see* Charters)
  handling of, 2–3, 45, 59, 178
  liquid or fluid cargoes, 49–50, 111, 114, 163
  petroleum (*see* Petroleum)
Bulkheads, 160–162
Bull Line, 89
Bunkering stations, 20, 52, 79, 80
Bunkers, use of coal for, 28, 51–52
  use of petroleum for, 52, 53
Buoys, 437–438

Bureau of the Census, 181, 425
Bureau of Customs, 326, 426
Bureau of Explosives, 436
Bureau Veritas, 160

C

C-type ships, 100, 260
C3-type ships, 49, 78, 109–110n., 163, 175, 206
C4-type ships, 100, 115, 123, 259
  (*See also* Mariners)
Cabotage, 92–93n., 430
Callaghan, Vice Admiral William M., 265, 266, 447–448, 459
Canada, 26, 27
  Great Lakes fleet of, 122
  petroleum in, 54–56
  as wheat exporter, 38–40, 73–74
Canal tolls, 78, 79, 388, 438
Canals and trade routes, 76–79
  (*See also* Panama Canal; Suez Canal)
Capacity, carrying (*see* Carrying capacity)
  cubic, 114, 163, 175, 385–386
  deadweight, 386–387
Capital reserve fund, 258, 270, 281, 294, 296–297, 423
Captain, duties and responsibilities of, 204–206, 311, 312, 327, 333–334, 344–345
  port, 207, 229, 233
Cargo, damage to, 177, 182–183, 385–386
  dangerous or hazardous, 177, 228, 427, 435-436
  deck, 177
  dry, 49n.
  and freight rates, 385–386, 388
  general, 49n.
  liquid or fluid, 49–50, 111, 163
  (*See also* Petroleum)
  "penalty," 303
  taxes on, 384
Cargo broker, 201, 203
Cargo handling, of bulk cargoes, 2–3, 45, 59, 178
  costs of, 101, 217–219, 232–233
  equipment and gear for, 165–166, 178–179
  paper work, 178–181
  and rates, 387
  steps in, for dry cargo, 178–179
Carloading, 170, 384
Carriage of Goods by Sea Act (COGSA), 185, 199, 200, 335–336
Carrier, common, 47, 334
  contract, 385n., 404
  meaning of, 101n.

INDEX 463

Carrying capacity, modern freighters, 49, 112
  modern tankers, 57, 112n.
  in relation to bunkers, 28, 80
Chamber of Commerce of the United States, 254, 280
Chamber of Shipping (British), 195, 275-276, 286
Charter hire, 192, 196
  insurance of, 353
Charter party, 185-187
Charter rates, 275-276, 384
Charter traffic, 44
  (See also Bulk shipments; Tramps)
Chartering of U.S. government vessels to private operators, 107-108, 116, 186, 188-190, 264, 417, 423
  (See also General agency agreements)
Charters, arbitration clause in, 193
  bareboat or demise, 186-190, 242
  time, 186, 190-193, 242
  voyage, 186-187, 193-200, 242
Chelentis case, 316-317
CIO (Congress of Industrial Organizations), 210-211
Citrus-fruit trade, 26, 36
Civil War, 41, 44, 252
Claims, collision, 373-375
  handling of cargo, 141, 181-183, 238-239
Claims department or division, 181-183, 237-239
Class of vessels, 160n., 188-189
Classification societies, 28, 160
Clearance, 329
Clermont, 27
Climatic conditions and trade routes, 80-81
Clipper ships, 22, 29
Coal, British supplies and trade, 25-26, 31, 34-37, 51-52, 114
  carriage of, 43, 45, 73
  U.S. exports, 52, 72-73
  use for bunkers, 28, 51-52
Coaling stations, 20, 52
Coast Guard (*see* U.S. Departments, Treasury)
Coastwise fleet and trade, U.S., 43-44, 93, 95-102
  (*See also* Domestic waterborne trade)
Cochrane, Vice Admiral E. L., 2, 32, 266, 419, 460
Coffee production and trade, 23, 26, 36, 42, 64-66
COGSA (Carriage of Goods by Sea Act), 185, 199, 200, 335-336

Colbert, 16, 19
Collins, E. K., 28, 48, 248-249
Collision, agreements and laws regarding, 338-340, 434, 437
Collision claims, 373-375
Collision insurance, 352, 354-355, 358-359
Combined Shipping Adjustment Board (World War II), 456-457
Common carrier, cargoes, 47-50, 185
  meaning of, 47, 334
  rates (*see* Ocean freight rates)
  (*See also* Liners)
Compass, 9, 10
Competition and freight rates, 388-389
Condenser, 28
Condliffe, J. B., 24n., 69
Conference system, 394-399
  pros and cons, 396-399
Conferences, contract with shippers, 396
  form of agreement, 394
  and freight rates, 140, 381, 391, 394-395, 397-398
  origin of, 389-390
  representative, operating to and from U.S. ports, 393-394
  and United States, 390-393
Congress of Industrial Organizations (CIO), 210-211
Constitution, 49, 86, 113, 121, 261-263, 271
Construction-differential subsidies, U.S., 119, 254, 298
  post-World War II experience with, 261-264, 271-272, 283-285
  provisions for, 258, 260
  (*See also* Long-Range Shipping Act of 1952)
Construction loans, U.S., 248-249, 256-258, 283
Construction reserve funds, 297
Contract carrier, 385n., 404
Conventions (*see* International maritime agreements)
Convoys, 113, 445
Coopering, 169, 387
Cost accounting, steamship (*see* Steamship accounting)
Costs, of ship construction (U.S.), Mariners, 123, 264, 266
  postwar freighters, 100, 284, 417
  postwar passenger ships, 113, 262-263, 274
  sailing ships, 21, 411
  tankers, 119n.

Costs, of ship operation, 78, 290–292
  labor, in total, 217–219
  and ocean freight rates, 387–388
  of ships to U.S. operators, of domestic fleet before World War II, 99
    after World War II (*see* ship construction *above*; Ship sales)
Cotton production and trade, 17, 23, 34–37, 41, 43–44
Crew, composition of, 304–310
  payrolls of, 301–302
  (*See also* Seamen)
Cuba Mail (Ward) Line, 89
Cubic capacity, 114, 163, 175, 385–386
Cubic ton, 303
Cunard Line, 28, 48, 49, 248
Currents, ocean, 80–81
Customhouse broker, 147

D

Damage to cargo, 177, 182–183, 385–386
Dangerous or hazardous cargo, 177, 228, 427, 435–436
Deadweight capacity, 386–387
Deadweight tonnage, 109–110n., 165
Death on the High Seas Act, Federal, 320, 339
Deck cargo, 177
Deck department, 206–207, 216
Decks of ship, 160–161
Deep tanks, 49–50, 114, 161–163
Defense (*see* National-defense features in U.S. ships; National-defense reserve fleet)
Defense Shipping Authority, 458
Deferred rebates, 390, 391
Delivery permit, 136
Demise (bareboat) charter, 186–190, 242
Demurrage, 171–172, 197
Denmark, 26, 37, 105–106
Desertion, 309, 313
Discharge of seamen, laws regarding, 312
Discharging of cargo, 181
Displacement tonnage, 165
Dock receipt, 133, 137–138, 176
Dockage, 171–172, 384
Documentation of vessels, U.S. laws regarding, 326, 410, 412, 413
Dollar shipping interests, 250–251, 277
  (*See also* American President Lines)
Domestic fleet (U.S.), postwar decline, 98–99, 118
  recent increase in tanker tonnage in, 97, 117–118
  in relation to total fleet (1850–1952), 93–94

Domestic operators (U.S.), current problems of, 99–102
  regulation of, 101, 279, 400–406
Domestic waterborne trade (U.S.), decreased volume, 95–97
  outlook, 102
  petroleum, 57, 97–98, 117
  reserved for American-flag ships, 92, 410
  routes, 92–93
Double-bottomed ships, 27, 160–162
Dry-cargo, definition of, 49n.
Dry-cargo carriers (*see* Common carrier; Liners)
Dual-rate system, 397–398
Dumping, 62n.
Dutch trade (*see* Netherlands)

E

Earned freight, 336, 353
Earning capacity of ships, 113–114
Earnings, current, of maritime labor, 215–218
  on early maritime ventures, 9n., 13
  unsatisfactory, of U.S. shipping companies, 100, 275–276
Economic Cooperation Administration (ECA), 68n., 72, 190
Economic nationalism, 69–71
Emergency Fleet Corporation (U.S.), 84n., 253, 413, 453–454
Emergency or relief shipments, U.S. postwar, 40, 72–74, 108, 116, 120
Empire preference (British), 24, 40
Engine department, 208–209, 216
Engines, marine, 112, 113
Enrollment of vessels, laws regarding, 326
Entry, 329
Essential trade routes (U.S.), 83–91
  early attempts to establish, 83–85, 250, 255–256
  growth after World War II, 90, 268
  services on, 86–90
  subsidized operators on (Jan. 1, 1953), 88–89
Explorations, 10, 12
Explosions, 357–358
Explosives, Bureau of, 436
  (*See also* Dangerous or hazardous cargo)
Extra lengths, 387

F

Fairplay, 112
Farrell, James A., Jr., 275

Farrell Lines, 88, 90
Farwell, Raymond F., 340
Federal Communications Commission, 208, 409
Federal Death on the High Seas Act of 1920, 320, 339
Federal Employers' Liability Act of 1908, 317
Federal Maritime Board, 140, 458, 460
  composition, 419
  functions, 87, 90, 154–155, 262–263, 397–399, 420
  (*See also* Maritime Administration)
Federal Maritime Lien Act, 331
Federal Ship Mortgage Act, 328
"Fighting ship," 390, 391
Finance department of steamship company, 234–236
  (*See also* Steamship accounting)
Fire prevention, 432, 435
Fleets (*see* Domestic fleet, U.S.; Merchant fleet; Tanker fleets)
Flying Enterprise, 342–343
Fog, 339, 340
Foreign flags, U.S.-owned ships under, 119, 251, 252, 285
Foreign trade zones, 425
Forwarding (*see* Freight forwarding)
France, 26, 31
  early commerce and colonies, 15, 16, 17–20
  modern merchant marine, 46, 105–106
Free-of-capture clause, 356
Free-trade policy (British), 24, 34
Freedom of the seas, 430, 432
Freight, 275, 336, 352
  earned, 336, 353
Freight contract, 132–133, 148
Freight forwarder, 129, 132
  compensation, 147, 152–153
  definition of, 146
  foreign versus domestic, 146–147
Freight forwarding, functions, 147–151
  general nature of, 146–147
  organization, 151–152
  regulation, 153–155
Freight insurance, 352–353, 357, 359
Freight rates (*see* Ocean freight rates; Tariffs)
Freight traffic department of steamship company, 225–229
  (*See also* Traffic department)
Freighters (*see* Liners)
Fuel, costs of, 80, 81
Furuseth, Andrew, 412, 434

G

Gallery, Rear Admiral D. V., 2
Garoche, Captain P., 217–218
Gatov, Albert W., 419
Gencon form of voyage charter, 194
General Accounting Office, U.S., 269, 429
General agency agreements, 187–188, 194–195, 203, 209, 241, 404, 451–452
General average, meaning of, 332, 364–365
  reference to, in hull policy, 351
  in protection and indemnity policy, 355–356
  (*See also* York-Antwerp rules)
General-average claims, 367–372
General cargo, 49*n*.
General traders (British), 47, 112, 158
Germany, 29, 30, 31, 39
  merchant marine, 46, 105–106
Government aid (U.S.), ineffective until World War I, 250–253
  reasons for, 247–248, 257, 277, 288
  (*See also* Capital reserve fund; Construction-differential subsidies; Construction loans; Ocean-mail subsidies; Operating-differential subsidy; Special reserve fund)
Government control of shipping in wartime (*see* Wartime merchant shipping)
Government ownership of merchant vessels, U.S. position regarding, 415
  (*See also* National-defense reserve fleet; Ship sales)
Government regulation (*see* Regulation of U.S. water carriers)
Grace Line, 87–90, 241, 399
Grain elevators, 45
Grain shipments, 45, 435
  (*See also* Wheat)
Grandfather clause, 404
Great Britain, commercial supremacy, rise of, 24–30, 35
  early trade and colonies, 11–13, 16–20
  free-trade policy, 24, 34
  public interest in merchant marine, 278
  trade wars with Dutch (1652–1674), 14–16
  United Kingdom merchant marine, 46, 105–106
Great Lakes fleet and shipping, 45, 79, 105, 122, 277
Great Western Railway Lines, 28
Greece, modern merchant fleet, 46
  shipping and trade in ancient, 7–9
Greek-controlled ships, 107, 113

466 INDEX

Gross tonnage, 109–110n., 163
Gulf & South American Steamship Co., 90
Gulf Stream, 81
Gunpowder, 8

H

Handling charges, 171, 384
  (*See also* Cargo handling)
Hanseatic cities, 9, 11–13
Harbors, 76, 115
Harter Act of 1893, 199, 335
Harvard report on U.S. merchant marine, 120, 276, 412, 414
Hatch list, 179
Hatches, 160–161, 166, 169
"Have-not" controversy, 70
Hawaii, 49, 50, 96–97, 401, 411
  (*See also* Domestic waterborne trade; Noncontiguous trade)
Heavy lifts, 387
Heilperin, M. A., 70
Hiring halls, 211–212
Hog Island ships, 112
Holds, 160–161
Holland (*see* Netherlands)
Honduras, 107, 119
Hoover, Herbert, 256
Hours, working, for maritime labor, 215–217
Hull, 158, 160–161
Hull insurance, 350–352, 357–360

I

Ice patrol, 427, 431, 434, 435, 441
IMCO (Intergovernmental Maritime Consultative Organization), 442–443
Immigration, 48, 252–253
Inchmaree clause, 350, 357–358
Increased-value insurance, 351–352, 357, 359
Independence, 49, 86, 113, 121, 261–262, 271
India, 12*ff.*
  cotton, 40–43
  emergency grain to (1951–1952), 74, 108
  sugar, 63–64
  wheat production and trade, 37–39
India tea companies, 65
Industrial carriers, 59–60, 242, 277, 384
Industrial Revolution, 25, 35
Inman Line, 48, 251
Inspection and survey laws, 329–331
Insurance (*see* Marine insurance)

Intercoastal Shipping Act of 1933, 380, 399–402, 405
Intercoastal Steamship Freight Conference, 400, 402
Intercoastal trade (U.S.), 93, 96, 98–99
  (*See also* Domestic waterborne trade)
Intergovernmental Maritime Consultative Organization (IMCO), 442–443
Internal Revenue Code, 297
International Convention for Safety of Life at Sea, 200, 409, 425, 431–432, 434–435, 437, 443
International Convention for Unification of Certain Rules Relating to Bills of Lading, 336, 433
International Hydrographic Bureau, 438, 441
International Ice Patrol, 427, 431, 434, 435, 441
International Labour Conference (1936), 313, 323
International Labour Office (or Organization), 425, 435, 438, 440
International Law Association, 431, 433, 441
International Load Line Convention, 409, 425
International maritime agreements, on admeasurement, 438–440
  classification of, 432
  limited nature of, 430–432
  in regard to, load lines, 436–437
  safety of goods, 435–436
  safety of life at sea, 200, 409, 425, 431–432, 434–435, 437, 443
International Maritime Committee, 431, 433, 441
International maritime organizations, 431, 440–443
International Rules for the Prevention of Collisions at Sea, 338–339
International Salvage Agreement, 200
International Seamen's Union, 322, 412, 434
International Shipping Conference, 431
International Union of Marine Insurance, 431, 433
International Wheat Agreement, 64n.
Interstate Commerce Commission, regulation of domestic water carriers, 101–102, 289–290, 380, 401, 403–404
Iron and steel, use of, in shipbuilding, 27–29, 111, 251–252, 446
Iron and steel industry, 59–60
Irregular carriers, 47
Isbrandtsen Company, 397–398

INDEX

Italy, 27*ff.*
  merchant marine, 46, 105–106

J

Japan, 27, 30, 31
  cotton and silk industries, 42–43
  merchant fleet, 46, 105
Jason clause, 193, 199, 333
Jettison, 205, 350, 357
Jones Act (*see* Merchant Marine Act of 1920)
Jones-White Act (*see* Merchant Marine Act of 1928)
Judiciary Act of 1789, 319, 320, 328
Jupp, William B., 409

K

Keystone Mariner, 112, 209
Kiel Canal, 432
Korean crisis, 107–108, 116, 120, 190, 217, 459–460

L

Labor, maritime (*see* Longshore labor; Seamen)
Labor-management relations in maritime industries, 101–102, 282
La Follette Act of 1915 (*see* Seamen's Act of 1915)
Laid-up ships (U.S.), 107–108
  (*See also* National-defense reserve fleet)
Lake Carriers' Association, 122*n.*, 440
Lakes, Great, fleet and shipping, 45, 79, 105, 122, 277
Land, Vice Admiral Emory S., 419, 455
Laws, regarding seamen, compensation for personal injury or death, 313–320
  wages, hours, and working conditions, 310–313
  (*See also* Seaman)
  regarding vessels, liens and mortgages, 330, 332
  nationality, 326
  registry, enrollment, and license, 326–327, 330
  security devices (bonds and mortgages), 327–328
  title and ownership, 327
Lay time, 196–197
League of Nations, 431, 432, 438–439, 440–441

Lend-lease, 68*n.*
Liability of shipowner, in case of injury or death of seamen, 312–320, 322–324
  under charter arrangements, 192–193, 198–200, 334
  limitation of, 345–346
  to cargo owners, 333–336
  in case of collision, 352
  for passengers, 337–338
Liberia, 107, 119
Liberty ships, 47, 100, 112, 123, 259, 274, 423
Licensed seamen, 206, 213–215
Liens and mortgages, vessel, 271, 328, 330–332, 433
Life boats, 437
Life-saving appliances, 434, 435
Light money, 330
Lighterage, 157*n.*, 171, 384, 387
Lighthouses, 8, 9
Lighting of coasts, 437–438
Limited Liability Act of 1851, 346, 352
  (*See also* Liability of shipowner)
Liners, characteristics of modern, 110–115
  explanation of, 49
  passenger, 49, 50, 113, 115, 121
  routes of, 50–51, 81–82, 87–90
  services of, 47–51, 111
Liquid or fluid cargoes, 49–50, 111, 114, 163
  (*See also* Petroleum)
Lloyd's, London, 28, 47, 350
Lloyd's Register of Shipping, 160, 362, 377, 437
Lloyd's Uniform Salvage Contract, 372
Load factor, 83
Load lines, 409, 425, 436–437
Loading of ship, 176–177
  (*See also* Stowage)
Loading and unloading charges, 172
Loans, British, abroad, 24–25, 67
Log, ship's, 87*n*, 207, 313
London as financial center, 24–25
Long-Range Shipping Act of 1952, 119*n.*, 203, 271–272, 284, 417–418
Longshore labor, 169, 210–213, 218–219
  laws relating to, 320–322
  (*See also* Stevedoring)
Longshoremen's and Harbor Workers' Compensation Act, 321
Losses, 360–362
Lumber and logs, 43, 44, 50, 95–96
Lurline, 49, 50
Lykes Bros. Steamship Co., 87–90, 241

M

Machinery, and Industrial Revolution, 25, 35
  propulsion, 115
  marine engines, 112, 113
McKay, Donald, 22
Magnuson report, 257, 259
Mahan, Admiral A. T., 19, 30
Mail subsidies (see Ocean-mail subsidies)
Management, steamship, 3-4, 156, 243-244
  (See also Organization of steamship company)
Manifest, ship's, 179-181
Manning scales, 206-210, 438
Manufactured goods, trade in, 35-37, 111
Marine engines, 112, 113
Marine exchange, 172-173
Marine hospitals, 314n.
Marine insurance, for charter operations, 189, 191, 353, 359
  collision, 352, 354-355, 358-359
  duration of coverage, 359-360
  main divisions, 351ff.
    freight, 352-353, 357, 359
    hull, 350-352, 357-360
    increased-value, 351-352, 357, 359
    protection and indemnity, 353-356, 359, 361, 374-375, 378-379
    war-risk, 356-357
  general nature of, 349-350
  International Union of Marine Insurance, 431, 433
  and ocean freight rates, 388
  program and its cost, 375-379
Marine insurance claims, general-average, 367-374
  particular-average or partial losses, 364-367
  protection and indemnity, 374-379
  salvage, 372-374
  total-loss and constructive-total-loss, 362-364
Marine insurance premiums, 359-360, 376-379
Marine losses, adjustment of, 360-362
Marine underwriters, 352-354
Mariners, 112, 113, 123, 209, 264-267, 423
Maritime Administration, 121, 214, 264, 290, 302, 305
  creation of, 419
  functions of, and essential trade routes, 87, 90-91
  general description, 421-424
  in regard to Korean crisis, 190, 458-460
  (See also Federal Maritime Board)

Maritime Administrator, 420-421
Maritime Board (see Federal Maritime Board)
Maritime Commission (see U.S. Maritime Commission)
Maritime labor (see Longshore labor; Seamen)
Maritime strikes, 204
Maritime training program, U.S., 213, 423
Maritime unions, 210-211
Master (see Captain)
Mates, 207
Matson Navigation Company, 49, 180, 277
Maury, Matthew Fontaine, 81n.
Mears, E. G., 34, 37
Measurement, of cargo (cubic) capacity, 114, 163, 175, 385-386
  of ships (see Tonnage)
Meat trade, 26, 36, 60-61
Merchant fleet, U.S., decline of, after Civil War, 250-253
  definition of merchant marine, 3
  domestic division, 94-98
  foreign-trade division, 120-121
  obsolescence, block, 123-124, 282-286, 417
  passenger ships, 118, 261
  replacements, 99-100, 123-124
  tanker division, 117-119
  since World War II, 115-124
  (See also National-defense reserve fleet)
  world, dry-cargo vessels in, 110-111
    increased tonnage (1900 to 1950), 104-105
    ownership of active, 105-107
    tankers in, 109-110
    and volume of world trade, 107-111
Merchant marine, Harvard report on U.S., 120, 276, 412, 414
  meaning of, 3
  policy of U.S., 253-254, 257-258, 277-282
Merchant Marine Act, of 1920, 160, 415
  loans and ship construction under, 122-123, 256, 264-265, 283
  ocean-mail subsidies and routes under, 84-85, 255
  purpose of, 253-254
  and seamen's rights, 317-320
  ship mortgage provisions, 328
  ship sales under, 84-85, 122, 254-255, 414
  (See also Emergency Fleet Corporation; U.S. Shipping Board)

Merchant Marine Act, of 1928, 415
  loans and ship construction under, 122–123, 256–257, 264–265, 283
  ocean-mail subsidies and routes under, 84–85, 255–256
  of 1936, 123, 154, 286, 403, 415
  administration of (*see* Federal Maritime Board; Maritime Administration; U.S. Maritime Commission)
  aid provisions (*see* Capital reserve fund; Construction-differential subsidies; Operating-differential subsidy; Special reserve fund)
  essential trade routes under (*see* Essential trade routes)
  and fleet modernization, 260–261, 416–417
  (*See also* Mariners)
  passage and main provisions of, 257–258
  seamen, provisions regarding, 206*n.*, 213, 288
Merchant navy, British, 450
Merchant Ship Sales Act of 1946, main provisions, 415, 417, 423
  passage of, 258–259, 417
  (*See also* Chartering of U.S. government vessels to private operators; National-defense reserve fleet; Ship sales)
Merchant-trader shipowners, 43, 47
Merritt-Chapman & Scott salvage form, 373
Metacenter, 176
Military Sea Transportation Service (MSTS), 190, 423, 428, 458–460
  (*See also* Callaghan, Vice Admiral William M.)
Mississippi Shipping Company, 88
Moore-McCormack Lines, 87–90, 277
Morgan, J. P., 251
Morgan Line, 48
Morison, S. E., 21*n.*, 22, 30
Morro Castle, 346, 432
Mortgages and liens, vessel, 271, 328, 330–332, 433
MSTS (*see* Military Sea Transportation Service)
Mutual Security Agency, 68*n.*, 72, 186

N

Napoleonic wars, 19–20, 24, 26
National Cargo Bureau, Inc., 436
National-defense features in U.S. ships, 113, 258, 262, 264–266, 428
National-defense reserve fleet, 107–109, 116, 123, 258–259, 415, 417, 423
National Federation of American Shipping (NFSA), 87*n.*, 100, 440
National power and sea power, 30–32
National Security Act of 1947, 427, 458, 459
National Security Resources Board (NSRB), 436, 458, 459
National Shipping Authority (NSA), 459, 460
Naval Overseas Transportation Service, 458–459
Navigation, aids to, 10
  rules of, 338–340, 431, 432, 434
Navigation Acts (British), 15, 22, 24, 410, 430
Navy, U.S., voyage of, around world, 411
  (*See also* U.S. Departments, Defense)
Negligence clause, 357–358
  Inchmaree clause, 350, 358–359
Net tonnage, 163
Netherlands, early commerce and colonies, 13–14, 18, 27, 65
  merchant marine, 46, 105–106
  trade wars with British, 14–16
New York, port of, legislation on rates at, 402–403
  loading charges at, 172
New York & Cuba Mail Steamship Co., 88
New York Shipping Association, 211
New Zealand, 26, 76
NFSA (National Federation of American Shipping), 87*n.*, 100, 440
"No cure—no pay" contract, 342
Noncontiguous trade, U.S., 93, 96–97, 99
  regulation of carriers in, 399, 401
  (*See also* Domestic waterborne trade)
North Atlantic & Gulf Steamship Co. (Norgulf Line), 89
North Atlantic Track Agreement, 432, 434
North Atlantic Treaty, 32, 120, 186, 190, 445, 458
North German Lloyd, 250
Norway, 26–27, 159, 439
  merchant fleet, 46, 105–106
NSA (National Shipping Authority), 459, 460
NSRB (National Security Resources Board), 436, 458, 459

O

Oars, 8–9
Obsolescence (*see* Block obsolescence)
Ocean currents, 80–81

Ocean freight rates, 100, 140, 171
  adjustment of, 395–396
  application, 383–384
  carrier in relation to, 384–385
  competition and, 388–389
  conferences and (see Conferences)
  factors determining, 385–389
  general nature of, 380–381
  regulation, of domestic carriers, 400–406
    of foreign carriers, 391–393
    of Pacific Coast coastwise carriers, 401
  types of, 381–383
Ocean Mail Act of 1891, 83, 250, 253, 255
Ocean-mail subsidies, British, 28, 248n.
  U.S., 83–85, 248–251, 255–257, 267
Ocean Steam Navigation Company, 248, 250
Oceanic Steamship Company, 89
Oceanography, Maury's work in, 81n.
Office of Defense Mobilization, 429, 458
Officers, ship's, 204–211
Oil (see Petroleum)
Oil pollution, 437
Operating costs (see Costs)
Operating department of steamship company, 156, 173–175, 230–234
  (See also Ship operation)
Operating-differential subsidy, U.S., 254, 258, 267–270, 279–281
  (See also Essential trade routes)
Ore carriers, 47, 59, 115, 158, 186, 271n., 277
Ores, trade in, 25, 36, 43, 59–60
Organization of steamship company, charts, 224, 227
  claims department, 181–183, 237–238
  finance department, 234–235
    (See also Steamship accounting)
  freight traffic department, 225–229
  operating department, 156, 173–175, 230–234
  passenger traffic department, 229–230, 242
  public relations, 236–237
  research department, 240
  service and supply (purchasing), 239–240
  variations in, 241–242
  (See also Management, steamship; Traffic department)
Osceola case, 313–314, 316
Overhead, allocation of, in steamship accounting, 305–306
Oyevaar, Dr. J. J., 442

P

Pacific American Steamship Association, 218
Pacific Argentine Brazil Line, 89, 90
Pacific Coast coastwise rate case, 101, 401–402, 405–406
Pacific Far East Line, 89–90, 121, 264, 268
Pacific Mail Line, 249–250
Pacific Maritime Association, 211, 410
Pacific Transport Lines, 89–90, 121, 268
Packaging, 182, 386, 436
Packet ships, 48
Paddle-wheelers, 27–28, 252
Palletizing, 168, 178–179, 219
Pan-American Union, 440–441
Panama, 105–107, 119
Panama Canal, 76–80, 96, 115, 165, 388, 409, 428, 432, 438–440
Panama Canal Act, 409, 428
Parcels, 50
Particular average, meaning of, 332–333, 364
  in relation to marine insurance, 364–367
Passenger ships, 49, 50, 113, 115, 121
Passenger traffic, 2, 50, 82, 206
  revenue from, versus freight revenue, 304–305
Passenger-traffic department of steamship company, 229–230, 242
Passengers, booking of, 230
  shipowner's liability in regard to, 337–338
"Penalty" cargo, 303
Peninsula & Oriental Steam Navigation Company, 28, 41
Perils clause, 350, 357
Petroleum, costs of moving, 2–3, 58–59
  overseas trade in, 53–57, 69, 117
  U.S. domestic waterborne trade, 57, 97–98
  use of, for bunkers, 52, 53
  (See also Tankers)
Philippines, 19, 62–64, 92n., 411
Phoenicians, 7–9
Piers, 166–168
Pilferage, 177, 179, 182, 385–386
Pilotage, 172, 344–345, 384
Pipe lines, 57, 97, 117
Planes, 2, 92, 99, 115, 337, 433
Plimsoll mark, 436
  (See also Load lines)
Policy, U.S. merchant marine, 253–254, 257–258, 277–282

INDEX 471

Pooling of ships in wartime, 445, 450–451, 455, 457
Pooling and rotation-of-sailing agreements, 398–399
Pope & Talbot (Pacific Argentine Brazil Line), 89, 90
Port captain, 207, 229, 233
Port charges and dues, 384, 388, 438, 441
Port congestion, 111, 445
Ports, 65, 76, 80
   freedom of, 432
   and terminals, charges of, 170–171, 384, 388
   influence on ship design, 113–115
   management of, 170–171
   and ocean freight rates, 388
Portugal, early commercial supremacy, 10–11, 14
Post Office Department, 428
   (*See also* Ocean-mail subsidies)
President's Advisory Committee on the Merchant Marine, 261, 418
Propulsion machinery, 115, 158
Protection and indemnity insurance (P&I), 353–356, 359, 361, 374–375, 378–379
Public Health Service, U.S., 314*n*.
Public relations, importance for traffic department, 130
   need for industry-wide program, 286–287
Public-relations department of steamship company, 236–237
Puerto Rico, 62–64, 97
   (*See also* Domestic trade; Noncontiguous trade)
Purchasing function, 183, 239–240
Purser, 208

Q

Queens (*Mary* and *Elizabeth*), British, 261

R

Radio, 208, 434
Rail-water rates, 140, 402, 405
Railroads, 27, 37, 38, 170
Rate wars, 401
Rates, rail-water, 140, 402, 405
   (*See also* Ocean freight rates)
Reactivation of U.S. reserve ships, 107
   (*See also* Chartering of U.S. government vessels to private operators; National-defense reserve fleet)
Rebates, deferred, 390, 391
Reciprocal trade agreements, 410, 426

Red Star Line, 48
Refrigerated ships (reefers), 60–61, 114–115, 163
Register tonnage, 163–165
Registry of vessels, laws regarding, 326
Regulation, of maritime affairs, by agreements (*see* International maritime agreements)
   by international maritime organizations, 431, 440–443
   of U.S. water carriers, domestic, by industry, 399–400
      under Intercoastal Steamship Act, 399–401
      by Interstate Commerce Commission since 1940, 101, 401–406
   foreign, 391–393
   (*See also* Federal Maritime Board; U.S. Maritime Commission)
   of maritime commerce, limited powers of states in, 328–330
Relief shipments (*see* Emergency or relief shipments)
Reorganization Plan 21, 417, 419, 424
Repatriation of seamen, 312, 425
Replacement reserves (*see* Reserve funds)
Replacements (*see* Ship replacements)
Requisition of privately owned ships during wartime, government power in, 258, 451
   World War I, 453
   World War II, 99, 122, 194, 451
Reserve fleet, U.S. (*see* National-defense reserve fleet)
Reserve funds, 100, 283
   capital, 258, 270, 281, 294, 296–297, 423
   construction, 297
   special, 258, 270, 281, 294, 297, 423
Respondentia bonds, 327–328, 364
Revenue, analysis of, for late 1952 voyage, 290–292
   (*See also* Earnings)
Revolutionary War, 20
Rice, 23, 26, 36, 76
Rigging, 166
Robin Line (Seas Shipping Company), 88, 90
Rome, ancient, shipping and trade in, 8–9
Roosevelt, Franklin D., 257, 416
Roosevelt, Theodore, 411
Rothschild, Louis S., 264
Routes, liner, 50, 79
   (*See also* Trade routes)
Royal Mail Steam Packet Company, 28, 48
Rubber, 66–67, 76
"Rules of the road," 338–340, 431

Russia, 12, 23, 26, 31, 37–40
(*See also* U.S.S.R.)

S

Safety of life at sea, 200, 409, 425, 431–432, 434–437, 443
Sailing ships, 8–10, 21–22, 109, 251–252
Sailings, scheduling of, 175
Sails, 8–10, 28
St. Lawrence Seaway, 79
Salvage, 341–343, 351, 372–373, 433, 437
Salvage Association (British), 362
Sanford, L. R., 280, 282
Savannah, 30
Sawyer, Charles, 263–264
Scandinavia, shipbuilding, 112
  trading, 116, 202
  (*See also* specific countries)
Scheduling of sailings, 175
Schools, U.S. maritime training, 213–215, 423
Schuyler Otis Bland, 264, 423
Scrapping of ships, 116, 423
Screw steamers, 27–29, 80
Sea power, 30–32
Seamen, certificates, licenses, and training of, 213–215, 423
  contract provisions for hiring, 210–213
  International Labour Organisation's work for, 438, 440
  laws regarding (*see* Laws)
  legal definition of, 310, 319–321
  legal remedies for, now superior to workmen's compensation, 322–324
  Merchant Marine Act of 1936 provisions for, 206n., 213, 288
  nature of employment, 212–213, 309–319
  repatriation of, 312, 425
  wages, hours, and working conditions, 215–219, 290
  "wages, maintenance, and cure," 314–315, 317–318, 323
  (*See also* Crew)
Seamen's Act of 1915, 250, 316–317, 412, 434
Seas Shipping Company, 88, 90
Seatrain Lines, 89
Seatrains, 123
Seaworthiness of vessels, 159–160, 176, 190, 191, 199
Service, 82–83
Service and supply department of steamship company, 239–240
Shape-up, 212
Ship broker, 129, 147, 201–202, 242

Ship brokerage, 201–203
Ship design, factors influencing, 113–115
  military, 113, 447
Ship operation, under charters, 201–203, 242
  components of, 157
  labor costs in total costs, 217–219
  process of, 175–181
  and the ship, 158–166
  supervision and administration, 173–175
  terminal in, 166–173
  (*See also* Operating department of steamship company)
Ship replacements, U.S. problem of, 99–100, 123–124
  (*See also* Block obsolescence)
Ship sales, U.S. government, after January, 1951, 264, 423
  after World War I, 84–85, 122, 254–255, 414
  after World War II, 100, 116, 121, 123, 258–259, 274, 415, 417, 423
  to noncitizens, 116, 123, 259n.
Ship-to-shore communications, 205, 208
Shipbuilders' Council of America, 280, 440
Shipbuilding, U. S., to about 1900, 20–22, 251–253
  interwar period, 122–123, 256–257, 260–261, 455
  low ebb of current, 119, 123, 261–264, 283–284
  World War I program, 107, 122, 254, 413–414, 453–454
  World War II program, 107, 116, 122
  (*See also* Merchant fleet, U.S.)
  use of iron and steel in, 25, 27–30, 111, 251–252
Shipper's papers, 132–139
  (*See also* Shipping papers)
Shipping in wartime (*see* Wartime merchant shipping)
Shipping Act of 1916, 47
  passage of, 253, 412–413
  regulatory provisions, 153, 285, 390–392, 401, 410
  (*See also* Emergency Fleet Corporation; U.S. Shipping Board)
Shipping Board (*see* U.S. Shipping Board)
Shipping Board Bureau, 391n., 392n., 416
Shipping capital, characteristics of, 274–278
  handicaps of, 278–282
Shipping Control Committee (British), 452–453
Shipping finance, problem of, 274–287

Shipping industry, complex nature of, 1, 3-4
  and trade, 34*ff.*
Shipping papers, 179*ff.*, 409
  (*See also* Shipper's papers)
Shipping permit, 132-133, 176
Shipping route, 82
  (*See also* Trade routes)
Ships, steam (*see* Steamships)
Signals at sea, 439
Silk, 36, 42-43, 66
Size of ships, increase in, since World War I, 43, 112-115, 158-159
Slave trade, 15, 330
Slop chest, 216-217, 312
South Atlantic Steamship Line, 90
Spain, early commerce and colonies, 10-12, 14, 18, 30
Special reserve fund, 258, 270, 281, 294, 297, 423
Speed of ships, as factor in ocean commerce, 83, 158
  increased, 112-115, 265-266
Sphericity of the earth, 79-80
Spice trade, 10, 11
Standard Oil of New Jersey, 277
Standardization of ships, 158-159
Steamship accounting, balance sheet, 296-298
  contrasted with other industries, 306
  cost accounting, 302-306
    allowance of overhead, 305-306
    joint passenger and freight, 304-305
    voyage costs and statistics, 302-304
  in finance department, 235-236
  methods and procedures, 298-302
  operating statements, 289-296
  voyage as unit in, 156, 289*ff.*
Steamships, appearance of, 27-30
  characteristics of modern, 111-115
  double-bottomed, 27, 160-162
  earning capacity of, 113-114
  screw, 27-29, 80
  size of, 43, 112-115, 158-159
  speed of (*see* Speed of ships)
Steel, use of, in shipbuilding, 29, 111, 446
Steel Designer, 209
Steel industry, 59-60
Sterling area, 67-68*n.*
Stevedoring, 168-169, 232-233
  under time charters, 197
  (*See also* Cargo handling; Longshore labor)
Steward's department, afloat, 210, 216
  ashore, 233-234
Stowage, 176-177, 233
  broken, 175, 303

Stowage, preplanning, 133, 229
Stowage factor, 114, 177
Stowage plan, 179-180, 229, 233
Strategic Planning Board, U.S., 455
Strikes, British coal, 40
  maritime, 204
Subsidies (*see* Construction-differential subsidies; Construction loans; Ocean-mail subsidies; Operating-differential subsidy)
Suez Canal, 25, 27, 38, 76-79, 115, 165, 409, 432, 438
Sugar, 17, 19, 23, 26, 50, 62-63, 96-97
Surplus-vessel tonnage, U.S., after World War I, 122
  after World War II, 110, 116, 122
  (*See also* National defense reserve fleet; Ship sales)
Survey of vessels, for adjustment of marine losses, 360-362
  laws regarding, 329-331
Swallow Tail, 48
Sweden, 25-27
  early Baltic trade, 17, 23
  modern fleet, 46, 105-106

T

T2 tankers, 112, 259
Talley sheets, 179
Tanker fleets, American-flag, domestic, 97-98
  total, 117-119
  companies owning large, 242, 277
  growth of world, 109-110
Tankers, development of, 57-58
  management of, 58-59, 186
  operation of, 58-59, 186
  size of, 58, 112-113, 117
  T2, 112, 259
  (*See also* Petroleum)
Tanks, bottom, 160-162
  deep, 49-50, 114, 161-163
Tariff, 61-62
  British, empire preference, 24, 40
  free-trade policy, 24, 34
  U.S., 252, 410-411
Tariffs, steamship, 101, 140, 334, 381, 395-495
  (*See also* Ocean freight rates)
Taxes, on cargo, 384
  no property, on vessels, 293
  tonnage, 172, 330, 410
Tea, 26, 36, 64-65
Terminal charges, 384
Terminals and ship operations, 166-173
  (*See also* Ports and terminals)
Territorial waters, 430, 432

474 INDEX

Time in port, 110–111, 115, 166n.
Time charters, 186, 190–193, 242
Titanic, 412, 431
Tobacco trade, 76
Tonnage, cargo, 303
   vessel, 109–110n., 163, 165
      admeasurement, 409, 438–440
      surplus- (*see* Surplus-vessel tonnage)
Tonnage tax, 172, 293–295, 330, 410
Towage, 172, 343–344, 384
Trade, and economic nationalism, 69–71
   government decisions affecting, 39–40, 42, 61–64, 66–69
   post-World War II, 71–74
      (*See also* Emergency or relief shipments)
   volume of, British and French during eighteenth century, 16–17
   increase in, during nineteenth century, 34–35
   seaborne (1928–1950), 72
   world (1938), 35–36
Trade routes, climatic conditions and, 80–81
   definition of, 81–82
   for movement, of cotton, 41–44
   of wheat, 38–40
   physical factors affecting, 76–81
   versus "service," 82–83
   U.S. essential (*see* Essential trade routes)
Traffic analysis, importance of, 140–141
   use of punch cards in, 140–141, 299
Traffic department, freight, 225–229
   general functions of, 129–130
   organization of, 143–144
   passenger, 229–230, 242
   rate functions of, 140
   relations with other departments, 140–142
Traffic management, 127–144
   explanation of, 127–128
Training of seamen, U.S., 213–215, 423
Tramps, decreased importance of, 45–47, 50, 114–115
   index numbers of freights (1949–1952), 275–276
   management of, 129, 242
   not common carriers, 47
   operations of, 43–45, 73, 384
      (*See also* Charters)
   origin, 43–44
   U.S. government aid to, 119n., 203, 271
Transportation Act of 1940, 101, 102, 380, 401, 403
   (*See also* Interstate Commerce Commission)

Treaties, maritime (*see* International maritime agreements)
Trim of ships, 176, 179–180
Truck transportation, 102, 172
Truck-water rates, 402
Truman, Harry S., 419
Tugs, 172, 343–344, 384
Turn-around, 110–111, 115, 166n.
Tydings-McDuffie Act of 1934, 92n.
Types of ships, 158
   (*See also* Liners; Ore carriers; Passenger ships; Refrigerated ships; Tankers; Tramps)

U

U.S.S.R., 31, 41, 64, 105n.
   (*See also* Russia)
Unions, maritime, 210–211
United Fruit Company, 60–61, 89, 242
United Kingdom merchant marine, 46, 105–106
United Maritime Authority, 441, 457
United Nations, 435, 438, 439, 441–443
United Nations Maritime Conference, 442–443
UNRRA, 190, 442, 457
United States, 49, 86, 113, 121, 261–263, 271
United States and Brazil Steamship Company, 249, 251
U.S. Coast Guard (*see* U.S. Departments, Treasury)
U.S. Congress, power of, to regulate commerce, 328
U.S. Departments, Commerce, 281–282, 424–425, 440
   Bureau of the Census, 181, 425
   Office of International Trade, 142, 425
   (*See also* Federal Maritime Board; Maritime Administration)
   Defense, 264, 427–428, 440, 460
   Department of the Navy, 428
   Military Sea Transportation Service, 190, 423, 428, 458–460
   national-defense features in U.S. ships, 113, 258, 262, 264–266, 428
   Justice, 428
   Labor, 428–429
   Post Office, 428
   (*See also* Ocean-mail subsidies)
   State, 295–296, 425–426, 440
   Treasury, 150, 281, 293, 297, 302, 426–427, 440
      Bureau of Customs, 326, 426
      Coast Guard, 177, 206, 213, 329, 409, 426–427, 434–436

United States Lines, 49, 87–88, 277
U.S. Maritime Commission, 167
  creation and composition of, 416
  functions of, modernization of American merchant marine, 260–261, 416–417
    regulatory, 154, 289, 403
    (*See also* Construction-differential subsidies; Essential trade routes; Operating-differential subsidy; Ship sales)
  1937 report, 47, 256, 260
  (*See also* Federal Maritime Board; Maritime Administration, War Shipping Administration)
U.S. Maritime Service, 213, 215
U.S. Public Health Service, 314*n.*, 409
U.S. Salvage Association, 360
U.S. Shipping Board, activities of, after World War I, 83–85, 254–257
  during World War I, 413–414
  (*See also* Ocean-mail subsidies; Ship sales)
  creation of, 253, 412–413
  inadequate administration of, 414–415
  (*See also* Shipping Act of 1916)
U.S. Shipping Board Bureau, 391*n.*, 392*n.*, 416
Unlicensed seamen, 206, 213–215

V

Venezuela, 54–56, 60
Venice, 8–11
Venture nature of early voyages, 309–310
Vessel, legal definition of, 325–326
Vessel day for allocation of overhead, 305–306
Vestris, 431–432
Victory ships, 49, 100, 112, 423
Vikings, 7, 9
Voyage as accounting unit, 156, 289*ff.*
Voyage charter, 186–187, 193–200, 242

W

W/M (weight or measure), 303, 381
"Wages, maintenance, and cure," 314–315, 317–318, 323
Wages, maritime, 215–217
War bonuses, 217

War-risk insurance, 356–357
War Shipping Administration, 188, 194–195, 404–405, 417
Ward Line, 89
Warship demise, 188
Warshipvoy (Rev.), 194–195, 197, 199
Wartime merchant shipping, administration of, 446–451
  claims on ships, 444–445
  functions, 451–452
  global aspects, 445–446
  inadequacy of supply, 444
  (*See also* Korean crisis; World War I; World War II)
Waterfront Employers' Association of Pacific Coast, 410
Waterman Steamship Corporation, 89, 209, 264
Weather and weather conditions, 78–81
West Indies, early trade, 13–15, 17, 23
Whalers, 48
Wharfage, 171–172, 384
Wheat, carriage of, 44–45, 50
  1949 agreement, 64*n.*
  trade in, 7, 24, 26, 34–40, 72–74
  (*See also* Grain shipments)
Williams, Robert W., 419
Windsor, 112
Wood, use of, in shipbuilding, 28, 29
Workmen's compensation, 322–324
World War I, control of merchant shipping during, 452–454
  requisitioning of merchant ships, 453
  U.S. shipbuilding program, 107, 122, 254, 413–414, 453–454
World War II, control of merchant shipping during, 454–458
  requisitioning of ships, 99, 122, 194, 451
  U.S. shipbuilding program, 107, 116, 122
  (*See also* War Shipping Administration)
Wrecks, 355

Y

York-Antwerp rules, 193, 200, 371, 433–434

Z

Zimmermann, E. W., 51, 56, 63*n.*, 66–67

www.ingramcontent.com/pod-product-compliance
Lightning Source LLC
Chambersburg PA
CBHW020631230426
43665CB00008B/131